D0408514

Hugh Johnson's
Pocket Wine Book

2005

MITCHELL BEAZLEY

Acknowledgments

This store of detailed recommendations comes partly from my own notes and mainly from those of a great number of kind friends. Without the generous help and cooperation of innumerable winemakers, merchants, and critics, I could not attempt it. I particularly want to thank the following for help with research or in the areas of their special knowledge:

Geoff Adams

Helena Baker

Charles Borden

Dr Ernö Péter Botos

Gregory Bowden

Stephen Brook

Bruce Cass

Michael Cooper

Rupert Dean

Michael Edwards

Jacqueline Friedrich

Rosemary George MW

Robert Gorjak

James Halliday

Darrel Joseph

Dr Annie Kay

Chandra Kurt

Gareth Lawrence

James Lawther MW

John Livingstone-
    Learmonth

Nico Manessis

Richard Mayson

Adam Montefiore

Jasper Morris MW

Vladimir Moskvan

Shirley Nelson

John and Erica Platter

Carlos Read

Jan and Maite Read

Daniel Rogov

Lisa Shara Hall

Stephen Skelton MW

Paul Strang

Bostjan Tadel

Marguerite Thomas

Daniel Thomases

Larry Walker

Simon Woods

Special thanks to Margaret Rand.

Hugh Johnson's Pocket Wine Book 2005

Edited and designed by Mitchell Beazley, an imprint of Octopus Publishing Group Limited, 2-4 Heron Quays, London E14 4JP.

© Octopus Publishing Group Limited, 1977–2004.

First edition published 1977
Revised editions published 1978, 1979, 1980, 1981, 1982, 1983, 1984, 1985, 1986, 1987, 1988, 1989, 1990, 1991, 1992, 1993, 1994, 1995, 1996, 1997, 1998, 1999, 2000, 2001, 2002(twice), 2003, 2004.

A CIP record for this book is available from the British Library.

ISBN 1 84000 895 4

Commissioning Editor: Hilary Lumsden
Editor: Julie Sheppard
Executive Art Editor: Yasia Williams
Design: Tim Pattinson
Production: Seyhan Esen

Printed and bound by Toppan Printing Company, China

Contents

Agenda 2005

I sign off each new edition of this little book (this is the 29th) in the
spring, with the news of the latest vintage received and considered,
but not yet tested. It is published in the autumn (books are not
newspapers) for use over the following twelve months. The
recommendations in this edition are therefore tuned to the period
September 2004 to September 2005 – which involves a certain
amount of informed guesswork, but not enough to give me nightmares.
Fine-tuning the entries is a constant process. How much changes from
one edition to another? Of vintage information, nearly all. Of other
information, maybe 15%. So readers who only buy me in alternate
years should aim off on their vintage choice, and have a roughly one
in three chance of out-dated data on the rest. Apart, that is, from the
subtle changes of emphasis, the lists of recommended wines and
producers, the ideas about wine with food, and the year's Agenda.

Does the world of wine really change in its broad outlines so much?
It looks the most stable of all businesses: Burgundy and Bordeaux
have been around since the Romans, Alsace since the Middle Ages,
and even New Zealand for twenty years now. There are wine-growing
families still tilling the same plots as they did in the 15th century.

Yes, but even they live in a different world today. Flavours are no
longer exclusive to regions, or knowledge to the experienced. The
same techniques are practised round the world. The New World
borrows ideas from the Old; the Old promptly returns the compliment.
You might think that with so much swapping going on, it scarcely
matters any more where your wine comes from: same grape varieties,
same tanks, same yeasts, same barrels – what's the fuss?

It is a powerful argument, and regularly aired by powerful buyers
looking to save a few cents. Buyers, especially for supermarkets, are
paid to be ruthless. The emergence of a new competitor – a new
region with plausible Chardonnays, let's say – hands the buyer a stick
to beat an established supplier. Healthy competition, they call it. But
is it really all positive? It makes producers 'realistic' in their pricing.
(Most realistic, of course, those icons whose wines have awaiting lists.
They can charge the earth.) But not so healthy, for those who love
wine, is the pressure it puts on producers to cut costs – which can
mean cutting corners.

I'll put the question to you. Would you rather – for the same money
– drink two glasses of something as good as its producer can possibly
make it, or three of a dumbed-down version? Do you shop for real
chickens, or the shrink-wrapped, long-life variety?

Of all the foods we buy wine is the one that has the most direct,
traceable links with its source. It is, after all, the water from the
ground of a real field, with its soil and stones, its slopes or lack of
them, its puddles and weeds, transmuted by the vine in to sweet juice,
and by yeasts into strong drink. Nothing is purer or more alive – alive
until the moment your stomach digests it. Why are we so precise about
which wine is which? This immediacy, from the vine to you, is at the
heart of it.

Anything new on this year's Agenda? In past editions I have written
about wines that are too highly seasoned to be good drinks. If Tex-Mex
cooking is your thing you may not agree. By over-seasoned I mean too

alcoholic, and/or too oaky. There are several reasons why alcohol levels are creeping up, in wine worldwide, from 12–13% to 14–15% or even more. Riper grapes is the most obvious. The mode is to pick them as late as possible, looking for smoother but stronger results. New yeast strains, too, have the capability to carry on fermenting sugar to levels of alcohol which asphyxiated the old ones. Wine of massive intensity and brain-numbing power is now easy to achieve in the right climate. All you need is sunshine. Can you drink it, though, with any pleasure – or at all, if you are driving home?

As for the fashion of giving every wine a supposedly luxurious taste of oak, the news is better. Common sense is beginning to prevail. With new French barrels costing over $500 each – or around $2 a bottle – the taste of grapes is on the way back.

When I started this book I used the abbreviation DYA – Drink Youngest Available – as exceptional advice for wines that could not be relied on to last even a couple of years in bottle. Today's fashion, in restaurants especially, is to demand the freshest wine every time, almost as if it were a fish, regardless of the benefit that comes to almost any good wine from the right resting-time between bottling and drinking.

Bad corks have encouraged the rather confused view that freshness is all. Australia and New Zealand are adopting screwcaps wholesale, with maximum freshness the ostensible reason. (It is a more powerful argument in the US, where shipping and storing conditions often leave a lot to be desired). Rieslings were first in line – summarily relegating the glorious flavours that fine ones acquire with maturity. Some good producers are proposing to follow with red wines. But since when has freshness been the desideratum with fine reds?

From the producers' and merchants' point of view, of course, the faster the turnover the better. But drinkers should not think this has to apply to them. The one instance when wine-lovers must move smartly is when a good new vintage is offered in the following spring, en primeur. It may be the only opportunity to make your choice from the whole range of good wines – certainly at their opening prices. Prices can go down, though, as well as up.

This is intended to be a practical guide; theory has no place here. It compresses all the useful information you can't possibly carry in your head – and neither can I. You are faced with a daunting restaurant wine list, or mind-numbing shelves of bottles in a store. Your mind goes blank; out comes your little book. You can start with what you propose to eat, see pp.17–31, or where you are by turning up a national section, or a grape variety. Establish which country a wine comes from, then look up the principal words on the label in that country's section. You should find enough information to guide your choice – and often a great deal more. Even after twenty-eight editions I can browse for hours...

How to use this book

The top line of most entries consists of the following information:

❶
❸

| Aglianico del Vulture | Bas | r dr (s/sw sp) | ★★★ | **96' 97** 98 99' 00 01' 02 (03) |

❷
❹

❶ Wine name and the region the wine comes from.

❷ Whether it is red, rosé or white (or brown/amber), dry, sweet or
sparkling, or several of these (and which is most important):

r	red
p	rosé
w	white
br	brown
dr	dry*
sw	sweet
s/sw	semi-sweet
sp	sparkling

( ) brackets here denote a less important wine
*assume wine is dry when **dr** or **sw** are not indicated

❸ Its general standing as to quality: a necessarily rough-and-ready
guide based on its current reputation as reflected in its prices:

★	plain, everyday quality
★★	above average
★★★	well known, highly reputed
★★★★	grand, prestigious, expensive

So much is more or less objective. Additionally there is a subjective rating:

★ etc   Stars are coloured for any wine which in my experience is usually
especially good within its price range. There are good everyday wines
as well as good luxury wines. This system helps you find them.

❹ Vintage information: which of the recent vintages can be recommended; of
these, which are ready to drink this year, and which will probably improve
with keeping. Your choice for current drinking should be one of the vintage
years printed in **bold** type. Buy light-type years for further maturing.

oo etc   recommended years that may be currently available
96'etc   vintage regarded as particularly successful for the property
in question
97 etc   years in **bold** should be ready for drinking (those not in bold
will benefit from keeping).
98 etc   vintages in colour are those recommended as first choice for
drinking in 2005. (See also Bordeaux introduction, p.80.)
(o2) etc   provisional rating

The German vintages work on a different principle again: see p.136.

Other abbreviations
DYA   drink the youngest available
NV   vintage not normally shown on label; in Champagne,
means a blend of several vintages for continuity
CHABLIS   properties, areas or terms cross-referred within the section

A quick-reference vintage chart appears on p.286–7

Vintage report 2003

For normally heat-starved northern Europeans, the summer of 2003 came as something of a shock. For day after day, week after week, month after month even, the sun shone. The thermometer rose to heights that made vines flag, and stayed there, with little relief until mid-September. In Bordeaux the extreme heat produced reds that fell into two broad styles: one alcoholic, tannic but light in flavour, from those who picked early; the other riper and far better balanced, from those who waited. Dry whites are rich and rather soft; sweet wines immensely concentrated, and with botrytis to match. A great year for some, an indifferent year for many.

Burgundy at its best is rich, even beefy, though not as beefy as in the Rhône. Generally old vines, with their deeper roots, did better; as they did in Alsace, with grower Olivier Humbrecht MW reporting a difference of three degrees of potential alcohol between adjacent blocks of Riesling, one young and one old. It wasn't a year for botrytis here; nor in the Loire, where there will certainly be sweet wines, but from grapes shrivelled in the heat, and the reds are on a scale unseen in fifty years.

If the fates were on the side of the Loire, they turned their back on Champagne. Frost cut the yield; drought cut it again, and hail, in some places, removed it altogether. Reserve wines will be drawn on heavily in order to keep supplies of non-vintage in the shops; few if any producers will have sufficient quantities of 2003 to venture a vintage wine.

Generally it was a year where late-picking paid off: it benefited from a cooling of temperature, the occasional spot of rain, and greater phenolic ripeness. That is true of Austria, where the weather cooled at the end of August and then turned into an Indian summer; it is true of Italy, where a cooler September helped many a Sangiovese and Cabernet to good ripeness. Germany is crowing about its fine vintage: the hottest since 1540, apparently; and they don't mean twenty to four in the afternoon, either.

Spain's prayers for rain were answered in mid-August, but even so ripening was irregular, and old-fashioned bush-trained vines managed best – which after all is why they were trained like that in the first place. Portugal, possibly praying to different saints, actually managed above-average yields in the Douro.

This was not the case in California, where freak heat was not a problem; the vintage was later than usual here. Australia, which can always be relied upon to produce exciting conditions somewhere, this year had bushfires in parts of Victoria and NSW and, in much of the country, the worst drought in decades followed, in places, by damaging rain. The usual quality hype is slightly muted this year, though more westerly regions had a calmer time of it, and Rutherglen is said to have had an excellent year.

New Zealand had its crop cut by frost, and rain at harvest time meant some emergency picking was necessary; quality seems patchy as a result. Meanwhile Argentina had an El Niño year, but a cool, dry one. Chile is delighted with the quality of its vintage, as is South Africa: "One of the finest of recent vintages", they say.

A closer look at 2002

In much of Europe 2002 was the year of the Great Rain. With the summer of 2003 just behind us it seems difficult to recall all those reports of floods – of whole vineyards, indeed, being washed away – although no doubt the owners of those vineyards remember all too well. It was a year when the European vintage seemed damned by drizzle, cold, and grey skies never to ripen; it seemed set to be the most depressing vintage on record.

In some places it was. If you lived in Piedmont and made your living from Dolcetto or Barbera you had a thin year of it, but Nebbiolo benefited from an Indian summer and turned out remarkably well, slightly more acidic and less powerful than in 2000 or 2001, but still very good. Tuscan reds were more marked by the cold and rain, and the best you can hope for here is ripe tannins and rather light wines. The best whites of the north, though, are very good indeed, with a freshness and balance that are notably lacking in years like 2000. Yields were down, which was no bad thing: in a difficult year it's easier to ripen a small crop than a big one.

A small crop was key in Bordeaux as well, where le tout Bordeaux endured a chilly August on the beaches of Arcachon before returning to their equally dismal vineyards. But then on September 10th the weather changed and an Indian summer began to put some proper ripeness into the grapes. But it came almost too late, which was why the size of the crop was so important. Tannins ripen slowly, and the lateness of the sunshine meant that they only ripened fully if the crop was small and selection rigorous. Big crops meant green tannins, and sometimes over-extracted ones, too, if the winemaking was not cautious. it turned out to be a Cabernet year, with some classic, elegant, balanced wines from the best Médoc appellations; but it's not a year for those who want their tannins absolutely silky-soft and melt-in-the-mouth.

Dry whites did well, though; they are fresh and zippy, not short of acidity, but not short of fruit either. And Sauternes is promising, if mixed in quality because of the erratic advance and spread of botrytis in the vineyards.

Burgundy had a superb year. First tastings of the wines at the beginning of 2004 revealed perfect balance and elegance; wines of great focus and perfume with seductive fruit and texture. One producer describes 2002 as 'a terroir year' for Pinot Noir: the differences between vineyards are particularly marked on the palate. Chardonnay is rich, with good acidity, and extremely seductive young, though it will age well in the medium term.

The Rhône, north and south, had what can only be described as a "difficult" year – though some producers might prefer the word "impossible". The only way to make anything decent at all was by rigorous selection – but in the event the results are surprisingly attractive. They're fairly light, and best drunk young, but the fruit is there, and the balance, too. As always, it will pay to be selective, but it is by no means a year to write off.

The other good news from France is the Loire and Champagne. In the Loire everything did well, from Muscadet to Sancerre

geographically, and from reds to sweet whites style-wise: quite
a coup in a region that normally requires different sorts of years
for different wines. It seems to be a classic vintage year in
Champagne, with the still wines already rich and flavoursome:
producers are comparing it to 1989, 1976, and 1959.

Comparisons were being made with 1976 in Germany, too,
until October rain turned a superb vintage into one that is instead
surprisingly good. It's a Kabinett and Spätlese year, with not much
above that, except for Eiswein, which nearly every region managed
to make.

"Better than expected" is also the verdict in Austria. Somehow,
and usually by means of strict selection and good viticulture,
some very nice wines have emerged from the drenching rains;
nobly rotten sweet wines are particularly good.

Turning to the New World, things went more smoothly in North
America. In California, where flavours are intense and ripe, helped
by a reduction in yields, which was in turn spurred on by a threat
of oversupply.

Australia's stars of this exceptionally cool vintage were Riesling,
and reds from warm, irrigated areas like the Riverland. In South
Australia it was the coldest summer for 100 years; autumn,
thankfully, was warmer, but it was the normally hot regions that
benefited from the chill, with wines having more restrained alcohol
and better acidity than usual. In premium regions like the Adelaide
Hills quality was often excellent, but quantities were way down
because of a difficult flowering. The cool conditions suited the
Barossa, too, where there's more finesse than usual, and Clare
Valley, Yarra Valley, and McLaren Vale also produced very good
flavours. Western Australia was also marked by good acidity and
plenty of aroma, especially from Margaret River. There was bad
news, however, from the Hunter, where only the Semillon seems
to have done well in a scorching summer followed by a soaking
vintage. The Mornington Peninsula had about as small a vintage
as is possible: cold weather during flowering meant that some
estates made no wine at all.

New Zealand revelled in good news. Yields were back to normal
after two thin years, and an Indian summer ensured plenty of
ripeness in both reds and whites.

South Africa had a patchy year, with some areas benefiting
from a cool growing season, which meant lower alcohol than
usual, but then a heatwave fattened up the whites; subsequent
cool weather meant that some late-ripening varieties didn't ripen
as well as they might have done. A cool summer, as one grower
pointed out, is not everything. It's a good year for Sauvignon
Blanc, though.

Chilean reds, at least those from more southerly regions like
Curicó and Maule, can be a bit dilute, thanks to harvest-time rain,
but whites escaped, and in any case the rain only affected certain
parts of the country. Argentina had a very good year, which served
to cheer up an industry afflicted on all sides by the country's
economic problems.

Grape varieties

In the past two decades a radical change has come about in all except the most long-established wine countries: the names of a handful of grape varieties have become the ready reference to wine. In senior wine countries, above all France and Italy (between them producing nearly half the world's wine), more complex traditions prevail. All wine of old prestige is known by its origin, more or less narrowly defined, not just the particular fruit-juice that fermented.

For the present the two notions are in rivalry. Eventually the primacy of place over fruit will become obvious, at least for wines of quality. But for now, for most people, grape tastes are the easy reference-point – despite the fact that they are often confused by the added taste of oak. If grape flavours were really all that mattered this would be a very short book.

But of course they do matter, and a knowledge of them both guides you to flavours you enjoy and helps comparisons between regions. Hence the originally Californian term "varietal wine" – meaning, in principle, from one grape variety.

At least seven varieties – Cabernet Sauvignon, Pinot Noir, Riesling, Sauvignon Blanc, Chardonnay, Gewurztraminer, and Muscat – have tastes and smells distinct and memorable enough to form international categories of wine. To these you can add Merlot, Malbec, Syrah, Semillon, Chenin Blanc, Pinots Blanc and Gris, Sylvaner, Viognier, Nebbiolo, Sangiovese, Tempranillo... The following are the best and/or most popular wine grapes.

Grapes for red wine

Agiorgitiko (St George) Versatile Greek (Nemea) variety with juicy damson fruit and velvety tannins. Sufficient structure for serious ageing.

Baga Bairrada (Portugal) grape. Dark and tannic. Has great potential, but hard to grow.

Barbera Widely grown in Italy, at its best in Piedmont, giving dark, fruity, often sharp wine. Fashionable in California and Australia; promising in Argentina.

Blaufränkisch Mostly Austrian; can be light and juicy but at best (in Burgenland) a considerable red. LEMBERGER in Germany, KEKFRANKOS in Hungary.

Brunello Alias for SANGIOVESE, splendid at Montalcino.

Cabernet Franc, alias Bouchet (Cab Fr) The lesser of two sorts of Cabernet grown in Bordeaux but dominant (as "Bouchet") in St-Emilion. The Cabernet of the Loire, making Chinon, Saumur, Champigny, and rosé. Used for blending with CABERNET SAUVIGNON, etc, or increasingly, alone, in California, Australia.

Cabernet Sauvignon (Cab Sauv) Grape of great character: spicy, herby, tannic, with characteristic blackcurrant aroma. The first grape of the Médoc; also makes most of the best California, South American, East European reds. Vies with Shiraz in Australia. Its wine almost always needs ageing; usually benefits from blending with eg MERLOT, CABERNET FRANC, SYRAH, TEMPRANILLO, SANGIOVESE etc. Makes aromatic rosé.

Cannonau GRENACHE in its Sardinian manifestation: can be very fine, potent.

Carignan In decline in France. Needs low yields, old vines; best in Corbières. Otherwise dull but harmless. Common in North Africa, Spain, and California.

Carmènere An old Bordeaux variety now virtually extinct in France. Widely used in Chile where until recently it was often mistaken for MERLOT.

Cinsault/Cinsaut Usually bulk-producing grape of Southern France; in South Africa crossed with PINOT NOIR to make PINOTAGE. Pale wine, but quality potential.

Dolcetto Source of soft seductive dry red in Piedmont. Now high fashion.

Gamay The Beaujolais grape: light, very fragrant wines, at their best young. Makes even lighter wine in the Loire Valley, in central France, and in Switzerland and Savoie. Known as "Napa Gamay" in California.

Grenache, alias Garnacha, Cannonau Useful grape for strong and fruity but pale wine: good rosé and *vin doux naturel* – especially in the South of France, Spain, and California – but also the mainstay of beefy Priorato. Old-vine versions are prized in South Australia. Usually blended with other varieties (eg in Châteauneuf-du-Pape).

Grignolino Makes one of the good everyday table wines of Piedmont.

Kadarka, alias Gamza Makes healthy, sound, agreeable reds in East Europe.

Kékfrankos Hungarian BLAUFRÄNKISCH; similar lightish reds.

Lambrusco Productive grape of the lower Po Valley, giving quintessentially Italian, cheerful, sweet, and fizzy red.

Lemberger See BLAUFRÄNKISCH. Württemberg's red.

Malbec, alias Côt Minor in Bordeaux, major in Cahors (alias Auxerrois) and especially in Argentina. Dark, dense, tannic wine capable of real quality.

Merlot Adaptable grape making the great fragrant and plummy wines of Pomerol and (with CABERNET FRANC) St-Emilion, an important element in Médoc reds, soft and strong (and à la mode) in California, Washington, Chile, Australia. Lighter but often good in North Italy, Italian Switzerland, Slovenia, Argentina, South Africa, New Zealand etc. Grassy when not fully ripe.

Montepulciano A good central-eastern Italian grape, and a Tuscan town.

Morellino Alias for SANGIOVESE in Scansano, southern Tuscany.

Mourvèdre, alias Mataro Excellent dark aromatic tannic grape used mainly for blending in Provence (but solo in Bandol) and the Midi. Enjoying new interest in, for example, South Australia and California.

Nebbiolo, alias Spanna and Chiavennasca One of Italy's best red grapes; makes Barolo, Barbaresco, Gattinara, and Valtellina. Intense, nobly fruity, perfumed wine but very tannic: improves for years.

Periquita Ubiquitous in Portugal for firm-flavoured reds. Often blended with CABERNET SAUVIGNON and also known as Castelão.

Petit Verdot Excellent but awkward Médoc grape, now increasingly planted in Cabernet areas worldwide for extra fragrance.

Pinot Noir (Pinot N) The glory of Burgundy's Côte d'Or, with scent, flavour, and texture that are unmatched anywhere. Makes light wines rarely of much distinction in Germany, Switzerland, Austria, and Hungary. But now also splendid results in California's Sonoma, Carneros, and Central Coast, as well as Oregon, Ontario, Yarra Valley, Adelaide Hills, Tasmania, and New Zealand's South Island.

Pinotage Singular South African grape (PINOT NOIR X CINSAUT). Can be very fruity and can age interestingly, but often jammy.

Primitivo Southern Italian grape making big, rustic wines, now fashionable because genetically identical to ZINFANDEL.

Refosco In northeast Italy possibly a synonym for Mondeuse of Savoie. Produces deep, flavoursome and age-worthy wines, especially when grown in warmer climates.

Sagrantino Italian grape found in Umbria for powerful cherry-flavoured wines.

Sangiovese (or Sangioveto) Main red grape of Chianti and much of central Italy. Aliases include BRUNELLO and MORELLINO. Interesting in Australia.

Saperavi Makes good, sharp, very long-lived wine in Georgia, Ukraine etc. Blends very well with CAB SAUV (eg in Moldova).

Spätburgunder German for PINOT N. Quality is variable, seldom wildly exciting.

St-Laurent Dark, smooth and full-flavoured Austrian speciality. Also in the Pfalz.

Syrah, alias Shiraz The great Rhône red grape: tannic, purple, peppery wine which matures superbly. Very important as Shiraz in Australia, and under either name in California, Washington State, South Africa, Chile, and elsewhere.

Tannat Raspberry-perfumed, highly tannic force behind Madiran, Tursan, and other firm reds from Southwest France. Also rosé. Now the star of Uruguay.

Tempranillo Aromatic fine Rioja grape, called Ull de Llebre in Catalonia, Cencibel in La Mancha, Tinto Fino in Ribera del Duero, Tinta Roriz in Douro, Aragonez in southern Portugal. Now Australia, too. Very fashionable; elegant in cool climates, beefy in warm. Early ripening.

Touriga Nacional Top port grape grown in the Douro Valley. Also makes full-bodied reds in south Portugal.

Zinfandel (Zin) Fruity adaptable grape of California (though identical to PRIMITIVO) with blackberry-like, and sometimes metallic, flavour. Can be structured and gloriously lush, but also makes "blush" white wine.

Grapes for white wine

Albariño The Spanish name for North Portugal's Alvarinho, making excellent fresh and fragrant wine in Galicia. Both fashionable and expensive in Spain.

Aligoté Burgundy's second-rank white grape. Crisp (often sharp) wine, needs drinking in 1–3 years. Perfect for mixing with cassis (blackcurrant liqueur) to make "Kir". Widely planted in East Europe, especially Russia.

Arinto White central Portuguese grape for crisp, fragrant dry whites.

Arneis Aromatic, high-priced grape, DOC in Roero, Piedmont.

Blanc Fumé Occasional (New World) alias of SAUVIGNON BLANC, referring to its smoky smell, particularly from the Loire (Sancerre and Pouilly). In California used for oak-aged Sauvignon and reversed to "Fumé Blanc". (The smoke is oak.)

Bourboulenc This and the rare Rolle make some of the Midi's best wines.

Bual Makes top-quality sweet madeira wines, not quite so rich as malmsey.

Chardonnay (Chard) The white grape of burgundy, Champagne, and the New World, partly because it is one of the easiest to grow and vinify. All regions are trying it, mostly aged (or, better, fermented) in oak to reproduce the flavours of burgundy. Australia and California make classics (but also much dross). Italy, Spain, New Zealand, South Africa, New York State, Argentina, Chile, Hungary and the Midi are all coming on strong. Called Morillon in Austria.

Chasselas Prolific early-ripening grape with little aroma, mainly grown for eating. AKA Fendant in Switzerland (where it is supreme), Gutedel in Germany.

Chenin Blanc (Chenin Bl) Great white grape of the middle Loire (Vouvray, Layon, etc). Wine can be dry or sweet (or very sweet), but with plenty of acidity. Bulk wine in California, but increasingly serious in South Africa. See also STEEN.

Clairette A low-acid grape, part of many southern French blends.

Colombard Slightly fruity, nicely sharp grape, makes everyday wine in South Africa, California, and Southwest France.

Fendant See CHASSELAS.

Fiano High quality grape giving peachy, spicy wine in Campania.

Folle Blanche High acid/little flavour make this ideal for brandy. Called Gros Plant in Brittany, Picpoul in Armagnac. Also respectable in California.

Furmint A grape of great character: the trademark of Hungary both as the principal grape in Tokáji and as vivid, vigorous table wine with an appley flavour. Called Sipon in Slovenia. Some grown in Austria.

Garganega The best grape in the Soave blend. Top wines, especially sweet ones, age well.

Gewurztraminer, alias Traminer (Gewurz) One of the most pungent grapes, distinctively spicy with aromas like rose petals and grapefruit. Wines are often rich and soft, even when fully dry. Best in Alsace; but also good in Germany (Gewürztraminer), East Europe, Australia, California, Pacific Northwest, and New Zealand.

Grauburgunder See PINOT GRIS.

Grechetto or Greco Ancient grape of central and south Italy noted for the vitality and stylishness of its wine.

Grüner Veltliner Austria's favourite. Around Vienna and in the Wachau and Weinviertel (also in Moravia) it can be delicious: light but dry, peppery and lively. Excellent young, but the best age five years or so.

Hárslevelü Other main grape of Tokáji (with FURMINT). Adds softness and body.

Kéknyelü Low-yielding, flavourful grape giving one of Hungary's best whites. Has the potential for fieriness and spice. To be watched.

Kerner The most successful of recent German varieties, mostly RIESLING X SILVANER, but in this case Riesling x (red) Trollinger. Early-ripening, flowery (but often too blatant) wine with good acidity. Popular in Pfalz, Rheinhessen, etc.

Laski Rizling Grown in northern Italy and Eastern Europe. Much inferior to Rhine RIESLING, with lower acidity, best in sweet wines. Alias Welschriesling, Riesling Italico, Olaszrizling (no longer legally labelled simply "Riesling").

Loureiro The best and most fragrant Vinho Verde variety in Portugal.

Macabeo The workhorse white grape of north Spain, widespread in Rioja (alias Viura) and in Catalan cava country. Good quality potential.

Malvasia A family of grapes rather than a single variety, found all over Italy and Iberia. May be red, white, or pink. Usually plump, soft wine. Malvoisie in France is unrelated.

Marsanne Principal white grape (with ROUSSANNE) of the northern Rhône (eg in Hermitage, St-Joseph, St-Péray). Also good in Australia, California, and (as Ermitage Blanc) the Valais. Soft full wines that age very well.

Moschofilero Good, aromatic pink Greek grape. Makes white or rosé wine.

Müller-Thurgau (Müller-T) Dominant in Germany's Rheinhessen and Pfalz and too common on the Mosel. It was thought to be a cross between RIESLING and Chasselas de Courtellier, but recent studies suggests otherwise. Soft aromatic wines for drinking young. Makes good sweet wines but usually dull, often coarse, dry ones. Should have no place in top vineyards.

Muscadelle Adds aroma to white Bordeaux, especially Sauternes. In Victoria as Tokay it is used (with MUSCAT, to which it is unrelated) for Rutherglen Muscat.

Muscadet, alias Melon de Bourgogne Makes light, refreshing, very dry wines with a seaside tang round Nantes in Brittany.

Muscat (Many varieties; the best is Muscat Blanc à Petits Grains.) Widely grown, easily recognized, pungent grapes, mostly made into perfumed sweet wines, often fortified (as in France's *vins doux naturels*). Superb in Australia. The third element in Tokáji Aszú. Rarely (eg Alsace) made dry.

Palomino, alias Listán Makes all the best sherry but poor table wine.

Pedro Ximénez, alias PX Makes very strong wine in Montilla and Málaga. Used in blending sweet sherries. Also grown in Argentina, the Canaries, Australia, California, and South Africa.

Petit (and Gros) Manseng The secret weapon of the French Basque country: vital for Jurançon; increasingly blended elsewhere in the Southwest.

Pinot Blanc (Pinot Bl) A cousin of PINOT NOIR, similar to but milder than CHARDONNAY: light, fresh, fruity, not aromatic, to drink young. Good for Italian spumante. Grown in Alsace, northern Italy, south Germany, and East Europe. Weissburgunder in Germany. See also MUSCADET.

Pinot Gris (Pinot Gr) At best makes rather heavy, even "thick", full-bodied whites with a certain spicy style. In Germany can be alias Ruländer (sweet) or GRAUBURGUNDER (dry); Pinot Grigio in Italy. Also found in Hungary, Slovenia, Canada, Oregon, New Zealand...

Pinot Noir (Pinot N) Superlative black grape (See p.12) used in Champagne and elsewhere (eg California, Australia) for making white, sparkling, or very pale pink "vin gris".

> ## Riesling (Ries)
> Riesling is making its re-entrance on the world-stage through, as it were, the back door. All serious commentators agree that Riesling stands level with Chardonnay as the world's best white wine grape, though in diametrically opposite style. Chardonnay gives full-bodied but aromatically discreet wines, while Riesling offers a range from steely to voluptuous, always positively perfumed, and with more ageing potential than Chardonnay. Germany makes the greatest Riesling in all styles. Yet its popularity is being revived in, of all places, South Australia, where this cool-climate grape does its best to ape Chardonnay. Holding the middle ground, with forceful but still steely wines, is Austria. While lovers of light and fragrant, often piercingly refreshing Rieslings have the Mosel as their exclusive playground. Also grown in Alsace (but nowhere else in France), Pacific Northwest, Ontario, California, New Zealand, and South Africa.

Roussanne Rhône grape of great finesse, now popping up in California and Australia. Can age well.

Sauvignon Blanc (Sauv Bl) Makes very distinctive aromatic grassy wines, pungent in New Zealand, often mineral in Sancerre, riper in Australia; also good in Rueda, Austria, north Italy, Chile's Casablanca Valley, and South Africa. Blended with SEMILLON in Bordeaux. Can be austere or buxom. May be called BLANC FUMÉ.

Savagnin The grape of *vin jaune* of Savoie: related to TRAMINER?

Scheurebe Spicy-flavoured German RIES x SILVANER (possibly), very successful in Pfalz, especially for Auslese. Can be weedy: must be very ripe to be good.

Semillon (Sem) Contributes the lusciousness to Sauternes and increasingly important for Graves and other dry white Bordeaux. Grassy if not fully ripe, but can make soft dry wine of great ageing potential. Superb in Australia: old Hunter Valley Sem, though light, can be great wine. Promising in New Zealand.

Sercial Makes the driest madeira (where myth used to identify it with RIESLING).

Seyval Blanc (Seyval Bl) French-made hybrid of French and American vines. Very hardy and attractively fruity. Popular and reasonably successful in eastern States and England but dogmatically banned by EU from "quality" wines.

Steen South African alias for CHENIN BLANC, not used for better examples.

Silvaner, alias Sylvaner Germany's former workhorse grape. Rarely fine except in Franken – where it is savoury and ages admirably – and in Rheinhessen and Pfalz, where it is enjoying a renaissance. Good in the Italian Tyrol; now declining in popularity in Alsace. Very good (and powerful) as Johannisberg in the Valais, Switzerland.

Tocai Friulano North Italian grape with a flavour best described as "subtle". No relation to TOKAY, but could be Sauvignonasse (see SAUVIGNON BLANC).

Tokay See PINOT GRIS. Also supposedly Hungarian grape in Australia and a table grape in California. The wine Tokay (Tokáji) is FURMINT, HARSLEVELU and MUSCAT.

Torrontes Strongly aromatic, MUSCAT-like Argentine speciality, usually dry.

Trebbiano Important but mediocre grape of central Italy (Orvieto, Soave etc). Also grown in southern France as Ugni Blanc, and Cognac as St-Emilion. Mostly thin, bland wine; needs blending (and more careful growing).

Ugni Blanc (Ugni Bl) See TREBBIANO.

Verdejo The grape of Rueda in Castile, potentially fine and long-lived.

Verdelho Madeira grape making excellent medium-sweet wine; in Australia, fresh soft dry wine of great character.

Verdicchio Potentially good dry wine in central-eastern Italy.

Vermentino Italian, sprightly with satisfying texture and ageing capacity.

Vernaccia Name given to many unrelated grapes in Italy. Vernaccia di San Gimignano is crisp, lively; Vernaccia di Oristano is sherry-like.

Viognier Ultra-fashionable Rhône grape, finest in Condrieu, less fine but still aromatic in the Midi. Good examples from California and Australia.

Viura See MACABEO.

Welschriesling See LASKI RIZLING.

Wine & food

The dilemma is most acute in restaurants. Four people have chosen different dishes. The host calculates. A bottle of white and then one of red is conventional, regardless of the food. The formula works up to a point. But it can be refined – or replaced with something more original, something to really bring out the flavours of both food and wine.

Remarkably little ink has been spilt on this byway of knowledge, but thirty years of experimentation and the ideas of many friends have gone into making this list. It is perhaps most useful for menu-planning at home. But used with the rest of the book, it may ease menu-stress in restaurants, too. At the very least, it will broaden your mind.

Before the meal – apéritifs

The conventional apéritif wines are either sparkling (epitomized by Champagne) or fortified (epitomized by sherry in Britain, port in France, vermouth in Italy, etc). A glass of white or rosé (or in France red) table wine before eating is presently in vogue. It calls for something light and stimulating, fairly dry but not acidic, with a degree of character; Chenin Blanc or Riesling rather than Chardonnay.

Warning: Avoid peanuts; they destroy wine flavours. Olives are also too piquant for many wines; they need sherry or a Martini. Eat almonds, pistachios or walnuts, plain crisps or cheese straws instead.

First courses

Aïoli A thirst-quencher is needed for its garlic heat. Rhône, sparkling dry white; Provence rosé, Verdicchio.

Antipasti Dry white: Italian (Arneis, Soave, Pinot Grigio, prosecco, Vermentino); light red (Dolcetto, Franciacorta, young Chianti); fino sherry.

Artichoke vinaigrette An incisive dry white: New Zealand Sauv Bl; Côtes de Gascogne or a modern Greek; young red: Bordeaux, Côtes du Rhône. **With hollandaise** Full-bodied slightly crisp dry white: Pouilly-Fuissé, Pfalz Spätlese, or a Carneros or Yarra Valley Chard.

Asparagus A difficult flavour for wine, being slightly bitter, so the wine needs plenty of its own. Sauv Bl echoes the flavour, but needs to be ripe, as in Chile. Sem beats Chard, esp Australian, but Chard works well with melted butter or hollandaise. Alsace Pinot Gr, even dry Muscat is gd, or Jurançon Sec.

Aubergine purée (Melitzanosalata) Crisp New World Sauv Bl eg from South Africa or New Zealand; or modern Greek or Sicilian dry white. Or try Bardolino red or Chiaretto.

Avocado with seafood Dry or slightly sharp white: Rheingau or Pfalz Kabinett, Grüner Veltliner, Wachau Riesling, Sancerre, Pinot Gr; Sonoma or Australian Chard or Sauv Bl, or a dry rosé. Or Chablis Premier Cru. **With vinaigrette** Manzanilla sherry.

Bisques Dry white with plenty of body: Pinot Gr, Chard, Gruner Veltliner. Fino or dry amontillado sherry, or montilla. West Australian Sem.

Boudin Noir (blood sausage) Local Sauv Bl or Chenin Bl – esp in the Loire. Or Beaujolais Cru, esp Morgon.

Bouillabaisse Savoury dry white, Marsanne from the Midi or Rhône, Corsican or Spanish rosé, or Cassis, Verdicchio, South African Sauv Bl.

Caesar Salad Spanish or southern French rosé; but when in Rome... please yourself.

Carpaccio, beef Seems to work well with the flavour of most wines. Top Tuscan is appropriate, but fine Chards are good. So are vintage and pink Champagnes. (See also Carpaccio under Fish.)

Caviar Iced vodka. If you prefer Champagne, it should be full-bodied (eg Bollinger, Krug).

Ceviche Try Australian Riesling or Verdelho; South African or New Zealand Sauv Bl.

Charcuterie Young Beaujolais-Villages, Loire reds such as Saumur, Swiss or Oregon Pinot N. Young Argentine or Italian reds. Sauv Bl can work well too.

Cheese fondue Dry white: Valais Fendant or any other Swiss Chasselas, Roussette de Savoie, Grüner Veltliner, Alsace Ries, or Pinot Gr. Or a Beaujolais Cru.

Chowders Big-scale white, not necessarily bone dry: Pinot Gr, Rhine Spätlese, Albariño, Australian Sem, buttery Chard. Or fino sherry.

Consommé Medium-dry amontillado sherry or sercial madeira.

Crostini Morellino di Scansano, Montepulciano d'Abruzzo, Valpolicella, or a dry Italian white such as Verdicchio or Orvieto.

Crudités Light red or rosé: Côtes du Rhône, Minervois, Chianti, Pinot N; or fino sherry. For whites: Alsace Sylvaner or Pinot Blanc.

Dim-Sum Classically, China tea. For fun: Pinot Grigio or Ries; light red (Bardolino or Sancerre). NV Champagne or good New World fizz.

Eggs See also Soufflés. Difficult: eggs clash with most wines and can spoil good ones. But local wine with local egg dishes is a safe bet. So ★→★★ of whatever is going. Try Pinot Bl or not too oaky Chard. As a last resort I can bring myself to drink Champagne with scrambled eggs.
Quail's eggs Blanc de Blancs Champagne.
Seagull's (or gull's) eggs Mature white burgundy or vintage Champagne.
Oeufs en meurette Burgundian genius: eggs in red wine calls for wine of the same.

Escargots Rhône reds (Gigondas, Vacqueyras), St-Véran, or Aligoté. In the Midi, very good Petits-Gris go with local white, rosé or red. In Alsace, Pinot Bl or Muscat.

Fish terrine Pfalz Ries Spätlese Trocken, Grüner Veltliner, Chablis Premier Cru, Clare Valley Ries, Sonoma Chard; or manzanilla.

Foie gras White. In Bordeaux they drink Sauternes. Others prefer a late-harvest Pinot Gr or Ries (inc New World), Vouvray, Montlouis, Jurançon Moelleux or Gewurz. Tokáji Aszú 5 puttonyos is a Lucullan choice. Old dry amontillado can be sublime. If the foie gras is served hot, mature vintage Champagne. But never Chard or Sauv Bl.

Gazpacho A glass of fino before and after. Or Sauv Bl.

Goat's cheese (warm) Sancerre, Pouilly-Fumé or New World Sauv Bl. Chilled Chinon, Saumur-Champigny, or Provence rosé. Australian sparkling Shiraz or strong east Mediterranean reds: Chateau Musar, Greek, Turkish.

Gravadlax Akvavit or iced sake. Grand Cru Chablis, or California, Washington, or Margaret River Chard, or Mosel Spätlese (not Trocken).

Guacamole California Chard, Sauv Blanc, dry Muscat or NV Champagne. Or Mexican beer.

Haddock, smoked, mousse or brandade A wonderful dish for showing off any stylish full-bodied white, inc Grand Cru Chablis or Chard from Sonoma or New Zealand .

Ham, raw or cured See also Prosciutto. Alsace Grand Cru Pinot Gr or good, crisp Italian Collio white. With Spanish *pata negra* or *jamon*, try fino sherry or tawny port.

Herrings, raw or pickled Dutch gin (young, not aged) or Scandinavian akvavit, and cold beer. If wine is essential, try Muscadet 2003.

Hors d'oeuvres See also Antipasti. Clean, fruity, sharp white: Sancerre or any Sauv Bl, Grüner Veltliner, Hungarian Leanyka, English white wine; or young light red Bordeaux, Rhône, or Corbières. Or fino sherry.

Houmous Pungent, spicy dry white, eg Furmint or modern Greek white.

Mackerel, smoked An oily wine-destroyer. Manzanilla sherry, proper dry Vinho Verde or Schnapps, peppered or bison-grass vodka. Or lager.

Mayonnaise Adds richness that calls for a contrasting bite in the wine. Côte Chalonnaise whites (eg Rully) are good. Try New Zealand Sauv Bl, Verdicchio or a Spätlese Trocken from the Pfalz.

Melon Strong sweet wine (if any): port, bual madeira, Muscat de Frontignan or *vin doux naturel*. Also dry, perfumed Viognier, Fiano di Avellino, or Australian Marsanne.

Minestrone Red: Chianti, Zin, Barbera, Côtes du Rhône, etc. Or fino.

Omelettes See Eggs.

Oysters, raw NV Champagne, Chablis Premier Cru, Muscadet, white Graves, Sancerre, or Guinness.
cooked Puligny-Montrachet, or good New World Chard. Champagne is good with either.

Pasta Red or white according to the sauce or trimmings:
cream sauce Orvieto, Frascati, or Alto Adige Chard.
meat sauce Montepulciano d'Abruzzo, Salice Salentino, or Merlot.
pesto (basil) sauce Barbera, Ligurian Vermentino, New Zealand Sauv Bl, Hungarian Hárslevelü, or Furmint.
seafood sauce (eg vongole) Verdicchio, Soave, top white Rioja, Cirò, or Sauv Bl.
tomato sauce Barbera, south Italian red, Zin, or South Australian Grenache.

Pastrami Alsace Ries, young Sangiovese, or Cab Fr.

Pâté
chicken liver Calls for pungent white (Alsace Pinot Gr or Marsanne), a smooth red like a light Pomerol or Volnay, or even amontillado sherry.
duck pâté Châteauneuf-du-Pape, Cornas, Chianti Classico, or Pomerol.
fish pâté Muscadet, Mâcon-Villages, or Australian Chard (unoaked).
Pâté de campagne A dry white ★★: Gd vin de pays, Graves, Pfalz Ries.

Peperonata Dry Australian Ries, Western Australia Sem or New Zealand

Sauv Bl. Red drinkers can try Tempranillo or Grenache.

Pipérade Navarra rosado, Provence or southern French rosés. Or dry South Australian Ries.

Pimentos, roasted New Zealand Sauv Bl, Spanish Chard, or Valdepeñas.

Pizza Any dry Italian red ★★ or Rioja, Australian Shiraz, southern French red, or Douro red.

Prawns, shrimps or langoustines Fine dry white: burgundy, Graves, New Zealand Chard, Pfalz Ries – even fine mature Champagne.
Indian-, Thai- or Chinese-style Rich Australian Hunter Valley Chard. ("Cocktail sauce" kills wine, and in time, the consumer.)

Prosciutto (also with melon, pears, or figs) Full dry or medium white: Orvieto, Lugana, Chenin Bl, Grüner Veltliner, Tokay Furmint, white Rioja, Australian Sem, or Jurançon Sec.

Quiches Dry full-bodied white: Alsace, Graves, Sauv Bl, dry Rheingau; or young red (Tempranillo, Periquita), according to ingredients.

Risotto, with seafood Pinot Gr from Friuli, Gavi, youngish Sem, Dolcetto, or Barbera d'Alba.
with mushrooms Cahors, Madiran, Barbera, or New World Pinot N.
with fungi porcini Finest mature Barolo or Barbaresco.

Ravioli See Pasta.
with wild mushrooms Dolcetto or Nebbiolo d'Alba, Oregon Pinot N, or red Rioja crianza.

Salade niçoise Very dry, ★★, not too light or flowery white or rosé: Provençal, Rhône, or Corsican; Catalan white; Fernão Pires, Sauv Bl.

Salads As a first course, esp with blue cheese dressing, any dry and appetizing white wine.
NB Vinegar in salad dressings destroys the flavour of wine. If you want salad at a meal with fine wine, dress the salad with wine or a little lemon juice instead of vinegar.

Salami Barbera, top Valpolicella, genuine Lambrusco, young Zin, Tavel or Ajaccio rosé, Vacqueyras, young Bordeaux, young Chilean Cab Sauv.

Salmon, smoked A dry but pungent white: fino sherry, Alsace Pinot Gr, Chablis Grand Cru, Pouilly-Fumé, Pfalz Ries Spätlese, or vintage Champagne. Also vodka, schnapps, or akvavit.

Seafood salad Fresh north Italian Chard or Pinot Gr. Mâcon Blanc, Australian Verdelho, or Clare Valley Ries.

Shark's fin soup Add a teaspoon of Cognac. Sip amontillado.

Shrimps, potted Fino sherry, Chablis, white Rioja, or Long Island Chard.

Soufflés As show dishes these deserve ★★★ wines.
fish Dry white: ★★★ Burgundy, Bordeaux, Alsace, Chard, etc.
cheese Red burgundy or Bordeaux, or mature Cab Sauv.
spinach (tougher on wine) Mâcon-Villages, St-Véran, or Valpolicella. Champagne can also be gd with many kinds of soufflé.

Spinach A challenge here. Can make reds taste of rust. Good Cab Sauvs usually survive, as do neutral whites like unoaked Chard.

Tapenade Manzanilla or fino sherry, or any sharpish dry white or rosé.

Taramasalata A rustic southern white with personality; not necessarily Retsina. Fino sherry works well. Try white Rioja or a Rhône Marsanne. The bland supermarket version goes well with any fine delicate white or Champagne.

Terrine As for Pâté, or similar reds: Mercurey, St-Amour, youngish St-Emilion, Tempranillo, Sangiovese; or Chilean Cab Sauv.

Tortilla Rioja crianza, fino sherry, or white Mâcon-Villages.

Trout, smoked Sancerre, California or South African Sauv Bl. Rully or Bourgogne Aligoté, Chablis or Champagne. But Mosel Spätlese is best.

Vegetable terrine Not a great help to fine wine, but California, Chilean, or South African Chards make a fashionable marriage; Chenin Bl such as Vouvray a lasting one.

Whitebait Crisp dry whites: Chablis, Verdicchio, Greek, Touraine Sauv Bl, or fino sherry.

Fish

Abalone Dry or medium white: Sauv Bl, Côte de Beaune Blanc, Pinot Gr, or Grüner Veltliner. Chinese style: try vintage Champagne.

Anchovies A robust wine: red, white, or rosé – try Rioja or fino sherry.

Beurre blanc, fish with A top-notch Muscadet-sur-lie, a Sauv Bl/ Sem blend, Chablis Premier Cru, Vouvray, or a Rheingau Riesling.

Brandade Chablis or Sancerre Rouge.

Bream (esp baked in a salt crust) Full-bodied white or rosé; Mersault, Rioja, Albariño, Sicily, Côtes de Lubéron, or Minervois.

Brill Very delicate: hence a top fish for fine old Puligny and the like.

Carpaccio of salmon or tuna Puligny-Montrachet, Condrieu, California Chard or New Zealand Sauv Bl.

Cod If roast, a good neutral background for fine dry–medium whites: Chablis, Meursault, Corton-Charlemagne, cru classé Graves, Grüner Veltliner, German Kabinett or dry Spätlesen, or a gd light red, eg Beaune.

Crab, cioppino Sauv Bl; but West Coast friends say Zin. Also California sparkling wine.
cold, with salad Alsace, Austrian, or Rhine Ries, dry Australian Ries, or Condrieu. Show off your favourite white.
softshell Top Chard or top-quality German Ries Spätlese.
Chinese, baked with ginger and onion German Ries Kabinett or Spätlese Halbtrocken. Tokay Furmint or Gewurz.
with Black Bean sauce A big Barossa Shiraz or Syrah.

Eel, jellied NV Champagne or a nice cup of (Ceylon) tea.
smoked Strong/sharp wine: fino sherry or Bourgogne Aligoté. Schnapps.

Fish and chips, fritto misto (or tempura) Chablis, white Bordeaux, Sauv Bl, Pinot Bl, Gavi, fino, montilla, Koshu, tea, or NV Champagne and Cava.

Fish pie (with creamy sauce) Albariño, Soave Classico, Pinot Gr d'Alsace.

Haddock Rich dry whites: Meursault, California or New Zealand Chard, Marsanne, or Albariño.

Hake Sauv Bl or any fresh fruity white: Pacherenc, Tursan, white Navarra.

Halibut As turbot.

Herrings Need a white with some acidity to cut their richness. Rully, Chablis, Bourgogne Aligoté, Greek, or dry Sauv Bl. Or try cider.

Kedgeree Full white, still or sparkling: Mâcon-Villages, South African Chard, or (at breakfast) Champagne.

Kippers A good cup of tea, preferably Ceylon (milk, no sugar). Scotch? Dry oloroso sherry is surprisingly good.

Lamproie à la Bordelaise 5-yr-old St-Emilion or Fronsac. Or Douro reds with Portuguese lampreys.

Lobster, richly sauced Vintage Champagne, fine white burgundy, cru classé Graves, California Chard or Australian Ries, Pfalz Spätlese.
salad NV Champagne, Alsace Ries, Chablis Premier Cru, Condrieu, Mosel Spätlese, Penedès Chard or Cava.

Mackerel Hard or sharp white: Sauv Bl from Touraine, Gaillac, Vinho Verde, white Rioja, or English white wine. Guinness is gd.

Monkfish Often roasted, which needs fuller rather than leaner wines. Try Australian/New Zealand Chard, Oregon Pinot N, or Chilean Merlot.

Mullet, red A chameleon, adaptable to gd white or red, esp Pinot N.

Mullet, grey Verdicchio, Rully, or unoaked Chard.

Mussels Muscadet-sur-lie, Chablis Premier Cru, or Chard.

Perch, sandre Exquisite freshwater fish for finest wines: top white burgundy, Alsace Ries Grand Cru, or noble Mosels. Or try top Swiss Fendant or Johannisberg.

Salmon, seared or grilled Fine white burgundy: Puligny- or Chassagne-Montrachet, Meursault, Corton-Charlemagne, Chablis Grand Cru; Grüner Veltliner, Condrieu, California, Idaho or New Zealand Chard, Rheingau Kabinett/Spätlese, Australian Ries. Young Pinot N can be gd. Salmon fishcakes call for similar, but less grand, wines.

Sand-dabs This sublime fish can handle your fullest Chard (not oaky).

Sardines, fresh grilled Very dry white: Vinho Verde, Soave, Muscadet, or modern Greek.

Sashimi If you are prepared to forego the wasabi, sparkling wines will go, or Washington or Tasmanian Chard, Chablis Grand Cru, Rheingau Ries, English Seyval Bl. Otherwise, iced sake, fino sherry or beer. Trials have matched 5-putt Tokáji with fat tuna, sea urchin, and anago (eel).

Scallops An inherently slightly sweet dish, best with finest whites.
in cream sauces German Spätlese, Montrachet, top Australian Chard, or dry Vouvray.
grilled or seared Hermitage Blanc, Grüner Veltliner, Entre-Deux-Mers, vintage Champagne, or Pinot N.
with Asian seasoning New Zealand, South African Sauv Bl, Verdelho, Australian Ries, or Gewurz.

Sea bass Weissburgunder from Baden or Pfalz. V.gd for any fine or delicate white: Clare Valley dry Ries, Chablis, or Châteauneuf-du-Pape.

Shellfish Dry white with plain boiled shellfish, richer wines with richer sauces. Crab and Ries are part of the Creator's plan. With *plateaux de fruits de mer*: Muscadet, Chablis, unoaked Chard, or dry Ries.

Skate with brown butter White with some pungency (eg Pinot Gr d'Alsace), or a clean straightforward wine like Muscadet or Verdicchio.

Snapper Sauv Bl if cooked with Oriental flavours; white Rhône with Mediterranean flavours.

Sole, plaice, etc: plain, grilled or fried Perfect with fine wines: white burgundy, or its equivalent.
with sauce Depending on the ingredients: sharp dry wine for tomato sauce, fairly rich for sole *véronique* with its sweet grapes, etc.

Sushi Hot wasabi is usually hidden in every piece. German QbA trocken wines, simple Chablis, or NV brut Champ. Or, of course, sake or beer.

Swordfish Full-bodied dry white of the country. Nothing grand.

Trout Delicate white wine, eg Mosel (Saar or Ruwer), Alsace Pinot Bl.
Tuna, grilled or seared White, red, or rosé of fairly fruity character; a top St-Véran, white Hermitage, or Côtes du Rhône would be fine. Pinot N or a light Merlot are the best reds to try.

Turbot Serve with your best rich dry white: Meursault or Chassagne-Montrachet, mature Chablis or its California, Australian or New Zealand equivalent. Condrieu. Mature Rheingau, Mosel or Nahe Spätlese or Auslese (not trocken).

Meat, poultry, etc

Barbecues The local wine would be Australian. Or south Italian, Tempranillo, Zin, or Argentine Malbec. Bandol for a real treat.

Beef, boiled Red: Bordeaux (Bourg or Fronsac), Roussillon, Gevrey-Chambertin, or Côte-Rôtie. Medium-ranking white burgundy is gd, eg. Auxey-Duresses. Or top-notch beer. Mustard softens tannic reds, and horseradish kills everything – but can be worth the sacrifice.
roast Ideal partner for fine red wine of any kind, esp Cab Sauv.

Beef stew Sturdy red: Pomerol or St-Emilion, Hermitage, Cornas, Barbera, Shiraz, Napa Cab Sauv, Ribera del Duero, or Douro red.

Beef Stroganoff Dramatic red: Barolo, Valpolicella Amarone, Cahors, Hermitage, late-harvest Zin – even Moldovan Negru de Purkar.

Boudin Blanc Loire Chenin Bl, esp when served with apples: dry Vouvray, Saumur, or Savennières. Mature red Côtes de Beaune, if without apple.

Cajun food Works well with Fleurie, Brouilly, or Sauv Bl. With gumbo: amontillado or Mexican beer.

Cassoulet Red from Southwest France (Gaillac, Minervois, Corbières, St-Chinian, or Fitou), or Shiraz. But best of all is Beaujolais Cru or young Tempranillo.

Chicken/turkey/guinea fowl, roast Virtually any wine, inc very best bottles of dry to medium white and finest old reds (esp burgundy). The meat of fowl can be adapted with sauces to match almost any fine wine

(eg *coq au vin* with red or white burgundy). Try sparkling Shiraz with strong, sweet, or spicy stuffings and trimmings.
Chicken Kiev Alsace or Pfalz Ries, Hungarian Furmint, young Pinot N.

Chilli con carne Young red: Beaujolais, Zin, or Argentine Malbec.

Chinese Food
Canton or Peking style Dry to medium-dry white – Mosel Ries Kabinett or Spätlese trocken – can be gd throughout a Chinese banquet. Gewurz is often suggested but rarely works (but brilliant with ginger), yet Chasselas and Pinot Gr are attractive alternatives. Dry or off-dry sparkling (esp cava) cuts the oil and matches sweetness. Eschew sweet and sour dishes but try St-Emilion ★★ (or Le Pin?), New World Pinot N, or Châteauneuf-du-Pape with duck. I often serve both white and red wines concurrently during Chinese meals. Champagne is popular.
Szechuan style Verdicchio, Alsace Pinot Blanc, or very cold beer.

Choucroute garni Alsace Pinot Blanc, Pinot Gris, Ries, or beer.

Cold meats Generally better with full-flavoured white than red. Mosel Spätlese or Hochheimer and Côte Chalonnaise are v.gd, as is Beaujolais. Leftover cold beef with leftover Champagne is bliss.

Confit d'oie/de canard Young tannic red Bordeaux Cru Bourgeois, California Cab Sauv and Merlot, and Priorato all cut the richness. Choose Alsace Pinot Gr or Gewurz to match it.

Coq au vin Red burgundy. In an ideal world, one bottle of Chambertin in the dish, two on the table.

Curry see Indian Food.

Duck or goose Rather rich white: Pfalz Spätlese or off-dry Alsace Grand Cru. Or mature gamey red: Morey-St-Denis, Côte-Rôtie, Bordeaux, or burgundy. With oranges or peaches, the Sauternais propose drinking Sauternes, others Monbazillac or Ries Auslese.
Peking See Chinese Food.
wild duck Big-scale red such as Hermitage, Bandol, California or South African Cab Sauv, or Barossa Shiraz – Grange if you can find it.
with olives Top-notch Chianti or other Tuscans.

Frankfurters German Ries, Beaujolais, or light Pinot N. Or Budweiser (Budvar) beer.

Game Birds, young birds plain-roasted The best red wine you can afford.
older birds in casseroles Red (Gevrey-Chambertin, Pommard, Santenay or Grand Cru St-Emilion, Napa Valley Cab Sauv, or Rhône.
well-hung game Vega Sicilia, great red Rhône, Lebanon's Chateau Musar.
cold game Mature vintage Champagne.

Game pie, hot Red: Oregon Pinot N.
cold Gd quality white burgundy, cru Beaujolais, or Champagne.

Goulash Flavoursome young red such as Hungarian Zin, Uruguayan Tannat, Morellino di Scansano, or a young Australian Shiraz.

Grouse See Game Birds – but push the boat right out.

Haggis Fruity red, eg young claret, Châteauneuf-du-Pape, or New World Cab Sauv. Or of course malt whisky.

Ham Softer red burgundies: Volnay, Savigny, Beaune; Chinon or Bourgueil; sweetish German white (Rhine Spätlese); Czech Frankovka; lightish Cab Sauv (eg Chilean), or California Pinot N. And don't forget the heaven-made match of Spanish *jamon* and sherry.

Hamburger Young red: Beaujolais or Australian Cab Sauv, Chianti, or Zin. Or Coke or Pepsi (not "Diet", but "Max").

Hare Jugged hare calls for flavourful red: not-too-old burgundy or Bordeaux, Rhône (eg Gigondas), Bandol, Barbaresco, Ribero del Duero, or Rioja Reserva. The same for saddle. Australia's Grange would be an experience.

Indian Food Medium-sweet white, very cold: Orvieto Abboccato, South African Chenin Bl, Alsace Pinot Bl, Indian sparkling, cava and NV Champagne. Or emphasize the heat with a tannic Barolo or Barbaresco, or deep-flavoured reds such as Châteauneuf-du-Pape, Cornas, Australian Grenache or Mourvèdre, or Valpolicella Amarone.

Kebabs Vigorous red: modern Greek, Corbières, Chilean Cab Sauv, Zinfandel, or Barossa Shiraz. If lots of garlic, then Sauv Bl.

Kidneys Red: St-Emilion or Fronsac: Nuits-St-Georges, Cornas, Barbaresco, Rioja, Spanish or Australian Cab Sauv, or top Alentejo.

Lamb, roast One of the traditional and best partners for v.gd red Bordeaux – or its Cab Sauv equivalents from the New World, esp Napa and Coonawarra. In Spain, the partner of the finest old Rioja and Ribera del Duero Reservas. New Zealand Pinot N for spicy lamb dishes. **cutlets or chops** As for roast lamb, but a little less grand.

Liver Choose a young red: Beaujolais-Villages, St-Joseph, Médoc, Italian Merlot, Breganze Cab Sauv, Zin, or Portuguese Bairrada. **Calf's** Red Rioja crianza, Salice Salentino Riserva, or Fleurie.

Meatballs Tangy medium-bodied red: Mercurey, Crozes-Hermitage, Madiran, Morellino di Scansano, Langhe Nebbiolo, Zin, Cab Sauv.

Spicy Middle-Eastern style Simple, crisp dry white, or rustic red.

Moussaka Red or rosé: Naoussa from Greece, Sangiovese, Corbières, Côtes de Provence, Ajaccio, or New Zealand Pinot N.

Osso buco Low tannin, supple red, such as Dolcetto d'Alba or Pinot N. Or dry Italian whites such as Soave and Lugana.

Oxtail Match with a rather rich red such as St-Emilion, Pomerol, Pommard, Nuits-St-Georges, Barolo, or Rioja Reserva, Ribera del Duero, California or Coonawarra Cab Sauv, or Châteauneuf-du-Pape.

Paella Young Spanish red, dry white, or rosé from Penedès, Somontano, Navarra, or Rioja.

Pigeons Lively reds: Savigny, Chambolle-Musigny; Crozes-Hermitage, Chianti Classico, or California Pinot N. Or try Franken Silvaner Spätlese.

Pork, roast A good rich neutral background to a fairly light red or rich white. It deserves ★★ treatment – Médoc is fine. Portugal's suckling pig is eaten with Bairrada Garrafeira. Chinese is gd with Pinot N.

Pot au feu, bollito misto, cocido Rustic red wines from the region of origin; Sangiovese di Romagna, Chusclan, Lirac, Rasteau, Portuguese Alentejo, or Yecla and Jumilla from Spain.

Quail As for squab. Carmignano, Rioja Reserva, mature claret, or Pinot N.

Rabbit Lively medium-bodied young Italian red or Aglianico del Vulture; Chiroubles, Chinon, Saumur-Champigny, or Rhône rosé. Le Pin in France.

Satay Australia's McLaren Vale Shiraz. Gewurz from Alsace or New Zealand.

Sauerkraut (German) Lager or Pils. But a Ries Auslese can be amazing.

Sausages See also Frankfurters, Salami. The British banger requires a young Malbec from Argentina (a red wine, anyway), or a traditional British ale.

Shepherd's pie Rough-and-ready red seems most appropriate, such as Sangiovese di Romagna. But beer or dry cider is the real McCoy.

Squab Fine white or red burgundy, Alsace Ries Grand Cru, or mature claret.

Steak
au poivre A fairly young Rhône red or Cab Sauv.
tartare Vodka or light young red: Beaujolais, Bergerac, or Valpolicella.
Korean Yuk Whe (The world's best steak tartare) Sake.
filet or tournedos Any red (but not old wines with Béarnaise sauce: top Californian Chard is better). My choice: Château Haut-Brion.
T-bone Reds of similar bone structure: Barolo, Hermitage, Australian Cab Sauv or Shiraz.
fiorentina (bistecca) Chianti Classico Riserva or Brunello.

Steak and kidney pie or pudding Red Rioja Reserva, Douro red, or mature Bordeaux.

Stews and casseroles Red burgundy comes into its own; otherwise lusty full-flavoured red, such as young Côtes du Rhône, Toro, Corbières, Barbera, Shiraz, or Zin.

Sweetbreads A grand dish, so grand wine, but not too dry: Rhine Ries or Franken Silvaner Spätlese, top Alsace Pinot Gr, or Condrieu, depending on the sauce.

Tagine These vary enormously, but fruity young reds are a gd bet: Beaujolais, Tempranillo, Sangiovese, Merlot, and Shiraz.

Tandoori chicken Sauv Bl, young red Bordeaux or light north Italian red served cool. Also cava or NV Champagne.

Tapas Perfect with fino sherry, which can cope with the wide range of flavours in both hot and cold dishes.

Thai food Ginger and lemongrass call for pungent Sauv Bl (Loire, South Africa, Australia, New Zealand) or Ries (German Spätlese or Australian).
coconut milk Hunter Valley or other ripe, oaked Chards; Alsace Pinot Bl for refreshment; Gewurz or Verdelho. And of course cava or NV Champagne.

Tongue Gd for any red or white of abundant character, esp Italian. Also Beaujolais, Loire reds, and full dry rosés.

Tripe Red (eg Corbières, Roussillon) or rather sweet white (eg German Spätlese). Better: Western Australian Sem/Chard, or cut with pungent dry white such as Pouilly-Fumé or fresh red such as Saumur-Champigny.

Veal, roast A good neutral background dish for any fine old red which may have faded with age (eg a Rioja Reserva), a German or Austrian Ries, or Vouvray, or Alsace Pinot Gr.

Venison Big-scale reds inc Mourvèdre – solo as in Bandol, or in blends – Rhône, Bordeaux or California Cab of a mature vintage; or rather rich whites (Pfalz Spätlese or Alsace Pinot Gr).

Vitello tonnato Full-bodied whites esp Chard; or light reds (eg young Bordeaux or Valpolicella) served cool.

Vegetarian dishes

Baked aubergine, lentil or mushroom dishes Sturdy reds such as Corbières, Zin, or Shiraz.

Baked pasta dishes Pasticcio, lasagne and cannelloni with elaborate vegetarian fillings and sauces: an occasion to show off a grand wine, esp finest Tuscan red, but also claret and burgundy.

Bubble-and-squeak Beer, stout, or Beaujolais-Villages Nouveau.

Cabbage, stuffed Try with Hungarian Cab Fr/Kadarka or village Rhônes. Salice Salentino, Primitivo, and other spicy south Italian reds also work well. Or Argentine Malbec.

Cauliflower cheese Crisp aromatic white: Sancerre, Ries Spätlese, Muscat, English Seyval Bl, or Schönburger.

Couscous with vegetables Young red with a bite: Shiraz, Corbières, Minervois, or well chilled rosé from Navarra or Somontano. Or try a robust Moroccan red.

Fennel-based dishes Sauv Bl: Pouilly-Fumé or one from New Zealand; English Schönburger or Seyval Blanc, or a Beaujolais.

Grilled Mediterranean vegetables Brouilly, Barbera, Greco di Tufo, or Shiraz .

Mezze A selection of hot and cold vegetable dishes. Sparkling is a gd all-purpose choice, as is rosé from the Languedoc or Provence. Fino sherry is in its element.

Mushrooms (in most contexts) Fleshy red; eg Pomerol, California Merlot, Rioja Reserva, top Burgundy or Vega Sicilia.
on toast Your best claret. Or even port.
wild mushroom risotto (ceps/porcini are best for wine) Ribera del Duero, Barolo or Chianti Rufina, or top claret: Pauillac or St-Estèphe.

Onion/leek tart Fruity off-dry or dry white: Alsace Pinot Gr or Gewurz, Canadian or New Zealand Ries, English whites, Jurançon, Australian Ries. Or Beaujolais or Loire red.

Peppers or aubergines (eggplant), stuffed Vigorous red wine: Nemea, Italian Chianti or Dolcetto, California Zin, Bandol, or Vacqueyras.

Pumpkin/Squash ravioli or risotto Full-bodied fruity dry or off-dry white: Viognier or Marsanne, demi-sec Vouvray, Gavi, or South African Chenin Bl.

Ratatouille Vigorous young red: Chianti, New Zealand Cab Sauv or Merlot; young red Bordeaux, Gigondas, or Coteaux du Languedoc.

Spiced vegetarian dishes See under Indian Food, Thai Food.

Spinach, ricotta and pasta bake/Spanacopitta Valpolicella (its bitterness helps); Greco di Molise, or white Sicilian/Sardinian.

Desserts

Apple pie, strudel, or tarts Sweet German, Austrian, Loire white, Tokáji Aszú, or Canadian Ice Wine.

Apples, Cox's Orange Pippins Vintage port (55 60 63 66 70 75 82).

Bread-and-butter pudding Fine 10-yr-old Barsac, Tokáji Azsú, or Australian botrytized Sem.

Cakes and gâteaux See also Chocolate, Coffee, Ginger, and Rum. Bual or malmsey madeira; oloroso or cream sherry.

Cheesecake Sweet white: Vouvray or Anjou or fizz, refreshing but nothing special.

Chocolate Generally only powerful flavours can compete. California Orange Muscat, Bual, Tokáji Aszú, Australian Liqueur Muscat, 10-yr-old tawny port; Asti for light, fluffy mousses. Experiment with rich, ripe reds: Syrah, Zin, even sparkling Shiraz. Médoc can match bitter black chocolate. Banyuls for a weightier partnership. Or a tot of good rum.

Christmas pudding, mince pies Tawny port, cream sherry, or liquid Christmas pudding itself, Pedro Ximénez sherry. Asti or Banyuls.

Coffee flavours Sweet Muscat inc Australia liqueur or Tokáji Aszú.

Creams, custards, fools, syllabubs See also Chocolate, Coffee, Ginger, and Rum. Sauternes, Loupiac, Ste-Croix-du-Mont, or Monbazillac.

Crème brûlée Sauternes or Rhine Beerenauslese, best Madeira or Tokáji. (With concealed fruit, a more modest sweet wine.)

Crêpes Suzette Sweet Champagne, Orange Muscat, or Asti spumante.

Fruit
fresh Sweet Coteaux du Layon or light sweet Muscat.
poached Sweet Muscatel: try Muscat de Beaumes- de-Venise, Moscato di Pantelleria, or Spanish dessert Tarragona.
dried fruit (and compotes) Banyuls, Rivesaltes, or Maury.
flans and tarts Sauternes, Monbazillac, or sweet Vouvray or Anjou.
salads A fine sweet sherry or any Muscat-based wine.

Ginger flavours Sweet Muscats, New World botrytized Ries and Sem.

Ice-cream and sorbet Fortified wine (Australian liqueur Muscat, Banyuls); sweet Asti spumante or sparkling Moscato. Amaretto liqueur with vanilla; rum with chocolate.

Lemon flavours For dishes like **Tarte au Citron**, sweet Ries from Germany or Austria, or Tokáji Aszú; the sharper the lemon, the sweeter the wine.

Meringues Recioto di Soave, Asti or Champagne doux.

Mille-feuille Delicate sweet sparkling white such as Moscato d'Asti or demi-sec Champagne.

Nuts Finest oloroso sherry, madeira, vintage or tawny port (nature's match for **walnuts**), Vin Santo, or Setúbal Moscatel.

Orange flavours Experiment with old Sauternes, Tokáji Aszú, or California Orange Muscat.

Panettone Jurançon moelleux, late-harvest Ries, Barsac, or Tokáji Aszú.

Pears in red wine A pause before the port. Or try Rivesaltes, Banyuls, or Ries Beerenauslese.

Pecan pie Orange Muscat or Australian liqueur Muscat.

Raspberries (no cream, little sugar) Excellent with fine reds which themselves taste of raspberries: young Juliénas, Regnié, even Pomerol.

Rum flavours (baba, mousses, ice-cream) Muscat – from Asti to Australian liqueur, according to weight of dish.

Strawberries and cream Sauternes or similar sweet Bordeaux, Vouvray Moelleux (90), or Jurançon Vendange Tardive.

Strawberries, wild (no cream) Serve with red Bordeaux (most exquisitely Margaux) poured over.

Summer pudding Fairly young Sauternes of a gd vintage (89 90 95 96 97).

Sweet soufflés Sauternes or Vouvray moelleux. Sweet (or rich) Champagne.

Tiramisú This Italian dessert works best with Vin Santo, but also with young tawny port, Muscat de Beaumes-de-Venise, or Sauternes and Australian liqueur Muscats.

Trifle Should be sufficiently vibrant with its internal sherry.

Zabaglione Light-gold marsala, Australian botrytized Sem, or Asti.

Wine & cheese

The notion that wine and cheese were married in heaven is not born out by experience. Fine red wines are slaughtered by strong cheeses: only sharp or sweet white wines survive. Principles to remember, despite exceptions, are first: the harder the cheese the more tannin the wine can have. And second: the creamier the cheese is the more acidity is needed in the wine. The main exception constitutes a third principle: wines and cheeses of a region usually sympathise. Cheese is classified by its texture and the nature of its rind, so its appearance is a guide to the type of wine to match it. Individual cheeses mentioned below are only examples taken from the hundreds sold in good cheese shops.

Fresh, no rind – cream cheese, crème fraîche, Mozzarella
Light crisp white – Simple Bordeaux Blanc, Bergerac, English unoaked whites; or rosé – Anjou, Rhône; or very light, very young, very fresh red such as Bordeaux, Bardolino, or Beaujolais.

**Hard cheeses, waxed or oiled, often showing marks from cheesecloth –
Gruyère family, Manchego and other Spanish cheeses, Parmesan, Cantal, Comté, old Gouda, Cheddar and most "traditional" English cheeses**
Particularly hard to generalize here; Gouda, Gruyère, some Spanish, and a few English cheeses complement fine claret or Cab Sauv and great Shiraz/Syrah wines. But strong cheeses need less refined wines, and preferably local ones. Sugary, granular old Dutch red Mimolette or Beaufort are good for finest mature Bordeaux. Also for Tokáji Aszú.

Blue cheeses Roquefort can be wonderful with Sauternes, but don't extend the idea to other blues. It is the sweetness of Sauternes, esp aged, which complements the saltiness. Stilton and port, preferably tawny, is a classic. Intensely flavoured old oloroso, amontillado, madeira, marsala, and other fortified wines go with most blues. The acidity of Tokáji Aszú also works well.

Natural rind (goat's or sheep's cheese) with bluish-grey mould (the rind is wrinkled when mature), sometimes dusted with ash – St-Marcellin Sancerre, Valençay, light fresh Sauv Bl, Jurançon, Savoie, Soave, Italian Chard, or English whites.

Bloomy rind soft cheeses, pure white rind if pasteurized, or dotted with red: Brie, Camembert, Chaource, Bougon (goat's milk 'Camembert') Full dry white burgundy or Rhône if the cheese is white and immature; powerful, fruity St-Emilion, young Australian (or Rhône) Shiraz/ Syrah, or Grenache if it's mature.

Washed-rind pungent soft cheeses, with rather sticky orange-red rind – Langres, mature Epoisses, Maroilles, Carré de l'Est, Milleens, Munster Local reds, esp for Burgundy cheeses; vigorous Languedoc, Cahors, Côtes du Frontonnais, Corsican, southern Italian, Sicilian, or Bairrada. Also powerful whites, esp Alsace Gewurz and Muscat.

Semi-soft cheeses, grey-pink thickish rind – Livarot, Pont l'Evêque, Reblochon, Tomme de Savoie, St-Nectaire Powerful white Bordeaux, Chard, Alsace Pinot Gr, dryish Ries, southern Italian and Sicilian whites, aged white Rioja, or dry oloroso sherry. But the strongest of these cheeses kill most wines.

Food & finest wine

With very special bottles, the wine sometimes guides the choice of food rather than the usual way around. The following suggestions are based largely on the gastronomic conventions of the wine regions producing these treasures, plus much diligent research. They should help bring out the best in your best wines.

Red wines

Red Bordeaux and other Cabernet Sauvignon-based wines (very old, light and delicate: eg pre-60)
Leg or rack of young lamb, roast with a hint of herbs (but not garlic); entrecôte; roast partridge or grouse, sweetbreads; or cheese soufflé after the meat has been served.

Fully mature great vintages (eg Bordeaux 59 61 70) Shoulder or saddle of lamb, roast with a touch of garlic, roast ribs, or grilled rump of beef.

Mature but still vigorous (eg 82 85 86 89) Shoulder or saddle of lamb (inc kidneys) with rich sauce. Fillet of beef *marchand de vin* (with wine and bone-marrow). Avoid Beef Wellington: pastry dulls the palate.

Merlot-based Bordeaux (Pomerol, St-Emilion) Beef as above (fillet is richest) or venison.

Côte d'Or red burgundy (Consider the weight and texture, which grow lighter/more velvety with age. Also the character of the wine: Nuits is earthy, Musigny flowery, great Romanées can be exotic, Pommard renowned for its four-squareness, etc.) Roast chicken, or better, capon, is a safe standard with red burgundy; guinea-fowl for slightly stronger wines, then partridge, grouse, or woodcock for those progressively more rich and pungent. Hare and venison (*chevreuil*) are alternatives.
great old reds The classic Burgundian formula is cheese: Epoisses (unfermented). A fabulous cheese but a terrible waste of fine old wines.
vigorous younger burgundy Duck or goose roasted to minimize fat.

Great Syrahs: Hermitage, Côte-Rôtie, Grange; or Vega Sicilia
Beef, venison, well-hung game; bone-marrow on toast; English cheese (esp best farm Cheddar) but also the newer hard goat's milk and ewe's milk cheeses such as Berkswell and Ticklemore.

Rioja Gran Reserva, Pesquera... Richly flavoured roasts: wild boar, mutton, saddle of hare, or whole suckling pig.

Barolo, Barbaresco Risotto with white truffles; pasta with game sauce (eg *pappardelle alle lepre*); porcini mushrooms; Parmesan.

White wines

Very good Chablis, white burgundy, other top quality Chards White fish simply grilled or *meunière*. Dover sole, turbot, halibut are best; brill, drenched in butter, can be excellent. (Sea bass is too delicate; salmon passes but does little for the finest wine.)

Supreme white burgundy (Le Montrachet, Corton-Charlemagne) or equivalent Graves Roast veal, organic chicken stuffed with truffles or herbs under the skin, or sweetbreads; richly sauced white fish or scallops as above. Or lobster or wild salmon.

Condrieu, Château-Grillet or Hermitage Blanc Very light pasta scented with herbs and tiny peas or broad beans.

Grand Cru Alsace
Ries Truite au bleu, smoked salmon or choucroute garni.
Pinot Gris Roast or grilled veal.
Gewurztraminer Cheese soufflé (Münster cheese).
Vendange Tardive Foie gras or Tarte Tatin.

Sauternes Simple crisp buttery biscuits (eg Langue-de-Chat), white peaches, nectarines, strawberries (without cream). Not tropical fruit. Pan-seared foie-gras. Experiment with blue cheeses.

Supreme Vouvray moelleux, etc Buttery biscuits, apples, or apple tart.

Beerenauslese/Trockenbeerenauslese Biscuits, peaches, greengages. Desserts made from rhubarb, gooseberries, quince, or apples.

Tokáji Aszú (4–6 putts) Foie gras is thoroughly recommended. Fruit desserts, cream desserts, even chocolate can be wonderful.

Great vintage port or madeira Walnuts or pecans. A Cox's Orange Pippin and a digestive biscuit is a classic English accompaniment.

Old vintage Champagne (not Blanc de Blancs) As an apéritif, or with cold partridge, grouse, or woodcock.

France

More heavily shaded areas
are the wine growing regions

The following abbreviations
of regional names
are used in the text:

Al   Alsace
Beauj   Beaujolais
Burg   Burgundy
B'x   Bordeaux
Champ   Champagne
Lo   Loire
Prov   Provence
Pyr   Pyrenees
N/S Rh   North/South Rhône
SW   Southwest

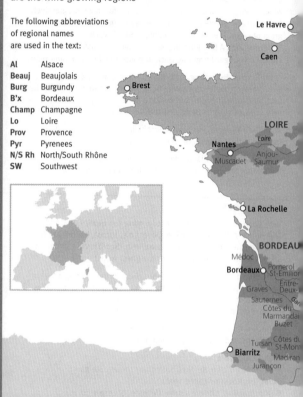

Le Havre

Caen

Brest

LOIRE

Loire

Nantes
Muscadet   Anjou-
                  Saumur

La Rochelle

BORDEAU

Médoc
Bordeaux   Pomerol
                  St-Emilion
                  Entre-
Graves   Deux-
Sauternes
                  Côtes du
                  Marmandai
                  Buzet

                  Côtes du
Tursan   St-Mom
Biarritz   Madiran
Jurançon

France is beginning to realize that it can afford to rest on its laurels
no longer. It is not just Australia that France has to watch but Chile,
Argentina, New Zealand, the USA, and South Africa. Quality and value
are uppermost in the mind of the 21st century wine consumer. Former
loyalties cannot be relied upon. The New World emulates the best of
France at almost all levels. However sublime the best French wines, the
fonctionnaires who run the system of Appellations Contrôlées (AC) must
abandon nit-picking restrictions and apply their minds to quality. The
danger of fossilization combined with commercialization is a sombre
prospect. The French genius for taste and style is on trial.

Appellations remain the key to French wine. An appellation defines
a type. It may apply to a single small vineyard or to a large district.

Burgundy, on the whole, has the most precise and smallest appellations, Bordeaux the widest and most general.

An appellation is the first thing to look for on a label, but more important still is the name of the winemaker. The best growers' and merchants' names are a vital ingredient of these pages. Regions without the overall quality and traditions required for an appellation can be ranked as *vins délimités de qualité supérieure* (VDQS), a shrinking category as its members gain AC status. Their place is being taken by the relatively new and highly successful *vins de pays*. *Vins de pays* are almost always worth trying. They include some brilliant originals and often offer France's best value for money – which still, despite all the competition, can mean the world's.

Recent vintages of the French classics

Red Bordeaux

Médoc/red Graves For some wines bottle-age is optional: for these it is indispensable. Minor châteaux from light vintages need only 2 or 3 years, but even modest wines of great years can improve for 15 or so, and the great châteaux of these years need double that time.

2003 Hottest summer on record. Some stress in the vineyards, but Cabernet Sauvignon looks tremendous. Rich, powerful wines to keep. Yields down.

2002 Saved by a dry, sunny Sept. The later-ripening Cabernet Sauvignon benefited most. Yields down. Some very good wines if selective.

2001 A cool Sept and rain at vintage meant Cabernet Sauvignon had difficulty in ripening fully. Some fine fresh wines to drink 2005–2012.

2000 Late flowering and a somewhat damp start to the summer looked worrying but the final product is outstanding – superb wines throughout. Keep.

1999 Vintage rain again diluted ripe juice, useful wines to drink now–2015.

1998 Rain at vintage *again*. But Aug heat ripened (even roasted) grapes. Good to very good. Drink 2006–2015.

1997 Uneven flowering and summer rain were a double challenge. Cabernet Sauvignon ripened best. Some good wines for the canny. Drink now–2010.

1996 Cool summer, fine harvest. Good to excellent. Drink 2006–2020.

1995 Heatwave and drought; saved by rain. Good to excellent. Now–2020+.

1994 Hopes of a supreme year; then heavy vintage rain. The best good, but be careful. Drink now–2010.

1993 Ripe grapes but a wet vintage. Attractive drinking now–2008.

1992 Rain at flowering, in Aug and at vintage. A huge crop; light wines, but some easy-drinking. Drink up.

1991 Frost in April halved crop and rain interrupted vintage. The northern Médoc did best. Drink soon. Now–2010?

1990 A paradox: a drought year with a threat of over-production. Self-discipline was essential. Its results are magnificent. To 2020+.

1989 Early spring, splendid summer. The top wines will be classics of the ripe, dark kind with elegance and length. Small chateaux uneven. To 2020.

1988 Generally very good; tannic, balanced, beginning to open. Keep top wines. To 2010.

1987 Much more enjoyable than seemed likely. Drink up.

1986 Another splendid, huge, heatwave harvest. A long-term prospect to 2020.

1985 Very good vintage, in a heatwave. Very fine wines now–2010.

1984 Poor. Originally overpriced. Avoid.

1983 A classic vintage, but many wines need drinking. To 2010 for the best.

1982 Huge, rich, strong wines are developing unevenly. Top will run to 2015.

1981 Admirable despite rain. Not rich, now a touch austere. Now–2005.

1980 Small late harvest: ripe but rained-on. Drink up.

Older fine vintages: 75 70 66 62 61 59 55 53 49 48 47 45 29 28.

St-Emilion/Pomerol

2003 Merlot suffered in the heat, but exceptional Cabernet Franc. Mixed.

2002 Sunny Sept but problems with rot and ripeness. Modest to good.

2001 Less rain than Médoc during vintage. Some powerful Merlot, but variable.

2000 Similar conditions to Médoc. Less kind to Merlot but a very good vintage.

1999 Careful, lucky growers made excellent wines but rain was again a problem.

1998 Earlier-ripening Merlot largely escaped the rain. Some excellent wines.

1997 Merlot suffered in the rain, but good for supple wines. Now–2010.

1996 Cool, fine summer. Vintage rain. Less consistent than Médoc. Now–2015.

1995 Perhaps even better than Médoc/Graves. Now–2015.
1994 Very good, especially Pomerol. Now–2015.
1993 Pomerol better than Médoc; good despite terrible vintage weather.
1992 Very dilute but some charming wines to drink quickly. Drink up.
1991 A sad story. Many wines not released.
1990 Another chance to make great wine or a lot of wine. Now–2020.
1989 Large, ripe, early harvest; an overall triumph. To 2020.
1988 Generally excellent. But some châteaux over-produced. Now–2005.
1987 Some very adequate wines (especially in Pomerol). Drink up.
1986 A prolific vintage; but top St-Emilions have a long life ahead.
1985 One of the great years, with a long future. To 2010+.
1984 A sad story. Most of the crop wiped out in spring. Avoid.
1983 Less impressive than it seemed. Drink soon.
1982 Enormously rich and concentrated wines, most excellent. Drink soon.
1981 A very good vintage, though not as great as it first seemed. Now or soon.
1979 A rival to 78, but not developing as well as hoped. Drink now.
1978 Fine wines, but some lack flesh. Drink soon.
Older fine vintages: 71 70 67 66 64 61 59 53 52 49 47 45.

Red burgundy

Côte d'Or Côte de Beaune reds generally mature sooner than bigger wines of Côte de Nuits. Earliest drinking dates are for lighter commune wines, eg Volnay, Beaune; latest for the biggest wines of eg Chambertin, Romanée. But even the best burgundies are much more attractive young than equivalent red Bordeaux.
2003 Exceptional conditions – but will they be exceptional wines? Reds coped with the heat better than the whites.
2002 Avoided the rains of southern France. Promises to be a very exciting, stylish vintage to drink and keep.
2001 A cool damp Sept took the edge off; still good though.
2000 Difficult. Fragile grapes in Côte de Beaune. Much better in Côte de Nuits.
1999 Big ripe vintage; good colour, bags of fruit, silky tannins. Wines to keep.
1998 Ripe fruit but dry tannins. Those in balance need keeping.
1997 Again the gods smiled. Very ripe grapes, with low acidity the main potential problem. Lovely wines mostly ready now.
1996 Fine summer and vintage. Fine ripe wines for keeping. Now–2020.
1995 Small, excellent crop, despite vintage rains. Grapes were very ripe.
1994 Compromised by vintage rain. Generally lean, but exceptions in Côte de Nuits. Drink up.
1993 An excellent vintage: concentrated. Now–2010. Drink up Côte de Beaune.
1992 Ripe, plump, pleasing. No great concentration. Drink up.
1991 Very small harvest; some wines very tannic. Côte de Nuits best. Drink soon.
1990 Great vintage: perfect weather compromised only by touches of drought and some over-production. Long life ahead but start to enjoy. To 2020.
1989 Year of great charm, not necessarily for long maturing. Drink up all but best.
1988 Very good, but tannic. Now–2015 (but only the best).
Older fine vintages: 85 78 71 69 66 64 62 61 59 (all mature).

White burgundy

Côte de Beaune Well-made wines of good vintages with plenty of acidity as well as fruit will improve and gain depth and richness for some years – up to 10. Lesser wines from lighter vintages are ready for drinking after 2 or 3 years.
2003 The heat may prove to have been too much of a good thing. Opulent wines to drink young.
2002 Ripe healthy grapes; medium-sized crop of great promise. Stylish wines.

2001 Generally good results despite lower sugar levels.
2000 Looks very exciting. A big crop of ripe, healthy grapes.
1999 Another generous vintage of good, fresh, well-balanced wines.
1998 Difficult year for white. Chassagne was successful. Drink soon.
1997 Overall an excellent vintage: forward and charming.
1996 A great vintage to lay down top wines. Often awkward now. 2007–2015.
1995 A potentially great vintage, diluted in places. Now–2010.
1994 Patchy. Top growers: very fine potent wines but not for keeping. Drink up.
1993 Poor reputation, but best wines have turned out really well.
1992 Ripe, aromatic, and charming. Mostly ready. Drink up.
1991 Mostly lack substance. Frost problems. Drink up.
1990 Starting to lose balance. Some excellent wines. Drink up.

The white wines of the Mâconnais (Pouilly-Fuissé, St-Véran, Mâcon-Villages) follow a similar pattern, but do not last as long. They are more appreciated for their freshness than their richness.

Chablis Grand cru Chablis of vintages with both strength and acidity can age superbly for up to 10 years; Premiers crus proportionately less.
2003 Small crop of ripe wines, but will they be in balance?
2002 Excellent; may be the equal of 2000.
2001 Too much rain. Relatively weak.
2000 Fine weather for harvesting ripe grapes – excellent.
1999 Another ripe vintage, some of it compromised by rain.
1998 Cool weather and some hail. Wines fair to good: not for long keeping.
1997 Another fine vintage; perhaps drink before the 96s.
1996 Ideal harvest but hail on top vineyards. Classic keeping Chablis. Drink now–2010.
1995 Very good to very, very good. Now–2006.
1994 Downpours on a ripe vintage. Easy wines; drink up.
1993 Fair to good quality; nothing great. Drink up.
1992 Ripe and charming wines. Grands crus splendid. Drink soon.
1991 Generally better than Côte d'Or. Useful wines. Drink now.
1990 Grands crus magnificent; others lack intensity and acidity. Now–2005.

Beaujolais 03: too much heat on the grapes. 02: too much rain for top quality. 01: very good if picked before the rain. 00: excellent. 99: splendid, rich, and deep. 98: very good, if patchy. Best Crus will keep. 97: very good. 95: excellent. Older wines should be finished.

Southwest France
2003 Little or no rain between March and Sept combined with the fiercest heat in France, resulted in small yields, high alcohol, low acidity. Hail in Gaillac ruined the vintage. A year that promised much, but delivered little.
2002 Indian summer saved late-picking vineyards (Madiran, Cahors, Jurançon). Otherwise disappointing.
2001 Hot summer and perfect vintage conditions. Perhaps too much sugar/alcohol.
2000 Better than forecast despite heavy rain in Sept. Better red wines should keep, perhaps longer than 01.
1999 Patchy weather spoiled the vintage for some, but far from disastrous.
1998 Outstanding everywhere. The reds should be at peak in 2004.
1997 Dismally wet, but sweet whites excellent after brilliant autumn. Otherwise patchy. Madiran good, will keep.
1996 Good "commercial year" in most areas. Madirans will still keep.
1995 & 1990 Fabulous for long-lived reds – Cahors, Pécharmant, Madiran.

The Midi

2003 The year of the heatwave, in sharp contrast to 02, often resulting in a greatly reduced crop, but also many fine wines from skilled winemakers.

2002 Not an easy year with heavy rain in early Sept causing problems. Varies widely from AC to AC, and grower to grower.

2001 Quantity lower than average. Quality generally very good with a hot summer making for ripe, concentrated wines.

2000 A warm summer throughout giving ripe fruity wines in Roussillon and Provence, and healthy grapes and balanced wines in Languedoc.

1999 Bad weather failed to ruin vintage in Roussillon; patchy in Languedoc (good in La Clape, not in Pic St-Loup). Good results in Provence.

1998 Drought in Roussillon meant small crop of concentrated wines. Wonderful vintage in Languedoc made ripe, fruity wines with great potential. Well-balanced fruity wines in Provence.

Northern Rhône

2003 A muscled, half-sized crop. Intense sun gave cooked "southern" flavours, high degrees, low acidity. Best (not all) reds show genuine richness.

2002 Poor Sept weather. Try before you buy. Best growers abandoned half their crop. Pretty good year for whites, especially Condrieu.

2001 Very good, lively year if picked before Sept rain. Fresh fruit, good acidity, can age well. Top year at Côte-Rôtie. Often very good whites.

2000 Decent density, quite warm and rich. Some stewed flavours. Hermitage good in parts, Cornas did well, Côte-Rôtie variable. Good Condrieu, sumptuous. Reds more simple than 99/01.

1999 Very successful. Full, ripe fruit. Delicious, likely to live long. More balance than the 98s. Harmony a key word. Ace Côte-Rôties. Sound whites.

1998 Big, robust vintage. More overt tannins than 99, but now fusing well, with rich oily textures. Tasty open flavours. Good Marsanne-based whites.

1997 Good to very good. Fat, fleshy wines that will evolve fast. Lower acidity means rich, smooth flavours. Drinking well now.

1996 Mineral, leathery, grainy textures with age. Acidity still evident. Can be complex – track progress for right moment. Drink top wines 2006–2008.

1995 Lots of full, ample flavour. Lesser names like Crozes delicious now. Top names need more time, maybe 2004–2006. Some have firm tannins.

1994 Good in general, very good in Côte-Rôtie. Well-framed wines with sound core. More mineral than the 95s. Top wines showing well now.

1991 Underestimated. Very good whites, with plenty of life.

Southern Rhône

2003 A classic, chunky, potent, and warm year from the best. Two-speed ripening, so not all balanced. Go fo the best names, best areas.

2002 Nature's payback. Floods around Châteauneuf. Simply-fruited reds (drink early) and acceptable whites. No super-cuvées this year.

2001 Excellent classic vintage, where grape, not oak, tannins prevail. Complex reds, lots of life ahead, be patient for top names.

2000 Tasty wines, led by fruit, juicy and fat. Not a very long-lived year. Go for leading names. Gigondas may edge Châteauneuf in quality.

1999 Very good overall. Ripe, open fruit with correct structure in the best wines.

1998 Excellent. Warm wines, at a funky, cooked-fruit, mineral stage now.

1997 Fruit can be cooked. Best to drink by 2007, unless top name and low yields.

1996 Uneven. Tannins are brusque. The best will age for 10+ years.

1995 Good, deeply flavoured wines. Evolving quickly. Best will live to 2012–2017.

1994 Good extract with noticeable tannins, now at secondary mineral stage.

Champagne

2003 An atypical year. Very small harvest, especially Chardonnay. Ripe, rich Pinots.

2002 Ideal harvest yielded rich, complex wines, especially Pinots. Potentially great.

2000 Fine harvest sun produced four-square wines. Good rather than great vintage year for many producers.

1999 Sporadic rain at harvest changed a great vintage into a good one. Some ripe expressive wines from Chardonnay.

1998 Well-constituted, sound wines. Probable vintage year.

1997 Brilliant Sept weather saved vintage. Ripe, low-acid wines for easy early drinking. Drink before the 96s.

1996 Champagnes of monumental structure, high in alcohol and acidity, real keepers. Drink 2004–2015.

1995 Classic, finely balanced wines; a Chardonnay year *par excellence*. Some superb prestige cuvées, eg Jacquesson Signature; Clicquot Grande Dame.

1993 The best vintage in the lean period 1991–95. Aromatic, delicate, and clean flavours. Excellent wines from Pol Roger and Jaccquesson.

Older fine vintages: 90 89 88 85 82 71

The Loire

2003 An atypical vintage. Some areas hit by spring frost. Wines are big and supple, though not flaccid. For early drinking. Good year for sweet wines.

2002 Best since 97. Vivid fruit and vibrant acidity in the dry whites. Some fine sweet Chenins. Where yields were kept low, the reds are juicy and deeply coloured. (Beware of rot in many of the Gamay-based wines.)

2001 Warm, wet winter left soils gorged with water. Best wines are from those who harvested late. But Muscadet perfect. Taste before buying.

2000 Muscadet, Sancerre, Touraine: satisfactory to good. Cabernet Franc deeply coloured but not rich. Drink within 6 years. Vouvray: good for sec, demi-sec.

1999 Looked to rival the great 89 until the rains came. Cabernet Franc marked by musky "animal" aromas. Vouvray: good for secs and demi-secs.

1998 End of the Loire's luck. Frost, hail, drought, and heavy rain during harvest. Wines are light, some Cabernet Sauvignon-based reds are overly tannic.

1997 Warm and sunny with a beautiful "*arrière saison*". The third excellent vintage. Supple reds and dry whites, and spectacular sweet wines.

1996 Excellent, though not as flattering as the 97s. Cabernet Sauvignon-based reds need time but will age beautifully (ultimately surpassing the 97s).

1995 An excellent vintage across the board. Long-lived, well-structured, delicious wines in every appellation.

Alsace

2003 Earliest harvest since 1893. Small crop of variable wines. Best are ripe, but with low acidity (hence acidification allowed for the first time ever).

2002 Better than most of France. Late-picked wines are good to very good.

2001 Unsettled weather in Sept. Well-balanced wines, good but not great.

2000 Superb – probably best since 90. Very good for Vendanges Tardives and Sélections des Grains Nobles.

1999 Growers who kept yields down made good, well-balanced wines.

1998 The fourth fine vintage in a row. Good wines despite heatwave.

1997 Almost perfect growing season ending with dry, sunny conditions produced concentrated dry wines and outstanding sweet ones.

1996 Harsh winter and late spring followed by hot July and Aug. Ideal conditions in Oct gave a ripe harvest. Fine dry wines, little Gewurztraminer.

1995 Thanks to an Indian summer, late-ripening varieties particularly successful (Pinot Gris, Gewurztraminer, and especially Riesling). Good sweet wines too.

Abelé Small Reims CHAMPAGNE house with v.gd NV.

Abel-Lepitre Middle-rank CHAMPAGNE house. V.gd BRUT Millésimé (**96**).

Abymes Savoie w ★ DYA Hilly area nr Chambéry; light, mild Vin de Savoie AC from Jacquère grape has alpine charm. SAVOIE has many such crus for local pleasure.

Agenais SW France r p (w) ★ DYA VIN DE PAYS of Lot-et-Garonne, mostly from co-ops at Goulens, Donzac, Monflanquin, Mézin. Also from Marmandais co-ops.

Ajaccio Corsica r p w ★→★★ 95 96 97 98 99 00 01 The capital of CORSICA. AC for some v.gd Sciacarello reds. Top grower: Peraldi (try his Vermentino). Also CLOS Capitoro, Jean Courrèges (Dom de Pratavone).

Aligoté Second-rank burgundy white grape and its wine. Should be pleasantly tart and fruity with local character when young. BOUZERON is the one commune to have an all-Aligoté appellation. The shining example is de Villaine's, but try others from gd growers. NB PERNAND-VERGELESSES.

Alliet, Philippe Lo r ★★★ 85 86 87 88 89 90 93 95 96 97 98 99 00 01 02 03 Top-notch producer of long-lived, barrel-aged Chinons: esp Coteau du Noire CUVÉE.

Aloxe-Corton Burg r w ★★→★★★ 90' 91 93' 95 96' 97 98 99' 01 02 03 Village at N end of CÔTE DE BEAUNE famous for two GRANDS CRUS: CORTON (red), CORTON-CHARLEMAGNE (white). Village wines are lighter but to try.

Alsace Al w (r sp) ★★→★★★ 95 96 97 98 99 00 01 02 Region comprising E foothills of Vosges mountains, esp Strasbourg-Mulhouse. Unique wines: aromatic, fruity, full-strength, normally dry and expressive of variety, but too often sweet these days. See VENDANGE TARDIVE, SÉLECTION DES GRAINS NOBLES. Mostly sold by variety (Pinot Bl, Ries, GEWURZTRAMINER). Matures well (except Pinot Bl, MUSCAT) 5–10 yrs; GRAND CRU even longer. Gd-quality and value CREMANT. Pinot N has gd varietal character; but not widely sold outside the region.

> ### Alsace: Wines to look for in 2005
>
> **Muscat** Josmeyer's exquisitely grapey Les Fleurons. Wonderfully aromatic Grand Cru Pfersigberg from Bruno Sorg.
> **Pinot Blanc** Martin Schaetzel's Reserve has lots of character. Gustave Lorentz makes a gd dry style. For sheer finesse try Domaine Mittnacht.
> **Riesling** Jean Becker's Grand Cru Frohn 2000 has a racy, lime character. Kuehn's Grand Cru Winneck-Schlossbery 2000 is intense and concentrated. The ultimate treat is Trimbach's Cuvée Frédéric Emile 1998.
> **Pinot Gris** Seppi Landmann's 2000 and Josmeyer's Grand Cru Brand 2000. Richer-style Grand Cru Kitterlé 1998 from Schlumberger.
> **Gewürztraminer** Léon Beyer's 2000 is a marvellous dry style. Hugel's Jubilee 2000 has intense fruit character. Zind-Humbrecht's Grand Cru Hengst 1998 is amazingly concentrated.

Alsace Grand Cru w ★★★→★★★★ 88 89' 90 93 95 96 97 98 99 00 01 02 AC restricted to 51 (Kaefferkopf is new) of the best-named v'yds (approx 4,000 acres, 2,025 in production) and 4 noble grapes (Ries, Pinot Gr, GEWURZTRAMINER, MUSCAT) mainly dry, some sweet. Not without controversy but generally v.gd, expressive of terroir.

Ampeau, Robert Burg ★★★ Exceptional grower and specialist in MEURSAULT and VOLNAY; also POMMARD. Perhaps unique in releasing only long-matured bottles.

André, Pierre Burg ★ NÉGOCIANT at Ch Corton-André, ALOXE-CORTON; 95 acres of v'yds in CORTON (Gd C-Charlemagne, Corton Blanc), SAVIGNY, GEVREY-CHAMBERTIN, etc. Also owns REINE PEDAUQUE.

d'Angerville, Marquis Burg ★★★ Top grower with immaculate 35-acre estate all in VOLNAY. Top wines: Champans and intense, potent CLOS des Ducs. 2003 sadly saw the passing of Jacques d'Angerville after over 50 yrs in charge.

Anjou Lo p r w (sw dr sp) ★→★★★★ Both region and Loire AC. Wide spectrum of styles: light red inc AC Anjou GAMAY; improving dry white. Gd ANJOU-VILLAGES; strong, usually dry, SAVENNIÈRES; luscious COTEAUX DU LAYON Chenin Bl.

Anjou-Coteaux de la Loire Lo w s/sw sw ★★→★★★ 89' 90' 93 94 95' 96 97 98 99 00 01 02 03 Tiny AC for forceful whites. DEMI-SEC/sw not as rich as COTEAUX DU LAYON, esp Musset-Roullier, Ch de Putille, Doms du Fresche, de Putille.

Anjou-Villages Lo r ★→★★★ 89 90 93 95 96 97 98 99 00 01 02 03 Superior central ANJOU AC for reds (mainly Cab Fr, some Cab Sauv). Juicy, tannic young; gd value esp: Bablut, RICHOU, Rochelles, PIERRE-BISE, Ogereau, Montigilet, Ch'x de Coulaine, de Tigné (Gérard Dépardieu's). New sub-AC to watch: Anjou-Villages-Brissac.

Appellation Contrôlée (AC or AOC) Government control of origin and production (*not* quality) of all the best French wines (see Introduction, p.32–33).

Apremont Savoie w ★★ DYA One of the best villages of SAVOIE for pale, delicate whites, mainly from Jacquère grapes, but recently inc CHARDONNAY.

Arbin Savoie r ★★ Deep-coloured lively red from MONDEUSE grapes, rather like a gd Loire Cab Sauv. Ideal après-ski. Drink at 1–2 yrs.

Arbois Jura r p w (sp) ★★→★★★ Various gd and original light but tasty wines; speciality is VIN JAUNE. On the whole, DYA except excellent VIN JAUNE.

l'Ardèche, Coteaux de Central France r p (w) ★→★★ Hilly area W of Rhône, buzzing along well. New DOMAINES; fresh oaked reds; Viognier (eg Mas de Libian) and Marsanne. Best from pure Syrah, Gamay, Cab Sauv (NB Serret). Powerful, almost burgundian CHARDONNAY "Ardèche" by LOUIS LATOUR (keep 1–2 yrs); "Grand Ardèche" is very oaked. Also Doms du Colombier, Flacher, Mazel, Vigier.

Ariège SW r ★ 00 01 (02) New VIN DE PAYS from 1998 plantings of Cab Sauv, Merlot, Côt, and Tannat under leadership of DOM DE RIBONNET. Will keep.

l'Arlot, Domaine de ★★★ Outstanding producer of excellent NUITS-ST-GEORGES, esp CLOS de l'Arlot, red and white. Owned by AXA Insurance.

Armagnac SW The alternative brandy; more tasty, rustic, and peppery than COGNAC. Table wines: CÔTES DE GASCOGNE, GERS, TERROIRS LANDAIS.

Armand, Comte Burg ★★★ Excellent POMMARD wines, from CLOS des Epéneaux.

Aube Southern extension of CHAMPAGNE. Now known as Côte des Bar.

Aujoux, J-M Beauj Substantial grower/merchant of BEAUJOLAIS. Swiss-owned.

Auxey-Duresses Burg r w ★★→★★★ 90' 93 95 96' 97 98 99' 02' 03 Second-rank (but very pretty) CÔTE DE BEAUNE village: affinities with VOLNAY, MEURSAULT. Best estates: Diconne, HOSPICES DE BEAUNE (CUVÉE Boillot), LEROY, M Prunier. Drink whites in 3–4 yrs. Top white: Leroy's Les Boutonniers.

Avize Champ One of the top Côte des Blancs villages. All CHARDONNAY.

Aÿ Champ One of the best Pinot N-growing villages of CHAMPAGNE.

Ayala Once-famous AŸ-based old-style CHAMPAGNE firm, now raising profile. V.gd vintage wines (esp BRUT 98) from own v'yds.

Bandol Prov r p (w) ★★★ 85' 86 88 89 90 91 92 93 94 95' 96 97 98' 99' 00 01 02 03 Little coastal region nr Toulon producing Provence's best wines; splendid, vigorous, tannic reds predominantly from Mourvèdre; esp Dom de Pibarnon, Ch Pradeaux, Mas de la Rouvière, DOM TEMPIER.

Banyuls Pyr br sw ★★→★★★ One of best VINS DOUX NATURELS, chiefly from Grenache (Banyuls GRAND CRU: over 75% Grenache, aged for 2 yrs+): a distant relation of port. The best are RANCIOS, eg those from Doms la Rectorie, du Mas Blanc (★★★), Vial Magnères, at 10–15 yrs old. Cheap NV wines end up in bars.

Barancourt One of many CHAMPAGNE marques bought by the acquisitive VRANKEN. Pinot N-led CHAMPAGNES, esp CUVÉE des Fondateurs. Gd BOUZY ROUGE.

Barrique The BORDEAUX (and COGNAC) term for an oak barrel holding 225 litres (300 bottles). Barrique-ageing to flavour almost any wine with oak was craze in late 1980s, with some sad results. Current price of oak should enjoin discretion.

Barsac B'x w sw ★★→★★★★ 70 71' 75 76' 79' 81 83' 86' 88' 89' 90' 95 96 97 98 99 01' 02 03' Neighbour of SAUTERNES with similar superb golden wines from different soil; generally less rich and more racy. Richly repays long ageing. Top ch'x: CLIMENS, COUTET, DOISY-DAËNE, DOISY-VÉDRINES.

Barthod, Ghislaine Burg ★★★ Impressive range of CHAMBOLLE-MUSIGNY.

Barton & Guestier BORDEAUX shipper since 18th C, now owned by Seagram.

Bâtard-Montrachet Burg w ★★★★ 79 85 86' 89' 90' 92 93 95 96' 97' 98 99 00 02' 03 Larger (55-acre) neighbour of MONTRACHET. Should be very long-lived: intense flavours, rich texture. Bienvenues-B-M: separate adjacent 9-acre GRAND CRU, 15 owners, thus no substantial bottlings; very rare. Criots-Bâtard-Montrachet (4 acres) even rarer. Seek out: BOUCHARD PÈRE ET FILS, J-M BOILLOT, CARILLON, DROUHIN, GAGNARD, L LATOUR, LEFLAIVE, MOREY, Pernot, RAMONET, SAUZET.

Baudry, Domaine Bernard Lo r p w ★★→★★★ 89 90 93 95 96 97 98 99 00 01 02 03 Impeccable CHINONS in a range of styles from Chenin Bl-based whites to rosés to several excellent CUVÉES of red, inc Les Grezeaux, CLOS Guillot, and Les Croix Boissées.

Baumard, Domaine des Lo ★★→★★★★ 75 76 78 81 85 86 88 89 90 93 94 95 96 97 98 99 00 01 02 03 Leading grower of ANJOU wine, esp SAVENNIÈRES, COTEAUX DU LAYON (CLOS Ste-Catherine), and QUARTS DE CHAUME. Baumard is making a tasty VIN DE TABLE from VERDELHO. Get it while it lasts.

Baux-en-Provence, Coteaux les Prov r p w ★→★★★ 95' 97' 98 99 01 03 Formerly joined with COTEAUX D'AIX, now AC in its own right (not for white). Best wine: DOM DE TREVALLON (Cab Sauv/Syrah) is VIN DE PAYS: no Grenache in v'yd so doesn't conform to AC (!) Also Mas Gourgonnier, Romanin, Mas Ste Berthe, Dom Hauvette.

Béarn SW France r p w ★→★★ w p DYA r 00 01 02 Low-key Basque AC centred on co-op at Bellocq. Also ★★ Dom de Guilhémas. JURANCON red (esp Dom Nigri) and MADIRAN rosé must be sold as Béarn or VIN DE PAYS PYRÉNÉES-ATLANTIQUES.

Beaujolais r (p w) ★ DYA Simple AC of the very big BEAUJOLAIS region: light short-lived fruity r from Gamay. BEAUJOLAIS Supérieur is little different.

Beaujolais de l'année The BEAUJOLAIS of the latest vintage, until the next.

Beaujolais Primeur (or Nouveau) Same as above, made in a hurry (often only 4–5 days fermenting) for release at midnight on the third Wednesday in November. Ideally soft, pungent, fruity, and tempting; too often crude, sharp, too alcoholic. BEAUJOLAIS-VILLAGES should be a better bet.

Beaujolais-Villages r ★★ 99 00 01 Wines from better (N) half of BEAUJOLAIS; should be much tastier than plain BEAUJOLAIS. The 10 (easily) best villages are the crus: FLEURIE, ST-AMOUR, JULIÉNAS, CHÉNAS, MOULIN-À-VENT, CHIROUBLES, MORGON, REGNIÉ, CÔTE DE BROUILLY, BROUILLY. Of the 30 others the best lie around Beaujeu. Crus cannot be released EN PRIMEUR before 15 December. Best kept until spring (or considerably longer).

Beaumes-de-Venise S Rh br r (r p w) DYA Widely regarded as France's best dessert MUSCAT, from S CÔTES DU RHÔNE; can be highly flavoured, subtle, lingering (eg Ch St Sauveur, Doms Coyeux, Durban, JABOULET, Pigeade, VIDAL-FLEURY). Mid-weight reds (Ch Redortier, Dom du Fenouillet, Durban, co-op) gd.

Beaumont des Crayères Champ Bijou Côte d'Epernay co-op making excellent Pinot Meunier-based Grande Réserve NV and very fine Fleur de Prestige (**95' 96**). Now well established on independents' lists in UK and USA.

Beaune Burg r (w) ★★★ 90' 91 93' 95 96' 97 98 99' 01 02' 03 Historic wine capital of Burgundy: walled town hollow with cellars. Wines: classic burgundy – but no GRAND CRU. Many fine growers. NÉGOCIANTS' CLOS wines (usually PREMIER CRU) often best; eg DROUHIN'S superb CLOS des Mouches (esp white), JADOT'S CLOS des Ursules. Beaune du Château is a BOUCHARD PÈRE ET FILS brand. Best v'yds: Bressandes, Fèves, Grèves, Marconnets, Teurons.

Becker, Caves J ★→★★ Proud old family firm at Zellenberg, ALSACE, now making even finer wines. Classic Ries Hagenschlauf and GRAND CRU Froehn MUSCAT. Second label: Gaston Beck.

Bellet Prov p r w ★★★ Fashionable, much-above-average local wines from Nice (Rolle grape). Serious producers: Ch de Bellet, Dom de la Source. Pricey.

Bergerac Dordogne r w p dr sw ★→★★★ (r) **00 01 02** Effectively, but not politically, an eastward extension of BORDEAUX with no clear break in style/quality. Top properties inc ★★★ La Tour des Gendres, CLOS de la Colline, CLOS des Verdots. Ch de Masburel. Otherwise ★★ Dom l'Ancienne Cure, Haut Montlong, Les Marnières, Ch'x Belingard-Chayne, Grinou, de la Jaubertie, du Constant, les Eyssards, Jonc Blanc, de la Mallevieille, les Marais, Les Miaudoux, le Paradis, le Raz, Thénac. See also MONBAZILLAC, ROSETTE, SAUSSIGNAC, PECHARMANT, MONTRAVEL.

Besserat de Bellefon Champ Grande Tradition NV; Cuvée des Moines Brut and Rosé NV; Grande Cuvée NV; BRUT and Rosé (**90 95 96**). CHAMPAGNE house in Epernay, known for lightish wines, not to keep. Owned by MARNE ET CHAMPAGNE.

Beyer, Léon ★★→★★★ Ancient ALSACE firm at Eguisheim. Forceful dry wines needing 5–10 yrs, esp Comtes d'Eguisheim Ries from GRAND CRU Pfersigberg, Comtes d'Eguisheim GEWURZTRAMINER. Beyer is militant against GRAND CRU.

Bichot, Maison Albert Burg One of BEAUNE'S largest growers/merchants. V'yds (32-acre Dom du CLOS Frantin ★★: excellent): CHAMBERTIN, RICHEBOURG, CLOS DE VOUGEOT; Dom Long-Depaquit (★★) in CHABLIS; also many other brand names.

Billecart-Salmon NV; Rosé NV; Nicolas François Billecart (**90' 95 96 97** 98); Blanc de Blancs (**95 96 97'** 98); Elizabeth Salmon Rosé (**97**); Grand Cuvée (**90' 95**). One of the best CHAMPAGNE houses, founded in 1818, still family-owned. Exquisite fresh-flavoured wines age beautifully. Part oak-fermented vintages from 2000. New single v'yd CLOS St-Hilaire BLANC DE NOIRS (**95** 96).

Bize, Simon Burg ★★★ Admirable red burgundy grower with 35 acres at SAVIGNY-LES-BEAUNE. Usually model wines in the racy and elegant Savigny style and some surprisingly gd whites.

Blagny Burg r w ★★→★★★ (w) **92 95 96' 97 99' 00'** 01 02' 03 Hamlet between MEURSAULT and PULIGNY-MONTRACHET: whites have affinities with both (and sold under both ACS), reds with VOLNAY (sold as AC Blagny). Gd ones need age; esp AMPEAU, JOBARD, LATOUR, LEFLAIVE, MATROT, G Thomas.

Blanc de Blancs Any white wine made from white grapes only, esp CHAMPAGNE. Not an indication of quality but should be of style.

Blanc de Noirs White (or slightly pink or "blush") wine from red grapes.

Blanck, Paul et Fils Al ★★→★★★ Versatile grower at Kientzheim. Gd Pinot Bl, GRANDS CRUS Furstentum (GEWURZTRAMINER, Pinot Gr, esp Ries), SCHLOSSBERG (Ries).

Blanquette de Limoux Midi w sp ★★ Gd-value fizz from nr Carcassonne with long local history. Very dry, clean, increasingly tasty: CHARDONNAY and Chenin Bl added to basic Mauzac, esp in newer AC CREMANT de Limoux.

Blaye B'x r w ★→★★★ DYA Simple dry whites from E of the Gironde and as of 2000 designation for region's top reds (lower yields, etc).

Boillot, J-M ★★★ POMMARD-based dom: though best known for very fine, oaky whites from PULIGNY-MONTRACHET, BATARD, and remarkable MONTAGNY.

Boisset, Jean-Claude Burg Far and away the biggest Burgundy merchant based in NUITS-ST-GEORGES. Owner of Bouchard-Aîné, Lionel Bruck, F Chauvenet, Delaunay, Jaffelin, Morin Père et Fils, de Marcilly, Pierre Ponnelle, Thomas-Bassot, Vienot, CELLIER DES SAMSONS (BEAUJOLAIS), MOREAU (CHABLIS), and a share in MOMMESSIN. Now involved in projects in Canada, California, Chile, Uruguay, and the Languedoc. Predictable commercial standards. From 1999 own v'yds separated as DOM DE LA VOUGERAIE (★★★). Potentially v.gd.

Boizel Quality Epernay family CHAMPAGNE house; brilliant, aged BLANC DE BLANCS NV and prestige Joyau de France (**95** 96). Also Grand Vintage Brut (**96** 98) and CUVÉE Sous Bois. Part of Boizel Chanoine.

Bollinger NV 'Special Cuvée'; Grande Année (**95 96'** 97); Rosé (**96**). Top CHAMPAGNE house at AŸ with distinct winey style. Luxury wines: RD (**85' 88 90** 95), VIEILLES VIGNES Françaises (**96'**) from ungrafted Pinot N vines, La Côte aux Enfants, AŸ.

Bonneau du Martray, Domaine Burg ★★★★ (w) ★★ (r) Biggest grower (22 acres) of CORTON-CHARLEMAGNE of highest quality; also red GRAND CRU CORTON all on a high since 90. Cellars at PERNAND-VERGELESSES. Whites have often outlived reds.

Bonnes-Mares Burg r ★★★→★★★★ 78' 85' 88' 89 90' 91 93 95 96' 97 98 99 00 01 02' 03 37-acre GRAND CRU between CHAMBOLLE-MUSIGNY and MOREY-ST-DENIS. Very sturdy long-lived wines, less fragrant than MUSIGNY; can rival CHAMBERTIN. Top growers: DUJAC, GROFFIER, JADOT, ROUMIER, DOM DES VAROILLES, DE VOGUE, VOUGERAIE.

Bonnezeaux Lo w sw ★★★→★★★★ 76' 78 85' 86 88' 89' 90' 93' 94 95' 96 97 98 99 00 01 03 Velvety, structured, complex sweet Chenin Bl, potentially best of COTEAUX DU LAYON. Esp: Angeli, Ch de Fesles, Dom du Petit Val. Ages well, but very tempting young.

Bordeaux B'x r w (p) ★→★★ 90 94 95 96 98 00' (for ch'x see pp.80–105) Catch-all AC for low-strength Bordeaux. Often despised: it may be light but cannot be imitated. If I had to choose one simple daily wine, gd Bordeaux would be it.

Bordeaux Supérieur ★→★★ As above, with more alcohol and ageing potential.

Borie-Manoux Admirable BORDEAUX shipper, ch'x-owner owned by Castéja family. Ch'x inc BATAILLEY, BEAU-SITE, DOM DE L'ÉGLISE, HAUT-BAGES-MONPELOU, TROTTE VIEILLE.

Bouchard Père et Fils Important Burgundy shipper (established in 1731) and grower; excellent v'yds (232 acres), mainly CÔTE DE BEAUNE; cellars at Ch de Beaune. Fine quality since 1996.

Bouches-du-Rhône Prov r p w ★ VINS DE PAYS from Marseille environs. Warming reds from southern varieties, plus Cab Sauv, Syrah, and Merlot.

Bourg B'x r (w) ★★ 86' 88' 89' 90' 94 95 96 98 99 00' 01 02 Un-fancy but consistent claret from E of the Gironde. For ch'x see CÔTES DE BOURG.

Bourgeois, Henri ★★→★★★ Lo 89 90 93 95 96 97 98 99 00 01 02 03 Leading SANCERRE grower/merchant in Chavignol; also owns Laporte. Also POUILLY-FUMÉ, MENETOU-SALON, and QUINCY. Top wines inc: Etienne Henri, MD de Bourgeois, La Bourgeoise, D'Antan Sancerrois, Sancerre Jadis, Le Chêne Etienne. Recently bought a v'yd in New Zealand.

Bourgogne is the generic word for the cheaper end of Burgundy. As well as some indifferent mass-produced wines, it also covers out-lying areas which have their own subdivisions within the AC Bourgogne. **Coulanges-la-Vineuse, Epineuil,** and **Vézélay** (Yonne département) **Chatillonais, Hautes Côtes de Beaune** and **Hautes Côtes de Nuits** (Côte d'Or) **Côte Chalonnaise** and **Couchois** (Saône et Loire). The best tip is to buy **Bourgogne Rouge** or **Blanc** from good growers in the famous villages of the Côte d'Or – they will be delicious simple wines with more style than négociant bottlings.

Bourgogne Burg r w (p) ★★ 00 01 02' Catch-all Burgundy AC, with higher standards than basic BORDEAUX. Light often gd flavour, best at 2–4 yrs. Top growers make bargain beauties from fringes of CÔTE D'OR villages; do not despise. BEAUJOLAIS crus (except Regnié) can also be labelled Bourgogne.

Bourgogne Grand Ordinaire r (w) ★ DYA Lowest Burgundy AC, also allowing GAMAY. Rare. White may inc ALIGOTÉ, Pinot Bl, Melon de Bourgogne.

Bourgogne Passe-Tout-Grains r (p) ★ Age 1–2 yrs, junior burgundy: min 33% Pinot N, the balance Gamay, mixed in vat. Not as heady as BEAUJOLAIS.

Bourgueil Lo r (p) ★★→★★★(★) 76' 89' 90' 95' 96 97 98 99 01 02 Brawny, fruity TOURAINE (mainly Cab Fr). Deep-flavoured, ageing like BORDEAUX in top yrs. ST-NICOLAS-DE-BOURGUEIL often lighter. Esp: Amirault, Audebert, Billet, Jacky Blot, Breton, Caslot, Cognard, Delaunay, Druet, Gambier, Lamé-Delisle-Boucard, Mailloches.

Bouvet-Ladubay Lo ★→★★★ Major sparkling SAUMUR house, controlled by TAITTINGER. Wines inc: vintage BRUT Saphir, oak-fermented deluxe Trésor (w p), CREMANT Excellence, Instinct. Also still wines (Les Nonpareils); gd sweet Grand Vin de Dessert. CUVÉES: Brut Zero, Trésor Rouge.

Bouzeron Burg w ★ CÔTE CHALONNAISE AC specifically for ALIGOTÉ. Age 1–2 yrs. Top grower: de Villaine. Also NB BOUCHARD PÈRE ET FILS.

Bouzy Rouge Champ r ★★★ 89 90 95 96 97 98 99 Still red of famous CHAMPAGNE Pinot N village. Like very light burgundy, but can last well in sunny vintages.

Brocard, J-M Burg ★★ CHABLIS grower to note for fine value, crisp, and typical wines, inc Montmains, Montée de Tonnerre. Expanding into new terroir.

Brouilly Beauj r ★★ 99 00 01 02 03 Biggest of the 10 crus of BEAUJOLAIS: fruity, round, refreshing wine, can age 3–4 yrs. CH DE LA CHAIZE is largest estate. Top growers: Michaud, Dom de Combillaty, Dom des Grandes Vignes.

Brumont, Alain SW ★★★ Best known, but expensive, producer in MADIRAN. One of the first to introduce oak-ageing and 100% Tannat wines. Revived the Co-op at Castelnau-Rivière-Basse. Flagship wines: Ch MONTUS, Dom Bouscassé, and gd-value MADIRAN Tonus.

Brut Term for the dry classic wines of CHAMPAGNE.

Brut Ultra/Zéro Term for bone-dry wines in CHAMPAGNE.

Buisse, Paul ★→★★ Quality Montrichard merchant. Range of, esp TOURAINE, wines.

Bugey Savoie r p w sp ★→★★ DYA VDQS for light sparkling, still, or half-sparkling wines from Roussette (or Altesse) and CHARDONNAY (gd). Best from Montagnieu; also Rosé de Cerdon, mainly Gamay.

Burguet, Alain Burg ★★→★★★ Superb GEVREY-CHAMBERTIN; esp VIEILLES VIGNES village wine.

Buxy Burg w Village in AC MONTAGNY with gd co-op for CHARDONNAY and Pinot N.

Buzet SW France r (w p) ★★ 99 00 01 02 Region SE of BORDEAUX; similar wines, sometimes a bit pruney. Dynamic co-op has bulk of production, inc some single properties (eg Châteaux de Gueyze, Mazelières). More local character from (independent) Dom de Pech, Ch'x du Frandat, Sauvagnères, Tournelles.

Cabardès Midi r (p w) ★→★★ 95 96 97 98' 99 00' 01 02 03 New AC NW of Carcassonne. MIDI and BORDEAUX grapes show promise at Ch'x Pennautier, Ventenac, Dom de Cabrol, Co-op de Conques sur Orbiel.

Cabernet See Grapes for red wine (pp.10–13).

Cabernet d'Anjou Lo p s/sw ★ DYA Delicate, grapey, med-sw rosé. Traditionally sw, ageworthy; a few venerable bottles survive. Esp from Bablut.

Cabrières Midi p (r) ★★ DYA COTEAUX DU LANGUEDOC.

Leading Cahors producers

★★★ CLOS DE GAMOT (inc Clos St Jean), Ch'x du Cèdre, Lamartine.

★★ Clos Coutale, Reysséguier Ch'x du Cayrou, La Coustarelle, La Caminade, Garinet, Gaudou, Les Hauts d'Aglan, La Reyne, Les Ifs, Les Lacquets, Latuc, De Lauze, Les Rigalets. Doms de la Bérangeraie, de Cause, Paillas, Pineraie, Savarines, Eugénie. Ch Lagrézette owned by MD of Cartier, priced accordingly.

Cahors SW France r ★→★★★ 88 89 90' 95 98 00' (01') (02) Fast-reviving v'yd mostly Auxerrois (Malbec). Ranges from tannic to atypical quick-drinking.

Cairanne S Rh r p w ★★ 90' 95' 96' 97 98' 99' 00' 01' 03 One of best CÔTES DU

RHONE-VILLAGES: solid, robust esp: Doms Aéria, Alary, Ameillaud, Brusset, l'Oratoire St-Martin, Rabasse-Charavin, Richaud. Some improving whites.

Canard-Duchêne CHAMPAGNE house owned by Alain THIÉNOT. Fair prices for lively, Pinot N-tasting wines. V.gd Charles VII prestige CUVÉE both BRUT and rosé.

Canon-Fronsac B'x r ★★→★★★ 85' 86 88 89' 90' 94 95 96 98 00' 01 Full tannic reds of increasing quality from W of POMEROL. Try Ch'x: Barrabaque, CANON-DE-BREM, Cassagne Haut-Canon, Gaby, Lamarche Canon Candelaire, Pavillon, La Fleur Caillou, Grand-Renouil, Mazeris, Moulin-Pey-Labrie, Vraye-Canon-Boyer.

Cantenac B'x r ★★★ Village of HAUT-MÉDOC entitled to the AC MARGAUX. Top ch'x inc BRANE-CANTENAC, PALMER, etc.

Cap Corse Corsica w br ★★→★★★ CORSICA's wild N cape. Splendid MUSCAT from CLOS Nicrosi (Rogliano); rare, soft, dry Vermentino w. *Vaut le détour*, if not *le voyage*.

Caramany Pyr r (w) ★ 95 96 97 98' 99 00' 01 02 03 Notionally superior AC for single-village CÔTES DU ROUSSILLON-VILLAGES.

Carillon, Louis Burg ★★★ PULIGNY-MONTRACHET dom now in top league. Esp PREMIER CRU Referts, Perrières, and tiny amount of GRAND CRU Bienvenues-Bâtard.

Cassis Prov w (r p) ★★ DYA Seaside village E of Marseille known for dry whites with a certain character, drunk with bouillabaisse (eg Dom de la Ferme Blanche, CLOS Ste Magdeleine, CLOS d'Albizzi). Not to be confused with cassis: blackcurrant liqueur made in Dijon.

Cave Cellar, or any wine establishment.

Cave coopérative Wine-growers' co-op winery; over half of all French production. Usually well-run, well-equipped, and wines reasonable value for money.

Cellier des Samsons ★ BEAUJOLAIS/MACONNAIS co-op at Quincié with 2,000 grower-members. Wines widely distributed; now owned by BOISSET.

Cépage Variety of vine, eg CHARDONNAY, Merlot.

Cérons B'x w dr sw ★★ 83' 85' 86' 88' 89' 90 95 96 97 98 99 01 02 (03) Neighbour of SAUTERNES with some gd sweet wine, eg Ch'x de Cérons et de Calvimont, Chantegrive, Grand Enclos. Ch Archambeau makes v.gd dry GRAVES.

Chablis

There is no better expression of the all-conquering Chardonnay than the full but tense, limpid but stony wines it makes on the heavy limestone soils of Chablis. Chablis terroir divides into three quality levels (four including Petit Chablis) with great consistency. Best makers use little or no new oak to mask the precise definition of variety and terroir: Barat, Bessin*, Billaud-Simon, Bouchard Père et Fils, Boudin*, J-M Brocard, J Collet*, D Dampt, R & V Dauvissat*, J Dauvissat, B, D et E, and J Defaix, Droin, Drouhin*, Duplessis, Durup, Fèvre*, Geoffroy, J-P Grossot*, Laroche, Long-Depaquit, Dom des Malandes, L Michel*, Picq*, Pupillon, Raveneau*, G Robin*, Servin, Tribut, Vocoret. Simple unqualified "Chablis" may be thin; best is premier or grand cru (see below). The co-op, La Chablisienne, has high standards (esp Grenouille*) and many different labels (it makes one in every three bottles). (* = outstanding)

Chablis Burg w ★★→★★★ 95 96' 97 99 00' 02' 03 Unique, flavoursome, dry minerally wine of N Burgundy, CHARDONNAY; a total of 10,000 acres for all levels.

Chablis Grand Cru Burg w ★★★→★★★★ 83 88 89 90' 92 93 95' 96' 97 98 99 00' 02' 03 In maturity a match for great white burgundy: often dumb in youth, at best with age combines mineral cut with hint of SAUTERNES. V'yds: Blanchots, Bougros, CLOS, Grenouilles, Preuses, Valmur, Vaudésir. See also MOUTONNE.

Chablis Premier Cru Burg w ★★★ 90' 92 95' 96' 97 98 99 00' 02' 03 Technically second-rank but at best excellent, more typical of CHABLIS than its GRANDS CRUS.

Can outclass more expensive MEURSAULT and other CÔTE DE BEAUNE. Best v'yds inc: Côte de Léchet, Fourchaume, Mont de Milieu, Montée de Tonnerre, Montmains, Vaillons. See box on previous page for producers.

Chai Building for storing and maturing wine, esp in BORDEAUX.

Chambertin Burg r ★★★★ 78' 85' 88 89 90' 91 93 95 96' 98 99' 00 01 02' 03 A 32-acre GRAND CRU; some of the meatiest, most enduring, best red burgundy. 20 growers inc: BOUCHARD, CHARLOPIN, Damoy, DROUHIN, LEROY, MORTET, PONSOT, Rebourseau, Rossignol-Trapet, ROUSSEAU, Trapet.

Chambertin-Clos de Bèze Burg r ★★★★ 78' 85 88 89 90' 91 93 95 96'98 99' 00 01 02' 03 37-acre neighbour of CHAMBERTIN. Similarly splendid wines. May legally be sold as Chambertin. 15 growers, inc: CLAIR (BRUNO), Damoy, DROUHIN, Drouhin-Laroze, FAIVELEY, GROFFIER, JADOT, ROUSSEAU.

Chambolle-Musigny Burg r ★★★→★★★★ 88 89 90' 91 93 95 96' 97 98 99' 00 01 02 420-acre CÔTE DE NUITS village: fabulously fragrant, complex, but never heavy wine. Best v'yds: Les Amoureuses, part of BONNES-MARES, Les Charmes, MUSIGNY. Growers to note: BARTHOD, DROUHIN, FAIVELEY, GROFFIER, HUDELOT-NOELLAT, JADOT, MUGNERET, MUGNIER, RION, ROUMIER, Serveau, DE VOGUE.

> **Champagne: growers to watch in 2005**
>
> **Alain Robert** – great Le Mesnil grower/winemaker with magnificent older cuvées: Mesnil Tête de Cuvée (**82' 85**).
>
> **Richard Cheurlin** – one of best grower/winemakers of the Aube. Rich but balanced Carte d'Or and vintage-dated Cuvée Jeanne.
>
> **Egly-Ouriet** – first-rate grower/winemaker in Ambonnay. Superb expressions of great Pinot Noir, especially Blanc de Noirs Vielles Vignes.
>
> **Claude Cazals** Prime Oger/Le Mesnil estate now run by daughter Delphine. Ace Clos de Cazals (**95'** 96).
>
> **Franck Bonville** – one of the great unsung estates of the Côte des Blancs. Superfine Blanc de Blancs from Grand Cru vineyards (part oak-fermented **98**), but less dosage would be welcome.
>
> **José Michel** – Doyen of Côte d'Epernay making fresh yet mature Carte Blanche NV. Also excellent Blanc de Blanc (**98 99**) and vintage (**96' 98** 99).
>
> **Pierre Gimmonet** – leading Côte des Blancs grower at Cuis. Superb bone-dry Cuvée Oenophile (**95' 96**) is ideal with oysters.
>
> **Henri Mandois** – Classy Pinot Meunier/Chardonnay wines with light touch.
>
> **Larmandier-Bernier** – Vertus; top-flight Blanc de Blanc grower-maker, especially Cramant Grand Cru.
>
> **Edmond Barnaut** Bouzy. Complex, fine Champagnes mainly from Pinot Noir culminate in first-rate Sélection Ultra Brut.
>
> **Pierre Cheval-Gatinois** Aÿ. Impeccable producer of monocru Champagnes and excellent still Aÿ Coteaux Champenois (**97'**).
>
> **Serge Mathieu** Avirey-Lingey. Outstanding Eco-friendly Aube domaine. Great value Blanc de Noirs.

Champagne Sparkling wine of Pinots N and Meunier and/or CHARDONNAY, and its region (70,000+ acres 90 miles E of Paris); made by MÉTHODE TRADITIONELLE. Bubbles from elsewhere, however gd, cannot be Champagne.

Champy Père et Cie Burg ★★→★★★★ Oldest NÉGOCIANT, in BEAUNE, rejuvenated by Meurgey family (also brokers "DIVA"). Range of very well chosen wines.

Chandon de Briailles, Domaine Burg ★★★ Small estate at SAVIGNY. Wonderful CORTON and v.gd PERNAND-VERGELESSES, esp PREMIER CRU Les Vergelesses.

Chanson Père et Fils Burg ★→★★★★ Old grower-NÉGOCIANT at BEAUNE (110 acres), now owned by BOLLINGER. Esp BEAUNE CLOS des Fèves, PERNAND-VERGELESSES, SAVIGNY, CORTON. Expect better quality now.

Chapelle-Chambertin Burg r ★★★ 85 88 89' 90' 91 93 95 96' 97 98 99' 00 01 02' 03 A 13-acre neighbour of CHAMBERTIN. Wine more "nervous", not so meaty. Top producers: Damoy, JADOT, Rossignol-Trapet, Trapet.

Chapoutier Rh ★★→★★★★ Long-established grower and trader of full Rhônes; bio-dynamic principles. Best: special CUVÉES CHÂTEAUNEUF Barbe Rac (Grenache), HERMITAGE: L'Ermite, Le Pavillon (r), L'Ermite, CUVÉE d'Orée (w). Also CROZES red Les Varonniers. Sound Meysonniers Crozes. New holdings in BANYULS, COLLIOURE, COTEAUX DU TRICASTIN, and COTEAUX D'AIX-EN-PROVENCE promising.

Chardonnay See Grapes for white wine (pp.12–16). Also the name of a MÂCON-VILLAGES commune. Hence Mâcon-Chardonnay.

Charlopin, Philippe Burg ★★★ Modern-style GEVREY-CHAMBERTIN estate.

Charmes-Chambertin Burg r ★★★ 85' 88 89' 90' 91 93 95 96' 97 98 99' 00 01 02' 03 CHAMBERTIN neighbour, inc AC MAZOYÈRES-CHAMBERTIN. More supple, rounder wines; esp Bachelet, DUGAT, DROUHIN, DUJAC, LEROY, Perrot-Minot, ROTY, ROUMIER, ROUSSEAU, VOUGERAIE.

Chassagne-Montrachet Burg w r ★★★→★★★★ r (★★★) 90' 93 95 96' 97 98 99' 01 02' 03; w 89' 90 92 95 96 97 98 99 00' 01 02' 03 750-acre CÔTE DE BEAUNE village. Sterling, hefty red; excellent rich, dry white rarely with quite the finesse of PULIGNY next door, but often costs less. Best v'yds inc part of MONTRACHET, BÂTARD-MONTRACHET, Boudriottes (r w), Caillerets, CRIOTS-B-M, Morgeot (r w), Ruchottes, CLOS ST-JEAN (r). Growers inc Amiot, Blain-Gagnard, COLIN-DELEGER, DROUHIN, Fontaine-Gagnard, J N Gagnard, GAGNARD-DELAGRANGE, Jouard, Lamy-Pillot, Ch de la Maltroye, MOREY, Morey-Coffinet, Niellon, Pillot, RAMONET.

Château

Means an estate, big or small, good or indifferent, particularly in Bordeaux (see pp.80–105). Elsewhere in France château tends to mean, literally, castle or great house, as in most of the following entries. In Burgundy, "domaine" is the usual term.

Château d'Arlay ★→★★ Major JURA estate; 160 acres in skilful hands with wines inc v.gd VIN JAUNE, VIN DE PAILLE, Pinot N, and MACVIN.

Château de Beaucastel S Rh r w ★★★ 78' 79 81' 83 85 86' 88 90' 93' 94' 95' 96' 97 98' 99' 00' 01' 03 One of biggest, best-run CHÂTEAUNEUF estates. Deep-hued, complex wines; unusual varietal mix inc one-third Mourvèdre. Small amount of wonderful Roussanne: keep 5–14 yrs. Leading CÔTES DU RHONE red and white Coudoulet de Beaucastel. V.gd organic Perrin Nature CÔTES DU RHÔNE plus NÉGOCIANT RASTEAU, VACQUEYRAS. Also see Tablas Creek, California, p.234.

Château du Cèdre SW r ★★★ 98' 00' (01') (02) Fashionable excellent CAHORS estate. Also delicious white VIN DE PAYS from Viognier.

Château de la Chaize Beauj r ★★★ Best-known BROUILLY estate.

Château de Fesles Lo r w sw p ★★→★★★ 93 94 95 96 97 98 00 02 Historic estate in Bonnezeaux producing the entire range of ANJOU wines. Inc COTEAUX DE LAYON Ch'x la Guimonière and la Roulerie.

Château Fortia S Rh r (w) ★★ 78' 81' 83 85 88 90 95' 96' 97 98' 99 00' 01' Traditional 72-acre CHÂTEAUNEUF property. Owner's father, Baron Le Roy, fathered the AC system in 1920s. Better form recently, inc Le Baron and whites.

Château Fuissé Burg w ★★→★★★ Now being challenged as the top estate in POUILLY-FUISSÉ. Numerous CUVÉES, made to mature more rapidly than before.

Château de Meursault Burg r w ★★★ 150-acre estate owned by PATRIARCHE, with gd v'yds and wines in BEAUNE, MEURSAULT, POMMARD, VOLNAY. Splendid cellars open to the public for tasting.

Château de Mont-Redon S Rh r w ★★★ 78 85 88 89 90' 94' 95' 97' 98' 99 01' Gd CHÂTEAUNEUF estate. Fine, complex red; v.gd aromatic, sometimes

FRANCE

substantial white (96 00). Also gd wines from Cantegril v'yd (LIRAC).

Château de Montaigne Dordogne w (sw) ★★ Home of great philosopher Michel de M, now making sweet COTES DE MONTRAVEL; part-owns CH PALMER (MARGAUX).

Château Montus ★★★ SW France **90 95' 96 97 98** (00) (01) (02) Top MADIRAN estate. Some 100% Tannat, long vinification, slow-maturing. Owner: A BRUMONT.

Château La Nerthe S Rh r (w) ★★★ 78' 81' 86 88 89' 90' 94 95' **96'** 97 98' 99' 00 01' 03 Very high-quality 222-acre CHÂTEAUNEUF estate. Solid modern-style wines, esp special CUVÉES Cadettes (r) and oaked Beauvenir (w). Take 5 yrs to show.

Château de Pierre-Bise Lo r w ★★→★★★★ 85 86 88 89 90 93 95 96 97 98 99 00 01 02 **03** Superb producer of ANJOU, esp COTEAUX DE LAYON, inc QUARTS DE CHAUME, vinifed and bottled by terroir. Also SAVENNIÈRES and ANJOU-VILLAGES under label CLOS de Coulaine.

Château Rayas S Rh r (w) ★★★ 78' 79 81' 83 85 86 88' 89 90' 93 94' 95' 96' 98' 99 00 01 Famous old-style 37-acre estate in CHÂTEAUNEUF. Concentrated Grenache ages superbly. Traditional white Rayas can be v.gd. Gd value second label: Pignan. V.gd Ch Fonsalette, CÔTES DU RHONE. All benefit from decanting.

Château Routas Prov r p w ★★ Dynamic estate making its mark in COTEAUX VAROIS. Wines inc Syrah, Cab Sauv, CHARDONNAY/Viognier, both AC and VIN DE PAYS.

Château de Selle Prov r p w ★★→★★★ 100-acre estate of OTT family nr Cotignac, Var. The original pace-setters for PROVENCE. CUVÉE Spéciale is largely Cab Sauv.

Château Simone Prov r p w ★★→★★★ Age 2–6 yrs or longer. Famous old property synonymous with AC PALETTE, nr Aix-en-Provence. The red is smooth but herby and spicy. White repays bottle age. Rosé exceptional.

Château de Villeneuve Lo r w ★★→★★★ 89 90 93 94 95 96 97 98 99 00 01 02 03 Dynamic SAUMUR estate. Exciting Saumur Blanc (esp Les Cormiers) and SAUMUR-CHAMPIGNY (esp VIEILLES VIGNES, Grand Clos).

Château-Chalon Jura w ★★★ Not a CHÂTEAU but AC and village. Unique dry, yellow, sherry-like wine (Savagnin grape). Develops *flor* (see p.181) while ageing in barrels for min 6 yrs. Ready to drink when bottled (62cl "Clavelin" bottle), but ages almost forever. A curiosity.

Château-Grillet N Rh w ★★ 91' 93' 95' 98' 00 A 9-acre terraced v'yd of Viognier; one of France's smallest ACS. Overpriced, but signs of revival. Always cask-reared. Less obvious floral aromas than CONDRIEU. Drink 6 yrs+. Decant first.

Châteaumeillant Lo r p ★→★★ DYA A tiny VDQS area nr SANCERRE. Gamay and Pinot N for light reds and rosés. Top producers: Lanoix and Cave des Vins de Châteaumeillant.

Châteauneuf-du-Pape S Rh r (w) ★★★ 78' 80 81' 83 85 86 88 89' 90' 94 95' 96 98' 99' 00' 01 03 8,200 acres nr Avignon with core of 30 or so doms for very fine wines (quality variable over remaining 90). Mix of up to 13 varieties led by Grenache, Syrah, Mourvèdre. Best are dark, strong, exceptionally long-lived. Whites fruity and zesty or rather heavy: many now DYA. Top growers inc: Ch'x DE BEAUCASTEL, FORTIA, Gardine, MONT REDON, LA NERTHE, RAYAS; Doms de Beaurenard, Bosquet des Papes, Les Cailloux, Font-de-Michelle, Pegaü, VIEUX TELEGRAPHE, Vieille Julienne, Villeneuve, Henri Bonneau, CLOS du Mont-Olivet, CLOS DES PAPES, CLOS St-Jean, Jean Versino, Vieux Donjon.

Châtillon-en-Diois Rh r p w ★ DYA Small AC E of Rhône. Adequate largely Gamay reds; white (some ALIGOTÉ) mostly made into CLAIRETTE DE DIE.

Chaume The first PREMIER CRU of Coteaux du Layon. 80 ha of S-facing slopes on the bank of the Loire. Applies to qualified wines from 2002 forward. 100% Chenin Bl wines are LIQUOREUX.

Chave, Gérard Rh ★★★ Superstar grower (with son Jean-Louis) of HERMITAGE. Nine hillside sites: 25 acres red; 12 acres white. Fleshy, very long-lived wines (inc gd ST-JOSEPH), and also VIN DE PAILLE. Very fruity new J-L Chave brand St-Joseph.

Chavignol Picturesque SANCERRE village with famous v'yd, Les Monts Damnés. Chalky soil gives vivid wines that age 4–5 yrs (or longer); esp from BOURGEOIS and Cotat. (Produces goats' cheese of same name.)

Chénas Beauj r ★★★ **99 00 01 02** 03 Smallest BEAUJOLAIS cru and one of the weightiest; neighbour to MOULIN-A-VENT and JULIENAS. Growers inc: Benon, Champagnon, Charvet, Ch Chèvres, DUBOEUF, Lapierre, Robin, Trichard, co-op.

Chenonceau, Ch de Lo ★→★★ DYA Architectural jewel of Loire makes gd to v.gd AC TOURAINE Sauv Bl, Cab Sauv, and Chenin Bl, still and sparkling. See vintages for CHEVERNY.

Chéreau-Carré ★→★★ **95 96 97 98 99 00 01 02** 03 Makers of some of top DOMAINE MUSCADETS (esp Ch'x du Chasseloir, du Coing, Comte Leloup de Chasseloir). A name to follow.

Chevalier-Montrachet Burg w ★★★★ 89' 90 92 95 96' 97 98 99' 00' 01 02' 03 17-acre neighbour of MONTRACHET making similar luxurious wine, perhaps less powerful. Inc 2.5-acre Les Demoiselles. Growers inc: LATOUR, JADOT, BOUCHARD PÈRE ET FILS, COLIN-DELEGER, LEFLAIVE, Niellon, PRIEUR.

Cheverny Lo r p w ★→★★ **95 96 97 98 99 00 01 02** 03 Loire AC nr Chambord. Dry crisp white from Sauv Bl and Chard. Also Gamay, Pinot N or Cab Sauv; light but tasty. "Cour-Cheverny" uses local Romorantin grape. Sparkling wines use CREMANT DE LOIRE and TOURAINE AC. Esp Cazin; CLOS Tue-Boeuf; Huards; OISLY ET THESEE; Doms de la Desoucherie and du Moulin (Herve Villemade).

Chevillon, R ★★★ 32-acre estate at NUITS-ST-GEORGES; soft and juicy wines.

Chidaine, Francois Lo dr sw w sp ★★ Serious young Montlouis producer who has recently taken over the v'yds of CLOS Baudoin (formerly Prince Poniatowski) in VOUVRAY. Biodynamic principles followed in both DOMAINES.

Chignin Savoie w ★ DYA Light, soft white from Jacquère grapes for alpine summers. Chignin-Bergeron (with Roussanne grapes) is best and liveliest.

Chinon Lo r (p w) ★★→★★★ 89' 90' 93' 95' 96 97 98 99 00 01 02 03 Juicy, variably rich TOURAINE Cab Fr. Drink cool, young; treat v.gd yrs like BORDEAUX. A little crisp, dry Chenin Bl. Top growers: Bernard Baudry, Alliet, Crespin, Ch de Coulaine, COULY-DUTHEIL (CLOS de l'Echo), Druet, Ch Grille, Joguet, Lambert, Loup, Raffault.

Chiroubles Beauj r ★★★ 00 01 02 03 Gd but tiny BEAUJOLAIS cru next to FLEURIE; freshly fruity silky wine for early drinking (1–3 yrs). Growers inc: Bouillard, Cheysson, DUBOEUF, Fourneau, Passot, Raousset, co-op.

Chorey-lès-Beaune Burg r (w) ★★ 95 96' 97 98 99' 01 02 Minor AC N of BEAUNE. Three fine growers: Arnoux, Germain (Ch de Chorey), and esp TOLLOT-BEAUT.

Chusclan S Rh r p w ★→★★ 98' 99' 00' 01' 03 CÔTES DU RHONE-VILLAGES with able co-op. Soft reds. Labels inc: CUVÉE de Marcoule, Les Genets, Seigneurie de Gicon. Also Ch Signac and special CUVÉES from André Roux. Drink young.

Cissac HAUT-MÉDOC village just W of PAUILLAC.

Clair, Bruno Burg ★★→★★★ Leading MARSANNAY estate. V.gd wines from there and GEVREY-CHAMBERTIN (esp CLOS DE BEZE), FIXIN, MOREY-ST-DENIS, SAVIGNY.

Clairet Very light red wine, almost rosé. BORDEAUX Clairet is an AC.

Clairette Traditional white grape of the MIDI. Its low-acid wine was a vermouth base. Revival by Terrasses de Landoc is full and zesty.

Clairette de Bellegarde Midi w ★ DYA Small AC nr Nîmes: fresh, neutral white.

Clairette de Die Rh w dr s/sw sp ★★ NV Popular dry or (better) semi-sweet Tradition MUSCAT-flavoured sparkling wine from pre-Alps in E Rhône; or straight dry CLAIRETTE, can age 3–4 yrs. Worth trying. Co-op, Achard-Vincent.

Clairette du Languedoc Midi w ★ DYA Nr Montpellier. Full white AC, more interest for late-harvest grapes, barrel ageing. Ch'x La Condamine Bertrand, St-André, and Cave d'Adissan are looking gd.

France entries also cross-refer to Châteaux of Bordeaux section, pp.80–105.

Clape, La Midi r p w ★★→★★★ Cru to note of AC COTEAUX DU LANGUEDOC. Full-bodied wines from limestone hills between Narbonne and the sea. Red gains character after 2–3 yrs, whites can last even longer. Esp: Châteaux Rouquette-sur-Mer, Mire l'Etang, Pech-Céléyran, Pech-Redon, Ch de l'Hospitalet.

Claret Traditional English term for all red BORDEAUX.

Climat Burgundian word for individually named v'yd, eg BEAUNE Grèves.

Clos A term carrying some prestige, reserved for distinct (walled) v'yds, often in one ownership (esp Burgundy and ALSACE). Les CLOS is CHABLIS' grandest cru.

Clos de Bèze See CHAMBERTIN-CLOS DE BÈZE.

Clos de Gamot SW France ★★★ 82 83' 85 89 90' 95 96 98 00 (01) (02) One of the most famous CAHORS estates. Ultra-traditional, long-lived benchmark wines. Top CUVÉE "CLOS St Jean" is outstanding.

Clos des Lambrays Burg r ★★★ 90' 93 95 97 99' 00 02' 03 15-acre GRAND CRU vineyard at MOREY-ST-DENIS. Great potential here, now at last being realized.

Clos des Mouches Burg r w ★★★ Splendid PREMIER CRU BEAUNE v'yd, largely owned by DROUHIN. White and red wines, spicy and memorable – and consistent.

Clos des Papes S Rh r w ★★★ Gd 79-acre (18 plots) CHÂTEAUNEUF estate. Usually long-lived, stylish red (mainly Grenache, Mourvèdre) and white (5–12 yrs).

Clos de la Roche Burg r ★★★ 78' 85' 88 89' 90' 91 93' 95 96' 97 98 99' 00 01 02' 03 MOREY-ST-DENIS GRAND CRU (38 acres). Powerful and complex, like CHAMBERTIN. Amiot, BOUCHARD PÈRE ET FILS, DUJAC, LEROY, H Lignier, PONSOT, ROUSSEAU.

Clos du Roi Burg r ★★★ Part of GRAND CRU CORTON. Also a BEAUNE PREMIER CRU.

Clos Rougeard Lo r (sw) ★★★ 85 86 87 88 89 90 93 94 95 96 97 98 99 00 01 02 **03** Controversial SAUMUR-CHAMPIGNY; cult following. Intense wines aged in new (or nearly new) BORDEAUX barrels. Also tiny amount of luscious COTEAUX DE SAUMUR.

Clos St-Denis Burg r ★★★ 78 85' 88 89' 90' 91 93' 95 96' 97 98 99' 00 01 02' 03 16-acre GRAND CRU at MOREY-ST-DENIS. Splendid sturdy wine growing silky with age. Growers inc: Bertagna, DUJAC, and PONSOT.

Clos Ste-Hune Al w ★★★★ Very fine austere Ries from TRIMBACH; perhaps best in ALSACE. Needs 5+ yrs age; comes from GRAND CRU Rosacker – doesn't need GRAND CRU status.

Clos St-Jacques Burg r ★★★ 78' 85' 88 89' 90' 91 95 96' 97 98 99' 00 01 02 03 17-acre GEVREY-CHAMBERTIN PREMIER CRU. Excellent, powerful, velvety long-ager, often better (and dearer) than some GRANDS CRUS, esp: ESMONIN, JADOT, CLAIR, Fourrier, and ROUSSEAU.

Clos St-Jean Burg r (w) ★★ 89' 90' 91 95 96' 97 98 99' 01 02' 03 36-acre PREMIER CRU of CHASSAGNE-MONTRACHET. V.gd reds more solid than subtle, eg Ch de la Maltroye. Try RAMONET.

Clos de Tart Burg r ★★★ 85' 88' 89' 90' 93 95 96' 97 98 99' 00 01 02 GRAND CRU at MOREY-ST-DENIS, owned by MOMMESSIN. At best wonderfully fragrant, young or old.

Clos de Vougeot Burg r ★★★ 78' 85' 88 89' 90' 91 93' 95 96' 97 98 99' 00 01 02' 03 A 124-acre COTE DE NUITS GRAND CRU with many owners. Variable, occasionally sublime. Maturity depends on the grower's philosophy, technique, and position. Top growers inc: CH DE LA TOUR, DROUHIN, ENGEL, FAIVELEY, GRIVOT, GROS, HUDELOT-NOELLAT, JADOT, LEROY, Chantal Lescure, MÉO-CAMUZET, MUGNERET, VOUGERAIE.

Coche-Dury Burg ★★★★ 21-acre MEURSAULT DOMAINE (plus over an acre of CORTON-CHARLEMAGNE) with the highest reputation for oak-perfumed wines. Even MEURSAULT Villages is great (with age). Also v.gd ALIGOTÉ and reds.

Cognac Town and region of the Charentes, W France, and its brandy.

Colin-Deléger Burg ★★★ Leading CHASSAGNE-MONTRACHET estate. Superb, but rare PULIGNY-MONTRACHET Les Caillerets.

Collines Rhodaniennes N Rh r w p ★ Popular, lively Rhône VIN DE PAYS. Also young vine CÔTE-RÔTIE. Mainly red: Merlot, Syrah, Gamay. Some Viognier, CHARDONNAY.

Collioure Pyr r ★★ 95 96 97 98' **99 00** 01 02 03 Strong, dry red from BANYULS area. Tiny production. Top growers inc: Le CLOS des Paulilles, Doms du Mas Blanc, de la Rectorie, La Tour Vieille, Vial-Magnères.

Comté Tolosan SW r p w ★ DYA VIN DE PAYS. Covers multitude of sins and whole of the SW. Mostly co-op wines. Pioneering ★★ DOM DE RIBONNET (Christian Gerber, S of Toulouse) for range of varietal wines, some long keepers.

Condrieu N Rh w ★★★ 99 00' 01' 02 (03) Soft fragrant white of great character (and price) from Viognier. Can be outstanding, but rapid growth of v'yd (now 250 acres; 90 growers) has made quality more variable and increased use of young oak is a doubtful move. Best: Y Cuilleron, DELAS, Dumazet, Gangloff, GUIGAL, JABOULET, André Perret, Niéro, C Pichon, Vernay (esp long-lived Coteau de Vernon), Verzier. Dubious move to VENDANGE TARDIVE by some growers.

Confuron, J-J Burg r ★★★ Tiny NUITS-ST-GEORGES estate to follow. Modern-style, full of fruit.

Corbières Midi r (p w) ★★→★★★ 95 96 97 98' **99 00'** 01 02 03 Vigorous bargain reds from warm, stony AC. Best: Ch'x Aiguilloux, la Baronne, Lastours, des Ollieux, Les Palais, de la Voulte Gasparet, Doms de Fontsainte, du Vieux Parc, de Villemajou. Co-ops: Embrès-et-Castelmaure, Camplong, Tuchan.

Cordier, Ets D Important BORDEAUX shipper and château-owner with wonderful track-record, now owned by Groupe Val d'Orbieu-Listel. Over 600 acres. Inc Ch'x CANTEMERLE, LAFAURIE-PEYRAGUEY, MEYNEY, etc.

Cornas N Rh r ★★→★★★ 83' 85' 86 88' 89' 90' 91' 93 94' 95' 96 **97'** 98' 99' 00' 01' 02 03 Sturdy, mineral-edged very dark Syrah from 215-acre steep granite v'yds S of HERMITAGE. Needs to age 5–15 yrs but always keeps its rustic character. Top: Allemand, Colombo (but beware new oak), Clape, Courbis, DELAS, Dumien-Serrette, Juge, Lionnet, JABOULET (esp St-Pierre CUVÉE), Tardieu-Laurent (modern, expensive), N Verset, Voge.

Corrèze Dordogne r ★ DYA VIN DE PAYS from Co-op de Branceilles, between Brive and Beaulieu. Also Dom de la Mégénie.

Corsica (Vin de Corse) Strong wines of all colours. ACS are: AJACCIO and PATRIMONIO, and better crus Cap Corse and Calvi. VIN DE PAYS: ILE DE BEAUTE.

Corton Burg r ★★★ 78' 85' 88 89' 90' 91 93 95 96' **97** 98 99' 00 01 02' 03 The only GRAND CRU red of the CÔTE DE BEAUNE. 200 acres in ALOXE-CORTON inc CLOS DU ROI, Les Bressandes. Rich and powerful, should age well. Many gd growers.

Corton-Charlemagne Burg w ★★★★ 85' 86 88 89' 90' 92' 95 96' 97 98 99' 00' 01 02 White section (one-third) of CORTON. Rich, spicy, lingering, the GRAND CRU Chablis of the Côte d'Or; ages like a red. Top growers: BONNEAU DU MARTRAY, Chapuis, COCHE-DURY, Delarche, Dubreuil-Fontaine, FAIVELEY, HOSPICES DE BEAUNE, JADOT, LATOUR, Rapet, Rollin, ROUMIER, Javillier, VOUGERAIE.

Costières de Nîmes S Rh r p w ★→★★ 96 98' **99'** 00' 01 03 Rhône delta AC; fast-improving quality, from best names (best reds: 6–8 yrs). Formerly Costières du Gard. Ch'x de Campuget, Grande Cassagne, Mas Neuf, Mourgues-du-Grès, de Nages (esp Joseph Torres), de la Tuilerie, Mas des Bressades, Tardieu-Laurent, Dom du Vieux Relais. Whites worth a look.

> **Côte(s)** Means hillside; generally a superior vineyard to those on the plain. Many ACs are prefixed by "Côtes" or "Coteaux", meaning the same. In St-Emilion, distinguishes valley slopes from higher plateaux.

Côte de Beaune Burg r w ★★→★★★★ Used geographically: the S half of the CÔTE D'OR. Applies as an AC only to parts of BEAUNE itself.

Côte de Beaune-Villages Burg r ★★ 96' 98 **99'** 01 02' 03 Regional APPELLATION for lesser wines of classic area. Cannot be labelled "Côte de Beaune" without either "-Villages" or village name added.

Côte de Brouilly Beauj r ★★ **99 00 01 02** 03 Fruity rich BEAUJOLAIS cru, one of the best. Esp: Dom de Chavanne, G Cotton, Ch Delachanel, J-C Nesme, Ch Thivin.

Côte Chalonnaise Burg r w sp ★★ V'yd area between BEAUNE and MÂCON. See also BOUZERON, GIVRY, MERCUREY, MONTAGNY, RULLY. Alias "Région de Mercurey".

Côte de Nuits Burg r (w) ★★→★★★★ N half of CÔTE D'OR. Mostly red wine.

Côte de Nuits-Villages Burg r (w) ★★ 96' 97 98 99' 00 01 02' 03 A junior AC for extreme N and S ends of CÔTE DE NUITS; well worth investigating for bargains.

Côte d'Or Département name applied to the central and principal Burgundy v'yd slopes: CÔTE DE BEAUNE and CÔTE DE NUITS. The name is not used on labels.

Côte Roannaise Central France r p ★→★★ 95 96 97 98 99 00 00 01 02 03 AC W of Lyon. Silky, focused Gamay. Doms Demon, Lapandéry, du Pavillon, des Millets, Serol.

Côte-Rôtie N Rh r ★★★→★★★★ 78' 83' 85' 88' 89' 90' 91' 94' 95' 96 97 98' 99' 00 01' 03 Finest Rhône red, from S of Vienne, mainly Syrah. Achieves rich, complex softness and finesse with age (esp 5–10+ yrs). Top growers inc: Barge, Bernard, Burgaud, Champet, CHAPOUTIER, Clusel-Roch, DELAS, Gaillard, J-M Gérin, GUIGAL (long oak-ageing, different and fuller), JABOULET, Jamet, Jasmin, Ogier (oak), ROSTAING (oak here, too), VIDAL-FLEURY.

Coteaux d'Affreux Aspiring to VIN DE PAYS status. Should perhaps use grapes as base.

Coteaux d'Aix-en-Provence Prov r p w ★→★★★ AC on the move. Top properties inc: Ch Calissanne, Ch Revelette, Dom des Béates (CHAPOUTIER-owned), Dom du Ch Bas. See also BAUX-EN-PROVENCE.

Coteaux d'Ancenis Lo r p w (sw) ★ DYA VDQS E Of Nantes. Light Gamay red and rosé, sharpish dry white (Chenin Bl). Semi-sweet from Malvoisie (ages well) – esp Guindon.

Coteaux de l'Ardèche See L'ARDÈCHE.

Coteaux de l'Aubance Lo w sw ★★→★★★★ 88' 89' 90' 93' 94' 95' 96 97 98 99 00 01 02 03 Similar to COTEAUX DU LAYON, nervy sweet wines from Chenin Bl. A few SELECTION DES GRAINS NOBLES. Esp from Bablut, Haute-Perche, Montgilet, RICHOU, Rochelles.

Coteaux des Baronnies S Rh r p w ★ DYA Rhône VIN DE PAYS nr Nyons. Syrah, Cab Sauv, Merlot, CHARDONNAY, plus traditional grapes. Fresh textures, promising. Doms du Rieu-Frais (gd Viognier) and Rosière (gd Syrah) worth noting.

Côteaux de Chalosse SW France r p w ★ DYA. Gd country wines from co-op at Mugron (Landes).

Coteaux Champenois Champ r w (p) ★★★ DYA AC for non-sparkling CHAMPAGNE. Vintages follow those for CHAMPAGNE. Not worth inflated prices.

Coteaux du Giennois Lo r p w ★ DYA Small area N of POUILLY promoted to AC in 1998. Light red: blend of Gamay and Pinot N; Sauv Bl à la SANCERRE. Top grower: Paulat.

Coteaux de Glanes SW France r ★ DYA Lively VIN DE PAYS from nr Bretenoux (Lot). Co-op only producer. Mostly drunk in local restaurants. Excellent value.

Coteaux du Languedoc Midi r p w ★★→★★★ 95' 96 97 98' 99 00' 01 02 03 Scattered well-above-ordinary MIDI AC areas. Best reds (eg LA CLAPE, FAUGERES, St-Georges-d'Orques, Quatourze, ST-CHINIAN, Montpeyroux, PIC ST-LOUP) age for 2–4 yrs. Now also some gd whites. Standards rising dizzily.

Coteaux du Layon Lo w s/sw sw ★★→★★★★ 75 76 85' 86 88' 89' 90' 93' 94 95 96 97 98 99 00 01 02 03 Heart of ANJOU: sweet Chenin Bl; admirable acidity, ages almost forever. New SELECTION DES GRAINS NOBLES; cf ALSACE. Seven villages can add name to AC. Top ACS: BONNEZEAUX, Ch du Layon-Chaume (first GRAND CRU), QUARTS DE CHAUME. Growers inc: Badouin, BAUMARD, Cady, Delhumeau (Dom de Brize), Delesvaux, des Forges, Dom de Juchepie, Richard Leroy, Ogereau, Papin (CH DE PIERRE-BISE), Jo Pithon, P-Y Tijou (Soucherie), du Breuil.

Coteaux du Loir Lo r p w dr sw ★→★★★ 95 96 97 98 99 00 01 02 03 Small region N of Tours, inc JASNIÈRES. Sometimes fine Chenin Bl, Gamay, Pineau d'Aunis, Cab Sauv. Top growers: Chaussard, de Rycke, Fresneau, Gigou, Nicolas, Robinot. The Loir is a minor tributary of the Loire.

Coteaux de la Loire See ANJOU-COTEAUX DE LA LOIRE.

Coteaux du Lyonnais Beauj r p (w) ★ DYA Junior BEAUJOLAIS. Best EN PRIMEUR.

Coteaux de Peyriac Midi r p ★ DYA One of the most-used VIN DE PAYS names of the Aude département. Huge quantities.

Coteaux de Pierrevert S Rh r p w sp ★ Gd, early drinking co-op reds, rosés, fresh whites (inc gd Viognier) from nr Manosque. Dom la Blaque, Ch Régusse Ch Rousset: fuller reds. Promoted to AC in 1998.

Coteaux du Quercy SW France r →★★ 98' 99 00' 01 02 S of CAHORS promoted to VDQS, now queuing for AC. Private growers working alongside v.gd co-op nr Monpezat inc Doms de la Combarade, la Garde, d'Aries, de Guyot, de Lafage, de Merchien.

Coteaux de Saumur Lo w sw ★★→★★★ 89 90 93 95' 96 97 98 99 02 03 Rare potentially fine semi-sweet Chenin Bl. VOUVRAY-like sweet (MOELLEUX) best. Esp CLOS ROUGEARD, Lavigne, Legrand.

Coteaux et Terrasses de Montauban SW France r p DYA ★→★★ Dominated by co-op at LAVILLEDIEU-LE-TEMPLE. Better from Doms de Biarnès and de Montels.

Coteaux du Tricastin S Rh r p w ★★ 95' 98' 99' 00' 01' 03 Fringe mid-Rhône AC of increasing quality. Attractively spiced red can age 8 yrs. Doms de Grangeneuve, de Montine, St-Luc, and Ch La Décelle are among best.

Coteaux Varois Prov r p w ★→★★ 98' 99' 00' 01 02 03 Substantial AC zone: California-style Dom de St-Jean de Villecroze makes v.gd red, also CH'X ROUTAS, la Calisse, Doms les Alysses, du Deffends.

Coteaux du Vendômois Lo r p w ★→★★ DYA Fringe Loire VDQS W of Vendôme. Pineau d'Aunis is the key grape alone or with others, in rosés, reds and with Chenin Bl in whites. Promoted to AC in 2000. Producers inc: Dom du Four à Chaux, Cave du Vendôme-Villiers, Patrice Colin, Emile Heredia.

Côtes d'Auvergne Central Fr r p (w) ★→★★ DYA Flourishing small VDQS. Mainly Gamay. Best: Bellard, Boulin-Constant, Cave St-Verny, Dom de Peyra.

Côtes de Blaye B'x w ★ DYA Run-of-the-mill BORDEAUX white from BLAYE. Mainly Colombard.

Côtes de Bordeaux St-Macaire B'x w dr sw ★ DYA From E of SAUTERNES.

Côtes de Bourg B'x r ★→★★ 89' 90' 94 95 96 98 99 00' 01 02 AC used for many of the better reds of BOURG. Ch'x inc DE BARBE, DU BOUSQUET, Brûlesécaille, Bujan, Falfas, Fougas, Grand-Jour, Garreau, Guerry, Haut-Guiraud, Haut-Maco, Haut-Mondésir, Mercier, Nodoz, Peychaud, Roc de Cambes, Rousset, Sociondo, Tayac, Tour de Guiet.

Côtes du Brulhois SW France r p (w) ★→★★ 98 99 00 01 Nr Agen. Mostly centred on Goulens and Donzac coops. Also Dom de Coujétou-Peyret.

Côtes de Castillon B'x r ★→★★ 89 90' 94 95' 96' 98 99 00' 01 02 Flourishing region E of ST-EMILION; similar wines. Best ch'x inc: de l'A, d'Aiguilhe, de Belcier, Cap de Faugères, La Clarière-Laithwaite, CLOS l'Eglise, CLOS Puy Arnaud, PITRAY, Poupille, Robin, Veyry, Vieux Château Champs de Mars.

Côtes de Duras Dordogne r w p ★→★★ 00' 01 02 BORDEAUX satellite; mostly lighter wines. Top producers inc Doms de Laulan (gd Sauv Bl), de Durand (bio), de la Solle, du Vieux Bourg, Amblard, Petit Malrome, Ch La Grave Béchade. Gd co-op.

Côtes de Forez Lo r p (sp) ★ DYA Uppermost Loire VDQS (Gamay), around Boën, N of St-Etienne. Promoted to AC in 2000, but hardly worth bothering with.

Côtes de Francs B'x r w ★★ 89' 90' 94 95 96 97 98 00' 01 Fringe BORDEAUX from E of ST-EMILION. Increasingly attractive tasty wines, esp from Châteaux Charmes-Godard, Laclaverie, de Francs, Marsau, PUYGUERAUD, La Prade.

Côtes de Gascogne SW w (r p) ★ DYA VIN DE PAYS branch of ARMAGNAC. Very popular, led by Plaimont co-op and Grassa family (Ch de Tariquet). Best-known for fresh fruity Colombard-based white. Best: Doms de Joy, Papolle, Bergerayre, Maubet, Sancet, Ch Monluc. Also from MADIRAN growers.

Côtes du Jura r p w (sp) ★ DYA Many light tints/tastes. ARBOIS more substantial.

Côtes du Lubéron S Rh r p w ★→★★ 97 98' 99' 00' 01' 03 Greatly improved country wines from S Rhône. A proliferation of new producers inc actors and media-magnates. Star is Ch de la Canorgue. Others inc: Ch'x Val-Joanis, La Verrerie, de l'Isolette, Dom de la Citadelle, Verget, Vieille Ferme (w), and reliable co-ops Cellier de Marrenon, Cave de Bonnieux.

Côtes de la Malepère Midi r ★ DYA Rising star VDQS on frontier of MIDI and SW, nr Limoux using grape varieties from both. Watch for fresh eager reds.

Côtes du Marmandais Dordogne r p w ★→★★★ Ever more serious AC. Cocumont co-op better than Beaupuy. Excellent Eliane da Ros (CLOS Bacqueys). V.gd: Dom des Geais (best are weighty, need ageing). Gd: La Verrerie, Ch de Beaulieu.

Côtes de Montravel Dordogne w dr sw ★★ dr DYA sw 97' 98 99 01 (02) Part of BERGERAC; traditionally med-sw, now often drier. Gd from Ch'x de Montaigne, Pique-Sègue, La Raye, La Resssaude, Doms de Golse, de Perreau. MONTRAVEL SEC is dry, HAUT-MONTRAVEL is sweet.

Côtes de Provence Prov r p w ★→★★★ r 95' 96 97 95' 98' 99 00 01 02 03 (p w DYA) Revolutionized by new attitudes and investment. Leaders: Castel Roubine, Commanderie de Peyrassol, Doms Bernarde, de la Courtade, OTT, des Planes, Rabiéga, Richeaume, Ch Ste Rosaline. See COTEAUX D'AIX, BANDOL.

> **Top Côtes du Rhône producers:** Ch'x Courac, La Courançonne, l'Estagnol, Fonsalette, Grand Moulas, Hugues, Montfaucon, St-Esteve, Trignon (inc Viognier); Clos Simian; Co-ops Chantecotes (Ste-Cécile-les-Vignes), Villedieu (esp white); Doms La Bouvade, Charvin, Coudoulet de Beaucastel (red and white), Cros de la Mûre, Espigouette, Fond-Croze, Gourget, Gramenon (Grenache, Viognier), Janasse, Jaume, Perrin, Réméjeanne, St-Georges, Vieille Julienne, Vieux Chêne; Guigal, Jaboulet.

Côtes du Rhône S Rh r p w ★ 98' 99 00' 01' 03 Basic Rhône AC. Best drunk young – even as PRIMEUR. Wide variations of quality: some heavy over-production. Look for estate bottlings. See CÔTES DU RHÔNE-VILLAGES.

Côtes du Rhône-Villages S Rh r p w ★→★★ 89' 90' 95' 96' 97' 98' 99' 00' 01' 03 Wine from 16 best S Rhône villages. Substantial, mainly reliable, sometimes delicious. Red base is Grenache; but more Syrah and Mourvèdre now used. Growing white quality, often with Viognier, Roussanne. See BEAUMES-DE-VENISE, CAIRANNE, CHUSCLAN, LAUDUN, RASTEAU, SABLET, SÉGURET, ST-GERVAIS. Sub-category with non-specified village name: gd value, eg Ch. Signac, Doms Cabotte, Grand Veneur, Montbayon, Rabasse-Charavin, Renjarde, Romarins, Ste-Anne, St Siffrein, Cave Estézargues.

Côtes du Roussillon Pyr r p w ★→★★ 95 96 97 98 99 00 01 02 03 E Pyrenees AC. Hefty Carignan red is best, can be very tasty (eg Gauby). Some whites.

Côtes du Roussillon-Villages Pyr r ★★ 95 96 97 98 99 00 01 02 03 Region's best reds, 28 communes inc CARAMANY, LATOUR DE FRANCE, LESQUERDE, Tautavel. Best labels: Co-op Baixas, Cazes Frères, Doms des Chênes, la Cazenove, Gauby (inc full, exotic white), Ch de Jau, Co-op Lesquerde, Dom Piquemal, Co-op Les Vignerons Catalans. Some now renounce AC status to make varietal VIN DE PAYS.

Côtes de St-Mont SW France r w p ★★ (r) 98 99 00' 01' Highly successful Gers VDQS still seeking AC status, imitating MADIRAN, PACHERENC. Co-op Plaimont all-powerful (Virgnes Retrouvées and Hauts de Bergelle ranges, Ch de

Sabazan) sweet CUVÉE Saint-Albert (★★★) is outstanding. Independent growers inc: Ch de Bergalasse, Dom de Bartat, Dom Maouries.

Côtes du Tarn SW France r w ★ DYA VIN DE PAYS overlaps GAILLAC; from same growers esp co-ops, Ch de Vigné-Lourac, Doms de Labarthe, d'Escausses.

Côtes de Thongue Midi r w ★ DYA Popular VIN DE PAYS from HERAULT. Dynamic area with some gd wines esp Doms Arjolle, les Chemins de Bassac, Coussergues, Croix Belle, Magellan, Montmarin.

Côtes de Toul E France (Lorraine) p r w ★ DYA Very light wines; mainly VIN GRIS.

Côtes du Ventoux S Rh r p (w) ★★ 95' 98' 00' 01' 03 Booming (15,000-acre) AC between Rhône and PROVENCE for tasty reds (café-style to much deeper flavours), easy rosés, and decent whites. Best: La Vieille Ferme (r) owned by J-P Perrin of CH DE BEAUCASTEL; Co-op Bedoin, Goult, St-Didier, Dom Anges, Brusset, Cascavel, Fondrèche, Font-Sane, Murmurium, Verrière, Ch'x La Croix des Pins, Pesquié, Pigeade, Valcombe, PAUL JABOULET.

Côtes du Vivarais S Rh r p w ★ 98' 99' 00' 01' 03 DYA 2,500 acres across several villages W of Montélimar; promoted to AC 1999. Improving simple CUVÉES; substantial oak-aged reds. Best: Boulle, Gallety, Dom de Belvezet.

Coulée de Serrant Lo w d sw ★★★★ 76' 78 79' 81 82 83' 85' 86 88 89' 90' 91 92 93 95' 96 97 98 99 00 01 02 03 A 16-acre Chenin Bl v'yd on Loire's N bank at SAVENNIERES. Run on ferociously biodynamic principles. Intense strong fruity/sharp wine, gd apéritif and with fish. Ages almost for ever; decant the day before drinking.

Couly-Dutheil Lo r p w ★★-→★★★ 85 86 87 88 89 90 93 95 96 97 98 99 00 01 02 03 Major CHINON grower/merchant; range of reliable wines. CLOS d'Olive and l'Echo are top wines. New CUVÉE, Crescendo (oak-aged).

Courcel, Dom ★★★ Leading POMMARD estate – top PREMIER CRU Rugiens.

Crémant In CHAMPAGNE meant "creaming" (half-sparkling). Since 1975, an AC for quality classic-method sparkling from ALSACE, Loire, BOURGOGNE, and most recently LIMOUX – often a bargain. Term no longer used in CHAMPAGNE.

Crémant de Loire Lo w sp ★★-→★★★ NV High-quality sparkler, esp SAUMUR and TOURAINE. Producers: BAUMARD Berger, Delhumeau (Dme de Brize), LANGLOIS-CHATEAU, Nerleux, and Passavant.

Crépy Savoie w ★★ DYA Light, soft, Swiss-style white from S shore of Lake Geneva. "Crépitant" has been coined for its faint fizz.

Crozes-Hermitage N Rh r (w) ★★ 88 89' 90' 91' 94 95' 96 97' 98' 99' 00' Nr HERMITAGE: larger v'yds. Syrah: some is fruity, early-drinking (2+ yrs); some cask-aged (wait 4–8 yrs). Gd examples from Belle, B Chave, Ch Curson, Desmeure, Doms du Colombier, des Entrefaux, du Pavillon-Mercurol, de Thalabert of JABOULET, CHAPOUTIER, Fayolle Fils & Fille, Alain Graillot. Drink whites (mostly Marsanne) young.

Cruse et Fils Frères Historic BORDEAUX shipper. Now owned by Pernod-Ricard. The Cruse family (not the company) owns CH D'ISSAN.

Cunac SW France ★ r DYA Part of GAILLAC area. Light, fruity, quaffable reds.

Cussac Village S of ST-JULIEN. (AC HAUT-MEDOC.) Top ch'x: BEAUMONT, LANESSAN.

Cuve Close Short-cut method of making sparkling wine in a tank. Sparkle dies away in glass much quicker than with MÉTHODE TRADITIONELLE wine.

Cuvée Wine contained in a *cuve*, or vat. A word of many uses, inc synonym for "blend" and first-press wines (as in CHAMPAGNE); in Burgundy interchangeable with "cru". Often just refers to a "lot" of wine.

Dagueneau, Didier Lo ★★★ 96 97 98 99 00 01 02 Top POUILLY-FUMÉ producer. Pouilly's *enfant terrible* has created new benchmarks for the AC and Sauv Bl. Top CUVÉE: barrel-fermented Silex. Didier's uncle Serge is also a top producer.

Daumas Gassac See MAS DE DAUMAS GASSAC.

De Castellane Brut NV; Blanc de Blancs; Brut (95 96 98); Prestige Florens de

Castellane (**90 95 96**). Traditional Epernay CHAMPAGNE house linked with LAURENT-PERRIER. Best for vintage wines; esp CUVÉE Commodore Brut (**90 95**).

Degré alcoolique Degrees of alcohol, ie per cent by volume.

Deiss, Domaine Marcel Fine ALSACE grower at Bergheim with 50 acres, wide range inc splendid Ries (GRAND CRU Schoenenberg), GEWURZTRAMINER (Altenburg de Bergheim), gd SELECTION DES GRAINS NOBLES and VIN DE PAILLE.

Delamotte Brut; Blanc de Blancs (**95 96** 98); CUVÉE Nicolas Delamotte. Fine small CHARDONNAY-dominated CHAMPAGNE house at Le Mesnil, owned by LAURENT-PERRIER.

Delas Frères ★→★★★ Old, worthy firm of Rhône specialists with v'yds at CONDRIEU, CÔTE-ROTIE, HERMITAGE. Top wines: CONDRIEU, Hermitage M de Tourette (r w), Bessards. St Joseph Challeys gd value. Owned by ROEDERER. Quality rising.

Delbeck Small fine CHAMPAGNE house revitalized by former partners Martin/Giraudière. Now in hands of Vranken Pommery group. Find remaining stocks of excellent Pinot N-led vintages (**90 95' 96** 99), GRAND CRU Aÿ and Cramant.

Delorme, André ★★ Leading CÔTE CHALONNAISE merchants and growers. Specialists in v.gd CREMANT DE BOURGOGNE and excellent RULLY, etc.

Demi-Sec Half-dry: in practice more than half sweet (eg of CHAMPAGNE).

Des Guelasses, Dom Source of much restaurant house wine, most in pubs and nearly all in theatre bars.

Deutz Brut Classic NV; Rosé NV; Brut (**95 96** 98); Blanc de Blancs (**95 96** 98). One of top small CHAMPAGNE houses, ROEDERER-owned. Very dry, classic wines. Superb CUVÉE William Deutz (**90 95 96**).

Dirler, J-P Al ★★→★★★ Producer of GRAND CRUS Kessler, Saering, Spiegel; esp Ries.

Dom Pérignon, Cuvée 88 90' 92 93 95 96; Rosé **90' 95 96** Luxury CUVÉE of MOËT & CHANDON (launched 1936), named after the legendary abbey cellarmaster who first blended CHAMPAGNE. Astonishingly consistent quality and creamy character, esp with 10–15 yrs bottle-age. Also wine library of late-disgorged limited release older vintages back to 62.

Domaine Property, particularly in Burgundy and rural France.

Dopff & Irion ★→★★ Famous Riquewihr (ALSACE) business. Esp MUSCAT les Amandiers, Ries Les Murailles, GEWURZTRAMINER Les Sorcières, Pinot Gr Les Maquisards: long-lived. Gd CRÉMANT d'Alsace. Now part of PFAFFENHEIM CO-op.

Dopff au Moulin ★★ Ancient top-class family wine house at Riquewihr, ALSACE. Best: GEWURZTRAMINER GRAND CRUS brand, Sporen; Ries SCHOENENBOURG; Sylvaner de Riquewihr. Pioneers of ALSACE sp wine; gd CUVÉES: Bartholdi and Julien.

Dourthe Frères BORDEAUX merchant with wide range: gd crus BOURGEOIS, inc BELGRAVE, MAUCAILLOU, TRONQUOY-LALANDE. Beau-Mayne is well-made brand.

Doux Sweet.

Drappier, André Leading AUBE region CHAMPAGNE house. Family-run. Vinous NV, BRUT Zéro, Rosé Saignée, Millésime d'Exception (**99**), Signature BLANC DE BLANCS (**95 96** 98), Sumptuous prestige CUVÉE Grande Sendrée (**90 95 96**).

Drouhin, J & Cie Burg ★★★→★★★★ Deservedly prestigious grower (150 acres) and merchant with highest standards. Cellars in BEAUNE; v'yds in Beaune, CHABLIS, CLOS DE VOUGEOT, MUSIGNY, etc, and Oregon, USA. Top wines inc (esp) (w) BEAUNE-CLOS DES MOUCHES, CHABLIS LES CLOS, CORTON-CHARLEMAGNE, PULIGNY-MONTRACHET, Les Folatières (r) GRIOTTE-CHAMBERTIN, MUSIGNY, GRANDS-ECHÉZEAUX.

Duboeuf, Georges ★★→★★★ The Grand Fromage of BEAUJOLAIS. Top-class merchant at Romanèche-Thorin. Region's leader in every sense; huge range of admirable wines. Also MOULIN-À-VENT atypically aged in new oak, white MÂCONNAIS, etc.

Dubos High-level BORDEAUX NÉGOCIANT.

Duclot BORDEAUX NÉGOCIANT; top-growth specialist. Linked with J-P MOUEIX.

Ducournau, Patrick Exclusive MADIRAN grower also known as inventor of MICROBULLAGE and now sadly trading in oak chips.

Dugat Burg ★★★ Cousins Claude and Bernard both make excellent, deep coloured wines in GEVREY CHAMBERTIN under their respective labels.

Dujac, Domaine ★★★ Burg grower (Jacques Seysses) at MOREY-ST-DENIS with v'yds in that village and BONNES-MARES, ECHEZEAUX, GEVREY-CHAMBERTIN, etc. Splendidly vivid and long-lived wines. Now also NÉGOCIANT for village wines and Dujac Fils et Père. Also venture with other grapes in COTEAUX VAROIS.

Dulong Highly competent BORDEAUX merchant. Breaking all the rules with unorthodox Rebelle blends. Also VINS DE PAYS.

Durup, Jean Burg ★★ One of the biggest CHABLIS growers with 375 acres, inc Dom de l'Eglantière and admirable Ch de Maligny.

Duval-Leroy Fleur de Champagne Brut NV; Extra Brut; Brut **95 96** 98; Blanc de Blanc **95' 96** 98; Rosé de Saignée NV; Prestige Cuvée des Rois **95' 96**. Rising Côte des Blanc house; fine quality, gd value. Many other labels.

Echézeaux Burg r ★★★ 78' 85' 88 89' 90' 91 93 95 96' 97 98 99' 00 01 02' 03 74-acre GRAND CRU between VOSNE-ROMANÉE and CLOS DE VOUGEOT. Can be superlative, fragrant, without great weight, eg Confuron-Cotetidot, DROUHIN, DUJAC ENGEL, GRIVOT, A F GROS, MUGNERET, DRC, RION, ROUGET.

Ecu, Dom de l' Lo dr w r ★★★ 85 86 87 88 89 90 93 95 96 97 98 99 00 01 02 03 Outstanding producer of MUSCADET DE SEVRE-ET-MAINE as well as delicious GROS PLANT DU PAYS NANTAIS. Cab Sauv rivals many SAUMUR-CHAMPIGNY. Biodynamic.

Edelzwicker Alsace w ★ DYA Modest blended light white.

d'Eguisheim, Cave Vinicole ★ V.gd ALSACE CO-OP: fine GRAND CRUS Hatschbourg, Hengst, Ollwiller, Spiegel. Owns Willm. Top label: WOLFBERGER. Best ranges: Grande Réserve, Sigillé, Armorié. Gd CRÉMANT and Pinot N.

Engel, R ★★★ Top-class grower of CLOS DE VOUGEOT, ECHÉZEAUX, GRANDS-ECHÉZEAUX, and VOSNE-ROMANÉE.

Entraygues SW France r p w DYA ★ Fragrant VDQS. Esp F Avallon's dry white.

Entre-Deux-Mers B'x w ★→★★ DYA Improving dry white BORDEAUX from between Rivers Garonne and Dordogne (aka E-2-M). Esp Ch'x BONNET, Fontenille, Moulin de Launay, Sainte-Marie, Tour de Mirambeau, Toutigeac, Turcaud

Esmonin, Sylvie Burg ★★★ Very classy GEVREY-CHAMBERTIN, esp CLOS ST-JACQUES.

Estaing SW France r p w ★ DYA Neighbour of ENTRAYGUES and similar in style.

L'Estandon Brand name of everyday wine of Nice (AC CÔTES DE PROVENCE): all colours.

l'Etoile Jura w dr sp (sw) ★★ Sub-region of the JURA known for stylish whites, inc VIN JAUNE, similar to CHÂTEAU-CHALON; gd sparkling.

Faiveley, J Burg ★★→★★★★ Family-owned growers and merchants at NUITS-ST-GEORGES, with v'yds (270 acres) in CHAMBERTIN-CLOS DE BEZE, CHAMBOLLE-MUSIGNY, CORTON, MERCUREY, NUITS (74 acres). Consistent high quality (rather than charm).

Faller, Théo/Domaine Weinbach ★★→★★★★ Top ALSACE grower (Kaysersberg) run by Colette Faller and her 2 daughters. Concentrated wines needing ageing up to 10 yrs. Esp GRAND CRUS SCHLOSSBERG (Ries), Furstentum (GEWURZTRAMINER).

Faugères Midi r (p w) ★★ 95 96 97 98' 99 00' 01 02 03 Isolated COTEAUX DU LANGUEDOC village with exceptional terroir. Wines gained AC status 1982. Esp Doms Alquier, Barral, du Météore, des Estanilles, Ch La Liquière.

Fessy, Sylvain Beauj ★★ Dynamic BEAUJOLAIS merchant with wide range.

Fèvre, William Burg ★★★ CHABLIS grower with biggest GRAND CRU holding, Dom de la Maladière (45 acres). Improved since bought by HENRIOT in 1998.

Fiefs Vendéens Lo r p w ★ DYA Up-and-coming VDQS for light wines from the Vendée, just S of MUSCADET on the Atlantic coast. Wines from CHARDONNAY, Chenin Bl, Colombard, Grolleau, Melon (whites), Cab Sauv, Pinot N, and Gamay for reds and rosés. Esp Coirier, Ferme des Ardillers, Michon.

Filliatreau, Domaine Lo r ★★→★★★ 89 90 93 95 96 97 98 00 01 02 03 Paul Filliatreau put SAUMUR-CHAMPIGNY on the map and in Paris restaurants. Supple, fruity, drinkable Jeunes Vignes. Other CUVÉES aged 2–5 yrs (VIEILLES VIGNES and La Grande Vignolle).

FRANCE

Fitou Midi r ★★ **95 96 97 98' 99 00'** 01 02 03 Superior CORBIERES-style reds; powerful, ageing well. Best from co-ops at Cascastel, Paziols, and Tuchan. Interesting experiments with Mourvèdre grapes in Leucate. Gd estates, inc Ch Nouvelles, Dom Lérys, Rolland.

Fixin Burg r ★★★ **89' 90' 91 93 95 96' 97** 98 99 01 02 Worthy and under-valued N neighbour of GEVREY-CHAMBERTIN. Often splendid reds. Best v'yds: CLOS du Chapitre, Les Hervelets, CLOS Napoléon. Growers inc Bertheau, R Bouvier, CLAIR, FAIVELEY, Gelin, Gelin-Molin, Guyard.

Fleurie Beauj r ★★★ **99 00 01 02** 03 The epitome of a BEAUJOLAIS cru: fruity, scented, silky, racy wines. Esp from Chapelle des Bois, Chignard, Depardon, Després, DUBOEUF, de Fleurie, Métras, the co-op.

Floc de Gascogne SW France r p w ARMAGNAC's answer to PINEAU DES CHARENTES. Apéritif from unfermented grape juice blended with ARMAGNAC.

Fortant de France Midi r p w ★→★★ VIN DE PAYS D'OC brand (dressed to kill) of reliable-quality single-grape wines from Sète neighbourhood. See SKALLI.

Frais Fresh or cool. **Frappé** Ice-cold. **Froid** Cold.

Fronsac B'x r ★→★★★ **85' 86' 88' 89' 90' 94 95 96 98** 00' 01 Picturesque area W of ST-EMILION; increasingly fine, often tannic red. Ch'x inc: de Carles, DALEM, LA DAUPHINE, Fontenil, La Grave, Mayne-Vieil, Moulin-Haut-Laroque, LA RIVIERE, La Rousselle, Les Trois Croix, La Vieille Cure, Villars. See also CANON-FRONSAC.

Fronton SW France r p ★★ **00' 01** 02 Called the "BEAUJOLAIS of Toulouse". DYA but Cab Sauv red needs longer. Gd growers: Doms de Caze, Joliet, du Roc; Ch'x Bellevue-la-Forêt, Boujac, Bouissel, Cahuzac, Coutinel, Plaisance, St-Guilhem.

Frontignan Midi golden sw ★★ NV Strong, sweet, liquorous MUSCAT of ancient repute. Quality steadily improving, esp from Ch'x Stony and La Peyrade.

Furstentum (ALSACE) GRAND CRU at Kientzheim and Sigolsheim renowned for superb ripening ability. See FALLER DOM WEINBACH and PAUL BLANCK.

Gagnard, Jean-Noel Burg ★★★ Jean Noel's daughter, Caroline l'Estimé, has pushed this DOMAINE to the top of the Gagnard clan. Beautifully expressive GRAND CRU, PREMIER CRU, and village wines in CHASSAGNE-MONTRACHET. Also cousins Gagnard-Delagrange, Blain-Gagnard, Fontaine-Gagnard.

A Guide to Gaillac

Good all-rounders Mas Pignou, Mas d'Aurel, Doms de Barreau, Labarthe, and d'Escausses, Ch de Mayragues, co-op at Técou (esp. "Passion" range).
Reds (★★) Doms de Cailloutis, Larroque, Pialentou, Salvy, and La Chanade.
Local varieties Robert Plageoles, Doms de Ramaye, Causse-Marines (all ★★★).
Sweet whites Doms de Causse-Marines, Rotier, Long Pech, Mas de Bicary.
Dry whites Dom de Causse-Marines, Chx d'Arlus, Vigné-Lourac. (★★→★★★)
Sparkling Doms Réné Rieux, La Tronque, and Canto Perlic.
Vins de pays Dom Borie-Vieille (Muscadelle) **Perlé** Dom de Salmes

---

Gaillac SW France r p w dr sw sp ★→★★★ Mostly DYA except oaked reds **98 00 01** 02. Also sweet whites (**97' 98 99 00' 01'**).

Garage Vins de Garage are (usually) BORDEAUX made on such a small scale your garage would be big enough. A bottle costs much the same as a full service.

Gard, Vin de Pays du Languedoc ★ The Gard département at the mouth of the Rhône is a centre of gd VIN DE PAYS production, inc Coteaux Flaviens, Pont du Gard, Cévennes, SABLES DU GOLFE DU LION, Salavès, Uzège, Vaunage.

Gers r w p ★ DYA Indistinguishable from nearby CÔTES DE GASCOGNE.

Gevrey-Chambertin Burg r ★★★ **88 90' 91 93 95** 96' **97** 98 99' 00 01 02' 03 Village containing the great CHAMBERTIN, its GRAND CRU cousins and many other noble v'yds (eg PREMIERS CRUS Cazetiers, Combe aux Moines, CLOS ST-JACQUES,

CLOS des Varoilles). Growers inc: Bachelet, L Boillot, Burguet, Damoy, DROUHIN, DUGAT, ESMONIN, FAIVELEY, Harmand-Geoffroy, Geantet-Pansiot, JADOT, Leclerc, LEROY, MORTET, ROTY, ROUSSEAU, SERAFIN, TRAPET, VAROILLES.

Gewurztraminer Speciality grape of ALSACE: 1 of 4 allowed for specified GRAND CRU wines. The most aromatic of ALSACE grapes: at best like rose petals to smell, grapefruit and/or lychees to taste.

Gigondas S Rh r p ★★→★★★ 78' 81' 85 88 89' 90' 94 95' 96 97 98' 99' 00' 01' 03 Worthy neighbour to CHÂTEAUNEUF. Strong, full-bodied, sometimes peppery, largely Grenache. Try: Ch de Montmirail, Redortier, Saint-Cosme, CLOS du Joncuas, Dom Boussière, du Cayron, Font-Sane, Goubert, Gour de Chaulé, Grapillon d'Or, Les Hauts de Montmirail, Pesquier, les Pallières, Piaugier, Raspail-Ay, Sta-Duc, St-Gayan, des Travers, du Trignon.

Ginestet Long-established BORDEAUX NÉGOCIANT now owned by Bernard Taillan, said to be second in turnover.

Girardin, Vincent Burg r w ★★→★★★ Quality grower in SANTENAY now dynamic merchant, specializing in CÔTE DE BEAUNE ACS. Modern, oak and fruit style.

Givry Burg r w ★★ 95 96' 97 98 99 00 02 Underrated CÔTE CHALONNAISE village: light but tasty and typical burgundy from eg DELORME, Dom Joblot, L LATOUR, T Lespinasse, CLOS Salomon, Sarrazin, BARON THENARD.

Gorges et Côtes de Millau SW France r p w ★ DYA Locally popular country wines: red best. Gd co-op at Aguessac. Some private growers for the brave.

Gosset Very old small CHAMPAGNE house at AŸ. Excellent full-bodied wine (esp Grand Millésime 96). Gosset Celebris (90 95 96) is prestige CUVÉE, with Celebris Rosé (95 96), launched in 1995 by owners, Cointreau family of COGNAC Frapin.

Gouges, Henri ★★★ Reinvigorated estate for rich, complex NUITS-ST-GEORGES, with great ageing potential.

Goût Taste. Goût anglais: as the English like it (ie dry for CHAMPAGNE, or well-aged).

Grand Cru One of top Burgundy v'yds with its own AC. In ALSACE one of the 50 top v'yds covered by ALSACE Grand Cru AC, but more vague elsewhere. In ST-EMILION the third rank of ch'x, inc about 200 properties.

Grande Champagne The AC of the best area of COGNAC. Nothing fizzy about it.

Grande Rue, La Burg r ★★★ 89' 90' 91 93 95 96' 97 98 99' 00 01 02' 03 VOSNE-ROMANÉE GRAND CRU, neighbour to ROMANÉE-CONTI. Owned by Dom Lamarche.

Grands-Echézeaux Burg r ★★★★ 78' 85' 88' 89' 90' 91' 93 95 96' 97 98 99' 00 01 02' Superlative 22-acre GRAND CRU next to CLOS DE VOUGEOT. Wines not weighty but aromatic. Viz: DROUHIN, ENGEL, DRC, GROS.

Gratien, Alfred and **Gratien & Meyer** ★★→★★★ Brut NV; Brut 95 96' 98; Prestige Cuvée Paradis Brut and Rosé (96). Excellent smaller family-run CHAMPAGNE house. Fine, very dry, long-lasting wine is still fermented in barrels. Gratien & Meyer is counterpart at SAUMUR. (V.gd CUVÉE Flamme.) Both owned by large German company but no lessening of standards.

Graves B'x r w ★★→★★★★ Region S of BORDEAUX city with excellent soft earthy red, dry white reasserting star status. PESSAC-LEOGNAN is inner zone.

Graves de Vayres B'x r w ★ 95 96 98 99 00' DYA ENTRE-DEUX-MERS; no special character.

Griotte-Chambertin Burg r ★★★★ 85' 88' 89' 90' 91 93 95 96' 97 98 99' 00 01 02' 03 A 14-acre GRAND CRU adjoining CHAMBERTIN. Similar wine, but less masculine, more "tender". Growers inc: DUGAT, DROUHIN, PONSOT.

Grivot, Jean Burg ★★★→★★★★ 35-acre COTE DE NUITS dom, in 5 ACS inc RICHEBOURG, Nuits PREMIERS CRUS, VOSNE-ROMANÉE, and CLOS DE VOUGEOT. Top quality.

Groffier, Robert Burg ★★★ Pure, elegant GEVREY-CHAMBERTIN, CHAMBOLLE-MUSIGNY, esp Les Amoureuses.

Gros, Domaines Burg ★★★→★★★★ Excellent family of vignerons in VOSNE-

ROMANÉE comprising (at least) Doms Jean, Michel, Anne, Anne-François Gros and Gros Frère et Soeur.

Gros Plant du Pays Nantais Lo w ★ DYA Junior VDQS cousin of MUSCADET, sharper, lighter; from the COGNAC grape, aka Folle Blanche, Ugni Blanc, etc.

Guffens-Heynen Burg ★★★ Belgian POUILLY-FUISSÉ grower. Tiny quantity, top quality. Heady Gamay. Also CÔTE D'OR wines (bought-in grapes) as VERGET.

Guigal, Ets E Celebrated grower (22-ha CÔTE-RÔTIE) HERMITAGE, ST-JOSEPH. Merchant (CONDRIEU, CÔTE-RÔTIE, HERMITAGE). Owns VIDAL-FLEURY, de Vallouit, Dom J-L Grippat. By ageing single-v'yd CÔTE-RÔTIE (La Mouline, La Landonne, La Turque) for 42 months in new oak, Guigal breaks local tradition to please (esp) American palates. Standard wines: gd value, reliable, esp red CÔTES DU RHONE. Also full oaky CONDRIEU La Doriane ; sweet Luminescence.

Guy Saget Lo ★★ Family firm with v'yds in the POUILLY-FUMÉ and Pouilly sur Loire appellations (Dom Saget), gradually buying up estates throughout the Loire to become one of the region's biggest proprietors. Saget's NÉGOCIANT line accounts for half the firm's annual production of 5 million bottles.

Haut-Poitou Lo w r ★→★★ DYA Up-and-coming VDQS S of ANJOU. V.gd whites from CAVE linked with DUBOEUF. Reds: Gamay, Cab Sauv, best age 4–5 yrs. Has rejected restrictions of AC status for freedom of choice.

Haut-Benauge B'x w ★ DYA AC for a limited area in ENTRE-DEUX-MERS.

Haut-Médoc B'x r ★★→★★★ 82' 83' 85' 86' 88' 89' 90' 95 96 98 00 01' 02 Big AC inc best parts of MÉDOC. Most of zone has communal ACS (eg MARGAUX, PAUILLAC). Some excellent ch'x (eg LA LAGUNE): simply AC HAUT-MÉDOC.

Haut-Montravel Dordogne w sw ★★ 90' 95 97' 98 99 01 02 Rare MONTRAVEL sweet white; rather like MONBAZILLAC. Look for Ch'x Le Bondieu, Moulin Caresse, Puy-Servain-Terrement, Roque-Peyre, also Doms de Libarde and de Gouyat.

Hautes-Côtes de Beaune Burg ★★ r 96 98 99' 00 01 02' 03 w 99' 00' 01 02' 03 AC for 12 villages in the hills behind the CÔTE DE BEAUNE. Light wines, worth investigating. Top growers: Cornu, Devevey, Jacob, Mazilly.

Hautes-Côtes de Nuits Burg ★★ r 96 98 99' 00 01 02' 03 w 99' 00' 01 02' 03 As above, for CÔTE DE NUITS. An area on the way up. Top growers: Duband, C Cornu, Jayer-Gilles, m ARGOS. Also has large BEAUNE co-op.

Heidsieck, Charles Brut Réserve NV; Brut 90' 95 96; Rosé 95 96 Major Reims CHAMPAGNE house, now controlled by Rémy Martin. Blanc des Millénaires (90' 95 96). Fine quality recently esp innovative Mis en Cave range of NV CUVÉES showing year of bottling. NV: real bargain. See also PIPER-HEIDSIECK.

Heidsieck, Monopole Brut NV Blue Top; Red Top; Gold Top (96 97 98). Once illustrious CHAMPAGNE house now owned by VRANKEN group. Red Top CUVÉE virtually BLANC DE NOIRS.

Hengst Wintzenheim (ALSACE) GRAND CRU. Excels with top-notch GEWURZTRAMINER from Albert Mann; also Pinot-Auxerrois, Chasselas (esp JOSMEYER'S) and Pinot N (esp A Mann's) with no GRAND CRU status.

Henriot Brut Souverain NV; Blanc de Blancs de Chardonnay NV; Brut 90 95 98; Brut Rosé 96 98; Luxury Cuvée: Cuvée des Enchanteleurs 88 90 95. Old family CHAMPAGNE house; regained independence in 1994. Very fine, fresh, creamy style. Joseph H also owns BOUCHARD PÈRE ET FILS (since 1995) and FEVRE.

Hérault Midi Biggest v'yd département: 263,000 acres. Some v.gd AC COTEAUX DU LANGUEDOC and pioneering VIN DE PAYS de l'Hérault, as well as VIN DE TABLE.

Hermitage N Rh r w ★★★→★★★★ 61' 66 72 78' 82 83' 85' 88 89' 90' 91' 94 95' 96' 97' 98' 99' 00 01' (02) 03 Dark, powerful, and profound. Truest example of Syrah from 312 acres on bank of Rhône. Needs long ageing. Heady and golden whites (Marsanne, some Roussanne); best mature for up to 25 yrs. Best: Belle, CHAPOUTIER, CHAVE, Dom du Colombier, DELAS, Desmeure, Faurie, GUIGAL, JABOULET, M Sorrel, Tardieu-Laurent. TAIN co-op also gd.

Hospices de Beaune Burg Historic hospital and charitable institution in BEAUNE, with excellent v'yds (known by CUVÉE names) in BEAUNE, CORTON, MEURSAULT, POMMARD, VOLNAY. Wines are auctioned on the third Sunday of each November.

Hudelot-Noëllat, Alain Under-appreciated VOUGEOT estate producing some excellent wines, in a light but fine style.

Huët L'Echansonne Lo ★★→★★★★ 47' 59' 76' 85' 88' 89' 90' 93 95' 96 97 98 99 00 01 03 (SEC/DEMI-SEC) 02 03 Leading estate in VOUVRAY, run on biodynamic principles. Now run by Huët's son-in-law Noel Pinguet. Wines for long ageing. Single-v'yd wines best: Le Haut Lieu, Le Mont, CLOS du Bourg.

Hugel et Fils ★★→★★★★ Best-known ALSACE company; founded at Riquewihr in 1639 and still in the family. "Johnny" H (retired 1997) is the region's beloved spokesman (Jean-Philippe and Etienne are in charge, Marc is winemaker). Quality escalates with Tradition and Jubilee ranges. Hugels are militantly against ALSACE GRAND CRU system. Hugel pioneered SELECTIONS DES GRAINS NOBLES and still makes some of finest examples. Also occasionally VIN DE PAILLE.

Ile de Beauté Name given to VINS DE PAYS from CORSICA. Mostly red.

Impériale BORDEAUX bottle holding 8 normal bottles (6 litres).

Irancy ("Bourgogne Irancy") Burg r (p) ★★ 96' 98 99' 00 02' 03 Gd light red made nr CHABLIS from Pinot N and the local César. The best vintages mature well. To watch. Growers inc Colinot.

Irouléguy SW France r p (w) ★★ 98' 00 01 02 Local wines of Basque country with a rustic twang. Dark dense Tannat/Cab Sauv reds to keep 5 yrs. Gd from Abotia; Doms Arretxea, Brana, Etchegaraya, Ilarria; co-op. Rivals MADIRAN.

Jaboulet Aîné, Paul Old family firm at TAIN, leading grower of HERMITAGE (esp La Chapelle ★★★★), CORNAS St-Pierre, CROZES Thalabert (v.gd value), Roure; merchant of other Rhône wines esp CÔTES DU RHONE Parallèle 45, CÔTES DU VENTOUX. Drink whites young.

Jacquart Brut NV; Brut Rosé NV (Carte Blanche and Cuvée Spéciale); Brut 90 95 96 Co-op-based CHAMPAGNE marque; in quantity the sixth-largest. Fair quality. Luxury brands: Cuvée Nominée Blanc 95 96 and Rosé 95 96. V.gd Mosaïque Blanc de Blancs 96' 98 and Rosé 96

Jacquesson Excellent small Dizy CHAMPAGNE house. V.gd Avize GRAND CRU 95 96; exquisite barrel-fermented "Grand Vin" Signature: white (88' 90 95') and rosé (95). Aÿ GRAND CRU Vauzelle Terme 96 and excellent NV CUVÉE 728.

Jadot, Louis Burg ★★→★★★★★ Top-quality merchant house with v'yds (155 acres) in BEAUNE, CORTON, Magenta, Ch des Jacques (MOULIN A VENT), etc. Wines to bank on.

Jardin de la France Lo w r p DYA One of France's 4 regional VINS DE PAYS. Covers Loire Valley: mostly single grape (esp CHARDONNAY, Gamay, Sauv Bl).

Jasnières Lo w dr (sw) ★★★ 76 78 79 83 85 86 88' 89' 90' 93 95' 96 97 98 99 00 01 02 03 Rare and almost immortal dry VOUVRAY-like wine (Chenin Bl) of N TOURAINE. Esp Aubert la Chapelle, Chaussard, Gigou, Nicolas, Robinot.

Jayer, Henri Near-legendary Burgundy figure. See ROUGET.

Jeroboam In BORDEAUX, a 6-bottle bottle (holding 4.5 litres) or triple MAGNUM; in CHAMPAGNE, a double MAGNUM.

Jobard, François Burg ★★★ Small MEURSAULT DOMAINE; classic, slow-evolving wines. Look out also for nephew Remi Jobard's more modern-style wines.

Jolivet, Pascal Lo ★★ →★★★ Considerable producer of gd SANCERRE and POUILLY-FUMÉ at several levels.

Joseph Perrier Cuvée Royale Brut NV; Cuvée Royale Blanc de Blancs NV; Cuvée Royale Rosé NV; Brut 95 96' 98. Excellent smaller CHAMPAGNE house at Chalons with gd v'yds in Marne Valley. Supple fruity style; v.gd prestige Cuvée Joséphine 89 90. Part-owned since 1998 by Alain THIÉNOT.

Josmeyer ★★→★★★★ Family house at Wintzenheim, ALSACE. V.gd long-ageing wines, esp GEWURZTRAMINER, Pinot Bl. Fine Ries from GRAND CRU Hengst. Wide range.

Juliénas Beauj r ★★★ **99 00 01** 02 03 Leading cru of BEAUJOLAIS: vigorous fruity wine to keep 2–3 yrs. Growers inc: Ch'x du Bois de la Salle, des Capitans, de Juliénas, des Vignes; Doms Bottière, R Monnet, Michel Tête, co-op.

Jura See CÔTES DU JURA.

Jurançon w sw dr ★→★★★ SW **90 95 97' 98 00** 01 (02) dr **98 00 01' 02** Racy long-lived speciality of Pau in Pyrenean foothills. Not to be missed: best like wildflower SAUTERNES. Sweet best, esp apéritif. Growers: Doms du Barrère, Bellegarde, Bordenave, Capdevielle, Castéra, de Souch, du Cinquau, Cauhapé, Gaillot, Jolys, Lamouroux, Lapeyre, Larredya, Nigri, de Rousse, Uroulat, Bousquet, Bellevue, Cabarrouy. Co-op's Grain Sauvage, BRUT d'Ocean, Peyre d'Or.

Kaefferkopf Alsace w dr sw ★★★ Ammerschwihr v'yd famous for blends rather than single-variety wines and denied GRAND CRU status for this reason.

Kientzheim-Kayserberg, Cave Vinicole de ★→★★ Important ALSACE co-op back to top quality. Esp GEWURZTRAMINER, Ries GRAND CRU Schlossberg and CRÉMANT.

Kientzler, André ★★→★★★ ALSACE Ries specialist in Geisburg GRAND CRU, esp VENDANGE TARDIVE and SGN. Equally gd from GCs Kirchberg de Ribeauvillé for GEWURZTRAMINER, Osterberg for occasional "vins de glaces" (Eisweins). Also v.gd Auxerrois, Chasselas.

Kreydenweiss Marc ★★→★★★ Fine ALSACE grower: 30 acres at Andlau, esp for Pinot Gr (v.gd GRAND CRU Moenchberg), Pinot Bl and Ries. Top wine: GRAND CRU Kastelberg (ages 20 yrs); also fine Auxerrois "Kritt Klevner" and gd VENDANGE TARDIVE. One of first in ALSACE to use new oak. Gd Ries/Pinot Gr blend "CLOS du Val d'Eléon". Great believer in terroir and in biodynamic viticulture.

Kriter Popular sparkler processed in Burgundy by PATRIARCHE. See the fountain on the Autoroute du Soleil.

Krug Grande Cuvée; Vintage **85' 88** 90 95; Rosé; CLOS du Mesnil (Blanc de Blancs) **85 88** 90; Krug Collection **62 64 66 69 71 73 76 79 81** Small and supremely prestigious CHAMPAGNE house. Dense, full-bodied very dry wines: long ageing, superlative quality. Owned since 1999 by MOËT-Hennessy.

Kuentz-Bas ★→★★★ Top-quality ALSACE grower/merchant at Husseren-les Châteaux, esp for Pinot Gr, GEWURZTRAMINER. Gd VENDANGES TARDIVES. Owned by Caves B Adam.

Labouré-Roi Burg ★★→★★★ Reliable, dynamic merchant at NUITS. Mostly white, but now also owns top red new-generation merchant Nicolas POTEL.

Ladoix-Serrigny Burg r (w) ★★ **95 96'** 97 98 99' 01 02' 03 Northernmost village of CÔTE DE BEAUNE below hills of CORTON. To watch for bargains.

Ladoucette, de ★★→★★★ 89 90 93 94 95 96 97 98 99 00 01 Leading producer of POUILLY-FUMÉ, based at Ch de Nozet. Luxury brand Baron de L can be wonderful. Also SANCERRE Comte Lafond, La Poussie, Marc Brédif (and PIC, CHABLIS).

Lafarge, Michel ★★★★ 25-acre CÔTE DE BEAUNE estate with excellent VOLNAYS.

Lafon, Domaine des Comtes Burg ★★★★ Top estate in MEURSAULT, LE MONTRACHET, VOLNAY. Glorious intense whites; extraordinary dark reds. Also in the Maconnais.

Laguiche, Marquis de Burg ★★★★ Largest owner of LE MONTRACHET. Superb DROUHIN-made wines.

Lalande de Pomerol B'x r ★★→★★★ **88' 89' 90' 94 95 96 98 99** 00' 01' Neighbour to POMEROL. Wines similar, but less mellow. General improvement in quality from 99. New investors and younger generation taking over. Top ch'x: Les Annereaux, DE BEL-AIR, Belles-Graves, Bertineau-St-Vincent, La Croix-St-André, La Fleur de Boüard, Garraud, Perron, La Sergue, SIAURAC, TOURNEFEUILLE. To try.

Lamartine, Château SW France r ★★★ 95 98 00 01 02 One of top new CAHORS estates. Powerful reds which also achieve some elegance and finesse.

Landron (Domaines) Lo dr w (also Dom de la Louvetrie) Excellent organic producer of MUSCADET DE SÈVRE ET MAINE with several CUVÉES, bottled by terroir, inc Fief du Breuil and Amphibolite.

Langlois-Château Lo ★→★★★ One of top SAUMUR sp houses (esp CRÉMANT).

Controlled by BOLLINGER. Also range of still wines, esp Saumur Bl VIEILLES VIGNES.

Lanson Père & Fils Black Label NV; Rosé NV; Brut **95 96' 97** 98 Important improving CHAMPAGNE house; cellars at Reims. Long-lived luxury brand: Noble CUVÉE BLANC DE BLANCS (**95'** 96). Black Label improved by longer ageing.

Laroche ★★→★★★★ Important grower (190 acres) and dynamic CHABLIS merchant, inc Doms La Jouchère and Laroche. Top wines: Blanchots (esp Réserve de l'Obédiencerie ★★★) and CLOS VIEILLES VIGNES. Also blends gd non-regional CHARDONNAY and now ambitious MIDI range, Dom La Chevalière.

Latour, Louis Burg ★★→★★★★ Famous merchant and grower with v'yds (120 acres) in BEAUNE, CORTON, etc. V.gd white: CHEVALIER-MONTRACHET Les Demoiselles, CORTON-CHARLEMAGNE, MONTRACHET, gd-value MONTAGNY and ARDECHE CHARDONNAY etc. Ch de Corton Grancey. Also Pinot N Valmoissine from the Var.

Latour de France r (w) r→★★ **95 96 97 98 99** 00 01 02 Supposedly superior village in AC CÔTES DE ROUSSILLON-VILLAGES.

Latricières-Chambertin Burg r ★★★ 85' 88' 89' **90' 93 95** 96' **97** 98 99' 00 01 02' 03 17-acre GRAND CRU neighbour of CHAMBERTIN. Similar wine but lighter and "prettier", eg from FAIVELEY, LEROY, PONSOT, TRAPET.

Laudun S Rh w r p ★ **99 00 01 03** Village of CÔTES DU RHONE-VILLAGES (W bank). Soft reds. Attractive wines from Serre de Bernon co-op, inc fresh whites. Dom Pelaquié best, esp white. Also Ch'x Courac, Duseigneur, Prieuré St-Pierre.

Laurent-Perrier Brut NV; Rosé NV; Brut **95** 96 98 99. Dynamic family-owned CHAMPAGNE house at Tours-sur-Marne. V.gd minerally NV; excellent luxury brands: Grand Siècle La CUVÉE Lumière du Millésime (**90**), CGS Alexandra Brut Rosé (**90' 95** 96). Also Ultra Brut. Owns SALON, DELAMOTTE, DE CASTELLANE.

Lavilledieu-du-Temple SW France r p w ★ DYA Fruity wines mostly from co-op nr Montauban, also experimenting with regional varieties. Also Dom de Rouch.

Leflaive, Domaine Burg ★★★★ Among the best white burgundy growers, at PULIGNY-MONTRACHET. Best v'yds: Bienvenues-, CHEVALIER-MONTRACHET, Clavoillons, Pucelles, and (since 1991) Le Montrachet. Ever-finer wines on biodynamic principles.

Leflaive, Olivier Burg ★★★ High-quality NÉGOCIANT at PULIGNY-MONTRACHET, cousin of the above. Reliable wines, mostly white, but drink them young.

Léognan B'x r w ★★★→★★★★ Top village of GRAVES with its own AC: PESSAC-LÉOGNAN. Best ch'x: DOM DE CHEVALIER, HAUT-BAILLY.

Leroy, Domaine Burg ★★★★ DOMAINE built around purchase of Noëllat in VOSNE-ROMANÉE in 1988 and Leroy family holdings (known as d'Auvenay). Extraordinary quality (and prices) from tiny biodynamic yields.

Leroy, Maison Burg ★★★★ The ultimate NÉGOCIANT-ELEVEUR at AUXEY-DURESSES with sky-high standards and the finest stocks of expensive old wine in Burgundy.

Lesquerde ★★ **95 96 97 98 99** 00 01 02 New superior AC village of CÔTES DU ROUSSILLON-VILLAGES.

Lichine, Alexis & Cie BORDEAUX merchants (once of the late Alexis Lichine). No connection now with CH PRIEURE-LICHINE.

Lie, sur "On the lees." MUSCADET is often bottled straight from the vat, for maximum zest and character.

Limoux Pyr r w ★★ AC for sparkling BLANQUETTE DE LIMOUX or better CRÉMANT de Limoux, oak-aged CHARDONNAY for Limoux AC. Pinot N for VIN DE PAYS as well as traditional grapes (Pinot N allowed in blend for Crémant). Growers: Doms de Fourn, des Martinolles; gd co-op. Also new AC for red from 2003.

Liquoreux Term for a very sweet wine: eg SAUTERNES, top VOUVRAY, JURANCON, etc.

Lirac S Rh r p w ★★ **90' 95' 96 98' 99' 00' 01'** 03 Next to TAVEL. Approachable gd value red (can age 5+ yrs) often soft, but firmer with increased use of Mourvèdre. Red overtaking rosé, esp Doms Cantegril, Devoy-Martine, Joncier, Lafond Roc-Epine, Maby (Fermade), André Méjan, de la Mordorée, Sabon, Ch d'Aquéria, de Bouchassy, Ségriès.

Listel Midi r p w ★→★★ DYA Vast (4,000-acre+) historic estate on Golfe du Lion. Owned by VAL D'ORBIEU. Pleasant, light "vins des sables", inc sparkling. Also Dom du Bosquet-Canet; Dom de Villeroy; rosé Gris de Gris; fruity, low-alcohol PETILLANT, Ch de Malijay; Abbaye de Ste-Hilaire; Ch La Gordonne.

Listrac-Médoc B'x r ★★→★★★ **90' 95 96 98** 00' 01 02 Village of HAUT-MÉDOC next to MOULIS. Grown-up clarets with tannic grip Best ch'x: CLARKE, FONREAUD, FOURCAS-DUPRE, FOURCAS-HOSTEN, Mayne-Lalande, and gd co-op.

Livinière, La See MINERVOIS-LA LIVINIÈRE.

Long-Depaquit Burg ★★★ V.gd CHABLIS DOMAINE (esp MOUTONNE), owned by BICHOT.

Lorentz, Gustave ★★ ALSACE grower and merchant at Bergheim. Esp GEWURZTRAMINER, Ries from GRAND CRUS Altenberg de Bergheim, Kanzlerberg. Also owns Jerome Lorentz. Equally gd for top estate and volume wines.

Loron & Fils ★→★★ Big-scale grower and merchant at Pontanevaux; specialist in BEAUJOLAIS and sound VINS DE TABLE.

Loupiac B'x w SW ★★ **86' 88' 89** 90 95 96 97 98 99 01' 02 (03) Across River Garonne from SAUTERNES and by no means to be despised. Top ch'x: CLOS-Jean, LOUPIAC-GAUDIET, Mémoires, Noble, RICAUD, Les Roques.

Lugny See MÂCON-LUGNY.

Lussac-St-Emilion B'x r ★★ **85 86' 88' 89' 90' 94 95 96 98** 00' 01 NE neighbour to ST-EMILION. Top ch'x inc Barbe Blanche, BEL AIR, Bellevue, de la Grenière, Mayne-Blanc, DU LYONNAT; co-op (at PUISSEGUIN) makes pleasant Roc de Lussac.

Macération carbonique Traditional fermentation technique: whole bunches of unbroken grapes in a closed vat. Fermentation inside each grape eventually bursts it, giving vivid, fruity, mild wine, not for ageing. Esp in BEAUJOLAIS; now much used in the MIDI and elsewhere, even CHÂTEAUNEUF.

The Mâconnais

The hilly zone just north of Beaujolais has outcrops of limestone where Chardonnay gives full, if not often fine, wines. The village of Chardonnay here may (or may not) be the home of the variety. Granite soils give light Gamay reds. The top Mâconnais AC is Pouilly-Fuissé, followed by Pouilly Vinzelles, St Véran and Viré-Clessé, then Mâcon-Villages with a village name. There is potential to produce lower-priced, typical Chardonnays to outdo the New World (and indeed the South of France). Currently, most wines are less than extraordinary but things are looking up.

Mâcon Burg r w (p) DYA Sound, usually unremarkable reds (Gamay best), tasty dry (CHARDONNAY) whites. Also MÂCON Superieur (similar).

Mâcon-Lugny Burg (r) w sp ★★ **99 00'** 01 Village next to VIRE with huge and v.gd co-op (4 million bottles). Les Genevrières is sold by LOUIS LATOUR.

Mâcon-Villages Burg w ★★→★★★ **00' 01 02'** 03 Increasingly well-made (when not over-produced). Named for their villages, eg Mâcon-Lugny, -Prissé, -Uchizy. Best co-op: Prissé, Lugny. Top growers: Vincent (Fuissé), THEVENET, Bonhomme, Guillemot-Michel, Merlin (La Roche Vineuse). See also VIRÉ-CLESSÉ.

Macvin Jura w SW ★★ AC for "traditional" MARC and grape-juice apéritif.

Madiran SW France r ★★ **88' 90'** 90 95' 96 97 98' 99 (00) (01) Dark, vigorous, characterful Gascon red, mainly from Tannat. Age need. Try MONTUS, Bouscassé, Bertheumieu, Chapelle Lenclos, Labranche-Laffont, Laffont, Laplace, Laffitte-Teston, Capmartin, Barréjat, du Crampilh, CLOS Fardet. Gd co-ops Crouseilles, Plaimont, Castelnau-Rivière-Basse. White AC PACHERENC DU VIC BILH.

Magnum A double bottle (1.5 litres).

Mähler-Besse First-class Dutch NÉGOCIANT in BORDEAUX. Has share in CH PALMER and owns Ch Michel de Montaigne. Brands inc Cheval Noir. (Total: 250 acres.)

Mailly-Champagne Top CHAMPAGNE co-op. Luxury wine: CUVÉE des Echansons.

Maire, Henri ★→★★ The biggest grower/merchant of JURA wines, with half of the entire AC. Some top wines, many cheerfully commercial. Fun to visit.

Mann, Albert ★→★★★ Growers at Wettolsheim admired for their rich, elegant wines. Excellent Pinot Bl Auxerrois, Pinot N. Fine Ries and GEWURZTRAMINER from GRANDS CRUS Schlossberg and Hengst respectively.

Maranges Burg r (w) ★★ **96 97 98 99'** 01 02 AC for 600+ acres of S CÔTE DE BEAUNE, beyond SANTENAY: one-third PREMIER CRU. Top NÉGOCIANTS: DROUHIN, Girardin.

Marc Grape skins after pressing; also the strong-smelling brandy made from them (the equivalent of Italian grappa, see p.120).

Marcillac SW France r p ★→★★ DYA (But CUVÉES prestiges will keep.) AC from 1990. Violet-hued with grassy red-fruit character. Gd co-op at Valady. J-L Matha, Doms du Cros, Costes, and Laurens.

Margaux B'x r ★★→★★★★ **78 81 82' 83' 85 86' 87 88' 89 90' 95 96** 98 99 00' 01 02 Village of HAUT-MÉDOC. Some of most elegant and fragrant red BORDEAUX. AC inc CANTENAC and several other villages. Top ch'x inc: MARGAUX, RAUZAN-SEGLA, PALMER, etc.

Marionnet, Henry Lo ★→★★★ **95 96 97 98 99 00 01 02** Leading TOURAINE property specializing in Gamay and Sauv Bl. Top CUVÉE Le M de Marionnet. Other CUVÉES: Provignage and Vinifera (ungrafted vines), Cépages Oubliés.

Marne et Champagne Recent but huge-scale CHAMPAGNE house, owner (since 1991) of LANSON and many smaller brands, inc BESSERAT DE BELLEFON. Alfred Rothschild brand v.gd CHARDONNAY-based wines.

Marque déposée Trademark.

Marsannay Burg p r (w) ★★ **96' 97 99' 00 01** 02' 03 (rosé DYA) Village with fine, light red and delicate Pinot N rosé. Inc villages of Chenôve, Couchey. Growers: CHARLOPIN, CLAIR, JADOT, MÉO-CAMUZET, ROTY, TRAPET.

Mas de Daumas Gassac Midi r w p ★★★ **93 94' 95 96 97 98** 99 00 01 02 03 The first "first-growth" estate of the LANGUEDOC, producing potent red on apparently unique soil. Extraordinary quality. Wines inc: new super CUVÉE Emile Peynaud, rosé Frisant, rich, fragrant white blend to drink at 2–3 yrs. Also quick-drinking red, Les Terrasses de Guilhem, from nearby co-op and traditional Languedoc varietals (Clairette, Cinsault, Aramon, etc) from old vines under Terrasses de Landoc label. VIN DE PAYS status. Intriguing sweet wine: Vin de Laurence (Sem, Muscats, and Sercial!).

Maury Pyr r sw ★★ NV Red VIN DOUX NATUREL of Grenache from ROUSSILLON. Taste the schist terroir. Much recent improvement, esp at Mas Amiel.

Mazis (or Mazy) Chambertin Burg r ★★★ **78' 85' 88' 89' 90' 91 93** 95 96' 97 98 99' 00 01 02' 03 A 30-acre GRAND CRU neighbour of CHAMBERTIN, sometimes equally potent. Best from FAIVELEY, HOSPICES DE BEAUNE, LEROY, Maume, ROTY.

Mazoyères-Chambertin See CHARMES-CHAMBERTIN.

Médoc B'x r ★★ **85 86' 88' 89' 90' 95 96 98 00'** 02 AC for reds of the less-gd (N) part of BORDEAUX's biggest top-quality district. Flavours tend to earthiness. HAUT-MÉDOC is much better. Top ch'x inc: LA CARDONNE, GREYSAC, LOUDENNE, LES ORMES-SORBET, POTENSAC, LA TOUR-DE-BY.

Meffre, Gabriel ★★ Biggest S Rhône estate, based at GIGONDAS. Variable quality, recent progress. Also bottles and sells for small CHÂTEAUNEUF doms.

Mellot, Alphonse Lo ★★→★★★ **94 95 96 97 98 99 00 01 02** 03 Leading SANCERRE grower. Esp for La Moussière and wood-aged CUVÉE Edmond, Génération XIX.

Menetou-Salon Lo r p w ★★ DYA Highly attractive similar wines from W of SANCERRE: Sauv Bl white full of charm, Pinot N light red. Top growers: Henri Pellé, Jean-Max Roger. Reds from Clément can age.

Méo-Camuzet ★★★★ Very fine DOMAINE in CLOS DE VOUGEOT, NUITS-ST-GEORGES, RICHEBOURG, VOSNE-ROMANÉE. JAYER-inspired. Esp VOSNE-ROMANÉE Cros Parantoux. Now also some less expensive NÉGOCIANT CUVÉES.

Mercier & Cie, Champagne Brut NV; Brut Rosé NV; Brut **98 99** One of biggest CHAMPAGNE houses at Epernay. Controlled by MOËT & CHANDON. Fair commercial quality, sold mainly in France. Gd powerful Pinot N-led CUVÉE Eugene Mercier.

Mercurey Burg r ★★→★★★ **90' 93 95 96' 97 98 99' 01** 02' 03 Leading red-wine village of CÔTE CHALONNAISE. Gd middle-rank burgundy, inc improving whites. Try Ch de Chamirey, FAIVELEY, M Juillot, Lorenzon, Raquillet, Dom de Suremain.

Mercurey, Région de The alternative name for the CÔTE CHALONNAISE.

Mérode, Domaine Prince de ★★★ Once more a top DOMAINE for CORTON and POMMARD.

Mesnil-sur-Oger, Le Champ ★★★★ One of the top Côte des Blancs villages. Structured CHARDONNAY for very long ageing.

Métaireau, Louis Lo w ★★→★★★ **89 90 91 92 93 94 95 96 97 98 99 00 01 02 03** A key figure in the MUSCADET quality revolution. His daughter Marie-Luce now runs the estate. Expensive well-finished wines: Number One, CUVÉES Grand Mouton and MLM.

Méthode champenoise Traditional laborious method of putting bubbles into CHAMPAGNE by refermenting wine in its bottle. Must use terms "classic method" or "méthode traditionnelle" outside region. Not mentioned on labels.

Méthode traditionnelle See entry above.

Meursault Burg w (r) ★★★→★★★★ **89' 90 91 92 95** 96' **97** 99' 00' 01 02' 03 CÔTE DE BEAUNE village with some of world's greatest whites: savoury, dry, nutty, mellow. Best v'yds: Charmes, Genevrières, Perrières. Also gd: Goutte d'Or, Meursault-Blagny, Poruzots, Narvaux, Tesson, Tillets. Producers inc: AMPEAU, J-M BOILLOT, M Bouzereau, Boyer-Martenot, CH DE MEURSAULT, COCHE-DURY, Ente, Fichet, Grivault, P Javillier, JOBARD, LAFON, LATOUR, O LEFLAIVE, LEROY, Manuel, Matrot, Mikulski, P MOREY, G ROULOT. See also BLAGNY.

Meursault-Blagny See BLAGNY.

Michel, Louis ★★★ CHABLIS DOMAINE with model unoaked, very long-lived wines, inc superb LES CLOS, v.gd Montmains, MONTÉE DE TONNERRE.

Microbullage Technique invented by Patrick DUCOURNAU: oxygen is injected into ageing wine to avoid racking, stimulate aeration, and accelerate maturity.

Midi General term for S of Fr, W of Rhône. Improving; brilliant promise. Top wines often based on variety (best tend to be blends). A melting pot.

Minervois Midi r (p w) br sw ★→★★ **95 96 97 98' 99 00'** 01 02' 03 Hilly AC region; gd, lively wines, esp Ch Bonhomme, Coupe-Roses, la Grave, Oupia, Villerembert-Julien, co-ops LA LIVINIÈRE, de Peyriac, Pouzols; La Tour Boisée, CLOS Centeilles. Sw Minervois Noble being developed. See ST-JEAN DE MINERVOIS.

Minervois-La Livinière, La Midi r (p w) ★→★★ Quality village (see last entry) the only sub-appellation or cru in Minervois. Best growers: Abbaye de Tholomies, Borie de Maurel, Combe Blanche, Ch de Gourgazaud, CLOS Centeilles, Laville-Bertrou, Doms Maris, Ste-Eulalie, Co-op La Livinière, Vipur.

Mis en bouteille au château/domaine Bottled at the CHÂTEAU, property or estate. NB "dans nos caves" (in our cellars) or "dans la région de production" (in the area of production) are often used but mean little.

Mittnacht Freres, Domaine ★★ Rising ALSACE star with v'yds in Riquewihr and Hunawihr. Lovely Pinot Bl, fine Ries (GRAND CRU ROSACKER), excellent Pinot Gr.

Moelleux "With marrow" Creamy-sweet. Sweet wines of VOUVRAY, COTEAUX DU LAYON.

Moët & Chandon Brut NV; Rosé **96 98** 99; Brut Imperial **96 98** 99. Largest CHAMPAGNE merchant/grower with cellars in Epernay; branches in Argentina, Australia, Brazil, California, Germany, Spain. Consistent quality, esp vintages. Prestige CUVÉE: DOM PERIGNON. Impressive multi-vintage Esprit du Siècle, GRANDS CRUS Aÿ and Sillery bottlings. Coteaux Champenois Saran: still wine.

Moillard Burg ★★→★★★ Big family firm (see THOMAS-MOILLARD) in NUITS-ST-GEORGES, making full range, inc dark and very tasty wines.

Mommessin, J ★→★★ Major BEAUJOLAIS merchant, merged with THORIN, now owned by BOISSET. Owner of CLOS DE TART. White wines less successful than reds.

Monbazillac Dordogne w sw ★★→★★★★ 90' 95' 97 98 99 01 (02) Golden SAUTERNES-style wine from BERGERAC. At best can equal Sauternes, as at Tirecul-la-Gravière. Top producers: L'Ancienne Cure, Ch'x de Belingard-Chayne, Bellevue, La Borderie, Le Fagé, Petit Paris, Poulvère, Theulet, Dom de la Haute-Brie et du Caillou, and La Grande Maison. Also Co-op de Monbazillac.

Mondeuse Savoie r ★★ DYA Red grape of SAVOIE. Potentially gd vigorous, deep-coloured wine. Possibly same as NE Italy's Refosco. Don't miss a chance.

Monopole V'yd under single ownership.

Montagne-St-Emilion B'x r ★★ 85 86' 88' 89' 90' 94 95 96 98 00' 01 NE neighbour and largest satellite of ST-EMILION: similar wines and APPELLATION regulations; becoming more important each year. Top ch'x: Calon, Faizeau, Maison Blanche, Montaiguillon, Roudier, Teyssier, DES TOURS, VIEUX-CH-ST-ANDRE.

Montagny Burg w ★★ 99' 00 01 02' 03 CÔTE CHALONNAISE village. Between MÂCON and MEURSAULT, both geographically and gastronomically. Top producers: Aladame, J-M BOILLOT, Cave de Buxy, Michel, Ch de la Saule.

Montée de Tonnerre Burg w ★★★ 90 93 95 96' 97 98 99 00' 02 Famous excellent CHABLIS PREMIER CRU. Esp BROCARD, Duplessis, L MICHEL, Raveneau, Robin.

Monthelie Burg r (w) ★★→★★★ 93 95 96' 97 98 99' 00 01 02' 03 Little-known VOLNAY neighbour, sometimes almost equal. Excellent fragrant red esp: BOUCHARD PÈRE ET FILS, COCHE-DURY, LAFON, DROUHIN, Garaudet, Ch de Monthelie (Suremain).

Montille, Hubert de Burg ★★★ VOLNAY and POMMARD DOMAINE to note. Etienne de Montille is now also responsible for Ch de Puligny.

Montlouis Lo w dr sw (sp) ★★→★★★ 85' 88' 89' 90' 93' 95' 96 97 98 99 00 01 02 03 (sec) Neighbour of VOUVRAY. Similar sweet or long-lived dry wines; also sparkling. Top growers: Berger, Chidaine, Deletang, Moyer, Frantz Saumon, Taille aux Loups.

Montrachet Burg w ★★★★ 78 79 82 85' 86 88 89' 90 91 92' 93 94 95 96' 97 98 99 00' 01 02' 03 (Both 't's in the name are silent.) 19-acre GRAND CRU v'yd in both PULIGNY- and CHASSAGNE-MONTRACHET. Potentially the greatest white burgundy: strong, perfumed, intense, dry yet luscious. Top wines from LAFON, LAGUICHE (DROUHIN), LEFLAIVE, RAMONET, ROMANÉE-CONTI, THÉNARD.

Montravel Dordogne ★★ p dr w DYA r 00' 01 02 (03) Now AC, similar to BERGERAC. Gd examples from Doms de Krevel, Gouyat, Perreau, Ch'x du Fouga, Masburel, Laulerie, Péchauriers, Pique-Sègue. Separate ACS for semi-sweet CÔTES DE MONTRAVEL and sweet HAUT-MONTRAVEL.

Morey, Domaines Burg ★★★ 50 acres in CHASSAGNE-MONTRACHET. V.gd wines by family members, esp Bernard, inc BATARD-MONTRACHET. Also Pierre M in MEURSAULT.

Morey-St-Denis Burg r ★★★ 85' 88 89' 90' 93 95 96' 97 98 99' 00 01 02' 03 Small village with 4 GRANDS CRUS between GEVREY-CHAMBERTIN and CHAMBOLLE-MUSIGNY. Glorious wine often overlooked. Inc: Amiot, DUJAC, H Lignier, Moillard-Grivot, Perrot-Minot, PONSOT, ROUMIER, ROUSSEAU, Serveau.

Morgon Beauj r ★★★ 95 96 97 98 99 00 01 02 The firmest cru of BEAUJOLAIS, needing time to develop its rich savoury flavour. Growers inc Aucoeur, Ch de Bellevue, Desvignes, J Foillard, Lapièrre, Ch de Pizay. DUBOEUF excellent.

Mortet, Denis ★★★ Splendid perfectionist GEVREY DOMAINE. Super wines since 93, inc a range of village Gevreys and excellent PREMIER CRU Lavaux St-Jacques.

Moueix, J-P et Cie B'x Legendary proprietor and merchant of ST-EMILION and POMEROL. Ch'x inc: LA FLEUR-PÉTRUS, MAGDELAINE, and PÉTRUS. Also in California: see Dominus, p.224. Alain Moueix, who owns Ch Saint-André-Corbin in St-Georges-St-Emilion, is cousin to Christian Moueix, who runs J-P Moueix.

Moulin-à-Vent Beauj r ★★★ 93 95 96' 98 99 00 01 02 03 The biggest and potentially best wine of BEAUJOLAIS. Can be powerful, meaty, and long-lived;

can even taste like fine Rhône or burgundy. Many gd growers, esp Ch du Moulin-à-Vent, Ch des Jacques, Dom des Hospices, Janodet, JADOT, Merlin.

Moulis B'x r ★★→★★★ **90 94 95 96 98** 00' 02 HAUT-MEDOC village with several leading Crus Bourgeois: CHASSE-SPLEEN, MAUCAILLOU, POUJEAUX (THEIL). Gd hunting ground.

Mousseux Sparkling.

Mouton Cadet Popular brand of blended (r w) BORDEAUX. Not a quality leader.

Moutonne ★★★ CHABLIS GRAND CRU honoris causa (between VAUDESIR and Preuses), owned by BICHOT.

Mugneret/Mugneret-Gibourg Burg ★★★ Superb reds from top CÔTE DE NUITS sites.

Mugnier, J-F Burg ★★★→★★★★ 10-acre Ch de Chambolle estate with first-class delicate CHAMBOLLE-MUSIGNY Les Amoureuses and MUSIGNY. Also BONNES-MARES.

Mumm, G H & Cie Cordon Rouge NV; Mumm de Cramant NV; Cordon Rouge **95 96** 98; Rosé NV Major CHAMPAGNE grower and merchant. NV much improved by new winemaker; new Special CUVÉE planned 2005. Also in California, Chile, Argentina, South Africa ("Cape Mumm").

Muré, Clos St-Landelin ★★→★★★ Very fine ALSACE grower and merchant at Rouffach with v'yds in GRAND CRU Vorbourg. Full-bodied wines: ripe (unusual) Pinot N, big Ries, also MUSCAT VENDANGES TARDIVES.

Muscadet Lo w ★→★★★ DYA (but see below) Popular, gd value, often delicious very dry wine from nr Nantes. Should never be sharp, but should have a faint iodine tang. Perfect with fish and seafood. Best are from zonal ACS: COTEAUX DE LA LOIRE, MUSCADET COTES DE GRAND LIEU, SEVRE-ET-MAINE. Choose a SUR LIE.

Muscadet Côtes de Grand Lieu ★→★★ 01 02 03 Recent (1995) zonal AC for MUSCADET named after the Lac de Grand Lieu in the middle of the zone. Best are SUR LIE, from eg Bâtard, Luc Choblet, Malidain.

Muscadet Coteaux de la Loire Lo w ★→★★ 01 02 03 Small MUSCADET zone E of Nantes (best SUR LIE). Esp Guindon, Luneau-Papin, Les Vignerons de la Noëlle.

Muscadet de Sèvre-et-Maine ★→★★★ 88 89 90 93 95 96 97 98 99 00 01 02 03 Wine from central (best) part of area. Top growers inc: Guy Bossard (ECU), CHEREAU-CARRE, Bruno Cormerai, Dom de la Haute Fevrie, Michel Delhomeau, Douillard, Landron, Luneau-Papin, METAIREAU. 2001 vintage can be perfection.

Muscat Distinctively perfumed and usually sweet wine, often fortified as VIN DOUX NATUREL. Made dry and not fortified in ALSACE where it is the main apéritif wine. For Muscat grape, see Grapes for white wine, (pp. 12–16).

Muscat de Beaumes-de-Venise See BEAUMES-DE-VENISE.

Muscat de Frontignan See FRONTIGNAN.

Muscat de Lunel Midi golden sw ★★ NV Ditto. A small area but gd, making real recent progress. Look for Dom CLOS Bellevue, Lacoste.

Muscat de Mireval Midi sw ★★ NV Ditto, from nr Montpellier. Dom La Capelle.

Muscat de Rivesaltes Midi golden sw ★★ NV Sweet MUSCAT wine from large zone near Perpignan. Esp gd from Cazes Frères, Ch de Jau.

Musigny Burg r (w) ★★★★ 85' 88' 89' 90' 91 93 95 96' 97 98 99' 00 01 02' 03 25-acre GRAND CRU in CHAMBOLLE-MUSIGNY. Can be the most beautiful, if not the most powerful, of all red burgundies. Best growers: DROUHIN, JADOT, LEROY, MUGNIER, PRIEUR, ROUMIER, DE VOGUE, VOUGERAIE.

Napoléon Brand name of family-owned Prieur CHAMPAGNE house at Vertus. Excellent Carte d'Or NV and first-rate vintages, esp **95 96**.

Nature Natural or unprocessed – esp of still CHAMPAGNE.

Négociant-éleveur Merchant who "brings up" (ie matures) the wine.

Nicolas, Ets Paris-based wholesale and retail wine merchant controlled by Castel Frères. One of the biggest in France.

Nuits-St-Georges Burg r ★★→★★★★ 88' 89' 90' 91 93 95 96' 97 98 99' 00 01 02' 03 Important wine town: wines of all qualities, typically sturdy, tannic, need time. Often shortened to "Nuits". Best v'yds: Les Cailles, CLOS des Corvées, Les Pruliers, Les St-Georges, Vaucrains. Many merchants and growers: L'ARLOT, Ambroise, J Chauvenet, R. CHEVILLON, CONFURON, FAIVELEY, GOUGES, GRIVOT, Lechéneaut, LEROY, Machard de Gramont, Michelot, RION, THOMAS-MOILLARD.

d'Oc (Vin de Pays d'Oc) Midi r p w ★→★★ Regional VIN DE PAYS for Languedoc and ROUSSILLON. Esp single-grape wines and VINS DE PAYS PRIMEURS. Tremendous technical advances recently. Top producers: VAL D'ORBIEU, SKALLI, Jeanjean, and numerous small growers.

Oisly & Thesée, Vignerons de ★★ 89 90 93 95 96 97 98 99 00 01 02 03 Go-ahead co-op in E TOURAINE (Loire), with gd Sauv Bl (esp CUVÉE Excellence), Cab Sauv, Gamay, Côt, and CHARDONNAY. Blends labelled Baronnie d'Aignan and gd DOMAINE wines.

Orléanais, Vin de l' Lo r p w ★ DYA Small VDQS for light but fruity wines, based on Pinots N and Meunier, Cab Sauv, and CHARDONNAY. Esp CLOS St-Fiacre.

Ostertag ★★ Small ALSACE DOMAINE at Epfig. Uses new oak for gd Pinot N; best Ries, Pinot Gr of GRAND CRU Muenchberg. GEWURZTRAMINER from lieu-dit Fronholz worth ageing.

Ott, Domaines Producer of PROVENCE, inc CH DE SELLE (rosé, red), CLOS Mireille (white), BANDOL Ch de Romassan.

Pacherenc du Vic-Bilh SW Fr w dr sw ★★ The white wine of MADIRAN. Dry DYA and (better) sweet (age up to 5 yrs for oaked versions). For growers see MADIRAN.

Paillard, Bruno Brut Première Cuvée NV; Rosé Première Cuvée; Chard Réserve Privée, Brut **90 95'** 96. New Vintage Blanc de Blancs **95'**. Superb Nec Plus Ultra Prestige Cuvée (**90'** 95). Young top-flight CHAMPAGNE house. Also owns Ch de Sarrin in Provence.

Palette Prov r p w ★★ Tiny AC nr Aix-en-Provence. Full reds, fragrant rosés, and intriguing whites from CH SIMONE.

Pasquier-Desvignes ★→★★ Very old firm of BEAUJOLAIS merchants nr BROUILLY.

Patriarche Burg ★→★★ One of the bigger burgundy merchants. Cellars in BEAUNE; also owns CH DE MEURSAULT (150 acres), sparkling KRITER. etc.

Patrimonio Corsica r w p ★★→★★★ 95 96 97 98 99 00 01 02 03 Wide range from dramatic chalk hills in N CORSICA. The island's best. Fragrant reds from Nielluccio, characterful whites. Top growers: Gentile, Leccia, Arena.

Pauillac B'x r ★★★→★★★★ 66' 70' 75 78' 79 81' 82' 83' 85' 86' 88' 89' 90' 93 94 95' 96' 98 99 00' 01 02 HAUT-MÉDOC village with 3 first growths (LAFITE, LATOUR, MOUTON) and many other fine ch'x, famous for high flavour; varied style.

Pécharmant Dordogne r ★★→★★★ 95' 98' 99 00 01 (02) Inner AC for top BERGERAC red, for ageing. Best: La Métairie, Doms du Haut-Pécharmant, des Costes, des Bertranoux; Ch'x Champarel, Terre Vieille, Les Grangettes, de Tiregand. Also (from Bergerac co-op) Doms Brisseau-Belloc, du Vieux Sapin, Ch le Charmeil.

Pelure d'oignon "Onion skin" – tawny tint of certain rosés.

Perlant or Perlé Very slightly sparkling.

Pernand-Vergelesses Burg r (w) ★★★ 90 93 95 96' 97 98 99' 00 01 02' 03 Village next to ALOXE-CORTON containing part of the great CORTON-CHARLEMAGNE and CORTON v'yds. One other top v'yd: Ile des Vergelesses. Growers: CHANDON DE BRIAILLES, CHANSON, Delarche, Dubreuil-Fontaine, JADOT, LATOUR, Rapet, Rollin.

Perrier-Jouët Brut NV; Blason de France NV; Blason de France Rosé NV; Brut **95 96 97** Excellent CHAMPAGNE grower at Epernay, the first to make dry CHAMPAGNE and once the smartest name of all; now best for vintage wines. Luxury brand: Belle Epoque **95 96 97** (Rosé **97**) in a painted bottle.

Pessac-Léognan B'x r w ★★★→★★★★ 90' 95 96 98 00' 01 02 AC for the best part of N GRAVES, inc area of most of the GRANDS CRUS, HAUT-BRION, PAPE CLÉMENT etc.

Pétillant Normally means slightly sparkling; but half-sparkling speciality in TOURAINE, esp VOUVRAY and MONTLOUIS.

FRANCE

Petit Chablis Burg w ★ DYA Wine from fourth-rank CHABLIS v'yds. Not much character but can be pleasantly fresh. Best: co-op La Chablisienne.

Pfaffenheim ★★ Top ALSACE co-op with 580 acres. Strongly individual wines, inc gd Sylvaner and v.gd Pinots (N, Gr, Bl). GRANDS CRUS: Goldert, Steinert and Hatschbourg. Hartenberger CREMANT d'Alsace is v.gd. Also owns DOPFF & IRION.

Pfersigberg Eguisheim (ALSACE) GRAND CRU with two parcels; very aromatic wines. GEWURZTRAMINER does very well. Ries, esp Paul Ginglinger, BRUNO SORG, and LEON BEYER Comtes d'Eguisheim. Top grower: KUENTZ-BAS.

Philipponnat NV; Rosé NV; Réserve Spéciale **95 96** 98; CLOS des Goisses **88 90 91'** **95** 96 Small family-run CHAMPAGNE house for well-structured wines. Remarkable single-v'yd CLOS des Goisses and charming rosé. Also Le Reflet BRUT NV.

Piat Père & Fils ★ Big-scale merchant of BEAUJOLAIS and MÂCON. Owned by Diageo.

Pic St-Loup Midi ★→★★ r (p) Improving COTEAUX DU LANGUEDOC cru. Growers: Ch'x de Cazeneuve, CLOS Marie, de Lancyre, Lascaux, Mas Bruguière, Dom de l'Hortus.

Picpoul de Pinet Midi w ★→★★ Improving AC exclusively for the old variety Picpoul. Best growers: Ch St Martin de la Garrigue, Co-op Pomérols, Félines-Jourdan.

Pineau des Charentes Strong, sweet apéritif: white grape juice and COGNAC.

Piper-Heidsieck Brut NV; Brut Rosé NV; Brut **90 95** CHAMPAGNE-makers of old repute at Reims. Rare (**90 95** 96) and Brut Sauvage (**90 96**) are best, but non-vintage CUVÉES much improved.

Plageoles, Robert Arch-priest of GAILLAC and defender of the lost grape varieties of the Tarn. Amazingly eccentric wines include a VIN JAUNE left to oxidize like sherry, an ultra-sweet dessert wine from Ondenc grapes left to dry in the sun. Outstanding range of wines from Mauzac, inc sparkler.

Pol Roger Brut White Foil NV; Brut **88' 90 93 95 96'**; Rosé **95 96'**; Blanc de Chard **93' 95 96'**. Top-ranking family-owned CHAMPAGNE house at Epernay, much loved in UK. Esp gd silky NV White Foil, Rosé, and CHARDONNAY. Sumptuous CUVÉE: Sir Winston Churchill (**90' 95**)

Pomerol B'x r ★★★→★★★★ 70 75' 81' 82' 83 85 86 88 89' 90' 94 95 96 98' 00' Next village to ST-EMILION: similar but more plummy, creamy wines, often mature sooner, reliable, delicious. Top ch'x inc: CERTAN-DE-MAY, L'EVANGILE, LA FLEUR, LA FLEUR-PETRUS, LATOUR-A-POMEROL, PETRUS, LE PIN, TROTANOY, VIEUX CH CERTAN.

Pommard Burg r ★★★ 85' 88' 89' 90 91 93 95 96' **97** 98 99' 01 02' 03 The biggest CÔTE D'OR village. Few superlative wines, but many potent and tannic ones to age 10 yrs+. Best v'yds: Epenots, HOSPICES DE BEAUNE CUVÉES, Rugiens. Growers inc COMTE ARMAND, Billard-Gonnet, J-M BOILLOT, DE COURCEL, Gaunoux, LEROY, Machard de Gramont, DE MONTILLE, Ch de Pommard, Pothier-Rieusset.

Pommery Brut NV; Rosé NV; Brut **90 91 95 96** 98. Historic CHAMPAGNE house, the brand now owned by VRANKEN. Outstanding luxury CUVÉE Louise (**90 95'** 96) and Rosé (**88 90 95**).

Ponsot ★★★★ Controversial 25-acre MOREY-ST-DENIS estate. Idiosyncratic high-quality GRANDS CRUS, inc CHAMBERTIN, CHAPELLE-CHAMBERTIN, CLOS DE LA ROCHE, CLOS ST-DENIS.

Portes de la Mediterranée New regional VIN DE PAYS from S Rhône/PROVENCE. Easy reds and interesting whites, inc Viognier.

Potel, Nicolas Burg ★★→★★★ Potel founded a small NÉGOCIANT after his father's Dom de la POUSSE D'OR was sold. Impressive reds, esp BOURGOGNE ROUGE, VOLNAY, NUITS-ST-GEORGES. Now owned by LABOURÉ-ROI.

Pouilly-Fuissé Burg w ★★→★★★ 92' 95 96 97 98 99 00 01 02' 03 The best white of the MÂCON region, potent and dense. At its best (eg Ch Fuissé VIEILLES VIGNES) outstanding, but usually over-priced compared with CHABLIS. Top growers: Ferret, Forest, VERGET, Luquet, Merlin, Ch des Rontets, Valette, Vincent.

Pouilly-Fumé Lo w ★★→★★★★ 90' 91' 92' 93' 94 95' 96 97 98 99 00 01 02 03 "Gun-flinty", fruity, often sharp white from upper Loire, nr SANCERRE. Must be Sauv Bl. Best CUVÉES can improve 5–6 yrs. Top growers inc: Cailbourin,

Chatelain, DAGUENEAU, Ch de Favray, Edmond and André Figeat, LADOUCETTE, Masson-Blondelet, Ch de Tracy, Tinel Blondelet, CAVE de Pouilly-sur-Loire, Redde. SANCERRE is currently more concentrated.

Pouilly-Loché Burg w ★ **99 00' 01** 02' 03 POUILLY-FUISSÉ's neighbour. Similar, cheaper; scarce. Can be sold as POUILLY-VINZELLES.

Pouilly-sur-Loire Lo w ★ DYA Neutral wine from the same v'yds as POUILLY-FUMÉ but different grapes (Chasselas). Rarely seen today, ever-diminishing.

Pouilly-Vinzelles Burg w ★★ **99 00' 01** 02' 03 Neighbour of POUILLY-FUISSÉ. Similar wine, worth looking for. Value. Best: Soufrandière.

Pousse d'Or, Domaine de la Burg ★★★ 32-acre estate in POMMARD, SANTENAY, and esp VOLNAY, where its MONOPOLES Bousse d'Or and CLOS des 60 Ouvrées are powerful, tannic, and were justly famous under Gérard Potel (manager 1964–96). Signs of gd wines under new ownership.

Premier Cru (1er Cru) First growth in BORDEAUX; second rank of v'yds (after GRAND CRU) in Burgundy.

Premières Côtes de Blaye B'x r w ★→★★ 88' 89' 90' 93 94 95 96 98 00' 01 Restricted AC for better BLAYE wines; greater emphasis on red. Ch'x inc: Bel Air la Royère, Bertinerie, Les Graves, Haut-Grelot, Haut-Sociando, Jonqueyres, Loumède, Mondésir-Gazin, Segonzac, des Tourtes.

Premières Côtes de Bordeaux B'x r w (p) dr sw ★→★★ 94 95 96 98 00' 01 Large hilly area E of GRAVES across the River Garonne. Upgrading sharply; gd bet for quality and value. Largely Merlot. Ch'x inc Carignan, Carsin, Chelivette, Fayau, Grand-Mouëys, du Juge, Lagarette, Lamothe de Haux, Lezongars, Plaisance, Puy Bardens, REYNON, Suau. To watch, esp in gd vintages.

Prieur, Domaine Jacques Burg ★★★ Splendid 40-acre estate all in top Burgundy sites, inc PREMIER CRU MEURSAULT, VOLNAY, PULIGNY-, and even LE MONTRACHET. Now 50% owned by RODET. Quality could still improve.

Primeur "Early" wine for refreshment and uplift; esp from BEAUJOLAIS; VINS DE PAYS too. Wine sold "En Primeur" is still in barrel for delivery when bottled.

Prissé See MÂCON-VILLAGES.

Propriétaire-récoltant Owner-manager.

Provence See CÔTES DE PROVENCE, CASSIS, BANDOL, PALETTE, COTEAUX DES BAUX-EN-PROVENCE, BOUCHES-DU-RHÔNE, COTEAUX D'AIX-EN-PROVENCE, COTEAUX VAROIS, PORTES DE LA MEDITERRANÉE.

Puisseguin St-Emilion B'x r ★★ 88' 89' 90' 94 95 96 98 00' 01 Satellite neighbour of ST-EMILION; wines similar – not so fine or weighty but often value. Ch'x inc: BELAIR, Durand-Laplagne, Fongaban, LAURETS, Soleil, Vieux-Ch-Guibeau. Also Roc de Puisseguin from co-op.

Puligny-Montrachet Burg w (r) ★★★→★★★★★ 89' 92 95 96' 97 99' 00 01 02' 03 Smaller neighbour of CHASSAGNE-MONTRACHET: potentially even finer, more vital and complex wine (apparent finesse can be result of over-production). V'yds: BATARD-MONTRACHET, Bienvenues-Bâtard-Montrachet, Caillerets, CHEVALIER-MONTRACHET, Clavoillon, Les Combettes, MONTRACHET, Pucelles. Producers: AMPEAU, J-M BOILLOT, BOUCHARD PÈRE ET FILS, L CARILLON, CHARTRON, Chavy, DROUHIN, JADOT, LATOUR, DOM LEFLAIVE, O LEFLAIVE, Pernot, SAUZET.

Pyrénées-Atlantiques SW France VIN DE PAYS for wines not qualifying for local ACS MADIRAN, PACHERENC DU VIC BILH or JURANCON.

Quarts de Chaume Lo w sw ★★★→★★★★ 75 76 78' 79' 82 85' 86 88' 89' 90' 91 92 93' 94 95 96 97 98 99 00 01 02 03 Famous COTEAUX DU LAYON plot. Chenin Bl grown for immensely long-lived intense, rich, golden wine. Esp from BAUMARD, Bellerive, Claude Papin (CH DE PIERRE-BISE)

Quatourze Midi r w (p) ★ 95 96 97 98 99 00 01 02 03 Minor cru of COTEAUX DE LANGUEDOC. Best: Dom Notre Dame du Quatourze (virtually sole producer).

Quincy Lo w ★→★★ DYA Small area: very dry SANCERRE-style Sauv Bl. Worth trying. Growers: Dom Mardon, Sorbe, Dom de Silice (wines can age).

Ramonet, Domaine Burg ★★→★★★★ Leading (legendary) estate in CHASSAGNE-MONTRACHET with 42 acres, inc some MONTRACHET. V.gd CLOS ST-JEAN.

Rancio Nutty tang of brown, wood-aged, fortified wine, eg VIN DOUX NATUREL, esp BANYULS. Indicates exposure to oxygen and/or heat: a fault in table wine.

Rangen High-class ALSACE GRAND CRU in Thann, Vieux Thann. Owes reputation to ZIND-HUMBRECHT. Other main grower: SCHOFFIT. Esp: Pinot Gr, GEWURZTRAMINER, Ries.

Rasteau S Rh r br sw (p w dr) ★★ 90' 95' 96 98' 99' 00' 01' 03 Village for sound, robust reds, esp Beaurenard, CAVE des Vignerons, Ch du Trignon, Doms Didier Charavin, Rabasse-Charavin, Girasols, Gourt de Mautens, St-Gayan, Soumade, Perrin. Grenache dessert wine is (declining) speciality.

Ratafia de Champagne Sweet apéritif made in CHAMPAGNE of 67% grape juice and 33% brandy. Not unlike PINEAU DES CHARENTES.

Récolte Crop or vintage.

Regnié Beauj r ★★ 99 00 01 02 03 Village between MORGON and BROUILLY, promoted to cru in 1988. About 1,800 acres. Try DUBOEUF, Aucoeur, or Rampon.

Reine Pédauque, La Burg ★ Long-established grower-merchant at ALOXE-CORTON. V'yds in ALOXE-CORTON, SAVIGNY, etc, and CÔTES DU RHONE. Owned by PIERRE ANDRE.

Remoissenet Père & Fils Burg ★★ Merchant (esp for whites and THENARD wines) with a tiny BEAUNE estate (5 acres). Give red time.

Rémy Pannier Important Loire wine merchant at SAUMUR.

Reuilly Lo w (r p) ★★ Neighbour of QUINCY. Similar white; rising reputation. Also rosé (Pinots N, Gr), red (Pinot N). Esp Claude Lafond, Beurdin, Sorbe, Vincent.

Ribonnet, Domaine de SW France ★★ Christian Gerber makes pioneering range of varietals (r p w) without benefit of AC in Haute Garonne and ARIÉGE.

Riceys, Rosé des Champ p ★★★ DYA Minute AC in AUBE for a notable Pinot N rosé. Principal producers: A Bonnet, Jacques Defrance.

Richeaume, Domaine Côte de Prov r ★★ Gd Cab Sauv/Syrah. Organic; a model.

Richebourg Burg r ★★★★ 78' 85' 88' 89' 90' 91 93' 95 96' 97 98 99' 00 01 02' 03 A 19-acre VOSNE-ROMANÉE GRAND CRU. Powerful, perfumed, expensive wine, among Burgundy's best. Growers: DRC, GRIVOT, J GROS, A GROS, LEROY, MÉO-CAMUZET.

Richou, Dom Lo ★→★★ 95 96 97 98 99 00 01 02 03 Long-established, quality ANJOU estate for wide range of wines, esp ANJOU-VILLAGES VIEILLES VIGNES, COTEAUX DE L'AUBANCE Les Trois Demoiselles.

Rion, Domaine Daniel et Fils Burg ★★★ Gd source for VOSNE-ROMANÉE (Les Chaumes, Les Beaumonts), Nuits PREMIER CRU Les Vignes Rondes and ECHEZEAUX. Former winemaker Patrice Rion now has his own dom (exceptional CHAMBOLLE-MUSIGNY Cras and CHARMES-CHAMBERTIN) and NÉGOCIANT label.

Rivesaltes Midi r w br dr sw ★★ NV Fortified wine of E Pyrenees. A tradition very much alive, if struggling these days. Top producers: Doms Cazes, Sarda-Malet, Vaquer, des Schistes, CH de Jau. See MUSCAT DE RIVESALTES.

Roche-aux-Moines, La Lo w sw ★★★ 76' 78 79 82 85 86 88' 89' 90' 93' 94 95' 96 97 98 99 00 01 02 03 A 60-acre v'yd in SAVENNIÈRES, ANJOU. Intense strong fruity/sharp wine, needs long ageing or drinking fresh.

Rodet, Antonin Burg ★★→★★★★ Quality merchant with 332-acre estate, esp in MERCUREY (Ch de Chamirey) and Dom d l'Aigle, nr Limoux. See also PRIEUR.

Roederer, Louis Brut Premier NV; Rich NV; Brut 90 93 95 96' 97; Blanc de Blancs 95 96' 97 98; Brut Rosé 96 97' 98. Top-drawer family-owned CHAMPAGNE-grower and merchant at Reims. Vanilla-rich NV with plenty of flavour. Sumptuous Cristal (may be greatest of all prestige CUVÉES) and Cristal Rosé (90' 95 96' 97). Also owns DEUTZ, DELAS, CH de PEZ. See also California, p.232.

Rolland, Michel Ubiquitous and fashionable consultant winemaker and Merlot specialist working in B'x and worldwide, favouring super-ripe flavours.

Rolly Gassmann ★★ Distinguished ALSACE grower at Rorschwihr, esp for Auxerrois and MUSCAT from lieu-dit Moenchreben. House style is usually off-dry.

Romanée, La Burg r ★★★★ 78' 85' 88' 89' 90' 91 93 95 96' 97 98 99' 00 01 02' 03 A 2-acre GRAND CRU in VOSNE-ROMANÉE. MONOPOLE of Liger-Belair, sold by BOUCHARD PÈRE ET FILS. Liger-Belair making wine for themselves from 2002.

Romanée-Conti Burg r ★★★★ 66' 76 78' 80' 82 83 85' 88' 89' 90' 91 93' 95 96' 97 98 99' 00 01 02 03 A 4.3-acre MONOPOLE GRAND CRU in VOSNE-ROMANÉE; 450 cases per annum. The most celebrated and expensive red wine in the world, with reserves of flavour beyond imagination. See next entry.

Romanée-Conti, Domaine de la (DRC) ★★★★ Grandest estate in Burgundy. Inc the whole of ROMANÉE-CONTI and LA TACHE, major parts of ECHEZEAUX, GRANDS ECHEZEAUX, RICHEBOURG, ROMANÉE-ST-VIVANT, and a tiny part of MONTRACHET. Crown-jewel prices (if you can buy them at all). Keep top vintages for decades.

Romanée-St-Vivant Burg r ★★★★ 85' 88' 89' 90' 91 93' 95 96' 97 98 99' 00 01 02' 03 A 23-acre GRAND CRU in VOSNE-ROMANÉE. Similar to ROMANÉE-CONTI but lighter and less sumptuous. Cathiard, DRC, DROUHIN, HUDELOT-NÖELLAT, LEROY.

Rosacker (ALSACE) GRAND CRU of 26 ha at Hunwihr. Produces best Ries in Alsace (See CLOS STE HUNE, SIPP-MACK and MITTNACHT).

Rosé d'Anjou Lo p ★ DYA Pale, slightly sweet rosé. CABERNET D'ANJOU is better.

Rosé de Loire Lo p ★→★★ DYA Wide-ranging AC for dry rosé (ANJOU is sweet).

Rosette Dordogne w s/sw ★★ DYA Pocket-sized AC for charming apéritif wines, eg CLOS Romain, CH Puypezat-Rosette and Dom de la Cardinolle.

Rostaing, René ★★★ N Rh Growing CÔTE-ROTIE estate with prime plots, notably La Blonde (soft, elegant), fuller, firmer La Viaillère and La Landonne (15–20 yrs). Accomplished style, some new oak. Also elegant CONDRIEU and Languedoc.

Roty, Joseph Burg ★★★ Small grower of classic GEVREY-CHAMBERTIN, esp CHARMES-CHAMBERTIN and MAZIS-CHAMBERTIN. Long-lived wines.

Rouget, Emmanuel Burg ★★★★ Inheritor of the legendary estate of Henri JAYER in ECHÉZEAUX, NUITS-ST-GEORGES, and VOSNE-ROMANÉE. Top wine: V-R-Cros Parantoux.

Roulot, Domaine G Burg ★★★ Range of 7 distinctive MEURSAULTS (2 PREMIER CRU).

Roumier, Georges Burg ★★★★ Christophe R makes exceptional long-lived wines in BONNES-MARES, CHAMBOLLE-MUSIGNY-Amoureuses, MUSIGNY etc. High standards.

Rousseau, Domaine A Burg ★★★★ Grower famous for CHAMBERTIN etc, of highest quality. Wines are intense (not deep-coloured), long-lived, mostly GRAND CRU.

Roussette de Savoie w ★★ DYA The tastiest fresh white from S of Lake Geneva.

Roussillon Midi Top region for VINS DOUX NATURELS (eg MAURY, RIVESALTES, BANYULS). Lighter MUSCATS and younger vintage wines are taking over from darker, heavier wines. See CÔTES DU ROUSSILLON (and Villages) for table wines.

Ruchottes-Chambertin Burg r ★★★★ 88' 89' 90' 91 93' 95 96' 97 98 99' 00 01 02' 03 A 7.5-acre GRAND CRU neighbour of CHAMBERTIN. Similar splendid lasting wine of great finesse. Top growers: LEROY, MUGNERET, ROUMIER, ROUSSEAU.

Ruinart "R" de Ruinart Brut NV; Ruinart Rosé NV; "R" de Ruinart Brut (**90 93 95 96'**). Oldest CHAMPAGNE house, owned by MOËT-Hennessy, with elegant wines, esp luxury brands: Dom Ruinart (**88 90 93** 95), Dom Ruinart Rosé (**88' 90 93 95' 96**). Minerally BLANC DE BLANCS NV. Also multi-vintage L'Exclusive de Ruinart.

Rully Burg r w (sp) ★★ (r) **99' 01 02** 03 (w) **99 00 01 02'** 03 CÔTE CHALONNAISE village. Still white and red are light but tasty. Gd value, esp white. Growers inc DELORME, FAIVELEY, Dom de la Folie, Jacquesson, A RODET.

Sables du Golfe du Lion Midi p r w ★ DYA VIN DE PAYS from Mediterranean sand-dunes: esp Gris de Gris from Carignan, Grenache, Cinsault. Dominated by LISTEL.

Sablet S Rh r w (p) ★★ **90' 95' 96 98' 99' 00'** 03 Admirable, improving CÔTES DU RHONE village, esp Dom de Boissan, Cabasse, Espiers, Les Goubert, Piaugier, Ch du Trignon, Dom de Verquière. Nicely full whites too.

St-Amour Beauj r ★★ **99 00 01 02** 03 Northernmost CRU of BEAUJOLAIS: light, fruity, irresistible (esp on Feb 14th). Growers to try: Janin, Patissier, Revillon.

St-Aubin Burg w r ★★★ (w) **96' 99** 00 01 02' 03 (r) **96' 98 99' 01** 02 03 Understated neighbour of CHASSAGNE-MONTRACHET. Several PREMIERS CRUS: light, firm, quite stylish wines; fair prices. Also sold as CÔTE DE BEAUNE-VILLAGES. Top growers: JADOT, H&O Lamy, Lamy-Pillot, H Prudhon, RAMONET, Roux, Thomas.

St-Bris Burg w ★ DYA Newly promoted appellation for Sauv Bl. Nr CHABLIS.

St-Chinian Midi r ★→★★ **95 96 97 98' 99 00'** 01 02 03 Hilly area of growing reputation in COTEAUX DU LANGUEDOC. AC since 1982. Tasty southern reds, esp co-ops Berlou, Roquebrun, Ch de Viranel, Dom Canet Valette.

St-Emilion B'x r ★★→★★★★ **70' 75 79' 81 82' 83' 85' 86' 88 89' 90' 94 95 96 98'** 00' 01 Biggest quality BORDEAUX district (13,300 acres); solid, rich, tasty wines from many ch'x inc: AUSONE, CANON, CHEVAL BLANC, FIGEAC, MAGDELAINE. Gd co-op.

St-Estèphe B'x r ★★→★★★★ **78' 81 82' 83' 85' 86 88' 89' 90' 94 95'** 96 98 00' 01 02 N village of HAUT-MÉDOC. Solid, structured, sometimes superlative wines. Top ch'x: COS D'ESTOURNEL, MONTROSE, CALON-SEGUR, etc, and more notable CRUS BOURGEOIS than any other HAUT-MÉDOC commune.

St-Gall Brut NV; Extra Brut NV; Brut Blanc de Blancs NV; Brut Rosé NV; Brut Blanc de Blancs **90 95** 96; Cuvée Orpale Blanc de Blancs **88 90 95** 96 Brand name used by Union-Champagne: top CHAMPAGNE growers' co-op at AVIZE. CUVÉE Orpale exceptionally gd value.

St-Georges-St-Emilion B'x r ★★ **82 83' 85' 86' 88' 89' 90' 94 95 96 98 00'** 01 Part of MONTAGNE-ST-EMILION with high standards. Best ch'x: Belair-Montaiguillon, Maquin-St-G, ST-GEORGES, Tour du Pas-St-G, Griffe de Cap d'Or.

St-Gervais S Rh r (w) **98 99 00 01'** 03 ★ W bank Rhône village. Sound co-op, excellent Dom Ste-Anne red (marked Mourvèdre flavours); white inc Viognier.

St-Jean de Minervois Min w sw ★★ Perhaps top French MUSCAT: sweet and fine. Much recent progress, esp Dom de Barroubio, Michel Sigé, co-op.

St-Joseph N Rh r w ★★ **90' 91 95' 96 97' 98' 99' 00' 01'** 03 AC stretching length of N Rhône (40 miles). Delicious, fruit-packed wines around Tournon; elsewhere quality variable. Often more structure than CROZES-HERMITAGE, esp from CHAPOUTIER (Les Granits), B Gripa, GUIGAL's Grippat; also CHAVE, Chèze, Courbis, Coursodon, Cuilleron, DELAS, B Faurie, P Faury, Gaillard, Gonon, JABOULET, Marsanne, Paret, Perret, Trollat. Gd aromatic white (mainly Marsanne).

St-Julien B'x r ★★★→★★★★ **70' 75 78' 81' 82' 83' 85' 86' 88' 89' 90' 93 94 95'** 96 98 99 00' 01 02 Mid-MÉDOC village with 12 of BORDEAUX's best ch'x, inc 3 LEOVILLES, BEYCHEVELLE, DUCRU-BEAUCAILLOU, GRUAUD-LAROSE, etc. The epitome of harmonious, fragrant, and savoury red wine.

St-Nicolas-de-Bourgueil Lo r p ★★ **89' 90' 95' 96 97 98 00 01** 02 **03** Next to BOURGUEIL: same lively, fruity Cab Fr. Try: Amirault, Cognard, Mabileau, Taluau.

St-Péray N Rh w sp ★★ **99' 00 01'** 03 W Rhône (mainly Marsanne), some sp. Curiosity worth trying. Top names: S Chaboud, B Gripa, Lionnet, J-L Thiers, TAIN co-op, du Tunnel, Voge. JABOULET planting here.

St-Pourçain-sur-Sioule Central Fr r p w ★→★★ DYA Niche wine of the Allier. Light red and rosé from Gamay and/or Pinot N, white from Tressalier and/or CHARDONNAY (increasingly popular), or Sauv Bl. Recent vintages improved. Growers inc: Ray, Dom de Bellevue, Pétillat, Barbara, and gd co-op.

St-Romain Burg w r ★★ (w) **99** 00' 02' 03 Overlooked village just behind CÔTE DE BEAUNE. Value, esp for firm fresh whites. Reds have a clean cut. Top growers: De Chassorney, FEVRE, Jean Germain, Gras, LATOUR, LEROY.

St-Véran Burg w ★★ **99 00' 01 02'** 03 Next door AC to POUILLY-FUISSE. Best nearly as gd; others on unsuitable soil. Try DUBOEUF, Doms Corsin, des Deux Roches, des Valanges, Demessey, Ch FUISSE.

Ste-Croix-du-Mont B'x w sw ★★ **83 86' 88' 89 90 95' 96 97 98 99** 01 02 (03) Neighbour to SAUTERNES with similar golden wine. Well worth trying, esp CH Loubens, Ch Lousteau Vieil, Ch du Mont. Often a bargain, esp with age.

Salon 82' 83 85 88' 90 95 The original BLANC DE BLANCS CHAMPAGNE, from Le Mesnil in the Côte des Blancs. Intense, very dry wine with long keeping qualities. Tiny quantities. Bought in 1988 by LAURENT-PERRIER.

Sancerre Lo w (r p) ★★★ 96 97 98 99 00 01 02 03 The world's model for fragrant Sauv Bl, almost indistinguishable from POUILLY-FUMÉ, its neighbour across the Loire. Top wines can age 5 yrs+. Also generally light Pinot N (best drunk at 2–3 yrs) and rosé (do not over-chill). Occasional v.gd VENDANGES TARDIVES. Top growers inc: BOURGEOIS, Cotat Frères, Lucien Crochet, André Dezat, Jolivet, MELLOT, Vincent Pinard, Roger, Vacheron.

Santenay Burg r (w) ★★★ 88' 90' 93 95 96' 99 98 99' 01 02' 03 Sturdy reds from village S of CHASSAGNE. Best v'yds: La Comme, Les Gravières, CLOS de Tavannes. Top growers: GIRARDIN, Lequin-Roussot, Muzard, POUSSE D'OR.

Saumur Lo r w p sp ★→★★★ 00 01 02 03 Fresh, fruity whites plus a few more serious, v.gd CREMANT and Saumur MOUSSEUX (producers inc: BOUVET-LADUBAY, Cave des Vignerons de Saumur, GRATIEN ET MEYER, LANGLOIS-CHATEAU, Dom St Just), pale rosés and increasingly gd Cab Fr (see next entry).

Saumur-Champigny Lo r ★★→★★★ 89' 95 97 98 99 00 01 02 03 Flourishing 9-commune AC for fresh Cab Fr ageing remarkably in sunny yrs. Look for Ch'x DU HUREAU, DE VILLENEUVE; Doms FILLIATREAU, Legrand, Nerleux, Roches Neuves, St Just, Val Brun; CLOS ROUGEARD.

Saussignac Dordogne w sw ★★→★★★ 97' 98 99 01 (02) MONBAZILLAC-style age-worthy wines. Producers of new ultra-sweet style, inc Dom de Richard, Ch'x les Miaudoux, Tourmentine, le Payral, le Chabrier, and CLOS d'Yvigne.

Sauternes B'x w sw ★★→★★★★ 67' 71' 75 76' 81 83' 85 86' 88' 89' 90' 95' 96 97 98 99 01' 02 03 District of 5 villages (inc BARSAC) which make France's best sweet wine, strong (14%+ alcohol), luscious and golden, demanding to be aged 10 yrs. Top ch'x are D'YQUEM, GUIRAUD, LAFAURIE-PEYRAGUEY, RIEUSSEC, SUDUIRAUT, etc. Dry wines cannot be sold as Sauternes.

Sauvignon de St-Bris Burg w ★★ DYA A new AC, cousin of SANCERRE, from nr CHABLIS. To try. Dom Saint Prix from Dom Bersan is gd. Goisot best.

Sauzet, Etienne Burg ★★★ Top-quality white burgundy estate and merchant at PULIGNY-MONTRACHET. Clearly defined, well-bred wines, better drunk young.

Savennières Lo w dr sw ★★★→★★★★ 75 76' 78' 85 86' 88 89' 90' 93 95' 96 97 98 99 00 01 02 03 Small ANJOU district for pungent, long-lived whites. Baumard, Ch de Chamboureau, Ch de Coulaine, Closel, Ch d'Epiré, Dom Laureau du CLOS Frémur. Top sites: COULÉE DE SERRANT, ROCHE-AUX-MOINES, CLOS du Papillon.

Savigny-lès-Beaune Burg r (w) ★★★ 90' 95 96' 97 98 99' 00 01 02' 03 Important village next to BEAUNE; similar mid-weight wines, often deliciously lively, fruity. Top v'yds: Dominode, Guettes, Lavières, Marconnets, Vergelesses; growers: BIZE, Camus, CHANDON DE BRIAILLES, CLAIR, Ecard, Girard, LEROY, Pavelot, TOLLOT-BEAUT.

Savoie E France r w sp ★★ DYA Alpine area with light, dry wines like some Swiss or minor Loires. APREMONT, CREPY, and SEYSSEL are best-known whites, ROUSSETTE is more interesting. Also gd MONDEUSE red.

Schlossberg Very successful ALSACE GRAND CRU for Ries in two parts: Kientzheim and small section at Kaysersberg. Best: FALLER/DOM WEINBACH & PAUL BLANCK.

Schlumberger, Domaines ★→★★★ ALSACE growers at Guebwiller and largest v'yd owners in region. Unusually rich wines, inc luscious GEWURZTRAMINER GRAND CRUS Kessler & Kitterlé (also SÉLECTION DES GRAINS NOBLES and VENDANGE TARDIVE). Fine Ries from GRAND CRUS Kitterlé, Saering. Also gd Pinot Gr.

Schlumberger, Robert de Lo SAUMUR sparkling wine made by Austrian method: fruity and delicate.

Schoffit, Domaine ★★→★★★ Colmar ALSACE house with GRAND CRU RANGEN Pinot Gr, GEWURZTRAMINER of top quality. Chasselas is unusual everyday delight.

Schröder & Schÿler Old BORDEAUX merchant, co-owner of CH KIRWAN.

Schoenenbourg Very rich successful Riquewihr GRAND CRU (ALSACE): Tokay/Pinot Gr, Ries, very fine VENDANGE TARDIVE and SÉLECTION DES GRAINS NOBLES. Esp from MARCEL DEISS and DOPFF AU MOULIN. Also v.gd MUSCAT.

Sciacarello Original grape of CORSICA for red and rosé, eg AJACCIO, Sartène.

Sec Literally means dry, though CHAMPAGNE so-called is medium-sweet (and better at breakfast, tea-time, and weddings than BRUT).

Séguret S Rh r w ★★ 98' 99' 00 01' 03 Gd S Rhône village nr GIGONDAS. Peppery, quite full reds; rounded, clean whites. Esp Ch La Courançonne, Dom de Cabasse, Garancière, Mourchon, Pourra.

Sélection des Grains Nobles (SGN) Term coined by HUGEL for ALSACE equivalent to German Beerenauslese and since 1984 subject to very strict regulations. Grains nobles are individual grapes with "noble rot".

Serafin Burg ★★★ Christian S has gained a cult following for his intense GEVREY CHAMBERTIN VIEILLES VIGNES and CHARMES-CHAMBERTIN GRAND CRU.

Sèvre-et-Maine The delimited zone containing the best v'yds of MUSCADET.

Seyssel Savoie w sp ★★ NV Delicate white, pleasant sp. NB Mollex-Corbonod.

Sichel & Co One of BORDEAUX'S most respected merchant houses. Peter A Sichel died in 1998; his 5 sons continue with the family's interests in ch'x D'ANGLUDET and PALMER, in CORBIÈRES, and as B'x merchants.

Sipp, Jean & Louis ★★ ALSACE growers in Ribeauvillé (Louis is also a NÉGOCIANT). Both make v.gd Ries GRAND CRU Kirchberg. Jean's is youthful elegance; Louis' is firmer when mature. V.gd GEWURZTRAMINER from Louis, esp GRAND CRU Osterberg.

Sipp-Mack ★★→★★★ Ries specialist in Hunawihr (since 1698). Outstanding Ries from GRANDS CRUS Rosacker and Osterberg (v.gd Pinot Gr from the latter).

Sirius Serious oak-aged blended BORDEAUX from Maison SICHEL.

Skalli ★→★★ Revolutionary producer of VINS DE PAYS D'OC from Cab Sauv, Merlot, CHARDONNAY, etc, at Sète in the LANGUEDOC, inspired by California's Mondavi. FORTANT DE FRANCE is standard brand. Style and value. Now Midi ACS as well.

Sorg, Bruno ★★→★★★ First-class small ALSACE grower at Eguisheim for GRAND CRUS Florimont (RIES) and PFERSIGBERG (MUSCAT). Also v.gd Auxerrois.

Sur Lie See LIE and MUSCADET.

Tâche, La Burg r ★★★★ 78' 85' 88' 89' 90' 93' 95 96' 97 98 99' 00 **01** 02' 03 A 15-acre (1,500-case) GRAND CRU of VOSNE-ROMANÉE and one of best v'yds on earth: big perfumed, luxurious wine. See Dom de la ROMANÉE-CONTI.

Tain, Cave Coopérative de 390 members in N Rhône ACS; owns one-quarter HERMITAGE. Red Hermitage improved since 91; modern style CROZES. Gd value.

Taittinger Brut NV; Rosé NV; Brut **88 90 95 96 98**; Collection Brut **82 85 88 90** 95. Fashionable (and excellent) Reims CHAMPAGNE grower and merchant; wines have distinctive silky, flowery touch. Luxury brand: Comtes de Champagne BLANC DE BLANCS (**82 85' 88 90 95** 96), also v.gd rich Pinot Prestige Rosé NV. See also California: Domaine Carneros, p.224.

Tastevin, Confrèrie des Chevaliers du Burgundy's cheerful promotion society. Wine with the Tastevinage label has been approved and is a fair standard. A "tastevin" is the traditional shallow silver wine-tasting cup of Burgundy.

Tavel Rh p ★★ DYA France's most famous, though not best, rosé: strong, very full, and dry. Best growers: CH d'Aquéria, Dom Corne-Loup, GUIGAL, Maby, Dom de la Mordorée, Prieuré de Montézargues, Lafond, Ch de Trinquevedel.

Tempier, Domaine r w p ★★★★ The top grower of BANDOL.

Terroirs Landais Gascony r p w ★ VIN DE PAYS an extension in the département of Landes of the COTES DE GASCOGNE. Dom de Laballe is most-seen example.

Thénard, Domaine Burg The major grower of the GIVRY appellation, but best known for his substantial portion (over 4 acres) of LE MONTRACHET. Could still try much harder with this jewel.

Thevenet, Jean Burg ★★★ Dom de la Bongran at Clessé stands out for rich, concentrated (even sweet!) white MÂCON. Expensive.

Thézac-Perricard SW Fr r p ★ **98' 00' 01** 02 VIN DE PAYS W of CAHORS. Same grapes but lighter style. Made by co-op at Thézac.

Thiénot, Alain Broker-turned-merchant; dynamic force for gd in CHAMPAGNE. Grande Cuvée **85' 90 95' 96**. New vintage Stanislas Blanc de Blancs (**99**). Also owns Marie Stuart and CANARD-DUCHÊNE in Champ, Ch Ricaud in LOUPIAC.

Thomas-Moillard Burg ★★★ Underrated NUITS-ST-GEORGES estate for slow-emerging wines; sister company is Moillard-Grivot NÉGOCIANT house.

Thorin, J Beauj ★ Grower and major merchant of BEAUJOLAIS.

Thouarsais, Vin de Lo w r p ★ DYA Light Chenin Bl (20% CHARDONNAY permitted), Gamay, and Cab Sauv from tiny VDQS S of SAUMUR. Esp Gigon.

Tokay d'Alsace Old name for Pinot Gr in ALSACE in imitation of Hungarian Tokay. Now changed to Tokay/Pinot Gr. Will be just Pinot Gr from 2007.

Tollot-Beaut ★★★ Stylish, consistent burgundy grower with 50 acres in CÔTE DE BEAUNE, inc v'yds at Beaune Grèves, CORTON, SAVIGNY- (Les Champs Chevrey), and at their CHOREY-LES-BEAUNE base.

Touraine Lo r p w dr sw sp ★→★★★ **95 97 98 99 00 01 02 03** Big mid-Loire region; huge range, inc Sauv Bl, Chenin Bl (eg VOUVRAY), red CHINON, and BOURGUEIL. Large AC with light Cab Fr, Gamay, gutsy Côt, or a blend of these; grassy Sauv Bl and MOUSSEUX; often bargains. Producers: MARIONNET, Dehelly, Puzelat/CLOS de Tue-Boeuf, Courtois, Oisly-Thesée, Ch de Petit Thouars, Jacky Marteau, Dom des Corbillieres, CLOS Roche Blanche, Dom de la Presle.

Up and coming producers from the Touraine appellations
Bourgueil Domaine des Ouches.
Cheverny Herve Villemade, Clos de Tue-Boeuf, Daridan/Cellier de la Marigonnerie.
Chinon Jean-Pierre Crespin, Coulaine, Dme de Bel Air.
Jasnières Eric Nicolas/Domaine de Belliviere, Jean-Pierre Robinot, Christian Chaussard.
Touraine Domaine de la Garreliere, Domaine des Cailloux du Paradis Vin de Pays de la Vienne: Ampelidae.

Touraine-Amboise Lo r w p ★→★★ Touraine sub-appellation. "François Ier" is engaging local blend (Gamay/Côt/Cab Fr). Dutertre, Xavier Frissant.

Touraine-Azay-le-Rideau Lo ★→★★ Chenin Bl-based dry, off-dry white and Grolleau-dominated rosé. Producers: Ch de la Roche, James Paget, Pibaleau Père et Fils.

Touraine-Mesland Lo r w p ★→★★ Best represented by its user-friendly red blends (Gamay/Côt/Cab Fr). Ch Gaillard, CLOS de la Briderie.

Touraine-Noble Joué Loire p ★→★★ DYA Ancient but recently revived rosé from 3 Pinots (N, Gr, Meunier) just S of Tours. Esp from ROUSSEAU and Sard. Granted AOC status (Touraine-Noble Joué) in 2000.

Trévallon, Domaine de Provence r w ★★★ **88' 90' 91 92 93 94 95 96'** 97 98 99 00 01 Fashionable estate at Les Baux. Intense Cab Sauv/Syrah to age.

Trimbach, F E ★★★→★★★★ Distinguished ALSACE grower and merchant at Ribeauvillé; supremely elegant if at times austere house style. Best wines inc Ries CLOS STE-HUNE, CUVÉE Frédéric-Emile (grapes mostly from GRAND CRU Osterberg). Also GEWURZTRAMINER. Opposed to GRAND CRU system like HUGEL.

Turckheim, Cave Vinicole de ★★ Important co-op in ALSACE. Large range of wines, inc GRANDS CRUS from 790 acres. Less exciting recently.

Tursan SW France r p w ★★→★★★★ (Most DYA) VDQS aspiring to AC. Easy drinking holiday-style wines. Mostly from co-op at Geaune, but Ch de Bachen (★★★) belongs to master-chef Michel Guérard. Super-ripe, oak-aged Sauv Bl is excellent. Also ★★ Dom de Perchade-Pourrouchet keeps better than most.

Vacqueyras S Rh r (w) ★★ 89' 90' 94 95' 96' 97 98' 99' 00' 01' 03 Full, peppery Grenache-based neighbour to GIGONDAS: finer structure, often cheaper. Try JABOULET, Armouriers, Chx de Montmirail, des Tours, Doms Archimbaud-Vache, Charbonnière, Couroulu, Font de Papier, Fourmone, Garrigue, Grapillon d'Or, Monardière, Montirius, Montvac, Pascal Frères, Sang des Cailloux.

Val d'Orbieu, Vignerons du Association of some 200 top growers and co-ops in CORBIÈRES, COTEAUX DU LANGUEDOC, MINERVOIS, ROUSSILLON, etc, marketing a first-class range of selected MIDI AC and VIN DE PAYS wines.

Valençay Lo r p w ★ DYA VDQS in E TOURAINE; light, easy-drinking sometimes sharp wines from similar range of grapes as TOURAINE, esp Sauv Bl.

Vallée du Paradis Midi r w p ★ VIN DE PAYS of local red varieties in CORBIÈRES.

Valmagne, Abbaye de Glorious Cistercian abbey nr Sète converted to cellar.

Valréas S Rh r (p w) ★★ 98' 99 00' 01 03 CÔTES DU RHÔNE village with big co-op. Gd mid-weight red (softer than CAIRANNE, RASTEAU) and improving white. Esp Emmanuel Bouchard, Dom des Grands Devers, Ch la Décelle.

Varichon & Clerc Principal makers and shippers of SAVOIE sparkling wines.

Vaudésir Burg w ★★★★ 85' 88 89' 90 92 93 95 96' 97 98 99 00' 02 03 Arguably the best of 7 CHABLIS GRANDS CRUS (but then so are the others).

VDQS Vins Délimités de Qualité Supérieure (see p.33).

Vendange Harvest. **Vendange Tardive** Late harvest. ALSACE equivalent to German Auslese, but usually higher alcohol.

Verget Burg ★★→★★★ The NÉGOCIANT business of J-M GUFFENS-HEYNEN with mixed range from MÂCON to MONTRACHET. Intense wines, often models, bought-in grapes. CHABLIS too oaky. New Lubéron venture: Verget du Sud. Follow closely.

Veuve Clicquot Yellow Label NV; White Label DEMI-SEC NV; Vintage Réserve 89' 90 93 95 96' 98; Rosé Reserve 85 90 95 96 Historic CHAMPAGNE house of highest standing, now owned by LVMH. Full-bodied, almost rich: one of CHAMPAGNE'S surest things. Cellars at Reims. Luxury brands: La Grande Dame (85' 90 95' 96), Rich Réserve (96 98), La Grande Dame Rosé (95' 96).

Veuve Devaux Premium CHAMPAGNE of powerful Union Auboise co-op in Bar-sur-Seine. V.gd aged Grande Réserve NV, Oeil de Perdrix Rosé, Prestige CUVÉE D.

Vidal-Fleury, J Rh ★→★★ Long-established GUIGAL-owned shipper of top Rhône wines and grower of CÔTE-RÔTIE, esp La Chatillonne. Steady quality.

Vieille Ferme, La S Rh r w ★★ V.gd brand of CÔTES DU VENTOUX (r) and CÔTES DU LUBERON (w) made by the Perrins, owners of CH DE BEAUCASTEL. Reliable.

Vieilles Vignes Old vines – therefore the best wine. Used by many, esp by BOLLINGER, DE VOGUE, and CH FUISSE.

Vieux Télégraphe, Domaine du S Rh r w ★★★ 78' 81' 83 85 88 89' 90 94' 95' 96' 97 98' 99' 00 01 A leader in vigorous, modern red CHÂTEAUNEUF, and tasty white (fuller style since 90s), which age well in lesser years. New gd value second wine: Vieux Mas des Papes. Second DOMAINE: de la Roquette, fruited wines. Owns GIGONDAS Dom des Pallières with US importer Kermit Lynch.

Vigne or vignoble Vineyard, vineyards. **Vigneron** Vinegrower.

Vin de l'année This year's wine. See BEAUJOLAIS, BEAUJOLAIS-VILLAGES.

Vin Doux Naturel (VDN) Sweet wine fortified with wine alcohol, so the sweetness is natural, not the strength. The speciality of ROUSSILLON, based on Grenache or MUSCAT. A staple in French bars, but the top wines can be remarkable.

Vin de garde Wine that will improve with keeping. The serious stuff.

Vin Gris "Grey" wine is very pale pink, made of red grapes pressed before fermentation begins – unlike rosé, which ferments briefly before pressing. Oeil de Perdrix means much the same; so does "blush".

Vin Jaune Jura w ★★★ Speciality of ARBOIS: odd yellow wine like fino sherry. Normally ready when bottled (after at least 6 yrs). Best is CH-CHALON.

Vin Nouveau See BEAUJOLAIS NOUVEAU.

Vin de Paille Wine from grapes dried on straw mats, consequently very sweet, like Italian passito (see p.217). Esp in the JURA. See also CHAVE.

Vin de Pays (VDP) Most dynamic category in France (140+). Zonal VDPs are best, eg Coteaux de l'Uzège, Côtes de Gascogne, Côtes de Thongue, among others.

Vin de Table Standard everyday table wine, not subject to particular regulations about grapes and origin. Choose VINS DE PAYS instead.

Vinsobres S Rh r (p w) ★ **95' 98' 99' 00 01'** 03 Contradictory name of gd village. Best are substantial, rounded, fruity reds. Look for: Doms les Aussellons, Bicarelle, Charme-Arnaud, Coriançon, Deurre, Jaume, Ch Rouanne.

Viré-Clessé Burg w ★★ **99 00' 01** 02 New AC based around 2 of the best white wine villages of MÂCON. Extrovert, exotic style esp: A Bonhomme, Bret Bros, CLOS du Chapitre, JADOT, Château de Viré, Merlin, and co-op.

Visan S Rh r p w ★ **98' 99 00 01** 03 Rhône village for gd medium-weight reds. Of note: Dom des Grands Devers and Roche-Audran.

Viticulteur Wine-grower.

Vogüé, Comte Georges de ("Dom les Musigny") ★★★★ First-class 30-acre BONNES-MARES and MUSIGNY DOMAINES at CHAMBOLLE-MUSIGNY. At best, esp since 90, the ultimate examples. Avoid most of the 80s.

Volnay Burg r ★★★→★★★★ **85' 88' 89' 90' 91 93 95** 96' **97** 98 99' 00 01 Village between POMMARD and MEURSAULT: often the best reds of the CÔTE DE BEAUNE, not dark or heavy but structured and silky. Best v'yds: Caillerets, Champans, CLOS des Chênes, Santenots, Taillepieds, etc. Best growers: D'ANGERVILLE, J M BOILLOT, HOSPICES DE BEAUNE, LAFARGE, LAFON, DE MONTILLE, POUSSE D'OR.

Volnay-Santenots Burg r ★★★ Excellent red wine from MEURSAULT is sold under this name. Indistinguishable from other PREMIER CRU VOLNAY. Best growers: AMPEAU, HOSPICES DE BEAUNE, LAFON, LEROY.

Vosne-Romanée Burg r ★★★→★★★★ **85' 88' 89' 90' 91 93 95** 96' **97** 98 99' 00 01 02' 03 Village with Burgundy's grandest crus (ROMANÉE-CONTI, LA TACHE etc). There are (or should be) no common wines in Vosne. Many gd growers inc: Arnoux, Cathiard, DRC, ENGEL, GRIVOT, GROS, JAYER, LATOUR, LEROY, Liger-Belair, MÉO-CAMUZET, Mongeard-Mugneret, Mugneret, RION.

Vougeot Burg r w ★★★ **90' 91 93 95'** 96' **97** 98 99' 00 01 02' 03 Some village and PREMIER CRU red (and white) wines. See CLOS DE VOUGEOT. Exceptional CLOS Blanc de Vougeot, white since 12th C. Bertagna and VOUGERAIE best.

Vougeraie, Dom de la Burg r ★★→★★★ DOMAINE uniting all BOISSET's v'yd holdings. Gd-value BOURGOGNE ROUGE up to fine MUSIGNY GRAND CRU.

Vouvray Lo w dr sw sp ★★→★★★★ 76' 82 83 85' 86 88' 89' 90' 93 95' 96 **97** 98 99 00 01 02 03 (SEC/DEMI-SEC) AC E of Tours: increasingly gd and reliable. Demi-sec is classic style but in great yrs MOELLEUX can be intensely sweet, almost immortal. Gd, dry sp: look out for PÉTILLANT. Best producers: Allias, Champalou, CLOS Baudoin, Dhoye-Deruet, Foreau, Fouquet, Ch Gaudrelle, HUËT, Lemaire & Renard, Pinon, Vigneau-Chevreau.

Vranken, Champagne Ever more powerful CHAMPAGNE group created in 1976 by Belgian marketing man. CHARDONNAY-led wines of gd quality. Leading brand Demoiselle. Owns HEIDSIECK MONOPOLE, POMMERY, and Bricout.

Wolfberger ★★ Principal label of Eguisheim co-op. Exceptional quality for such a large-scale producer. Very important for CRÉMANT.

"Y" (pronounced: "ygrec") B'x **78' 79' 80' 85 86 88 94 96 00** Intense dry wine produced occasionally at Ch D'YQUEM. Most interesting with age.

Zind-Humbrecht, Domaine ★★★★ Outstanding 99-acre ALSACE estate in Thann, Turckheim, Wintzenheim. First-rate, single-v'yd wines (esp CLOS St-Urbain), and very fine from GRANDS CRUS from Rangen, Goldert, Brand, and Hengst. Very rich, ultra-concentrated style, sometimes at the expense of elegance.

Châteaux of Bordeaux

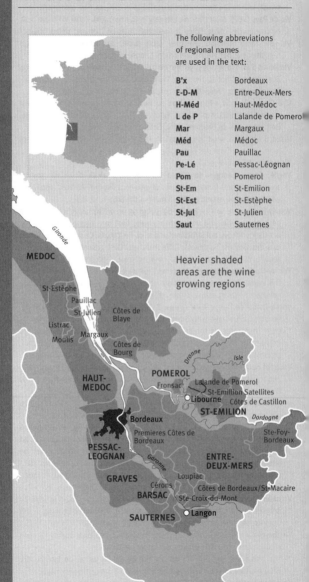

The following abbreviations
of regional names
are used in the text:

B'x	Bordeaux
E-D-M	Entre-Deux-Mers
H-Méd	Haut-Médoc
L de P	Lalande de Pomerol
Mar	Margaux
Méd	Médoc
Pau	Pauillac
Pe-Lé	Pessac-Léognan
Pom	Pomerol
St-Em	St-Emilion
St-Est	St-Estèphe
St-Jul	St-Julien
Saut	Sauternes

Heavier shaded
areas are the wine
growing regions

Gironde

MEDOC

St-Estèphe

Pauillac

St-Julien

Côtes de Blaye

Listrac

Margaux

Moulis

Côtes de Bourg

Dronne

Isle

HAUT-MEDOC

POMEROL

Fronsac

Lalande de Pomerol

St-Emilion Satellites

Libourne

Côtes de Castillon

ST-EMILION

Dordogne

Bordeaux

Premieres Côtes de Bordeaux

Ste-Foy-Bordeaux

PESSAC-LEOGNAN

Garonne

ENTRE-DEUX-MERS

GRAVES

Loupiac

Cérons

Côtes de Bordeaux/St-Macaire

BARSAC

Ste-Croix-du-Mont

SAUTERNES

Langon

Which Bordeaux vintages to drink now, and which to keep? There is little need or temptation to stock up on the most recent vintages now, either for drinking or investment, except for the more modest châteaux of 2000, which are consistently ripe and pleasing without inflated prices. There is plenty of wine to enjoy at all stages of maturity at similar or lower prices in the pipeline.

Anything older than 82 is speculative: storage conditions will be decisive to its state of health. But 82, a great vintage all round, does not look overpriced today. Nor do 85 and 86 – the latter a classic Cabernet vintage and still a keeper for Médocs of quality. 88 is relatively undervalued; 89 fully valued but excellent for drinking or keeping. 90 is a banker; an easy choice. No need to buy anything from 91 to 94, but 95 is an all-rounder beginning to be splendid drinking. Buy 96 from the northern Médoc, 97 selectively for pleasant drinking now, 98 from the Right Bank, and 00 as you need them. 01 will give great pleasure in two or three years. Leave "garage" wines to boy racers.

In case of doubt the term Left Bank is wine trade short-hand for the Médoc and Graves, lying on the west side of the north-flowing river Garonne and its estuary the Gironde. Right Bank means St-Emilion, Pomerol, Fronsac, and vineyards to the east. In this listing we have picked out in colour the vintages that proprietors themselves may be serving this year as their first choices: their own wines in the state of maturity they prefer. Their choices, for older or younger wines or both, remind us that there are no absolutes – least of all in the glorious diversity of Bordeaux.

d'Agassac H-Méd r ★★ 82' 85' 86 88 89' 90' 93 94 95 96 98 99 00' 02 "Sleeping Beauty" 14th-C moated fort. 86 acres very nr BORDEAUX suburbs. New owners and improved quality since 1996.

Andron-Blanquet St-Est r ★★ 82 85' 86 88 89' 90 91 93 94 95 96 98' 00'. Sister ch to COS-LABORY. 40 acres. Toughish wines showing more charm lately.

Angélus St-Em r ★★★★ 85' 86 87 88 89' 90' 92' 93 94 95 96 97 98' 99 00' 01 02 (03) A 57-acre classed-growth on ST-EMILION Côtes. A current star with some sumptuous wines. Promoted to Premier Grand Cru Classé status in 1996.

d'Angludet Cantenac-Mar r ★★★ 82 83' 85 86 88' 89' 90 94 95 96' 97' 98' 00 02 A 75-acre Cru Bourgeois of classed-growth quality run by Benjamin Sichel. Lively long-living MARGAUX of great style popular in UK. Gd value.

Archambeau Graves r w dr (sw) ★★ (r) 85 86 88 89 90 93 94 95 96 98 00 (w) 95 96 97 98 99 00 01 02 Up-to-date 54-acre property at Illats. V.gd fruity dry white; fragrant barrel-aged reds (three-quarters of v'yd).

d'Arche Saut w sw ★★ 83' 85 86' 88' 89' 90 95 96 97 98 99 01' 02 (03) Classed-growth of 88 acres rejuvenated since 1980. Modern methods. Rich, juicy wines to follow with pleasure.

d'Arcins H-Méd r ★★ 90 94 95 96 98 00 01 185-acre Castel family property (Castelvin: famous VIN DE TABLE). Sister to neighbour Barreyres (160 acres).

d'Armailhac Pau r ★★★ 82' 85 86' 88' 89 90' 93 94 95' 96' 98 99 00 01 02 Formerly CH MOUTON BARONNE PHILIPPE. Substantial fifth-growth under Rothschild

Vintages shown in light type should only be opened now out of curiosity to gauge their future. Vintages shown in **bold type** are deemed (usually by their makers) to be ready for drinking. Remember though that the French tend to enjoy the vigour of young wines, and that many 88s, 89s, and 90s have at least another decade of development in front of them. Vintages marked thus' are regarded as particularly successful for the property in question. Vintages in colour are the first choice for 2005.

ownership. 125 acres: wine much less rich and luscious than MOUTON ROTHSCHILD, but outstanding in its class.

l'Arrosée St-Em r ★★★ 82 83 85' 86' 88 89' 90' 92 93 94' 95 96 97 98' 00 02 A 24-acre Côtes estate. The name means diluted, but wine is top-flight: opulent and structured.

Ausone St-Em r ★★★★ 75 76 78' 79 82' 83' 85 86' 88 89 90 93 94 95' 96' 97' 98' 99 00' 01 02 (03) Illustrious first-growth with 17 acres (about 2,500 cases); best position on the Côtes with famous rock-hewn cellars. Priciest ST-EMILION. For a long time behind CHEVAL BLANC or FIGEAC in performance, but not any more. Second wine: La Chapelle d'Ausone. Now superb.

Bahans-Haut-Brion Pe-Lé r ★★★ NV and 82 85 86' 88 89' 90 93 94 95 96' 97 98 99 00 01 02 The second wine of CH HAUT-BRION. Worthy of its noble origin; softly earthy yet intense.

Balestard-la-Tonnelle St-Em r ★★ 85 86' 88' 89 90' 93 94 95 96 98' 00' Historic 30-acre classed-growth on the plateau. Big flavour and finesse.

de Barbe Côtes de Bourg r (w) ★★ 90 94 95 96 98 99 00 01 02 The biggest (148 acres) and best-known ch of BOURG. Light, fruity Merlot.

Barde-Haut St-Em r ★★ 98 99 00 01 02 The 42-acre sister property of CLOS L'EGLISE and HAUT-BERGEY. VALANDRAUD influence: opulent.

Baret Pe-Lé r w ★★ (r) 85 86 88 89' 90' 95 96 98 00 02 Famous name recovered from a lull. Now run by BORIE-MANOUX. White well-made too.

Bastor-Lamontagne Saut w sw ★★ 85 86 88' 89' 90' 95 96' 97 98' 99 01 02 (03) Large Preignac sister to BEAUREGARD. Classed-growth quality; excellent rich wines. Second label: Les Remparts de Bastor. Also Ch St-Robert at Pujols: red and white growers. 10,000 cases.

Batailley Pau r ★★★ 82' 83' 85' 86 88' 89' 90' 93 94 95 96 98 00 02 The bigger of the famous pair of fifth-growths (with HAUT-BATAILLEY) on the borders of PAUILLAC and ST-JULIEN. 110 acres. Fine, firm, strong-flavoured, and gd value PAUILLAC, to age. Home of the Castéja family of BORIE-MANOUX.

Beaumont Cussac (H-Méd) r ★★ 82 85 86' 88 89' 90' 93' 94 95 96 98' 00 02 200-acre+ Cru Bourgeois Supérieur, well known in France for easily enjoyable wines from maturing vines. Second label: Ch Moulin d'Arvigny. 35,000 cases. In the same hands as BEYCHEVELLE.

Beauregard Pom r ★★★ 85 86 88 89' 90' 94' 95' 96' 97 98' 00' 01 02 A 42-acre v'yd; fine 17th-C ch nr LA CONSEILLANTE. Top-rank rich wines. Advice from consultant Michel ROLLAND. Second label: Benjamin de Beauregard.

Beau-Séjour-Bécot St-Em r ★★★ 82' 85 86' 88' 89' 90' 94 95' 96 97 98' 99 00' 01 02 Other half of BEAUSEJOUR-DUFFAU; 45 acres. Controversially demoted in class in 1985 but properly re-promoted to Premier Grand Cru Classé in 1996. The Bécots also own GRAND-PONTET. Now also LA GOMERIE: 1,000 cases, 100% Merlot, garagiste.

Beau-Site St-Est r ★★ 82 85 86' 88 89' 90 94 95 96 98 00 A 55-acre Cru Bourgeois in same hands as BATAILLEY etc. Recent wines rather "easy" for ST-ESTÈPHE.

Beauséjour-Duffau St-Em r ★★★ 82 83 85 86 88 89' 90' 93' 94 95 96 97' 98 99 00 01 02 Part of the old BEAU-SÉJOUR-BÉCOT Premier Grand Cru estate on W slope of the Côtes. 17 acres in old family hands; only 2,000+ cases of firm-structured, concentrated, even hedonistic wine.

de Bel-Air L de P r ★★ 82' 85 86 88' 89' 90 94' 95 96 98 00 A well-known estate of LALANDE DE POMEROL, just N of POMEROL. Similar wine. 37 acres.

Bel-Air Marquis d'Aligre Soussans-Mar r ★★ 82' 85 86 88 89 90 95 96 97 98' 00 02 Organically run MARGAUX with 42 acres of old vines giving only 3,500 cases. Concentrated but supple; a sleeper.

Bel-Orme-Tronquoy-de-Lalande St-Seurin-de-Cadourne (H-Méd) r ★★ 85 86 88

89 90 94 95 96 97' 98' 00 02 A 60-acre Cru Bourgeois N of ST-ESTÈPHE. Old v'yd previously known for tannic wines. More tempting since new management in 1997.

Belair St-Em r ★★★ **82' 83' 85' 86' 87 88' 89' 90' 94 95' 96 97** 98 99 00' 01 02 Neighbour of AUSONE. Fine wine but simpler; less tightly wound. Also NV Roc-Blanquant (magnums only). Biodynamic approach since 1994.

Belgrave St-Laurent r ★★ **82 85 86' 88 89 90' 94 95 96'** 98' 00' 01 02 Fifth-growth well-managed by DOURTHE in ST-JULIEN's back-country. 107 acres. Second label: Diane de Belgrave.

Belles-Graves L de P r ★★ **82 85 86 88 93 94 95 96 99** 00 01 Confusing name, but one of the reasons to watch LALANDE DE POMEROL.

Berliquet St-Em r ★★ **86 88 89' 90 91 93 94 95 96 97** 98' 99 00' 01 02 A 23-acre Grand Cru Classé. Has been very well run recently.

Bernadotte H-Méd-r ★★ **98 99** 00' 01 02 Small ch managed by PICHON-LALANDE. One to watch.

Bertineau St-Vincent L de P r ★★ **98 99** 00' 01 Top oenologist Michel ROLLAND owns this 10 acre estate. (See also LE BON PASTEUR.)

Beychevelle St-Jul r ★★★ **82' 85 86' 88 89' 90' 93 94' 95 96 97** 98 99 00 01 02 170-acre fourth-growth with historic mansion, owned by an insurance company; now also Japanese Suntory. Wine should have elegance and power, just below top-flight ST-JULIEN. Second wine: Amiral de Beychevelle.

Biston-Brillette Moulis r ★★ **95 97** 98 00 01 02 Another attractive MOULIS wine. Making 7,000 cases.

le Bon Pasteur Pom r ★★★ **82' 85 86' 88 89' 90' 93' 94' 95 96' 97** 98' 99 00 01 Excellent small property on ST-EMILION boundary, owned by oenologist Michel ROLLAND. Concentrated, even creamy wines can be virtually guaranteed. (See also BERTINEAU ST-VINCENT.)

Bonalgue Pom r ★★ **89 90 93 94 95 96' 97** 98' 99 00 Ambitious little estate recently off form. Les Hautes-Tuileries is sister ch. Also manages CLOS DU CLOCHER in POMEROL.

Bonnet E-D-M r w ★★ (r) **90 94 95 96 97 98' 00** (w) DYA Owned by André Lurton. Big producer (600 acres!) of some of the best ENTRE-DEUX-MERS. Watch out for new Cuvée Prestige "Dominus" (00).

le Boscq St-Est r ★★ **85 86 88 89' 90 93 95' 96' 97'** 98 00 01 Leading Cru Bourgeois giving excellent value in tasty ST-ESTÈPHE.

le Bourdieu Vertheuil H-Méd r ★★ **82 85 86 88 89 90' 94 95 96 98** 00 Vertheuil estate with sister ch Victoria (134 acres in all); ST-ESTÈPHE-style wines.

Bourgneuf-Vayron Pom r ★★ **85' 86 88 89' 90 94 95' 96' 97** 98' 99 00 01 A 22-acre v'yd on sandy, gravel soil, its best wines with typically plummy POMEROL perfume. 5,000 cases.

Bouscaut Pe-Lé r w ★★ (r) **82' 85 86' 88 89 90 94 95 96** 98 00 01 02 (w) **96 97 98 99 00** 01 02 Underperforming classed-growth at Cadaujac bought in 1980 by Lucien Lurton of BRANE-CANTENAC etc. 75 acres red (largely Merlot); 15 acres white. Sophie Lurton is making steady improvements.

du Bousquet Côtes de Bourg r ★★ **85 86 88 89 90' 95 96 98 99 00 01** 02 Reliable estate with 148 acres making attractive, solid wine.

Boyd-Cantenac Mar r ★★★ **82' 85 86' 88 89 90 94' 95 96' 98'** 00 02 A 44-acre third-growth often producing attractive wine, full of flavour, if not of third-growth class. Second wine: Jacques Boyd. See also POUGET.

Branaire St-Jul r ★★★ **82' 85 86 88 89' 90' 93' 94 95** 96 98 99 00 01 02 Fourth-growth of 125 acres. Reliable source of smooth, typical ST-JULIEN. Second label: Duluc.

Brane-Cantenac Cantenac-Mar r ★★★ **82' 85 86' 88 89 90 95 96** 98 99 00 01' 02 Big (211-acre) second-growth. At best rich, even gamey wines of strong character. Also owned by the Lurton family. Second label: Baron de Brane. Much improved from late 1990s.

du Breuil Cissac (H-Méd) r ★★ **89 90 93 94 95 96 98** 99 00 01 02 Historic ch being restored by CISSAC's owners.

Brillette Moulis r ★★ **85' 86 88 89' 90 95 96 97 98** 99 00 02 70-acre Cru Bourgeois Supérieur. Reliable and attractive. Second label: Berthault Brillette.

la Cabanne Pom r ★★ **82' 88' 89' 90' 94' 95 96** 98' 00 Well-regarded 25-acre property. Recently modernized. Second wine: Dom de Compostelle. See also CH HAUT-MAILLET.

Cadet-Piola St-Em r ★★ 82 **85' 86 88 89' 90 93' 94' 95 97** 98 00 01 Distinguished small property (17.5 acres) N of ST-EMILION town. 3,000 cases of tannic wine. FAURIE-DE-SOUCHARD: same owner; less robust.

Caillou Saut w sw ★★ 75 76 79 **81 83 85 86 87 88' 89' 90' 95 96 97** 98 99 01 02 (03) Well-run second-rank 37-acre BARSAC v'yd for firm fruity wine. Private CUVÉE (86 88 89' 97) is a top selection.

Calon-Ségur St-Est r ★★★ **82' 85 86' 88' 89' 90' 93 94 95** 96' 98 99 00' 01 02 Big (123-acre) third-growth with great historic reputation. Greater consistency since 1995. Second label: Marquis de Ségur.

Cambon La Pelouse H-Méd r ★★ **94 95 96' 97 98' 99** 00 01 02 Big, accessible Cru Bourgeois Supérieur. A sure bet for rich typical MÉDOC.

Camensac St-Laurent (H-Méd) r ★★ **82' 85 86' 88 89 90 95** 96' **97'** 98' 00 01 149-acre fifth-growth. Quite lively if not exactly classic wines. Second label: La Closerie de Camensac.

Canon St-Em r ★★★ **82' 85' 86 88' 89' 90' 93' 94 95 97** 98' 99 00 01 02 Famous first-classed-growth with 44-plus acres on plateau W of the town bought in 1996 by (Chanel) owners of RAUZAN-SEGLA. Conservative methods, the v'yd is being restructured. Steady progress. Second label: Clos J Kanon.

Canon-de-Brem Canon-Fronsac r ★★ **82' 85 86 88 89' 90 94 95 96 98** 99 00 01 One of the top FRONSAC v'yds for vigorous wine. Formerly a MOUIEX property now under new ownership (DE LA DAUPHINE). Massive recent investment. To watch.

Canon La Gaffelière St-Em r ★★★ **82 85 86' 88' 89' 90' 93' 94' 95** 96 97 98' 99 00 01 **02** A 47-acre classed-growth on the lower slopes of the côtes. Same ownership as CLOS DE L'ORATOIRE and LA MONDOTTE. Produces stylish, upfront, impressive wines.

Cantegril Graves r ★★ **94 95 96 97 98 99** 00 Gd earthy red from CH DOISY-DAENE.

Cantemerle Macau (H-Méd) r ★★★ **82 85 88 89' 90 95 96' 97 98'** 00 01 02 Romantic southern MÉDOC estate, a ch in a wood (sadly battered in 1999 gales) with 150 acres of vines. Fifth-growth capable of great things. Second label: Les Allées de Cantemerle.

Cantenac-Brown Cantenac-Mar r ★★–★★★ **82 85 86' 88 89 90' 94 95** 96 97 98 99 00 01 02 Formerly old-fashioned 77-acre third-growth. Now owned by AXA Millésimes (same as PICHON-LONGUEVILLE). Its investment is starting to pay off. Tannic wines. Second label: Canuet.

Cap de Mourlin St-Em r ★★ **82' 85 86 88 89 90 93 94 95 96 97** 98' 99 00 01 Well-known 37-acre property of the Cap-de-Mourlin family, also owners of CH BALESTARD and Ch Roudier, MONTAGNE-ST-EMILION. Should be a rich tasty ST-EMILION.

Capbern-Gasqueton St-Est r ★★ **86 88 89 90 94 95 96** 98 00 02 Gd 85-acre Cru Bourgeois; same owner as CALON-SEGUR.

Carbonnieux Pe-Lé r w ★★★ **82 85 86' 88 89' 90' 93 94 95 96 98** 99 00 02 Historic estate at LÉOGNAN for sterling r and w. The whites, 65% Sauv Bl (eg **92' 94' 95 96 97 98** 00 01 02), can have the structure to age 10 yrs. Ch'x Le Pape and Le Sartre are also in the family. Second label: La Tour-Léognan.

de Cardaillan Graves r ★★ **94 95 96 98 99** 00 The trusty red wine of the distinguished CH DE MALLE (SAUTERNES).

la Cardonne Blaignan (Méd) r ★★→★★★ **94 95 96 97 98 99** 00 02 Fairly large (125-acre) Cru Bourgeois Supérieur of N MEDOC.

de Carles Fronsac r ★★ 86 **88 89 90 94 95 96 97' 98** 99 00 01 02 Ancient ch (named after Charlemagne). Steadily well-made, quite juicy FRONSACS. Haut Carles is the top selection.

les Carmes-Haut-Brion Pe-Lé r ★★★ 85 **86 88' 89 90' 93' 94 95 96 97** 98 99 00 01 02 Small (11-acre) neighbour of HAUT-BRION with classed-growth standards. Old vintages show its potential. Produces 2,000 cases.

Caronne-Ste-Gemme St-Laurent (H-Méd) r ★★→★★★ **83 85 86 89' 90 94' 95** 96' 98 99 00 01 02 Cru Bourgeois Supérieur (100 acres). Steady, stylish quality repays patience. At minor CRU CLASSÉ level (esp 96).

Carsin Premières Côtes r w ★★ (r) **94 95 96 97 98' 99 00 01** (w) **95 96 97 98 99 00** 01 02 Ambitious enterprise: Finnish-owned, Australian-designed winery. Very attractive (esp "Cuvée Prestige" and white "Etiquette Grise"). To follow.

Carteau Côtes-Daugay St-Em r ★★ 85 **88 89 90 94 95 96' 97 98'** 99 00 01 02 Emerging 5,000-case GRAND CRU; full-flavoured wines maturing fairly early.

Certan-Guiraud Pom r ★★ 82 83' 85 86 88 89' 90' 93' 94 95 96 98 99 00 01 Small (17-acre) property. Has underperformed but was bought in 1999 by J-P MOUEIX. Renamed Ch HOSANNA in 2000.

Certan-de-May Pom r ★★★ 82' 83' 85' 86 87 88' 89' 90' 94 95 96' 98 00' 01 Tiny property (1,800 cases) with full-bodied, rich, tannic wine.

Chambert-Marbuzet St-Est r ★★→★★★ **82 85 86 88 89' 90' 93 94' 95 96 97'** 98 99 00 01 02 HAUT-MARBUZET's tiny (20-acre) sister ch. V.gd predominantly Cab Sauv, aged in new oak. M Duboscq likes his wine well hung.

Chantegrive Graves r w ★★→★★★ **88 89 90 94 95 96** 98' 99' 00 01 02 A 215-acre estate, half white, half red; modern GRAVES of very fair quality. Cuvée Caroline is top white selection (**93 94 95 96 97 98' 99 00** 01 02); top reds (**85 88 89 90 94 95 96 98** 99 00 01 02). Other labels inc Mayne-Lévêque, Mayne-d'Anice, Bon-Dieu-des-Vignes.

Chasse-Spleen Moulis r ★★★ 78' 82' 83' 85 86 88 89' 90' 93 94 95 96 98 99 00 01 02 A 180-acre Cru Bourgeois Exceptionnel at classed-growth level. Consistently gd, often outstanding (eg **90'**), long-maturing wine. Second label: Ermitage de C-S. One of the surest things in B'x. See also LA GURGUE and HAUT-BAGES-LIBÉRAL.

Chauvin St-Em r ★★ 88 89 90 93 94 95 96 98' 99 00 01 Steady performer; increasingly serious stuff. New v'yds purhased in 1998.

Cheval Blanc St-Em r ★★★★ 75' 76 78 79 82' 83' 85' 86 88 89 90' 93 94 95 96' 97 98' 99 00' 01 02 This and AUSONE are the first growths of ST-EMILION. Until recent vintages, Cheval Blanc has been consistently richer, more full-blooded, intensely vigorous, and perfumed, from 100 acres. Delicious young; lasts a generation. For many *the* first choice in B'x. Second wine: Le Petit Cheval.

Chevalier, Domaine de Pe-Lé r w ★★★ 79'83' 85 86' 88' 89' 90' 93 94' 95' 96' 97 98' 99 00' 01 02 Superb estate of 94 acres at LÉOGNAN. Red is stern at first, softly earthy with age. White matures slowly and develops rich flavours (**83' 85' 87' 88 89 90' 93 94 95** 96' 97 98' 99 00 01 02). Second wine: Esprit de Chevalier. Also look out for Dom de la Solitude, PESSAC-LÉOGNAN.

Cissac Cissac-Méd r ★★ 82' 83' 86' 88 89 90 93 94' 95 96' 98 00 02 Pillar of the bourgeoisie. 80-acre Cru Bourgeois Supérieur: steady record for tasty, long-lived wine. New winery 00. Second wine: Les Reflets du Ch Cissac. Also, since 1987, CH DU BREUIL.

Citran Avensan (H-Méd) r ★★ **82 85 86 88 89' 90' 94' 95 96 97** 98 99 00 02 Cru Bourgeois Supérieur of 178 acres, back in the possession of Villars-Merlaut family since 1996 after a Japanese interlude of dark, tannic wines.

Much of the v'yd was replanted in 1999. Second label: Moulins de Citran. This is one to watch.

Clarke Listrac r (p w) ★★★ 82 85' 86' 88 89' 90' 95 96' 97 98' 99 00 01 02 Huge (350-acre) Cru Bourgeois Supérieur Rothschild development, inc visitor facilities and neighbouring Ch'x Malmaison and PEYRE-LEBADE. Also a dry white "Le Merle Blanc du Ch Clarke".

Clerc Milon Pau r ★★★ 82' 85 86' 88 89' 90' 93 94 95 96' 97 98' 99 00 01 02 Once-forgotten fifth-growth bought by the late Baron Philippe de Rothschild in 1970. Now 73 acres and a top performer, weightier than ARMAILHAC.

Climens Saut w SW ★★★★ 71' 75' 76 78 79 80' 83' 85' 86' 88' 89 90' 95 96 97' 98 99 01' 02 03 A 74-acre BARSAC classed-growth making some of the world's most stylish wine (but not the sweetest) for a gd 10 yrs' maturing. (Occasional) second label: Les Cyprès. Owned by Berenice Lurton.

Clinet Pom r ★★★★ 82 83 85 86 88' 89' 90' 93' 94 95 96 97' 98' 99 00 01 02 17-acre property in central POMEROL making intense, sumptuous wines from old vines. Since 1988 one of the models for Pomerol. Since 1998 owned by Groupe Jean Louis Laborde. Second label: Fleur de Clinet.

Clos l'Eglise Pom r ★★★ 85 86 88 89 90' 93 94 95 96 97 98 99 00' 01 02 A 15-acre v'yd on one of the best sites in POMEROL. Fine wine with more depth since 1998. Michel ROLLAND consults. The same family owns HAUT-BERGEY.

Clos Floridène Graves r w ★★ (r) 95 96 97 98' 99 00 01 02 (w) 93 94 95 96' 97 98' 99 00 01 02 A sure thing from one of B'x's most famous white-winemakers, Denis Dubourdieu. Oak-fermented Sauv Bl/Sem to keep 5 yrs; fruity red. See also CH REYNON. New winery 2000.

Clos Fourtet St-Em r ★★★ 82' 83 85 86 88 89 90 94 95 96 97 98 99 00 01 02 Well-placed 42-acre first-growth on the plateau, cellars almost in town. Back on form after a middling patch. Acquired by Philippe Cuvelier in 2001. Second label: Dom de Martialis.

Clos Haut-Peyraguey Saut w SW ★★ 75 76 79 82 83' 85 86' 88' 89 90' 95' 96 97 98 99 00 01' 02 (03) Tiny production of excellent medium-rich wine. Haut-Bommes is the second label.

Clos des Jacobins St-Em r ★★ 82' 83' 85 86 88' 89' 90' 94 95 96 98 00 01 02 Well-known and well-run little (18-acre) classed-growth. New ownership from 2001; new creamy style. To watch.

Clos du Marquis St-Jul r ★★→★★★ 82 85 86' 88 89' 90 94 95 96 97 98 99 00 01 02 The second wine of LÉOVILLE-LAS-CASES, cut from the same cloth and regularly a match for many highly classed growths.

Clos de l'Oratoire St-Em r ★★ 90 94 95 96 97 98 99 00 01 Serious performer on the NE slopes of ST-EMILION. Same stable as CANON-LA-GAFFELIÈRE and LA MONDOTTE, but lighter than either.

Clos René Pom r ★★ 82' 85 86 88 89 90 94 95 96 98 00 Leading ch W of POMEROL. 38 acres. Increasingly concentrated wines. Alias Château Moulinet-Lasserre.

Clos Toumilon Graves r w ★★ 96 97 98 99 00 01 02 Little ch in St-Pierre-de-Mons to note. Fresh and charming red and white.

la Closerie du Grand-Poujeaux Moulis r ★★ 85 86 88 89 90 94' 95 96 98' 00 Small but respected middle-MÉDOC property with emphatic wines. Also owners of neighbouring Ch'x Bel-Air-Lagrave and Haut-Franquet.

la Clotte St-Em r ★★ 82 83' 85 86 88 89 90' 93' 94 95' 96' 97 98' 99 00' 01 02 Tiny CÔTES GRAND CRU CLASSÉ: pungent, supple wine. Drink at owners' restaurant, Logis de la Cadène, in ST-EMILION. Second label: Clos Bergat Bosson.

Colombier-Monpelou Pau r ★★ 86' 88 90' 94 95 96 97 98 99 00 Reliable small Cru Bourgeois Supérieur; fair standard.

la Conseillante Pom r ★★★★ 70' 75' 81' 82' 83 85 86 87 88 89 90' 93 94 95'

96' 97 98' 99 00 01 02 A 29-acre historic property on the plateau between PÉTRUS and CHEVAL BLANC. Some of the noblest and most fragrant POMEROL, worthy of its superb position; drinks well young or old.

Corbin St-Em r ★★ 82' 83 **85** 86 **88 89** 90' **95 96 98 99** 00 A 28-acre classed-growth. A cluster of Corbins occupy the plateau edge. The top vintages are very rich.

Corbin-Michotte St-Em r ★★ 82 85 88 89' 90 93 94' 95 96 97 98' 99 00 01 Well-run, modernized, 19-acre property; generous, POMEROL-like wine. In same hands as Ch'x Calon and Cantelauze.

Cordeillan-Bages Pau r ★★ A mere 1,000 cases of rather lean PAUILLAC. Better known as a luxury wealth-spa for wine writers.

Cos d'Estournel St-Est r ★★★★ 82' **85' 86'** 87 88' **89' 90'** 93' **94 95** 96' 97' 98' 00 01 02 (03) A 140-acre second-growth with eccentric chinoiserie CHAI. Most refined ST-ESTÈPHE and regularly one of the best wines of the MÉDOC. Second label: Les Pagodes de Cos. Managed by Jean-Guillaume Prats.

Cos-Labory St-Est r ★★ 82 85 86 **87 88 89'** 90' 93 94 95 96' 98' 99 00 02 Little-known fifth-growth neighbour of COS-D'ESTOURNEL with 37 acres. Efforts since 1985 have raised it steadily to classed-growth form (esp since 1990). ANDRON-BLANQUET is sister ch.

Coufran St-Seurin-de-Cadourne (H-Méd) r ★★ 82' 85 86' 88 89 90 94 95 96' **98** 99 00 01 Coufran and VERDIGNAN, in the extreme N of the HAUT-MÉDOC, are co-owned. Coufran is mainly Merlot for supple wine. 148 acres. SOUDARS is another, smaller ch.

Couhins-Lurton Graves w ★★→★★★ 93 94 95 96 97' **98'** 99 00 01 02 Tiny quantity of fine oaky Sauv Bl. Classed-growth ch.

la Couspaude St Em r ★★★ **89 90** 93 94 95 96 97 98 99 00 01 02 Another to watch closely. Modern methods and full-flavoured wine.

Coutet Saut w SW ★★★ 71' 75' 76 79 81' 83' **85** 85 86' 88' 89' 90' (no 93 94) 95 **96** 97 98' 99 01' 02 (03) Traditional rival to CLIMENS; 91 acres in BARSAC. Usually slightly less rich; at its best equally fine. "Cuvée Madame" is a very rich selection in the best vintages. A dry GRAVES is sold under the same name.

Couvent des Jacobins St-Em r ★★ 82' 85 86 87 **88 89** 90 94 95 **96' 97 98' 99** 00 Well-known 22-acre v'yd on E edge of town. Among the best of its kind. Splendid cellars. Second label: Ch Beau-Mayne.

le Crock St-Est r ★★ 82 85 86 **88 89 90'** 93 95 96 97 98 99 00 01 02 Outstanding Cru Bourgeois Supérieur of 74 acres in the same family as LÉOVILLE-POYFERRÉ. Among the best Crus Bourgeois of the commune.

La Croix Pom r ★★ **83** 85' **86 88** 89 90 93 94 95 **96 97** 98 99 00 01 Well-reputed property of 32 acres. Appealing plummy POMEROL. Also La Croix-St-Georges, La Croix-Toulifaut, Castelot, Clos des Litanies, and HAUT-SARPE (ST-EMILION).

la Croix-de-Gay Pom r ★★★ 85 86 88' **89 90** 93 94' **95** 96 98 99 00 01 02 30 acres in the best part of the commune. Recently on fine form. Has underground cellars (rare in POMEROL). LA FLEUR-DE-GAY is the best selection.

la Croix du Casse Pom r ★★ 89 90 **93 94 95 96 97 98** 99 00 01 Up-and-coming property to look out for. Same owner as CLINET.

Croizet-Bages Pau r ★★ 82' 85 86 **88 89** 90' **95 96'** 98' 00 01 02 A 52-acre fifth-growth. Same owners as RAUZAN-GASSIES. The 98 may indicate better things to come.

Croque-Michotte St-Em r ★★ 82' **83** 85 86 88 89' 90' **94 95 96 98** 00 01 A 35-acre GRAND CRU on the POMEROL border. Gd steady wines but not grand enough to be classé.

To decipher codes, please refer to "Key to symbols" on front flap of jacket, or to "How to use this book" on p.6.

de Cruzeau Pe-Lé s r w ★★ (r) **86 88 89 90 94 95 96** 99 00 01 02 A 100-acre PESSAC-LÉOGNAN v'yd recently developed by André Lurton of LA LOUVIERE etc. To try. Oak-fermented white keeps 2–5 years.

Dalem Fronsac r ★★ **85 86 88 89 90 94 95 96' 97** 98' 99 00 01 02 Leading full-blooded FRONSAC. 36 acres: 85% Merlot.

Dassault St-Em r ★★ **82 85 86 88 89 90 94 95 96 97 98'** 99 00 01 02 A consistent, early-maturing, middle-weight GRAND CRU CLASSÉ. 58 acres. Could be more exciting.

de la Dauphine Fronsac r ★★ **85 86 88 89' 90' 94 95 96 98' 99 00** 01 Old star rejuvenated by J-P MOUEIX and sold to owners of CANON-DE-BREM in 00. New winery and cellars in 2002 – to watch.

Dauzac Labarde-Mar r ★★→★★★ **82' 85 86 88' 89' 90' 93' 94 95** 96 98' 99 00 01 02 A 120-acre fifth-growth nr the river S of MARGAUX; underachiever for many yrs, now improving. New owner (insurance company) in 1989; began to achieve in the 1990s. Second wine: La Bastide Dauzac.

Desmirail Mar r ★★→★★★ **82 85 86 88 89 90** 94 95' 96' 97 98 00 01 02 Third-growth, 45 acres. Wines for drinking fairly young, but higher ambitions.

Doisy-Daëne Barsac w (r) sw dr ★★★ **76' 80 82 83** 85 86 88' 89' 90' 95 96 97 98' 99 01 02 (03) Forward-looking, even experimental, 34-acre estate producing a crisp, oaky, dry white and a red, CH CANTEGRIL, but above all renowned for its notably fine (and long-lived) sweet BARSAC. L'Extravagance (**90** 96 97 01 02) is a super-cuvée.

Doisy-Dubroca Barsac w sw ★★ **75' 76 78 79** 83 85 86 88' 89 90' 95 96 97 99 01 (03) Tiny (8.5-acre) BARSAC classed-growth allied to CH CLIMENS.

Doisy-Védrines Saut w sw ★★★ **75' 76' 79 80 83' 85 86 88' 89' 90 95 96 97** 98' 99 01 (03) A 50-acre classed-growth at BARSAC, nr CLIMENS and COUTET. Delicious, sturdy, rich: for keeping. A sure thing for many yrs.

la Dominique St-Em r ★★★ **79 81 82' 83 86' 87 88' 89' 90' 93 94 95 96 97** 98 99 00 01 A 45-acre classed-growth for fruity wines. Second label: St Paul de Dominique.

Ducluzeau Listrac r ★★ **82 85 86 88 89 90 94 95 96'** 00 01 Tiny sister property of DUCRU-BEAUCAILLOU. 10 acres, unusually 90% Merlot.

Ducru-Beaucaillou St-Jul r ★★★★ **61 66' 70' 75' 78' 81 82' 83' 85' 86' 89 90 93 94** 95 96' **97** 98 99 00' 01 02 (03) Outstanding second-growth on excellent form; 120 acres overlooking the river. Classic cedar-scented claret suited to long ageing. See also GRAND-PUY-LACOSTE, HAUT-BATAILLEY, LALANDE-BORIE.

Duhart-Milon Rothschild Pau r ★★★ **82' 85 86 88 89 90 93 94 95** 96' 98 00' 01 02 Fourth-growth neighbour of LAFITE, under same management. 110 acres. Maturing vines; increasingly fine quality and reputation. 00 is the best yet. Second label: Moulin de Duhart.

Duplessis Moulis r ★★ **82 85 86 88'** 89 90 93 95 96 98 00 02 CRU BOURGEOIS run by Marie Laure Lurton-Roux. Wines typical of MOULIS. See also VILLEGEORGE.

Durfort-Vivens Mar r ★★★ **82' 85' 86 88' 89' 90 94 95 96** 98 99 00 01 02 Relatively small (49-acre) second-growth owned and being improved by Gonzague Lurton. Recent wines have structure (lots of Cab Sauv) and class.

Dutruch Grand-Poujeaux Moulis r ★★ **82' 85 86 88 89 90 93 94 95 96' 98'** 99 00 01 02 One of the leaders of MOULIS making full-bodied and tannic wines.

de l'Eglise, Domaine Pom r ★★ **82' 85 86 88 89 90 95 96 98** 99 00 02 Small property: stylish, resonant wine distributed by BORIE-MANOUX.

l'Eglise-Clinet Pom r ★★★★ **82' 83' 84 85' 86 88' 89 90' 93' 94** 95 96 97' 98' 99 00 01 02 An 11-acre estate. Ranked very nr the top; full, concentrated, fleshy wine. A ch to follow, but expensive. 1,700 cases produced. Second label: La Petite Eglise.

l'Enclos Pom r ★★★ **82' 85 86 88 89' 90' 93 94 95 96** 98' 99 00 01

Excellent 26-acre property on W side of POMEROL. Usually big, well-made, long-flavoured wine.

l'Evangile Pom r ★★★★ 75' 82' 83' 85' 86 87 88' 89' 90' 93 95' 96' **97** 98' 99 00 01 02 33 acres between PÉTRUS and CHEVAL BLANC. Deep-veined but elegant style in a POMEROL classic. Bought in 1990 by Domaines (LAFITE) Rothschild. New equipment in 2000.

de Fargues Saut w sw ★★★ 70' 71' 75' 76' 78 79 81 83 85' 86 88 89 90 95 96 97 98 99'A 25-acre v'yd by ruined ch owned by Luc-Saluces of YQUEM fame. Fruity and extremely elegant wines, maturing earlier than Yquem.

Faurie-de-Souchard St-Em r ★★ 85 86 88 89 90 93 94 95 96 98' 00 01 Small GRAND CRU CLASSÉ on the Côtes. See also CADET-PIOLA.

de Ferrand St-Em r ★★ 85 86 88 89 90' 93' 94 95 96 98 00 01 Big (75-acre) plateau estate. Rich oaky wines, with plenty of tannin.

Ferrande Graves r (w) ★★95 96 98 00 Major estate at Castres: over 100 acres. Easy, enjoyable red and gd white wine, at their best at 1–4 yrs.

Ferrière Mar r ★★→★★★ 89 90 93 94 95 96 97' 98 99 00 01 02 In same capable hands as LA GURGUE and HAUT-BAGES-LIBÉRAL. New equipment 2000.

Feytit-Clinet Pom r ★★ 82' 85' 86 90' 94 95 96 97' 98 99 00 Little property. At best fine, lightish wines. In 2000, the owning Chasseuil family took back management from J-P MOUEIX.

Fieuzal Pe-Lé r (w) ★★★ 82' 85' 86' 88 89 90' 93 94 95 96' 97 98' 99 00 01 02 A 75-acre classed-growth at LÉOGNAN. Finely made, memorable wines of both colours. Classic whites since 85 are 10-yr keepers. Ch Le Bonnat is sister ch vinified at FIEUZAL.

Figeac St-Em r ★★★★ 70' 75 82' 83 85' 86' 88 89' 90' 94' 95' 96 98 99 00 01 02 First-growth, 98-acre gravelly v'yd gives one of B'x's most stylish, rich, but elegant wines, lovely to drink relatively quickly, but lasting indefinitely. Second label: Grangeneuve.

Filhot Saut w sw dr ★★ 82' 83' 85 86' 88' 88 90 95 96 97 98 99 01 02 (03) Second-rank classed-growth with splendid ch, 148-acre v'yd. Lightish and rather simple (Sauv Bl) sweet wines for fairly early drinking, a little dry, and red. V.gd Crème de Tête (**90** extremely rich).

la Fleur St-Em r ★★ 82' 85 86 88 89' 90' 94 95 96 98 00 01 16-acre Côtes estate; deliciously fruity wines. Managed by J-P MOUEIX.

la Fleur-de-Gay Pom r ★★★ 1,000-case super-cuvée of CH LA CROIX DE GAY.

la Fleur-Pétrus Pom r ★★★★ 82 83' 85 86 87 88' 89' 90' 93 94 95 96' 97 98' 99 00 01 A 32-acre v'yd flanking PÉTRUS, with the same management. Exceedingly fine, densely plummy wines. This is POMEROL at its most stylish (and expensive).

Fombrauge St-Em r ★★→★★★ 88' 89 90 94' 95 96 98 00 01 02 A 120-acre estate at St-Christophe-des-Bardes, E of ST-EMILION; Mainstream ST-EMILION making great efforts. Second label: Ch Maurens. Magrez-Fombrauge is its GARAGE wine.

Fonbadet Pau r ★★ 85 86 88 89 90' 94 95 96' 98' 00 02 Cru Bourgeois Supérieur of solid reputation. 50 acres. Old vines; wine needs long bottle-age. Value.

Fonplégade St-Em r ★★ 82' 85 86 88 89 90' 94 95 96 98 00 A 48-acre GRAND CRU CLASSÉ on the Côtes W of ST-EMILION. At best firm and long-lasting.

Fonréaud Listrac r ★★ 82' 83 85' 86' 88 89 90 94 95 96 98 00 02 One of the bigger (96 acres) and better Crus Bourgeois of its area. Investment since 1998. 5 acres of white: Le Cygne, barrel-fermented. See also LESTAGE.

Fonroque St-Em r ★★★ 75' 78 82 83' 85' 86 87 88 89' 90' 94 95 96 98 00 01 02 A 48 acres on the plateau N of ST-EMILION. Was J-P MOUEIX property until 2000, now Alain Moueix. Major investment and organic ideas. Big, deep, dark wine: drink or (better) keep.

Fontenil Fronsac r ★★ 88 89 90 **94 95 96 97** 98 99' 00 01 02 A new FRONSAC leader started by Michel ROLLAND in 1986. Dense, oaky, new-style.

Fontmarty Pom r ★★ 82 83 85 86 88' 89 90 94 95' 96 **98'** 00 Small property owned by Bernard Moueix group (also TAILLEFER); 1,500 cases.

Forts de Latour Pau r ★★★ 70' 78' 82' 83 85 86 88 89' 90' 93 94 95' 96' **97** 98 99 00 01 02 The (worthy) second wine of CH LATOUR; the authentic flavour in slightly lighter format. Until 1990 unique in being bottle-aged at least 3 yrs before release; now offered EN PRIMEUR.

Fourcas-Dupré Listrac r ★★ 82' 83' 85' 86' 88 89' 90 94 95 96' 98' 99 00 01 02 Top-class 100-acre Cru Bourgeois Supérieur making consistent wine in the tight LISTRAC style. To follow. Second label: Château Bellevue-Laffont. Complete renovation in 2000.

Fourcas-Hosten Listrac r ★★→★★★ 82' 83' 85 86' 87 88 89' 90' 94 95' 96' 98' 00 01 02 A 96-acre Cru Bourgeois Supérieur often the best of its (underestimated) commune. Firm wine with a long life. New gear in 1998.

Franc-Mayne St-Em r ★★ 85 86 88 89' 90' 94 95 96 97 98' 99 00 01 An 18 acre-GRAND CRU CLASSÉ. Ambitious new owners since 1996. Michel ROLLAND consults. To watch. Continuing renovation started in 1998.

de France Pe-Lé r w ★★ (r) 89 90' 95' 96' 98 99 00 02 (w) 95 96 97 98 99 01 02 Well-known GRAVES property (the name helps) with Michel ROLLAND consulting. Try a top vintage.

du Gaby Canon-Fronsac r ★★ Perhaps the finest situation in France. Serious wines from new owner.

la Gaffelière St-Em r ★★★ 82' 83' 85 86' 88' 89' 90' 94 95 96 98' 99 00 01 A 61-acre first-growth at the foot of the Côtes. Elegant, not rich wines. Re-equipped and improved since 1998.

Galius St-Em r ★★ 95 96 **98** 00 01 Oak-aged selection from ST-EMILION co-op, to a high standard. Formerly Haut Quercus.

La Garde Pe-Lé r w ★★ 90 94 95' 96' 97' 98' 99 00 01 02 Substantial property of 120 acres owned by NÉGOCIANT CVBG-Dourthe; reliable red and improving. More Merlot planted 2000.

le Gay Pom r ★★★ 75' 76' 82' 83' 85 86 88 89' 90' 95 96 97 98 99 00 01 Fine 14-acre v'yd on N edge of POMEROL. Same owner as CH LAFLEUR until 2002. Major investment, with Michel ROLLAND now consulting. Usually impressive tannic wines.

Gazin Pom r ★★★ 82 85 86 87' 88 89' 90' 94' 95 96 97 98' 99 00 01 02 Large property (for POMEROL): 58 acres, recently shining. Second label: l'Hospitalet de Gazin.

Gilette Saut w SW ★★★ 49 53 55 59 61 67 70 75 76 78 79 81 82 83 Extraordinary small Preignac ch stores its sumptuous wines in concrete vats to a great age. Only about 5,000 bottles of each. Ch Les Justices is its sister (**96** 97 99 01 02).

Giscours Labarde-Mar r ★★★ 70 75' 78' 82 85 88 89' 90 94 95 96' 98 99 00 01 02 Splendid 182-acre third-growth property S of CANTENAC. Excellent vigorous wine in 1970s; but 1980s very wobbly; some revival during 1990s esp under new owner since 1995, but should do better. Second labels: Ch Cantelaude, Grand Goucsirs (!) and La Sirène de Giscours. Ch La Houringue is its baby sister.

du Glana St-Jul r ★★ 89 90 94 95 96 97' 98 99 00 02 Big Cru Bourgeois Supérieur. Undemanding; undramatic; value. Second wine: Ch Sirène.

Gloria St-Jul r ★★→★★★ 82 85 86 88 89 90 95' 96 98 99 00 01 02

NB The vintages printed in colour are the ones you should choose first for drinking in 2005.

A 110-acre ST-JULIEN estate, which didn't apply for the recent Cru Bourgeois Classification (see p.97). Same ownership as ST-PIERRE. Wines of vigour, with a recent return to long-maturing style. Second label: Peymartin.

la Gomerie See BEAU-SÉJOUR-BÉCOT.

Grand Barrail Lamarzelle Figeac St-Em r ★★ 85 86 88 89 90 94 95 96 98 00
A 48-acre property S of FIGEAC. Well-reputed and popular, if scarcely exciting.

Grand-Corbin-Despagne St-Em r ★★→★★★ 82' 83 85 88 89 90' 93 94 95 96 97 98 99 00 01 One of the bigger and better GRANDS CRUS on CORBIN plateau. New generation in 1993, determined to get reinstated as GRAND CRU CLASSÉ after being demoted in 1996. Now fashionably thick wines. Also Ch Maison Blanche, MONTAGNE ST-EMILION.

Grand-Mayne St-Em r ★★★ 82 85 86 88 89' 90' 94 95 96 97 98 99 00 01 02 40-acre GRAND CRU CLASSÉ on W Côtes. Noble old ch with wonderfully rich, tasty wines recently.

Grand-Pontet St-Em r ★★★ 82' 86' 88 89 90' 93 94 95' 96 97 98' 99 00 01 02 A 35-acre estate revitalized since 1985. Quality improving.

Grand-Puy-Ducasse Pau r ★★★ 82' 85 86 88 89' 90 94 95 96' 98' 99 00 01 02 Fifth-growth enlarged to 90 acres under expert management, but lacks the vigour of the next entry. Second label: Ch Artigues-Arnaud.

Grand-Puy-Lacoste Pau r ★★★ 70' 75 78' 79' 81' 82' 83 85' 86' 88' 89' 90' 93 94 95 96' **97** 98 99 00 01 Leading fifth-growth famous for excellent full-bodied, vigorous examples of PAUILLAC. 110 acres, owned by the Borie family (see DUCRU-BEAUCAILLOU). Second label: Lacoste-Borie.

Gravas Saut w sw ★★ 96 97 00 Small BARSAC property; impressive, firm, sweet. Recommended: Cuvée Spéciale.

La Grave à Pomerol Pom r ★★★ 82' 85 86' 88 89' 90 93 94 95 96 98' 00 01 Verdant ch with small but first-class v'yd owned by CHRISTIAN MOUEIX. Beautifully structured POMEROL of medium richness.

Gressier-Grand-Poujeaux Moulis r ★★→★★★ 82 83' 85 86 88 89 90 94 95 96 98 00 01 V.gd Cru Bourgeois Supérieur. Fine firm wine with gd track record. Repays patient cellaring. Since 2003, same ownership as CHASSE-SPLEEN.

Greysac Méd r ★★ 95 96 00 02 Elegant 140-acre property. Easy, early maturing wines popular in US.

Gruaud-Larose St-Jul r ★★★★ 61 70 75 78' 82' 83' 85 86' 88' 89 90' 93 95 96' 98 99 00 01 02 One of the biggest and best-loved second-growths. 189 acres. Smooth, rich, stylish claret, yr after yr; ages for 20+ yrs. Owned by Societé Bernard Taillan since 1997. V.gd second wine: Sarget de Gruaud-Larose.

Guadet-St-Julien St-Em ★★ 82 85 86 88 89 90' 94 95 96' 98 00 01 Extremely well-made wines from very small GRAND CRU CLASSÉ.

Guiraud Saut w (r) sw (dr) ★★★ 79 81 83' 85 86' 88' 89' 90' 95 96' 97' 98 99 01' 02 (03) Restored classed-growth of top quality. 250+ acres. At best excellent sweet wine of great finesse; also small amount of red and dry white.

la Gurgue Mar r ★★ 82 83' 85' 86 87 88 89' 90 93 94 95' 96' 98 00 01 02 Small, well-placed v'yd for MARGAUX of the fruitier sort. Same management as HAUT-BAGES-LIBERAL. Winery renovated in 2000.

Hanteillan Cissac r ★★ 95 96 98 00 02 Huge v'yd: very fair Cru Bourgeois Supérieur, conscientiously made. Ch Laborde is the second label.

Haut-Bages Averous Pau r ★★ 82' 85' 86 88 89' 90 94 95 96 98 99 00 02 The second wine of LYNCH-BAGES. Should be tasty drinking.

Haut-Bages-Libéral Pau r ★★★ 82' 85 88 89 90' 93 94' 95 96' 97' 98 99 00 01 02 Lesser-known fifth-growth of 70 acres (next to LATOUR) in same stable as LA GURGUE. Results are excellent, full of PAUILLAC vitality.

Haut-Bages-Monpelou Pau r ★★ 85 86 88 89' 90 94 95 96 98 99 00

A 25-acre Cru Bourgeois Supérieur stable-mate of CH BATAILLEY on former DUHART-MILON land. Gd minor PAUILLAC.

Haut-Bailly Graves r ★★★ 82 83 85' 86 88' 89' 90' 92 93' 94 95 96 97 98' **99'** 00 01 02 A 70-acres+ estate at LÉOGNAN. American-owned since 1998, but old family still directing. Since 1979 some of the best savoury, round, intelligently made red GRAVES have regularly come from this ch. Second label is La Parde de Haut-Bailly.

Haut-Batailley Pau r ★★★ 70' 75' 78 82' 83 85 86 88 89' 90' 95 96' 97 98 99 00 02 Smaller part of divided fifth-growth BATAILLEY: 49 acres. Gentler than sister ch GRAND-PUY-LACOSTE. Second wine: La Tour-d'Aspic.

Haut-Beauséjour St-Est r ★★ 95 97 98 99 00 01 Another Cru Bourgeois performing well. Owned by CHAMPAGNE house ROEDERER.

Haut-Bergey Pessac-L r ★★ 98 99 00 01 02 A 65-acre estate, largely Cab Sauv; fragrant, delicate GRAVES. Also a little dry white. Completely renovated in the 1990s. Same ownership as BARDE-HAUT and CLOS L'ÉGLISE.

Haut Bommes See CLOS HAUT-PEYRAGUEY.

Haut-Brion Pessac (Graves) r (w) ★★★★ 59' 61' 66' 70' 71' 75' 76 78' 79' 81 82' 83' 85' 86' 87 88' 89' 90' 91 92 93 94 95 96' 97 98' 99 00 01 02 (03) The oldest great ch of B'x and the only non-MÉDOC first-growth of 1855. 108 acres. Deeply harmonious, never-aggressive wine with endless, honeyed, earthy complexity. Consistently great since 75. A little full dry white: 82 83 85 87 88 89' 90 91 92 93 94 95 96 97 98 99 00 01 02. See BAHANS HAUT-BRION, LA MISSION HAUT-BRION, LAVILLE-HAUT-BRION.

Haut-Condissas Méd r ★★ 99 00 01 02 Aspiring new cru at Bégadan. To watch.

Haut Carles See DE CARLES.

Haut-Maillet Pom r ★★ 98' 00 12-acre sister of LA CABANNE. Well-made gentle wines.

Haut-Marbuzet St-Est r ★★→★★★ 82' 85' 86' 88 89' 90' 91 93' 94 95 96' 97 98 99 00 01 02 The best of many gd ST-ESTÈPHE CRUS BOURGEOIS. Now Cru Bourgeois Exceptionnel. M Dubosq has reassembled the ancient Dom de Marbuzet, in total 175 acres. Also owns CHAMBERT-MARBUZET, MACCARTHY, Tour de Marbuzet. Haut-Marbuzet is 60% Merlot. New oak gives the wines a distinctive, if not subtle, style of great appeal.

Haut-Pontet St-Em r ★★ 98 00 Reliable 12-acre v'yd of the Côtes deserving its GRAND CRU status. 2,500 cases.

Haut-Sarpe St-Em r ★★ 82 83' 85 86 88 89 90' 93 94 95 96 98 00 01 GRAND CRU CLASSÉ (6,000 cases) with elegant ch and park, 70% Merlot. Same owner as CH LA CROIX, POMEROL.

Why do the Châteaux of Bordeaux have such a large section of this book devoted to them? Wine-lovers love to snipe at them and complain about their prices, but collectively they form by far the largest supply of high-quality wine on earth. A single typical Médoc château with 150 acres (some have far more) makes approximately 26,000 dozen bottles of identifiable wine each year – the production of two or three California boutique wineries. Moreover, between the extremes of plummy Pomerol, grainy Graves and tight, restrained Médocs – not to mention crisp, dry whites and unctuous golden ones – Bordeaux offers a wider range of tastes than any other homogeneous region.

The tendency over the last two decades has been to buy more land. Many classed-growths have expanded quite considerably since their classification in 1855. The majority have also raised their sights and invested their recent profits in better technology.

Hortevie St-Jul r ★★ **90 95 96** 98 00 02 One of the few non-classified ST-JULIENS. This tiny v'yd and its bigger sister TERREY-GROS-CAILLOU are shining examples. Now hand-harvesting only.

Hosanna Pom r ★★★★ 00 01 The new name for MOUEIX-owned CERTAN-GUIRAUD. Stellar ambitions.

Houissant St-Est r ★★ **90 95 96** 98 00 02 Typical robust well-balanced ST-ESTÈPHE Cru Bourgeois also called Ch Leyssac; well-known in Denmark.

d'Issan Cantenac-Mar r ★★★ **85 86 88 89 90' 95** 96' 98 99 00 01 02 Beautifully restored moated ch nr the Gironde with 75-acre third-growth v'yd; lightish, fragrant wines. Second label: Ch de Candale.

Kirwan Cantenac-Mar r ★★★ **82' 85 86 88 89' 90' 93' 94 95** 96 **97** 98 99 00 01 02 An 86-acre third-growth; from 1997 majority owned by SCHRODER & SCHYLER. Michel ROLLAND advises. Mature v'yds now giving classy wines.

Labégorce Mar r ★★ **82' 85 86 88 89' 90' 94 95 96** 98 99 00 01 02 Substantial 95-acre property N of MARGAUX; long-lived wines of true MARGAUX quality. Recent investment. Making every effort.

Labégorce-Zédé Mar r ★★→★★★ **82' 83' 85 86' 88 89' 90' 93 94 95** 96' **97** 98 99 00 01 02 Cru Bourgeois Exceptionnel on road N from MARGAUX. 62 acres. Typically delicate, fragrant, classic. Same family as VIEUX-CHÂTEAU-CERTAN. Second label: Dom Zédé. Also 23 acres of AC BORDEAUX: "Z".

Lacoste-Borie The second wine of GRAND-PUY-LACOSTE.

Lafaurie-Peyraguey Saut w sw ★★★ **78 82 83' 85 86' 88' 89' 90' 95 96' 97** 98 99 01 02 (03) Fine classed-growth of only 49 acres at Bommes, belonging to CORDIER. Now one of best buys in SAUTERNES. Second wine: La Chapelle de Lafaurie.

Lafite Rothschild Pau r ★★★★ **59 76' 78 79 81' 82' 83 85 86' 87 88' 89' 90' 91 93** 94 95 96' 97 98 99 00' 01 02 (03) First-growth of famous elusive perfume and style, but never huge weight. Great vintages keep for decades. Recent vintages are well up to form. Amazing circular cellars. Joint ventures in Chile (1988), California (1989), Portugal (1992). Second wine: Carruades de Lafite. 225 acres. Also owns CH'X DUHART-MILON, L'EVANGILE, RIEUSSEC.

Lafleur Pom r ★★★★ **70' 75' 79' 82' 83 85' 86' 88' 89' 90' 93 94** 95 96 **97** 98 99 00' 01 02 Superb 12-acre property. Resounding wine of the turbo-charged, tannic, less fleshy kind for long maturing and investment. Second wine: Les Pensées de Lafleur.

Lafleur-Gazin Pom r ★★ **82' 83 85' 86 88' 89** 90 93 **94 95 96** 98 00 Distinguished small J-P MOUEIX estate on the NE border of POMEROL.

Lafon-Rochet St-Est r ★★★ **70' 78 82 83' 85 86 88' 89' 90' 94 95** 96' **97** 98 00 01 02 Fourth-growth neighbour of COS D'ESTOURNEL, 110 acres. Gd hard, full-bodied ST-ESTÈPHE, slow to give. Same owner as CH PONTET-CANET. New equipment in 1998. Second label: Numéro 2. Renovation in 2000.

Lagrange Pom r ★★ **82' 83 85' 86 88 89' 90' 94 95 96** 98 00 01 A 20-acre v'yd in the centre of POMEROL run by the ubiquitous house of J-P MOUEIX. Rising profile for flavour/value.

Lagrange St-Jul r ★★★ **82 85' 86' 88' 89' 90' 93 94 95** 96 **97** 98 99 00 01 02 Formerly neglected third-growth inland from ST-JULIEN, bought by Japanese Suntory in 1983. 280 acres now in tip-top condition with wines to match (and lots of oak). Second wine: Les Fiefs de Lagrange.

la Lagune Ludon (H-Méd) r ★★★ **82' 83' 85 86' 88' 89' 90' 94 95** 96' 98 00 01 02 Ultra-modern 160-acre third-growth in southernmost MÉDOC. Rich wines with marked oak and steady high quality. Owned by CHAMPAGNE AYALA.

Châteaux entries also cross-refer to France section, pp.32–79.

Lalande-Borie St-Jul r ★★ A baby brother of the great DUCRU-BEAUCAILLOU created from part of the former v'yd of CH LAGRANGE. Gracious, easy-drinking wine.

de Lamarque Lamarque (H-Méd) r ★★ **82 85 86' 88 89** 90' **94 95** 96 97 98 99 00 02 Splendid medieval fortress in central MÉDOC. 113 acres giving admirable wine of high BOURGEOIS standard. Second wine: Donjon de L.

Lamothe Bergeron H-Méd r ★★ **88 89 90 93 94** 95 96' **98'** 00 02 A 150-acre estate at CUSSAC making 25,000 cases of reliable claret. Run by GRAND-PUY-DUCASSE.

Lanessan Cussac (H-Méd) r ★★78' **81 82 83 85 86' 88' 89' 90'** 93 94 95 96' 98 00 02 Distinguished 108-acre Cru Bourgeois Supérieur just S of ST-JULIEN. Fine rather than burly, but ages well. Same family owns Ch'x de Ste-Gemme, Lachesnaye, La Providence.

Langoa-Barton St-Jul r ★★★ 78' **82' 83 85 86' 88' 89' 90' 93 94'** 95 96 98 99 00 01 02 The 49-acre third-growth sister ch to LÉOVILLE-BARTON. Very old Barton-family estate with impeccable standards and generous value. Second wine: Réserve de Léoville-Barton

Larcis-Ducasse St-Em r ★★ 85 86 **88' 89' 90'** 94 95 96 98' 00 02 Top property of St-Laurent, eastern neighbour of ST-EMILION, on Côtes. 30 acres in a fine situation; wines could be better. New management from 2002 (PAVIE-MACQUIN and PUYGUERAUD).

Larmande St-Em r ★★★ **82 83' 85 86 88' 89'** 90' **93 94 95'** 96 97 98' 00 01 Substantial 60-acre property. Replanted, re-equipped, and now making rich, strikingly scented wine, silky in time. Second label: Ch des Templiers.

Laroque St-Em r ★★→★★★ **82' 85 86 88** 89 90 **94 95** 96 **97** 98 99 00 01 02 Important 108-acre v'yd on the ST-EMILION Côtes in St-Christophe. Promoted to GRAND CRU CLASSÉ in 1996.

Larose-Trintaudon St-Laurent (H-Méd) r ★★ **89 90' 94' 95 96' 98** 00 01 02 The biggest v'yd in the MÉDOC: 425 acres. Modern methods make reliable, fruity, and charming Cru Bourgeois wine to drink young. Second label: Larose St-Laurent. Special Cuvée: Larose Perganson.

Laroze St-Em r ★★ 90' **94 95** 96' **98'** 99 00 Large v'yd (74 acres) on W Côtes. Fairly light wines from sandy soils, more depth from 1998; approachable when young.

Larrivet-Haut-Brion Pe-Lé r (w) ★★ **82' 83** 85 86 87 **88 89** 90 94 95 96' 98' 00 01 02 LÉOGNAN property with perfectionist standards; Michel ROLLAND consulting. Also 500 cases of fine, barrel-fermented white (**93 94 95 96' 98' 99 00** 01 02). New plantings in 1999.

Lascombes Mar r (p) ★★★ 70' **82 83' 85 86 88 89' 90' 95 96'** 98' 99 00 01 02 A 240-acre second-growth owned since 2001 by an American pension fund. Wines have been wobbly, but real improvements in recent vintages. Second label: Ch Segonnes.

Latour Pau r ★★★★ 49' 59' 61' **62** 64 66' 70' **75 78' 79 81** 82' **83 85 86' 87 88' 89' 90' 91 92 93** 94' 95' 96' 97 98 99 00 01 02 (03) First-growth considered the grandest statement of the MÉDOC. Profound, intense, almost immortal wines in great yrs; even weaker vintages have the characteristic note of terroir and run for many years. 150 acres sloping to R Gironde. Latour always needs 10 yrs to show its hand. British-owned from 1963 to 1993, now again in (private) French hands. New CHAI (2003) will allow more precise selection. Second wine: LES FORTS DE LATOUR; third wine: PAUILLAC.

Latour-Martillac Pe-Lé r w ★★ (r) **82' 85' 86 88'** 89 90 **93 94 95 96** 98' 00 01 02 Small but serious property at Martillac. 10 acres of white grapes; 37 of black. The white can age admirably (**94' 95 96 97 98' 99 00** 01 02).

Latour-à-Pomerol Pom r ★★★ 61' **70'** 82 83 85' 86 87 88' 89' 90' 93 94 95 96

98' 99 00 01 Top growth of 19 acres under MOUEIX management. POMEROL of great power and perfume, yet also ravishing finesse.

des Laurets St-Em r ★★ **89' 90' 94 95 96 98 00 01** Major property in PUISSEGUIN-ST-EMILION and MONTAGNE-ST-EMILION (to the E) with 160 acres of v'yd on the Côtes (40,000 cases). Sterling wines sold by J-P MOUEIX.

La Lauzette Listrac r ★★ 82 **85 86 88 89 90 95 96** 98 99 00 A 38-acre Cru Bourgeois, previously named Ch Bellegrave, making full-flavoured wine. Why the name change? There are about a dozen Bellegraves in B'x.

Laville-Haut-Brion Pe-Lé w ★★★★ **85' 86 88** 89' **90 92 93' 94** 95' 96 **97** 98 99 00 01 02 A tiny production of the very best white GRAVES for long, succulent maturing, made at CH LA MISSION-HAUT-BRION. The 89, 95, and 96 are off the dial.

Léoville-Barton St-Jul r ★★★★ 78 **82' 83** 85' **86' 88' 89' 90' 93'** 94' 95 96' **97** 98 99 00 01 02 A 90-acre portion of the great second-growth LÉOVILLE v'yd in Anglo-Irish hands of the Barton family for over 150 years. Powerful, classic claret; traditional methods, very fair prices. Major investment raised already high standards to super-second. See also LANGOA-BARTON.

Léoville-Las-Cases St-Jul r ★★★★ 66' 75' 78' 79' 81' **82' 83' 84** 85' 86' **87 88 89'** 90' **91 93'** 94 95 96 **97** 98 99 00 01 02 The largest LÉOVILLE; 210 acres with daunting reputation. Elegant, complex, powerful, austere wines, for immortality. Second label CLOS DU MARQUIS is also outstanding.

Léoville Poyferré St-Jul r ★★★ 82' 83' **85 86' 88 89' 90' 94 95** 96 98 99 00 01 02 For yrs the least outstanding of the LÉOVILLES; high potential rarely realized. Michel ROLLAND consults here; things should be better. 156 acres. Second label: Ch Moulin-Riche.

Lestage Listrac r ★★ 86' **88 89' 90' 95 96 98** 00 A 130-acre Cru Bourgeois Supérieur in same hands as CH FONREAUD. Light, stylish wine, oak-aged since 85. Second wine: Ch Caroline. Also La Mouette (white).

Lilian Ladouys St-Est r ★★ **89 90 94 95** 96 97 98 00 01 02 Created in the 1980s: a 50-acre Cru Bourgeois Supérieur with high ambitions and early promise. There have been problems, but early and recent wines are looking gd.

Liot Barsac w sw ★★ 75' **76 82 83 85 86 88** 89' 90' **95 96 97** 98 99 00 01 02 Consistent, fairly light golden wines from 50 acres. How they last!

Liversan St-Sauveur (H-Méd) r ★★ **82' 85 86' 88' 89' 90' 93 94 95** 96 98 00 02 A 116-acre Cru Bourgeois Supérieur inland from PAUILLAC. The Polignac family have had steadily high standards. Same owners as PATACHE D'AUX. Second wine: Ch Fonpiqueyre.

Livran Méd r ★★ **82' 86 88' 89' 90' 94' 95 96 98** 00 Big estate at St-Germain in the N MÉDOC. Consistent round wines (half Merlot).

Loudenne St-Yzans (Méd) r ★★ **82' 85 86' 88 89' 90 94 95** 96' **98** 00 01 02 Beautiful riverside ch owned by Gilbeys 1975–2000. New owners, and Michel ROLLAND is consulting, so wines are getting bigger, blacker, and denser. Well-made Cru Bourgeois Supérieur red and Sauv Bl white from 155 acres. The new oak-scented white is best at 2–4 yrs (**95 96 97 98 99' 00 01**).

Loupiac-Gaudiet Loupiac w sw ★★ **85 86 88 89 95 96 97 98'** 99 01 02 A reliable source of gd value "almost-SAUTERNES", just across R Garonne.

la Louvière Pe-Lé r w ★★★ (r) **82' 85 86' 88' 89' 90' 94' 95 96' 97** 98' 99 00 01 02 (w) **93' 94 95' 96' 97' 98' 99 00** 01 02 A 135-acre LÉOGNAN estate with classical mansion restored by André Lurton. Excellent white and red of classed-growth standard. See also BONNET, DE CRUZEAU, COUHINS-LURTON, and DE ROCHEMORIN.

de Lussac St-Em r ★★ **85 86 88 89' 90 94 95** 96 97 98 99 00 One of the best estates in LUSSAC-ST-EMILION (to the NE). New technical methods since 2000.

Lynch-Bages Pau r (w) ★★★★ 59 61 70 **79** 82' **83' 84** 85' **86' 88' 89' 90' 91 94**

BORDEAUX

95 96 **97** 98 99 00 01 02 Always popular, now a regular star. 200 acres. Rich, robust wine: deliciously dense, brambly; aspiring to greatness. See also HAUT-BAGES-AVEROUS. From 1990, v.gd intense oaky white – Blanc de Lynch-Bages. Same owners (Cazes family) as LES ORMES-DE-PEZ.

Lynch-Moussas Pau r ★★ 89 90' **94 95' 96' 98** 00 01 02 Fifth-growth restored by the director of CH BATAILLEY. Could be on the up, at last.

Lyonnat Lussac-St-Em r ★★ **95 96 98 00 01** A 120-acre estate; well-distributed, reliable wine.

MacCarthy St-Est r ★★ The second label of CHAMBERT-MARBUZET.

Macquin-St-Georges St-Em r ★★ 89 90' **94 95 96 97 98 99** 00 01 Steady producer of delicious, not weighty, satellite ST-EMILION at ST-GEORGES.

Magdelaine St-Em r ★★★ 82' 83' **85 86 88** 89' 90' 93 94 95 96 **97** 98' 99 00 01 Leading Côtes first-growth: 28 acres owned by J-P MOUEIX. Top-notch, Merlot-led wine; recently powerful and fine.

Magence Graves r w ★★ (r) **90 94 95 96 98** 00 (w) **96 97 98 00 01** 02 Go-ahead 93-acre property in S GRAVES. Sauv Bl-flavoured dry white and fruity red. Both age well 2–6 yrs.

Malartic-Lagravière Pe-Lé r (w) ★★★ (r) 82' **85 86'** 88 89 90' 94 95 96 98 99 00 01 02 (w) **93 94 95 96 97 98 99 00** 01 02 LÉOGNAN classed-growth of 53 acres. Rich, modern red wine since late 1990s and a little long-ageing Sauv Bl white. New Belgian owner (1996). Michel ROLLAND and Denis Dubourdieu now consulting. To watch.

Malescasse Lamarque (H-Méd) r ★★ **82 85 86 88 89 90** 93' **94 95'** 96 98 00 01 02 Renovated Cru Bourgeois Supérieur with 100 well-situated acres. Second label: Le Tana de M. Wines steadily improving.

Malescot-St-Exupéry Mar r ★★★ 61 70 82' 83' **86 88 89** 90' 94 95 96 97 98' 99 00 01 02 Third-growth of 59 acres returned to fine form in the 1990s. Can be tough when young, but eventually fragrant MARGAUX.

de Malle Saut w r sw dr ★★★ (w sw) 75 76 78 79 81' 82' 83 85 86' **88 89' 90'** **94 95 96'** 97 98' 99 01 02 (03) Beautiful Preignac ch. 124 acres. V.gd SAUTERNES; also M de Malle dry white. See also CH DU CARDAILLAN.

Marbuzet St-Est r ★★ **85 86 88 89 90 93 94 95'** 96' 98 99 00 01 02 Second label of COS-D'ESTOURNEL until 1994. Now a Cru Bourgeois.

Margaux, Château Mar r (w) ★★★★ 53 61' 78' 79 80 81' 82' 83' 84 85' 86' **87 88' 89' 90' 91 93'** 94 95' 96' **97'** 98' 99 00' 01' 02 (03) First-growth (209 acres), the most seductive and fabulously perfumed of all in its frequent top vintages. PAVILLON ROUGE **(86 88 89 90'** 93 94 95 96 97 98 99 00 01 02) is second wine. PAVILLON BLANC is best white (Sauv Bl) of MÉDOC: keep 5 yrs-plus **(88 89 90 91 93 95 96 98 99** 00 02). Now under full Mentzelopoulos ownership again.

Marojallia Mar r ★★★ 99 00 01 02 New micro-château with 5 acres, looking for big prices for big, beefy, un-MARGAUX-like wines. Second wine Clos Margalaine.

Marquis-d'Alesme-Becker Mar r ★★ **85 86 88'** 89 90 94 95 96 98 00 01 02 Tiny (17-acre) third-growth. An underperforming CRU CLASSÉ, once highly regarded. Potential here for classic MARGAUX.

Marquis de St-Estèphe St-Est r ★ The growers' co-op; bigger but not as interesting as formerly.

Marquis-de-Terme Mar r ★★→★★★ 82 83' **85 86' 88'** 89' 90' 95 96' 97 98 99 00 01 02 Renovated fourth-growth of 84 acres. Fragrant, lean style has developed since 1985, with more Cab Sauv and more flesh.

Martinens Mar r ★★ **86 88 89 90** 95 96 97 98 99 00 01 02 Worthy 75-acre Cru Bourgeois of the mayor of CANTENAC.

Maucaillou Moulis r ★★ **82 83' 85' 86' 88' 89' 90' 94' 95** 96 98' 00 01 02

A 130-acre Cru Bourgeois Supérieur with gd standards, property of DOURTHE family. Richly fruity Cap de Haut-Maucaillou is second wine.

Mazeyres Pom r ★★ **95 96' 97'** 98' **99** 00 01 Consistent, if not exciting lesser POMEROL. 50 acres. Better since 1996. Alain Moueix manages. See FONROQUE.

Méaume r ★★ **90 96 98** 00 An Englishman's domaine, N of POMEROL. Solid reputation for v.gd daily claret to age 4–5 yrs. B'x Supérieur. 7,500 cases.

Médoc: The new classification of the Crus Bourgeois

The Médoc has 60 crus classés, ranked in 1855 in five classes (first to fifth growth). A new official classification of the Crus Bourgeois of the Médoc was announced in June 2003. The previous list was originally established in 1932 but without any legal sanction.

From a total of 490 candidates drawn from the eight appellations of the Médoc only 247 were selected. These have been ranked into three categories: CB Exceptionnel (nine châteaux), CB Supérieur (87 châteaux), and plain CB (151 châteaux). The new designations will be permitted on labels from the 2003 vintage. The selections were made over a period of 18 months by a jury of wine professionals who studied each estate (history, vineyard, vinification, investment, notoriety, etc) and tasted samples from six vintages (1999 to 1994). Needless to say there are still plenty of arguments.

The nine elite CB Exceptionnels are now Châteaux Chasse-Spleen, Haut-Marbuzet, Labégorce-Zédé, Les Ormes de Pez, de Pez, Phélan-Ségur, Potensac, Poujeaux, and Siran. Two significant estates absent from the new list, Gloria and Sociando-Mallet, did not apply for classification.

Apart from the first-growths, the five classes of 1855 are now hopelessly jumbled in quality, with some second-growths making wine of fifth-growth level and vice versa. They also overlap in quality with the top Crus Bourgeois. The French always do things logically.

Meyney St-Est r ★★→★★★ **82' 85 86' 88' 89' 90' 94** 95 96 98 00 01 02 Big (125-acre) riverside property in a superb situation; among many steady long-lived CRUS BOURGEOIS in ST-ESTÈPHE. Owned by CORDIER. Second label: Prieur de Meyney.

Millet Graves r w (p) ★★ **98 00** Useful GRAVES. Second label, Clos Renon: drink young. Cuvée Henri: oak-aged white.

la Mission-Haut-Brion Pe-Lé r ★★★★ 59' 61' 66' 75' 78' 82' **83** 85' **86 88 89'** 90' **93' 94' 95** 96' **97** 98' 99 00 01 02 Neighbour and long-time rival to HAUT-BRION; since 1984 in same hands. Consistently grand-scale, full-blooded, long-maturing wine; even bigger than Haut-Brion and sometimes more impressive. 30 acres. Second label is La Chapelle de la Mission. White is LAVILLE-HAUT-BRION.

Monbousquet St-Em r (w) ★★★ **82 85' 86 88' 89' 90' 93 94 95 96 97** 98 99 00 01 02 A familiar old property on gravel revolutionized by new owner. Now super-rich, concentrated, and voluptuous wines. New owners also acquired PAVIE and PAVIE-DECESSE in 1998.

Monbrison Arsac-Mar r ★★→★★★ **82 83 85 86 88' 89' 90 95 96'** 97 98 99 00 01 02 A name to follow. High standards make it MARGAUX's most modish Cru Bourgeois. 4,000 cases and 2,000 of second label, Ch Cordet.

la Mondotte St-Em r ★★★→★★★★ 96' 97' 98 99 00 01 02 Intense garagiste wines from micro-property owned by Comte Stephen von Neipperg (CANON-LA GAFFELIERE, CLOS DE L'ORATOIRE).

Montrose St-Est r ★★★→★★★★ **61 70' 75' 82' 85 86' 88 89'** 90' **91 93 94** 95 96' **97** 98 99 00 01 02 A 158-acre family-run second-growth famous for deeply coloured, forceful, old-style claret. Vintages 79–85 (except 82) were lighter, but recent Montrose is almost ST-ESTÈPHE's answer to LATOUR. Second wine: La Dame de Montrose.

Moulin du Cadet St-Em r p ★★ 89' 90' 94 95 96 97 98 00 Little v'yd on the Côtes, owned by J-P MOUEIX. Fragrant medium-bodied wines.

Moulin de la Rose St-Julien r ★★ 95 96 98 00 01 02 Tiny Cru Bourgeois Supérieur; high standards. To watch.

Moulin Pey-Labrie Canon-Fronsac r ★★ 89 90 94 95 96 97 98' 99 00 01 Increasingly well-made, drinker-friendly FRONSAC. To follow.

Moulin-St-Georges St-Em r ★★ 95 96 97 98 99 00 01 02 Stylish and rich wine.

Moulin-à-Vent Moulis r ★★ 82' 85' 86 88 89 90' 94 95 96' 98 00 A 60-acre property in the forefront of this booming AC. Lively, forceful wine. LA TOUR-BLANCHE (MÉDOC) has the same owners.

Moulinet Pom r ★★ 85 88 89' 90 95 96 98 00 01 One of POMEROL's bigger ch'x; 45 acres on lightish soil, wine lightish too.

Mouton Baronne Philippe See D'ARMAILHAC.

Mouton Rothschild Pau r (w) ★★★★ 59 61 62' 66' 70' 75' 76 78 81 82' 83' 85' 86' 88' 89' 90' 91 93' 94 95' 96 97 98' 99 00' 01 02 (03) Officially a first-growth since 1973, though in reality far longer. 175 acres (87% Cab Sauv) can make majestic, rich wine, often MÉDOC's most opulent (also, from 91, white Aile d'Argent). Artists' labels and the world's greatest museum of art relating to wine. Second wine: Le Petit Mouton from 97. See also OPUS ONE (California) and ALMAVIVA (Chile).

Nairac Saut w sw ★★ 76' 82 83' 85 86' 88 89 90' 95' 96 97 98 99 01 02 (03) Perfectionist BARSAC classed-growth. 2,000 cases of oak-fermented and scented wine to lay down for a decade.

Nenin Pom r ★★★ 82 85' 86 88' 89 90 94' 95 96 97 98 99 00 01 02 Well-known 66-acre estate, one of POMEROL's biggest; on a (very necessary) but slow up-swing since 1985. LÉOVILLE-LAS-CASES involvement since 1997.

Olivier Graves r w ★★★ (r) 82 86 88 89' 90' 95 96 98 00 01 02 (w) 93 94 95 96 97 98' 00 01 A 90-acre classed-growth, surrounding a moated castle at LÉOGNAN. Makes 9,000 cases of oaky red; 6,000 of oaky white. Recent wines promise more charm.

les Ormes-de-Pez St-Est r ★★→★★★ 82' 85 86' 88 89' 90' 93 94 95 96 97 98 99 00 01 02 Outstanding 72-acre Cru Bourgeois Exceptionnel owned by LYNCH-BAGES. Consistently one of the most likeable ST-ESTÈPHES.

les Ormes-Sorbet Méd r ★★ 82' 85' 86' 88 89 90' 94 95 96 98' 99 00 01 02 A 10,000-case Couquèques producer of gd stylish red aged in new oak. A leader in N MÉDOC. Second label: Ch de Conques.

Palmer Cantenac-Mar r ★★★★ 61' 62 66' 70 71' 75' 76 78' 79' 81 82 83' 85 86' 87 88' 89 90 93 94 95 96' 98' 99 00 01' 02. The star of CANTENAC: a third-growth occasionally outshining first-growths. Wine of power, flesh, delicacy, and much Merlot. 110 acres with Dutch, British (the SICHEL family), and French owners. Second wine: Alter Ego de Palmer (a steal for early drinking).

Pape Clément Pe-Lé r (w) ★★★→★★★★ 70 75' 83 85 86' 88' 89' 90' 93' 94' 95 96 97 98 99' 00 01 02 Ancient PESSAC v'yd; record of seductive, scented, not ponderous reds. Early 1980s not so gd: dramatic improvement (and more white) since 1985. Ambitious new-wave direction and more concentration from 2000. Watch very closely. Also Ch Poumey at Gradignan.

de Parenchère r (w) ★★ 98 99 00 01 Steady supply of useful AC Ste-Foy BORDEAUX and AC BORDEAUX SUPÉRIEUR from handsome ch with 125 acres.

Patache d'Aux Bégadan (Méd) r ★★ 89' 90' 95 96 98 99 00 02 A 90-acre Cru Bourgeois Supérieur of the N MÉDOC. Fragrant, largely Cab Sauv wine with the earthy quality of its area. See also LIVERSAN.

Paveil-de-Luze Mar r ★★ 82' 85 86' 88' 89' 90 95 96' 98 00 Old family estate at Soussans. Small but highly regarded. Investment in 2000.

Pavie St-Em r ★★★ 82' 83' 85 86' 88' 90' 94' 95 96' 98 99 00 01 02 Splendidly sited first-growth; 92 acres mid-slope on the Côtes. Great track record. Bought by owners of MONBOUSQUET, along with adjacent PAVIE-DECESSE and La Clusière. This is new-wave ST-EMILION: thick, intense, sweet, mid-Atlantic, and the subject of heated debate.

Pavie-Decesse St-Em r ★★ 82 86 88 89 90 94 95 96 97 98 99' 00 01 02 A 24-acre estate. Brother to the above and on form since 1998.

Pavie-Macquin St-Em r ★★★ 85' 86 88 89' 90' 93 94 95 96' 97 98' 99 00' 01 02 Another PAVIE; this time the neighbours up the hill. A 25-acre Côtes v'yd E of ST-EMILION. Steadily fine organic winemaking by Nicolas Thienpont of PUYGUERAUD. Second label: Les Chênes.

Pavillon Rouge (Blanc) du Château Margaux See CH MARGAUX.

Pedesclaux Pau r ★★ 82' 85 86 88 89' 90' 94 95' 96 98' 99 00 02 A 50-acre fifth-growth on the level of a Cru Bourgeois. Wines mostly go to Belgium. Second labels: Bellerose, Grand-Duroc-Milon.

Petit-Village Pom r ★★★ 75' 82' 83 85' 86 88 89' 90' 91 93 94' 95 96 97 98' 99 00 01 Top property revived. 26 acres; same owner (AXA Insurance) as PICHON-LONGUEVILLE since 1989. Powerful plummy wine. Second wine: Le Jardin de Petit-Village.

Pétrus Pom r ★★★★ 61 62 64 66 67 70' 71' 73 75' 76 78 79' 81 82' 83 84 85' 86 87 88' 89' 90 93' 94 95' 96 97 98' 99 00 01 02 The (unofficial) first-growth of POMEROL: Merlot solo in excelsis. 28 acres of gravelly clay giving 5,000 cases of massively rich and concentrated wine, on allocation to the world's millionaires. Each vintage adds lustre. (NB no 91 produced.)

Peyrabon St-Sauveur (H-Méd) r ★★ 98 99 00 Serious 132-acre Cru Bourgeois popular in the Low Countries. Also La Fleur-Peyrabon (only 12 acres).

Peyre-Lebade Listrac r p ★ Second label of CH CLARKE. Investment in 2000.

Peyreau St-Em r ★★ 90 94 95 96 98 99' 00 Sister ch of CLOS DE L'ORATOIRE.

de Pez St-Est r ★★→★★★ 82' 85 86' 88 89 90' 93' 94 95' 96' 97 98' 99 00 01 02 Outstanding Cru Bourgeois Exceptionnel of 60 acres. As reliable as any of the classed-growths of the village, if not quite so fine. Bought in 1995 by CHAMPAGNE house ROEDERER.

Phélan-Ségur St-Est r ★★→★★★ 88' 89' 90' 94 95 96' 97 98 99 00 01 02 Big and important Cru Bourgeois Exceptionnel (125 acres): rivals the last as one of ST-ESTÈPHE's best. From 1986 has built up a strong reputation.

Pibran Pau r ★★ 88 89' 90' 94 95 96 00 01 Small Cru Bourgeois Supérieur allied to PICHON-LONGUEVILLE. Classy wine with PAUILLAC drive.

Pichon-Longueville Comtesse de Lalande Pau r ★★★★ 61 62 66 70' 75' 76 78' 79' 80 81 82' 83 85' 86' 88' 89' 90' 93 94 95 96 97 98 99 00 01 02 Super-second-growth neighbour to LATOUR; 148 acres. Consistently among the very top performers; a long-lived, Merlot-marked wine of fabulous breed, even in lesser yrs. Second wine: Réserve de la Comtesse. Rivalry across the road (next entry) worth watching. Other property Ch Bernadotte.

Pichon-Longueville (formerly Baron de Pichon-Longueville) Pau r ★★★★ 82' 83 85 86' 88' 89' 90' 93 94' 95 96 97 98 99 00 01 02 A 77-acre second-growth. Since 1987 owned by AXA Insurance. Revitalized winemaking matches aggressive new buildings. Second label: Les Tourelles de Longueville

le Pin Pom r ★★★★ 82 83 85 86 88 89 90' 94 95 96 97 98' 99 00 01 02 The original of the new BORDEAUX cult mini-crus. A mere 500 cases of Merlot, with same family behind it as VIEUX-CHÂTEAU-CERTAN (a much better buy). Almost as rich as its drinkers, but prices well beyond PÉTRUS are ridiculous.

de Pitray Castillon r ★★ 85 86 88 89 90 94 95 96' 98' 00 Large (77-acre) v'yd on CÔTES DE CASTILLON E of ST-EMILION. Flavoursome wines, once the best-known of the AC.

Plince Pom r ★★ **82 85 86 88 89' 90 93 94 95 96 98'** 99 00 Reliable 20-acre property nr Libourne. Lightish wine from sandy soil.

la Pointe Pom r ★★→★★★ **89' 90' 94 95 96 97** 98 99 00 01 Prominent 63-acre estate; wines recently plumper and more pleasing. LA SERRE is in same hands.

Pontac-Monplaisir Pe-Lé r (w) ★★ **90 94 95 96** 98 99 00 02 Offers useful white and fragrant red.

Pontet-Canet Pau r ★★★ **82' 85 86' 88 89' 90 93 94'** 95 96' **97** 98 99 00 01 02' A 182-acre neighbour to MOUTON-ROTHSCHILD. Dragged its feet for many years. Old hard tannins were a turn-off. Since mid-1990s very fine results.

Potensac Méd r ★★ **82' 85' 86 88 89' 90' 94 95 96 97** 98 99 00 01 02 Biggest and best-known Cru Bourgeois of N MÉDOC. Now a Cru Bourgeois Exceptionnel.

Smaller Bordeaux châteaux to watch for:
The detailed list of châteaux on these pages is limited to the prestigious classified parts of the Bordeaux region. But this huge vineyard by the Atlantic works on many levels. Standard Bordeaux AC wine is claret at its most basic – but it is still recognizable. The areas and representative châteaux listed below are an important resource; they are potentially distinct and worthwhile variations on the claret theme to be investigated and enjoyed.

Bordeaux Supérieur Ch'x Mouton, Penin, Bouillerot, de Seguin, Trocard.
Canon-Fronsac Ch'x Barrabaque, Cassagne-Haut-Canon (La Truffière), Canon-de-Brem, La Fleur Caillou, Grand Renouil, Moulin-Pey-Labrie, Vraye-Canon-Boyer, du Gaby.
Côtes de Bourg Ch'x Bujan, Brûlésécaille, Falfas, Fougas, Guerry, Haut-Maco, Mercier, Nodoz, Roc de Cambes, Rousset, Tayac Cuvée Prestige.
Côtes de Castillon Ch'x d'Aiguilhe, de Belcier, Cap de Faugères, Cantegrive, La Clarière-Laithwaite (NB Le Prieuré), Clos l'Eglise, Clos Puy Arnaud, Côte Montpezat, Peyrou, Poupille, Robin, Roque le Mayne, Vieux Château Champs de Mars.
Côtes de Francs Ch'x Les Charmes Godard, de Francs, Laclaverie, Lauriol, Marsau, Pelan, La Prade, Puygueraud.
Entre-Deux-Mers Ch'x de Fontenille, Launay, Moulin de Launay, Nardique la Gravière, Sainte-Marie, Tour de Mirambeau, Toutigeac, Turcaud.
Fronsac Ch'x Dalem, Fontenil, Mayne-Vieil, Moulin-Haut-Laroque, La Rousselle, Tour du Moulin, Les Trois Croix, La Vieille Cure, Villars.
Lalande de Pomerol Chx Les Annereaux, La Croix-St-André, Les Cruzelles, La Fleur de Boüard, Garraud, Grand Ormeau, Haut Chaigneau, La Sergue Perron, Sergant, Tournefeuille, de Viaud.
Lussac St-Emilion Ch'x Barbe-Blanche, Bellevue, de la Grenière, Mayne-Blanc, des Roches.
Montagne St-Emilion Ch'x Calon, Croix Beanséjour, Faizeau, Roudier.
Premières Côtes de Blaye Chx Bel Air la Royère, Bertinerie, Charron, Haut-Sociando, Jonqueyres, Loumède, Mondésir-Gazin, Prieuré Malesan (formerly Pérenne), Roland-la-Garde, Segonzac, des Tourtes.
Premières Côtes de Bordeaux Chx Carignan, Chelivette, Clos Ste-Anne, Grand-Mouëys, Haux, du Juge, Jonchet, Lamothe de Haux, Lezongars, Mont-Pérat, Pic, Plaisance, Puy Bardens, Reynon, Suau.
Ste-Croix du Mont Chx Loubens, Lousteau-Vieil, du Mont, Pavillon, La Rame.

Run and part-owned by Delon family. Class shows, in the form of rich, silky, balanced wines.

Pouget Mar r ★★ 82' 85 86 88 89 90 94 95 96 98' 00 02 A 27-acre fourth-growth attached to BOYD-CANTENAC. Similar wines. New CHAI in 2000.

Poujeaux (Theil) Moulis r ★★ 82' 85' 86 88' 89' 90' 93' 94' 95' 96' 97 98 99 00 01 02 Family-run Cru Bourgeois Exceptionnel of 120 acres, with CHASSE-SPLEEN and MAUCAILLOU the high-point of Moulis. 20,000-odd cases of characterful tannic and concentrated wine for a long life, yr after yr. Second label: La Salle de Poujeaux. Also Ch Arnauld.

Prieuré-Lichine Cantenac-Mar r ★★★ 82' 83' 85 86' 88 89' 90' 94' 95 96 97 98' 99 00 01 02 A 143-acre fourth-growth brought to the fore by the late Alexis Lichine, now advised by Michel ROLLAND. Fragrant MARGAUX currently on fair form: to follow. Second wine: Clairefont. A gd Bordeaux Blanc, too.

Puy-Blanquet St-Em r ★★ 82' 85 86 88 89' 90' 94 95 96 98 00 A major property in St-Etienne-de-Lisse, E of ST-EMILION, with 50 acres.

Puygueraud Côtes de Francs r ★★ 88 89' 90 95' 96 97' 98 99 00 01 02 Leading ch of this tiny AC. Wood-aged wines of surprising class. Ch'x Laclaverie and Les Charmes-Godard follow the same lines. Special Cuvée George from 2000. Same winemaker as PAVIE-MACQUIN (ST-EMILION).

Rabaud-Promis Saut w sw ★★→★★★ 83' 85 86' 87 88' 89' 90 94 95 96 97 98 99 01 02 (03) 74-acre classed-growth at Bommes. Since 1986 it has been nr top rank. Rich stuff.

Rahoul Graves r w ★★ (r) 82 85 86 88 89' 90' 94 95 96 98' 00 01 02 This 37-acre v'yd at Portets is still a sleeper despite long record of gd red (80%) and v.gd (Sem) white (94 95 96 97 98 99 00 01 02).

Ramage-la-Bâtisse H-Méd r ★★ 89' 90 95 96' 98 99 00 02 Potentially outstanding Cru Bourgeois Supérieur; 130 acres at ST-SAUVEUR, N of PAUILLAC. Ch Tourteran is second wine.

Rauzan-Gassies Mar r ★★ 88 89' 90' 95 96 98 99 00 01 02 The 75-acre second-growth neighbour of RAUZAN-SÉGLA that has long lagged behind it. Is something stirring? The 02 looks gd.

Rauzan-Ségla Mar r ★★★★ 70' 82 83' 85 86' 88' 89' 90' 94' 95 96 97 98 99 00 01 02 106-acre second-growth famous for its fragrance; a great MÉDOC name back at the top. New owners in 1994 (Chanel) have rebuilt the ch and CHAIS. Second wine: Ségla. This should be the top second-growth of all.

Raymond-Lafon Saut w sw ★★★ 75' 76 79 80' 82 83' 85 86' 88 89' 90' 95 96' 97 98 99 01 02 Serious little SAUTERNES estate (44 acres) owned by YQUEM ex-manager. Splendid wines for ageing.

Rayne Vigneau Saut w sw ★★★ 76' 83 85 86' 88' 90' 95 96 97 98 99 01 02 164-acre classed-growth at Bommes. V.gd. Sweet wine and dry Rayne SEC.

Respide Médeville Graves w (r) ★★ (w) 90 92' 93 94 95' 96' 99 00 01 02 One of the better unclassified properties, but current whites are disappointing. Should be full-flavoured wines for ageing. Drink the reds at 4–6 yrs – longer for the better vintages. Recommended: Cuvée Kauffman.

Reynon Premières Côtes r w ★★ 100 acres for fragrant white from old Sauv Bl vines (VIEILLES VIGNES) 98' 99 00 01 02; also serious red (88' 89 90 94 95 96 97 98 99 00 01 02). Second wine (red): Ch Reynon-Peyrat. From 1996 v.gd Ch Reynon Cadillac liquoreux, too. See also CLOS FLORIDÈNE.

Reysson Vertheuil (H-Méd) r ★★ 95 96 00 02 Recently replanted 120-acre Cru Bourgeois Supérieur; same owners as GRAND-PUY-DUCASSE.

Ricaud Loupiac w sw (r dr) ★★ 95 96 97 99 01 02 Substantial grower of SAUTERNES-like ageworthy wine just across the river.

Rieussec Saut w sw ★★★★ 67 71' 75' 79 82 83' 85 86' 88' 89' 90' 95 96' 97 98' 99 01 02 (03) Worthy neighbour of D'YQUEM with 136 acres in Fargues, bought in 1984 by the (LAFITE) Rothschilds. Vinified in oak since 96. Fabulously opulent wine. Also producing a dry "R" and super-wine Crème de Tête.

Ripeau St-Em r ★★ **95 98** 00 01 Steady GRAND CRU CLASSÉ with the right idea in the centre of the plateau. 40 acres.

de la Rivière Fronsac r ★★ **85' 86 88' 89 90 94 95 96' 97** 98' 99 00 01 02 The biggest and most impressive FRONSAC property, with a Wagnerian castle and cellars. Formerly big tannic wines seem to have lightened recently. New winery in 1999 – Michel ROLLAND consults.

de Rochemorin Pe-Lé r (w) ★★→★★★ **89' 90' 93 94 95** 96 **97** 98' 99 00 01 02 An important restoration at Martillac by the Lurtons of LA LOUVIERE: 165 acres of maturing vines. Oaky whites to keep 4–5 yrs.

Rol Valentin St-Em r ★★★ **95 96 97** 98 **99** 00 01 02 New 10-acre estate going for modestly massive style (and price). Owned by former footballer.

Rouet Fronsac r ★★ **90 95 96** 98 **99 00** Well-made, full of life and fruit.

Rouget Pom r ★★ **85' 86 88 89' 90 95** 98' **99** 00 01 Attractive old estate on the N edge of POMEROL. New owners are doing well. Track-record is for solid long-agers. To watch.

Royal St-Emilion Brand name of important, dynamic growers' CO-OP. See GALIUS.

Ruat-Petit-Poujeaux Moulis r ★★ **95 96** 98 00 02 A 45-acre v'yd with local reputation for vigorous wine, keep for 5–6 yrs.

St-André-Corbin St-Em r ★★ **95 96** 97 98' **99 00** 01 A 54-acre estate in MONTAGNE- and ST-GEORGES-ST-EMILION: above-average wines.

St-Georges St-Georges-St-Em r ★★ **88' 89' 90' 94 95' 96' 98'** 00 01 Noble 18th-C ch overlooking the ST-EMILION plateau from the hill to the N. 125 acres (25% of St-Georges AC). Gd wine sold direct to the public.

St-Georges-Côte-Pavie St-Em r ★★ **82 85' 86 88' 89' 90' 94 95 96'** 98' 00 Perfectly placed little v'yd on the Côtes. Run with dedication.

St-Pierre St-Jul r ★★★ **82' 85 86' 88' 89' 90' 93 94 95'** 96' **97** 98 99 00 01 02 Small (42-acre) fourth-growth. Very stylish and consistent classic ST-JULIEN. Also see GLORIA.

St-Emilion: the class system

St-Emilion has its own class system, revised every ten years, the last in 1996. At the top are two Premiers Grands Crus Classés "A": Châteaux Ausone and Cheval Blanc. Then come 11 Premiers Grands Crus Classés "B'. 55 châteaux were elected as Grands Crus Classés. To be considered for classification the ch'x must have obtained the AC St Emilion Grand Cru certificate, which is renewable every year.

---

de Sales Pom r ★★ **82' 85 86 88 89' 90' 94 95 98** 00 Biggest v'yd of POMEROL (116 acres), attached to grandest ch. Never poetry: recently below form. Second labels: Ch'x Chantalouette, du Delias.

Sansonnet St-Em r ★★ **99** 00 01 02 A 17-acre estate ambitiously run in the new ST-EMILION style (rich, fat) since 1999.

Saransot-Dupré Listrac r (w) ★★ **86 88 89** 90 **95 96'** 98' 99 00 01 02 Small property performing tremendously well since 1986. Also one of LISTRAC'S little band of whites.

Sénéjac H-Méd r (w) ★★ **82' 85 86' 88 89' 90' 94 95** 96 98 99 00 01 02 A 60-acre Cru Bourgeois Supérieur in S MÉDOC recently bought by the same family as TALBOT. Tannic reds to age and unusual all-Sem white, also to age (**96 97 98** 99 00 01 02). Second label: Artigue de Sénéjac.

la Serre St-Em r ★★ **82 85 86 88'** 89 90 **94 95** 96 98 **99** 00 Small GRAND CRU, same owner as LA POINTE. Pleasant stylish wines.

Sigalas-Rabaud Saut w sw ★★★ **75 76' 80 82 83 85 86 88 89' 90' 95' 96'** 97'

98 99 01 02 (03) The smaller part of the former RABAUD estate: 34 acres in Bommes run by CORDIER. At best very fragrant and lovely. Top-ranking now. Since 1995 second wine: Le Cadet de Sigalas Rabaud.

Siran Labarde-Mar r ★★→★★★ 82' 83 85 86 88 89' 90' **95** 96 98 99 00 02 A 77-acre property of passionate owner who resents lack of CLASSÉ rank. Given Cru Bourgeois Exceptionnel status in 2003. To follow for full-flavoured wines to age. Property is continually striving.

Smith-Haut-Lafitte Pe-Lé r (w p) ★★★ (red) **82' 85** 86 89' 90' 94 95 96 98 99 00 01 02 (white) **93 94 95 96 97 98 99' 00** 01 02 Classed-growth at Martillac: 122 acres (14 acres makes oaky white). Ambitious owners (since 1990) continue to spend hugely to spectacular effect, inc a luxurious wine therapy (external!) clinic. Second label: Les Hauts de Smith. Also look out for their Ch Cantelys, PESSAC-LÉOGNAN.

Sociando-Mallet H-Méd r ★★★ 82' **85' 86'** 88' **89' 90'** 94 95 96' **97** 98 99 00 01 02 Splendid, widely followed estate at St-Seurin. Classed growth quality; 65 acres. Conservative big-boned wines to lay down for years. Second wine: Demoiselles de Sociando.

Soudars H-Méd r ★★ 86 89 90 **94 95** 96' **98** 99 00 01 Sister to COUFRAN; recent Cru Bourgeois Supérieur doing pretty well.

Soutard St-Em r ★★★ 82' **85' 86** 88' **89' 90'** 93 94 95 **96 97** 98' 99 00 01 02 Potentially excellent 48-acre classed-growth, 70% Merlot. Potent wines: can be long-lived to suit Anglo-Saxon drinking; also exciting when young to French palates. Forward-thinking viticultural practices. Second label: Clos de la Tonnelle.

Suduiraut Saut w sw ★★★★ 67 75 76' 78 79' 81 82 83 85 86 88' **89' 90'** 95 96 97 98 99 01 02 (03) One of the best SAUTERNES, in its best vintages supremely luscious. 173 acres potentially are of top class. See PICHON-LONGUEVILLE.

du Tailhas Pom r ★★ 89 90 94 95 96' 98' **99** 00 5,000 cases. POMEROL of the lighter kind, nr FIGEAC.

Taillefer Pom r ★★ 82 85 86 88' 89 90 94 95' 96 98' 00 01 02 A 28-acre v'yd on the edge of POMEROL in the Bernard Moueix family (see also FONTMARTY).

Talbot St-Jul r (w) ★★★ 78' 82' 83' **85' 86' 88' 89'** 90 94 95 96' 98' 99 00 01 02 Important 240-acre fourth-growth, for many years younger sister to GRUAUD-LAROSE. Wine similarly attractive: rich, consummately charming, reliable; gd value. V.gd second label: Connétable Talbot. White: Caillou Blanc matures as well as a gd GRAVES. Oenologist also oversees TOUR DE MONS.

Tayac Soussans-Mar r ★★ **95** 96 **98** 00 02 MARGAUX's biggest Cru Bourgeois. Reliable if not noteworthy.

de Terrefort-Quancard B'x r w ★ **98 99** 00 Huge producer of gd value wines at ST-ANDRE-DE-CUBZAC on the road to Paris. Very drinkable quality. 33,000 cases. Also B'x Supérior: Ch Canada.

Terrey-Gros-Caillou St-Jul r ★★ 82' 86' 88 89 90 94 95 96 98 99 00 02 Sister ch to HORTEVIE; at best, equally noteworthy and stylish.

du Tertre Arsac-Mar r ★★★ 82' 83' 85 86 88' 89' 90' 94 95 96' 98' 99 00 01 02 Fifth-growth isolated S of MARGAUX. History of undervalued fragrant and fruity wines. Since 1997, same owner as CH GISCOURS. To watch. New techniques and investment in 2000 have produced a really concentrated wine.

Tertre Daugay St-Em r ★★★ 82' 83' 85 86 88' 89' 90' 94 95 96 97 98 **99** 00 01 Small, spectacularly sited GRAND CRU CLASSÉ. Currently being restored to gd order. Potent and stylish wines. Same owner as LA GAFFELIÈRE.

Tertre-Rôteboeuf St-Em r ★★★★ 85 86 88' 89' 90' 93 94 95 96 97 98' 99 00 01 02 A cult star making concentrated, even dramatic, largely Merlot wine since 1983. The prices are frightening. The roast beef of the name gives the right idea. Also CÔTES DE BOURG property, Roc de Cambes.

Thieuley E-D-M r p w ★★ Supplier of consistent quality red and white AC B'x; fruity CLAIRET; oak-aged red and white CUVÉE Francis Courselle. Also owns Clos Ste-Anne in PREMIÈRES CÔTES DE BORDEAUX.

la Tour-Blanche Saut w (r) SW ★★ 83' 85 86 88' 89' 90' 95 96 97 98 99 01 02 (03) Historic leader of SAUTERNES, now a government wine college. Coasted in 1970s; hit historic form again in 1988.

La Tour-de-By Bégadan (Méd) r ★★ 82' 85' 86 88' 89' 90' 94 95 96' 98 00 01 02 Very well-run 182-acre Cru Bourgeois Supérieur in N MÉDOC with a name for the most attractive, sturdy wines of the area.

la Tour-Carnet St-Laurent (H-Méd) r ★★ 82 85 86 89' 90 94' 95 96 98 99 00 01 02 Fourth-growth with medieval fortress, long neglected. New ownership and investment from 2000 have produced richer wines with more polish. Second wine: Sire de Comin.

la Tour Figeac St-Em r ★★ 82' 83 85 86 88 89' 90' 94' 95 96' 97' 98' 99 00 01 02 A 36-acre GRAND CRU CLASSÉ between FIGEAC and POMEROL. California-style ideas since 1994. Biodynamic methods. Keep an eye on this one.

la Tour Haut Brion Graves r ★★★ 85 88 89 90 94 95 96' 97 98' 99 00 01 02 Formerly second label of LA MISSION-HAUT-BRION. Up to 1983, a plainer, very tannic wine. Now a separate 12-acre v'yd: wines stylish, to keep.

Tour Haut-Caussan Méd r ★★ 95 96 98 00 01 02 Ambitious 40-acre estate at Blaignan to watch for full, firm wines.

Tour-du-Haut-Moulin Cussac (H-Méd) r ★★ 82' 85' 86' 88' 89' 90' 94 95 96 98 00 02 Conservative grower: intense Cru Bourgeois Supérieur to mature.

la Tour de Mons Soussans-Mar r ★★ 82' 83 85 86 88 89' 90' 94 95 96' 98' 99 00 01 02 Famous Cru Bourgeois Supérieur of 87 acres, in the same family for 3 centuries. A long dull patch but new (1995) TALBOT influence is returning to the old fragrant, vigorous, ageworthy style.

Tour-du-Pas-St-Georges St-Em r ★★ 86 88 89 90 94 95 96 97 98 99 00 01 Wine from 40 acres of ST-GEORGES-ST-EMILION made by BELAIR winemaker.

la Tour-du-Pin-Figeac St-Em r ★★ 98 00 A 26-acre GRAND CRU CLASSÉ worthy of restoration.

la Tour du Pin Figeac Moueix St-Em r ★★ 82 83 85 86 88' 89' 90' 94 95 96 98 00 Another 26-acre section of the same old property, owned by the Armand Moueix family. Splendid site; should be powerful wines.

Tour-St-Bonnet Méd r ★★ 86 89' 90' 95 96 98 99 00 02 Consistently well-made potent N MÉDOC from St-Christoly. 100 acres.

Tournefeuille Lalande de Pom r ★★ 82' 83' 85 86 88 88 89 90' 94 95' 98' 99 00 01 02 Well-known Néac ch. 43 acres. On the up-swing since 1998 with new owners.

des Tours Mont-St-Em r ★★ 98 99 00 01 Spectacular ch; modern 170-acre v'yd. Sound, easy wine.

Tronquoy-Lalande St-Est r ★★ 82' 85 86 88 89 90' 94 95 96 98 99 00 02 A 40-acre Cru Bourgeois Supérieur: high-coloured wines to age, but no thrills. DOURTHE-distributed.

Troplong-Mondot St-Em r ★★★ 82' 83 85' 86 88' 89' 90' 94' 95 96' 97 98' 99 00' 01 02 Well-sited 75 acres on the Côtes. One of ST-EMILION's hottest things. Second wine: Mondot.

Trotanoy Pom r ★★★★ 61' 70' 71' 75' 81 82' 85' 88 89 90' 93 94 95 96 97 98' 99 00 01 02 Potentially the second POMEROL, after PÉTRUS, from the same stable. Only 27 acres; but at best (eg **82**) a glorious fleshy, perfumed wine. Ten wobbly years since; now resurgence under J-P MOUEIX control.

Trottevieille St-Em r ★★★ 82' 85 86 89' 90 94 95 96 98 99 00 01 02 First-growth of 27 acres on the Côtes. Dragged its feet for yrs. Same owners as BATAILLEY have raised its game.

> ### Vins de garage
>
> The concept of garage wine started in Bordeaux as a joke; the name
> at least: production was so small that a garage was big enough to
> make it in. With small production went rarity; hence the chance of
> a high price. It is now stylistic. Garage wines are made with very
> small crops, preferably from old vines, and have the dark colour,
> thick texture, rich mouthfeel, and coffee/vanilla/chocolate flavours
> associated with toasted new oak. The current runners are massively
> concentrated in St-Emilion, where the stylistic change is becoming
> widely influential. Not all are over-priced. In **St-Emilion** Andréas, Barde
> Haut, Clos Badon-Thunévin, Croix de Labrie, Clos St Martin, Le Fer,
> Ferrand-Lartigue, Magrez-Fombrauge, Gracia, Péby-Faugères, Quinault-
> l'Enclos, Rol Valentin, Le Dôme, La Gomerie, La Mondotte, Valandraud;
> in **Pomerol** Beau Soleil; in **Graves** Branon; in **Margaux** Marojallia; in
> **Côtes de Castillon** Domaine de l'A and Le Presbytère; in **Premières
> Côtes de Blaye** Gigault-Cuvée Viva; in **Entre-Deux-Mers** Balestard.

le Tuquet Graves r w ★★ (r) **95 96' 98' 99** 00 02 (w) **93 94 95 96 97 98' 99 00** 02 Big estate at Beautiran. Light, fruity red; the white is better. (Cuvée Spéciale oak-aged.)

de Valandraud St-Em r ★★★★ 92 **93 94 95** 96 97 98 99 00 01 02 Leader among garagiste micro-wines fulfilling aspirations to glory. But silly prices for the sort of thick, vanilla-scented wine California can make. V'yds expanded in 1998; better terroir now. Second and third wines available in even smaller quantities: Virginie and Axelle.

Valrose St-Est r ★★ A newcomer since 1999, co-owned with CLINET. To watch.

Verdignan Méd r ★★ **86 89' 90 94 95' 96 98 99** 00 01 02 Substantial Bourgeois sister to COUFRAN. More Cab than Coufran. Second label: Ch Plantey de la Croix.

la Vieille Cure Fronsac r ★★ 94 95 **96 97 98 99** 00 01 02 A 50-acre property, US-owned, leading the commune.

Vieux-Château-Certan Pom r ★★★★ 78 79 81 82' 83' 85 86' 88' 89 90' 93 **94** 95' 96' **97** 98' 99 00 01 02 Traditionally rated close to PÉTRUS in quality, but totally different in style; almost HAUT-BRION build. 34 acres. Same (Belgian) family owns LABEGORCE-ZEDE and tiny LE PIN.

Vieux Château St-André St-Em r ★★ 82' 85' 86 88' 89' 90' 93' 94' 95 98 99 00 01 Small v'yd in MONTAGNE-ST-EMILION owned by winemaker of PÉTRUS until 2002. To follow. 2,500 cases.

Villegeorge Avensan (H-Méd) r ★★ 82 85 86 88 89 90 94 95 96' 98' 99 00 02 A 24-acre Cru Bourgeois Supérieur N of MARGAUX. Enjoyable rather tannic wine. Sister ch: DUPLESSIS.

Villemaurine St-Em r ★★ 82' 85' 86 88 89 90 95 96 98 99 00 01 02 Small GRAND CRU CLASSÉ with splendid cellars well-sited on the Côtes by the town. Firm wine with a high proportion of Cab Sauv. Also Ch'x du Cartillon, Timberlay.

Vray Croix de Gay Pom r ★★ 82' 85 86 88 89 90 95 96 98 00 Very small but ideally situated v'yd in the best part of POMEROL. Could do a lot better.

Yon-Figeac St-Em r ★★ 85 86 88 89 90 95 96 98 **99** 00 01 59-acre GRAND CRU for savoury supple wine at best.

d'Yquem Saut w sw (dr) ★★★★ 67' 70 71' 75' 76' 79 80' 81' 83' 85 86' 88' 89' 90' **93 94** 95' 96 97 98 99 The world's most famous sweet wine estate. 250 acres; only 500 bottles per acre of very strong, intense, luscious wine, kept 4 yrs in barrel. Most vintages improve for 15 yrs+; some live 100 yrs+ in transcendent splendour. Sadly, after centuries in the Lur-Saluces family, in 1998 control was surrendered to Bernard Arnault of LVMH. Also makes dry "Y" (YGREC).

Italy

More heavily shaded areas
are the wine growing regions

The following abbreviations
are used in the text:

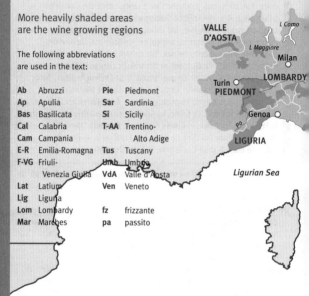

Ab	Abruzzi	**Pie**	Piedmont
Ap	Apulia	**Sar**	Sardinia
Bas	Basilicata	**Si**	Sicily
Cal	Calabria	**T-AA**	Trentino-
Cam	Campania		Alto Adige
E-R	Emilia-Romagna	**Tus**	Tuscany
F-VG	Friuli-	**Umb**	Umbria
	Venezia Giulia	**VdA**	Valle d'Aosta
Lat	Latium	**Ven**	Veneto
Lig	Liguria		
Lom	Lombardy	**fz**	frizzante
Mar	Marches	**pa**	passito

Wine is central to Italy's traditional way of life. The vine is cultivated in almost every region and province with a variety of intentions and results that only France can rival. Until recently in Italy, a meal without wine was virtually unthinkable.

Italy produces a massive fifty-five million hectolitres each year, making it, along with France, the dominant player on the world wine stage. Italians are now drinking less than they used to, but the wine they do drink is of higher quality. The long conflict in the national psyche between wine as a basic essential and as a pleasurable choice is resolving itself in favour of the latter. But tension remains, and nowhere so visibly as in the proliferation of wines with indecipherable names and few clear links to their *terroir*. Often of excellent quality and having a lasting impact on their region, they have generated constant complaint about the confusion they create.

The first Italian appellations (DOCs) were created in the 1960s. They were not designed to assure quality, simply to protect "tradition" – yields, varieties, viticulture, and ageing practices were absurdly proscriptive. Houses with greater ambition were forced to operate outside their appellations, thereby creating the parallel production system which exists to this day. If consumers are fazed when presented with the challenge of a very long list of names to memorize, there may be some consolation in the fact that never before have so many fantastic choices been available.

Italy's two most important regions, Piedmont and Tuscany, have long produced wines with unambiguous links to precise, easily identifiable zones. This is where the quality revolution began. Now it is spreading to other parts of the country: first to Soave and Friuli-Venezia Giulia, where an excessively technological approach had led to a dull standardization in white wines. But

no longer. Central Italy – Umbria, then the Marches – was next to feel the winds of change; then Emilia-Romagna, once known only for its abundance. And perhaps the most encouraging sign of all is the Brussels-sponsored revolution bringing quality and character to the South and the islands.

Italy, after a brief flirtation with international varieties, is also returning to its native grapes. They include many original, ancient, and individual kinds that have never, before the advent of modern winemaking, had the airing they deserve.

Recent Vintages

Tuscany

2003 Considerable vine stress from searing heat and three months of drought. Success with late-ripening varieties (Cabernet Sauvignon, Sangiovese); less so with Merlot. Young vineyards particularly penalized by hot summer.

2002 Cool Aug, frequent rains in Sept/Oct. Dilution and rot widespread.

2001 A scorching Aug, unusually cool in early Sept, then humid when warm weather returned. Some excellent wines, but much irregularity.

2000 Very hot, dry late summer/early autumn, one of earliest vintages in memory. Full, alcoholic wines, some impressive, some unbalanced.

1999 An excellent vintage in all major zones.

1998 Very good along the coast, irregular elsewhere.

1997 Rich, round, full wines; an outstanding vintage.

Older fine vintages: 95 90

Piedmont

2003 Sweltering summer, but nonetheless very positive for Barbera, Dolcetto, and Moscato. Nebbiolo more irregular, with late pickers more successful.

2002 Cool, damp growing season, heavy rain in Sept/Oct and serious hail damage in Barolo. First off-vintage after seven winners in a row.

2001 Classy and firm Nebbiolo and Barbera, other grapes less successful.

2000 Excellent Barolo, Barbaresco, Barbera. Fifth sound vintage in a row.

1999 Balanced and elegant Barbaresco and Barolo; Barbera more spotty due to irregular end-of-season weather; lovely Dolcetto.

1998 Very good whites, excellent reds. For Barolo and Barbaresco, third fine vintage in a row after difficulties in 91, 92, and 94.

1997 Hot, dry summer and early autumn. Superlative Barbera; rich, round, and alcoholic; very good Barolo and Barbaresco with unusually soft tannins.

Older fine vintages: 90 89

Amarone

2003 The hottest and driest vintage of the post-war period. Very concentrated and sugar-rich grapes; could be outstanding.

2002 Heavy rains throughout the ripening season, dilution and mould in the vineyards. A vintage to forget for Amarone.

2001 Very balanced weather in the growing season. Promising and classic.

2000 Very hot late summer, cooler early autumn which saved the grapes from a damaging excessive ripeness. Shaping up as a vintage of powerful wines.

1999 Rain in Sept, some dilution. Less successful than in other parts of Italy.

1998 Balanced grapes; powerful wines with good freshness.

1997 Rich grapes even before drying; full and alcoholic wines.

Marches & Abruzzo Reds

2003 One of the most successful areas in Italy in 2003, as the Montepulciano grape stood up to the heat and drought, giving first-rate results.

2002 Cool, damp year; only fair results.

2001 Ideal weather, fine balance of power and elegance in the wines, which are fragrant with much complexity and depth.

2000 Properly hot in late Aug and early Sept, a return of the heat after a cooler interval; ripe grapes of good balance; ample and classy wines.

1999 Rain in Sept; wines of a certain style, lack the usual depth and fullness.

1998 Warm and dry in early Oct, superior results for those who waited to pick.

1997 Very ripe grapes, perhaps some loss of aroma and finesse.

Campania & Basilicata

2003 Scorching and drought-stressed growing conditions, but the altitude of
the vineyards worked in Aglianico's favour. Generally a success.

2002 Heavy rains here as elsewhere; part of the crop salvaged by the lateness
of the harvest, but little to crow about.

2001 Hot, dry and very regular from July to the end of Oct, textbook weather.
Intense, perfumed, and ageworthy wines.

2000 Hotter than 1999, a powerful impetus to the ripening of the grapes.
Potent and alcoholic wines built to last.

1999 Warm and dry throughout the growing season, excellent conditions.

1998 Irregular weather, rather austere wines; doubts about future evolution.

1997 Plenty of warmth for the Aglianico. Large crop, rather forward wines,
though the best will certainly last.

Abbazia Sant Anastasia ★★→★★★ New Sicilian producer of excellent reds.

Abboccato Semi-sweet.

Aglianico del Vulture Bas DOC r dr (s/sw sp) ★★★ 90' 93' 94' 95 97' 98 99 00'
01' Among the best wines of S Italy. Ages well to rich aromas. Called VECCHIO
after 3 years, RISERVA after 5 yrs. Top growers: Basilium, Cantina del Notaio,
Elena Fucci, Di Palma, PATERNOSTER, Le Querce, Torre degli Svevi, and Sasso.

Alba Major wine city of PIEDMONT, on River Tanaro, SE of Turin.

Albana di Romagna E-R DOCG w dr s/sw (sp) ★★→★★★ DYA Italy's first DOCG
for white wine, though it was hard to see why. Albana is the
(undistinguished) grape. AMABILE is usually better than dry. ZERBINA and
Giovanna Madonia's botrytis-sweet PASSITO are outstanding.

Alcamo Si DOC w ★ Soft whites and reds. Rapitalà, Ceuso are best brands.

Aleatico Red Muscat-flavoured grape for sweet, aromatic, often fortified
wines, chiefly in the S. Aleatico di Puglia DOC (best grower is CANDIDO) is
better and more famous than Aleatico di Gradoli (Latium) DOC. Gd Aleatico
from Falesco, v.gd from Jacopo Banti in VAL DI CORNIA and Sapereta on ELBA.

Alessandria, Gianfranco ★★★ Small producer of high-level ALBA wines at
Monteforte d'Alba, esp BAROLO San Giovanni, BARBERA Vittoria, DOLCETTO.

Alezio Ap DOC p (r) ★★ Salento DOC esp for full, flavourful reds and delicate
rosés. The top growers are Giuseppe Calò with fine, barrel-aged
NEGROAMARO Portulan and Michele Calò with Negroamaro IGT Spano.

Allegrini ★★★ Top-quality Veronese producer; outstanding single v'yd IGT
wines (Palazzo della Torre, Grola, and Poja), AMARONE, and RECIOTO.

Altare, Elio ★★★ Small producer of gd, very modern BAROLO. Look for BAROLO
Arborina, BAROLO Brunate, LANGHE DOC Larigi (BARBERA), La Villa, VDT L'Insieme
and DOLCETTO D'ALBA – always one of the best in the appellation.

Alto Adige T-AA DOC r p w dr sw sp ★→★★★ Alto Adige or SÜDTIROL DOC
inc almost 50 types of wine: different grapes of different zones (inc
varietals of VALLE ISARCO/EISACKTAL, TERLANO/TERLANER, Val Venosta/Vinschgau,
AA STA MAGDALENA, AA Bozner Leiten, AA MERANESE DI COLLINA/Meraner).

Ama, Castello di, (Fattoria di Ama) ★★★ One of the best and most consistent
modern CHIANTI CLASSICO estates, nr Gaiole. La Casuccia and Bellavista are top
single-v'yd wines. Gd IGTS, CHARDONNAY, MERLOT (L'Apparita), PINOT NOIR (Il Chiuso).

Amabile Means semi-sweet, but usually sweeter than ABBOCCATO.

Amaro Bitter. When prominent on label, contents are not wine but "bitters".

Amarone della Valpolicella (formerly Recioto della Valpolicella Amarone) Ven
DOC r ★★★ 85' 86 88' 90' 93 94 95' 97' 98' 00' 01 Dry version of RECIOTO
DELLA VALPOLICELLA: from air-dried VALPOLICELLA grapes; concentrated, long-
lived, very impressive from: Stefano Accordini, Serego Alighieri, ALLEGRINI,
Begali, BERTANI, Bolla, BOSCAINI, BRUNELLI, BUSSOLA, Campagnola, Corteforte,

Corte Sant Alda, CS VALPOLICELLA, DAL FORNO, Guerrieri-Rizzardi, LE SALETTE, MASI, Mazzi, Novaia, QUINTARELLI, LE RAGOSE Villa Monteleone, Speri, TEDESCHI, Trabucchi, Viviani, ZENATO.

Ambra, Fattoria di ★★ Fine CARMIGNANO (Tusc) producer with two v.gd single-v'yd DOCG wines, Elzana and Vigne Alte.

Angelini, Tenimenti ★★→★★★ Owner of Val di Suga BRUNELLO estate in MONTALCINO, Tre Rose in MONTEPULCIANO, and San Leonino in CHIANTI CLASSICO.

Anselmi, Roberto ★★★ A leader in SOAVE with his single-v'yd Capitel Foscarino and exceptional sweet dessert RECIOTO i Capitelli, now both IGT.

Antinori, Marchesi L & P ★★→★★★★ Very influential, long-established Florentine house of highest repute (mostly justified), owned by Piero A, sharing management with oenologist Renzo Cotarella. Famous for CHIANTI CLASSICO (esp Tenute Marchese Antinori and Badia a Passignano), Umbrian (CASTELLO DELLA SALA), and PIEDMONT (PRUNOTTO) wines. Pioneer of new IGT, eg TIGNANELLO, SOLAIA (TUSCANY), CERVARO DELLA SALA (Umbria). Marchese Piero A was the "Voice of Italy" in wine circles in 1970s and 1980s. Expanding into S TUSCAN MAREMMA, MONTEPULCIANO (La Braccesca), MONTALCINO, in ASTI (for BARBERA), in FRANCIACORTA (Lombardy), and in APULIA ("Vigneti del Sud"). V.gd DOC BOLGHERI Guardo al Tasso (Cab Sauv/MERLOT). See PRUNOTTO.

Apulia Puglia. Italy's heel, producing almost a sixth of Italy's wine, most bottled in N Italy/France. Region to follow in increasing quality/value. Best DOC: CASTEL DEL MONTE, MANDURIA (PRIMITIVO DI), SALICE SALENTO. Producers: D'Alfonso del Sordo, ANTINORI, Botromagno, CANDIDO, Casale Bevagna, Castel di Selva, Co-op Copertino, Co-op Due Palme, Conti Zecca, La Corte, D'Alfonso del Sordo, DE CASTRIS, Fatalone, Felline, I Pástini, Masseria Monaci, Masseria Pepe, Michele Calò, Mille Una, Pasquale Petrera, Pervini, Resta, RIVERA, Rubino, ROSA DEL GOLFO, Santa Lucia, Sinfarosa, TAURINO, Torre Quarto, Valle dell'Asso, VALLONE.

Aquileia F-VG DOC r w ★→★★ (r) **95 96 97** 99' 00 01 A group of 12 single-grape wines from around the town of Aquileia. Gd REFOSCO, SAUVIGNON BLANC. Ca Bolani and Denis Montanara are the ones to watch.

Argiano Top BRUNELLO estate. Castello di Agiano next door is equally fine.

Argiolas, Antonio ★★→★★★ Important SARDINIAN producer. High-level CANNONAU, NURAGUS, VERMENTINO, Bovale, and red IGTS Turriga (★★★) and Korem.

Arneis Pie w ★★ DYA Fairly gd white from nr ALBA: revival of an ancient grape to make fragrant, light wine. DOC: ROERO Arneis, a zone NW of ALBA, normally better than LANGHE Arneis. Try: Almondo, Bric Cencurio, Ca' du Russ, Cascina Chicco, Correggia, BRUNO GIACOSA, Malvirà, Monchiero-Carbone, PRUNOTTO.

Assisi Umb r (w) ★→★★ DYA IGT ROSSO and BIANCO di Assisi: very attractive. Sportoletti particularly gd.

Asti Major wine centre of PIEDMONT.

Asti Spumante Pie DOCG w sw sp ★→★★ NV Charming sweet, white Muscat fizz. Unfortunately, the big Asti houses are not remotely interested in making production of 80 million bottles better than routine. Despite its unique potential, Asti is a cheap, fairly proper product for supermarket shelves. Few producers care: WALTER BERA, Dogliotti-Caudrina, CASCINA FONDA, Vignaioli di Santo Stefano (see also MOSCATO D'ASTI).

Avignonesi ★★★ Noble MONTEPULCIANO house; highly ambitious, with a very fine range: VINO NOBILE, blended red Grifi, 50:50 – a SANGIOVESE/MERLOT joint venture with CAPANNELLE, a white blend, and superlative VIN SANTO (★★★★).

Azienda agricola/agraria Estates (large and small) making wine from own grapes.

Azienda/casa vinicola Négociants making wine from bought-in and own grapes.

Azienda vitivinicola A (specialized) wine estate.

Badia a Coltibuono ★★★ Fine CHIANTI-maker in lovely old abbey at Gaiole with a restaurant and collection of old vintages. Best wine: IGT SANGIOVETO.

Badia di Morrona ★★ Nr Pisa (Tus). Gd CHIANTI, outstanding IGT N'Antia (Cab Sauv/SANGIOVESE), and IGT VIGNA Alta (SANGIOVESE/Canaiolo).

Banfi (Castello or Villa) ★★ →★★★ Space-age MONTALCINO CANTINA of biggest US importer of Italian wine. Huge plantings at Montalcino, mostly SANGIOVESE; also Syrah, PINOT NOIR, Cab Sauv, CHARDONNAY, SAUVIGNON BLANC, etc: part of a drive for quality plus quantity. Poggio all'Oro and Poggio alle Mura are ★★★ BRUNELLOS. Centine is ROSSO DI MONTALCINO. In PIEDMONT also produces gd Banfi Brut, BRACCHETTO D'ACQUI, GAVI, PINOT GRIGIO. See also North America.

Barbaresco Pie DOCG r ★★→★★★★ 89' 90' 93 95' 96' 97' 98' 99' 00 01' Neighbour of BAROLO; the other great NEBBIOLO wine. Perhaps marginally less sturdy. At best, palate-cleansing, deep, subtle, fine. At 4 yrs becomes RISERVA. Producers inc: Antichi PODERI di Gallina, Ca' del Baio, Piero Busso, Cascina Luisin, CERETTO, CIGLIUTI, La Contea, Cortese, Fontanabianca, Fontanafredda, GAJA, BRUNO GIACOSA, MARCHESI DI GRESY, MOCCAGATTA, Montaribaldi, Morassino, Fiorenzo Nada, Paitin, Giorgio Pelissero, PIO CESARE, PRODUTTORI DEL BARBARESCO, PRUNOTTO, Prunset, Ressia, Roagna, Albino Rocca, BRUNO ROCCA, RIVETTI, Ronchi, Sottimano, Varaldo.

Barbatella, Cascina La ★★★ Top producer of BARBERA D'ASTI: excellent single-v'yd. VIGNA dell'Angelo and MONFERRATO Rosso Sonvico (BARBERA/Cab Sauv).

Barbera d'Alba Pie DOC r ★★ →★★★ 97' 98' 99 00' 01' Tasty, fragrant red. Best age up to 7 yrs. Many excellent wines, often from fine producers of BAROLO and BARBARESCO. Top producers: Gianfranco Alessandria, Almondo, Boroli, Cascina Chicco, ALDO CONTERNO, Giovanni CONTERNO, Cordero di Montezemolo, Corino, Correggia, Ghisolfi, ELIO GRASSO, Silvio Grasso, MANZONE, Massolino, Molino, Paolo Monti, OBERTO, PARUSSO, Pelissero, Gianmatteo Pira, Principiano, PRUNOTTO, Revello, Rivetti, Albino Rocca, Rocche Costamagna, SCAVINO, Vajra, VIETTI, ROBERTO VOERZIO.

Barbera d'Asti Pie DOC r ★★ →★★★ 97 98' 99 00' 01' 03 For real BARBERA-lovers: BARBERA alone, tangy and appetizing, drunk young or aged up to 7–10 yrs. Top growers: L'Arbiola, LA BARBATELLA, BAVA, BERA, Berta, BERTELLI, Alfiero Boffa, BRAIDA, Brema, Cantina Soc Vinchio e Vaglio, Cascina Ferro, Castino, CHIARLO, Contratto, COPPO, Ferraris, Garetto, HASTAE, Hohler, La Lune del Rospo, Marchesi Alfieri, Martinetti, La Morandina, Pico Maccario, PRUNOTTO, RIVETTI, Scrimaglio, Scagliola, La Tenaglia, Tenute dei Vallarino, VIETTI.

A Barole of honour

The classic style: Anselma, Borgogno, Brovia, Cappellano, Cavallotto, Aldo Conterno, Giovanni Conterno, Paolo Conterno, Fontanafredda, Bruno Giacosa, Bartolo Mascarello, Giuseppe Mascarello, Massolino, Monchiero, Prunotto, Renato Ratti, Giuseppe Rinaldi, Schiavenza, Vietti.

A promising new generation: Gianfranco Alessandria, Altare, Boglietti, Bongiovanni, Boroli, Bruna Brimaldi, Cabutto, Camerano, Cascina del Monastero, M Chiarlo, Clerico, Conterno Fantino, Cordero di Montezemolo, Corino, Damilano, Ettore Germano, Ghisolfi, Elio Grasso, Silvio Grasso, Davide Rosso Paolo Manzone, Giovanni Manzone, Molino, Oberto, Parusso, Luigi Pira, Porro, Principiano, Revello, Rocche Costamagna, Rocche dei Manzoni, Sandrone, Scavino, Fratelli Seghesio, Vajra, Gianni Voerzio, Roberto Voerzio, many others.

Barbera del Monferrato Pie DOC r ★ →★★ DYA Easy-drinking BARBERA from Alessandria and ASTI. Pleasant, slightly fizzy, sometimes sweetish. Delimited area is almost identical to BARBERA D'ASTI but style was simpler, less ambitious. Now more serious wines from Accornero, Bricco Mondalino, Cave di Moleto, La Tenaglia.

Barco Reale Tus DOC r ★★ **97 98 99** 00 01 DOC for junior wine of CARMIGNANO; using the same grapes.

Bardolino Ven DOC r (p) ★→★★ DYA Pale, summery, slightly bitter red from E shore of Lake Garda. Bardolino CHIARETTO: paler and lighter. Top makers: Cavalchina, Guerrieri-Rizzardi, MONTRESOR, Le Vigne di San Pietro, ZENATO, Zeni.

Barolo Pie DOCG r ★★★→★★★★ 89' 90' 93' 95' 96' 97' 98' 99' 00 01' Small area S of ALBA with one of Italy's supreme reds: rich, tannic, alcoholic (min 13%), dry but wonderfully deep and fragrant (also crisp and clean) in the mouth. From NEBBIOLO grapes. Ages for up to 20–25 yrs (RISERVA after 5).

Barolo Chinato A dessert wine made from BAROLO DOCG, alcohol, sugar, herbs, spices, and Peruvian bark. Producers: Cappellano, CERETTO, Guilio Cocchi.

Basciano ★★ Producer of gd DOCG CHIANTI RUFINA and IGT wines.

Bava ★★→★★★ Producer of v.gd BARBERA D'ASTI Piano Alto and Stradivarius, MONFERRATO BIANCO, BAROLO CHINATO; the Bava family controls the old firm Guilio Cocchi in Asti, where it produces gd sparkling METODO CLASSICO.

Bellavista ★★★ FRANCIACORTA estate with brisk SPUMANTE (Gran Cuvée Franciacorta is top). Also Satèn (a crémant-style sparkler). Terre di Franciacorta DOC and Sebino IGT Solesine (both Cab Sauv/MERLOT blends). Owner Vittorio Moretti also expanding into TUSCAN MAREMMA, Val di Cornia, and Monteregio.

Bera, Walter ★★→★★★ Small estate nr BARBARESCO. V.gd MOSCATO D'ASTI, ASTI, BARBERA D'ASTI, and LANGHE NEBBIOLO .

Berlucchi, Guido ★★★ Italy's biggest producer of sparkling METODO CLASSICO.

Bersano Historic wine house in Nizza MONFERRATO with BARBERA D'ASTI Generala, and BAROLO Badarina, most PIEDMONT DOC wines inc: BARBARESCO, MOSCATO D'ASTI, ASTI SPUMANTE.

Bertani ★★→★★★ Well-known, quality wines from VERONA, esp traditional AMARONE.

Bertelli ★★★ Superb wines from a family of medical researchers near ASTI, esp BARBERA D'ASTI, CHARDONNAY, Cab Sauv; very interesting experiments with SAUVIGNON BLANC, Sem, Nebbiolo, Syrah, and Marsanne/Roussanne.

Bianco White.

Bianco di Custoza Ven DOC w (sp) ★→★★ DYA Twin of SOAVE from VERONA'S other side (W). Corte Sant'Arcadio, Le Tende, Le VIGNE di San Pietro, MONTRESOR all gd.

Bibi Graetz Important reds from hills of Fiesole nr Florence, old-vine SANGIOVESE, Canaiolo, and Colorino of character and depth.

Biondi-Santi ★★★★ The original producer of BRUNELLO DI MONTALCINO, from 45-acre Il Greppo estate. Absurd prices, but some old vintages are very fine.

Boca Pie DOC r ★★ **95 96' 97'** 98' 99' 00 01 Another NEBBIOLO from N of PIEDMONT. Look for Le Piane and Poderi ai Valloni (Vigneto Cristiana ★★★).

Boccadigabbia ★★★ Top Marches producer of IGT wines: SANGIOVESE, Cab Sauv, PINOT NOIR, CHARDONNAY. Proprietor Elvidio Alessandri also owns fine Villamagna estate in Rosso Piceno DOC.

Bolgheri Tus DOC r p w (sw) ★★→★★★★ Ultra-modish recent region on the coast S of Livorno. Inc 7 types of wine: BIANCO, VERMENTINO, SAUVIGNON BLANC, ROSSO, ROSATO, VIN SANTO and Occhio di Pernice, plus top IGTS. Newish DOC Bolgheri Rosso: Cab Sauv/MERLOT/SANGIOVESE blend. Top producers: Giovanni Chiapinni: DOC Guado de Gemoli; Le Macchiole: DOC Paleo, TOSCANA IGTS Scrio (Syrah), Messorio (MERLOT); Micheletti: DOC Guardione; Enrico Santini: DOC Montepergoli, ORNELLAIA: DOC Ornellaia, Toscana IGT Masseto (MERLOT); SAN GUIDO: DOC SASSICAIA; ANTINORI: DOC Guado al Tasso; Meletti-Cavallari: DOC Grattamacco; Michele Satta: DOC Piastraia, I Castagni, Toscana IGT VIGNA al Cavaliere (SANGIOVESE). Much new investment and forthcoming wines from GAJA (Ca' Marcanda) and Ambrogio Folonari.

Bolla ★★ Famous VERONA firm for VALPOLICELLA, AMARONE, SOAVE, etc. Also RECIOTO.

Top wines: Castellaro, Creso (red and white), Jago. Wines, particularly AMARONE and SOAVE selections, are once again on the upswing.

Bonarda Minor and confusing red grape or grapes (can be Croatia) widely grown in PIEDMONT, Lombardy, Emilia-Romagna, and blended with BARBERA.

Bonarda Lom DOC r ★★ **97** 98 00 01 03 Soft, fresh FRIZZANTE and still wines from OLTREPÒ PAVESE, actually made from Croatina grapes.

Borgo del Tiglio ★★★ FRIULI estate for one of NE Italy's top MERLOTS, ROSSO della Centa; also superior COLLIO CHARDONNAY, TOCAI, and BIANCO.

Boscaini Ven ★★ VERONA producer of VALPOLICELLA, AMARONE, SOAVE.

Boscarelli, Poderi ★★★ Small estate with v.gd VINO NOBILE DI MONTEPULCIANO and barrel-aged IGT Boscarelli.

Brachetto d'Acqui Pie DOCG r sw (sp) ★★ DYA Sweet, sparkling red with enticing Muscat scent. Can be much better than it sounds. Or dire.

Braida ★★★ The late Giacomo Bologna's estate; for top BARBERA D'ASTI (BRICCO dell'Uccellone, Bricco della Bigotta, Ai Suma).

Bramaterra Pie DOC r ★★ **96 97'** 98' 99' 00 01 Neighbour to GATTINARA. NEBBIOLO grapes predominate in a blend. Gd producer: SELLA.

Breganze Ven DOC ★→★★★ (r) **97'** 98 99 00 01 Catch-all for many varieties nr Vicenza. Best: Cab Sauv, CHARDONNAY. Top producers: MACULAN, Miotti, Zonta.

Bricco Term for a hilltop (and by implication v.gd) v'yd in PIEDMONT.

Brindisi Ap DOC r ★★ **94 95 97** 99 00 01 Strong NEGROAMARO, esp from Vallone, Due Palme, Rubino, and forthcoming wines from ZONIN.

Brolio, Castello di ★★→★★★ After a sad period under foreign ownership, the RICASOLI family has taken this legendary 900-yr-old estate in hand again. Results are heartening. V.gd CHIANTI CLASSICO (NB 97) and IGT Casalferro (SANGIOVESE/Cab Sauv/MERLOT).

Brunelli ★★→★★★ V.gd quality of AMARONE and RECIOTO.

Brunello di Montalcino Tus DOCG r ★★★→★★★★ 88' 90' 93 95' 97' With BAROLO, Italy's most celebrated red: strong, full-bodied, high-flavoured, tannic and long-lived. Four years' ageing; after 5 yrs becomes RISERVA. Quality ever improving. Montalcino is 25 miles S of Siena.

> **Brunello di Montalcino to buy**
>
> Altesino, Argiano, Banfi, Barbi, Biondi-Santi, Brunelli, La Campana, Campogiovanni, Canalicchio di Sopra, Caparzo, Casanova di Neri, Case Basse, Castelgiocondo, Castello di Argiano, Castello di Camigliano, Cerbaiona, Col d'Orcia, Collelceto, Collesorbo, Costanti, Eredi Fuligni, Fanti-San Filippo, La Fiorita, La Fuga, La Gerla, Gorelli, Lambardi, Lisini, Marroneto, Oliveto, Siro Pacenti, Franco Pacenti, Palazzo, Pertimali, Ciacci Piccolomini, Pieve di Santa Restituta, La Poderina, Poggio Antico, Poggione, La Rasina, Salvioni-Cerbaiola, Scopetone, La Serena, Sesta, Talenti, Tiezzi, La Torre, Uccelliera, Valdicava, and Verbena.

Bussola, Tommaso ★★★ Emerging leading producer of AMARONE and RECIOTO in VALPOLICELLA.

Ca' dei Frati ★★→★★★ The best producer of DOC LUGANA: and v.gd, dry white blend IGT Pratto, sweet Tre Filer, and red IGT Ronchedone.

Ca' del Bosco ★★★★ FRANCIACORTA estate; some of Italy's best sparklers (outstanding DOCG Annamaria Clementi ★★★★), v.gd CHARDONNAY, and excellent Cab Sauv blend (Maurizio Zanella), PINOT NOIR (Pinèro).

Cacchiano, Castello di ★★→★★★ CHIANTI CLASSICO estate at Gaiole, owned by Barone Giovanni RICASOLI-Firidolfi, cousin of the Brolio Ricasolis.

Cafaggio, Villa ★★★ Very reliable CHIANTI CLASSICO estate with excellent IGTS San Martino (SANGIOVESE) and Cortaccio (Cab Sauv).

Calatrasi SI ★★→★★★ Gd producer of r and w IGT labels, esp D'Istinto line of better wines (Syrah, NERO D'AVOLA, SANGIOVESE/MERLOT, Magnifico red blend).

Caldaro (Lago di Caldaro) T-AA DOC r ★ DYA Alias Kalterersee. Light, soft, bitter-almond SCHIAVA. From a huge area. CLASSICO – smaller area – is better.

Candido, F ★★→★★★ Important grower in Salento, APULIA. Gd reds: Cappello di Prete, Duca d'Aragona, SALICE SALENTINO, and dessert wine ALEATICO DI PUGLIA.

Cannonau di Sardegna Sar DOC r (p) dr s/sw ★★ 95 96 97 98 99 00 01 02 Cannonau (Grenache) is the basic red grape of the S. Ranges from very potent to fine and mellow. Look for: ARGIOLAS, CS di Jerzu, Contini, Giuseppe Gabbas, Dettori.

Cantalupo, Antichi Vigneti di ★★→★★★ Top GHEMME wines, esp single-v'yd Breclemae and Carellae.

Cantina Cellar or winery.

Cantina Sociale (CS) Cooperative winery.

Capannelle ★★★ V.gd producer of IGT and CHIANTI CLASSICO, plus 50:50 SANGIOVESE/MERLOT joint venture with AVIGNONESI nr Gaiole.

Capezzana, Tenuta di (or Villa) ★★★ The TUSCAN estate (W of Florence) of the Contini Bonacossi family. Gd CHIANTI Montalbano, excellent CARMIGNANO (esp Villa Capezzagna, Villa Trefiano). Also v.gd B'x-style red, Ghiaie Della Furba.

Capichera ★★★ No 1 producer of VERMENTINO DI GALLURA, esp VENDEMMIA Tardiva. Now with excellent red Mantènghja from Carignano grapes.

Caprai ★★★ Widely copied, superb DOCG SAGRANTINO, v.gd DOC ROSSO DI MONTEFALCO. Highly rated.

Capri Cam DOC r p w ★→★★ Legendary island with widely abused name. Only interesting wines are from La Caprense.

Cartizze Famous, frequently too expensive, and too sweet DOC PROSECCO of top sub-zone of Valdobbiadene.

Carema Pie DOC r ★★→★★★ 89' 90' 93 95 96' 97' 98 99' 00 01 Old speciality from Nebbiolo grapes in N PIEDMONT. Best from Luigi Ferrando (or the CANTINA SOCIALE).

Carignano del Sulcis Sar DOC r p ★★→★★★ 90 91 93 94 95 96 97 98 99' 00 01' 02 Well-structured, age-worthy red. Best are Terre Brune and Rocca Rubia from CANTINA SOCIALE di SANTADI.

Carmignano Tus DOCG r ★★★ 90' 93 94 95 96 97' 98 99' 00 01' Region W of Florence. CHIANTI grapes plus 15% Cab Sauv make distinctive, reliable, even excellent reds. Best inc: AMBRA, CAPEZZANA, Farnete, La Piaggia, Pratesi.

Carpenè Malvolti Leading producer of classic PROSECCO and other sparkling wines at Conegliano, Veneto. Seen everywhere in Venice.

Carso F-VG DOC r w ★★→★★★ (r) 94 97' 99' 00 01 02 03 DOC nr Trieste inc gd MALVASIA. Terrano del C is a REFOSCO red. Top growers: EDI KANTE, Zidanich.

Casanova di Neri ★★★ BRUNELLO DI MONTALCINO, Pietradonice (SANGIOVESE/Cab Sauv) and v.gd ROSSO DI M from Neri family.

Cascina Fonda ★★★ Brothers Marco and Massimo Barbero have risen to the top in MOSCATO D'ASTI DOC. Look for VENDEMMIA Tardiva and METODO CLASSICO ASTI SPUMANTE.

Case Basse ★★★★ Pace-setter at MONTALCINO with sublime BRUNELLO and single-v'yd BRUNELLO Intistieti.

Castel del Monte Ap DOC r p w ★★→★★★ (r) 93' 94 95 96 97' 98 99 00 01 Dry, fresh, well-balanced wines. The red is RISERVA after 3 yrs. Rosé best known. Gd Pietrabianca and excellent Bocca di Lupo from Vigneti del Sud (ANTINORI). V.gd Il Falcone, Puer Apuliae, and Cappellaccio RISERVAS from RIVERA.

Castelgiocondo ★★★ FRESCOBALDI estate in MONTALCINO: v.gd BRUNELLO and IGT MERLOT Lamaïone.

Castell' in Villa ★★★ V.gd CHIANTI CLASSICO estate.

Castellare ★★→★★★ Small but admired CHIANTI CLASSICO producer. First-rate SANGIOVESE IGT I Sodi di San Niccoló and sprightly GOVERNO di Castellare: old-style CHIANTI updated. Also Poggio ai Merli (MERLOT) and Coniale (Cab Sauv).

Castello Castle. (See under name: eg Albola, Castello d'.)

Castello della Sala See ANTINORI.

Castello di Albola See ZONIN.

Castelluccio ★★→★★★ Pioneering producer of quality SANGIOVESE of Romagna: IGT RONCO dei Ciliegi and RONCO dei Ciliegi. New wine Massicone.

Castris, Leone de ★★ Large, reliable producer to follow for APULIAN wines. Estate at SALICE SALENTO, near Lecce. Four Roses is one of Italy's best ROSATOS.

Caudrina-Dogliotti Romano ★★★ Top MOSCATO D'ASTI: La Galeisa and Caudrina.

Cavalleri ★★→★★★ V.gd reliable FRANCIACORTA producer. Esp sparkling.

Cavicchioli E-R ★→★★ Large producer of LAMBRUSCO and other sparkling wines: Lambrusco di Sorbara VIGNA del Cristo is best. Also TERRE DI FRANCIACORTA.

Ca'Vit (Cantina Viticoltori) Group of co-ops nr Trento. Top wines: Brune di Monte (r w) and sp Graal.

Cecchi Tus ★→★★ Bottler, producer; La Gavina, Spargolo, CHIANTI CLASSICO RISERVA.

Cerasuolo Ab DOC p ★ The ROSATO version of MONTEPULCIANO D'ABRUZZO.

Cerasuolo di Vittoria Si DOC p ★★ **97 98** 99 00 01 Garnet, full-bodied, aromatic (Frappato and NERO D'AVOLA grapes); can be interesting, esp from Valle dell'Acate and COS.

Ceretto ★★★ V.gd grower of BARBARESCO (BRICCO Asili), BAROLO (Bricco Rocche, Brunate, Prapò), LANGHE Rosso Monsordo, and ARNEIS. Also v.gd METODO CLASSICO SPUMANTE La Bernardina.

Chardonnay Permitted for several northern DOCS (eg T-AA, FRANCIACORTA, F-VG, PIEDMONT). Some of the best (eg from ANTINORI, BOCCADIGABBIA, CAPANNELLE, PLANETA, and REGALEALI) are still only IGT. Now being tried almost everywhere.

Chianti Tus DOCG r ★→★★★ **95' 97' 99'** 00 01 03 Chianti Annata DYA The lively local wine of Florence and Siena. At best fresh, fruity, and tangy. Of the sub-districts, RUFINA (★★→★★★) and COLLI Fiorentini (★→★★★) can make CLASSICO-style RISERVAS. Montalbano, COLLI Senesi, Aretini, and Pisani: lighter wines. New sub-district since 1997 is Chianti Montespertoli; wines similar to Colli Fiorentini.

> ### Who makes really good Chianti Classico?
>
> AMA, ANTINORI, Bossio, CACCHIANO, CAFAGGIO, Capaccia, CAPANNELLE, Carobbio, BROLIO, Casa Emma, Casale dello Sparviero, Casaloste, Castel Ruggero, CASTELLARE, Castell'in Villa, Collelungo, Colombaio di Cencio, COLTIBUONO, Le Corti, FELSINA-BERARDENGA, Le Filigare, FONTERUTOLI, FONTODI, ISOLE E OLENA, Ispoli, LA MASSA, Lucignano, LE CINCIOLE, Le Macie, Le Masse di San Leolino, MONSANTO, Giovanna Morganti, NITTARDI, PALAZZINO, PANERETTA, Panzanello, Petroio-Lenzi, Poggerino, Poggiolino, Poggio al Sole, Quercecto, QUERCIABELLA, RAMPOLLA, RIECINE, Rocca di Montegrossi, Rocca di Castagnoli, RUFFINO, SAN FELICE, SAN GIUSTO A RENTENNANO, Selvole, Vecchie Terre di Montefili, VERRAZZANO, VOLPAIA.

Chianti Classico Tus DOCG r ★★→★★★★ **95' 97' 99'** 00 01 (RISERVA and single-v'yd) **88' 90' 93 95 97'** 99 01 Senior CHIANTI from central area. Its old, pale style is now rarer as top estates opt for darker, richer, firmer wines. Some are among the best wines of Italy, but too much Cab Sauv can spoil the style. Members of the CONSORZIO use the badge of a black rooster, but many top firms do not belong.

Chiarlo, Michele ★★→★★★ Gd PIEDMONT producer (BAROLOS Cerequio and Cannubi, BARBERA D'ASTI, LANGHE, and MONFERRATO Rosso). Also BARBARESCO.

Chiaretto Rosé (the word means "claret") produced esp around Lake Garda. See BARDOLINO, RIVIERA DEL GARDA BRESCIANO.

Chionetti ★★→★★★ Makes top DOLCETTO di Dogliani (look for Briccolero).

Cigliuti, Renato ★★★ Small, high-quality estate for BARBARESCO and BARBERA D'ALBA.

Cinqueterre Lig DOC w dr sw ★★ Fragrant, fruity white from precipitous coast nr La Spezia. PASSITO is known as SCIACCHETRA (★★→★★★). Gd from Co-op Agricola di Cinqueterre and Forlini Cappellini.

Cirò Cal DOC r (p w) ★ →★★★ 95 96 97 98 99 00 01 Strong red from Gaglioppo grapes; light, fruity w (DYA). Best: Caparra, Ippolito, LIBRANDI (Duca San Felice ★★★), San Francesco (Donna Madda, RONCO dei Quattroventi), and Siciliani.

Classico Term for wines from a restricted area within the limits of a DOC. By implication, and often in practice, the best of the district. Applied to sparkling wines it denotes the classic method (as for Champagne).

Clerico, Domenico ★★★ Constantly evolving PIEDMONT wines; the aim is for international flavour. Esp gd for BAROLO.

Col d'Orcia ★★★ Top MONTALCINO estate. Best wine: BRUNELLO.

Colli Hills. Occurs in many wine names.

Colli Berici Ven DOC r p w ★★ 97 99 00 01 Hills S of Vicenza. Best wine is Cab Sauv. Top producer: Villa Dal Ferro.

Colli Bolognesi E-R DOC r w ★★ SW of Bologna, 8 wines, 5 varieties. TERRE ROSSE, the pioneer, now joined by Bonzara (★★→★★★), Santarosa, Vallona.

Colli del Trasimeno Um DOC r w ★→★★★ (r) 97 98 99' 00 01 Lively white wines from near Perugia, but now more important reds as well. Best: Duca della Corgna, La Fiorita, Pieve del Vescovo, Poggio Bertaio.

Colli Euganei Ven DOC r w dr s/sw (sp) → →★★★ DYA DOC SW of Padua for 7 wines. Adequate red; white and sparkling are pleasant. Best producers: VIGNALTA, Ca' Lustra, La Montecchia, Riolite, Speaia.

Colli Orientali del Friuli F-VG DOC r w dr sw ★★→★★★★★ (r) 95 97 99' 00 01 Hills E of Udine. A group of 20 wines (18 named after their grapes). Both white and red can be v.gd. Top growers: Bastianich, Rosa Bosco, Castello di Buttrio, DORIGO, Dri, LE DUE TERRE, LIVIO FELLUGA, Meroi, Miani, Midolini, Moschioni, Perusini, Rocca Bernarda, Ronchi di Cialla, Ronchi di Manzano, RONCO DEL GNEMIZ, SCHIOPETTO, Scubla, Specogna, Le Viarte, VIGNA Traverso, LE VIGNE DI ZAMÒ, Volpe Pasini.

Colli Piacentini E-R DOC r p w ★→★★ DYA DOC inc traditional GUTTURNIO and Monterosso Val d'Arda among 11 types grown S of Piacenza. Gd fizzy MALVASIA. Most wines FRIZZANTE. New French and local reds: Montesissa, Mossi, Romagnoli, Solenghi, La Stoppa, La Tosa.

Colline Novaresi Pie DOC r w ★→★★ DYA New DOC for old region in Novara province. 7 different wines: BIANCO, ROSSO, NEBBIOLO, BONARDA, Vespolina, Croatina, and BARBERA. Inc declassified BOCA, FARA, GHEMME, and SIZZANO.

Collio F-VG DOC r w ★★→★★★★ 97 99' 00 01 Makes 19 wines, 17 named after their grapes, nr Slovenian border. V.gd whites, esp SAUVIGNON BLANC, PINOTS BLANC and GRIGIO from: BORGO DEL TIGLIO, Il Carpino, La Castellada, CASTELLO di Spessa, Damijan, MARCO FELLUGA, Fiegl, GRAVNER, Renato Keber, LIVON, Aldo Polencic, Primosic, Princic, RONCO dei Tassi, RUSSIZ SUPERIORE, SCHIOPETTO, Tercic, Terpin, Toros, Venica & Venica, VILLA RUSSIZ, Zuani.

Colterenzio CS (or Schreckbichl) T-AA ★★→★★★ Pioneering quality leader among ALTO ADIGE co-ops. Look for: Cornell line of selections; Lafoa Cab Sauv and SAUVIGNON BLANC; Cornelius red and white blends.

Consorzio In Italy there are two types of association recognized by wine law. One is dedicated to the observance of DOC regulations (eg Consorzio Tutela del CHIANTI CLASSICO). The second promotes the wines of their members (eg Consorzio del Marchio Storico of CHIANTI CLASSICO, previously Gallo Nero).

Conterno, Aldo ★★★★ Legendary grower of BAROLO, etc, at Monforte d'Alba. V.gd CHARDONNAY Printanier and Bussiadoro, gd BARBERA d'Alba Conca Tre Pile. Best BAROLOS: Gran Bussia, Cicala, and Colonello. Langhe Nebbiolo Favot and Langhe Rosso Quartetto both v.gd.

Conterno, Giacomo ★★★★ Top grower of BAROLO, etc, at Monforte d'Alba. Monfortino BAROLO is long-aged, rare, outstanding.

Conterno-Fantino ★★★ Two young families for v.gd BAROLO, etc, at Monforte d'Alba.

Contini, Attilio ★ ›★★★ Famous producer of VERNACCIA DI ORISTANO; best is vintage blend Antico Gregori. Also gd Cannonau.

Contrada Castelletta Pioneering MONTEPULCIANO/Syrah blend from v'yd of director of Saladini Pilastri in ROSSO PICENO DOC, juicy and rich.

Contratto ★★ At Canelli (owned by GRAPPA-producing family Bocchino), produces v.gd BARBERA D'ASTI, BAROLO, SPUMANTE, ASTI (De Miranda), MOSCATO D'ASTI.

Copertino Ap DOC r (p) ★★ **97** 99 00 01 Savoury, ageeable, strong red of NEGROAMARO from the heel of Italy. Look for CANTINA SOCIALE's RISERVA and Masseria Monaci, esp new barrel-aged Le Braci.

Coppo ★★ ›★★★ Ambitious producers of BARBERA D'ASTI (Pomorosso), CHARDONNAY.

Corini New house in remote area of Umbria. Produces intriguing, innovative blend of SANGIOVESE/MONTEPULCIANO/MERLOT.

Corsero di Montezemolo-Monfalletto ★★ ›★★★ Historic maker of gd BAROLO, now with fine BARBERA D'ALBA and CHARDONNAY.

Cortese di Gavi See GAVI. (Cortese is the grape.)

Corzano & Paterno, Fattoria di ★★★ Dynamic CHIANTI COLLI Fiorentini estate. V.gd RISERVA, red IGT Corzano, and outstanding VIN SANTO.

COS ★★ Small estate: three friends making top Sicilian wines.

Dal Forno, Romano ★★★★ Very high-quality VALPOLICELLA, AMARONE, and RECIOTO from perfectionist grower, bottling only best: 14,000 bottles from 20 acres.

Del Cerro, Fattoria ★★★ Estate with v.gd DOCG VINO NOBILE DI MONTEPULCIANO (esp RISERVA and Antica Chiusina), red IGTS Manero (SANGIOVESE), and Poggio Golo (MERLOT). Controlled by insurance co SAI. Also owns La Poderina (BRUNELLO DI MONTALCINO) and Colpetrone (MONTEFALCO SAGRANTINO).

Denominazione di Origine Controllata (DOC) Means much the same as *appellation d'origine contrôlée* (see France).

Denominazione di Origine Controllata e Garantita (DOCG) Like DOC but with an official "guarantee" of origin shown by an officially numbered neck-label on the bottle indicating limited production.

> **Italy's DOCG wines: the complete list (guaranteed)**
> Albana di Romagna, Asti and Moscato d'Asti, Barbaresco, Bardolino Superiore, Barolo, Brachetto d'Acqui, Brunello di Montalcino, Carmignano, Chianti, Chianti Classico, Colline Teramane, Franciacorta, Gattinara, Gavi, Ghemme, Montefalco Sagrantino, Sforzato, Soave Recioto, Taurasi, Torgiano Rosso Riserva, Valtellina Superiore, Vermentino di Gallura, Vernaccia di San Gimignano, and Vino Nobile di Montepulciano.

Di Majo Norante ★★ ›★★★ Lone star of Molise, S of Abruzzo with v.gd Biferno ROSSO, Molise Montepulciano, Ramitello Don Luigi, and AGLIANICO Contado, white blend Falanghina-Greco and Moscato Passiton Apianae.

DOC, DOCG See DENOMINAZIONE DI ORIGINE CONTROLLATA (E GARANTITA).

Dogliotti Romano See CAUDRINA.

Dolce Sweet.

Dolceacqua See ROSSESE DI DOLCEACQUA.

Dolcetto ★→★★★ PIEDMONT's earliest-ripening red grape, for very attractive everyday wines: dry, youthful, fruity, and fresh with deep purple colour. Gives its name to several DOCs: D d'Acqui; D di Diano d'Asti; D di Diano d'Alba (also Diano DOC), esp Alari, Bricco Maiolica, Cascina Flinion, and FONTANAFREDDA; D di Dogliani (esp from M & E Abbona, Francesco Boschis, CHIONETTI, Gillardi, Pecchenino, Poderi Luigi Einaudi, San Fereolo, San Romano); D delle Langhe Monregalesi (look for Barome Ricatti); and D di Ovada (best from La Guardia, Rossi Contini). D d'Alba: ALESSANDRIA, ALTARE, AZELIA, Baudana, Brovia, Cabutto, Ca' Viola, CLERICO, ALDO CONTERNO, CONTERNO-FANTINO, Corino, Gastaldi, Germano, GRESY, MANZONE, GIUSEPPE MASCARELLO, Massolino, Mossio, OBERTO, Luigi Pira, Gianmatteo Pira, PRUNOTTO, Rocche Costamanga, SANDRONE, SCAVINO, Schiavenza, Fratelli Seghesio, VAJRA, ROBERTO VOERIO.

Donnafugata Si w r ★★→★★★ Zesty Sicilian whites (best from Chiaranda and VIGNA di Gabri). Also solid, improving reds, esp Mille e Una Notte and Tancredi, fine Moscato Passito di Pantelleria Ben Rye. Wines, once VDT, now in DOC Contessa Entellina.

Dorigo, Girolamo ★★→★★★ Gd COLLI ORIENTALI producer for white Ronc di Juri, CHARDONNAY, dessert PICOLIT, red Pignolo (★★★), REFOSCO, Schioppettino, and Monsclapade (Cab Sauv/MERLOT).

Duca Enrico See DUCA DI SALAPARUTA.

Duca di Salaparuta Si ★★ Vini Corvo. Popular Sicilian wines. Sound, dry reds; pleasant, soft whites. Excellent Duca Enrico (★★★) is one of Sicily's best reds. Valguarnera is premium oak-aged white.

Elba Tus r w (sp) ★→★★ DYA The island's white is very drinkable with fish. Try Acquabona. Napoléon in exile here loved the sweet red ALEATICO. Me too. Promising new wines from Sapereta, both reds and dessert.

Enoteca Wine library; also wine shop or restaurant with extensive wine list. There are many, the impressive original being the Enoteca Italiana of Siena.

Eredi Fuligni ★★★ V.gd producer of BRUNELLO and ROSSO DI MONTALCINO.

Est! Est!! Est!!! Lat DOC w dr s/sw ★ DYA Unextraordinary white from Montefiascone, N of Rome. Trades on its oddball name. See FALESCO.

Etna Si DOC r p w ★★ (r) **95 97** 98 99 00 01 Wine from volcanic slopes. New investment in zone from Andrea Franchetti (Trinoro) and broker Marc De Grazia. Gd producers: Benanti, Cambria, Bonaccorsi.

Falchini ★★★ Producer of gd DOCG VERNACCIA DI SAN GIMIGNANO (esp Castel Selva and VIGNA a Solatio). Some of the area's best reds, eg IGT Campora (★★★).

Falerno del Massico ★★→★★★ Cam DOC r w ★★ (r) **90 93 94 95 97'** 98 99 00' 01 As in Falernum (or Falernian), the best-known wine of ancient times. Times change. Elegant red from AGLIANICO, fruity white from Falanghina. V.gd producer: VILLA MATILDE. Masseria Felice is a promising new face.

Falesco ★★→★★★ Latium estate, v.gd MERLOT Montiano and Cab Sauv Marciliano (both ★★★). Gd red IGT Vitiano and DOC EST! EST!! EST!!!

Fara Pie DOC r ★★ **90 95' 96' 97** 98 99 00' 01 Gd NEBBIOLO from Novara, N PIEDMONT. Fragrant; worth ageing; esp Dessilani's Caramino and Lochera.

Farnetella, Castello di ★★→★★★ Estate nr MONTEPULCIANO where Giuseppe Mazzocolin of FELSINA makes gd SAUVIGNON BLANC and CHIANTI COLLI Senesi. Also v.gd PINOT NOIR "Nero di Nubi" and red blend Poggio Granoni.

Faro Si DOC r ★★ **97 98** 99 00 01 Interesting full-bodied red from Messina. Gd producer: Palari.

Fattoria Central Italian term for an agricultural property, normally wine-producing, of a certain size.

Fazi-Battaglia ★★ Well-known producer of VERDICCHIO, best selections: Le Moie, Massaccio, San Sisto. Owns Fassati (producer of VINO NOBILE DI MONTEPULCIANO).

Felluga, Livio ★★★ Substantial estate, consistently fine COLLI ORIENTALI DEL FRIULI wines, esp PINOT GRIGIO, SAUVIGNON BLANC, TOCAI, PICOLIT, and MERLOT/REFOSCO blend.

Felluga, Marco ★★→★★★ The brother of Livio (see previous entry) owns a négociant house bearing his name plus RUSSIZ SUPERIORE in COLLIO DOC, Castello di Buttrio in COLLI ORIENTALI DOC. Marco's daughter Patrizia is now owner of Zuani estate in Collio.

Felsina-Berardenga ★★★ CHIANTI CLASSICO estate; famous RISERVA VIGNA Rancia, IGT Fontalloro; the regular CHIANTI CLASSICO and RISERVA, although less fashionable and less expensive, are more traditional. Gd IGT CHARDONNAY and Cab Sauv as well.

Ferrari T-AA ★★→★★★ Cellars making dry sparkling wines nr Trento. Giulio Ferrari RISERVA is best. Sizeable production, steadily improving quality.

Feudi di San Gregorio ★★★ Top Campania producer, with DOCG TAURASI, DOC FIANO, Flangina, Greco di Tufo. Red IGT Serpico and Patrimo (MERLOT), white IGT Campanaro.

Fiano di Avellino Cam w ★★→★★★ (DYA) Considered the best white of Campania. Can be intense, slightly honeyed, memorable. Best producers: Caggiano, COLLI di Lapio, FUEDI DI SAN GREGORIO, MASTROBERARDINO, Villa Raiano.

Florio The major volume producer of MARSALA, controlled by Illva-Saronno.

Folonari Ambrogio Folonari and son Giovanni have split off from RUFFINO to create their own house. Will continue to make Cabreo (a CHARDONNAY and a SANGIOVESE/Cab Sauv), wines of NOZZOLE (inc Cab Sauv Pareto), BRUNELLO DI MONTALCINO La Fuga, VINO NOBILE DI MONTEPULCIANO Gracciano Svetoni, with new offerings from BOLGHERI and COLLI ORIENTALI DEL FRIULI.

Fontana Candida ★★ One of the biggest producers of FRASCATI. Single-v'yd Santa Teresa stands out. See also GRUPPO ITALIANO VINI.

Fontanafredda ★★→★★★ Historic producer of PIEDMONT wines on former royal estates, inc: single-v'yd BAROLOS and range of ALBA DOCS. V.gd SPUMANTE Brut (esp ★★★ GATTINARA).

Fonterutoli ★★★ Historic CHIANTI CLASSICO estate of the Mazzei family at Castellina. Notable new selection CASTELLO di Fonterutoli (dark, oaky, fashionable CHIANTI), IGT Siepi (SANGIOVESE/MERLOT). Mazzei also own Tenuta di Belguardo in MAREMMA, gd MORELLINO DI SCANSANO.

Fontodi ★★★ Top Panzano CHIANTI CLASSICO estate for CHIANTI and RISERVA, esp RISERVA del Sorbo. V.gd red IGT Flaccianello, Case Via PINOT NERO, ˈCase Va Syrah.

Foradori ★★★ Elizabetta F makes best TEROLDEGO. Also oak-aged Teroldego Granato, red IGT Karanar, white IGT Myrto. New estate in TUSCAN MAREMMA.

Forte, Podere Pasquale Forte's Val d'Orcia estate, just S of MONTALCINO, puts cutting-edge technology at the service of ambitious SANGIOVESE and Cab Sauv/MERLOT/Petit Verdot wines.

Forteto della Luja ★★★ Lone star in LOAZZOLO; v.gd BARBERA/PINOT NOIR Le Grive.

Fossi, Enrico ★★★ High-level small estate in Signa, W of Florence, very fine SANGIOVESE, Cab Sauv, Syrah, Malbec, and CHARDONNAY.

Franciacorta Lom DOCG w (p) sp ★★→★★★★ Small sparkling wine centre growing in quality and renown. Wines exclusively bottle-fermented. Top producers: Barone Pizzini, BELLAVISTA, CA' DEL BOSCO, Castellino, CAVALLERI, Gatti, UBERTI, VILLA; also v.gd: Contadi Gastaldi, Cornaleto, Il Mosnel, La Montina, Majolini, Monte Rossa, Monzio Compagnoni, Ricci Curbastri, Ronco Calino, Vezzoli. For white and red, see TERRE DI FRANCIACORTA.

Frascati Lat DOC w dr s/sw sw (sp) ★→★★ DYA Best-known wine of Roman hills: should be soft, limpid, golden, tasting of whole grapes. Most is disappointingly neutral today: look for Conte Zandotti, Villa Simone, or Santa Teresa from FONTANA CANDIDA. Sweet is known as Cannellino. The best place to drink it is from the jug in a *trattoria* in Rome.

Freisa Pie r dr s/sw sw (sp) ★★ DYA Usually very dry (except nr Turin), often

FRIZZANTE red, said to taste of raspberries and roses. With enough acidity it can be highly appetizing, esp with salami. Gd wines from CIGLIUTI, Clerico, ALDO CONTERNO, COPPO, PARUSSO, Pecchenino, Pelissero, Sebaste, Trinchero, VAJRA, and VOERZIO.

Frescobaldi ★★→★★★★ Ancient noble family, leading CHIANTI RUFINA pioneer at NIPOZZANO, E of Florence. Also POMINO (w) and Mormoreto (r). See MONTESODI. Owner of CASTELGIOCONDO (★★★). Joint TUSCAN venture with Mondavi of California nr MONTALCINO producing LUCE and Lucente. New v'yds in COLLIO DOC and MAREMMA. Important development of v'yds to SE of Florence nr Montespertoli.

Friuli-Venezia Giulia The NE region on the Slovenian border. Many wines; the DOCS ISONZO, COLLIO, and COLLI ORIENTALI inc: most of the best.

Frizzante (fz) Semi-sparkling. Used to describe wines such as LAMBRUSCO.

Gaja ★★★★ Old family firm at BARBARESCO under meteoric direction of Angelo Gaja. Top-quality – and price – wines, esp BARBARESCO (single-v'yds SORI Tildin, Sorì San Lorenzo, Costa Russi), BAROLO Sperss. Trend-setting, excellent CHARDONNAY (Gaia and Rey), Cab Sauv Darmagi. Latest acquisition: Marengo-Marenda estate (BAROLO), commercial Gromis label, PIEVE DI SANTA RESTITUTA (BRUNELLO); recently planted v'yd, Ca Marcanda, at BOLGHERI. Single-v'yd BARBARESCOS and BAROLO now marked LANGHE DOC.

Galardi ★★★ Producer of Terra di Lavoro, a mind-boggling blend of AGLIANICO and Piedirosso, in N Campania nr FALERNO DEL MASSICO DOC.

Galestro Tus w ★ Very light white from eponymous shaley soil in CHIANTI country.

Gambellara Ven DOC w dr s/sw (sp) ★ DYA Neighbour of SOAVE. Dry wine similar. Sweet (RECIOTO DI G), nicely fruity. Top producer: La Biancara.

Gancia Famous ASTI house also producing dry sparkling.

Garganega Principal white grape of SOAVE and GAMBELLARA.

Garofoli ★★→★★★ One of quality leaders in the Marches (nr Ancona). Notable style in VERDICCHIO Podium, Macrina, and Serra Fiorese. ROSSO CONERO Piancarda and v.gd Grosso Agontano.

Gattinara Pie DOCG r ★★★ 89' 90' 93 95 96' 97' 98 99' 00 01 Very tasty NEBBIOLO-based red, historically the finest from N PIEDMONT. Best are TRAVAGLINI (RISERVA), Antoniolo (single-v'yd wines). Others inc Bianchi, Nervi, SERGIO GATTINARA.

Gavi Pie DOCG w ★→★★★★ DYA At (rare) best, subtle dry white of CORTESE grapes. LA SCOLCA is best-known, gd from BANFI (esp VIGNA Regale), Castellari Bergaglio, Franco Martinetti, Broglia, Cascina degli Ulivi, CASTELLO di Tassarolo, CHIARLO, La Giustiniana, PODERE, Saulino, Villa Sparina are also fair.

Geografico ★★ Co-op with rising-quality CHIANTI CLASSICO; gd riserva Montegiachi. IGTS Pulleraia and Ferraiolo.

Ghemme Pie DOCG r ★★ 89 90' 93 95 96 97' 98 99' 00 01 Neighbour of GATTINARA but not as gd. Best: Antichi Vigneti di Cantalupo and Rovellotti.

Giacosa, Bruno ★★→★★★★ Inspired loner: outstanding BARBARESCO, BAROLO, and PIEDMONT wines at Neive. Remarkable ARNEIS white and PINOT NOIR sparkler.

Governo Old TUSCAN custom, enjoying mild revival. Dried grapes or must are added to young wine to induce second fermentation and give a slight prickle, sometimes instead of using must concentrate to increase alcohol.

Gradi Degrees (of alcohol), ie per cent by volume.

Grappa Pungent and potent spirit made from grape pomace (skins, etc, after pressing), sometimes excellent. Best grappa comes from PIEDMONT (Ugo Marolo, Paolo Marolo, Distilleria Artigiana, Berta), Trentino (POJER & SANDRI, Pilzer, Giovanni Poli), Friuli (Nonino), Veneto (Carlo Gobetti, Vittorio Capovilla, Jacopo Poli), Tuscany (Nannoni), Sicily (Giovi).

Grasso, Elio ★★★ V.gd BAROLO (look for Runcot, Gavarini, and Casa Maté), full, barrel-aged BARBERA D'ALBA VIGNA Martina, DOLCETTO D'ALBA, and CHARDONNAY Educato, etc.

Grattamacco ★★ ·★★★ Pioneering producer nr BOLGHERI, on TUSCAN coast. V.gd DOC BOLGHERI red.

Grave del Friuli F-VG DOC r w ★·★★ (r) **95 97 99** 00 01 DOC covering 15 different wines, 14 named after their grapes, from central part of region. Gd REFOSCO, MERLOT, and Cab Sauv. Best producers: Borgo Magredo, Le Fredis, Di Leonardo, Le Monde, Plozner, Vicentini-Orgnani, Villa Chiopris.

Gravner, Josko ★★★ Visionary COLLIO producer, leading drive for low yields, oak ageing, and age-worthy wines. Tirelessly self-critical in his search for new concepts and methods.

Grechetto White grape, with more flavour than the ubiquitous TREBBIANO. Increasingly popular in Umbria.

Greco di Bianco Cal DOC w sw ★★ **97** 98 99 00 01 Original, smooth and fragrant sweet wine from Italy's toe; worth ageing. Best from Ceratti. See MANTONICO.

Greco di Tufo Cam DOC w (sp) ★★·★★★ (DYA) One the best whites from the S: fruity and slightly wild in flavour. V.gd examples from Benito Ferrara, FEUDI DI SAN GREGORIO, MASTROBERARDINO (Nuovaserra & Vignadangelo), Villa Raiano.

Gresy, Marchesi de (Cisa Asinari) ★★★ Consistent producer of fine BARBARESCO. Also v.gd LANGHE Rosso, SAUVIGNON BLANC, CHARDONNAY, MOSCATO D'ASTI.

Grevepesa CHIANTI CLASSICO co-op – quality now rising.

Grignolino d'Asti Pie DOC r ★ DYA Lively light red of PIEDMONT.

Grignolino del Monferrato Casalese Much like Grignolino d'Asti but firmer. Look for: Bricco Mondalino, Colonna, La Tenaglia.

Gruppo Italiano Vini (GIV) Complex of co-ops and wineries inc Bigi, Conti Serristori, FOLONARI, FONTANA CANDIDA, LAMBERTI, Macchiavelli, MELINI, Negri, Santi, and since 1997 controls Ca' Bianca (PIEDMONT) and Vignaioli di San Floriano (FRIULI). Now moving into S with recent investments in Sicily and Basilicata.

Guerrieri-Gonzaga ★★★ Top TRENTINO estate; esp San Leonardo blend.

Gutturnio dei Colli Piacentini E-R DOC r dr ★·★★ DYA BARBERA/BONARDA blend from the hills of Piacenza, often FRIZZANTE.

Haas, Franz ★★★ ALTO ADIGE producer of v.gd PINOT NOIR, LAGREIN, and IGT red and white blends.

Hastae ★★★ New Super-BARBERA from ASTI from group of producers: BRAIDA, CHIARLO, COPPO, PRUNOTTO, VIETTI.

Hofstätter ★★★ ALTO ADIGE producer of top PINOT NOIR. Look for S Urbano, LAGREIN, Cab Sauv/Petit Verdot, Gewurz.

IGT (Indicazione Geografica Tipica) New category for quality wines unable to fit into DOC zones or regulations; replaces the anomaly of glamorous VDTS.

Ischia Cam DOC w (r) ★·★★ DYA Wine of the island off Naples. Top producer d'Ambra makes gd DOC red Dedicato a Mario D'Ambra, IGT red Tenuta Montecorvo, IGT white Tenuta Frassitelli, and Piellero. Gd wines from Pietratorcia as well.

Isole e Olena ★★★ ·★★★★ Top CHIANTI CLASSICO estate of great beauty with fine red IGT Cepparello. V.gd VIN SANTO, Cab Sauv, CHARDONNAY, and L'Eremo Syrah.

Isonzo F-VG DOC r w ★★★ (r) **95 97'** 98 **99** 00' 01 DOC covering 19 wines (17 varietals) in NE. Best white and MERLOT compare to COLLIO wines. Esp from Masut da Rive, LIS NERIS, Pierpaolo Pecorari, RONCO del Gelso, Borgo San Daniele, VIE DI ROMANS, Sant'Elena.

Jermann, Silvio ★★★ Family estate with v'yds in COLLIO and ISONZO: top white VDT, inc blend VINTAGE TUNINA, oak-aged Capo Martino, and "Were dreams, now is just wine" (yes, really). Now joined by important red Pignacoluse.

Kalterersee German (and local) name for LAGO DI CALDARO.

Kante, Edi ★★·★★★ Leading light of CARSO; fine DOC CHARDONNAY, SAUVIGNON BLANC, MALVASIA; gd red Terrano.

Lacryma (or Lacrima) Christi del Vesuvio Cam r p w dr (sw fz) ★·★★ DYA

Famous but ordinary wines in great variety from Vesuvius (DOC Vesuvio). MASTROBERARDINO and Caputo wines suggest untapped quality.

La Fiorita Lamborghini family property nr Lake Trasimeno in Umbria with touchstone SANGIOVESE/MERLOT blend Campoleone.

Lageder, Alois ★★→★★★ Top ALTO ADIGE producer. Exciting wines inc oak-aged Löwengang CHARDONNAY and Römigberg Cab Sauv. Single-v'yd SAUVIGNON BLANC is Lehenhof, PINOT GRIGIO Benefizium Porer, PINOT NOIR Krafuss, Lagrein Lindenberg, TERLANO Tannhammer. Also owns Cason Hirschprunn for v.gd IGT red and white blends.

Lago di Caldaro See CALDARO.

Lagrein T-AA DOC r p ★★→★★★ 95' 96 97' 98 99 00' 01 02 A grape with a bitter twist. Gd, fruity wine – at best very appetizing. The rosé: "Kretzer", the dark: "Dunkel". Best from Colterenzio co-op, Gries, Gojer, HAAS, HOFSTÄTTER, LAGEDER, Laimburg, Josephus Mayr, Thomas Mayr, Muri Gries, NIEDERMAYR, Niedrist Estates, St Magdalena, TERLANO CO-OP.

An Italian choice for 2005

Barolo Villero 1999 Boroli (Piedmont)

Langhe Rosso Dialogo 2001 Tenute dei Vallarino (Piedmont)

Franciacorta Cuvée Annamaria Clementi 1996 Ca' del Bosco (Lombardy)

Alto Adige Pinot Nero Krafuss 2000 Alois Lageder (Alto Adige)

Collio Bianco Studio di Un Bianco 2001 Borgo del Tiglio (Friuli)

Vito Arturo 2001 Le Fonti (Tuscany)

Brunello di Montalcino 1999 Pian delle Vigne (Tuscany)

Villa Fidelia Rosso 2001 Sportoletti (Umbria)

Montefalco Sagrantino 2000 Perticaia (Umbria)

Irpinia Rosso Serpico 2001 Feudi di San Gregorio (Campania)

Salento Rosso Re 2001 La Corte (Puglia)

Contessa Entellina Mille e Una Notte 2000 Donnafugata (Sicily)

La Massa ★★★ Highly rated producer of v.gd CHIANTI CLASSICO; Giorgio Primo.

Lamberti ★★ Large producer of SOAVE, VALPOLICELLA, BARDOLINO, etc, at Lazise on the E shore of Lake Garda.

Lambrusco E-R DOC (or not) r p dr s/sw ★→★★ DYA Popular fizzy red, best known in industrial s/sw version. Best is SECCO, traditional with second fermentation in bottle (with sediment). DOCs: L Grasparossa di Castelvetro, L Salamino di Santa Croce, L di Sorbara. Best from: Bellei, Caprari, Casali, CAVICCHIOLI, Graziano, Lini Oreste, Medici Ermete (esp Concerto), Rinaldo Rinaldini, Venturini Baldini. Forget your prejudices – try it!

La Morandina ★★★ Small family estate with top MOSCATO and BARBERA D'ASTI.

Langhe The hills of central PIEDMONT, home of BAROLO, BARBARESCO, etc. Has become name for recent DOC (r w ★★→★★★) for 8 different wines: ROSSO, BIANCO, NEBBIOLO, DOLCETTO, FREISA, ARNEIS, Favorita, and CHARDONNAY. Barolo and Barbaresco can now be declassified to DOC Langhe Nebbiolo.

La Scolca ★★ Famous GAVI estate for gd Gavi and SPUMANTE.

Latisana F-VG DOC r w ★→★★ (r) 99 00 01 02 DOC for 13 varietal wines from 50 miles NE of Venice. Best wine is Tocai Friulano.

Le Cinciole ★★★ DOCG CHIANTI CLASSICO (the best is RISERVA Petresco).

Le Due Terre Small producer in COLLI ORIENTALI DEL FRIULI for choice MERLOT, PINOT NOIR, Sacrisassi Rosso (Refosco-Schioppettino), and white Sacrisassi Bianco.

Le Fonti ★★★ V.gd CHIANTI CLASSICO house in Poggibonsi; look for RISERVA and IGT Vito Arturo (SANGIOVESE).

Le Macchiole ★★★ Outstanding red DOC BOLGHERI Paleo, TOSCANA IGTs Macchiole Rosso (SANGIOVESE/Cab Fr), Messorio (MERLOT), and Scrio (Syrah).

Le Pupille ★★★ Top producer of MORELLINO DI SCANSANO (look for Poggia Valente), excellent IGT blend Saffredi (Cab Sauv/MERLOT/ALICANTE).

Le Salette ★★→★★★ Small VALPOLICELLA producer: look for v.gd AMARONE Pergole Vece and RECIOTO Le Traversagne.

Le Vigne di Zamò ★★★ First-class FRIULI estate for PINOT BLANC, TOCAI, Pignolo, Cab Sauv, and MERLOT from v'yds in 3 areas of COLLI ORIENTALI DEL FRIULI DOC: Buttrio, MANZANO, Premariacco.

Lessona Pie DOC r ★★ 94 95 96' 97' 98 99' 00 01 Soft, dry, claret-like wine from Vercelli province. NEBBIOLO, Vespolina, BONARDA grapes. Best producer: SELLA.

Librandi ★★★ Top Calabria producer. V.gd red CIRO (RISERVA Duca San Felice is ★★★), IGT Gravello (Cab Sauv/Gaglioppo blend), and Magno Megonio from Magliocco grape. New IGT from Efeso from Mantonico grape most impressive.

Liquoroso Means strong; usually sweet and always fortified.

Lis Neris ★★★ Top ISONZO estate with bevy of high-quality wines: CHARDONNAY, PINOT GRIGIO, SAUVIGNON BLANC, a MERLOT-based red, an aromatic Confini white blend, and lovely VDT dessert VERDUZZO.

Lisini ★★★ Historic small estate for some of the finest BRUNELLO.

Livon ★★→★★★ Substantial COLLIO producer, also some COLLI ORIENTALI wines like VERDUZZO. Expanded into the CHIANTI CLASSICO and Montefalco DOCGs.

Loazzolo Pie DOC w sw ★★★ 95 96' 97' 98' 99' 00 01' DOC for MOSCATO dessert wine from botrytized, air-dried grapes: expensive and sweet. Gd from Forteto della Luja.

Locorotondo Ap DOC w (sp) ★ DYA Pleasantly fresh southern white.

Lugana Lom and Ven DOC w (sp) ★→★★ DYA Whites of S Lake Garda: can be fragrant, smooth, full of body and flavour. Gd from CA' DEI FRATI, ZENATO.

Luce ★★★ Ambitious Mondavi (see California) joint venture launched in 1998 with FRESCOBALDI. SANGIOVESE/MERLOT blend. Could become Italy's Opus One.

Lungarotti ★★→★★★ Leading producer of TORGIANO, with cellars, hotel, and museum nr Perugia. Gd IGT Sangiorgio (SANGIOVESE/Cab Sauv), Aurente (CHARDONNAY) and Giubilante. See TORGIANO.

Macchiavelli See GRUPPO ITALIANO VINI.

Maculan ★★★ Excellent Cab Sauv (Fratta, Ferrata), CHARDONNAY (Ferrata), MERLOT (Marchesante), and Torcolato (esp RISERVA Acininobili).

Malvasia Widely planted grape; chameleon-like: white or red, sparkling or still, strong or mild, sweet or dry, aromatic or neutral; often IGT, sometimes DOC.

Manduria (Primitivo di) Ap DOC r s/sw ★★→★★★ 97' 98 99 00 01 Dark red, naturally strong, sometimes sweet from nr Taranto. Gd producers: Casale Bevagna, Felline, Masseria Pepe, Pervini, Pozzopalo, Sinfarosa.

Mantonico Cal w dr sw fz ★★ 95 97 99 00 01 Fruity, deep-amber sweet wine from Reggio Calabria. Can age remarkably well. Ceratti's is gd. Notable new dry version from LIBRANDI. See GRECO DI BIANCO.

Manzone, Giovanni ★★★ V.gd ALBA wines of much personality from Ciabot del Preve estate nr Manforte d'Alba. Single-v'yd BAROLO, BARBERA D'ALBA, DOLCETTO.

Marchesi di Barolo ★★ Important ALBA house: BAROLO (esp Cannubi and Sarmassa), BARBARESCO, DOLCETTO D'ALBA, BARBERA, FREISA D'ASTI, and GAVI.

Maremma Southern coastal area of TUSCANY in provinces of Livorno and Grosseto. DOCS inc BOLGHERI and VAL DI CORNIA (Livorno), MONTEREGIO, MORELLINO DI SCANSANO, PARRINA, SOVANA (Grosseto). Now attracting much interest and new investments for high-quality potential demonstrated by wines.

Marino Lat DOC w dr s/sw (sp) ★→★★ DYA A neighbour of FRASCATI with similar wine; often a better buy. Look for Di Mauro.

Marsala Si DOC br dr s/sw sw fz ★→★★★ NV Sicily's sherry-type wine, invented by the Woodhouse Bros from Liverpool in 1773; excellent apéritif or for dessert, but mostly used in the kitchen for *zabaglione*, etc. Dry ("virgin"), sometimes made by the *solera* system, must be 5 yrs old. Top producers: FLORIO, Pellegrino, Rallo, VECCHIO SAMPERI. Very special old vintages ★★★★.

Martini & Rossi Vermouth and sparkling wine house now controlled by Bacardi group. (Has a fine wine-history museum in Pessione, nr Turin.)

Marzemino (Trentino) T-AA DOC r ★→★★ 00 01 03 Pleasant local red. Fruity and slightly bitter. Esp from: Bossi Fedrigotti, CA'VIT, Gaierhof, Letrari, Longariva, Simoncelli, E Spagnolli, De Tarczal, Vallarom.

Mascarello The name of two top producers of BAROLO, etc: Bartolo M and Giuseppe M & Figli. Look for the latter's supreme BAROLO Monprivato.

Masi ★★→★★★ Well-known, conscientious, reliable VALPOLICELLA, AMARONE, RECIOTO, SOAVE, etc, inc fine red Campo Fiorin. Also v.gd barrel-aged red IGT Toar.

Mastroberardino ★★→★★★ Campania's historic house has split into two parts: M and Terredora, but with very few changes. Wines inc FIANO DI AVELLINO, GRECO DI TUFO, LACRYMA CHRISTI, TAURASI (look for Radici), IGT Avalon wines from Vesuvius, IGT Historia Naturalis, new top blend of AGLIANICO and Piedirosso.

Melini ★★ Long-established producers of CHIANTI CLASSICO at Poggibonsi. Gd quality/price; look for single-v'yd CHIANTI CLASSICO Selvanella and RISERVAS La Selvanella and Masovecchio. See GRUPPO ITALIANO VINI.

Meranese di Collina T-AA DOC r ★ DYA Light red of Merano.

Merlot Adaptable red grape widely grown in N (esp) and central Italy. Merlot DOCS are abundant. Best producers: BORGO DEL TIGLIO, LIVIO FELLUGA (Sossò), Renato Keber, LE DUE TERRE, Miani, Radikon, VILLA RUSSIZ (De la Tour) in FRIULI-VENEZIA GIULIA; Bonzara (Rocca di Bonacciara) in E-R; BOCCADIGABBIA in the Marches; FALESCO (Montiano) in Latium; PLANETA in Sicily; FEUDI DI SAN GREGORIO (Patrimo) in Campania; and TUSCAN Super-IGTS AMA (L'Apparita), FRESCOBALDI (Lampione), La Cappella (Cantico), Cantine Leonardo da Vinci (Artisi), Macchiole (Messorio), ORNELLAIA (Masseto), Petrolo (Galatrona), RODANO (Lazzicante), San Giusto a Rentennano (La Ricolma), Tua Rita (Redigaffi).

Metodo classico or tradizionale Now mandatory terms to identify classic method sparkling wines. "Metodo Champenois" banned since 1994 and now illegal. (See CLASSICO.)

Mezzacorona ★★ TRENTINO co-op with gd DOC TEROLDEGO, METODO CLASSICO sp Rotari.

Moccagatta ★★→★★★ Specialist in impressive single-v'yd BARBARESCO: Basarin, Bric Balin (★★★), and VIGNA Cole. Also BARBERA D'ALBA and LANGHE.

Molino ★★★ Talented producer of elegant ALBA wines at La Morra; look for BAROLOS Gancia and Conca, BARBERA Gattere, and DOLCETTO

Monacesca, La ★★→★★★ Fine producer of VERDICCHIO DI MATELICA. Top wine: Mirus.

Moncaro ★★ Marches co-op: gd VERDICCHIO DEI CASTELLI DI JESI, Rosso Conero and Rosso Piceno.

Monferrato Pie DOC r p w sw ★★ Hills between River Po and Apennines. Name of new DOC; inc ROSSO, BIANCO, CHIARETTO, DOLCETTO, Casalese, FREISA, and CORTESE.

Monica di Sardegna Sar DOC r ★→★★ DYA Monica is the grape of a light, dry red.

Monsanto ★★★ Esteemed CHIANTI CLASSICO estate, esp for Il Poggio v'yd and IGTS Fabrizio Bianchi (SANGIOVESE) and Nemo (Cab Sauv).

Montalcino Small town in province of Siena (TUSCANY), famous for concentrated, expensive BRUNELLO and more approachable, better-value ROSSO DI MONTALCINO.

Montecarlo Tus DOC w r ★★ DYA (w) White, and increasingly red, wine area nr Lucca in N TUSCANY. Whites are smooth, neutral blend of TREBBIANO with range of better grapes; basic reds are CHIANTI-style. Gd producers: Buonamico (red IGTS Cercatoja Rosso and Fortino), Carmignani (v.gd red IGT "For Duke"), red IGTS of La Torre, Montechiari, Wandanna, Fattoria del Teso.

Montecucco New TUSCAN DOC between MONTALCINO and MORELLINO DI SCANSANO. Look for Fattoria di Montecucco. Much new investment: FOLONARI, MASI, Pertimali, RIECINE, Talenti.

Montefalco (Rosso di) Umb DOC r ★★→★★★ 93 94 95 96 97' 98 99' 00' 01 SANGIOVESE/TREBBIANO/SAGRANTINO blend. For producers, see MONTEFALCO SAGRANTINO.

Montefalco Sagrantino Umb DOCG r dr (sw) ★★★→★★★★ 90 91 93 94 95' 96 97' 98 99' 00' 01 Strong interesting SECCO or sweet PASSITO red from Sagrantino grapes only. Gd from Benincasa, CAPRAI, Colpetrone, Perticaia, Scacciadiavoli, Terra di Trinci.

Montellori, Fattoria di ★★→★★★ TUSCAN producer making SANGIOVESE/Cab Sauv IGT blend Castelrapiti, Cab Sauv/MERLOT blend Salamartano, white IGTS Montecupoli (blend) and Sant'Amato (SAUVIGNON BLANC), and METODO CLASSICO SPUMANTE.

Montepulciano An important red grape of E central Italy as well as the famous TUSCAN town (see next entries).

Montepulciano d'Abruzzo Ab DOC r p ★→★★★ 90 92 94 95 97' 98' 00' 01 At its best, one of Italy's tastiest reds, full of flavour and warmth, from Adriatic coast nr Pescara. Best: Barone Cornacchia, Nestore Bosco, Cataldi-Madonna, Feuduccio, Filomusi-Guelfi, Illuminati, Masciarelli, Monti, Montori, Nicodemi, Orlandi Contucci Ponno, Terre d'Aligi, Torre dei Beati, La Valentina, VALENTINI, Valle Reale, Valori. Farnese is the big-value brand. See also CERASUOLO.

Montepulciano, Vino Nobile di See VINO NOBILE DI MONTEPULCIANO.

Monteregio Emerging DOC zone nr Massa Marittima in MAREMMA, high-level SANGIOVESE and Cab Sauv wines from MORIS FARMS, Massa Vecchia, Montebelli, La Pierotta, Suveraia. New investors (inc ANTINORI, BELLAVISTA, Erik Rothschild, ZONIN) flocking in.

Montescudaio Tus DOC r w ★★ 95 97 98 99 00 01 DOC between Pisa and Livorno; best are SANGIOVESE or SANGIOVESE/Cab Sauv blends. Try Aione, Merlini, Poggio Gagliardo, Sorbaiano.

Montesodi Tus r ★★★ 90 93 95 97 99 01' Tip-top CHIANTI RUFINA RISERVA from FRESCOBALDI.

Montevertine Radda estate, once a leading force in the renaissance of TUSCAN wine in the 1970s and 1980s. IGT Le Pergole Torte a pioneering example of small-barrel-aged SANGIOVESE.

Montevetrano ★★★ Small Campania producer; superb IGT Montevetrano (Cab Sauv/MERLOT/AGLIANICO).

Montresor ★★ VERONA wine house: gd LUGANA, BIANCO DI CUSTOZA, VALPOLICELLA.

Morellino di Scansano Tus DOC r ★→★★★ 90' 93 94 95 97 98 99' 00 01 Local SANGIOVESE of the MAREMMA, the S TUSCAN coast. Cherry-red, should be lively and tasty young or matured. Belguardo, Col di Bacche, Colli dell'Uccellina, Fattoria di Magliano, Fattorie LE PUPILLE, La Carletta, Malfatti, MORIS FARMS, Mantellasi, Banti, Poggio Argentiera, Poggiolungo, and Cantina di Scansano are producers to try.

Moris Farms ★★★ Gd producer in Monteregio and MORELLINO DI SCANSANO, respectively to N and S of Grosseto; look for RISERVA and IGT Avvoltore, a rich SANGIOVESE/Cab Sauv/Syrah blend.

Moscadello di Montalcino Tus DOC w sw (sp) ★★ DYA. Revived traditional wine of MONTALCINO, once more important than BRUNELLO. Sweet white fizz and sweet to high-octane MOSCATO PASSITO. Best producers: COL D'ORCIA, La Poderina, Poggio Salvi.

Moscato Fruitily fragrant ubiquitous grape for a diverse range of wines: sparkling or still, light or full-bodied, but always sweet.

Moscato d'Asti Pie DOCG w sp sw ★★→★★★ DYA Similar to DOCG ASTI, but usually better grapes; lower in alcohol, sweeter, fruitier, often from small producers. Best DOCG MOSCATO from: L Armangia, Bera Walter, Ca'd'Gal, CASCINA FONDA, Caudrina, Il Falcheto, Icardi, Marino, Marco Negri, La Morandina, Perrone, Rivetti, Saracco, Scagliola, Vignaioli di Sante Stefano, Viticoltori Acquese.

Moscato Giallo Aromatic ALTO ADIGE grape made into irresistible dry white, esp LAGEDER, CS CALDARO.

Müller-Thurgau Variety of some interest in TRENTINO-ALTO ADIGE and FRIULI. Leading producers: Lavis, LAGEDER, POJER & SANDRI, Zeni.

Murana, Salvatore ★★★ V.gd MOSCATO and PASSITO di PANTELLERIA.

Muri Gries ★★ V.gd producer of DOC ALTO ADIGE, best is DOC LAGREIN.

Nada, Fiorenzo ★★★ Fine producer of smooth, elegant DOCG BARBARESCO.

Nebbiolo The best red grape of PIEDMONT. Also in VALTELLINA (Lombardy).

Nebbiolo d'Alba Pie DOC r dr (s/sw sp) ★★ 96 97 98 99 00 01 From ALBA (but not BAROLO, BARBARESCO). Often like lighter BAROLO but more approachable. Best from Alario, BRICCO Maiolica, Cascina Chicco, La Contea, Correggia, De Marie, FONTANAFREDDA, GIACOSA, Gianmatteo, Hilberg, MASCARELLO, PRUNOTTO, SANDRONE, VAL DI PRETE. See also ROERO.

Negri See GRUPPO ITALIANO VINI.

Negroamaro Literally "black bitter"; APULIAN red grape with high quality potential. See ALEZIO, BRINDISI, COPERTINO, and SALICE SALENTINO.

Nero d'Avola Sicilian dark red grape (Avola is S of Siracusa) with real promise, alone or in blends.

Niedermayr ★★★ V.gd DOC ALTO ADIGE, esp LAGREIN, PINOT NOIR. Gewurz, SAUVIGNON BLANC, and IGT Euforius (LAGREIN/Cab Sauv) and Aureus (sweet white blend).

Niedrist, Ignaz ★★★ Small, gifted producer of white and red ALTO ADIGE wines (esp LAGREIN, PINOT NOIR, PINOT BLANC, RIESLING).

Nipozzano, Castello di ★★★ FRESCOBALDI estate in RUFINA E of Florence making MONTESODI CHIANTI. The most important outside the CLASSICO zone.

Nittardi ★★→★★★ Up-and-coming CHIANTI CLASSICO estate.

Nosiola (Trentino) T-AA DOC w dr sw ★ DYA Light, fruity white from Nosiola grapes. Also gd VIN SANTO. Best from Castel Noarna, POJER & SANDRI, Giovanni Poli, Pravis, Zeni.

Nozzole ★★→★★★ Famous estate now owned by AMBROGIO FOLONARI, in heart of CHIANTI CLASSICO, N of Greve. Also v.gd Cab Sauv Pareto.

Nuragus di Cagliari Sar DOC w ★★ DYA Lively Sardinian white.

Oasi degli Angeli Benchmark all-MONTEPULCIANO wines from small producer in southern Marches; lush and mouth-filling.

Oberto, Andrea ★★→★★★ Small La Morra producer: top BAROLO, BARBERA D'ALBA.

Oddero Pie ★★→★★★ Well-known La Morra estate for excellent BAROLO (look for Mondocco di Bussia, Rocche di Castiglione, and VIGNA Rionda).

Oltrepò Pavese Lom DOC r w dr sw sp ★→★★★ 14 wines from Pavia province, most named after grapes. Sometimes v.gd PINOT NOIR and SPUMANTE. Top growers: Anteo, Barbacarlo, Casa Re, Frecciarossa, Le Fracce, La Versa co-op, Monsupello, Mazzolino, Ruiz de Cardenas, Travaglino, Vercesi del Castellazzo.

Ornellaia Tus ★★★★ Lodovico ANTINORI-founded estate nr BOLGHERI on the Tuscan coast, now owned by MONDAVI-FRESCOBALDI, with a long list of prestigious wines: excellent Bolgheri DOC Ornellaia, superb IGT Masseto (MERLOT), v.gd Bolgheri DOC Le Serre Nuove and VDT Le Volte.

Orvieto Umb DOC w dr s/sw ★→★★ DYA The classic Umbrian golden white, smooth, substantial; once very dull but recently more interesting, esp when sw. Orvieto CLASSICO is better. Only finest (eg Barberani, Co.Vi.O, Decugnano del Barbi, La Carraia, Palazzone, Vi.C.Or) age well. But see CASTELLO DELLA SALA.

Pacenti, Siro ★★★ Very international-style BRUNELLO and ROSSO DI MONTALCINO.

Pagadebit di Romagna E-R DOC w dr s/sw ★ DYA Pleasant traditional "payer of debts" from around Bertinoro.

Pagani de Marchi New face N of Bolgheri, impressive IGT varietal wines from Cab Sauv, SANGIOVESE and, in particular, MERLOT.

Palazzino, Podere Il ★★★ Small estate with admirable CHIANTI CLASSICO.

Paneretta, Castello della ★★→★★★ To follow for very fine CHIANTI CLASSICO, IGTS Quatrrocentenario, Terrine.

Pancrazi, Marchese ★★→★★★ Estate nr Florence: some of Italy's top PINOT NOIR.

Panizzi ★★→★★★ Makes top VERNACCIA DI SAN GIMIGNANO. Also CHIANTI COLLI Senesi.

Pantelleria Island off the Sicilian coast noted for MOSCATO, particularly PASSITO. Watch for Abraxas, DONNAFUGATA, Nuova Agricoltura.

Parrina Tus DOC r w ★★ Grand estate nr classy resorts of Argentario. Gd white Ansonica, improving reds (SANGIOVESE/Cab Sauv and MERLOT) from MAREMMA.

Parusso ★★★ Marco and Tiziana Parusso make fine BAROLO (eg single-v'yd Bussia VIGNA Rocche and Bussia VIGNA Munie), BARBERA D'ALBA, and DOLCETTO.

Pasqua, Fratelli ★★ Gd producer and bottler of VERONA wines: VALPOLICELLA, AMARONE, SOAVE. Also BARDOLINO and RECIOTO.

Passito (pa) Strong, mostly sw wine from grapes dried on the vine or indoors.

Paternoster ★★★ Top AGLIANICO DEL VULTURE producer, esp Don Anselmo, Villa Rotondo.

Patriglione ★★★ Dense, strong red IGT (NEGROAMARO/MALVASIA Nera). See TAURINO.

Piave Ven DOC r w ★→★★ (r) **97 99'** 00 01 (w) DYA Flourishing DOC NW of Venice for 4 red and 4 white wines named after their grapes. Cab Sauv, MERLOT, and RABOSO reds can all age. Gd examples from Molon, Loredan Gasparini.

Picolit (Colli Orientali del Friuli) F-VG DOC w s/sw sw ★★→★★★★ **95 97** 99 00 01 03 Delicate sweet wine, but with an exaggerated reputation. A little like France's Jurançon. Ages up to 6 yrs, but very overpriced. Best: DORIGO, FELLUGA, Meroi, Perusini, Specogna, VILLA RUSSIZ.

Piedmont (Piemonte) With TUSCANY, the most important Italian region for top-quality wine. Turin is the capital, ASTI and ALBA the wine centres. See BARBARESCO, BARBERA, BAROLO, DOLCETTO, GRIGNOLINO, MOSCATO, etc.

Piemonte Pie DOC r w p (sp) ★→★★ New all-PIEDMONT blanket-DOC inc BARBERA, BONARDA, BRACHETTO, CORTESE, GRIGNOLINO, CHARDONNAY, SPUMANTE, MOSCATO.

Pieropan ★★★ Outstanding SOAVE and RECIOTO: deserving its fame, esp Soave La Rocca and Calvarino, sweet PASSITO della ROCCA.

Pieve di Santa Restituta ★★★ Estate for admirable BRUNELLO DI MONTALCINO, esp Sugarille. Owned by GAJA.

Pigato Lig DOC w ★★ DOC under Riviera Ligure di Ponente. Often outclasses VERMENTINO as Liguria's finest white, with rich texture and structure. Gd from: Bruna, COLLE dei Bardellini, Durin, Feipu, Foresti, Lupi, TERRE ROSSE, Vio.

Pinocchio p w sw ★ Popular in youth, famous for its nose.

Pinot Bianco (Pinot Bl) Popular grape in NE for many DOC wines, generally bland and dry. Best from ALTO ADIGE (top growers: Colterenzio, HOFSTÄTTER, LAGEDER, NIEDRIST, TERLANO, Termeno), COLLIO ★★→★★★ (v.gd from Renato Keber, Aldo Polencic, RUSSIZ SUPERIORE, SCHIOPETTO, VILLA RUSSIZ), and COLLI ORIENTALI ★★→★★★ (best from Zamò & Zamò). ISONZO ★★ (from Masut da Rive).

Pinot Grigio Tasty, low-acid white grape popular in NE. Best from DOCS ALTO ADIGE (SAN MICHELE APPIANO, CALDARO, LAGEDER, Termeno), COLLIO (Renato Keber, LIVON, Aldo Polencic, RUSSIZ SUPERIORE, SCHIOPETTO, Tercic, Terpin, Venica, VILLA RUSSIZ), COLLI ORIENTALI (LIVIO FELLUGA), and ISONZO (Borgo San Daniele, LIS NERIS, Masut da Rive, Pierpaolo Pecorari, VIE DI ROMANS).

Pinot Nero (Pinot Noir) Planted in much of NE Italy. DOC status in ALTO ADIGE (co-op Caldaro, Colterenzio co-op, co-op Cortaccia, HAAS, Haderburg, HOFSTÄTTER, LAGEDER, Laimburg, NIEDERMAYR, Niedrist, SAN MICHELE APPIANO CO-OP, Termeno co-op) and in OLTREPÒ PAVESE (Frecciarossa, Ruiz de Cardenas). Promising trials elsewhere, eg FRIULI (LE DUE TERRE, Masut da Riva), TUSCANY (Ama, FARNETELLA, FONTODI, Pancrazi), and on Mount Etna in SICILY. Also fine from several regions: TRENTINO (Lunelli, Maso Cantanghel, POJER & SANDRI), Lombardy (CA' DEL BOSCO, Ronco Calino), Umbria (ANTINORI), Marches (BOCCADIGABBIA).

Pio Cesare ★★→★★★ Long-established ALBA produce. Esp BAROLO, BARBARESCO.

Planeta ★★★ Top Sicilian estate: Segreta Bianco blend, Segreta ROSSO; outstanding CHARDONNAY, Cab Sauv, Fiano, MERLOT, NERO D'AVOLA (Santa Cecilia).

Podere Small TUSCAN farm, once part of a big estate.

Poggio Antico (Montalcino) ★★★ Admirably consistent, top-level BRUNELLO.

Poggione, Tenuta Il ★★★ Very reliable estate for BRUNELLO, ROSSO DI MONTALCINO.

Pojer & Sandri ★★→★★★ Top TRENTINO producers: red and white, inc SPUMANTE.

Poliziano ★★★→★★★★ Montepulciano estate. Federico Carletti makes superior VINO NOBILE (esp Asinine) and superb IGT Le Stanze (Cab Sauv/MERLOT).

Pomino Tus DOC w r ★★★ r **95 97** 98 99' 01 Fine red and white blends (esp Il Benefizio). Esp from FRESCOBALDI and SELVAPIANA.

Primitivo V.gd red grape for far S, identified with California's Zin. See MANDURIA.

Produttori del Barbaresco ★★→★★★ Co-op and one of DOCG's most reliable producers. Often-outstanding single-v'yd wines (Asili, Montestefano, Ovello).

Prosecco Shorthand in wide use for a glass of dry fizz. But see next.

Prosecco di Conegliano-Valdobbiàdene Ven DOC w s/sw sp (dr) ★★ DYA White grape for light, very dry sp wine. Slight fruity nose: the dry, nicely bitter; the sweet fruity. Sweetest are called Superiore di Cartizze. CARPENE-MALVOLTI: best-known; also Adami, Bisol, Bortolin, Canevel, Case Bianche, Le Colture, Col Salice, Col Vetoraz, Nino Franco, Gregoletto, Ruggeri, Zardetto.

Prunotto, Alfredo ★★★→★★★★ Very serious ALBA company with top BARBARESCO, BAROLO, NEBBIOLO, BARBERA D'ALBA, DOLCETTO, etc. Since 1999 Prunotto (now controlled by ANTINORI) also produces BARBERA D'ASTI (look for Costamiole).

Puglia See APULIA.

Puiatti ★★ Reliable, important producer of COLLIO; also METODO CLASSICO SPUMANTE. Puiatti also owns a FATTORIA in CHIANTI CLASSICO (Casavecchia).

Querciabella ★★★ Leader in CHIANTI CLASSICO. Fine RISERVA, excellent IGT Camartina (SANGIOVESE/Cab Sauv), barrel-fermented white Batàr, new SANGIOVESE/MERLOT.

Quintarelli, Giuseppe ★★★★ True artisan producer of VALPOLICELLA, RECIOTO, and AMARONE, at the top in both quality and price.

Raboso del Piave (now DOC) Ven r ★★ **95 97** 99' 00 01 Powerful, sharp, interesting country red; needs age. Look for Molon.

Ragose, Le ★★→★★★ Family estate, one of VALPOLICELLA's best. AMARONE and RECIOTO top quality; Cab Sauv and VALPOLICELLA v.gd, too.

Rampolla, Castello dei ★★★→★★★★ Fine estate in Panzano in CHIANTI CLASSICO, notable Cab Sauv-based IGT wines Sammarco and Alceo.

Recioto
Wine made of half-dried grapes. Speciality of Veneto since the days of the Venetian empire; has roots in classical Roman wine, Raeticus. Always sweet; sometimes sparkling (drink young). Sweet, concentrated, can be kept for a long time.

Recioto di Gambellara Ven DOC w sw (sp s/sw DYA) ★ Mostly half-sparkling and industrial. Best is strong and sweet. Look for La Biancara.

Recioto di Soave Ven DOCG w s/sw (sp) ★★★ **90 91 92 93 94 95** 97 98 99 00 01 03 SOAVE made from selected half-dried grapes: sweet, fruity, slightly almondy; high alcohol. Outstanding from ANSELMI, Gini, PIEROPAN, Tamellini.

Recioto della Valpolicella Ven DOC r s/sw (sp) ★★→★★★ **95 97** 98 00 01 Potentially excellent rich and tangy red. V.gd from Stefano Accordini, Serègo Alighieri, ALLEGRINI, Baltieri, BOLLA, BRUNELLI, BUSSOLA, Campagnola, Castellani, DAL FORNO, LE RAGOSE, QUINTARELLI, LE SALETTE, Speri, TEDESCHI, Trabucchi, CS VALPOLICELLA, Villa Bellini, Villa Monteleone, and Viviani.

Recioto della Valpolicella Amarone See AMARONE.

Refosco (dal Peduncolo Rosso) r ★★→★★★ 95 96 97' 99' 00 01 Interesting, full, dark, tannic red for ageing. Possibly the same grape as Mondeuse of Savoie. Best comes from FRIULI-VENEZIA GIULIA DOC COLLI ORIENTALI: v.gd from FELLUGA (LIVIO) and Miani; gd from Dorigo, Moschioni, Ronchi di Manzano, Venica, Ca Bolani and Denis Montanara in Aquileia DOC. Often gd value.

Regaleali See TASCA D'ALMERITA.

Ribolla (Colli Orientali del Friuli and Collio) F-VG DOC w ★→★★ DYA Highly acidic NE white. The best comes from COLLIO. Top estates: La Castellada, Damijan, Fliegl, GRAVNER, Il Carpino, Primosic, Radikon, Tercic, Terpin.

Ricasoli Famous TUSCAN family, "inventors" of CHIANTI, whose CHIANTI CLASSICO is named after its BROLIO estate and castle. Other Ricasolis own Castello di Cacchiano and Rocca di Montegrossi.

Riecine Tus r ★★★ First-class CHIANTI CLASSICO estate at Gaiole, created by its late English owner, John Dunkley. Also fine IGT La Gioia SANGIOVESE.

Riesling Used to mean Riesling Italico or Welschriesling. German (Rhine) Riesling now ascendant. Best: DOC ALTO ADIGE ★★ (esp HOFSTÄTTER, Laimburg Ignaz Niedrist, Kuenhof, co-op La Vis, Unterortl); DOC OLTREPÒ PAVESE (Lom) ★★ (Brega, Frecciarossa, Le Fracce); excellent from RONCO del Gelso and Vie di Romans (DOC ISONZO). V.gd from Le Vigne di San Pietro (Ven), JERMANN, Vajra (Pie).

Ripasso VALPOLICELLA re-fermented on AMARONE grape skins to make a more complex, longer-lived and fuller wine. First-class is MASI's Campo Fiorin.

Riserva Wine aged for a statutory period, usually in casks or barrels.

Riunite One of the world's largest co-op cellars, nr Reggio Emilia, producing huge quantities of LAMBRUSCO and other wines.

Rivera ★★→★★★ Reliable winemakers at Andria in APULIA. ★★★ CASTEL DEL MONTE Il Falcone RISERVA; v.gd Cappellaccio; VIGNA al Monte; Puer Apuliae.

Riviera del Garda Bresciano Lom DOC w p r (sp) ★→★★ r 97 99 00 01 Simple, sometimes charming cherry-pink CHIARETTO, neutral white from SW Garda. Esp from: Ca' dei Frati, Comincioli, Costaripa, Monte Cigogna.

Rivetti, Giorgio (La Spinetta) ★★★→★★★★ Fine MOSCATO d'Asti, excellent BARBERA, interesting IGT Pin, series of top single-v'yd BARBARESCOS. Now owner of v'yds both in the BAROLO and the CHIANTI Colli Pisane DOCGS.

Rocca, Bruno ★★★ Young producer with admirable BARBARESCO (Rabajà) and other ALBA wines.

Rocca delle Macìe ★★ Large CHIANTI CLASSICO winemaker nr Castellina.

Rocche dei Manzoni ★★★ Modernist estate at Monforte d'Alba. V.gd oaky BAROLO (esp VIGNA Big, VIGNA d'la Roul, Cappella di Stefano, Pianpolvere), BRICCO Manzoni (pioneer BARBERA/NEBBIOLO blend), Valentino Brut.

Roero Pie DOC r ★★ 96 97' 98' 99' 00 01' Evolving former "drink-me-quick" NEBBIOLO. Can be delicious. Best: Almondo, Ca' Rossa, Cascina Chicco, Correggia, Funtanin, Malvirà, Monchiero-Carbone, Taliano, Val de Prete.

Roero Arneis See ARNEIS.

Ronco Term for a hillside v'yd in N Italy, esp FRIULI-VENEZIA GIULIA.

Ronco del Gnemiz ★★★ Small estate, very fine COLLI ORIENTALI DEL FRIULI.

Rosato Rosé.

Rosato del Salento Ap p ★★ DYA From nr BRINDISI; can be strong, but often really juicy and gd. See COPERTINO, SALICE SALENTO for producers.

Rossese di Dolceacqua Lig DOC r ★★ DYA Quite rare, fragrant, light red of the Riviera. Gd from Foresti, Giuncheo, Guglielmi, Lupi, Terre Bianche.

Rosso Red.

Rosso Cònero Mar DOC r ★★→★★★ 94 95 97' 98 00' 01' Some of Italy's best MONTEPULCIANO (the grape, that is: GAROFOLI's Grosso Agontano, Moroder's RC Dorico, Le Terrazze's Sassi Neri, Visioni di J. Also gd: Fazi-Battaglia, Lanari, Leopardi Dittajuti, Malacari, Moncaro, Poggio Morelli, UMANI RONCHI.

Rosso di Montalcino Tus DOC r ★★→★★★ **97' 99'** 00 01' DOC for younger wines from BRUNELLO grapes. For growers see BRUNELLO DI MONTALCINO.

Rosso di Montepulciano Tus DOC r ★★ **97' 98' 99'** 00 Equivalent of the last for junior VINO NOBILE. For growers see VINO NOBILE DI MONTEPULCIANO. While ROSSO DI MONTALCINO is increasingly expensive, Rosso di Montepulciano offers value.

Rosso Piceno Mar DOC r ★★ **95 97'** 98' 00' 01' Stylish MONTEPULCIANO/SANGIOVESE, SUPERIORE from classic zone nr Ascoli. Best inc: Boccadigabbia, Bucci, COLLI Ripani, De Angelis, Fonte della Luna, Forano, Laila, Le Caniette, Laurentina, Saladini Pilastri, San Savino, Velenosi Ercole, Villamagna, Villa Ragnola.

Rubesco ★★ The excellent popular red of LUNGAROTTI; see TORGIANO.

Ruchè (also Rouchè/Rouchet) Rare old grape of French origin; fruity, fresh, rich-scented red wine (s/sw). Ruchè di Castagnole Monferrato is recent DOC. Look for Borgogone, Dezzani, Garetto. SCARPA'S Rouchet Briccorosa: dry (★★★).

Ruffino ★→★★★ Outstanding CHIANTI merchant at Pontassieve, E of Florence. Best are RISERVA Ducale and Santedame. V.gd IGT CHARDONNAY Solatia, SANGIOVESE/Cab Sauv Modus. Owns Lodola Nuova in MONTEPULCIANO for VINO NOBILE DI MONTEPULCIANO, and Greppone Mazzi in MONTALCINO for BRUNELLO DI MONTALCINO. Excellent new SANGIOVESE/Colorino blend Romitorio from Santedame estate. Recent purchase: Borgo Conventi estate in FRIULI-VENEZIA GIULIA.

Rufina ★★★ Important sub-region of CHIANTI in the hills E of Florence. Best wines from Basciano, CASTELLO del Trebbio, CASTELLO DI NIPOZZANO (FRESCOBALDI), Colognole, Frascole, SELVAPIANA, Tenuta Bossi, Travignoli.

Russiz Superiore (Collio) See FELLUGA (MARCO).

Sagrantino di Montefalco See MONTEFALCO.

Sala, Castello della ★★→★★★ ANTINORI estate at ORVIETO. Campograde is the regular white. Top wine is Cervaro della Sala, oak-aged CHARDONNAY/GRECHETTO. Muffato della Sala is one of Italy's best botrytis wines. PINOT NOIR also gd.

Salice Salento Ap DOC r ★★→★★★ **93 94' 95** 97' **97'** 99 00 01 Resonant but clean and quenching red from NEGROAMARO grapes. RISERVA after 2 yrs. Top makers: CANDIDO, LEONE DE CASTRIS, Due Palme, TAURINO, Valle dell'Asso.

San Felice ★★→★★★ Picturesque CHIANTI resort/estate. Fine CLASSICO RISERVA Poggio ROSSO. Also red IGT Vigorello and BRUNELLO DI MONTALCINO Campogiovanni.

San Gimignano Famous TUSCAN city of towers and its dry white VERNACCIA. Also very fine red wines: Cesani, Cusona, FALCHINI, Fontaleoni, La Rampa di Fugnano, Le Calcinaie, Mormoraia, Palagetto, Palagione, PARADISO.

San Giusto a Rentennano ★★★→★★★★ One of the best CHIANTI CLASSICO producers (★★★). Delicious but very rare VIN SANTO. Superb SANGIOVESE IGT Percarlo (★★★★).

San Guido, Tenuta See SASSICAIA.

San Leonardo ★★★ Top estate in TRENTINO with outstanding San Leonardo (Cab Sauv) and gd Trentino DOC MERLOT.

San Michele Appiano Top ALTO ADIGE co-op. Look for Sanct Valentin (★★★) selections: CHADONNAY, PINOT GRIGIO, SAUVIGNON BLANC, Cab Sauv, PINOT NOIR, Gewurz.

Sandrone, Luciano ★★★ Exponent of new-style BAROLO vogue with v.gd BAROLO Cannubi Boschi, Le Vigne, DOLCETTO, BARBERA D'ALBA, LANGHE ROSSO, and NEBBIOLO D'ALBA.

Sangiovese (Sangioveto) Principal red grape of central Italy. Top performance only in TUSCANY, where there are many forms inc CHIANTI, VINO NOBILE, BRUNELLO, MORELLINO, etc. Very popular: S di Romagna, San Valentino, Terragens, Trer (E-R DOC), a pleasant standard red. V.gd from La Berta, Berti, Calonga, Drei Donà, Madonia, Poderi dei Nespoli, San Patrignano, Tre Monti, Zerbina, IGT Ronco del Ginestre, Ronco dei Ciliegi from CASTELLUCCIO. V.gd MONTEFALCO ROSSO and TORGIANO (Umbria), sometimes gd from the Marches.

Santa Maddalena (or St-Magdalener) T-AA DOC r ★→★★ DYA Typical SCHIAVA ALTO ADIGE red. Sometimes light with bitter aftertaste; or warm, smooth and fruity, esp: CANTINA SOCIALE St-Magdalena (Huck am Bach), Gojer, Hans Rottensteiner (Premstallerhof), Heinrich Rottensteiner, Georg Ramoser, Josephus Mayr.

Santa Margherita Large Veneto (Portogruaro) merchants: Veneto (Torresella), ALTO ADIGE (Kettmeir), TUSCANY (Lamole di Lamole and Vistarenni), and Lombardy (CA' DEL BOSCO).

Santadi ★★★ Consistently fine wines from SARDINIAN co-op, esp DOC CARIGNANO DEL SULCIS Grotta Rossa, TERRE BRUNE, ROCCA Rubia and IGT Baie Rosse (Carignano), Vermentino Villa Solais, Villa di Chiesa (VERMENTINO/CHARDONNAY).

Santi See GRUPPO ITALIANO VINI.

Saracco, Paolo ★★★ Small estate with top MOSCATO D'ASTI.

Sardinia (Sardegna). Major potential, at times evidenced in excellent wines, eg TERRE BRUNE from SANTADI, Turriga from ARGIOLAS, Arbeskia and Dule from Gabbas, VERMENTINO of CAPICHERA, CANNONAU RISERVAS of Jerzu, and SELLA & MOSCA.

Sartarelli ★★★ One of top VERDICCHIO DEI CASTELLI DI JESI producers, (Tralivio), outstanding, rare Verdicchio VENDEMMIA Tardiva (Contrada Balciana).

Sassicaia Tus r ★★★★ 85' 88' 90' 93 95' 96 97' 98 99 01 One of the first Cab Sauvs, outstanding in 1970s and 1980s. Extraordinarily influential, from the Tenuta San Guido of Incisa della Rocchetta family at BOLGHERI. Promoted from SUPER TUSCAN VDT to special sub-zone status in Bolgheri DOC, but quality wobbling now.

Satta, Michele ★★★ V.gd DOC BOLGHERI, IGT red blend Piastraia.

Sauvignon Blanc White variety working well in the NE, best from the following DOCS: ALTO ADIGE, COLLIO, COLLI ORIENTALI, ISONZO.

Savuto Cal DOC r p ★★ 95 97' 98 99 00 01 Fragrant, juicy red from the provinces of Cosenza and Catanzaro. Best producer is Odoardi.

Scarpa ★★→★★★ Old-fashioned house with BARBERA D'ASTI (La Bogliona), rare Rouchet (RUCHÈ), v.gd DOLCETTO, BAROLO, BARBARESCO.

Scavino, Paolo ★★★ Successful modern-style BAROLO producer. Sought-after single-v'yd wines: Bric del Fiasc, Cannubi, Carobric, and Rocche dell'Annunziata; also oak-aged BARBERA and Langhe Corale.

Schiava High-yielding red grape of TRENTINO-ALTO ADIGE, used for light reds such as LAGO DI CALDARO, SANTA MADDALENA, etc.

Schiopetto, Mario ★★★→★★★★ Legendary late COLLIO pioneer with 25,000-case winery; v.gd DOC SAUVIGNON BLANC, PINOT BIANCO, TOCAI, IGT blend Blanc de Rosis, etc. Also operates with customary elegance in COLLI ORIENTALI DEL FRIULI.

Sciacchetrà See CINQUETERRE.

Secco Dry.

Sella & Mosca ★★ Major SARDINIAN grower and merchant with very pleasant white TORBATO and light, fruity VERMENTINO Cala Viola (DYA). Gd Alghero DOC Marchese di Villamarina (Cab Sauv) and Tanca Farrà (CANNONAU/Cab Sauv). Also interesting port-like Angheiu Ruju. A safe bet.

Selvapiana ★★★ Top CHIANTI RUFINA estate. Best wines are RISERVA Bucerchiale and IGT Fornace. Also fine red DOC POMINO.

Sforzato See VALTELLINA.

Sicily Island in full creative ferment, both with native grapes (NERO D'AVOLA, Frappato, Inzolia, Grecanico) and international varieties. To watch: Benanti, Bonaccorsi, Ceusi, Colosi, COS, Cottanera, Cusumano, De Bartoli, DONNAFUGATA, DUCA DI SALAPARUTA, Fatasci, Firriato, Fondo Antico, Gulfi-Ramada, Morgante, MURANA, Principe di Butera (ZONIN), PLANETA, Rapitalà, Santa Anastasia, SIV, Spadafora, TASCA D'ALMERITA, VECCHIO SAMPERI, Zemmer.

Sizzano Pie DOC r ★★ 90 93 95 96' 97' 98 99' 00 01 Full-bodied red from Sizzano, (Novara); mostly NEBBIOLO. Ages up to 10 yrs. Esp: Bianchi, Dessilani.

Soave Ven DOC w ★→★★ DYA Famous white. Should be fresh, smooth, limpid. Standards rising (at last). Soave CLASSICO: at best intense fruit/mineral flavours. Esp PIEROPAN; also Bolla, La Cappuccina, Fattori & Graney, Gini, Guerrieri-Rizzardi, Inama, Portinari, Pra, Tamellini, TEDESCHI, Ca' Rugate.

Solaia Tus r ★★★★ 85 88 90 93 94' 95 96 97' 98 99' 00 01' Very fine B'x-style VDT of Cab Sauv and a little SANGIOVESE from ANTINORI; first made in 1978. Italy's best Cab Sauv in the 1990s and great wine by any standards.

Solopaca Cam DOC r w ★ 94 95 97 99 00 01 Rather sharp red and soft, dry white from nr Benevento. Some promise: esp Antica Masseria Venditti.

Sorì Term for a high S-, SE- or SW-oriented v'yd in PIEDMONT.

Sovana New MAREMMA DOC; inland nr Pitigliano. Look for SANGIOVESE, Ciliegiolo from Tenuta Roccaccia, Pitigliano, Ripa, Sassotondo, Cab Sauv from ANTINORI.

Spanna Local name for NEBBIOLO in a variety of N PIEDMONT zones (BOCA, BRAMATERRA, FARA, GATTINARA, GHEMME, LESSONA, SIZZANO).

Sportoletti ★★★ V.gd wines from Spello, nr ASSISI in Umbria. Esp Villa Fidelia.

Spumante Sparkling, as in sweet ASTI or many gd dry wines, inc both METODO CLASSICO (best from TRENTINO, ALTO ADIGE, FRANCIACORTA, PIEDMONT, OLTREPÒ PAVESE, some v.gd also from FRIULI and Veneto) and tank-made cheapos.

Stravecchio Very old.

Südtirol The local name of German-speaking ALTO ADIGE.

Super Tuscans Term coined for innovative wines from TUSCANY, often involving pure SANGIOVESE or international varieties, barriques, and elevated prices.

Superiore Wine with more ageing than normal DOC and 0.5–1% more alcohol.

Tasca d'Almerita ★★★ Historic SICILIAN producer owned by noble family (between Palermo and Caltanissetta to the SE). Gd IGT red, white, and ROSATO Regaleali, v.gd ROSSO, impressive CHARDONNAY and Cab Sauv.

Taurasi Cam DOCG r ★★★ 90' 93' 94' 95 97' 98 99 00 01 The best Campanian red. Tannic when young. RISERVA after 4 yrs. V.gd from FEUDI DI SAN GREGORIO, Gaggiano, Mastroberardino, Molettieri, and Villa Raiano.

Taurino, Cosimo ★★★ Tip-top producer of Salento-APULIA, v.gd SALICE SALENTO, VDT Notarpanoro, and IGT PATRIGLIONE ROSSO.

Tedeschi, Fratelli ★★→★★★ Very reliable and v.gd producer of VALPOLICELLA, AMARONE, RECIOTO. Gd Capitel San Rocco red IGT.

Tenute dei Vallarono New project of Gancia family, high-class BARBERA D'ASTI and LANGHE ROSSO near Canelli in ASTI SPUMANTE territory.

Terlano T-AA w ★★→★★★ DYA Terlano DOC incorporated into ALTO ADIGE. AA Terlano DOC is applicable to 8 varietal whites, esp SAUVIGNON BLANC. Terlaner in German. Esp from CS Terlano, LAGEDER, NIEDERMAYR, NIEDRIST.

Teroldego Rotaliano T-AA DOC r p ★★→★★★ 95 97 99 00 01 02 Attractive blackberry-scented red; slightly bitter aftertaste; can age very well. Esp FORADORI'S. Also gd from CA'VIT, Dorigati, Endrizzi, MEZZACORONA'S RISERVA, Zeni.

Terre Brune Sard r ★★★ Splendid earthy Carignano/Bovelladda blend from SANTADI, a flag-carrier for SARDINIA.

Terre di Franciacorta Lom DOC r w ★★ 97 99 00 01 Usually pleasant reds (blends of Cab Sauv, BARBERA, NEBBIOLO, MERLOT); quite fruity and balanced whites (CHARDONNAY, PINOT GRIGIO). Best producers: see FRANCIACORTA DOCG.

Terre Rosse ★★ Pioneering small estate nr Bologna. Its Cab Sauv, CHARDONNAY, PINOT BIANCO, RIESLING, even Viognier, were trail-blazing wines for the region.

Terre da Vino ★→★★★ Association of 27 PIEDMONT co-ops and private estates inc most local DOCS. Best: Barbaresco La Casa in Collina, BAROLO Podere Parussi, BARBERA d'Asti La Luna e I Falò.

Terriccio, Castello di ★★★ Estate S of Livorno: excellent IGT Lupicaia, v.gd IGT Tassinaia, both Cab Sauv/MERLOT blends. Impressive new IGT Terriccio, an unusual blend of various French grapes.

Tignanello Tus r ★★★→★★★★ 88 90 93 95 96 97' 98 99' 00 01' Pioneer and leader of international-style TUSCAN reds, made by ANTINORI. Needs bottle-age.

Tocai Mild, smooth white (no relation of Hungarian Tokay) of NE. DOC also in Ven and Lom (★→★★), but producers are most proud of it in FRIULI-VENEZIA GIULIA (esp COLLIO and COLLI ORIENTALI) ★★→★★★. Best producers: Aldo Polencic, BORGO DEL TIGLIO, Borgo San Daniele, LE VIGNE DI ZAMO, LIVIO FELLUGA, Masut da Rive, Meroi, Mirani, Renato Keber, RONCO del Gelso, RONCO DI GNEMIZ, RUSSIZ SUPERIORE, SCHIOPETTO, Venica & Venica, VILLA RUSSIZ.

Tommasina Vestini Campagnano Small producer N of Naples specializing in forgotten local grapes, excellent results from Casavecchia, Pallagrello Bianco, and Pallagrello Rosso.

Torgiano Umb DOC r w p (sp) ★★ and **Torgiano, Rosso Riserva** Umb DOCG r ★★→★★★ 90 93 94 95 97 99 00 01 Gd red from Umbria, resembles CHIANTI CLASSICO in style. RUBESCO: standard. RISERVA VIGNA Montecchi has been outstanding in vintages such as 75, 79, 85; keeps for many yrs.

Traminer Aromatico T-AA DOC w ★★→★★★ DYA (German: Gewürz) Delicate, aromatic, soft. Best from: various co-ops (Caldaro, Colterenzio, Prima & Nuova, SAN MICHELE APPIANO, TERLANO, Termeno) plus Abbazia di Novacella, HAAS, HOFSTÄTTER, Kuenhof, LAGEDER, Laimberg, NIEDERMAYR.

Trebbiano Principal white grape of TUSCANY, found all over Italy. Ugni Blanc in French. Sadly, a waste of gd v'yd space, with very rare exceptions.

Trebbiano d'Abruzzo Ab DOC w ★→★★ DYA Gentle, neutral, slightly tannic white from region of Pescara. Best producer: VALENTINI (also MONTEPULCIANO D'ABRUZZO), but challenged by Masciarelli; Nicodemi, Valentina, and Valori also v.gd.

Trentino T-AA DOC r w dr sw ★→★★★ DOC for 20 wines, most named after grapes. Best: CHARDONNAY, PINOT BIANCO, MARZEMINO, TEROLDEGO. Region's capital is Trento.

Triacca ★★→★★★ V.gd producer of VALTELLINA; also owns estates in TUSCANY (CHIANTI CLASSICO: La Madonnina; MONTEPULCIANO: Santavenere. All ★★).

Trinoro, Tenuta di ★★★ Isolated and exceptional TUSCAN red wine estate (B'x varieties) in DOC Val d'Orcia between MONTEPULCIANO and MONTALCINO. Early vintages of Cab Sauv/Petit Verdot TRINORO are jaw-dropping. Andrea Franchetti is now developing another project on Mount Etna in SICILY.

Tuscany (Toscana) Italy's central wine region, inc DOCS CHIANTI, MONTALCINO, MONTEPULCIANO, etc, regional IGT Toscana and of course SUPER TUSCANS.

Uberti ★★→★★★ Producer of DOCG FRANCIACORTA. V.gd Terre di Franciacorta (r w).

Umani Ronchi ★★→★★★ Leading Marches merchant and grower, esp for VERDICCHIO (Casal di Serra, Plenio), ROSSO CONERO Cumaro white IGT Le Busche, red IGT Pelago.

Vajra, Giuseppe Domenico ★★★ V.gd consistent BAROLO producer, esp for BARBERA, BAROLO, DOLCETTO, LANGHE, etc. Also an interesting (not fizzy) FREISA.

Valcalepio Lom DOC r w ★→★★ From nr Bergamo. Pleasant red; lightly scented fresh white. Gd from Brugherata, CASTELLO di Grumello, Monzio.

Val di Cornia Tus DOC r p w ★★→★★★ 95 97 98 99' 00 01' New DOC nr Livorno, competing in quality with BOLGHERI. Many v.gd wines from SANGIOVESE, Cab Sauv, MERLOT, and MONTEPULCIANO. Look for: Ambrosini, Jacopo Banti, Botrona, Bulichella, Il Bruscello, Gualdo del Re, Incontri, Montepeloso (Gabbro, Nardo), Petra, Le Pianacce, Russo, San Giusto, San Luigi, San Michele, Suveraia, Tenuta Vignale, Tua Rita (Redigaffi), and Villa Monte Rico.

Valdadige T-AA DOC r w dr s/sw ★ Name for the simple wines of the ADIGE Valley – in German "Etschtaler".

Valentini, Edoardo ★★★ The grand tradition and, with Gianni Mascerelli, the best maker of MONTEPULCIANO and TREBBIANO D'ABRUZZO.

Valgella See VALTELLINA.

Valle d'Aosta VdA DOC r w p ★★ Regional DOC for more than 20 Alpine wines inc: Premetta, Fumin, Blanc de Morgex et de La Salle, Chambave, Nus Malvoisie, Arnad Montjovet, Torrette, Donnas, and Enfer d'Arvier.

Valle Isarco (Eisacktal) T-AA DOC w ★★ DYA AA Valle Isarco DOC is applicable to 7 varietal wines made NE of Bolzano. Gd Gewürz, MÜLLER-THURGAU, RIESLING, and SILVANER. Top producers: CS Eisacktaler, Abbasid di Novacella, Kuenhof.

Vallone Ap w→★★★ Always better DOC BRINDISI and DOC SALICE SALENTO; outstanding, very concentrated red IGT from dried NEGROAMARO grapes (Gratticaia).

Valpolicella Ven DOC r ★→★★★ (Superiore) **95 97 98** 00 01 03 (Others) DYA Attractive red from nr VERONA; best young. Can be very light, but the best are concentrated, complex and merit higher prices. Delicate nutty scent, slightly bitter taste (but beware junk sold in big bottles). CLASSICO more restricted; SUPERIORE is 12% abv and 1 yr of age. Best (★★★) DAL FORNO and QUINTARELLI. Gd from Stefano Accordino, Bertani, BOLLA, Brunelli, BUSSOLA, Campagnola, Michele Castellani, Guerrieri-Rizzardi, MASI, Mazzi, Pasqua, LE RAGOSE, LE SALETTE, Sant' Antonio, Speri, TEDESCHI, Tommasi, CS VALPOLICELLA Villa Monteleone, and ZENATO. Interesting IGTs developing new Valpolicella style: MASI's Toar and Osar, ALLEGRINI's La Grola, La Poja, Palazzo della Torre (★★★).

Valtellina Lom DOC r ★★→★★★ **90 95 96 97** 98 99' 00 01 03 DOC for tannic wines: mainly from Chiavennasca (NEBBIOLO) in N Alpine Sondrio province. V.gd SUPERIORE DOCG from Grumello, Inferno, Sassella, Valgella v'yds. Best: Caven Camuna, Conti Sertoli-Salis, Fay, Nera, Nino Negri, Rainoldi, TRIACCA. Sforzato is the most concentrated type of Valtellina; similar to AMARONE.

Vecchio Old.

Vecchio Samperi Si ★★★ MARSALA-like VDT from outstanding estate. Best is barrel-aged 30 yrs, not unlike amontillado sherry. The owner, Marco De Bartoli, also makes the best DOC MARSALAS and a gd dry Cattarato.

Vendemmia Harvest or vintage.

Verdicchio dei Castelli di Jesi Mar DOC w (sp) ★★→★★★ DYA Ancient fresh, pale white from nr Ancona, now fruity, well-structured, gd value. Also CLASSICO. Esp Bonci-Vallerosa, Brunori, Bucci, Casalfarneto, Cimarelli, Colonnara, Coroncino, FAZI-BATTAGLIA, Fonte della Luna, GAROFOLI, Laila, Lucangeli Aymerich di Laconi, Mancinelli, Monte Shiavo, Sta Barbara, SARTARELLI, UMANI RONCHI.

Verdicchio di Matelica Mar DOC w (sp) ★★→★★★ DYA Similar to above, smaller, less known, longer lasting. Esp Belisario, Bisci, San Biagio, La Monacesca.

Verduno Pie DOC r ★★ (DYA) Pale red with spicy perfume, from Pelaverga grape. Gd producers: Alessandria and Castello di Verduno.

Verduzzo (Colli Orientali del Friuli) F-VG DOC w dr s/sw sw ★★→★★★ Full-bodied white from a native grape. Ramandolo is highly regarded sub-zone. Top makers: Dario Coos, DORIGO, Giovanni Dri. Superb sw VDT from LIS NERIS in ISONZO.

Verduzzo (del Piave) Ven DOC w ★★ DYA A dull little white wine.

Vermentino Lig w ★★ DYA Best seafood white of Riviera, esp from Pietra Ligure and San Remo. DOC is Riviera Ligure di Ponente. See PIGATO. Esp gd: Colle dei Bardellini, Durin, Lambruschi, La Rocca di San Niccolao, Lunae Bosoni, Lupi, Picedi Benettini. Also Tuscan coast: ANTINORI, SATTA, Tenuta Vignale.

Vermentino di Gallura Sar DOCG w ★★→★★★ DYA Soft, dry, strong white of N Sardinia. Esp from CS di Gallura, CS del Vermentino, CAPICHERA.

Vernaccia di Oristano Sar DOC w dr (sw fz) ★→★★★ **71' 80' 85' 86' 87 88 90'** 91' 93' 94' 95' 97' 98 99 00 01 Sardinian speciality, like light sherry, a touch bitter, full-bodied. SUPERIORE 15.5% alcohol, 3 yrs of age. Top producer: CONTINI.

Vernaccia di San Gimignano Tus DOCG w ★→★★ DYA Renaissance favourite, then ordinary tourist wine. Much recent improvement (renaissance even), now newly DOCG with tougher production laws. Best: Cusona, Cesani, FALCHINI, Fontaleoni, Le Calcinaie, Il Paradiso, Montenidoli, Palagetto, Palagione, PANIZZI, Rampa di Fugnano, TERUZZI E PUTHOD.

Verona Capital of the Veneto region (home of VALPOLICELLA, BARDOLINO, SOAVE, etc) and seat of Italy's splendid annual April wine fair "Vinitaly".

Verrazzano, Castello di ★★→★★★ V.gd CHIANTI CLASSICO estate nr Greve.

Vicchiomaggio ★★→★★★ CHIANTI CLASSICO estate nr Greve.

Vie di Romans ★★★ Gifted young producer Gianfranco Gallo has built up his father's ISONZO estate to top FRIULI status. Excellent Isonzo CHARDONNAY, PINOT GRIGIO, SAUVIGNON BLANC, RIELSING, and white blend called Flors di Uis.

Vietti ★★★ Exemplary producer of characterful PIEDMONT wines, inc BAROLO, BARBARESCO, BARBERA D'ALBA and D'ASTI at Castiglione Falletto in BAROLO region.

Vigna or vigneto A single v'yd (but unlike elsewhere in the world, higher quality than that for generic DOC is not required in Italy).

Vignalta ★★ Top producer in COLLI EUGANEI near Padova (Veneto); v.gd COLLI Euganei Cab Sauv RISERVA and MERLOT/Cab Sauv "Gemola".

Vignamaggio ★★→★★★ Historic, beautiful, v.gd CHIANTI CLASSICO estate nr Greve.

Villa ★★→★★★ Top producer of DOCG FRANCIACORTA, also v.gd red DOC TERRE DI FRANCIACORTA (Gradoni).

Villa Matilde ★★★ Top Campania producer of IGT VIGNA Camarato, Eleusi PASSITO, Falerno ROSSO and BIANCO (VIGNA Caracci).

Villa Russiz ★★★ Impressive w DOC COLLIO Goriziano: v.gd SAUVIGNON BLANC and MERLOT (esp "de la Tour" selections), PINOT BIANCO, PINOT GRIGIO, TOCAI, CHARDONNAY.

Vin Santo or Vinsanto, Vin(o) Santo Term for certain strong, sweet wines, esp in TUSCANY: usually PASSITO. Can be very fine both in TUSCANY and TRENTINO.

Vin Santo Toscano Tus w s/sw ★→★★★ Aromatic, rich, and smooth. Aged in very small barrels called *caratelli*. Can be as astonishing as expensive, but a gd one is very rare and top producers are always short of it. Best from AVIGNONESI, CAPEZZANA, CORZANO & PATERNO, Fattoria del Cerro, FELSINA, ISOLE E OLENA, ROCCA DI MONTEGROSSI, SAN GIUSTO A RENTENNANO, SAN GERVASIO, SELVAPIANA.

Vino da arrosto "Wine for roast meat" – ie gd, robust dry red.

Vino Nobile di Montepulciano Tus DOCG r ★★★ 90 93 95' 97' 98 99' 00 01 Impressive SANGIOVESE with bouquet and style but often very tannic, now making its name and fortune. RISERVA after 3 yrs. Best estates inc AVIGNONESI, Bindella, BOSCARELLI, Canneto, Le Casalte, Fattoria del Cerro, Contucci, Dei, Fassati, Le Berne, La Bracesca, La Calonica, La Ciarliana, I Cipressi, Icario, Macchione, Nottola, Paterno, POLIZIANO, Romeo, Salcheto, Trerose, Valdipiatta, Vecchia Cantina (look for Briareo), Villa Sant'Anna. So far reasonably priced.

Vino novello Italy's equivalent of France's *primeurs* (as in Beaujolais).

Vino da tavola (vdt) "Table wine": the humblest class of Italian wine. No specific geographical or other claim to fame, but occasionally some excellent wines which do not fit into official categories. See IGT.

Vintage Tunina F-VG w ★★★ A notable blended white from JERMANN estate.

Vivaldi-Arunda ★★→★★★ Winemaker Josef Reiterer makes top SUDTIROL sparkling wines. Best: Extra Brut RISERVA, Cuvée Marianna.

Voerzio, Roberto ★★★→★★★★ Young BAROLO pace-setter. Top single-v'yd BAROLOS: Brunate, Cerequio, Sarmassa, Serra; impressive BARBERA D'ALBA.

Volpaia, Castello di ★★→★★★ First-class CHIANTI CLASSICO estate at Radda.

VQPRD "Vini di Qualità Prodotti in Regione Delimitata" on DOC labels.

Zanella, Maurizio Creator of CA' DEL BOSCO. His name is on his top Cab Sauv/ MERLOT blend, one of Italy's best.

Zenato Ven ★★→★★★ Very reliable estate for VALPOLICELLA, SOAVE, AMARONE.

Zerbina, Fattoria ★★★ New leader in Romagna; best ALBANA DOCG to date (rich PASSITO: Scacco Matto), gd SANGIOVESE; barrique-aged IGT Marzieno.

Zibibbo Si ★★ Local PANTELLERIA name for Muscat of Alexandria. Gd: Murana.

Zonin ★→★★★ One of Italy's biggest private estates, based at GAMBELLARA, with DOC and DOCG VALPOLICELLA, etc. Also found in ASTI, CHIANTI CLASSICO (Castello di Albola), SAN GIMIGNANO, FRIULI, Sicily, Apulia, and throughout Italy. And now in Virginia (US). Quality on the rise under chief winemaker Franco Giacosa.

ITALY

Germany

More heavily shaded
areas are the wine
growing regions

The following abbreviations of
regional names are used in the text:

Bad	Baden
Frank	Franken
M-M	Mittelmosel
M-S-R	Mosel-Saar-Ruwer
Na	Nahe
Rhg	Rheingau
Rhh	Rheinhessen
Pfz	Pfalz
Würt	Württemberg

Hamburg

Bremen

Berlin ○

Hanover

Leipzig ○

SAALE-UNSTRUT   **SACHSEN**

Erfurt ○   Dresden ○

Bonn ○

AHR   **MITTELRHEIN**

Koblenz ○   **RHEINGAU**

MOSEL-   Frankfurt ○

SAAR-RUWER   **RHEINHESSEN**   **FRANKEN**

Trier ○   Mannheim ○   Würzburg ○

NAHE   **HESSISCHE-**

PFALZ   **BERGSTRASSE**   Nürnberg ○

WÜRTTEMBERG

Stuttgart ○

Baden Baden ○   Danube

BADEN

Freiburg ○   München ○

Bodensee

Rhine

Elbe

Weser

Main

German wines should be enjoying a worldwide boom today. New ideas, easier labelling on many wines, reasonable prices, and an unprecedented string of sixteen good-to-great vintages are all in their favour. Yet in most places outside Germany they are still a hard sell. What is wrong? Pure, penetrating flavours and low-to-moderate alcohol should be ideal for modern tastes. Instead, Germany has everyone confused. Kabinett, Spätlese, and Auslese might all be sweet, dry, or in the middle. Their appellations might mean single vineyards, whole communes, or entire regions. This, and the failure to create excitement for their wines, is a turn-off for the average consumer.

This is a pivotal time in the politics of German wine. With the 2000 vintage two new designations were introduced nationally. "Classic" denotes dry wines from a single variety intended for good, everyday drinking. "Selection" is intended as the top designation for dry wines; the rules include a maximum yield and a blind tasting test. But the international impact of these new categories has been almost zero. The German craze for dry German wines is not shared by the cognoscenti abroad. Most German wines are still classified according to grape ripeness levels. Most wines (like most from France) need sugar added before fermentation to make up for missing sunshine. But unlike in France, German wine from grapes ripe enough not to need extra sugar is made and sold as a separate product: *Qualitätswein mit Prädikat*, or QmP. Within this top category, natural sugar content is expressed by traditional terms in ascending order of ripeness: *Kabinett, Spätlese, Auslese, Eiswein, Beerenauslese, Trockenbeerenauslese.*

QbA (*Qualitätswein bestimmter Anbaugebiete*), the second level, is for wines that needed additional sugar. The third level, *Tafelwein*, like Italian *vino da tavola*, is free of restraints. Officially it is the lowest grade, but impatience with the outdated law can make it the logical resort for innovative producers who set their own high standards.

Though there is much more detail in the laws, this is the gist of the quality grading. In theory, all any German vineyard has to do to make the best wine is to grow the ripest grapes – even of inferior varieties – which is patent nonsense.

The law does distinguish between degrees of geographical exactness – but in a way that just leads to confusion. In labelling "quality" wine, growers or merchants are given a choice. They can (and still generally do) label their best wines with the name of a single vineyard or *Einzellage*. Germany has about 2,600 *Einzellage* names. Obviously, only a few are famous enough to help sell the wine, so the 1971 law created another grouping: the *Grosslage*. This is a group of *Einzellagen* of supposedly similar character. Because there are fewer *Grosslage* names, and far more wine from each, they have the advantage of familiarity – a poor substitute for hard-earned fame. What's more, a *Grosslage* such as Niersteiner Gutes Domtal need not, and probably won't, contain a single drop of wine from Nierstein itself. This is entirely legal, but treats the consumer with contempt.

Thirdly, growers or merchants may choose to sell their wine under a *Bereich* or regional name. These are so broadly defined as to be meaningless. Thus "Bereich Johannisberg" covers the entire 3,000 hectare Rheingau: this is another avenue to consumer disappointment that should be closed.

In 2002, the leading German growers association, the VDP, established its own vineyard classification system, which non-members are also free to join. The idea is to identify and validate the true Grosses Gewächs, the German equivalents of the Burgundian *grands crus*. Strict quality criteria specifying grape varieties, yield, styles (usually dry or nobly sweet), plus strict tasting panels, will ensure that standards are very high. It is hoped this will usher in an international renaissance of German wine appreciation. Only time will tell whether this hope will be realised. (The Rheingau has established a different classification system. See p.154.) Make a vow to drink a fine German wine once a month at least. It will change your perception of purity and finesse, and make most Chardonnay taste gross.

Recent vintages

Mosel-Saar-Ruwer

Mosels (including Saar and Ruwer wines) are so attractive young that their keeping qualities are not often enough explored, and wines older than about 8 years are unusual. But well-made Riesling wines of *Kabinett* class gain from at least 5 years in bottle and often much more, *Spätlese* from 5 to 20, and *Auslese* and *Beerenauslese* anything from 10 to 30 years.

As a rule, in poor years the Saar and Ruwer make sharp, lean wines, but in the best years, above all with botrytis, they can surpass the whole world for elegance and thrilling, steely "breed".

2003 Hot weather brought high ripeness levels but rather low acidity. Ironically, some great sites suffered from drought, while less-esteemed cooler sites often fared better. So there will be considerable variation in quality, with the best superb.

2002 It is a small miracle how the Riesling grapes survived one of the wettest harvests on record to give ripe, succulent, lively wines (mostly Kabinett and Spätlese) which will be very attractive drunk young or mature.

2001 Golden Oct resulted in the best Mosel Riesling since 1990. Saar and Ruwer less exciting but still perfect balance. Lots of Spätlesen and Auslesen.

2000 Riesling stood up to harvest rain here better than most other places. Dominated by good QbA and Kabinett. Auslesen rarer, but exciting.

1999 Excellent in Saar and Ruwer, lots of Auslesen; generally only good in the Mosel due to high yields. Best will both drink well young and will age.

1998 Riesling grapes came through a rainy autumn to give astonishingly good results in the Middle Mosel; the Saar and Ruwer were less lucky, with mostly QbA. Plenty of Eiswein.

1997 A generous vintage of consistently fruity, elegant wines from the entire region. Marvellous Auslesen in the Saar and Ruwer.

1996 A very variable vintage with fine Spätlesen and Auslesen from top sites, but only QbA and Tafelwein elsewhere. Many excellent Eiweins.

1995 Excellent vintage, mainly of Spätlesen and Auslesen of firm structure and long ageing potential. Try to resist drinking too early.

1994 Another good vintage, mostly QmP with unexceptional QbA and Kabinett, but many Auslesen, Beerenauslesen, and Trockenbeerenauslesen. Rich fruit and high acidity. Drinking well now but will keep.

1993 Small, excellent vintage: lots of Auslesen/botrytis; near perfect harmony. Ready to drink except top Auslesen.

1992 A very large crop. Mostly good QbA, but 30 per cent QmP. To drink soon.

1991 A mixed vintage. Bad frost damage in the Saar and Ruwer, many tart QbA wines but also fine Spätlesen. To drink soon.

1990 Superb vintage, though small. Many QmP wines were the finest for 20 years. Try to resist drinking them all too soon.

1989 Large and often outstanding, with noble rot giving many Auslesen, etc. Saar wines best; the Mittelmosel overproduced, causing some dilution. Except for top Auslesen, ready to drink.

1988 Excellent vintage. Much ripe QmP, esp in the Mittelmosel. For long keeping. Lovely now but no hurry.

Fine older vintages: 76 71 69 64 59 53 49 45 37 34 21.

Rheinhessen, Nahe, Pfalz, Rheingau

Even the best wines can be drunk with pleasure when young, but Kabinett, Spätlese, and Auslese Riesling gain enormously in character by keeping for longer. Rheingau wines tend to be longest-lived, improving for 15 years or more, but best wines from the Nahe and Pfalz can last as long. Rheinhessen wines usually mature sooner, and dry Franken and Baden wines are generally best at 3–6 years. Rheingau and Nahe are the longest-living.

2003 Very hot weather led to rich wines in the Rheingau; some could lack acidity. The Pfalz produced superb Rieslings, and red wines fared well everywhere.

2002 Few challenge the best from 01, but should prove very good for both classic style Kabinett/Spätlese and for dry; balance very good. Excellent Pinot Noir.

2001 Though more erratic than in the Mosel, here, too, this was often an exciting vintage for both dry and classic styles; excellent balance.

2000 The further south, the more difficult was the harvest, the Pfalz catching worst of harvest rain. However, all regions have islands of excellence.

1999 Quality was average where yields were high, but for top growers an excellent vintage of rich, aromatic wines with lots of charm.

1998 Excellent: rich, balanced wines, many good Spätlesen and Auslesen with excellent ageing potential. Slow-maturing; many wines still a bit closed.

1997 Very clean, ripe grapes gave excellent QbA, Kabinett, Spätlese in dry and classic styles. Little botrytis, so Auslese and higher are rare.

1996 An excellent vintage, particularly in the Pfalz and the Rheingau, with many fine Spätlesen that will benefit from long ageing. Great Eiswein.

1995 Rather variable, but some excellent Spätlesen and Auslesen maturing well – like the 90s. Weak in the Pfalz due to harvest rain.

1994 Good vintage, mostly QmP, with abundant fruit and firm structure. Some superb Auslesen, Beerenauslesen and Trockenbeerenauslesen. Except for them, beginning to drink.

NB On the German vintage notation

Vintage notes after entries in the German section are given in a different form from those elsewhere, to show the style of the vintage as well as its quality. Three styles are indicated:

Bold type (eg **93**) indicates classic, super-ripe vintages with a high proportion of natural (QmP) wines, including Spätlesen and Auslesen.

Normal type (eg 92) indicates "normal" successful vintages with plenty of good wine but no great preponderance of sweeter wines.

Italic type (eg *91*) indicates cool vintages with generally poor ripeness but a fair proportion of reasonably successful wines, tending to be over-acidic. Few or no QmP wines, but correspondingly more selection in the QbA category. Such wines sometimes mature more favourably than expected.

Where no mention is made, the vintage is generally not recommended, or most of its wines have passed maturity.

1993 A small vintage of very good to excellent quality. Plenty of rich Spätlesen and Auslesen, which are just beginning to reach their peak.

1992 Very large vintage, would have been great but for Oct cold and rain. A third were QmP of rich, stylish quality. Most drinking well now.

1991 A good, middling vintage, though light soils in the Pfalz suffered from drought. Some fine wines are emerging. Most drinking well.

1990 Small and exceptionally fine. High percentage QmP; will keep many years.

1989 Summer storms reduced crop in Rheingau. Very good quality elsewhere, up to Auslese level. Most wines mature, but no hurry to drink.

Fine older vintages: 83 76 71 69 64 59 53 49 45 37 34 21.

Achkarren Bad w (r) ★★ Village on the KAISERSTUHL, known esp for GRAUBURGUNDER. First Class v'yd: Schlossberg. Wines generally best drunk during first 5 yrs. Gd wines: DR HEGER and co-op (WG).

Ahr Ahr r ★→★★ 90 91 93 94 95 96 97 98 99 00 01 02 03 Traditional specialized red-wine area, S of Bonn. Light, at best elegant, SPÄTBURGUNDER, esp from Adeneuer, Deutzerhof, Kreuzberg, MEYER-NÄKEL, Nelles, Stodden.

Amtliche Prüfungsnummer See PRÜFUNGSNUMMER.

APNr Abbreviation of AMTLICHE PRÜFUNGSNUMMER.

Assmannshausen Rhg r ★→★★★ 76 89 90 93 94 95 96 97 98 99 00 01 02 03 RHEINGAU village known for its usually pale, light SPÄTBURGUNDERS. First Class v'yd: Höllenberg. Growers inc Johanninger, AUGUST KESSELER, Robert König, Hotel Krone, and the STATE DOMAIN.

Auslese Wines from selective harvest of super-ripe bunches, the best affected by noble rot (*Edelfäule*) and correspondingly unctuous in flavour. Dry Auslesen are usually too alcoholic and clumsy for me.

Avelsbach M-S-R (Ruwer) w ★★★ 71 75 76 83 85 88 89 90 92 93 94 95 96 97 98 99 00 01 02 03 Village near TRIER. At (rare) best, lovely delicate wines. Esp BISCHÖFLICHE WEINGUTER, Staatliche Weinbaudomäne (see STAATSWEINGUT).

Ayl M-S-R (Saar) w ★★★ 71 75 76 83 85 88 89 90 91 93 94 95 96 97 98 99 00 01 02 03 One of the best villages of the SAAR. First Class v'yd: Kupp. Growers inc BISCHÖFLICHE WEINGUTER, Lauer, DR WAGNER.

Bacchus Modern, perfumed, often kitsch, grape found mostly in FRANKEN. Best for KABINETT wines.

Bacharach ★→★★★ 83 88 89 90 92 93 94 95 96 97 98 99 00 01 02 03 Main wine town of MITTELRHEIN, in new BEREICH LORELEY. Racy, austere RIESLINGS, some very fine. First Class v'yds: Hahn, Posten, Wolfshöhle. Growers inc BASTIAN, JOST, Randolph Kauer, Helmut Mades, RATZENBERGER.

Bad Dürkheim Pfz w (r) ★★→★★★ 76 88 89 90 92 93 94 95 96 97 98 99 00 01 02 03 Main town of MITTELHAARDT, with the world's biggest barrel and an ancient September wine festival, the *Würstmarkt* (sausage market). First Class v'yds: Michelsberg, Spielberg. Growers: Kurt Darting, Fitz-Ritter, Karst, Pflüger, Karl Schäfer.

Bad Kreuznach Nahe w ★★→★★★ 76 79 83 85 86 88 89 90 92 93 94 95 96 97 98 99 00 01 02 03 Pleasant spa town with fine v'yds. First Class: Brückes, Kahlenberg, and Krötenpfuhl. Growers inc ANHEUSER, Anton Finkenauer, Carl Finkenauer, VON PLETTENBERG.

Baden Huge SW area of scattered v'yds with a rapidly growing reputation for substantial, generally dry but supple wines that are gd with food. Fine Pinots, SPÄTBURGUNDER, RIESLING, GEWÜRZTRAMINER. The best areas are: KAISERSTUHL, ORTENAU.

Badische Bergstrasse/Kraichgau (Bereich) Widespread district of N BADEN. WEISSBURGUNDER and GRAUBURGUNDER make best wines.

Badischer Winzerkeller Germany's (and Europe's) biggest co-op, at BREISACH;

25,000 members with 12,000 acres, producing almost half of BADEN's wine: dependably unambitious.

Badisches Frankenland See TAUBERFRANKEN.

Barriques Small new-oak casks arrived tentatively in Germany 20 yrs ago. Results are still rather mixed. Oak aromatics can add substance to the white Pinots, SPÄTBURGUNDER, and LEMBERGER. But they ruin RIESLING.

Bassermann-Jordan ★★★ 76 79 83 86 88 **89** 90 **96** 97 **98 99** 00 01 02 **03** 104-acre MITTELHAARDT family estate with many of the best v'yds in DEIDESHEIM, FORST, RUPPERTSBERG, etc. Winemaker Ulrich Mell has put this historic estate back on top. Now one of the most dependable large estates.

Bastian, Weingut Fritz ★★ 14-acre BACHARACH estate. Racy, austere RIESLINGS with MOSEL-like delicacy, best from the First Class Posten v'yd.

Becker, J B ★★→★★★ Dedicated family estate and brokerage house at WALLUF. 30 acres in ELTVILLE, MARTINSTHAL, Walluf. Specialist in dry RIESLING.

Beerenauslese (BA) Luscious sweet wine from exceptionally ripe, individually selected berries, usually concentrated by noble rot. Rare, expensive.

Bensheim See HESSISCHE BERGSTRASSE.

Bercher ★★★ KAISERSTUHL estate; 40 acres of white and red Pinots at Burkheim. Excellent CHARDONNAY, etc, and some of Germany's best SPÄTBURGUNDER.

The Mosel-Saar-Ruwer: Germany's most dynamic region

Nowhere else in Germany are there so many exciting new producers to be discovered as in the Mosel-Saar-Ruwer. Perhaps this is the result of the special mentality of the *Moselaner* as much as the international interest in the elegant and subtly aromatic Rieslings that this archetypal cool-climate region produces. These are four names to watch for:

Clemens Busch Clemens and Rita Busch's organic estate in Pünderich is situated in one of the least well-known sections of the Mosel Valley and produces unusually powerful, dry Rieslings as well as great Auslese.

Herrenberg A tiny Saar estate owned and run by Claudia and Manfred Loch. The styles of wine vary according to vintage conditions: some years give mostly sweet wines, other years give rich dry wines of surprising power and complexity.

Daniel Vollenweider A young Swiss who bought vines in the forgotten Mosel top site of Wolfer Goldgrube in 2000 and specializes in classic-style Spätlese and Auslese inspired by famous names of Middle Mosel.

Van Volxem An historic Saar estate brought back to life by owner Roman Niewodniczanski and winemaker Gernot Kollmann. Good classic Kabinett and Spätlese, but it is the vineyard-designated dry wines that stand out.

Bernkastel M-M w ★→★★★ 71 75 76 **83** 85 86 **88** 89 90 92 **93** 94 **95** 96 **97** 98 **99** 00 **01** 02 **03** Top wine town of the MITTELMOSEL; the epitome of RIESLING. Great First Class v'yd: Doctor, 8 acres; First Class v'yds: Graben, Lay. Top growers inc KERPEN, LOOSEN, Markus Molitor, PAULY-BERGWEILER, PRÜM, Studert-Prüm, THANISCH, WEGELER.

Bernkastel (Bereich) Wide area of deplorably dim quality and superficial flowery character. Mostly MÜLLER-THURGAU. Inc all the MITTELMOSEL. Avoid.

Biffar, Josef ★★ Important DEIDESHEIM estate. 40 acres (also WACHENHEIM) of RIESLING. Dependable, classic wines.

Bingen Rhh w ★→★★★ 76 **83** 85 88 **89 90** 92 **93** 94 95 96 **97** 98 99 00

> **Warning notice: *Bereich***
> District within an *Anbaugebiet* (region). "Bereich" on a label should be treated as a flashing red light. Do not buy. See Introduction and under Bereich names, eg Bernkastel (Bereich).

01 02 **03** Rhine/NAHE town; fine v'yds: First Class: Scharlachberg. Best grower: Villa Sachsen.

Bingen (Bereich) District name for NW RHEINHESSEN.

Bischöfliche Weingüter ★★→★★★ Famous M-S-R estate at TRIER, a union of the cathedral property with two other charities, the Bischöfliches (Dom) Priesterseminar and the Bischöfliches Konvikt. 240 acres of top v'yds, esp in SAAR and RUWER. Recent vintages returning to former fine form.

Bocksbeutel Squat, flask-shaped bottle used for FRANKEN wines.

Bodensee (Bereich) Idyllic district of S BADEN, on Lake Constance. Dry wines are best drunk within 5 yrs. RIESLING-like MÜLLER-THURGAU a speciality.

Boppard ★→★★★ 76 83 88 90 92 **93** 94 **95** 96 97 **98** 99 00 **01** 02 **03** Important wine town of MITTELRHEIN where quality is rapidly improving. Best sites all in amphitheatre of vines called Bopparder Hamm. Growers: Heinrich Müller, August Perll, Weingart. Unbeatable value for money.

Braunberg M-M w **★★★★ 71 75 76 83 85 88** 89 **90** 91 **92 93** 94 **95** 96 **97** 98 99 00 **01** 02 **03** Top M-S-R village nr BERNKASTEL (750 acres), unbroken tradition for excellent full-flavoured RIESLING – Grand Cru if anything on the Mosel is. Great First Class v'yd: Juffer-SONNENUHR. First Class v'yd: Juffer. Growers: Bastgen, FRITZ HAAG, WILLI HAAG, Paulinshof, RICHTER.

Breisach Frontier town on Rhine near KAISERSTUHL. Seat of the largest German co-op, the BADISCHER WINZERKELLER.

Breisgau (Bereich) Little-known BADEN district. Gd reds and pink WEISSHERBST.

Breuer, Weingut Georg ★★★ Family estate of 36 acres in RÜDESHEIM: 6 acres of Berg Schlossberg, also 12.5-acre monopole RAUENTHALER Nonnenberg. Both have given superb quality, full-bodied dry RIESLING in recent years. Also excellent AUSLESEN, BEERENAUSLESEN, TROCKENBEERENAUSLESEN since 1995.

Buhl, Reichsrat von ★★★ Historic PFALZ family estate, returning to historic form as of 1994. 160 acres (DEIDESHEIM, FORST, RUPPERTSBERG). Leased by Japanese firm.

Bundesweinprämierung The German State Wine Award, organized by DLG (see opposite): gives great (*grosse*), silver, or bronze medallion labels.

Bürgerspital zum Heiligen Geist ★★ Ancient charitable WÜRZBURG estate. 275 acres: Wurzburg, RANDERSACKER, etc. Rich, dry wines, esp SILVANER, RIESLING; can be v.gd.

Bürklin-Wolf, Dr ★★★→★★★★ Famous PFALZ family estate. 234 acres in FORST, DEIDESHEIM, RUPPERTSBERG, and WACHENHEIM, inc many First Class sites. The full-bodied dry wines from these are often spectacular.

Castell'sches Fürstlich Domänenamt ★→★★★ Historic 142-acre princely estate in STEIGERWALD. SILVANER, RIESLANER. Back on form since 1999. Superb 01.

Chardonnay Now grown throughout Germany; with over 1,800 acres. A few gd wines from recent vintages. Best growers: K H JOHNER, REBHOLZ, Wittman.

Christmann ★★★ A 35-acre estate in Gimmeldingen (PFALZ) making rich, dry RIESLING from First Class v'yds, notably Königsbacher Idig. Impressive quality since 1995.

Christoffel, J J ★★★ Tiny domain in ERDEN, URZIG. Polished, elegant RIESLING.

Clevner (or Klevner) Synonym in WÜRTTEMBERG for Blauer Frühburgunder red grape, a mutation of Pinot N or Italian Chiavenna (early ripening black Pinot). Confusingly also ORTENAU (BADEN) synonym for TRAMINER.

Crusius ★★→★★★ 33-acre family estate at TRAISEN, NAHE. Vivid RIESLING from Bastei and Rotenfels of Traisen and SCHLOSSBÖCKELHEIM. Top wines age very well. Also gd SEKT and fresh fruity SPÄTBURGUNDER dry rosé.

Deidesheim Pfz w (r) ★★→★★★★ 71 **76** 83 **85** 88 **89** 90 **92** 93 94 95 **96** 97 **98** 99 00 01 02 **03** Largest top-quality village of the PFALZ (1,000 acres). Richly flavoured, lively wines. Also SEKT. First Class v'yds: Grainhübel, Hohenmorgen, Kalkofen, Kieselberg, Langenmorgen, Leinhöhle. Esp BASSERMANN-JORDAN, BIFFAR, BUHL, BÜRKLIN-WOLF, DEINHARD, WOLF.

Deinhard In 1997 the Wegeler family sold the 200-yr-old merchant house and SEKT producer Deinhard to sparkling wine giant Henkell-Söhnlein. But the splendid Deinhard estates remain in family ownership (see WEGELER).

Deinhard, Dr ★★★ Fine 74-acre family estate: some of DEIDESHEIM's best v'yds.

Deutscher Tafelwein Officially the term for very humble German wines. Now, confusingly, the flag of convenience for some costly novelties as well (eg BARRIQUE wines). The law will have to change, as it did in Italy.

Deutsches Weinsiegel A quality seal (ie neck label) for wines that have passed a statutory tasting test. Seals are: yellow for dry, green for medium-dry, red for medium-sweet. Means little; proves nothing.

Diel, Schlossgut ★★★ Fashionable 30-acre NAHE estate; made its name by ageing GRAUBURGUNDER and WEISSBURGUNDER in French BARRIQUES. Its traditional RIESLING is among the finest of NAHE wines. Makes delectable AUSLESE and EISWEIN.

DLG (Deutsche Landwirtschaftgesellschaft) The German Agricultural Society at Frankfurt. Awards national medals for quality – far too generously.

Domäne German for "domain" or "estate". Sometimes used alone to mean the "State domain" (STAATSWEINGUT or Staatliche Weinbaudomäne).

Dönnhoff, Weingut Hermann ★★★★ 88 **89** 90 92 93 94 **95** 96 97 **98** 99 **00** 01 02 **03** 31-acre leading NAHE estate with exceptionally fine RIESLING from NIEDERHAUSEN, Oberhausen, SCHLOSSBÖCKELHEIM. Produces some of Germany's greatest wines.

Dornfelder Red grape making deep-coloured, usually rustic wines. An astonishing 15,000 acres are now planted throughout Germany.

Durbach Baden w (r) ★★→★★★ **90** 93 **94** 95 **96** 97 **98** 99 00 01 02 03 Village with 775 acres of v'yds inc a handful of First Class sites. Top growers: A LAIBLE, H Männle, SCHLOSS STAUFENBERG, WOLFF METTERNICH. Choose their KLINGELBERGERS (RIESLING) and CLEVNERS (TRAMINER).

Edel Means "noble". *Edelfäule* means "noble rot".

Egon Müller zu Scharzhof ★★★★ 75 76 *78 79* 80 81 82 **83** *84* 85 86 *87* 88 **89** 90 91 *92* **93 94** 95 96 **97** 98 **99** 00 **01** 02 **03** Top SAAR estate of 30 acres at WILTINGEN. Its rich and racy SCHARZHOFBERGER RIESLING in AUSLESEN vintages is among the world's greatest wines; best are given gold capsules. Vintages: 93 95 97 99 01 are sublime, honeyed, immortal. Le Gallais is a second estate in WILTINGER Braune Kupp.

Eiswein Dessert wine made from frozen grapes with the ice (ie water content) discarded, thus very concentrated in flavour, acidity, and sugar – of BEERENAUSLESE ripeness or more. Alcohol content can be as low as 5.5%. Very expensive. Sometimes made as late as Jan/Feb of following year. 02 looks to be the best Eiswein vintage since 96, possibly since 83.

Eitelsbach M-S-R (Ruwer) w ★★→★★★★ 71 75 **76** 83 **85** 88 **89** 90 92 **93** 94 95 *96* **97** 98 **99** 00 01 02 **03** RUWER village bordering TRIER, inc superb Great First Class KARTHAUSERHOFBERG v'yd site. Grosslage: Römerlay.

Elbling Grape introduced by the Romans, widely grown on upper MOSEL. Can be sharp and tasteless, but capable of real freshness and vitality in the best conditions (eg at Nittel or SCHLOSS THORN in the OBERMOSEL).

To decipher codes, please refer to "Key to symbols" on front flap of jacket, or to "How to use this book" on p.6.

Eltville Rhg w ★★ ·★★★ **71 76 83** 88 **89 90** 92 **93** 94 **95** 96 **97** 98 **99** 00 01 02 **03** Major wine town with cellars of RHEINGAU STATE DOMAIN, FISCHER, and VON SIMMERN estates. First Class v'yd: Sonnenberg.

Emrich-Schönleber ★★★ Located in the obscure NAHE village of Monzingen, Werner Schönleber, but since the late 1980s has shown that his RIESLING can match those of any other producer in the region, esp his sumptuous EISWEIN.

Enkirch M-M w ★★ ·★★★ **71 76 85 88 89 90 93** 94 95 *96* **97** 98 99 00 **01** 02 **03** Little-known MITTELMOSEL village, often overlooked but with lovely light, tasty wine. The best grower is Immich-Batterieberg.

Germany's quality levels

The official range of qualities in ascending order are as follows:

1 Deutscher Tafelwein: sweetish light wine of no specified character. (From certain producers, can be very special.)

2 Landwein: dryish Tafelwein with some regional style.

3 Qualitätswein: dry or sweetish wine with sugar added before fermentation to increase its strength, but tested for quality and with distinct local and grape character.

4 Kabinett: dry or dryish natural (unsugared) wine of distinct personality and distinguishing lightness. Can occasionally be sublime.

5 Spätlese: stronger, often sweeter than Kabinett. Full-bodied. Today many top Spätlesen are *trocken* or completely dry.

6 Auslese: sweeter, sometimes stronger than Spätlese, often with honey-like flavours, intense and long. Occasionally dry and weighty.

7 Beerenauslese: very sweet, sometimes strong, intense. Can be superb.

8 Eiswein: (Beeren- or Trockenbeerenauslese) concentrated, sharpish, and very sweet. Can be very fine or too extreme, unharmonious.

9 Trockenbeerenauslese: intensely sweet and aromatic; alcohol slight. Extraordinary and everlasting.

Erbach Rhg w ★★★ **71 76 83** 85 86 88 **89 90 92 93** 94 95 **96** 97 98 99 *00* 01 02 **03** RHEINGAU area: big, perfumed, age-worthy wines, inc First Class v'yds Hohenrain, MARCOBRUNN, Siegelsberg, Steinmorgen, Schlossberg. Major estates: SCHLOSS REINHARTSHAUSEN, SCHLOSS SCHÖNBORN. Also BECKER, JAKOB JUNG, KNYPHAUSEN, VON SIMMERN, etc.

Erben Word meaning "heirs", often used on old-established estate labels.

Erden M-M w ★★★ **71 75 76 83** 85 88 **89 90** 92 **93** 94 **95** 96 **97** 98 99 *00* **01** 02 **03** Village between Urzig and Kröv: noble, full-flavoured, vigorous wine (more herbal and mineral than the wines of nearby BERNKASTEL and WEHLEN but equally long-living). Great First Class v'yds: Prälat, Treppchen. Growers inc BISCHÖFLICHE WEINGÜTER, CHRISTOFFEL, LOOSEN, Meulenhof, Mönchhof, Peter Nicolay.

Erstes Gewächs Literally translates as "first growth". See box on p.154.

Erzeugerabfüllung Bottled by producer. Being replaced by "GUTSABFÜLLUNG", but only by estates. Co-ops will continue with Erzeugerabfüllung.

Escherndorf Frank w ★★ ·★★★ **76** 83 **88** *89* **90 92 93** 94 *95* 96 97 **98 99** 00 01 02 **03** Important wine town near WÜRZBURG. Similar tasty, dry wine. First Class v'yd: Lump. Grosslage: Kirchberg. Growers inc: Michael Fröhlich, JULIUSSPITAL, Horst SAUER, Rainer Sauer, Egon Schäffer.

Eser, Weingut August ★★ 20-acre RHEINGAU estate at OESTRICH. V'yds also in Hallgarten, RAUENTHAL (esp Gehrn, Rothenberg), WINKEL. Variable wines.

Faul, Fritz Prolific producer of MÜLLER-THURGAU under fashionable BEREICH label.

Filzen M-S-R (Saar) w ★★ ·★★★ **76** 83 **88 89 90 93** 94 **95** 96 **97** 98 **99** 00 **01** 02 **03** Small SAAR village near WILTINGEN. First Class v'yd: Pulchen. Grower to note: Piedmont.

Fischer Erben, Weingut ★★★ 18-acre RHEINGAU estate at ELTVILLE, with high traditional standards. Long-lived classic wines.

Forschungsanstalt Geisenheim See HESSISCHE FORSCHUNGSANSTALT.

Forst Pfz w ★★→★★★ 71 76 83 **89 90** 92 93 94 95 **96** 97 **98** 99 *00* 01 02 **03** MITTELHAARDT village with 500 acres of Germany's best v'yds. Ripe, richly fragrant, full-bodied but subtle wines. First Class v'yds: Jesuitengarten, Kirchenstück, FREUNDSTÜCK, Pechstein, Ungeheuer. Top growers inc: BASSERMANN-JORDAN, BURKLIN-WOLF, DEINHARD, MOSBACHER, Eugen Müller, H Spindler, Werlé, WOLF.

Franken Franconia region of distinctive dry wines, esp SILVANER, always bottled in round-bellied flasks (BOCKSBEUTEL). The centre is WURZBURG. Bereich names: MAINDREIECK, STEIGERWALD. Top producers: BURGERSPITAL, CASTELL'SCHES, FÜRST, JULIUSSPITAL, LÖWENSTEIN, Ruck, Horst Sauer, STAATLICHER HOFKELLER, WIRSCHING, etc.

Friedrich-Wilhelm Gymnasium ★★ Important 82-acre charitable estate based in TRIER, with v'yds in BERNKASTEL, GRAACH, OCKFEN, TRITTENHEIM, ZELTINGEN, etc, all M-S-R. Since 1995 much improved after poor patch.

Fuhrmann See PFEFFINGEN.

Fürst ★★★ Small estate in Bürgstadt making some of the best wines in FRANKEN, particularly Burgundian SPÄTBURGUNDER and oak-aged WEISSBURGUNDER.

Gallais Le See EGON MÜLLER.

Geisenheim Rhg w ★★→★★★ 71 76 85 88 **89 90** 92 **93** 94 95 **96** 97 98 **99** *00* 01 02 **03** Village famous for Germany's best-known wine school and v.gd aromatic wines. First Class v'yds: Kläuserweg, Rothenberg. Top growers: JOHANNISHOF, SCHLOSS SCHÖNBORN, WEGELER, VON ZWIERLEIN.

Gemeinde A commune or parish.

Gewürztraminer (or Traminer) Highly aromatic grape, speciality of Alsace, also impressive in Germany, esp in PFALZ, BADEN, SACHSEN, and WÜRTTEMBERG.

Gimmeldingen Pfz w ★★ **76 85** 88 **89 90 92 93** 94 95 **96 97 98** 99 *00* 01 02 **03** Village just S of MITTELHAARDT. At best, rich succulent wines. Grosslage: Meerspinne. Growers inc: CHRISTMANN, MÜLLER-CATOIR.

Graach M-M w ★★★ 71 75 76 83 **85** 88 **89 90** 92 93 94 95 **96** 97 **98 99** *00* 01 02 **03** Small village between BERNKASTEL and WEHLEN. First Class v'yds: Domprobst, Himmelreich, Josephshofer. Many top growers: VON KESSELSTATT, LOOSEN, PRÜM, SCHAEFER, SELBACH-OSTER, WEINS-PRÜM.

Grans-Fassian ★★★ Fine 25-acre MOSEL estate at Leiwen. V'yds there and in TRITTENHEIM. EISWEIN a speciality. Dependable high quality since 1995.

Grauburgunder Synonym of RULÄNDER or Pinot Gr: grape giving soft full-bodied wine. Best in BADEN and S PFALZ.

Grosser Ring Group of top (VDP) MOSEL-SAAR-RUWER estates, whose annual September auction regularly sets world-record prices.

Grosses Gewächs Translates as "great/top growth". This is the top tier in the v'yd classification launched in 2002 by the growers' association VDP, except in the RHEINGAU, which has its own Erstes Gewächs classification. Wines released as Grosses Gewächs must meet very strict quality criteria.

Grosslage See Introduction, p.137.

Gunderloch ★★★→★★★★ 88 89 **90** 91 92 **93** 94 95 **96 97 98** 99 *00* **01** 02 **03** 30-acre NACKENHEIM estate making some of the finest RIESLING on the entire Rhine, inc spectacular BEERENAUSLESEN and TROCKENBEERENAUSLESEN. Also owns well-known Balbach estate in NIERSTEIN.

Remember that vintage information for German wines is given in a different form from the ready/not ready distinction applying to other countries. Read the explanation at the bottom of p.139.

GERMANY

Guntrum, Louis ★★ Large (67-acre) family estate in NIERSTEIN, OPPENHEIM, etc. Gd SILVANER and GEWÜRZTRAMINER as well as RIESLING.

Gutedel German name for the ancient Chasselas grape, used in S BADEN. Fresh, but neutral, white wines.

Gutsabfüllung Estate-bottled. Term for genuinely estate-bottled wines.

Haag, Weingut Fritz ★★★★ 69 70 71 73 75 76 77 78 79 80 81 82 83 84 85 86 87 88 89 90 91 92 93 94 95 96 97 98 99 00 01 02 03 Top estate in BRAUNEBERG run by Wilhelm Haag, president of GROSSER RING. MOSEL RIESLING of crystalline purity and racy brilliance for long ageing. Haag's son runs the SCHLOSS LIESER estate.

Haag, Weingut Willi ★★ 7-acre BRAUNEBERG estate. Full, old-style RIESLING. Some fine AUSLESE. Improving quality since 1995.

Haart, Reinhold ★★★ The best estate in PIESPORT, and growing in repute. Refined, aromatic wines capable of long ageing.

Halbtrocken Medium-dry (literally "semi-dry"). Containing fewer than 18 but more than 9 grams per litre unfermented sugar. Popular category of wine intended for mealtimes, usually better balanced than TROCKEN.

Hattenheim Rhg w ★★→★★★★ 71 76 83 89 90 92 93 94 95 96 97 98 99 00 01 02 03 Superlative 500-acre wine town, though not all producers achieve its full potential. The First Class v'yds are Engelmannsberg, Mannberg, Nussbrunnen, Pfaffenberg, Wisselbrunnen, and most famously STEINBERG (ORTSTEIL). MARCOBRUNN: on ERBACH boundary. Estates inc: KNYPHAUSEN, Lang, RESS, SCHLOSS SCHÖNBORN, VON SIMMERN, STATE DOMAIN.

Henkell See DEINHARD.

Heger, Dr ★★★ Leading estate of KAISERSTUHL in BADEN with excellent dry WEISSBURGUNDER, GRAUBURGUNDER, and powerful oak-aged SPÄTBURGUNDER reds.

Heilbronn Würt w r ★→★★ 90 93 94 96 97 98 99 00 01 02 03 Wine town with many small growers and gd co-op. Best wines are RIESLING and LEMBERGER. Seat of DLG competition. Top growers inc: Amalienhof, Drautz-Able, Schäfer-Heinrich.

Hessen, Prinz von ★★→★★★ Famous 75-acre estate in JOHANNISBERG, KIEDRICH, and WINKEL. Rapidly improving quality since 1995 vintage.

Hessische Bergstrasse w ★★→★★★ 90 92 93 94 95 96 97 98 99 00 01 02 03 Smallest wine region in W Germany (1,000 acres), N of Heidelberg. Pleasant RIESLING from STATE DOMAIN v'yds at BENSHEIM, Bergsträsser co-op, Simon-Bürkle, and Stadt Bensheim.

Hessische Forschungsanstalt für Wein-Obst & Gartenbau Famous wine school and research establishment at GEISENHEIM, RHEINGAU. Gd wines inc reds. The name on the label is Forschungsanstalt.

Heyl zu Herrnsheim ★★★ Leading 92-acre NIERSTEIN estate, 60% RIESLING. Since fine 96 vintage owned by Ahr family. Dry RIESLING, SILVANER, WEISSBURGUNDER of classical elegance.

Heymann-Löwenstein ★★★ Young estate in Lower or "Terrace Mosel" with most consistent dry RIESLING in MOSEL-SAAR-RUWER and some remarkable AUSLESE and TROCKENBEERENAUSLESEN. Spectacular wines in 01. A rapidly rising star.

Hochgewächs Supposedly superior level of QBA RIESLING, esp in MOSEL-SAAR-RUWER.

Hochheim Rhg w ★★→★★★★ 71 75 76 79 83 85 86 88 89 90 92 93 94 95 96 97 98 99 00 01 02 03 600-acre wine town 15 miles E of main RHEINGAU area, once thought of as best on Rhine. Wines with an earthy intensity, body, and fragrance of their own. First Class v'yds: Domdechaney, Hölle, Kirchenstück, Königin Viktoria Berg (12-acre monopoly of Hupfeld of OESTRICH). Grosslage: Daubhaus. Growers inc Hupfeld, FRANZ KUNSTLER, WJ SCHAEFER, SCHLOSS SCHÖNBORN, STAATSWEINGUT, WERNER.

Hock Traditional English term for Rhine wine, derived from HOCHHEIM.

Hoensbroech, Weingut Reichsgraf zu ★★ Top KRAICHGAU estate. 37 acres. Dry WEISSBURGUNDER, GRAUBURGUNDER, SILVANER, eg Michelfelder Himmelberg.

Hohenlohe-Oehringen, Weingut Fürst zu ★★ Noble 47-acre estate in Oehringen and WURTTEMBERG. Earthy, bone-dry RIESLING and powerful reds from SPÄTBURGUNDER and LEMBERGER grapes.

Hövel, Weingut von ★★★ Very fine SAAR estate at OBERMOSEL (Hütte is 12-acre monopoly) and in SCHARZHOFBERG. Superb wines since 1993.

Huber, Bernhard ★★★ Rising star of Breisgau area of BADEN with powerful oak-aged SPÄTBURGUNDER reds and Burgundian-style WEISSBURGUNDER, CHARDONNAY.

Ihringen Bad r w ★→★★★ **86** 88 **89 90** 92 **93** 94 95 **96 97 98 99** 00 **01** 02 03 One of the best villages of the KAISERSTUHL, BADEN. Proud of its SPÄTBURGUNDER red, WEISSHERBST, and GRAUBURGUNDER. Top growers: DR HEGER, Stigler.

Ingelheim Rhh r w ★★ **90 93** 94 95 96 **97** 98 **99** 00 01 **02 03** Town opposite RHEINGAU historically known for its SPÄTBURGUNDER. Few wines today live up to reputation. Top v'yds are Horn, Pares, Sonnenberg, and Steinacker.

Iphofen Frank w ★★→★★★ **76 79 83 85 88** 89 **90** 92 **93** 94 95 96 **97** 98 **99** 00 **01** 02 Village nr WURZBURG. Superb First Class v'yds: Julius-Echter-Berg, Kalb. Grosslage: Burgweg. Growers: JULIUSSPITAL, Ruck, WIRSCHING.

Jahrgang Year – as in "vintage".

Johannisberg Rhg w ★★→★★★★ **71 75** **76 83 85** 86 88 **89 90** 92 **93** 94 **95 96 97** 98 **99** 00 **01** 02 A 260-acre classic RHEINGAU village with superlative subtle RIESLING. First Class v'yds: Hölle, Klaus, SCHLOSS JOHANNISBERG. Grosslage: Erntebringer. Top growers: JOHANNISHOF, SCHLOSS JOHANNISBERG.

Johannisberg (Bereich) District name for the entire RHEINGAU. Avoid.

Johannishof ★★★ JOHANNISBERG family estate, aka HH Eser. 45 acres. RIESLINGS that justify the great Johannisberg name. Since 1996 also fine RÜDESHEIM wines.

Johner, Karl-Heinz ★★★ Small BADEN estate at Bischoffingen, in the front line for New World-style SPÄTBURGUNDER and oak-aged WEISSBURGUNDER.

Josephshöfer First Class v'yd at GRAACH, the sole property of VON KESSELSTATT.

Jost, Toni ★★★ Perhaps the top estate of the MITTELRHEIN. 25 acres, mainly RIESLING, in BACHARACH, and also in the RHEINGAU.

Juliusspital ★★★ Ancient WÜRZBURG religious charity with 374 acres of top FRANKEN v'yds and many superb wines. Look for its dry SILVANERS and RIESLING.

Kabinett See "Germany's quality levels" box on p.144.

Kaiserstuhl (Bereich) One of the top BADEN districts, with notably warm climate and volcanic soil. Villages inc ACHKARREN, IHRINGEN. Grosslage: Vulkanfelsen.

Kallstadt Pfz w (r) ★★→★★★ **83 85 88** 89 **90** 92 **93** 94 **95 96** 97 **98** 99 00 **01** 02 **03** Village of N MITTELHAARDT. Often underrated fine, rich, dry RIESLING and Pinot N. First Class v'yd: Saumagen. Grosslagen: Feuerberg, Kobnert. Growers inc Henninger, KOEHLER-RUPRECHT, Schüster.

Kanzem M-S-R (Saar) w ★★★ **71 76 88 89 90** 92 **93** 94 **95** 96 **97** 98 **99** 00 **01** 02 **03** Small neighbour of WILTINGEN. First Class v'yd: Altenberg. Grosslage: SCHARZBERG. Growers inc Othegraven, J P Reinert, Reverchon.

Karlsmühle ★★★ Small estate with Lorenzhöfer monopoly site in RUWER making classic Ruwer RIESLING, also wines from First Class KASEL v'yds sold under Patheiger label. Consistently excellent quality since 1994.

Karthäuserhofberg ★★★★ Top RUWER estate of 46 acres at Eitelsbach. Easily recognized by bottles with only a neck-label. Since 1993 estate has been back on top form. Also gd TROCKEN wines.

Kasel M-S-R (Ruwer) w ★★→★★★ **71 76 83 85 88 89 90** 92 **93** 94 **95** 96 **97** 98 **99** 00 **01** 02 **03** Stunning flowery RIESLING. First Class v'yds: Kehrnagel, Nies'chen. Top growers: KARLSMÜHLE, VON KESSELSTATT.

Keller Wine cellar.

Kellerei Winery (ie a big commercial bottler).

GERMANY

Kerner Modern aromatic grape variety, earlier ripening than RIESLING. Makes wines of fair quality but without the inbuilt grace and harmony of RIESLING. Best in SACHSEN.

Kerpen, Weingut Heribert ★★ Small gd estate in BERNKASTEL, GRAACH, WEHLEN.

Kesseler, Weingut August ★★★ 35-acre estate making the best SPÄTBURGUNDER reds in ASSMANNSHAUSEN. Also v.gd classic-style RIESLING.

Kesselstatt, von ★★★ The largest private MOSEL estate, 650 yrs old. Now belongs to Reh family. Some 150 acres in GRAACH, KASEL, PIESPORT, WILTINGEN, etc, producing aromatic, generously fruity MOSELS. Consistently high quality, often magnificent, wines from JOSEPHSHÖFER monopoly v'yd and SCHARZHOFBERG.

Kesten M-M w ★→★★★ **76 83** 88 89 **90 92 93** 94 **95** 96 **97** 98 **99** 00 **01** 02 **03** Neighbour of BRAUNEBERG. Best wines (from Paulinshofberg v'yd) similar. Top growers: Bastgen, Kees-Kieren, PAULINSHOF.

Kiedrich Rhg w ★★→★★★★ **71 76 83** 89 **90 92 93** 94 95 **96** 97 **98 99** 00 01 02 **03** Neighbour of RAUENTHAL; equally splendid and high-flavoured. First Class v'yds: Gräfenberg, Wasseros. Growers inc: FISCHER, KNYPHAUSEN, Speicher-Schuth. R WEIL now top estate.

Klingelberger ORTENAU (BADEN) term for RIESLING, esp at DURBACH.

Kloster Eberbach Glorious 12th-C Cistercian abbey in HATTENHEIM forest. Monks planted STEINBERG, Germany's Clos de Vougeot. Now the label of the STATE-DOMAIN with a string of great v'yds in ASSMANNSHAUSEN, RÜDESHEIM, RAUENTHAL, etc. The new director has the right ideas.

Klüsserath M-M w ★→★★★ **76 83 88 90** 92 **93** 94 **95** 96 97 **98** 99 00 **01** 02 **03** Little-known MOSEL village whose wine growers have joined forces to classify its top site, Brüderschaft. Growers: Bernhard Kirsten, FRIEDRICH-WILHELM-GYMNASIUM, Regnery.

Knyphausen, Weingut Freiherr zu ★★→★★★ Noble 54-acre estate on former Cistercian land (see KLOSTER EBERBACH) in ELTVILLE, ERBACH, HATTENHEIM, KIEDRICH, and MARCOBRUNN. Classic RHEINGAU wines, many dry.

Koehler-Ruprecht ★★★★ **76 79** 80 **81** 82 **83** 84 **85** 86 87 **88 89 90** 91 92 **93** 94 95 **96 97 98** 99 00 **01** 02 **03** Highly rated KALLSTADT grower. Traditional winemaking; very long-lived dry RIESLING from K Saumagen. Outstanding SPÄTBURGUNDER and striking BARRIQUE-aged wines under the Philippi label.

Kraichgau Small BADEN region S of Heidelberg. Top grower: HOENSBROECH.

Liebfraumilch

Much-abused name, once accounting for 50% of all German wine exports – to the detriment of Germany's better products. Legally defined as a QBA "of pleasant character" from RHEINHESSEN, PFALZ, NAHE, or RHEINGAU, of a blend with at least 51% RIESLING, SILVANER, KERNER, or MÜLLER-THURGAU. Most is mild, semi-sweet wine from Rheinhessen and the Pfalz. Rules now say it must have more than 18 grams per litre unfermented sugar. Its definition makes a mockery of the legal term Quality Wine. With sales falling fast everywhere, this category is in the process of disappearing.

Kröv M-M w ★→★★★ **88 90** 92 **93** 94 95 *96* **97 98** 99 *00* 01 **03** Popular tourist resort famous for its Grosslage name: Nacktarsch, or "bare bottom". Be very careful. Best grower: Martin Müllen.

Künstler, Franz ★★★★ HOCHHEIM estate expanded in 1996 to 50 acres by purchase of well-known Aschrott estate. Superb dry RIESLING, esp from First Class Domdechaney, Hölle, and Kirchenstück; also excellent AUSLESE.

Kuntz, Sybille M-S-R ★★ Successful protagonist of untypical dry MOSEL RIESLING of AUSLESE strength.

Laible, Weingut Andreas ★★★ 10-acre DURBACH estate. Fine sweet and dry RIESLING, SCHEUREBE, GEWÜRZTRAMINER (First Class Plauelrain v'yd). Klingelberger can be utter joy. Superb quality since 1997.

Landespreismünze Prizes for quality at state, rather than national, level.

Landwein See "Germany's quality levels" box on p.144.

Leitz, J ★★★ Fine RÜDESHEIM family estate for elegant, dry RIESLING. A rising star.

Lemberger Red variety imported to Germany and Austria in the 18th C, from Hungary, where it is known as Kékfrankos. Blaufränkisch in Austria. Deep-coloured, moderately tannic wines; can be excellent. Or rosé.

Liebfrauenstift A 26-acre v'yd in city of Worms; origin of LIEBFRAUMILCH.

Lieser M-M w ★★ **76 83 88 89 90** 92 **93** 94 **95** 96 **97** 98 99 00 **01** 02 **03** Little-known neighbour of BERNKASTEL. Lighter wines. First Class v'yd: Niederberg-Helden. Top grower: SCHLOSS LIESER.

Lingenfelder, Weingut ★★ Small innovative Grosskarlbach (PFALZ) estate: gd dry and sweet SCHEUREBE, full-bodied RIESLING, etc.

Loewen, Carl ★★★ Top grower of Leiwen on MOSEL making ravishing AUSLESE from town's First Class Laurentiuslay site. Also fine EISWEIN.

Loosen, Weingut Dr ★★★★ 71 73 75 **76** 77 79 80 81 82 83 84 85 86 87 **88** 89 **90** 91 92 **93** 94 **95** 96 **97** 98 99 00 01 02 **03** Dynamic 24-acre St-Johannishof estate in BERNKASTEL, ERDEN, GRAACH, URZIG, WEHLEN. Deep, intense RIESLINGS from old vines in great First Class v'yds. Also WOLF in the Pfalz since 1996. Superlative quality since 1990. Joint-venture RIESLING in Washington State with Ch Ste Michele: Eroica (dry) first vintage 99. A joint venture with Jasper Hill (Australia) is being planned.

Lorch Rhg w (r) ★→★★ **76 83 85** 88 **89 90** 92 **93** 94 **95** 96 **97 98** 99 00 01 02 **03** Extreme W of RHEINGAU. Some fine MITTELRHEIN-like RIESLING. Best grower: von Kanitz.

Loreley (Bereich) New BEREICH name for RHEINBURGENGAU and BACHARACH.

Löwenstein, Fürst ★★★ Top FRANKEN estate. Excellent 01. Intense savoury SILVANER from Homberger Kallmuth, very dramatic slope. Also 45-acre Hallgarten estate long rented by SCHLOSS VOLLRADS, independent since 1997.

Maindreieck (Bereich) District name for central FRANKEN, inc WÜRZBURG.

Marcobrunn Historic RHEINGAU v'yd; one of Germany's very best. See ERBACH.

Markgräflerland (Bereich) District S of FREIBURG, BADEN. Typical GUTEDEL wine can be delicious refreshment when drunk very young, but best wines are the BURGUNDERS: WEISS-, GRAU-, and SPÄT-. Also SEKT.

Maximin Grünhaus M-S-R (Ruwer) w ★★★★ 71 75 76 79 **83 85** 86 **88 89 90** 92 **93** 94 **95** 96 **97** 98 99 00 01 02 **03** Supreme RUWER estate of 80 acres at Mertesdorf. Wines of firm elegance and great subtlety to mature 20 yrs+.

Meyer-Näkel, Weingut ★★★ 15-acre AHR estate. Fine SPÄTBURGUNDERS in Dernau and Bad Neuenahr exemplify modern oak-aged German reds.

Mittelhaardt The N central and best part of the PFALZ, inc DEIDESHEIM, FORST, RUPPERTSBERG, WACHENHEIM, largely planted with RIESLING.

Mittelhaardt-Deutsche Weinstrasse (Bereich) Name for N and central PFALZ.

Mittelmosel The central and best part of the MOSEL, inc BERNKASTEL, PIESPORT, WEHLEN, etc. Its top sites are (or should be) entirely RIESLING.

Mittelrhein Northern Rhine area of domestic importance (and great beauty), inc BACHARACH and BOPPARD. Some attractive, steely RIESLING.

Morio-Muskat Stridently aromatic grape variety now on the decline.

Mosbacher, Weingut ★★★ Fine 23-acre estate for some of best dry and sweet RIESLING of FORST. Best wines are dry GROSSES GEWÄCHS.

GERMANY

To decipher codes, please refer to "Key to symbols" on front flap of jacket, or to "How to use this book" on p.6.

Mosel The TAFELWEIN name of the area. All quality wines from the Mosel must be labelled MOSEL-SAAR-RUWER. (Moselle is the French – and English – spelling.)

Mosel-Saar-Ruwer (M-S-R) 26,000-acre QUALITÄTSWEIN region between TRIER and Koblenz; inc MITTELMOSEL, RUWER, and SAAR. The natural home of RIESLING.

Moselland, Winzergenossenschaft Huge MOSEL-SAAR-RUWER co-op, at BERNKASTEL, inc Saar-Winzerverein at WILTINGEN. Its 5,200 members produce 25% of M-S-R wines (inc classic method SEKT), but little above average.

Müller zu Scharzhof, Egon See EGON MÜLLER.

Müller-Catoir, Weingut ★★★★ 76 78 **79** 81 82 **83** 85 86 *87* 88 **89 90** 91 **92 93** 94 *95* **96** 97 **98 99** 00 **01** 02 **03** Outstanding 40-acre NEUSTADT estate. Very aromatic powerful wines (RIESLING, SCHEUREBE, GEWÜRZTRAMINER, RIESLANER, WEISSBURGUNDER, GRAUBURGUNDER, and MUSKATELLER). Consistent quality and gd value; dry/sweet equally impressive.

Müller-Thurgau Fruity, early ripening, usually low-acid grape; most common in PFALZ, RHEINHESSEN, NAHE, BADEN, and FRANKEN; decreasingly planted in favour of RIESLING over the past 8 yrs. Should be banned from all top v'yds by law.

Münster Nahe w ★ →★★★ **71 75 76 83** 88 **89 90** 92 **93** 94 95 **96** 97 **98** 99 00 **01** 02 **03** Best N NAHE village; fine, delicate wines. First Class V'yds: Pittersberg, Dautenpflänzer, Kapellenberg. Top growers: Göttelmann, Kruger-Rumpf.

Muskateller Ancient aromatic white grape with crisp acidity. A rarity in the PFALZ, BADEN, and WÜRTTEMBERG, where it is mostly made dry.

Nackenheim Rhh w ★ →★★★★ **76 83 89 90** 92 **93** 94 95 **96 97 98** 99 00 **01** 02 NIERSTEIN neighbour also with top Rhine terroir; similar best wines (esp First Class Rothenberg). Top grower: GUNDERLOCH.

Nahe Tributary of the Rhine and high-quality wine region. Balanced, fresh, clean but full-bodied, even minerally wines; RIESLING best. BEREICH: NAHETAL.

Nahetal (Bereich) BEREICH name for amalgamated BAD KREUZNACH and SCHLOSS-BÖCKELHEIM districts.

Neckar The river with many of WÜRTTEMBERG's finest v'yds, mainly between STUTTGART and HEILBRONN.

Neipperg, Graf von ★★ →★★★ Noble 70-acre estate in Schwaigern, WÜRTTEMBERG: elegant dry RIESLING and TRAMINER, and gd reds, esp from LEMBERGER.

Neumagen-Dhron M-M w ★★ Fine neighbour of PIESPORT. Top grower: Heinz Schmitt.

Neustadt Central town of PFALZ with a famous wine school. Top growers: MÜLLER-CATOIR, Weegmüller.

Niederhausen Nahe w ★★→★★★★ **71 75 76 83** 85 86 88 **89 90** 93 94 95 **96** 97 **98** 99 **00 01** 02 **03** Neighbour of SCHLOSSBÖCKELHEIM. Graceful, powerful wines. First Class V'yds inc Hermannsberg, Hermannshöhle. Esp from CRUSIUS, DÖNNHOFF, Gutsverwaltung Niederhausen-Schlossböckelheim, Mathern.

Nierstein Rhh w ★→★★★★ **71 75 76 83 85** 86 **88 89 90 92 93** 94 95 **96** 97 **98** 99 00 **01** 02 03 Famous but treacherous village name. 1,300 acres. Superb First-Class v'yds: Brüdersberg, Glöck, Heiligenbaum, Hipping, Oelberg, Orbel, Pettenthal. Notorious Grosslagen: Auflangen, Rehbach, Spiegelberg, Gutes Domtal. Ripe, aromatic, elegant wines. Beware Grosslage Gutes Domtal: a supermarket deception now disappearing from shelves. Try GUNDERLOCH, GUNTRUM, HEYL ZU HERRNSHEIM, ST-ANTONY, SCHNEIDER, Strub.

Nierstein (Bereich) Large E RHEINHESSEN district of ordinary quality.

Nierstein Winzergenossenschaft ★ →★★ The leading NIERSTEIN co-op, with above-average standards. (Formerly traded under the name Rheinfront.)

Nobling New white grape: light fresh wine in BADEN, esp MARKGRÄFLERLAND.

Norheim Nahe w ★★ →★★★ **71 76 83** 88 **89 90 91 92 93** 94 95 **96 97 98** 99 00 **01** 02 Neighbour of NIEDERHAUSEN. First Class v'yds: Dellchen, Kafels, Kirschheck. Grosslage: Burgweg. Growers: CRUSIUS, DÖNNHOFF, Mathern.

Oberemmel M-S-R (Saar) w ★★→★★★ 71 75 76 83 85 88 **89 90** 92 **93** 94 **95** 96 **97** *98* **99** 00 **01** 02 **03** Next village to WILTINGEN. Very fine from First Class v'yd Hütte, etc. Grosslage: SCHARZBERG. Growers: VON HÖVEL, VON KESSELSTATT.

Obermosel (Bereich) District name for the upper MOSEL above TRIER. Wines from the ELBLING grape, generally uninspiring unless very young.

Ockfen M-S-R (Saar) w ★★→★★★ 71 75 76 **83 85** 86 **88 89 90** *91* 92 **93** 94 **95** 96 **97** 98 **99** 00 01 02 Superb fragrant, austere wines. First Class v'yd: Bockstein. Grosslage: SCHARZBERG. Growers: DR FISCHER, Jankt Urbans-Hof, WAGNER, ZILLIKEN.

Oechsle Scale for sugar content of grape juice (see p.283).

Oestrich Rhg w ★★→★★★ 71 75 76 83 **88 89 90** 92 **93** 94 95 **96** 97 98 **99** 00 01 02 **03** Big village; variable but some splendid RIESLING, esp AUSLESE. First Class v'yds: Doosberg, Lenchen. Top growers: AUGUST ESER, Peter Jakob Kühn, Querbach, Spreitzer, WEGELER.

Offene weine Wines by the glass: the way to order it in wine villages.

Oppenheim Rhh w ★→★★★ 76 83 **88 89 90** 92 **93** 94 95 96 **97** 98 99 00 01 02 **03** Town S of NIERSTEIN; spectacular 13th-C church. First Class Herrenberg and Sackträger v'yds: top wines. Growers inc: GUNTRUM, C Koch, Kühling-Gillot. None of these, though, is realizing the full potential of these sites.

Ortenau (Bereich) District just S of Baden-Baden. Gd KLINGELBERGER (RIESLING), SPÄTBURGUNDER, and RULÄNDER. Top village: DURBACH.

Ortsteil Independent part of a community allowed to use its estate v'yd name without the village name, eg SCHLOSS JOHANNISBERG, STEINBERG.

Palatinate English for PFALZ.

Pauly-Bergweiler, Dr ★★★ Fine 31-acre BERNKASTEL estate. V'yds there and in WEHLEN, etc. Peter Nicolay wines from URZIG and ERDEN are usually best.

Perlwein Semi-sparkling wine.

Pfalz 56,000-acre v'yd region S of RHEINHESSEN (see MITTELHAARDT and SÜDLICHE WEINSTRASSE). Warm climate: grapes ripen fully. The classics are rich wines, with dry RIESLING increasingly fashionable and well-made. Biggest RIESLING area after MOSEL-SAAR-RUWER. Formerly known as the Rheinpfalz.

Pfeffingen, Weingut ★★★ Messrs Fuhrmann and Eymael make v.gd RIESLING and SCHEUREBE on 26 acres of UNGSTEIN. Back on fine form since 1999.

Piesport M-M w ★→★★★★ 71 75 76 83 **88 89 90** 92 **93** 94 95 96 **97** 98 99 00 **01** 02 **03** Tiny village with famous vine amphitheatre: at best glorious rich aromatic RIESLING. Great First Class v'yds: Goldtröpfchen & Domherr. Treppchen far inferior. Grosslage: Michelsberg (mainly MÜLLER-THURGAU; avoid). Esp Grans Fassian R HAART, Kurt Hain, KESSELSTATT, St Urbans-Hof, Weller-Lehnert.

Plettenberg, von ★★ 100-acre estate at BAD KREUZNACH. Mixed quality.

Portugieser Second-rate red-wine grape now often used for WEISSHERBST.

Prädikat Special attributes or qualities. See QMP.

Prinz, Fred Rhg w ★★ Best RIESLING in the village of Hallgarten.

Prüfungsnummer The official identifying test-number of a quality wine.

Prüm, J J ★★★★ **69** *70* 71 73 **75 76** *78* **79** *80* 81 82 **83** *84* 85 **86** 87 **88 89 90** 91 92 *93* 94 **95** 96 **97** 98 **99** 00 01 02 **03** Superlative and legendary 34-acre MOSEL estate in BERNKASTEL, GRAACH, WEHLEN, ZELTINGEN. Delicate but long-lived wines, esp in Wehlener SONNENUHR: 81 KABINETT is *still* young. Plain Prüm RIESLING is a bargain.

Qualitätswein bestimmter Anbaugebiete (QbA) The middle quality of German wine, with sugar added before fermentation (as in French chaptalization), but controlled as to areas, grapes, etc.

Qualitätswein mit Prädikat (QmP) Top category, for all wines ripe enough to be unsugared (KABINETT to TROCKENBEERENAUSLESE). See p.137 and p.144.

GERMANY

Randersacker Frank w ★★→★★★ **76 83 88** 89 **90** 92 **93** 94 **95** 96 **97** **98** 99 00 **01** 02 Leading village for distinctive dry wine. First Class v'yds: Marsberg, Pfülben, Sonnenstuhl. Grosslage: Ewig Leben. Growers inc BURGERSPITAL, STAATLICHER HOFKELLER, JULIUSSPITAL, Robert Schmitt, Schmitt's Kinder.

Ratzenberger, Jochen ★★ 20-acre estate making racy dry and off-dry RIESLING in BACHARACH; best from First Class Posten and Steeger St-Jost v'yds.

Rauenthal Rhg w ★★★→★★★★ **71 75 76 83** 88 **89 90 92 93** 94 95 96 **97 98 99** 00 **01** 02 **03** Supreme village: spicy, complex wine. First Class v'yds: Baiken, Gehrn, Nonnenberg, Rothenberg, Wülfen. Grosslage: Steinmächer. Top grower: BREUER.

Rebholz ★★★→★★★★ Top SÜDLICHE WEINSTRASSE estate for 50 yrs. Many varieties on 33 acres. Makes the best dry MUSKATELLER, GEWÜRZTRAMINER, CHARDONNAY (Burgundian style), and SPÄTBURGUNDER in Pfalz.

Ress, Balthasar ★★ RHEINGAU estate (74 gd acres), cellars in HATTENHEIM. Also runs SCHLOSS REICHARTSHAUSEN. Variable quality; original artists' labels.

Restsüsse Unfermented grape sugar remaining in (or in cheap wines added to) wine to give it sweetness. TROCKEN wines have very little, if any.

Rheinburgengau (Bereich) District name for MITTELRHEIN v'yds around the Rhine Gorge. Wines with steely acidity needing time to mature.

Rheingau Best v'yd region of Rhine, W of Wiesbaden. 7,000 acres. Classic, substantial but subtle RIESLING, yet on the whole recently eclipsed by brilliance elsewhere. BEREICH name for whole region: JOHANNISBERG.

Regions to watch out for in 2005

Mittelrhein had a string of poor vintages to contend with, but with 2001 it proves that it is capable of producing great classic Rieslings.

Rheinhessen is producing a wave of new-style, clean, harmonious dry white wines that are often excellent value for money.

Saale-Unstrut has finally shaken off the legacy of its communist past and is starting to make some surprisingly full-bodied, supple dry whites.

Sachsen too, has overcome the same problems and is making sleeker and more aromatic dry whites than Saale-Unstrut.

Rheinhessen Vast region (61,000 acres of v'yds) between Mainz and Worms, bordered by River NAHE, mostly second rate, but inc top RIESLINGS from NACKENHEIM, NIERSTEIN, OPPENHEIM, etc.

Rheinhessen Silvaner (RS) New uniform label for earthy dry wines from SILVANER – designed to give a modern quality image to the region.

Rheinpfalz See PFALZ.

Richter, Weingut Max Ferd ★★★ Top 37-acre MITTELMOSEL family estate, at Mülheim. Fine barrel-aged RIESLING produced from First Class v'yds: BRAUNEBERG Juffer-SONNENUHR, GRAACH Domprobst, Mülheim (Helenenkloster), WEHLEN Sonnenuhr.

Rieslaner Cross between SILVANER and RIESLING; makes fine AUSLESEN in FRANKEN, where most is grown. Also superb from MÜLLER-CATOIR.

Riesling The best German grape: fine, fragrant, fruity, long-lived. Only CHARDONNAY can compete as the world's best white grape.

Rüdesheim Rhg w ★★→★★★★ **71 75 76** 79 82 **83** 84 **85** 86 87 88 **89 90** 91 **92 93** 94 95 **96 97 98 99** 00 **01** 02 **03** Rhine resort with First Class v'yds; the three best are called Rüdesheimer Berg-. Full-bodied wines, fine-flavoured, often remarkable in off years. Many of the top RHEINGAU estates own some Rüdesheim v'yds. Best growers: BREUER, JOHANNISHOF, August Kesseler, LEITZ, SCHLOSS SCHONBORN, STATE DOMAIN.

Ruländer Pinot Gris: now more commonly known as GRAUBURGUNDER.

Ruppertsberg Pfz w ★★→★★★ 89 **90** 92 **93** 94 95 **96** 97 **98** 99 00 01 02 **03** Southern village of MITTELHAARDT. First Class v'yds inc: Linsenbusch, Nussbein, Reiterpfad, Spiess. Growers inc: BASSERMANN-JORDAN, BIFFAR, BUHL, BÜRKLIN-WOLF, DEINHARD.

Ruwer 76 83 88 **89 90** 92 93 94 95 96 **97** 98 **99** 00 01 02 **03** Tributary of MOSEL nr TRIER. Very fine, delicate but highly aromatic and well-structured wines. Villages inc EITELSBACH, KASEL, MERTESDORF.

Saale-Unstrut 93 94 95 96 **97** 98 99 **00 01** 02 **03** Region in former E Germany, 1,300 acres around confluence of these two rivers at Naumburg, nr Leipzig. The terraced v'yds of WEISSBURGUNDER, SILVANER, GEWÜRZTRAMINER, RIESLING, etc, and red PORTUGIESER have Cistercian origins. Quality leaders: Lützkendorf, Landesweingut Kloster Pforta, Pawis, Thüringer Weingut.

Saar 75 76 79 80 81 82 **83** 84 85 86 87 88 **89 90** 91 92 **93** 94 **95** 96 **97** 98 **99** 00 01 02 **03** Hill-lined tributary of the MOSEL S of RUWER. The most brilliant, austere, steely RIESLING of all. Villages inc: AYL, OCKFEN, Saarburg, SERRIG, WILTINGEN (SCHARZHOFBERG). Grosslage: SCHARZBERG. Many fine estates here.

Saar-Ruwer (Bereich) District covering these two regions.

Sachsen 94 95 96 97 98 99 **00 01** 02 Former E German region (900 acres) in Elbe Valley around Dresden and Meissen. MÜLLER-THURGAU dominant, but WEISSBURGUNDER, GRAUBURGUNDER, TRAMINER, RIESLING give dry wines with real character. Best growers: SCHLOSS PROSCHWITZ, Vincenz Richter, Klaus Seifert, Schloss Wackerbarth, Klaus Zimmerling.

St-Antony, Weingut ★★★ Excellent 57-acre estate. Rich, intense, dry and off-dry RIESLING from First Class v'yds of NIERSTEIN.

St-Ursula Well-known merchants at BINGEN.

Salm, Prinz zu Owner of SCHLOSS WALLHAUSEN in NAHE and Villa Sachsen in RHEINHESSEN. President of VDP.

Salwey, Weingut ★★★ Leading BADEN estate at Oberrotweil, esp for RIESLING, WEISSBURGUNDER, and RULÄNDER.

Samtrot Red WÜRTTEMBERG grape. Makes Germany's closest shot at Beaujolais.

Sauer, Horst ★★★ Escherndorfer Lump is one of FRANKEN's top sites, and no one makes better SILVANER and RIESLING from here than Sauer. Notable dry wines, and sensational TROCKENBEERENAUSLESEN.

Schaefer, Willi ★★★ The finest grower of GRAACH (but only 5 acres).

Scharzhofberg M-S-R (Saar) w ★★★★ 71 75 76 83 88 **89 90** 91 92 **93** 94 **95** 96 **97** 98 **99** 00 **01** 02 **03** Superlative 67-acre SAAR v'yd: austerely beautiful wines, the perfection of RIESLING, best in AUSLESEN. Top estates: BISCHÖFLICHE WEINGÜTER, EGON MÜLLER, VON HÖVEL, VON KESSELSTATT, Van Volxem.

Schaumwein Sparkling wine.

Scheurebe Aromatic grape of high quality (and RIESLING parentage), esp used in PFALZ. Excellent for botrytis wine (BEERENAUSLESEN, TROCKENBEERENAUSLESEN).

Schillerwein Light red or rosé QBA; speciality of WÜRTTEMBERG (only).

Schloss Johannisberg Rhg w ★★★ 76 83 85 86 **88 89 90** 91 92 93 94 95 96 97 98 **99** 00 **01** 03 Famous RHEINGAU estate of 86 acres owned by Princess Metternich and the Oetker family. The original Rhine first growth. Wines inc fine SPÄTLESE, KABINETT TROCKEN. Since 1996 there has been a dramatic return to form. The 01 vintage are the best wines since 75 and 76.

Schloss Lieser ★★★ Small estate run by Thomas Haag, from FRITZ HAAG estate, making pure racy RIESLINGS from underrated v'yds of Lieser.

Schloss Neuweier ★★★ Leading producer of dry RIESLING in BADEN.

Schloss Proschwitz ★★ A resurrected princely estate at Meissen, which leads former E Germany in quality, esp with dry WEISSBURGUNDER and GRAUBURGUNDER.

Schloss Reichartshausen 10-acre HATTENHEIM v'yd run by RESS.

Schloss Reinhartshausen ★★ Fine 250-acre estate in ERBACH, HATTENHEIM, KIEDRICH, etc. Originally property of Prussian royal family, now in private hands. Model RHEINGAU RIESLING. The mansion beside the Rhine is now a luxury hotel. The last few vintages were nothing special.

Schloss Schönborn ★★★ One of biggest RHEINGAU estates, based at HATTENHEIM. Full-flavoured wines, variable, at best excellent. Also v.gd SEKT.

Schloss Thorn Ancient OBERMOSEL estate, remarkable ELBLING, RIESLING, and castle.

Schloss Vollrads Rhg w ★★→★★★ **71 76 83 85 88 89** 90 *92* 93 94 95 96 97 **98 99** 00 01 02 One of the greatest historic RHEINGAU estates, owned by a bank since the sudden death of owner Erwein Count Matuschka in 1997. Since 1998 vintage quality is much improved.

Erstes Gewächs

From 1 September 2000, the Rheingau's vineyard classification came into force and with it the designation "Erstes Gewächs" or "First Growth". It applies to wines produced according to strict rules (including maximum yield and blind-tasting test). The weakness of the scheme is that the classification takes in just over 35 per cent of the region's vineyards, including some rather poor sites. The scheme is open for Spätburgunder and Riesling, which may be dry or sweet. So far, few Erstes Gewächs wines have been released.

Schloss Wallhausen ★★ The 25-acre NAHE estate of the PRINZ ZU SALM, one of Germany's oldest. 65% RIESLING. V.gd TROCKEN. Variable quality.

Schlossböckelheim Nahe w ★★→★★★★ **75 76** 79 **83 85** 86 88 **89 90** 91 92 **93** 94 **95** 96 **97 98** 99 00 **01** 02 Village with top NAHE v'yds, inc First Class Felsenberg, In den Felsen, Königsfels, Kupfergrube. Firm yet delicate wine. Top growers: CRUSIUS, DÖNNHOF, Gutsverwaltung Niederhausen-Schlossböckelheim.

Schneider, Weingut Georg Albrecht ★★ Impeccably run 32-acre estate. Classic off-dry and sweet RIESLING in NIERSTEIN, the best from Hipping Vineyard.

Schoppenwein Café (or bar) wine, ie wine by the glass.

Schwarzer Adler, Weingut ★★★ Franz Keller and his son Fritz make top BADEN dry GRAU-, WEISS-, and SPÄTBURGUNDER on 35 acres at Oberbergen.

Schweigen Pfz w r ★★ **89 90 92 93** 94 *95* **96 97 98** 99 00 01 02 **03** Southern PFALZ village. Best growers: Fritz Becker, esp for SPÄTBURGUNDER, Bernhart.

Sekt German (QBA) sparkling wine, best when the label specifies RIESLING, WEISS-BURGUNDER, or SPATBURGUNDER. Sekt BA (BEERENAUSLESE) is the same but comes from a specified area.

Selbach-Oster ★★★ 26-acre ZELTINGEN estate among MITTELMOSEL leaders.

Serrig M-S-R (Saar) w ★★→★★★ **71 75 76** 83 **85 88 89 90 93** 94 95 96 **97** *98* 99 00 01 02 **03** Village giving steely wines, excellent in sunny years. First Class v'yds: Herrenberg, Saarstein, WÜRZBERG. Top grower: SCHLOSS SAARSTEIN.

Silvaner Third most-planted German white grape variety, generally underrated; best examples in FRANKEN: the closest thing to Chablis in Germany. Worth looking for in RHEINHESSEN and KAISERSTUHL too.

Simmern, Langwerth von ★★★ Famous ELTVILLE family estate. Top v'yds: Baiken, Mannberg, MARCOBRUNN. After disappointing quality during the 1990s back on form with 01.

Sonnenuhr Sundial. Name of several v'yds, esp First Class one at WEHLEN.

Spätburgunder Pinot N: the best red-wine grape in Germany – esp in BADEN and WÜRTTEMBERG and increasingly V.gd PFALZ – generally improving quality, but most still underflavoured or over-oaked.

Spätlese Late harvest. One better (riper, with more alcohol, more substance and usually more sweetness) than KABINETT. Gd examples age at least 5 yrs, often longer. TROCKEN Spätlesen can be very fine with food.

Staatlicher Hofkeller ★★→★★★ The Bavarian STATE DOMAIN. 370 acres of the finest FRANKEN v'yds with spectacular cellars under the great baroque Residenz at WÜRZBURG.

Staatsweingut (or Staatliche Weinbaudomäne) The state wine estates or domains; esp KLOSTER EBERBACH.

State Domain See STAATSWEINGUT.

Steigerwald (Bereich) District name for E part of FRANKEN.

Steinberg Rhg w ★★★ **71 75 76** 79 **83** 86 88 89 **90** 92 **93** 94 **95** 96 97 98 **99** 00 **01** 02 **03** Famous 79-acre HATTENHEIM walled v'yd, planted by Cistercian monks 700 yrs ago. Now owned by STATE DOMAIN, ELTVILLE. Some glorious wines; some in the past were sadly feeble.

Steinwein Wine from WÜRZBURG's best v'yd, Stein.

Südliche Weinstrasse (Bereich) District name for S PFALZ. Quality has improved tremendously in last 25 yrs. See ILBESHEIM, REBHOLZ, SCHWEIGEN.

Tafelwein See "Germany's quality levels" box on p.144.

Tauberfranken (Bereich) New name for minor Badisches Frankenland BEREICH of N BADEN: FRANKEN-style wines.

Thanisch, Weingut Dr H ★★→★★★ BERNKASTEL estate, inc part of the Doctor v'yd. Confusingly two estates share the same name.

Traben-Trarbach M-M w ★★ 76 **83** 88 89 **90** 93 **95** 96 **97** 98 99 00 **01** 02 **03** Major wine town of 800 estates, 87% of it RIESLING. Top v'yds: Ungsberg, Würzgarten. Top growers: Louis Klein, Martin Müller, and RICHTER.

Traisen Nahe w ★★★ **71 75 76** 79 **83 85** 86 **88 89 90** 91 92 **93** 94 **95 96** 97 98 99 00 **01** 02 **03** Small village inc First Class Bastei and Rotenfels v'yds, capable of making RIESLING of concentration and class. Top grower: CRUSIUS.

Traminer See GEWÜRZTRAMINER.

Trier M-S-R w ★★→★★★ Great wine city of Roman origin, on MOSEL, nr RUWER, now also inc AVELSBACH and EITELSBACH. Big Mosel charitable estates have cellars here among imposing Roman ruins.

Trittenheim M-M w ★★ **71 75 76 85 89 90** 92 **93** 94 **95** 96 97 98 99 00 **01** 02 **03** Attractive S MITTELMOSEL light wines. Top v'yds were Altärchen, Apotheke, but now inc second-rate flat land; First Class v'yds are Felsenkopf, Leiterchen. Grosslage: Michelsberg (avoid). Growers inc: E Clüsserath, Clüsserath-Weiler, GRANS-FASSIAN, Milz.

Trocken Dry. Trocken wines have max 9 grams per litre unfermented sugar. Some are austere, others (better) have more body and alcohol.

Trockenbeerenauslese (TBA) Sweetest, most expensive category of German wine, extremely rare, with concentrated honey flavour. Made from selected shrivelled grapes affected by noble rot (botrytis). See also EDEL. *Edelbeerenauslese* would be a less confusing name.

Trollinger Pale red grape variety of WÜRTTEMBERG; over-cropped but locally very popular.

Ungstein Pfz w ★★ ·★★★ 76 **83 85 88 89 90** 91 92 **93** 94 95 **96** 97 98 **99 00** **01** 02 **03** MITTELHAARDT village with fine harmonious wines. First Class v'yds: Herrenberg, Weilberg. Top growers: Darting, FITZ-RITTER, PFEFFINGEN, Pflüger, Karl Schäfer.

Ürzig M-M w ★★★★ **71 75 76 83** 88 89 **90** 92 **93** 94 **95** 96 **97** 98 **99** 00 01 02 **03** Village on red sandstone and red slate famous for firm, full, spicy wine unlike other MOSELS. First Class v'yd: Würzgarten. Growers inc: CHRISTOFFEL, LOOSEN, Mönchhof, Peter Nicolay, WEINS-PRÜM.

VDP Verband Deutscher Prädikats und Qualitätsweingüter. The pace-making association of premium growers. Look for its eagle insignia on wine labels. President: PRINZ ZU SALM.

Vereinigte Hospitien ★★ "United Hospices". Ancient charity at TRIER with large holdings in PIESPORT, SERRIG, TRIER, WILTINGEN, etc; wines recently well below their wonderful potential.

Wachenheim Pfz w ★★★→★★★★ **71 76 83** 88 **89 90** 92 **93** 94 95 **96 97 98** 99 00 **01** 02 **03** 840 acres, inc exceptionally fine RIESLING. First Class v'yds: Belz, Gerümpel, Goldbächel, Rechbächel, etc. Top growers: BIFFAR, BÜRKLIN-WOLF, WOLF.

Wagner, Dr ★★★ Saarburg estate. 20 acres of RIESLING. Many fine wines inc TROCKEN.

Walluf Rhg w ★★★ **75 76 83 88 89 90 92** 93 94 95 96 **97** 98 **99** 00 **01 02 03** Neighbour of ELTVILLE; formerly Nieder- and Ober-Walluf. Underrated wines. First Class v'yd: Walkenberg. Growers inc BECKER, JOST.

Walporzheim Ahrtal (Bereich) District name for the whole AHR Valley.

Wawern M-S-R (Saar) w ★★→★★★ **71 75 76 83** 85 88 **89 90** 92 **93** 94 95 96 **97 98 99** 00 01 02 **03** Small village, fine RIESLING. First Class v'yd: Herrenberg.

Wegeler ★★ Important family estates in OESTRICH, MITTELHARDT, and BERNKASTEL. The Wegelers owned the merchant house of Deinhard until 1997.

Wehlen M-M w ★★★→★★★★ **71 75 76 83** 85 86 **88 89 90** 92 **93** 94 **95** 96 **97** 98 **99** 00 **01** 02 Neighbour of BERNKASTEL with equally fine, somewhat richer wine. Location of great First Class v'yd: SONNENUHR. Grosslage: Münzlay. The top growers are: Heribert Kerpen, LOOSEN, PRÜM, S A Prüm, Studert-Prüm, SELBACH-OSTER, WEGELER, and WEINS-PRÜM.

Weil, Weingut Robert ★★★★ *71* 76 83 85 *86 87* 88 89 **90** 91 92 93 **94** 95 **96** 97 98 99 00 01 02 **03** Outstanding 145-acre estate in KIEDRICH; now owned by Suntory of Japan. Superb QMP, EISWEIN, TROCKENBEERENAUSLESEN, BEERENAUSLESEN; standard wines also v.gd since 1992. Widely considered to be RHEINGAU'S No 1.

Weingut Wine estate.

Weinkellerei Wine cellars or winery. See KELLER.

Weins-Prüm, Dr ★★→★★★ Classic MITTELMOSEL estate; 12 acres at Wehlen. WEHLENER SONNENUHR is usually top wine.

Weinstrasse Wine road: a scenic route through v'yds. Germany has several.

Weintor, Deutsches See SCHWEIGEN.

Weissburgunder Pinot Blanc. Most reliable grape for TROCKEN wines: low acidity, high extract. Also much used for SEKT.

Weissherbst Usually a pale pink wine, QBA or above and occasionally BEERENAUSLESE, from a single variety. Speciality of BADEN, PFALZ, and WÜRTTEMBERG.

Werner, Domdechant ★★★ Family estate on best HOCHHEIM slopes: top wines excellent, others only fair.

Wiltingen M-S-R (Saar) w ★★→★★★★ **71 75 76 83** 85 86 **88 89 90** 92 **93** 94 **95** 96 **97** 98 **99** 00 **01 02 03** The centre of the SAAR. 790 acres. Beautifully subtle, austere wine. Great First Class v'yd is SCHARZHOFBERG (ORTSTEIL); and First Class are Braune Kupp, Hölle. Top growers: EGON MÜLLER, VON KESSELSTATT, Von Volxem, etc.

Winkel Rhg w ★★★ **71 75 76 83 88 89 90** 92 **93** 94 95 **96** 97 98 **99** 00 01 02 **03** Village famous for full, fragrant wine. First Class v'yds inc Hasensprung, Jesuitengarten, SCHLOSS VOLLRADS, Schlossberg. Growers inc PRINZ VON HESSEN, Von Mumm, BALTHASAR RESS, SCHLOSS SCHÖNBORN, etc.

Winningen M-S-R w ★★ Lower MOSEL town near Koblenz: unusually full RIESLING for region. Excellent dry wines. First Class v'yds: Röttgen, Uhlen. Top growers: Heymann-Löwenstein, Knebel, Richard Richter.

Wintrich M-M w ★★→★★★ 71 76 83 88 89 90 92 93 94 95 *96* 97 98 99 00 01 02 **03** Neighbour of PIESPORT; similar wines. First Class v'yd: Ohligsberg. Top grower: REINHOLD HAART.

Winzergenossenschaft (WG) Wine-growers' co-operative, often making sound and reasonably priced wine. Referred to in this text as "co-op".

Winzerverein The same as above.

Wirsching, Hans ★★★ Estate in IPHOFEN and FRANKEN. Wines can be firm, elegant, and dry, but quality is variable. 170 acres in First Class v'yds: Julius-Echter-Berg, Kalb, etc.

Wonnegau (Bereich) District name for S RHEINHESSEN.

Wolf J L ★★★ Formerly run-down estate in WACHENHEIM acquired by Ernst Loosen (see LOOSEN) of Bernkastel. From first vintage (1996) strong, dry PFALZ wines with a MOSEL-like finesse. Superb quality since 1998.

Wolff Metternich ★★ Noble DURBACH estate: some gd RIESLING.

Württemberg 83 85 86 *87* 88 **89** 90 92 **93** 94 95 96 **97** 98 **99** 00 01 02 03 Vast southern area, little known for wine outside Germany despite some v.gd RIESLING (esp NECKAR Valley) and frequently unrealized potential to make gd reds: LEMBERGER, SAMTROT, TROLLINGER.

Würzburg Frank ★★→★★★★ 71 76 81 83 85 86 88 89 90 92 **93** 94 96 **97** 98 99 00 **01** 02 03 Great baroque city on the Main, centre of FRANKEN wine: fine, full-bodied, dry. First Class v'yds: Abtsleite, Innere Leiste, Stein. See MAINDREIECK. Growers: BÜRGERSPITAL, JULIUSSPITAL, STAATLICHER HOFKELLER.

Zell M-S-R w ★→★★★ 83 88 89 90 93 94 **95** 96 **97** 98 99 00 01 02 03 Best-known lower MOSEL village, esp for awful Grosslage: Schwarze Katz (Black Cat). RIESLING on steep slate gives aromatic wines. Top grower: KALLFELZ.

Zell (Bereich) District name for whole lower MOSEL from Zell to Koblenz.

Zeltingen M-M w ★★→★★★★ 71 75 76 79 83 85 86 88 89 90 92 93 94 **95** 96 **97 98** 99 00 **01** 02 03 Top MOSEL village near WEHLEN. Lively crisp RIESLING. First Class v'yd: SONNENUHR. Top growers: Markus Molitor, PRÜM, and SELBACH-OSTER.

Zilliken, Forstmeister Geltz ★★★ Former estate of Prussian royal forester with 25 acres at Saarburg and OCKFEN, SAAR. Racy, minerally RIESLINGS, inc superb AUSLESE, EISWEIN with excellent ageing potential.

Zwierlein, Freiherr von ★★ 55-acre family estate in GEISENHEIM. 100% RIESLING.

Luxembourg

Luxembourg has 3,285 acres of vineyards on limestone soils on the Moselle's left bank. High-yielding Elbling and Rivaner (Müller-Thurgau) vines dominate, but there are also significant acreages of Riesling, Gewürztraminer and (usually best) Auxerrois, Pinot Blanc, and Pinot Gris. These give light to medium-bodied (10.5–11.5%), dry, Alsace-like wines. The highly competent Vins Moselle co-op makes 70% of the total, including quantities of very fair fizz. Domaine et Tradition estates association, founded in 88, promotes quality from noble varieties. The following vintages were all good: 89 90 92 95; 97 outstanding; 98 average; 99 similar but softer; 2000 poor; 2001 much better; 2002 and 2003 look good for Pinot Noir. Best from: Aly Duhr et Fils, M Bastian, Caves Gales, Bernard Massard (surprisingly good Cuvée de l'Ecusson classic method sparkling), Clos Mon Vieux Moulin, Ch de Schengen, Sunnen-Hoffmann.

Spain & Portugal

More heavily shaded areas
are the wine growing regions

The following abbreviations are used in the text:

Amp	Ampurdán/Empordà-Costa Brava
Alen	Alentejo
Bair	Bairrada
Bul	Bullas
Cos del S	Costers del Segre
El B	El Bierzo
Est	Estremadura
La M	La Mancha
Mont-M	Montilla-Moriles
Nav	Navarra
Pen	Penedès
Pri	Priorato/Priorat
Rib del D	Ribera del Duero
Rib del G	Ribera del Guadiana
R Ala	Rioja Alavesa
R Alt	Rioja Alta
RB	Rioja Baja
Set	Setúbal
Som	Somontano
U-R	Utiel-Requena

MADEIRA (off west coast of Africa)

Spain and Portugal joined the EU (and, as far as most of their wine is concerned, the 20th century) only 19 years ago. Both made rapid progress, Euro-grants encouraging massive re-equipping. Ferment continues: splendid new wines continue to appear. But some makers are asking (and indeed getting) silly prices.

Currently in Spain (apart from the sherry country), the North, Rioja, Navarra, Galicia, Rueda, Catalonia, and Ribera del Duero hold most interest; those in Portugal (apart from the port vineyards and Madeira) are the Douro, Ribatejo, Alentejo, the central coast, and the North. In Portugal especially, newly delimited areas have successfully challenged old, traditional appellations. Portugal is now concentrating on its huge range of indigenous grape varieties, often blendng them with international ones, especially Syrah in the South. There is quite a lot of Syrah coming on stream in the Alentejo.

The following list includes the best and most interesting makers, types, and regions of each country, whether legally delimited or not. Geographical references (see map above) are to demarcated regions (DOs and DOCs), autonomies, and provinces.

Sherry, Port, and Madeira have a separate chapter on p.176.

Spain

Recent vintages of the Spanish classics
Rioja

2003 Irregular weather and an extremely hot, dry summer posed problems for harvesting and vinification. But the yields and quality are officially rated good.

2002 Cold and drought affected development of the fruit, and yields in Rioja Alta and Alavesa were low. Quality is doubtful, but wait and see.

2001 Smaller harvest and good-quality fruit. Excellent potential.

2000 Generally favourable conditions. Huge harvest, but abnormally high summer and autumn temperatures led to uneven quality.

1999 The worst April frost in memory delayed maturation, and summer rain resulted in mildew. Average.

1998 Biggest-ever vintage. Lack of sun and rain in the autumn delayed picking. Very good.

1997 Little sun and much rain gave a large and patchy vintage. Average/poor.

1996 An unusually cold spring and cool summer resulted in well-structured but fairly immediate wines. Very good.

1995 Good alcoholic strength and acidity. Excellent.

Ribera del Duero

2003 A very cold winter, mild spring, scorching summer, and timely October rains resulted in a tricky harvest. The best of the wines are of good colour, glycerine, and alcohol, but low in acidity.

2002 Hot weather followed by heavy rain in late summer led to a large harvest, but with quality often below normal.

2001 April frost reduced the crop, otherwise an almost perfect growing season and quality is outstanding.

2000 Very large harvest but ripening was uneven. Some bodegas made spectacular wines; but in general good.

1999 Almost perfect weather and bumper harvest, but rainfall around harvest time resulted in lack of acidity. Very good.

1998 Torrential rain in early autumn and record grape prices. Good.

1997 Cool and wet with spring and summer frosts. Poor.

1996 Dry summer and autumn. Good acidity; long-lived reservas. Excellent.

1995 April frost, but late sun resulted in rich, structured wines. Excellent.

Navarra

2003 The hot, dry summer was followed by extended torrential rain and outbreaks of botrytis and mildew. As in 2002, only the best and most professional producers obtained decent results.

2002 Torrential August rains affected the quality of wines from the south of the region; others are excellent.

2001 An excellent year with big, ripe, well-balanced wines.

2000 Very dry year of prolific yields, calling for rigorous selection. Best wines are big and fleshy, with good potential for ageing. Very good.

1999 Most frost-afflicted vintage of the decade, with soaring grape prices. Wines are well-structured and long-ageing. Excellent.

1998 Spring frosts but dry, hot summer. Well-structured wines with excellent colour and elegant aromas. Very good.

1997 Dank, overcast summer. Short-lived wines. Poor.

1996 Cold, wet summer. Wines spare, but notably fresh and aromatic with adequate acidity and concentration. Good.

1995 Very small crop due to major frost in April. Wines similar to those of 94, but longer-lived because of superior acidity. Excellent.

Penedès

2003 A very dry and long summer, refreshed with rains in Aug, then cool nights and sunny days in Sept, resulted in a great vintage.

2002 Aug rain ruined part of the crop; but a splendid Sept gave wines of good quality.

2001 April frosts reduced the yield but warm summer produced very good wines.

2000 Dry winter, some spring rain, and very dry summer. Perfect ripening of the grapes gave well-balanced wines. Very good.

1999 Dry summer but abundant harvest. Very good.

1998 Very good whites and excellent reds.

1997 Large harvest. Good white wines and very good reds.

1996 Heavy August rains resulted in a prolific harvest. Very good.

1995 Dry and mild winter. Summer alternately wet and hot. Very good.

Abadia Retuerta Castilla y León r ★★★ 96 97 98 99 00 01 02 One of the most modern BODEGAS in Spain. Non-DO, but with top B'x help is making exceptional Temp, Cab Sauv, and Merlot with prices to match. Esp Pago Valdebellón (**99**).

Agapito Rico Jumilla r ★★★ 95 98 99 01 02 Young BODEGA making some of Spain's best VINOS JOVENES in the unlikely region of JUMILLA, esp 98 99 Carchelo wines (Syrah, Merlot, or Monastrell with Temp and Merlot) Also excellent CRIANZA.

Agramont See PRÍNCIPE DE VIANA, BODEGAS.

Albariño High-quality, aromatic white grape of GALICIA. Perhaps the most highly regarded white. See RÍAS BAIXAS, CERVERA, GRAN BAZÁN, PAZO DE BARRANTES.

Albet y Noya Pen r w p ★★→★★★ 97 98 99 Leading producer of gd but pricey organic wines. Reliable Col-leccio whites and reds. Excellent barrel-fermanted Chard and outstanding red blend Marti (**97**).

Alella r w (p) dr sw ★★ DYA Small, demarcated region N of Barcelona. Pleasantly fruity wines. (See MARQUÉS DE ALELLA, PARXET.)

Alicante r (w) ★ 98 99 00 01 DO. Most wines still earthy and over-strong – with shining exceptions such as Syrah from Enrique Mendoza.

Alión Rib del D r ★★★ 95 96 99 00 Since discontinuing the 3-yr-old VALBUENA in 1997, VEGA SICILIA has acquired this second BODEGA to make 100% Temp; impressive results. Vigorous; gd to mid-term keeping.

Allende, Finca R Ala r ★★★→★★★★ 96 97 98' 99 00 01 Much-praised BODEGA: elegant, oak-aged Temp. Vastly expensive Aurus (96 97 98) and single-estate Calvario (01').

Alvaro Palacios Pri r ★★★★ 98 99 00 01 Gifted emigré from RIOJA making some of the most expensive and fashionable red wine in Spain, inc Finca Dofi (98), L'Ermita (94), Les Terrasses. One of the few PRIORATOS to repay bottle-age.

Ampurdán/Empordà-Costa Brava Amp r w p ★→★★ Demarcated region abutting Pyrenees. Mainly co-op-made rosés and reds.

Año Year: 4° Año (or Años) means 4 yrs old when bottled. Was common on labels, now largely discontinued in favour of vintages, or terms such as CRIANZA.

Artadi See COSECHEROS ALAVESES.

Arzuaga, Bodegas Rib del D r ★★★ 94 95 96 97 98 99 Architecturally showy new BODEGA with 370 acres aiming for luscious, modern wines.

Bach, Masía Pen r w dr sw res ★★ 98 99 00 Once gloriously independent winery renowned for its sensational sweet, white, oaky Extrísimo. Now just another average PENEDÈS producer, albeit belonging to CAVA giant CODORNÍU.

Barbier, René Pen r w res ★★ 96 98 01 Owned by FREIXENET, known for fresh white Kraliner, red RIOJA BAJA RESERVAS.

Barón de Ley RB r (w) res ★★★ 95 99 00 Newish RIOJA BODEGA linked with EL COTO: gd single-estate wines, esp Finca del Monasterio (00).

Baso r w ★★ Brand name for reliable Garnacha from NAVARRA made by young winemaker TELMO RODRÍGUEZ, formerly of LA GRANJA REMELLURI.

Berberana, Bodegas See BODEGAS UNIDAS.

Berceo, Bodegas R Alt r w p res ★★→★★★ 95 98 00 02 Cellar in HARO with gd Gonzalo de Berceo GRAN RESERVA.

Beronia, Bodegas R Alt r w res ★★→★★★ 94 96 98 99 Modern BODEGA making reds in traditional, oaky style and fresh, modern whites. Owned by GONZÁLEZ-BYASS.

Bilbaínas, Bodegas R Alt r w (p) w dr sw sp res ★★ 94 95 96 97 98 99 Historic Haro BODEGA, well-known for its red Viña Pomal and lighter Zaco. New owners CODORNÍU have some way to go in introducing less oaky modern-style wines. Best are Res La Vicalanda (95 99) and gd Royal Carlton CAVA.

SPAIN

Binissalem r w ★★ **98 99 00 01** Best-known MALLORCA DO. See also FRANJA ROJA.

Blanco White.

Bodega Spanish term for (i) a wineshop; (ii) a concern occupied in the making, blending, and/or shipping of wine; and (iii) a cellar.

Bodegas de Crianza Castilla la Vieja Rueda w dr sp ★★→★★★ The Sanz family makes some of RUEDA's liveliest whites under a variety of labels (eg PALACIO DE BORNOS) using Verdejo, Viura, Sauv Bl. Reds inc concentrated, oaky Medina del Campo, Almirantazgo de Castilla, and wines from new BODEGA in DO TORO.

Bodegas Unidas Umbrella organization controlling MARQUÉS DE GRIÑÓN, MARQUÉS DE MONISTROL, BODEGAS BERBERANA (still producing old favourites like Carta de Oro), and Vinícola Mediterráneo with its holiday wines. A new departure are the *haciendas* situated in the v'yds, both making wine and putting up visitors, eg Hacienda Durius (Alto Duero) and Hacienda Concordia (Rioja). Unidas also owns the winery of late Prince Hohenlohe in Ronda, famous for its pure Petit Verdot (oo).

Bodegas y Bebidas Part of Allied-Domecq, owns wineries all over Spain. Mainly mid-market brands. Also controls various prestigious firms, eg AGE, CAMPO VIEJO, Marqués del Puerto.

Bodegas y Viñedos del Jalón Calatayud r (w dr p) ★★ **99 00 01 02** 03 Leading brands are the very drinkable Castillo Maluenda and Marqués de Aragón.

Bornos, Palacio de Bornos Rueda w sp ★★★ **99 00 01 02** First-rate Sauv Bl and Verdejo wines. See BODEGAS DE CRIANZA CASTILLA LA VIEJA.

Bretón, Bodegas R Alt r res ★★★ **90** 91 94 95 96 98 Respected Loriñon range and little-seen, expensive, concentrated Dominio de Conté (**96**) and Alba de Bretón (**98**). Current wines are disappointingly astringent.

Calatayud ★→★★ **94 97 98 99 00 01 02** Aragón DO (1 of 4): esp Garnacha. VINOS Y VIÑEDOS DE JALON holds sway.

Campillo, Bodegas R Ala r (p) res ★★★ **91 92 94 95 96 97 99** Affiliated with FAUSTINO MARTÍNEZ, a young BODEGA with gd, if unspectacular, wines.

Campo Viejo, Bodegas RAlt r (w) res ★→★★★ **95 97 99** 00 100% Temp Alcorta; big, fruity red RESERVAS, esp Marqués de Villamagna. See BODEGAS Y BEBIDAS.

Can Rafols dels Caus Pen r p w ★★ **94 96 97 98 00** 01 Young, small PENEDÈS BODEGA: own-estate, fruity Cab Sauv, pleasant Chard/Xarel-lo/Chenin Bl; Gran Caus and less expensive Petit Caus ranges. Best red is Caus Lubis.

Canary Islands (Islas) r w p g ★→★★ Until recently there were few wines of any quality other than dessert Malvasías (BODEGAS El Grifo and BODEGAS Mozaga on Lanzarote). No fewer than 8 DOS have been created, and modernized BODEGAS, esp on TENERIFE, are making better, lighter wines. The tourist trade may keep prices high, but the flavours have real interest. To investigate.

Caralt, Cavas Conde de Pen r w sp res ★★→★★★ CAVA wines from outpost of FREIXENET, esp gd, vigorous Brut NV; also pleasant still wines.

Cariñena r (w p) ★ **91 92 93 96 98 99 00 01 02** Co-op-dominated DO: large-scale supplier of strong, everyday wine. Being invigorated and wines lightened.

Casa Castillo Jumilla r (w p) ★★→★★★ **98 99 00 01** Some of the best wines from JUMILLA made by Julia Roch e Hijos, but Parker-esque: designed for immediate, brambly oak impact.

Casa Gualda La M r ★★→★★★ **99 00 01** Cencibel (Temp), Cab Sauv, Crianza, and young Merlot (**99**) of unbeatable quality/value from the co-op Nuestra Sra de la Cabeza in Cuenca.

Casa de la Viña Valdepeñas r (w p) ★★ **98 99 00 01** 02 BODEGAS Y BEBIDAS-owned estate, since 1980s: sound and fruity Cencibel, CRIANZAS, and JOVENES (**00**).

Castaño, Bodegas Yecla (w dr) r res ★★ **98 99 00 01 02** Trail-blazer in remote YECLA making sound and pleasant blends of Monastrell with Cab Sauv, Temp, and Merlot under the names of Castaño, Colección, Hecula, and Pozuelo.

Castell del Remei Cos del S r w p ★★→★★★ 99 00 01 Historic v'yds/winery revived, re-equipped, and replanted since 1983. Best wines: Gotim Bru (Temp/Cab Sauv/Merlot), new designer-style Oda, and top Merlot 1780 (01).

Castellblanch Pen w sp ★★ PENEDÈS CAVA firm, owned by FREIXENET. Look for Brut Zero and Gran Castell GRAN RESERVAS.

Castillo de Monjardín Nav r w ★★→★★★ 97 98 99 00 Newish winery making fragrant, oaky Chard Res (**99**) and v.gd reds and rosé (**01**), esp blends of Merlot (**97 98**). Has recently reverted to much oakier wines in response to Spanish tastes.

Castillo de Ygay R Alt r w ★★★★ (r) 25 52 64 68 75 78 82 85 87 89 94 A legend. The **64** is still superb. See MARQUÉS DE MURRIETA.

Castillo de Perelada, Caves Amp r w p res sp ★★→★★★ 94 95 98 99 01 Large range of both still wines and CAVA, inc Chard, Sauv Bl, Cab Sauv (esp Gran Claustro **94 95 96**), and sparkling Gran Claustro Extra Brut.

Cataluña 00 01 DO covering the whole Catalan area. Wines may be registered as from an existing DO or from the new global DO, but not from both.

Cava Official term for any classic-method Spanish sparkling wine, and the DO covering the areas up and down Spain where it is made, though Rueda and Galicia are not included.

Celler de Capçanes Montsant r ★★→★★★ 99 00 01 Large ex-co-op in MONTSANT with some of the best new-wave wine from the Tarragona area. Typical is the **99**: meaty, concentrated, and somewhat tannic.

Centro Españolas, Bodegas La M r w p ★★ 96 97 99 01 Large modern BODEGA best known for creditable red Allozo, 100% Temp.

Cervera, Lagar de Rías Baixas w ★★★ DYA Maker of one of best ALBARIÑOS: flowery and intensely fruity with subdued bubbles and a long finish.

Chacolí País Vasco w (r) ★→★★ DYA Alarmingly sharp, often sparkling wine from the Basque coast; two DOS for all 700 acres. 9–11% alcohol. Best producers: Txomin Etxaniz (Guetaria), Aretxondo (Viscaya).

Chivite, Bodegas Julián Nav r w (p) dr sw res ★★★ 95 96 97 98 99 00 The biggest and best NAVARRA BODEGA. Now some of Spain's top reds, deep-flavoured, very long-lived; flowery, well-balanced white, esp Chivite Colección 125 (**01**), v.gd rosé (**02**), and superb Vendemia Tarde Moscatel (**01**), the best from Spain. See GRAN FEUDO.

Cigales r p ★→★★ 99 00 01 Recently demarcated region N of Valladolid, esp for light reds (traditionally known as *claretes* – a term banned by the EU).

Clos Mogador Pri r ★★★→★★★★ 99 00 01 René Barbier (no connection with FREIXENET) produces first-rate new-wave Clos Mogador PRIORATO.

Old Vintages

Extended lists of old vintages, still occasionally available at a price, are given for wines such as Vega Sicilia, Lopez de Heredia, and Castillo de Ygay from Murrieta. At their best these wines are memorable and of great complexity, but a great deal depends on their provenance and cellerage, and they must be acquired from entirely reliable sources. Faking of old vintages, especially of Vega Sicilia, is rife.

Codorníu Pen w sp ★★→★★★ One of the two largest firms in SAN SADURNÍ DE NOYA making gd CAVA: very high-tech, 10 million bottles ageing in cellars. Mature Non Plus Ultra, fresh Anna de Codorníu or premium Jaume de Codorníu RESERVA. Also owns RAÍMAT, BILBAINAS.

Compañía Vinícola del Norte de España (CVNE) R Alt r w dr (p) ★★→★★94 95 96 97 98 99 01 Famous RIOJA BODEGA. In spite of (or because of?) a revolutionary new vinification plant, young wines are less gd than formerly, though some of the older Viña Real and Imperial RESERVAS are spectacular. See also CONTINO.

Con Class, Bodegas Rueda w dr ★★→★★★ DYA Despite the dreadful brand name, exciting Verdejo/Viura and Sauv Bl from the Sanz family.

Conca de Barberà w (r p) **98 99 00** Catalan DO region growing Parellada grapes for making CAVA. But its best wines are the superb MILMANDA Chard and red Grans Muralles, both from TORRES.

Condado de Haza Rib del D r ★★★ **94 95 96 97 98 00 01** Pure, oak-aged Tinto Fino. Similar to PESQUERA but more consistent and better value.

Conde de Valdemar See MARTÍNEZ-BUJANDA.

Consejo Regulador Official organization for the control, promotion, and defence of a DENOMINACIÓN DE ORIGEN.

Contino R Ala r res ★★★ **94 95 96' 97 98 99** 00 Very fine single-v'yd red made by a subsidiary of COMPAÑIA VINICOLA DEL NORTE DE ESPANA. Look for 100% Graciano (**94' 99**) and premium Viña del Olivo (**96' 99**).

Cosecha Crop or vintage.

Cosecheros Alaveses R Ala r (w p) ★★★ **94 95 96 97 98 01 02** Up-and-coming former co-op, esp for gd, young, unoaked red Artadi, Viñas de Gain, Viña El Pisón, and Pagos Viejos RESERVAS.

Costers del Segre Cos del S r w p sp ★★→★★★ **92 95 96 97 98 99 00 01** Small, demarcated area around city of Lleida (Lérida), famous for v'yds of RAÍMAT.

Costers del Siurana Pri r (sw) ★★★→★★★★ **99 01'** A star of Priorato. Carlos Pastrana makes the prestigious Clos de l'Obac, Misere, and Usatges from Garnacha/Cab Sauv, sometimes plus Syrah, Merlot, Temp, and Cariñena. Wonderful sweet Dolç de l'Orbac.

CoViDes Pen r w p sp res ★★ **96 99** 00 01 Large co-op; gd Duc de Foix white and Cab Sauv, Cab Sauv/Temp; also first-rate Duc de Foix CAVA.

Criado y embotellado por... Grown and bottled by...

Crianza Literally "nursing"; the ageing of wine. New or unaged wine is *sin crianza* or *joven* ("young"). Reds labelled *crianza* must be at least 2 yrs old (with 1 yr in oak, in some areas 6 months), and must not be released before the third year.

Denominación de Origen (DO) Official wine region (see p.156).

Denominación de Origen Calificada (DOCa) Classification for wines of the highest quality; so far only RIOJA benefits (since 1991).

Denominació de Origen Qualificada (DOQ) The Catalan equivalent of DOCa (see above), applied to the wines of PRIORAT from the 02 vintage onwards.

Domecq R Ala r (w) res ★★→★★★ **94 95 97 98 99** RIOJA outpost of sherry firm. Excellent Marqués de Arienzo RESERVAS, fragrant, and medium-bodied.

Don Darias/Don Hugo Alto Ebro r w ★ Huge-selling, modestly priced wines, very like RIOJA, from undemarcated BODEGAS Vitorianas. Sound red and white.

Dulce Sweet.

El Bierzo El B DO **91 92 94 96 98 99** 00 01 N of León. Top wine: Luna Berberida RESERVA.

El Coto, Bodegas R Ala r (w) res ★★★ **94 95 97 98 99** BODEGA best-known for light, soft, red El Coto and Coto de Imaz RESERVAS (**94**).

Elaborado y añejado por... Made and aged by...

Enate Som DO r w p res ★★★ **95 96 97 98 99** Gd wines from SOMONTANO in the N: light, clean, fruity, inc barrel-fermented Chard (**02**) and Cab Sauv blends (the CRIANZA is full and juicy). Wonderful **00** Merlot.

Espumoso Sparkling (but see CAVA).

Fariña, Bodegas Toro r w res ★★→★★★ **95 98 99** 00 Best-known BODEGA of DO TORO, but being overtaken by younger rivals. Gd spicy reds. Gran Colegiata is cask-aged; Colegiata not. Young Primero. Recent vintages overpriced and disappointing.

Faustino, Bodegas R Ala r w (p) res ★★→★★★ **93 94 95 97 98 99** 00 Long-established BODEGA, formerly F Martínez, with gd reds. GRAN RESERVA is Faustino I. Top is Faustino de Autor (**95**).

Fillaboa, Granxa Rías Baixas w ★★★ DYA Small firm; delicately fruity ALBARIÑO.

> **A Spanish choice for 2005**
> **Agustín Blázquez Carta Blanca** Fino Jerez
> **Emilio Hildago Privilgio 1860** Palo Cortado Jerez
> **Gramona Impérial 98 Brut Natur** Cava
> **Torres Esmeralda Blanco 02** Penedès
> **Viña Mein Blanco 02** Ribeira
> **Artadi Viña el Pisón 00** Rioja Alavesa
> **Mas Martinet Clos Martinet 00** Priorato
> **Marqués de Griñón Valdepusa Syrah 99** Toledo
> **Alión 99** Ribera del Duero
> **Bodegas Maurodos Viña San Román 99** Toro

Franja Roja Binissalem-Mallorca r res ★★ **97** 98 99 00 Best-known MALLORCA BODEGA at Binissalem, making improving José L Ferrer wines, esp Especial Miró (**99**).

Freixenet, Cavas Pen w sp ★★→★★★ Huge CAVA firm, rivalling CODORNÍU in size. Gd sparklers, notably bargain Cordón Negro in black bottles, Brut Barroco, RESERVA Real, and Premium Cuvée DS. Also owns Gloria Ferrer in California, Champagne Henri Abelé (Reims), and a sparkling-wine plant in Mexico.

Galicia Rainy NW Spain: esp for fresh, aromatic but pricy whites, eg ALBARIÑO.

Generoso Apéritif or dessert wine rich in alcohol.

Gramona Pen r w d sw res ★★→★★★ 00 01 02 Established and sizeable family firm makes gd Chard, Sauv Bl, Gewurz, Pinot N, and Merlot. Also excellent CAVA.

Granbazán w dr ★★★ DYA Agro de Bazán produces a classic, fragrant ALBARIÑO with mouth-cleansing acidity.

Gran Feudo Nav w Res ★★ →★★★ **95 96 98 99** 00 Brand name of fragrant white, refreshing rosé (**02**); soft, plummy red; the best-known wines from CHIVITE.

Gran Reserva See RESERVA.

Gran Vas Pressurized tanks (French *cuves closes*) for making cheap sparkling wines; also used to describe this type of wine.

Guelbenzu, Bodegas Non-DO r (w) res ★★→★★★ **98 99 00 01** Family estate in Navarra making concentrated, full-bodied reds: Azul, EVO, and top wine Lautus (**99**).

Guitán Godello Valdeorras w ★★★→★★★★ **01 02** Made by BODEGAS Tapada, these splendidly fruity, fragrant, and complex 100% Godello wines, rated among the top whites in Spain, typify renaissance of native grapes in GALICIA. The barrel-fermented type has the edge.

Haro Wine centre of the RIOJA ALTA, a small but stylish old town.

Hill, Cavas Pen w r sp res ★★→★★★ **93 96 97 98 99** Old PENEDÈS firm: fresh, dry white Blanc Cru, gd Gran Civet, and Gran Toc reds, first-rate young Masía Hill Temp, and delicate RESERVA Oro Brut CAVA.

Iljalba, Viña R Alt r w dr p ★→★★★ **94 95 96 98 99** 00 A newish BODEGA with a reputation for organically made younger wines and a rare 100% Graciano.

Josep Anguera Beyme Montsant r ★★→★★★ **98 00** Small family firm on verges of PRIORATO making superior fruity Finca L'Argata wines from Syrah, Cab Sauv, Garnacha, and Cariñena blends.

Joven (vino) Young, unoaked wine. Also see CRIANZA.

Jumilla r (w p) ★→★★★ **91 93 96 98 99 00 01** DO in mountains N of Murcia. Its traditionally overstrong wines are being lightened by earlier picking and better winemaking. The Monastrell grape can yield dark and fragrant wines to rival those of RIBERA DEL DUERO. See AGAPITO RICO and CASA CASTILLO.

Juvé y Camps Pen w sp ★★★ **97 98 99** Family firm. Top-quality CAVA from free-run juice only, esp RESERVA de la Familia and Gran Juvé y Camps (**98**).

LAN, Bodegas R Alt r (p w) res ★★→★★★ **95 96 97 98 99 01** Huge, modern BODEGA. Recently reorganized; making improved Lan, Lanciano, new-style Ediciones Limitados, and premium Culmen de Lan (**94'**).

Lanzarote Canary Island with very fair, dry Malvasía, eg El Grifo.

Lar de Lares Rib del G r res ★★ **97 98 99 00** Meaty GRAN RESERVA from BODEGAS INVIOSA, in remote Extremadura (in SW). And younger, lighter Lar de Barros. Also gd Bonaval CAVA.

León, Jean Pen r w res ★★★ **90 91 93 96 97 99** Small firm; TORRES-owned since 1995. Gd oaky Chard (**99**). Earlier Cab Sauv was huge, repaid long ageing; lighter since 90. Also outstanding Merlot (**97**).

López de Heredia R Alt r w (p) dr sw res ★★→★★★ **54 57 61 64 68 70 73 78 81 87 93 94 97** Old-established HARO BODEGA: very long-lasting, very traditional wines. Best are really old RESERVAS from 54 onwards; still marvellous 64S.

Los Llanos Valdepeñas r (p w) res ★★ **95 96 98 99** One of growing number of VALDEPEÑAS BODEGAS to age wine in oak. RESERVA, GRAN RESERVA; premium Pata Negra Gran Reserva: 100% Cencibel (Temp). Clean, fruity, white Armonioso.

Málaga Almost nothing left, but see TELMO RODRIGUEZ.

Mallorca Interesting things are happening on the island at last, inc fresh Chard (better unoaked), Merlot, Syrah, Cab Sauv. Also traditional varieties and blends. Anima Negra, FRANCA ROJA, Herens de Ribas, Miguel Oliver, Pere Seda, Son Bordils, and Jaume Mesquida are leaders.

Vinos de Alta Expresión

Within the last few years a new generation of select and very pricey wines has appeared in Spain. The full potential of the grape is realized by using fruit from old vines, picking at the optimum point, hand sorting, and fermenting in small batches. From Rioja; Allende Aurus; Artadi el Pisón; Marqués de Riscal Barón de Chirel; Remírez de Ganuza; Cirsión; Muga Torre Muga. From Conca de Barberà: Torres Grans Muralles. From Priorato: Clos Mogador Reserva; Alvaro palacio Finca Dolfi. From Ribera del Duero; Vega Sicilia Unico. From Navarra: Guelbenzu Lautus. Expect to pay.

Mancha, La La M r w ★→★★ **92 93 94 96 97 98 99 00** 01 Vast demarcated region N and NE of VALDEPEÑAS. Mainly white wines; the reds lack the liveliness of the best Valdepeñas but show signs of improvement. To watch.

Marqués de Alella Alella w (sp) ★★→★★★ DYA Light, fragrant white ALELLA wines from PARXET, some Chard (inc barrel-fermented Allier). Also CAVA.

Marqués de Cáceres, Bodegas R Alt r p w res ★★★ **91 92 94 96 98 01** Gd red RIOJAS made by modern French methods inc premium Gaudium (**96**) and MC (**01**); surprisingly light, fragrant, white (DYA), barrel-fermented Antea (**01**), and sweet Santinela.

Marqués de Griñón Dominio de Valdepusa r w ★★★ **94 95 96 97 98 99** Enterprising nobleman initiated very fine Cab Sauv, delicious (**99 01**) Syrah (**01**), and Petit Verdot at his Dominio de Valdepusa nr Toledo, S of Madrid, not formerly known for wine. Fruity wines to drink fairly young. Also gd RIOJAS and Durius. See BODEGAS UNIDAS.

Marqués de Monistrol, Bodegas Pen p r sp dr sw res ★★→★★★ **92 94 95' 98 99** Old BODEGA now owned by BODEGAS UNIDAS. Reliable CAVAS. Fresh blends of Cab Sauv, Merlot, and Temp.

Marqués de Murrieta R Alt r p w res ★★★→★★★★ **25 42 50 52 54 60 68 70 75 78 87 89 94 95 96 97 99** Historic, revered BODEGA nr Logroño. Famous for red CASTILLO DE YGAY and old-style, oaky white. Magnificent premium Dalmau, a blend of Temp/Cab Sauv/Graciano (**99**).

Marqués de Riscal R Ala r (p w) res ★★★→★★★★ **91 92 94 95 96 97 99** Best-known RIOJA ALAVESA BODEGA. Fairly light, dry red. Old vintages: very fine, some more recent ones variable; now right back on form. Barón de Chirel, 50% Cab Sauv (**94' 95' 99**) is magnificent. RUEDA whites inc Sauv Bl (**02**) and oak-aged RESERVA Limousin (**00**).

Marqués de Vargas, Bodegas y Viñedos R Ala ★★★ **92 93 94 95 96 97** Spectacular newcomer making a RESERVA and a Privada (**96' 97**), both with magnificent concentration and balance.

Martínez-Bujanda R Ala r p w res ★★★ **90 91 92 93 94 95 96 97 98 99** Refounded (1985), family-run RIOJA BODEGA, remarkably equipped. Superb wines, inc fruity *sin* CRIANZA, irresistible ROSADO; noble Valdemar RESERVAS (**95**), 100% Garnacha, and splendid premium 100% Temp single-v'yd Finca Valpiedra (**94 96**).

Mascaró, Antonio Pen r p w sp ★★→★★★ **90 91 92 93 94 96** 97 Top brandy maker, gd CAVA; fresh, lemony, dry white Viña Franca and Anima Cab Sauv.

Mas Martinet Pri r ★★★→★★★★ **99 00** Maker of Clos Martinet and a pioneer of the exclusive boutique PRIORATOS.

Mauro, Bodegas r ★★→★★★ **94 95 96 97 98 99** Young BODEGA in Tudela del Duero; v.gd, round, fruity TINTO del País (Temp) red and superb Vendimia Seleccionado (**99**). Not DO, as some of the fruit is from outside RIBERA DEL DUERO. Now making excellent TORO San Roman (01).

Milmanda ★★★ Premium barrel-fermented Chard from TORRES.

Montecillo, Bodegas R Alt r w (p) res ★★ **95 97 00** RIOJA BODEGA owned by OSBORNE. Old GRAN RESERVAS are magnificent.

Montsant Tiny, new DO (since 2001) in an enclave of PRIORATO, sharing much in common with its wines.

Muga, Bodegas R Alt r (w sp) res ★★★ **91 94 95 96 99 00** Small family firm in HARO, known for some of RIOJA's best strictly traditional reds. Wines are light but highly aromatic, with long, complex finish. Best is Prado Enea and now extraordinary concentrated Torre Muga (**94' 95 96 98 00**). Whites and CAVA less gd. Fresh white Viura fermented in barrel (**00**).

Navajas, Bodegas R Alt r w res ★★★→★★★ **95 96 98 99 00 01** 02 Small firm: bargain reds, CRIANZAS, RESERVAS. Also excellent oak-aged white Viura (**00 02**).

Navarra Nav r p (w) ★★→★★★ **92 94 95 96 97 98 99 00** 01 02 Demarcated region. Stylish Temp and Cab Sauv reds, rivalling RIOJAS in quality and trouncing many in value. See CHIVITE, GUELBENZU, PALACIO DE LA VEGA, OCHOA, PRÍNCIPE DE VIANA.

Nuestro Padre Jésus del Perdón, Co-op de La M r w ★→★★ **94 96 98 99 00 01** Bargain fresh white Lazarillo and more-than-drinkable Yuntero; 100% Cencibel (alias Temp) and Cencibel/Cab Sauv aged in oak.

Ochoa Nav r p w res ★★→★★★ **91 92' 93 94 96 97 99 00** Small family BODEGA; excellent Moscatel (**02**), but better-known for well-made red and rosés, inc 100% Temp and 100% Merlot (**99**).

Organic Wines Spain's most prestigious and long-standing producer is ALBET I NOYA in PENEDÈS.

Pago A v'yd or area of limited size giving rise to exceptional wines. The term now has legal status, eg DO Dominio de Valdepusa (see MARQUÉS DE GRIÑÓN).

Pago de Carraovejas Rib del D r res ★★→★★★ **99 00 01** New estate; some of the region's most stylish, densely fruity TINTO Fino/Cab Sauv in minimal supply.

Palacio, Bodegas R Ala r p w res ★★★ **94' 95 96 97 98 99 00** Gd old BODEGA rescued from Seagram ownership. Very sound RESERVA Privada (**94**) and Cosme Palacio (**95**).

Palacio de Fefiñanes Rías Baixas w dr ★★★ DYA Oldest-established of the BODEGAS in RÍAS BAIXAS, now making excellent, modern-style ALBARIÑOS.

SPAIN

> **Important note:**
> Most large Spanish wineries make a range of red, white, and rosé. The vintages at the top of an entry refer to the best of a bodega's red *crianzas* and reservas, and are only a rough guide, since the vintages and degree of maturity may well vary from one wine to another. When individual wines are named in the text, preferred vintages are given in brackets.

Palacio de la Vega Nav r p w res ★★→★★★ 93 95 96 97 98 00 New BODEGA with juicy Temp JOVEN, Cab Sauv, Merlot, and much promise. Gd Chard (01).

Parxet Alella w p sp ★★→★★★ Excellent fresh, fruity, exuberant CAVA (only one produced in ALELLA): esp Brut Nature. Elegant w ALELLA (DYA): MARQUÉS DE ALELLA.

Paternina, Bodegas R Alt r w (p) dr sw res ★→★★★ Known for its standard red brand Banda Azul. Conde de los Andes label was fine, but the famous 78 is strictly for fans of oak/volatile acidity. Recent vintages, as of its other RIOJAS, are disappointing. Most consistent is Banda Dorada white (DYA).

Pazo Ribeiro r p w ★★ DYA Brand name of the RIBEIRO CO-OP, whose wines are akin to VINHOS VERDES. Rasping red is local favourite. Pleasant, slightly fizzy Pazo whites are safer; white Viña Costeira and Amadeus have quality.

Pazo de Barrantes Rías Baixas w ★★★ DYA New ALBARIÑO from RIAS BAIXAS; estate owned by late Conde de Creixels of MURRIETA. Delicate, exotic, top quality.

Pazo de Señorans Rías Baixas w dr ★★★ DYA Exceptionally fragrant wines from a BODEGA considered a benchmark of the DO.

Penedès Pen r w sp ★→★★★ 91 93 94 95 96 98 99 00 01 Demarcated region inc Vilafranca del Penedès and SAN SADURNI DE NOYA. See also TORRES.

Pérez Pascuas Hermanos Rib del D r res ★★★ 91 92 94 95 96 97 99 00 01 Immaculate, tiny BODEGA. In Spain, its fruity and complex red VIÑA Pedrosa is rated one of the best.

Pesquera Rib del D r ★★★ 90 91 92 93 94 95' 97 99 00 Small quantities of RIBERA DEL DUERO from Alejandro Fernández. Robert Parker rated it level with finest B'x, and it has never forgotten. Janus Gran Reserva (95). Also CONDADO DE HAZA.

Pingus, Dominio de Rib del D r ★★★ Temp-based (only 450 cases). Winemaker/owner: Peter Sisseck. Spain's answer to "garage" wines of B'x. Absurdly expensive, their keeping qualities being unknown.

Piqueras, Bodegas Almansa r (w dr p) ★★→★★★ 96 98 00 02 Family BODEGA. Some of LA MANCHA's best: Castillo de Almansa CRIANZA, Marius GRAN RESERVA.

Pirineos, Bodega Som w p r ★★→★★★ 96 97 98 99 00 01 Former CO-OP and SOMONTANO pioneer. Gd Gewurz (02) and excellent red Marboré (99).

Príncipe de Viana, Bodegas Nav r w p ★★ 98 00 01 02 Large firm (formerly Cenalsa), blending and maturing CO-OP wines and shipping a range from NAVARRA, inc flowery, new-style white and fruity red Agramont.

Priorato/Priorat Pri br r ★★★ 92 93 94 95 96 98 99 00 01 DO enclave of TARRAGONA, traditionally known for alcoholic RANCIO and huge-bodied, almost black red. At its brambly best, one of Spain's triumphs. COSTERS DE SIURANA, MAS MARTINET, and ROTLLAN TORRA rightly rank among Spain's stars. DOQ since 02 vintage.

Raïmat Cos del S r w p sp ★★→★★★ (Cab) 94 95 96 97 98 99 00 Clean, structured wines from DO nr Lérida, planted by CODORNÍU with Cab Sauv, Chard, other international vines. Gd 100% Chard CAVA. Value.

Raventós i Blanc Pen w sp ★★→★★★ Excellent CAVA aimed at top of market. Also fresh El Preludi white and 100% Chard.

Remelluri, La Granja R Ala w dr r res ★★★ 95 96 99 00' Small estate (since 1970), making v.gd traditional red RIOJAS but future less certain after departure of Telmo Rodriguez. Avoid the disappointing 97.

Reserva (res) Gd-quality wine matured for long periods. Red Reservas must spend at least 1 yr in cask and 2 in bottle; Gran Reservas 2 in cask and 3 in bottle. Thereafter many continue to mature for yrs.

Rías Baixas w ★★→★★★ 95 96 97 98 00 01 DYA NW DO embracing sub-zones Val do Salnés, O Rosal, and Condado do Tea, now for some of the best (and priciest) cold-fermented Spanish whites, mainly from ALBARIÑO grapes.

Ribera del Duero Rib del D 91 94 95 96 98 99 00 01 Fashionable, fast-expanding DO E of Valladolid (the Duero becomes the Portuguese Douro). Excellent for TINTO Fino (Temp) reds. Many excellent wines, but high prices. See ARZUAGA, PAGO DE CARRAOVEJAS, PÉREZ PASCUAS, PESQUERA, TORREMILANOS, VEGA SICILIA. Also non-DO MAURO.

Rioja r p w sp ★★→★★★★ 64 70 75 78 81 82 85 89 91 92 94 95 96 98 99 00 01 N upland region along River Ebro for many of Spain's best red table wines in scores of BODEGAS *de exportación*. Temp predominates. Sub-divided into the following three areas:

Rioja Alavesa N of the R Ebro, produces fine red wines, mostly light in body and colour, but particularly aromatic.

Rioja Alta S of the R Ebro and W of Logroño, grows most of the finest, best-balanced red and white wines; also some rosé.

Rioja Baja Stretching E from Logroño, makes stouter red wines, often from Garnacha and high in alcohol, and often used for blending.

La Rioja Alta, Bodegas R Alt r w (p) dr (sw) res ★★★ 89 90 94 95 96 98 99 Excellent RIOJAS, esp red RESERVA viña Alberdi, velvety Ardanza RESERVA, lighter Araña Reserva, splendid Reserva 904, and marvellous Reserva 890 (82) – but the wines are not lasting as long as they used to.

Riojanas, Bodegas R Alt r (w p) res ★★★ 64 73 94 95 96 98 Old BODEGA. Traditional viña Albina; big, mellow Monte Real RESERVAS (96).

Roda, Bodegas R Alt r ★★★ 92 94' 95' 96 98 99 00 01 Founded in 1989 by a Catalan couple who decided that only in HARO could they make their dream wines. Superb costly Roda I (which has the edge) and Roda II. Cirsión (98').

Rosado Rosé.

Rotllan Torra Pri r (r&w sw) ★★★ 99 00 Premium Amadis, Balandra, sweet Amadis Dolç, and Moscatel RESERVA Especial PRIORATOS.

Rovellats Pen w p sp ★★→★★★ Small family firm making only gd (and expensive) CAVAS, stocked in some of Spain's best restaurants.

Rueda br w ★★→★★★ 96 97 98 99 00 01 Small, historic DO W of Valladolid. Traditional *flor*-growing, sherry-like wines up to 17% alcohol; now for fresh whites, esp MARQUÉS DE RISCAL. Secret weapon is the Verdejo grape, but the region is under threat from a massive influx of mercenary outsiders, seeking to exploit its success.

Ruíz, Santiago Rías Baixas w ★★→★★★ DYA Small, prestigious RIAS BAIXAS company, now owned by LAN: fresh, lemony ALBARIÑOS, not quite up to former standards.

San Sadurní de Noya Pen w sp ★★→★★★ Town S of Barcelona, hollow with CAVA cellars. Standards can be very high, though the flavour (of Parellada and other grapes) never gets close to Champagne.

Sangría Cold red-wine cup traditionally made with citrus fruit, fizzy lemonade, ice, and brandy. But too often repulsive commercial fizz.

Scala Dei, Cellers de Pri r w p res ★★→★★★ 99 00 01 Original PRIORATO BODEGA owned by CODORNÍU. Dark, powerful Garnacha. Cartoixa RESERVAS, concentrated, blackberry-rich young Negre.

Schenk, Bodegas Valencia, U-R r w sw dr p ★★ 99 00 01 Large concern making decent Estrella Moscatel, gd Monastrell/Garnacha Cavas Murviedro, and Los Monteros. Also from UTIEL-REQUENA, reliable Las Lomas red and fresh Bobal ROSADO.

Seco Dry.

Segura Viudas, Cavas Pen w sp ★★→★★★ CAVA from SAN SADURNI (FREIXENET-owned). Buy the Brut Vintage **99**, Galimany **98**, or esp RESERVA Heredad **98**.

Solís, Félix w dr p r ★★ **93 97 98 99** 02 BODEGA in VALDEPEÑAS making sturdy, oak-aged reds, VIÑA Albali RESERVAS, and fresh white.

Somontano Som ★★→★★★ **91 94 95 96 98 99 00 01** 02 Fashionable DO in Pyrenean foothills. Given the cool conditions, future could lie with whites and Pinot N. Best-known BODEGAS: old French-established Lalanne (esp Viña San Marcos (Moristel/Tem/Cab Sauv); white Macabeo, Chard), BODEGA PIRINEOS, VIÑAS DEL VERO. Also Viñedos y CRIANZAS del Alto Aragón (excellent ENATE range).

Tarragona r w br dr sw ★→★★★ **95 96 97 98 99 00 01** Table wines from demarcated region (DO); previously of little note; now greatly improved.

Telmo Rodríguez, Compañía de Vinos r w ★★→★★★ HQ in Logroño, controlled by gifted oenologist Telmo Rodríguez, formerly of REMELLURI. Excellent DO wines in TORO, RUEDA, NAVARRA (see BASO), ALICANTE. His Molina Real 100% Moscatel from MÁLAGA is exceptional.

Tenerife r w ★→★★ DYA Now 4 DOs; sometimes more than merely drinkable young wines. Best BODEGAS: Flores, Monje, Insulares (VIÑA Norte label).

Tinto Red.

Toro r ★★★ **90 91 93 94' 95 96 98 99 00 01** 02 This increasingly fashionable DO 150 miles NW of Madrid still produces powerful, fairly basic reds. VEGA SICILIA has now built a BODEGA there; and spectacular wines like San Román from MAURO and Numanthia from Vega de Toro are showing what the region can do.

Torremilanos Rib del D r (p) res ★→★★★ **94 95 96 97 99** Label of BODEGAS Peñalba López, a fast-expanding family firm nr Aranda de Duero. TINTO Fino (Temp) is smoother, more RIOJA-like than most.

Torres, Miguel Pen r w p dr s/sw res ★★→★★★★ **90 92 93 94 95 96 97 98 99 00** World-famous family company among the stars of the wine world. Makes most of the best PENEDÈS wines; flagship for all Spain. Wines are flowery white VIÑA Sol (**02**), Green Label Fransola Sauv (**02**), Gran Viña Sol (**01**) Parellada, MILMANDA oak-fermented Chard (**00**), off-dry aromatic Esmeralda (**02**), Waltraud Ries (**02**), red Sangre de Toro, Gran Sangre de Toro (**96 97**), v.gd Mas la Plana Gran Coronas (Cab Sauv) RESERVAS (**89 93 94 96 98 99**), fresh, soft Atrium Merlot (**02**), and VIÑA Magdala Pinot. Mas Borrás (**98**): 100% Pinot N. Superb new Grans Muralles (**98**), full-bodied, made from native grapes inc reintroduced Garot, is noble. Also in Chile, California, and China. The new Nerola wines, with DO Catalunya, are innovative blends of Mediterranean grapes. Also superb new Praedium (**03**) from grapes grown in PRIORATO.

Unión de Cosecheros de Labastida R Ala r p w dr ★→★★★ **94 95 96 97 98 99 00** Old-established and first-rate RIOJA co-op. Young, juicy Montebuna, gd Solagüen CRIANZAS and RESERVAS, and top Manuel Qintano RESERVAS (**98**).

Utiel-Requena U-R r p (w) ★→★★ **92 93 94 98 99 00 01** 02 Region W of VALENCIA. Sturdy reds and hyper-tannic wines for blending; also light, fragrant rosé.

Valbuena Rib del D r ★★★ **89 90 91 92 95' 97 99** Formerly made with the same grapes as VEGA SICILIA but sold when 5 yrs old. Best at about 10 yrs, but the 94 has been recalled because of cork taint. Some prefer it to its elder brother, but see ALIÓN.

Valdeorras Galicia r w ★→★★★ **97 98 99 00** DO E of Orense. Fresh, dry wines; at best, Godellos rated among top white wines in Spain. See GUITÁN GODELLO.

Valdepeñas La M r (w) ★→★★★ **90 91 95 96 98 99 00 01** 02 Demarcated region nr Andalucían border. Mainly reds, high in alcohol but surprisingly soft in flavour. Best wines (eg LOS LLANOS, FELIX SOLIS, CASA DE LA VIÑA) now oak-matured.

Valduero, Bodegas Rib del D r (w p) ★★→★★★ **90 91 95 96 98** Now more than 10 yrs old; growing reputation for well-made wine and v.gd-value RESERVAS.

Valencia r w ★ **98 99 00 01** Demarcated region exporting vast quantities of clean and drinkable table wine; also refreshing whites, esp Moscatel.

Vega Sicilia Rib del D r res ★★★★ **53 60 62 64 66 68 70 73 75 76 80 81 82 83 85 86 89 90 91** Top Spanish wine: full, fruity, piquant, rare, and fascinating. Up to 16% alcohol; best at 12-15 yrs. RESERVA Especial: a blend, chiefly of 62 and 79 (!). Also VALBUENA, ALION. Also owns Oremus in Tokáji, Hungary.

Vendimia Vintage.

Viña Literally, a v'yd. But wines such as Tondonia (LOPEZ DE HEREDIA) are not necessarily made only with grapes from the v'yd named.

Viñas del Vero Som w p r res ★★→★★★ **92 93 94 95 96 97 99** 01' SOMONTANO estate. Gd varietal wines: Chard, Ries, Gewurz. Best red: Gran Vos (**97 98**).

Vinícola de Castilla La M r p w ★★ **92 96 97 98 00** 02 One of largest LA MANCHA firms. Red and white Castillo de Alhambra are palatable. Top are Cab Sauv, Cencibel (Temp), Señorío de Guadianeja GRAN RESERVAS.

Vinícola Navarra Nav r p w dr res ★★ **97 98 99 00 01** Old-established firm, now part of BODEGAS Y BEBIDAS, but still thoroughly traditional. Best wines Castillo de Javier rosé (**02**), Las Campañas RESERVA (**97**).

Vino común/corriente Ordinary wine.

Yecla r w ★→★★ DO to the N of Murcia. Decent red from BODEGAS CASTAÑO.

Portugal

Recent vintages

2003 Hot summer produced soft, ripe, early-maturing wines, especially in the South. Best Bairrada for a decade.

2002 Challenging vintage with heavy rain during picking. Better in the South.

2001 Large vintage throughout. Those producers who undertook careful selection made very good wines.

2000 Small harvest in fine weather led to ripe-flavoured wines from all regions.

1999 Another small year with prospects dashed by rain during the vintage. Wines from the South better than those from the North.

1998 Tiny yields, potentially excellent wines in the North diluted by late September rain. Inland areas and the Alentejo fared better.

Adega A cellar or winery.

Alenquer r w ★→★★★ Aromatic wines from IPR just N of Lisbon. Gd estate wines from PANCAS, CARNEIRO, and MONTE D'OIRO (Syrah).

Alentejo r (w) ★→★★★ **97 98 99 00' 01** 02 Vast tract of SE Portugal with only sparse v'yds, over the River Tagus from Lisbon, but rapidly emerging potential for excellent wine and expanding v'yds. To date the great bulk has been co-op-made. Estate wines from CARTUXA, CORTES DE CIMA, HERDADE DE MOUCHAO, JOÃO RAMOS, JOSE DE SOUSA, CARMO (part Rothschild-owned), and ESPORÃO have potency and style. Best co-ops are at BORBA, REDONDO, and REGUENGOS. Now classified as a DOC in its own right with BORBA, REDONDO, REGUENGOS, PORTALEGRE, EVORA, Granja-Amareleja, Vidigueira, and Moura entitled to their own sub-appellations. Also VINHO REGIONAL Alentejano.

Algarve r w ★ Wines of the holiday area are covered by DOCS Lagos, Tavira, Lagoa, and Portimão. Nothing special apart from the fact that Sir Cliff Richard has a v'yd nr Albufeira.

Aliança, Caves Bair r w sp res ★★ Large BAIRRADA-based firm making classic-method sparkling. Reds and whites inc gd Bairrada wines and mature DÃOS. Also interests in ALENTEJO and the DOURO.

Alorna, Quinta de Ribatejo r w ★→★★ DYA Enterprising estate with a range of gd varietals: CASTELÃO, TRINCADEIRA, and Cab Sauv.

Altano Douro **00 01** Gd new red from the Symington family (Dow's port). Look out for future releases.

Alvarinho White grape planted in the extreme N of Portugal making fragrant and attractive white wines. Known as ALBARIÑO in neighbouring Galicia.

Ameal, Quinta do w ★★★ DYA One of best VINHOS VERDES available. 100% LOUREIRO.

Aragonez Successful red grape in ALENTEJO for varietal wines. See TINTA RORIZ.

Arinto White grape. Best from central and S Portugal, where it retains acidity and produces fragrant, crisp, dry, white wines.

Arruda r w ★ DOC in ESTREMADURA with large co-op.

Avaleda, Quinta da w ★→★★ DYA Reliable VINHO VERDE made on the Avaleda estate of the Guedes family. It is sold dry in Portugal but slightly sweet for export. There are also gd varietal wines from LOUREIRO, ALVARINHO, and Trajadura. Reds: Charamba (DOURO) and Aveleda (ESTREMADURA).

Azevedo, Quinta do w ★★ DYA Superior VINHO VERDE from SOGRAPE. 100% LOUREIRO grapes.

Bacalhoa, Quinta da Set r res ★★★ **98 99 00 01** Estate nr SETUBAL. Its fruity, reliable, mid-weight Cab Sauv is made by J P VINHOS.

Bairrada Bair r w sp ★→★★★ **90' 94 97' 98 99** 00 01 DOC in central Portugal for solid (astringent) reds from the tricky Baga grape. Best wines: CASA DE SAIMA, LUIS PATO, and CAVES SÃO JOÃO will keep for yrs. Most white used by local sparkling wine industry.

Barca Velha Douro r res ★★★★ **52 54 58 64 65 66' 78 81 82 85 91' 95** Portugal's most renowned red, made in very limited quantities in the high Douro by the port firm of FERREIRA (now owned by SOGRAPE). Powerful, resonant wine with deep bouquet, but facing increasing competition from other Douro reds. Second wine known as RESERVA Ferreirinha.

Beiras ★→★★ VINHO REGIONAL inc DÃO, BAIRRADA, and granite mountain ranges of central Portugal.

Beira Interior ★ DOC incorporating former IPRS of Castelo Rodrigo, Pinhel, and Cova da Beira. Huge potential from old v'yds.

Boavista, Quinta da Est ★★ DYA Large property nr ALENQUER making increasingly gd range of red and white: Palha Canas, Quinta das Sete Encostas, Espiga, and a Chard, Casa Santos Lima. Winemaker: José Neiva.

Borba Alen r ★→★★ Small DOC in central ALENTEJO; well-managed co-op making fruity reds.

Branco White.

Brejoeira, Palácio de w (r) ★★ The best-known ALVARINHO from Portugal, but now facing increasingly stiff competition from neighbouring VINHO VERDE estates around Moncão.

Bright Brothers ★★ DYA Australian flying winemaker based in Portugal: interests as far-flung as Argentina, Sicily, and Spain. Range of well-made wines from DOURO, RIBATEJO, ESTREMADURA, and BEIRAS. See also FIUZA BRIGHT.

Buçaco Beiras r w (p) res ★★★★ (r) **53 59 62 63 70 78 82 85 89 92** (w) **91 92 93** Recent vintages disappointing. Legendary speciality of the Palace Hotel at Buçaco near Coimbra, not seen elsewhere. An experience worth the journey. So are the palace and park.

Bucelas Est w ★★ Tiny demarcated region N of Lisbon with 3 main producers. Quinta da Romeira makes attractive wines from the ARINTO grape.

Cadaval, Casa Rib r w ★★ **99 00 01** Gd varietal reds esp TRINCADEIRA. Also Pinot N, Cab Sauv, and Merlot.

A general rule for Portugal: choose youngest vintages of whites available.

Carcavelos Est br sw ★★★ Normally NV. Minute DOC W of Lisbon. Rare, sweet apéritif or dessert wines average 19% alcohol and resemble honeyed MADEIRA. The only producer is now Quinta dos Pesos, Caparide.

Carmo, Quinta do Alen r w res ★★ **97 98 99** 00' Beautiful, small ALENTEJO ADEGA, partly bought in 1992 by Rothschilds (Lafite). 125 acres, plus cork forests. Fresh white; red better. Second wine: Dom Martinho.

Carneiro, Quinta do Alenquer r ★★ **99 00 01 02** w DYA New-wave estate; gd, mid-weight reds (PERIQUITA, Trincadeira Preta, TINTA RORIZ, and TOURIGA NACIONAL).

Cartaxo Ribatejo r w ★ District in RIBATEJO N of Lisbon, now a DOC area making everyday wines popular in the capital.

Cartuxa, Herdade de Alen ★★→★★★ r **97 98** 00' 01 w DYA 500-acre estate nr Evora. Big reds, esp Pera Manca (**94 95 97 98**) one of ALENTEJO's best (and most pricey); creamy whites. Also Foral de Evora, Fundação Eugenio de Almeida.

Carvalhais, Quinta dos Dão ★★★ r **99 00 01** w DYA Excellent single-estate SOGRAPE wine. Gd red varietals (TOURIGA NACIONAL, Alfronchiero Preto) and white Encruzado.

Casal Branco, Quinta de Ribatejo r w ★★ Large family estate making gd red and white wines. Best red: Falcoaria (**99 00 01**).

Casal García w ★★ DYA Big-selling VINHO VERDE, made at AVELEDA.

Casal Mendes w ★ DYA The VINHO VERDE from CAVES ALIANÇA.

Castelão The official name for PERIQUITA, a grape planted throughout S Portugal, but particularly in TERRAS DO SADO. Makes firm-flavoured, raspberryish reds which take on a tar-like quality with age. Also known as João de Santarem.

Chryseia Douro r ★★★→★★★★ 00 01 Bruno Prats from B'x has come together with the Symington family to produce a dense, yet elegant, wine from port grapes. A star in the making.

Colares r ★★ Small DOC on the sandy coast W of Lisbon. Its antique-style, dark-red wines, rigid with tannin, are from ungrafted vines. They need ageing, but TOTB (the older the better) no longer. Look for Paulo da Silva.

Consumo (vinho) Ordinary wine.

Cortes de Cima r ★★★ 98' 00 01 02 Estate nr Vidigueira (ALENTEJO) owned by Danish family. Gd reds from ARAGONEZ, TRINCADEIRA, and PERIQUITA grapes. Chamine: second label. Also Syrah bottled under Incognito label.

Côtto, Quinta do Douro r w res ★★★ r **99 00 01** w DYA Pioneer table wines from port country; v.gd red Grande Escolha (**90 94 95 00**) and also do Côtto are dense fruity, tannic wines for long keeping. Also port.

Crasto, Quinta do Douro r dr sw ★★→★★★★ **99 00 01 02** (03') Top estate nr Pinhão for port and excellent oak-aged reds. Excellent varietal wines (TOURIGA NACIONAL, TINTA RORIZ) and RESERVA. Vinha do Ponte and María Theresa (**98 00'**) are outstanding wines from low-yielding plots of old vines.

Dão r w res ★★→★★★ 97 00' 01 02 DOC region round town of Viseu. Too many dull, earthy wines produced in the past but region is improving, if not rapidly, with single-QUINTAS making headway: solid reds of some subtlety with age; substantial, dry whites. Most sold under brand names. But see ROQUES, MAIAS, TERRAS ALTAS, GRÃO VASCO, DUQUE DE VISEU, etc.

DFJ Vinhos r w ★→★★ DYA Successful partnership making well-priced wines, mainly in RIBATEJO and ESTRAMADURA. Look out for these labels: Ramada (r w), Segada (r w), Manta Preta (r), and Grand'Arte (r w).

DOC (Denominação de Origem Controlada) Official wine region. There are now 27 in total, a number of mergers having taken place in recent years. See also IPR, VINHO REGIONAL.

Doce (vinho) Sweet (wine).

Douro r w ★★→★★★★ **95 96 97 98 99 00' 01** 02 (03') N river valley producing port and some of Portugal's most exciting table wines. Look for BARCA VELHA, CÔTTO,

174 |

Redoma, and Symington's new wines (see ALTANO). Watch this space.

Duas Quintas Douro ★★★ r **00 01** 02 (03') w DYA Rich red from port shipper RAMOS PINTO. V.gd RESERVA and outstanding Reserva Especial (**99**).

Duque de Viseu Dão ★★★ r **00 01 02** w DYA High-quality red DÃO from SOGRAPE.

Esporão, Herdade do Alen w DYA r ★★→★★★ **99 00 01 02** Impressive estate owned by Finagra. Wines made (since 1992) by Aussie David Baverstock: rich, ripe, gently oaked white; fruity, young red Alandra; superior red Esporão: one of ALENTEJO's best. Also Monte Velho gently oaked red and fruity white. Gd varietals: ARAGONEZ, TRINCADEIRA, TOURIGA NACIONAL, Alicante Bouchet, Syrah.

Espumante Sparkling.

Esteva Douro r ★ DYA Very drinkable DOURO red from port firm FERREIRA.

Estremadura ★→★★★ VINHO REGIONAL on W coast, sometimes called "Oeste". Large co-ops. Alta Mesa, Ramada, Portada: gd, inexpensive wines from local estates and co-ops. IPRS: Encostas d'Aire. DOCS: ALENQUER, ARRUDA, Obidos, TORRES VEDRAS.

Fernão Pires White grape making ripe-flavoured, slightly spicy whites in RIBATEJO. (Known as María Gomes in BAIRRADA.)

Ferreira Douro r ★→★★★★ Port shipper making a range of gd to v.gd red DOURO wines: Esteva, Vinha Grande, Callabriga, Quinta de Leda, RESERVA Ferreirinha, and BARCA VELHA.

Fonseca, José María da Est r w dr sw sp res ★★→★★★ Venerable firm in Azeitão nr Lisbon. Huge range of wines inc brands Periquita, Pasmados, Quinta de Camerate, Garrafeiras, and the famous dessert SETÚBAL (Alambre). Impressive range of reds from new winery opened in 2001: Septimus, Vinya, Primum, and the Domingos Soares Franco Seleccão Privado. Top of range: Optimum. Also with interests in DÃO (TERRAS ALTAS), ALENTEJO, (JOSE DE SOUSA and d'Avillez), DOURO (Domini). Also see LANCERS.

Foz de Arouce, Quinta de Beiras r ★★ **96 98 99 00 01** w DYA Big, cask-aged red from heart of BEIRAS.

Franqueira, Quinta da w ★★ DYA Typically dry, fragrant VINHO VERDE made by Englishman Piers Gallie.

Fuiza Bright Ribatejo r w ★★ DYA Joint venture with Peter Bright (BRIGHT BROTHERS). Gd inexpensive Chard, Merlot, and Cab Sauv.

Gaivosa, Quinta de Douro r ★ **95 97 99 00** Important estate nr Regua. Deep, concentrated, cask-aged reds from port grapes. Second wine Quinta do Vale da Raposa (DYA) is lighter, fruity red. Third wine: QUINTA da Estação (DYA).

Garrafeira Label term: merchant's "private reserve", aged for minimum of 2 yrs in cask and 1 in bottle, often much longer. Usually their best, though traditionally often of indeterminate origin. Now has to show origin on label.

Gatão w ★ DYA Standard BORGES & IRMÃO VINHO VERDE; fragrant but sweetened.

Gazela w ★★ DYA Reliable VINHO VERDE made at Barcelos by SOGRAPE.

Generoso Apéritif or dessert wine rich in alcohol.

Grão Vasco Dão r w ★★ DYA One of the best and largest brands of DÃO, from a new high-tech ADEGA at Viseu. Fine red GARRAFEIRA; fresh, young white. Owned by SOGRAPE.

IPR Indicação de Proveniência Regulamentada.

José de Sousa Alen r res ★★→★★★ **99 00** Small firm acquired by JOSÉ MARÍA DA FONSECA. The most sophisticated of the full-bodied wines from ALENTEJO (solid, foot-trodden GARRAFEIRAS, although now slightly lighter in style), fermented in earthenware amphoras and aged in oak. GARRAFEIRA Major (**94 97 98**).

J P Vinhos Set r w sp res ★→★★★ An enterprising and well-equipped winery. Wide range of well-made reds inc: BACALHOA, inexpensive JP, Serras de Azeito, TINTO DA ANFORA, Só (varietal Syrah), JP Garrafeira. Also Cova da Ursa Chard, SETÚBAL dessert wine, Lorridos sparkling wine from ESTREMADURA.

Lancers Est p w sp ★ Sweet, *frizante* (semi-sparkling) Rosé and white

Branco, extensively shipped to the US by JOSÉ MARÍA DA FONSECA. Also Lancers ESPUMANTE Brut, a decent sparkler made by a continuous process of Russian invention.

Lagoalva, Quinta da r w ★★ 99 00 01 02 Important RIBATEJO property making gd reds from local grapes and Syrah. Second label: Monte da Casta.

Lavadores de Feitoria Douro r Enterprising amalgam of a number of small quality-conscious estates. Principal label: Três Bagos.

Loureiro Best VINHO VERDE grape variety after ALVARINHO: crisp, fragrant whites.

Madeira br dr sw ★★→★★★★ Portugal's Atlantic island making famous fortified dessert and apéritif wines. See pp.178–185.

Maias, Quinta das Dão ★★ r 00 01 DYA New-wave QUINTA: reds to age.

Portuguese wines to look out for in 2005

Douro reds Batuta and Charme from Niepoort; Quinta Vale do Meão, Vinha do Ponte, and Maria Theresa from Quinta do Crasto; Chryseia from Prats/Symington.

Alentejo reds Especially wines made from Trincadeira and/or Syrah.

Dão Single quinta especially Carvalhas, Roques, Pellada & Saes. Duque de Viseu (value).

Indigenous varietals Touriga Nacional, Tinta Roriz/Aragonez, Trincadeira.

Mateus Rosé Bair p (w) ★ World's biggest-selling, medium-dry, carbonated rosé, from SOGRAPE. Now made at Anadia in BAIRRADA.

Messias r w ★→★★ Large BAIRRADA-based firm; interests in DOURO (inc port). Old-school reds best.

Minho River between N Portugal and Spain – lends its name to a VINHO REGIONAL.

Monte d'Oiro, Quinta do Est r ★★★→★★★★ 99' 00 Makes outstanding Rhône-style reds from Syrah with a touch of Viognier. Second wine, Vinha da Nora, also gd.

Morgadio de Torre w ★★ DYA Top VINHO VERDE from SOGRAPE. Largely ALVARINHO.

Mouchão, Herdade de Alen r res ★★★ 96 98 99 00 Perhaps top ALENTEJO estate, ruined in 1974 revolution; since replanted and fully recovered. Gd, powerful second wine under the Dom Rafael label.

Mouro, Quinta do Alen r ★★★→★★★★ 98 99 00 Fabulous old-style reds, mostly from traditional ALENTEJO grapes. Dry farmed, low yields and very concentrated. From nr Estremoz.

Murganheira, Caves ★ Largest producer of ESPUMANTE. Now owns RAPOSEIRA.

Niepoort Douro r w ★★★→★★★★ Family port shipper making even better DOURO wines. Redoma (r w p) 99 00 01; Batuta (r) 00 01'; Charme (r) 00 02. Reds age very well.

Palmela ★→★★★ Terras do Sado r w Sandy soil IPR. Reds can be long-lived. Now a promising DOC incorporating the limestone hills of the Serra d'Arrabida and the sandy plains around the eponymous town. Reds from PERIQUITA can be long-lived. Very sucessful Cooperativa de Pegões (best wine: Colheita Seleccionada).

Pancas, Quinta das Est r w res ★★→★★★ 99 00' 01 w DYA Go-ahead estate nr ALENQUER. Outstanding red Premium (00') and varietals from ARAGONEZ, Syrah, Cab Sauv, and CASTELÃO.

Pato, Luís Bair r sp ★★→★★★★ 95' 97 99 00 01 02 (03') Top estate of BAIRRADA. Tannic reds inc tremendous RIBEIRINHO and João Pato. The 95 reds are notable, esp QUINTA do Ribeirinho Pé Franco. Vinha Formal is Pato's fresh, aromatic dry white. Although still technically within the Bairrada DOC, Pato has declassified all his wines to VINHO REGIONAL BEIRAS after disagreeing with the authorities. Also classic-method ESPUMANTE.

PORTUGAL

Pegos Claros r **97 98 99 00 01** Solid, traditionally made red from PALMELA area. Proof at last that PERIQUITA can make substantial wine.

Pellada, Quinta de Dão r **00'** 01 02 Small mountain estate making fine, polished reds. Pape is one of the best DÃO wines around. Quinta de Saes is under the same ownership and also makes wines to a high standard.

Periquita The nickname for the CASTELÃO grape. Periquita is also a brand name for a successful red wine from JOSÉ MARÍA DA FONSECA (DYA). Robust, old-style red bottled under Periquita Classico label (**94 95**).

Pires, João w DYA Fragrant, off-dry, Muscat-based wine from J P VINHOS.

Planalto Douro w ★★ DYA Gd white wine from SOGRAPE.

Ponte de Lima, Cooperativa de VV r w ★ Maker of one of the best bone-dry red VINHOS VERDES, and first-rate dry and fruity white.

Portal, Quinta do Douro r w p ★→★★★ **99 00 01** Estate that once belonged to SANDEMAN now making increasingly gd red as well as ports.

Portalegre Alen r w ★→★★★ DOC on Spanish border. Strong, fragrant reds with potential to age. Alcoholic whites. Best red wine JOSÉ MARÍA DA FONSECA's full-flavoured d'Avillez. Promising wines from local co-op.

Quinta Estate.

Ramos, João Portugal Alen r w DYA Vila Santa (**00 01 02**) and Marqués de Borba. RESERVAS of the latter fetch a high price.

Raposeira Douro w sp ★★ Well-known fizz made by the classic method at Lamego. Ask for the Bruto.

Real Companhia Velha ★★→★★★ r **00 01 02** w DYA Giant of the port trade (see p.184); also produces increasingly gd range of DOURO wines: EVEL, Quinta dos Aciprestes, QUINTA de Cidro. Also sweet Granjó from botrytis-affected Sem.

Redondo Alen r w ★ DOC in heart of ALENTEJO with well-managed co-op.

Reguengos Alen r (w) res ★→★★★ Important DOC nr Spanish border. Inc JOSÉ DE SOUSA and ESPORÃO estates, plus large co-op for gd reds.

Ribatejo r w The second-largest wine-producing region in Portugal. Now promoted to DOC with a number of sub-regions entitled to village appellations: ALMEIRIM, CARTAXO, CORUCHE, Chamusca, Tomar, Santarem. Mid-weight reds inc a range made from international grapes: Cab Sauv, Pinot N, Chard, and Sauv Bl. Also VINHO REGIONAL Ribatejano.

Ribeirinho, Quinta do See PATO.

Roques, Quinta dos Dão r ★★→★★★ **97 99 00 01** w DYA Promising estate for big, solid, oaked reds. Gd varietal wines from TOURIGA NATIONAL, TINTA RORIZ, Tinta Cão, and Alfrocherio Preto.

Roriz, Quinta de Douro r ★★★ **99 00'** 01 02 (03') One of the great QUINTAS of the DOURO, now making fine reds (and vintage port) with the Symingtons

Rosa, Quinta de la Douro r ★★ **99 00 01 02** (03') Firm, oak-aged red from port v'yds. RESERVA is esp worthwhile. Amarela: lighter Second wine.

Rosado Rosé.

Saima, Casa de Bair r (w DYA) ★★★ **99 00 01** 02 (03') Small, traditional estate; big, long-lasting, tannic reds (esp GARRAFEIRAS **90' 91 95' 97' 01**) and some astounding whites.

Santar, Casa de Dão r ★★★ **98 00 01** 02 Well-established estate now making welcome comeback. Reds much better than old-fashioned whites.

São Domingos, Comp dos Vinhos de Est r w ★ DYA Reds (Espiga, Palha-Canas), from estate managed by José Neiva.

São João, Caves Bair ★★→★★★ r **95 98** 00 Res **95** w DYA Small, traditional firm making top-class wines the old-fashioned way. Reds can age for decades. BAIRRADA: Frei João; DÃO: Porta dos Cavaleiros. Poço do Lobo: well-structured Cab Sauv.

Seco Dry.

Serradayres ★ DYA Everyday red and enjoying something of a comeback having been taken over by TEODOSIO, CAVES DOM.

Setúbal Set br (r w) sw (dr) ★★★ Tiny demarcated region S of the River Tagus. Dessert wines made predominantly from the Moscatel (Muscat) grape. Two main producers: JOSÉ MARÍA DA FONSECA and J P VINHOS.

Sezim, Casa de w ★★ DYA Beautiful estate making v.gd VINHO VERDE.

Silva, Antonio Bernardino Paulo da Colares r (w) res ★★ **89 90 92** His COLARES Chitas is one of the very few of these classics still made.

Sogrape ★→★★★★ Largest wine concern in the country, making VINHO VERDE, DÃO, BAIRRADA, ALENTEJO, MATEUS ROSÉ, and now owners of FERREIRA, Sandeman port, and Offley port. See also BARCA VELHA.

Tamariz, Quinta do VV w ★ Fragrant VINHO VERDE from LOUREIRO grapes only.

Teodósio, Caves Dom r w ★→★★ Large producer in the RIBATEJO now making a welcome comeback. Everyday wines under the SERRADAYRES label, but delicious red from Quinta de Almargem made from TRINCADEIRA grape.

Terras Altas Dão r w res ★ DYA Brand of red and white DÃO from JOSÉ MARÍA DA FONSECA.

Terras do Sado VINHO REGIONAL covering sandy plains around Sado Estuary.

Tinta Roriz A major port grape (alias Temp) making gd DOURO table wines. It is being increasingly planted for similarly full reds. Also known as ARAGONEZ in ALENTEJO.

Tinto Red.

Tinto da Anfora Alen r ★★ **00 01** New heavyweight red: Tinto da Anfora Grande Escolha **99 01**. Lighter wines: Montes das Anforas.

Torres Vedras ★ Est r w DOC N of Lisbon, famous for Wellington's "lines". Major supplier of bulk wine.

Touriga Nacional Top red grape used for port and DOURO table wines; now increasingly elsewhere, esp DÃO, ALENTEJO, and ESTREMADURA.

Trás-os-Montes VINHO REGIONAL covering mountains of NE Portugal. Reds and whites from international grape varieties grown in the DOURO. Also IPRS: Chaves, Mirandes, Valpaços.

Trincadeira V.gd red grape in ALENTEJO for spicy, single-varietal wines.

Tuella r w ★★ DYA Gd-value DOURO red from Cockburn.

Vale D Maria, Quinta do r **99 00 01** 02 Small, highly regarded QUINTA run by Cristiano VAN ZELLER. Gd solid reds and value port.

Vale Meão, Quinta do Douro r ★★★★ **99** 00 01' Once the source of the legendary BARCA VELHA, now making great wine in its own right. Second wine: Meandro.

Vallado ★★ r **98 99 00' 01** 02 (RESERVA) **01** w DYA Family-owned DOURO estate; v.gd wines.

Van Zeller Cristiano Van Zeller (former owner of NOVAL see p.183) is now making excellent port under a new label, Vale da Miña, and Domini red with FONSECA.

Ventozello, Quinta do Douro r **99 00 01** Huge Spanish-owned property in the heart of the DOURO, making gd reds and port.

Verde Green (see VINHO VERDE).

Vidigueira Alen w r ★→★★★ DOC for traditionally made, unmatured whites and plummy reds from the hottest part of Portugal. Best producer: CORTES DE CIMA.

Vinho Regional Larger provincial wine region, with same status as French Vin de Pays: they are: ALGARVE, ALENTEJO, BEIRAS, ESTREMADURA, RIBATEJANO, MINHO, TRÁS-OS-MONTES, TERRAS DO SADO. See also DOC, IPR.

Vinho Verde w ★→★★★ r ★ DOC between River DOURO and N frontier, for "green wines" (white or red): made from grapes with high acidity and (originally) undergoing a secondary fermentation to leave them slightly sparkling. Today the fizz is usually just added carbon dioxide. Ready for drinking in spring after harvest.

Sherry, Port, & Madeira

Sherry, port, and madeira are the three classic fortified wines of Spain and Portugal – and the world. They are reinforced with alcohol up to 15.5% (for fino) and 22% (for vintage port).

Sherry is the most famous of Spanish fortified wines, and since 1996 its name has been legally recognized as belonging to Spain alone. Like other fortified wines, sherry has suffered a decline in popularity over recent years, but remains an excellent preliminary to a meal and of all thoroughbred wines is certainly the best value. And more people are now discovering sherry with food.

The port trade underwent a major restructuring in 2001 leaving three major players (Symingtons, Fladgate Partnership, and Sogrape) with ownership of most of the big names. The millennium saw the third small vintage in a row for port. Both 1998 and 1999 produced some good single-quinta wines (though 1998 is better than 1999) and 2000 was declared a Vintage across the board; 2001 has produced some good single-quinta wines and 2003 looks very promising indeed.

In Madeira the relatively new *colheita* or "harvest" wines are now starting to emerge onto the market. Bottled after six years in wood (as opposed to the minimum twenty years for "vintage" Madeira) and from a single year, they are intended to be more accessible. The suspension of bulk shipments of Madeira in 2002 led to a restructuring of the Madeira business, with the emphasis on better-quality wines.

Recent Declared Port Vintages

2000 A very fine vintage, universally declared. Rich, well-balanced wines for the long-term. Drink from 2015.

1997 Fine, potentially long-lasting wines with tannic backbone. Most shippers declared. Drink 2012 onwards.

1994 Outstanding vintage with ripe, fleshy fruit disguising underlying structure at the outset. Universal declaration. Drink 2010–2030.

1992 Favoured by a few (especially Taylor and Fonseca) over 91. Richer, more concentrated, a better year than 91. Drink from 2008–2025.

1991 Favoured by most shippers (especially Symingtons with Dow, Graham, and Warre) over 92; classic, firm but a little lean in style. Drink now – 2020.

1987 Dense wines for drinking over the medium term, but only a handful of shippers declared. Drink now – 2015.

1985 Universal declaration which looked good at the outset but has thrown up some disappointments in bottle. Now – 2020 for the best wines.

1983 Powerful wines with sinewy tannins. Most shippers declared. Now – 2020.

1982 Rather simple, early maturing wines declared by a few shippers. Drink up.

1980 Lovely fruit-driven wines, perfect to drink now and over the next 15 years. Most shippers declared.

1977 Big, ripe wines declared by all the major shippers except Cockburn, Martinez, and Noval. Lovely now, but don't keep too long.

1975 Soft and early maturing. Drink up.

1970 Classic, tight-knit wines – only just reaching their peak. Now – 2020+.

1966 Wines combine power and elegance. The best rival 1963. Now – 2020+.

1963 Classic vintage, one of the best of the 20th century (with prices to match). Some bottle variation. Now; no need to keep them.

Almacenista Individual matured but unblended sherry; usually dark, dry wines for connoisseurs. Often superb quality and value. See LUSTAU.

Alvear Largest producer of v.gd sherry-like apéritif and sweet wines in MONTILLA.

Barbadillo, Antonio Much the largest SANLÚCAR firm with a wide range of MANZANILLAS and sherries, inc: Muy Fina FINO, Solear MANZANILLA PASADA, austere Principe AMONTILLADO, Cuco dry OLOROSO, Eva Cream, and superb but vastly expensive Reliquia PALO CORTADO, OLOROSO SECO, and PX. Also young Castillo de San Diego table wines, for some reason.

Barbeito Very enterprising firm managed by Ricardo de Freitas. Bottles delicious single-cask COLHEITAS, eg 1995 Bual Cask 81a.

Barros Almeida Large, family-owned port house with several brands (inc Feist, Feuerheerd, KOPKE): excellent 20-yr-old TAWNY and many COLHEITAS.

Barros e Sousa Tiny, family-owned madeira producer with old lodges in centre of Funchal. Extremely fine but now rare vintages, plus gd 10-yr-old wines.

Blandy The top name of the MADEIRA WINE COMPANY. Duke of Clarence Rich Madeira is the most famous wine. 10-yr-old reserves (VERDELHO, BUAL, MALMSEY, SERCIAL) are gd. Many glorious old vintages (eg MALMSEY 1978, BUAL 1920, SERCIAL 1940, BUAL 1958), though mostly nowadays at auctions. New COLHEITAS from 95. New 5-yr-old blend of BUAL and Malvasia called Alvada.

Blázquez DOMECQ-owned BODEGA at PUERTO DE SANTA MARIA. Outstanding FINO, Carta Blanca, very old SOLERA OLOROSO Extra; Carta Oro AMONTILLADO (unsweetened).

Borges, H M Family company making full range. Vintages: SERCIAL 79, BOAL 77.

Bual (Sometimes spelt Boal.) One of the best grapes of Madeira, making a soft, smoky, sweet wine, usually lighter and not as rich as MALMSEY (see p.182).

Burmester Family port house now owned by cork giant Amorim, with fine, soft, sweet 20-yr-old TAWNY; also v.gd range of COLHEITAS and single-QUINTA: Quinta Nossa Sra do Carmo. Vintages: **70 77 80 85 89 91 92** 94 95 97 00.

Burdon English-founded sherry BODEGA owned by CABALLERO. Puerto FINO, Don Luis AMONTILLADO, and raisiny Heavenly Cream are top lines.

Caballero Important sherry shipper at PUERTO DE SANTA MARIA. Pavón FINO, Mayoral Cream OLOROSO, excellent BURDON sherries, PONCHE orange liqueur. Also owns LUSTAU.

Sherry Styles

Fino The lightest, finest sherries. Completely dry, very pale, delicate but pungent. Should be drunk cool and fresh. Deteriorates rapidly once opened (use half bottles if possible). Eg Tio Pepe by González-Byass.

Manzanilla A pale, dry wine (not strictly a sherry), often more delicate than a fino, matured in the cooler maritime conditions of Sanlúcar de Barrameda (as opposed to inland Jerez). Eg Hidalgo's La Gitana.

Amontillado A fino aged in cask to become darker, more powerful, and pungent. Naturally dry wines. Eg Lustau's Almancenistas.

Oloroso Heavier, less brilliant than fino when young, but matures to richness and pungency. Naturally dry, often sweetened for sale. Eg Rio Viejo from Domecq.

Palo Cortado A rare style close to oloroso with some amontillado character. Dry, rich and soft – worth looking for. Eg Domecq's Sibarita.

Cream Sherry Sweet style from oloroso. Eg Harvey's Bristol Cream.

Other styles Manzanilla Pasada – half way between fino and amontillado; Pale Cream – sweetened fino; Amoroso, Brown Sherry, East India Sherry – variations on cream sherry.

Age-dated Sherries Two new categories – **VOS** (Very Old Sherry more than 20 yrs) and **VORS** (Very Old Sherry more than 30 yrs). Also very expensive.

Cálem Old port house; had fine reputation, but recent vintages not as gd. Vintages: **63 66 70 75 77 80 83 91** 94 97 00' Reliable light TAWNY; gd range of COLHEITAS. Sold in 1998, but family still owns QUINTA da Foz (**86 87**).

Churchill **82 85 91** 94 97 00 Port shipper founded in 1981 and already highly respected. Bought its own QUINTA in 1999/2000. V.gd traditional LBV. Quinta da Agua Alta and Quinta da Gricha are Churchill's single-QUINTA ports: **87** 90 92 01. V.gd aged white port too.

Cockburn British-owned (Allied-DOMECQ) port shipper with gd range of wines inc popular, fruity Special Reserve. Fine VINTAGE PORT from v'yds predominantly in the Douro Superior: sometimes deceptively forward when young. Vintages: **63 67 70 75 83** 91 94 97 00. Gd single-QUINTA wines from QUINTA dos Canais.

Colheita Vintage-dated port of a single yr, but aged at least 7 winters in wood: in effect a vintage TAWNY. The bottling date is shown on the label. Excellent examples: KOPKE, CALEM, NIEPOORT, Krohn, C DA SILVA (Dalva). *Colheita* now also applies to a category of madeiras from a single yr (see introduction p.178).

Cossart Gordon One-time leading madeira shipper, founded 1745; with BLANDY, now one of the 2 top-quality labels of the MADEIRA WINE COMPANY. Wines slightly less rich than BLANDY's. Best known for Good Company Finest Medium Rich. Also 5-yr-old reserves, old vintages (latest 74), and SOLERAS (esp BUAL 1845). Malvasia COLHEITA 1989, older vintages inc 1958 BUAL and 1908 BOAL, plus old wines from 19th-C SOLERAS.

Crasto, Quinta do Ports improving, esp LBV. Vintages: **85 87 91** 94 95 97 00.

Croft One of the oldest firms, shipping VINTAGE PORT since 1678. Now part of the Fladgate partnership alongside DELAFORCE. Well-balanced vintage wines tend to mature early (since 66). Vintages: **66 67 70 75 77 82 85** 91 94 00. Lighter QUINTA da Roeda (**83 87**). "Distinction": most popular blend. Also produces sherry, and brandy popular in Portugal.

Croft Jerez Founded only in 1970 and recently bought by GONZÁLEZ-BYASS. One of the most successful sherry firms. Best known for the sweet Croft Original PALE CREAM and drier Croft Particular. Also dry and elegant Delicado FINO and first-rate and moderately priced PALO CORTADO.

Crusted Vintage-style port, usually blended from several vintages. Bottled young and then aged so it throws a deposit, or "crust". Needs decanting.

Cruz Biggest single port brand. Mostly light, inexpensive TAWNIES sold to France.

Delaforce Port shipper also part of the Fladgate Partnership, is best known in Germany. His Eminence's Choice is a very pleasant 10-yr-old TAWNY; VINTAGE CHARACTER is also gd. VINTAGE PORTS dipped in quality in the 1980s, but have been getting steadily better since 1992: **63 66 70' 75 82 85** 92' 94 00.

Delgado, Zuleta Old-established SANLÚCAR firm, best known for marvellous La Goya Manzanilla Pasada (a matured MANZANILLA).

Domecq Giant family-run sherry BODEGA at JEREZ, merged with Allied-DOMECQ, famous also for Fundador and other brandies. Double Century Original OLOROSO, its biggest brand, now replaced by Pedro CREAM SHERRY; La Ina is excellent FINO. Other famous wines inc Celebration Cream, Botaina (old AMONTILLADO), and magnificent Rio Viejo (very dry OLOROSO) and Capuchino (PALO CORTADO). Recently: a range of wonderful old SOLERA sherries (dry Sibarita OLOROSO, AMONTILLADO 51-1a, and venerable PX). Also in Rioja and Mexico.

Don Zoilo Luxury sherries, inc velvety FINO. Now sold by Bodegas Internacionales to the MEDINA group.

Douro The port country river, known in Spain as the Duero. All the best port comes from the spectacular Upper Douro. Port country divides into 3, with the best coming from Cima Corgo and Douro Superior, both well upriver. Table wines are also important and Douro is a DOC for unfortified wines made from port grapes.

Dow Brand name of port house Silva and Cozens. Celebrated bicentenary in 1998. Belongs to Symington family alongside GRAHAM, WARRE, SMITH WOODHOUSE, GOULD CAMPBELL, QUARLES HARRIS, and QUINTA DO VESUVIO, but deliberately drier style than other shippers in group. V.gd range of ports, inc single-QUINTA Bomfim (86' 87' 88 89 90 92 95 98) and outstanding Vintages: **63 66 70 72 75 77 80 83** 85 91 94 97 00'. New v'yd: Quinta da Senhora da Ribeira 98 99 01.

Duff Gordon Sherry shipper best-known for El Cid AMONTILLADO. Gd FINO Feria; Niña Medium OLOROSO. OSBORNE-owned; name also second label for Osborne's ports.

Emilio Hildago Small sherry bodega making the exquisite Privilegio 1860 PALO CORTADO and Santa Ana PX. Jerez Cortado is gd value.

Ferreira One of the biggest Portuguese-owned port growers and shippers (since 1751). Largest-selling brand in Portugal. Known for old TAWNIES and juicily sweet, relatively light vintages: **63 66 70 75 77 78 80 82 85 87 91** 94 95 97 00. Also Doña Antónia Personal Reserve, splendidly rich tawny Duque de Bragança and occasional single-QUINTA wines from Quinta do Seixo.

Flor A floating yeast peculiar to FINO sherry and certain other wines that age slowly and tastily under its influence.

Fonseca Guimaraens British-owned port shipper with a stellar reputation; connected with TAYLOR'S. Robust, deeply coloured vintage wine, among the very best. Vintages: Fonseca **63' 66' 70 75 77 80 83 85** 92 94' 97 00'; Fonseca Guimaraens 76' 78 82 84 86 87 88 91 95' 98'. Quinta do Panascal is a single-QUINTA wine **88** 91'. Also delicious VINTAGE CHARACTER Bin 27.

Forrester Port shipper and owner of the famous Quinta da Boa Vista, now owned by SOGRAPE. The vintage wines tend to be round, fat, and sweet, gd for relatively early drinking. Baron de Forrester is v.gd TAWNY. Vintages: (Offley Forrester) **63 66 67 70 72 75 77 80 82 83 85 87 89** 94 95 97 00'.

Garvey Famous old sherry shipper at JEREZ, now owned by José María Ruiz Mateos. The finest wines are deep-flavoured FINO San Patricio, Tio Guillermo Dry AMONTILLADO, and Ochavico Dry OLOROSO. San Angelo Medium AMONTILLADO is the most popular. Also Bicentenary PALE CREAM.

González-Byass Enormous family-run sherry firm with most famous and one of very best FINOS: TIO PEPE. Brands inc La Concha medium AMONTILLADO, Elegante dry FINO, new El Rocío MANZANILLA Fina, San Domingo PALE CREAM, Nectar Cream, Alfonso sweet OLOROSO. AMONTILLADO del Duque, Matúsalem OLOROSO, and Apóstoles PALO CORTADO are on a higher plane. Magnificent Millennium is choicest old OLOROSO. Also top-selling Soberano and exquisite Lepanto brandies.

Gould Campbell Port shipper belonging to the Symington family. Gd-value VINTAGE PORTS **70 77 80 83 85** 91 94 97 00.

Graham Port shipper famous for some of the richest, sweetest, and best VINTAGE PORT, largely from its own Quinta dos Malvedos (**86 87 88** 92 95'). Also excellent brands, inc Six Grapes RUBY, LBV, and 10- and 20-yr-old TAWNIES. Vintages: **63 66 70 75 77 80 83 85** 91 94 97 00'.

Gracia Hermanos Mont-M Firm within the same group as PEREZ BARQUERO and Compañia Vinícola del Sur making gd-quality MONTILLAS. Its labels inc María del Valle FINO, Montearruit AMONTILLADO, OLOROSO CREAM, and Dulce Viejo PX.

Guita, La Esp fine Pasada (matured MANZANILLA) made by Pérez Marín in SANLÚCAR.

Hartley & Gibson See VALDESPINO.

Harvey's Important sherry pillar of the Allied-DOMECQ empire, along with TERRY. World-famous Bristol shippers of Bristol Cream (sweet), Club AMONTILLADO and Bristol Dry (medium), Luncheon Dry, and Bristol FINO (not very dry).

Henriques & Henriques Independent madeira shipper, with wide range of well-structured, rich wines – 10-yr-olds are medal-winners. Outstanding 15-yr-old wines. Gd, extra-dry apéritif Monte Seco, and very fine old reserves and vintages inc 1944 SERCIAL, 1934 VERDELHO, 1957 BUAL, and MALMSEYS from 1954

SHERRY, PORT, & MADEIRA

1934, and 1900. The joke goes: "There are only two names in Madeira..."

Henriques, Justino Madeira shipper. Most wine sold in France under the CRUZ label. Gd 10-yr-old and vintage, eg 1934 VERDELHO.

Hidalgo, La Gitana Old family sherry firm in SANLÚCAR DE BARRAMEDA Excellent pale MANZANILLA La Gitana, fine OLOROSO Seco, lovely soft, deep Jerez Cortado and first-rate new Pastrana MANZANILLA PASADA.

Jerez de la Frontera Centre of sherry industry, between Cádiz and Seville. "Sherry" is a corruption of the name, pronounced in Spanish "hereth". In French, Xérès.

Jordões, Casal dos One of few certified organic port producers – decent LBV.

Kopke The oldest port house, founded by a German in 1638. Now belongs to BARROS ALMEIDA. Fair-quality vintage wines, but some excellent (70 74 75 77 78 79 80 82 83 85 87 89 91 94 9700), and excellent COLHEITAS.

Krohn Small family-owned port shipper with an excellent range of COLHEITAS, some dating back to the 19th century.

Late-bottled vintage (LBV) Port from a single vintage kept in wood for twice as long as VINTAGE PORT (about 5 yrs), therefore lighter when bottled and ages more quickly. Don't expect miracles. Some LBVs bottled unfiltered have the capacity to age for 10 yrs or more (WARRE, SMITH WOODHOUSE, NIEPOORT, CHURCHILL, FERREIRA, NOVAL).

Leacock One of the oldest madeira shippers, now a label of the MADEIRA WINE COMPANY. Basic St-John range is very fair; 10-yr-old Special Reserve MALMSEY and 15-yr-old BUAL excellent. Older vintages available: BUAL 34, VERDELHO 54.

Lustau One of the largest family-run sherry bodegas in JEREZ (now controlled by CABALLERO), making many wines for other shippers, but with a v.gd Dry Lustau range (esp FINO and OLOROSO) and Jerez Lustau PALO CORTADO. Pioneer shipper of excellent ALMACENISTA and "landed age" wines; AMONTILLADOS and OLOROSOS aged in elegant bottles before shipping.

Madeira Wine Company Formed in 1913 by two firms as the Madeira Wine Association, subsequently to inc all the British madeira firms (26 in total) amalgamated to survive hard times. Remarkably, 3 generations later, the wines, though cellared together, preserve their house styles. BLANDY and COSSART GORDON are top labels. Now controlled by the Symington group (see DOW) which runs it in partnership with the BLANDY family.

Malmsey The sweetest and richest form of madeira; dark amber, rich, and honeyed, yet with madeira's unique sharp tang. Word is English corruption of "Malvasia" (or the Greek "Monemvasia"). See box on p.184.

Martinez Gassiot Port firm, subsidiary of COCKBURN, known esp for excellent rich, and pungent Directors 20-yr-old TAWNY, CRUSTED, and LBV. Vintages: 63 67 70 75 82 85 87 91 94 97 00. V.gd single QUINTA wines from Quinta da Eira Velha.

Marqués del Real Tesoro Old firm with a spanking new bodega – the first in yrs. Recently acquired the historic firm of VALDESPINO. Tío Mateo is a v.gd FINO (now histamine-free!).

Miles Formerly Rutherford & Miles. Madeira shipper: Old Trinity House Medium Rich, etc. Latest vintage 78 Malvasia. Now a MADEIRA WINE COMPANY label.

Medina, José Originally a SANLÚCAR bodega, now a major exporter, esp to the Low Countries. Now owns Bodegas Internacionales and WILLIAMS & HUMBERT, also Pérez Megia and Luis Paez: probably the biggest sherry grower and shipper, with some 25% of total volume.

Montecristo Mont-M Brand of big-selling MONTILLAS by Compañía Vinícola del Sur.

Montilla-Moriles Mont-M DO nr Córdoba. Not sherry, but close. Its soft FINO and AMONTILLADO, and luscious PX contain 14–17.5% natural alcohol and remain unfortified. At best, singularly toothsome apéritifs.

Niepoort Small Dutch family-run port house with long record of fine vintages (63 66 70' 75 77 78 80 82 83 87 91 92 94 97 00') and exceptional

COLHEITAS. Also excellent single-QUINTA port, Quinta do Passadouro (91 99).

Noval, Quinta do Historic port house now French (AXA) owned. Intensely fruity, structured, and elegant VINTAGE PORT; a few ungrafted vines in the QUINTA make small quantity of Nacional – extraordinarily dark, full, velvety, slow-maturing. V.gd 20-yr-old TAWNY. Vintages: **63 66 67** 70 **75 78 82 85** 87 91 94' 95 97' 00'. Second label: Silval. Also (unfiltered) LBV.

Port & Madeira to look out for in 2005
White port Churchill
Good value single quinta ports Fonseca Quinta do Pascal 91, Dow's Quinta do Bomfim 95, Taylor's Quinta de Vargellas 92 and 95, Fonseca Guimarens 95, Graham's Malvedos 95.
Outstanding vintage ports Fonseca 63, Taylor 63, Fonseca 66, Graham 70, Taylor 70, Smith Woodhouse 77, Graham 80, Taylor 92, Quinta do Noval 94, Fonseca 94.
Madeiras Blandy's Alvada, Barbeito's Single Cask Colheita 95, Henriques & Henriques 15-year-old Bual.
Other ports Warre's 94 LBV (unfiltered), Ramos Pinto 20- and 30-year-old Tawnies, Dow's Crusted (bottled 99)
Vintage madeiras Leacock 78 Malvasia, Pereira d'Oliveira Verdelho 66, Cossart Gordon Bual 58, Justino Henriques Verdelho 34, Justino Henriques Malmsey 33, Pereira d'Oliveira Bual 22.

Offley Forrester See FORRESTER.

Osborne Huge Spanish firm producing sherry, brandy, gin, etc, and quality port. Sherries inc FINO QUINTA, Coquinero dry AMONTILLADO, 10 RF medium OLOROSO and a range of very fine rare sherries, eg Solera India sweet OLOROSO. Has recently taken over Bobadilla sherries and brandies. DUFF GORDON used as second label for both sherries and ports. Declared gd VINTAGE PORTS in 95 97 00'.

Paternina, Federico Marcos Eguizabel from Rioja acquired the sherry firm Diez-Merito, retaining 3 wines to be marketed under his Paternina label. FINO Imperial, OLOROSO, Victoria Regina, and PX Vieja SOLERA.

Pereira d'Oliveira Vinhos Family-owned madeira company established in 1850. V.gd basic range as well as 5- and 10-yr-olds; fine old reserve VERDELHO 1890, BUAL 1908, Malvasia 1895. 1987 COLHEITA Malvasia. Vintages: 1973 VERDELHO, 1968 BOAL, 1922 BOAL, 1900 Moscatel.

Pérez Barquero Mont-M Another firm like GRACIA HERMANOS once part of Rumasa. Its excellent MONTILLAS inc Gran Barquero FINO, AMONTILLADO, and OLOROSO.

Poças Improving family port firm specializing in TAWNIES and COLHEITAS. Gd LBV and Vintage (97 00'). Single-QUINTA wines from Quinta Sta Barbera.

Ponche Aromatic digestif made with old sherry and brandy, flavoured with herbs and presented in eye-catching silvered bottles. See CABALLERO, JOSÉ DE SOTO.

Puerto de Santa María The second city and former port of sherry, with important bodegas.

PX Pedro Ximénez, grape part sun-dried: used in JEREZ for sweetening wines.

Quarles Harris One of the oldest port houses, since 1680, now owned by the Symingtons (see DOW). Small quantities of LBV, mellow, and well-balanced. Vintages: **63 66** 70 **75 77 80 83** 85 91 94 97 00'.

Quinta Portuguese for "estate". Also traditionally used to denote VINTAGE PORTS which are usually (legislation says 100%) from estate's v'yds, made in gd but not exceptional vintages. Now several excellent *quintas* produce wines from top vintages in their own right, esp VESUVIO, LA ROSA, Passadouro (NIEPOORT).

Rainwater A fairly light, medium-dry blend of madeira – traditional in US.

Ramos Pinto Dynamic, small port house specializing in single-QUINTA TAWNIES of style and elegance. Also outstanding aged TAWNIES, esp Quinta do Bom Retiro 20-yr-old. Vintages on sweeter side. Some, like 60 and 83, have developed well. Owned by Champagne house Louis Roederer.

Real Companhia Vinícola do Norte de Portugal Aka Royal Oporto Wine Co and REAL COMPANHIA VELHA (see p.176); large port house, with long political history. Many brands and several QUINTAS, inc Quinta dos Carvalhas for TAWNIES and COLHEITAS. VINTAGE PORTS have been dismal, but 97 and 00 look promising. Some aged TAWNIES are gd.

Régua Main town in Douro Valley, centre for port producers and growers.

Reserve The new name for "Vintage Character". Reserve port is similar to RUBY, but made from better-quality grapes and aged for 4–7 yrs before bottling.

Rosa, Quinta de la Fine single-QUINTA port from the Bergqvist family at PINHÃO. Recent return to traditional methods and stone *lagares*. Look for **92 94 95** vintages and wines from a small plot of old vines called Vale do Inferno.

Royal Oporto See REAL COMPANHIA VINÍCOLA DO NORTE DE PORTUGAL.

Rozès Port shipper owned by Champagne house Vranken. RUBY very popular in France; also TAWNY. Vintages: **63 66 67 77 83 85 87 91** 94' 95 97 00.

Ruby Youngest (and cheapest) port style: simple, sweet, and red. The best are vigorous, full of flavour; others can be merely strong and rather thin.

Sanchez Romate Family firm in JEREZ since 1781. Best-known in Spanish-speaking world, esp for brandy Cardenal Mendoza. Gd sherry: OLOROSO La Sacristía de Romate, PX Duquesa, AMONTILLADO NPU ("Non Plus Ultra").

Sandeman Large firm founded by Scot George Sandeman who set up twin establishments in Oporto and JEREZ. Scrupulously made sherries inc medium AMONTILLADO, Don FINO, and Armada CREAM. Also rare and exceptional Royal Esmeralda PALO CORTADO, dry and sweet Imperial Corregidor, and Royal Ambrosante OLOROSOS. Gd aged TAWNIES, esp 20-yr-old. Vintage has been very patchy in recent years (**63 66 70 75 77 80 82 85** 94 97 00) Second label: Vau Vintage.

Sanlúcar de Barrameda Historic seaside sherry town (see MANZANILLA).

Santa Eufemia, Quinta de Family port estate with v.gd old TAWNIES.

> Since 1993, madeiras labelled sercial, verdelho, bual, or malmsey must be at least 85% from that grape variety. The majority, made using the chameleon Tinta Negra Mole grape, which purports to imitate each of these grape styles, may only be called *seco* (dry), *meio seco* (medium-dry), *meio doce* (medium-rich), or *doce* (rich) respectively. Meanwhile, replanting is building up supplies of the (rare) classic varieties.

Sercial Madeira grape for the driest of the island's wines – supreme apéritif (see panel above).

Silva, C da Port shipper owned by Ruiz Mateos of GARVEY fame. Mostly inexpensive RUBIES and TAWNIES, but gd aged TAWNIES and outstanding COLHEITAS under Dalva label.

Smith Woodhouse Port firm founded in 1784, now owned by Symingtons (DOW). GOULD CAMPBELL is a subsidiary. Relatively light, easy wines inc Old Lodge TAWNY, Lodge Res RUBY (widely sold in US). Vintages (very fine): **63 66 70 75 77' 80 83** 85 91 94 97 00'. Single-QUINTA wine: Madalena for secondary vintages.

Solera System used in making sherry. Consists of topping up progressively more mature barrels with slightly younger wine of same sort, the object being to attain continuity in final wine. Most sherries are blends of several *solera* wines. Used to be applied to madeiras. Although no longer used there are many very fine old *solera* wines in bottle.

Soto, José de Best-known for inventing PONCHE, this family firm, which now belongs to the former owner of Rumasa, José María Ruiz Mateos, also makes a range of gd sherries, esp delicate FINO and a fuller-bodied MANZANILLA.

Tawny Style of port aged for many yrs in wood (VINTAGE PORT is aged in bottle) until tawny in colour. Many of the best are 20 yrs old. Low-price tawnies are merely attenuated RUBIES, sometimes mixed with WHITE PORT.

Taylor, Fladgate & Yeatman (Taylor's) Often considered the best of the port shippers, esp for full, rich, long-lived VINTAGE PORT and TAWNIES of stated age (40-yr-old, 20-yr-old, etc). Its Vargellas estate is said to give Taylor's distinctive scent of violets. Vintages: **63 66 70 75 77 80 83 85** 92' 94 97 00'. Quinta de Vargellas is shipped unblended in lesser years (**86 87 88** 91' 95' 96 98). Also now Terra Feita single-QUINTA wine (**82 86 87 88** 91' 95 96).

Terry, SA Magnificent sherry bodega at PUERTO DE SANTA MARÍA, part of Allied-DOMECQ. Makers of Maruja MANZANILLA and range of popular brandies. Blending and bottling of all HARVEY'S sherries is at the vast modern El Pino plant.

Tío Pepe The most famous of FINO sherries (see GONZÁLEZ-BYASS).

Toro Albalá, Bodegas Mont-M Family firm located in a 1920s' power station and aptly making Eléctrico FINOS, AMONTILLADOS, and a PX which is among the best in MONTILLA and Spain.

Valdespino Famous family bodega at JEREZ, recently taken over by José Ertévez of MARQUÉS DEL REAL TESORO. Owner of Inocente v'yd and making excellent aged FINO of that name. Tío Diego is its dry AMONTILLADO, Solera 1842 an OLOROSO, Don Tomás its best AMONTILLADO. Matador is a popular range. In the US, its sherries rank second in sales volume and are still sold as "Hartley & Gibson".

Vale D Maria, Quinta do Estate in the Torto Valley – gd value VINTAGE PORT.

Ventozelo, Quinta de Huge, beautifully situated estate recently acquired by a Spanish family. Gd single-QUINTA ports: 00.

Verdelho Madeira grape for medium-dry wines, pungent but without the searing austerity of SERCIAL (see box opposite). Pleasant apéritif and gd, all-purpose madeira. Some glorious old vintage wines.

Vesúvio, Quinta de Enormous 19th-C FERREIRA estate in the high DOURO. Owned by Symingtons. 130 acres planted. Esp **91 92** 94 95' 00' 01.

Vila Nova de Gaia City on the S side of the River DOURO from Oporto where the major port shippers mature their wines in "lodges".

Vintage Character See RESERVE.

Vintage Port The best port of exceptional vintages is bottled after only 2 yrs in wood and matures very slowly for up to 20 yrs or more in bottle. Always leaves a heavy deposit and therefore needs decanting.

Warre Oldest of British port shippers (since 1670), owned by the Symington family (see DOW) since 1905. Fine, elegant, long-maturing vintage wines, gd TAWNY, VINTAGE CHARACTER (Warrior), excellent LBV; 10-yr-old Otima has been huge sucess. Single-v'yd Quinta da Cavadinha (**88 89 92** 95 98). Vintages: **63 66 70' 75 77' 80 83** 85 91 94 97 00'.

White port Port made with white grapes, occasionally sweet (*lagrima*) but mostly off-dry and drunk as an apéritif. Look for wines with cask age: BARROS, NIEPOORT, CHURCHILL. Younger, paler wines can be drunk long with tonic.

Williams & Humbert Famous First-class sherry bodega, now owned by MEDINA group. Dry Sack (medium AMONTILLADO) is best-seller; Pando is an excellent FINO; Canasta CREAM and Walnut Brown are gd in their class; Dos Cortados is its famous dry, old PALO CORTADO. Also the famous Gran Duque de Alba brandy acquired from Diez-Merito.

Wisdom & Warter Not a magic formula for free wine, but an old bodega (controlled by GONZÁLEZ-BYASS) with gd sherries, esp AMONTILLADO Tizón and very rare SOLERA. Also FINO Olivar.

Switzerland

More heavily shaded areas are the wine growing regions

The high price of living, combined with cost-intensive wine production, means that Switzerland's wines find it difficult to compete on the world market and, in any case, are rarely seen outside the domestic arena. Those areas producing international-style wines are Ticino (Merlot), Valais (Pinot Noir, Amigne, Arvigne), and Bündner Herrschaft (Pinot Noir). The most important vineyards (28,550 out of 37,280 acres) are in French-speaking areas: along the south-facing slopes of the upper Rhône Valley (Valais) and Lake Geneva (Vaud, Geneva). Wines from German- and Italian-speaking zones are treasured and mostly drunk locally. Wines are known by place, grape names, and legally controlled type names, and tend to be drunk young. The Swiss cantonal and federal appellation system, set up in 1988, still governs wine production.

Aargau 01 02 03 Wine-growing canton in E Switzerland (976 acres). Best for fragrant Müller-THURGAU and rich BLAUBURGUNDER.

Aigle Vaud r w ★★→★★★ Well-known for elegant whites and supple reds.

Amigne Traditional VALAIS white grape, esp of VETROZ. Full-bodied, tasty, often sweet. Best producer: André Fontannaz ★★ 01 02 03.

Ardon Valais r w ★★→★★★ Wine commune between SION and MARTIGNY.

Arvine Old VALAIS white grape (also Petite Arvine): dry and sweet, elegant, long-lasting wines with a salty finish. Best in SIERRE, SION, Granges, FULLY. Top producers: Benoît Dorsaz, René Favre et Fils, Marie Thérèse Chappaz.

Auvernier Neuchâtel r p w ★★→★★★ Old wine village on Lake NEUCHÂTEL and biggest wine growing commune of the canton.

Basel Second-largest Swiss town and canton with many vines: divided into Basel-Stadt and Basel-Land. Best wines: Müller-THURGAU, BLAUBURGUNDER.

Beerliwein Originally wine of destemmed BLAUBURGUNDER (E). Today name for wine fermented on skins traditionally rather than SÜSSDRUCK. Drink young.

Bern Swiss capital and canton. V'yds in W (BIELERSEE: CHASSELAS, PINOT NOIR, white SPÉCIALITÉS) and E (Thunersee: BLAUBURGUNDER, Müller-THURGAU); 648 acres.

Bielersee r p w ★★→★★★ **01 02** 03 Wine region on N shore of the Bielersee (dry light CHASSELAS, PINOT NOIR) and at the foot of Jolimont (SPÉCIALITÉS).

Blauburgunder German name for PINOT NOIR. (Aka Clevner.)

Recent vintages

2003 A style which is more elegant than full-bodied.

2002 Not the best year for everybody. Stick to the best producers.

2001 Low yields but characteristic, full-bodied wines with ageing potential.

2000 Fourth good vintage in a row. One of the best for years for reds.

1999 Despite difficult weather, quality was very good, with remarkable fruit and colour (red wines). White have good acidity.

1998 High-quality wines. Drink both reds and whites now.

Bündner Herrschaft Grisons r p w ★★→★★★ Best German-Swiss region inc top villages: Fläsch, Jenins, Maienfeld, Malans. BLAUBUNDER ripens esp well due to warm Föhn wind, cask-aged v.gd. Also Chard, Müller-THURGAU, SPÉCIALITÉS. Best producers: Gantenbein ★★★, Davaz ★★, Fromm ★★★, Studach ★★ 00 01 02 03'.

Calamin Vaud w ★★→★★★ LAVAUX v'yds next to DEZALEY: lush, fragrant whites.

Chablais Vaud r w ★★→★★★ **02** 03 Sunny wine region on right bank of Rhône and upper end of Lake GENEVA, inc villages: AIGLE, Bex, Ollon, VILLENEUVE, YVORNE. Robust, full-bodied reds and whites.

Chamoson Valais r w ★★→★★★ Largest VALAIS wine commune, esp for SYLVANER.

Chasselas (Gutedel) French cantons, top white grape: neutral flavour, takes on local character: elegant (GENEVA), refined, full (VAUD), exotic, racy (VALAIS), pétillant (lakes Bienne, NEUCHÂTEL, Murtensee). Only E of BASEL. Called FENDANT in VALAIS. 37% of Swiss wines are Chasselas. More and more Chasselas will be replaced.

Completer Native white grape, mostly used in GRISONS, making aromatic, generous wines with high acidity that keep well. Increasing experimentation. ("Complet" was a monk's final daily prayer, or "nightcap".) Best: Adolf Boner, Malans ★★ 00 01 02 03'.

Cornalin ★★→★★★ **01 02** 03' Local VALAIS speciality; dark, spicy, very strong red. Best: Denis and Ann Mercier, SIERRE ★★.

Côte, La Vaud r p w ★→★★★ Largest VAUD wine area between LAUSANNE and GENEVA (N shore of Lake). Whites with elegant finesse; fruity, harmonious reds. Esp from MONT-SUR-ROLLE, Vinzel, Luins, FECHY, MORGES, etc.

Côtes de l'Orbe Vaud r p w ★→★★ N VAUD appellation between Lake NEUCHÂTEL and Lake GENEVA esp for light, fruity reds.

Dézaley Vaud w (r) ★★→★★★ Celebrated LAVAUX v'yd on slopes above Lake GENEVA, once tended by Cistercian monks. Unusually potent CHASSELAS, develops esp after ageing. Red Dézaley is a GAMAY/PINOT NOIR/MERLOT/Syrah rarity.

Dôle Valais r ★★→★★★ Appellation for PINOT NOIR, more often a PINOT NOIR-dominated blend with GAMAY (at least 85%) and other red varieties from the VALAIS: full, supple, often v.gd. Lightly pink Dôle Blanche is pressed immediately after harvest. Eg from MARTIGNY, SIERRE, SION, etc. **01 02** 03'.

Epesses Vaud w (r) ★→★★★ **02** 03 LAVAUX AC: supple, full-bodied whites.

Ermitage Alias the Marsanne grape; a VALAIS SPÉCIALITÉ. Concentrated, full-bodied dry white, sometimes with residual sugar. Esp from FULLY, SION, Noble Contrée.

Féchy Vaud ★→★★ Famous appellation of LA CÔTE, esp elegant whites.

Federweisser German-Swiss name for white wine from BLAUBURGUNDER.

Fendant Valais w ★→★★★ VALAIS appellation for CHASSELAS. Fuel of the ski slopes;

not for wimps. Wide range of wines; best now use village names only.

Flétri/Mi-flétri Late-harvested grapes for sw/slightly sw wine (respectively).

Fribourg Smallest French-Swiss wine canton (285 acres, nr Jura). Esp for PINOT NOIR, CHASSELAS, GAMAY, SPÉCIALITÉS from VULLY, Lake Murten, S Lake NEUCHÂTEL.

Fully Valais r w ★★→★★★ Village nr MARTIGNY: excellent ERMITAGE and GAMAY. Best producer: Marie-Thérèse Chappaz sw ★★→★★★ 99 00 01 02.

Gamay Beaujolais grape; abounds in French cantons. Mainly thin wine used in blends (SALVAGNIN, DÔLE). Gamay accounts for 14% of grapes in Switzerland.

Geneva Capital, and French-Swiss wine canton; the third largest (3,370 acres). Key areas: Mandement, Entre Arve et Rhône, Entre Arve et Lac. Mostly CHASSELAS, GAMAY, Chard, PINOT NOIR, Muscat, and gd Aligoté. Best: Jean-Michel Novelle ★★★

Gewurztraminer Grown in Switzerland as a SPÉCIALITÉ variety esp in VALAIS. Best producer: Jean-Michel Novelle, Satigny 01 02 03.

Germanier, Jean-René VETROZ winemaker; Cayas (100% Syrah) ★★★ 99 00 01 02; Mitis (sweet) ★★★ 99 00 01.

Glacier, Vin du (Gletscherwein) Fabled oxidized, wooded white from rare Rèze grape of Val d'Anniviers; offered by the thimbleful to visiting dignitaries. See also VISPERTERMINEN. Best producer: St Jodern-Kellerei ★ 01 02 03.

Grand Cru Quality designation. Implication differs by canton: in VALAIS, GENEVA, and VAUD used where set requirements fulfilled.

Grisons (Graubünden) Mountain canton, mainly in German Switzerland (BÜNDNER HERRSCHAFT, Churer Rheintal; esp BLAUBURGUNDER) and partly S of Alps (Misox, esp MERLOT). 928 acres, primarily red, also Müller-Thurgau and SPÉCIALITÉS.

Heida (Païen) Old VALAIS white grape (Jura's Savagnin) for country wine of upper Valais (VISPERTERMINEN v'yds at 1,000 metres plus). Successful in lower VALAIS, too. Best producer: Josef-Marie Chanton ★★ 00 01 02 03'.

Humagne Strong native white grape (VALAIS SPÉCIALITÉ). Humagne Rouge (unrelated, from Aosta Valley) also. Esp from CHAMOSON, LEYTRON, MARTIGNY.

Johannisberg Synomyn for SYLVANER in the VALAIS.

Landwein (Vin de pays) Traditional light white and esp red BLAUBURGUNDER from E.

Lausanne Capital of VAUD. No longer with v'yds in town area, but long-time owner of classics: Abbaye de Mont, Château Rochefort (LA CÔTE); Clos des Moines, Clos des Abbayes, Dom de Burignon (LAVAUX). Pricey.

Lavaux Vaud w (r) ★→★★★ DYA Scenic region on N shore of Lake GENEVA between Montreux and LAUSANNE. Delicate, refined whites, gd reds. Best: CALAMIN, Chardonne, DÉZALEY, EPESSES, Lutry, ST-SAPHORIN, VEVEY-MONTREUX, Villette.

Leytron Valais r w ★★→★★★ Commune nr SION/MARTIGNY, esp Le Grand Brûlé.

Malvoisie See PINOT GRIS.

Martigny Valais r w ★★ Lower VALAIS commune esp for HUMAGNE ROUGE and Syrah.

Merlot Grown in Italian Switzerland (TICINO) since 1907 (after phylloxera destroyed local varieties): soft to very powerful wines. Also used with Cab Sauv.

Mont d'Or, Domaine du Valais w s/sw sw ★★→★★★ 01 02 03' Well-sited property nr SION: rich, concentrated demi-sec and sweet wines, notable SYLVANER.

Mont-sur-Rolle Vaud w (r) ★★ DYA Important appellation within LA CÔTE.

Morges Vaud r p w ★→★★ DYA Largest LA CÔTE/VAUD AOC: CHASSELAS, fruity reds.

Neuchâtel 01 02 03 City and canton; 1,519 acres from Lake Neuchâtel to BIELERSEE. CHASSELAS: fragrant, lively (sur lie, sp). Gd PINOT NOIR (OEIL DE PERDRIX), PINOT GRIS, Chard. Best producer: Grillette Domaine de Cressier ★★.

Nostrano Word meaning "ours", applied to red wine of TICINO, made from native and Italian grapes (Bondola, Freisa, Bonarda, etc).

Oeil de Perdrix Pale PINOT NOIR rosé. DYA Esp NEUCHÂTEL's; also VALAIS, VAUD.

Pinot Blanc (Weissburgunder) New variety producing full-bodied, elegant wines.

Pinot Gris (Malvoisie) Widely planted white grape for dry and residually sweet wines. Makes very fine late-harvest wines in VALAIS (called Malvoisie).

Pinot Noir (Blauburgunder) Top red grape (31% of Swiss v'yds). Esp: BÜNDNER HERRSCHAFT, NEUCHÂTEL, THURGAU, VALAIS, ZÜRICH. Try: Philippe Constantin (Salgesch), Christian Hermann (Flàsch), Peter Wegelin (Malans) ★★ 99 00 **01** 02 03'.

Rauschling Old white ZÜRICH grape; discreet fruit and elegant acidity. Best: Urs Picher, Eglisau.

Riesling (Petit Rhin) Mainly in the VALAIS. Excellent botrytis wines.

Riesling-Sylvaner Old name for Müller-THURGAU (top white of E; a SPÉCIALITÉ in W). Typically elegant wines with nutmeg aroma and some acidity. Best producers: Hermann Schwarzenbach, Daniel Marugg, Hans Weisendanger. All: ★★ **02 03**.

St-Gallen E wine canton (553 acres). Esp for BLAUBURGUNDER (full-bodied), Müller-THURGAU, SPÉCIALITÉS. Inc Rhine Valley, Oberland, upper Lake ZÜRICH.

St-Saphorin Vaud w (r) ★★→★★★ **01** Famous LAVAUX AC for fine, light whites.

Salvagnin Vaud r ★→★★★ **02** GAMAY and/or PINOT NOIR appellation. (See also DÔLE.)

Schaffhausen German-Swiss canton and wine town on River Rhine. Esp BLAUBURGUNDER; also Müller-THURGAU and SPÉCIALITÉS. Best: Baumann ★★.

Schenk Europe-wide wine giant, founded and based in Rolle (VAUD). Owns firms in France (Burg and B'x), Germany, Italy, and Spain.

Sierre Valais r w ★★→★★★ Sunny resort and famous wine town. Known for FENDANT, PINOT NOIR, ERMITAGE, Malvoisie. V.gd DÔLE.

Sion Valais r w ★★→★★★ Capital/wine centre of VALAIS. Esp FENDANT de Sion.

Sylvaner (Johannisberg, Gros Rhin) White grape esp in warm VALAIS v'yds. Heady, spicy: some with marked sweetness.

Spécialités (Spezialitäten) Wines of unusual grapes: vanishing local Gwäss, Himbertscha, Bondola, etc, ARVINE and AMIGNE, or modish Chenin Bl, Sauv Bl, Cab Sauv, Syrah. Eg VALAIS: 43 of its 47 varieties are considered spécialités.

Süssdruck Dry rosé/bright-red wine: grapes pressed before fermentation.

Thurgau German-Swiss canton beside Bodensee (678 acres). Wines from Thur Valley: Weinfelden, Seebach, Nussbaum, and Rhine. S shore of the Untersee. Typical: BLAUBURGUNDER, also gd RIESLING-SYLVANER (aka Müller-Thurgau: Dr Müller was born in the region). SPÉCIALITÉS inc Kerner, PINOT GRIS, Regent. Best producer: Hans Ulrich Kesselring ★★★ 99 00 **01** 02 03'.

Ticino Italian-speaking S Switzerland (with Misox), growing mainly MERLOT (gd from mountainous Sopraceneri region) and SPÉCIALITÉS. Trying Cab Sauv (oaked B'x style), Sauv Bl, Sem, Chard, Merlot white, and rosé. (2,347 acres.) Best producers: Luigi Zanini, Werner Stucky, Daniel Huber, Adriano Kaufmann, Christian Zündel. All: ★★★ **98 99** 00 01 02 03'.

Valais (Wallis) Rhône Valley from German-speaking upper-Valais to French lower-Valais. Largest and most varied wine canton in Switzerland (13,162 acres; source of 30% Swiss wine), now seeing a revival of quality, and ancient grapes. Near-perfect climatic conditions. Wide range: 47 grape varieties, plus many SPÉCIALITÉS. Esp white; FLETRI/MI-FLETRI wines.

Vaud (Waadt) French Switzerland's second largest wine canton inc: CHABLAIS, LA CÔTE, LAVAUX, BONVILLARS, CÔTES DE L'ORBE, VULLY. CHASSELAS stronghold.

Vétroz Valais w r ★★→★★★ Top village nr SION, esp famous for AMIGNE.

Vevey-Montreux Vaud r w ★★ Up-and-coming appellation of LAVAUX. Famous wine festival held about every 30 yrs.

Villeneuve Vaud w (r) ★★→★★★ Nr Lake Geneva: powerful yet refined whites.

Visperterminen Valais w (r) ★→★★ Upper VALAIS v'yds esp for SPÉCIALITÉS.

Vully Vaud w (r) ★→★★ Refreshing white from Lake Murten/FRIBOURG area.

Yvorne Vaud w (r) ★★ **02** 03 Top CHABLAIS AC for strong, fragrant wines.

Zürich Capital of largest German-speaking wine canton (of the same name). Mostly BLAUBURGUNDER; also PINOT GRIS, GEWURZTRAMINER, and esp Müller-THURGAU, RAUSCHLING (1,591 acres).

SWITZERLAND

Austria

More heavily shaded areas are the wine growing regions

In less than twenty years Austria has emerged as a vigorous, innovative producer of dry white and dessert wines up to the very finest quality, though entry-level wines can also be very good. Red wines (20% of vineyards) are starting to make an international reputation, too. Strict laws, first passed in 1985, with the latest revisions made in 2004, include curbs on yields and impose levels of ripeness for each category that reflect the Austrian climate. Many regional names, introduced under the 1985 law, are still unfamiliar outside Austria. All are worth trying; there are dramatic discoveries to be made.

Recent vintages

2003 Early harvest after long, hot summer. Very good for Grüner Veltliner and Burgenland reds, especially Blaufränkisch and Zweigelt. Little botrytis for dessert wines.

2002 Though Grüner Veltliner was hit by harvest rains, Riesling and the white Pinots did well. A difficult red-wine vintage, but excellent dessert wines.

2001 Another top vintage for dry whites and very good for late-harvest wines. Red are more erratic.

2000 Very good vintage in Lower Austria. Mixed in Styria due to harvest rains. In Burgenland, possibly the greatest vintage since 1945.

1999 A great vintage whose dry white wines combine concentration and elegance. The best to date for the reds.

1998 A superb vintage for late-harvest wines, a very good one for the dry whites, but rather disappointing for reds.

1997 Very few late-harvest wines (wrong conditions for botrytis), but top dry whites and reds are rich and powerful.

Ausbruch PRÄDIKAT wine (very sweet) between Beerenauslese and Trockenbeerenauslese in quality. Traditionally produced in RUST.

Ausg'steckt ("hung out") HEURIGEN are not open all year. To show potential visitors wine is being served, a green bush is hung up above the door.

Bergwein Legal designation for wines made from grapes grown on slopes with an incline of over 26%.

Blauburger Austrian red grape variety. A cross between BLAUER PORTUGIESER and BLAUFRÄNKISCH. Dark-coloured but light-bodied; simple wines.

Blauer Burgunder (Pinot Noir) A rarity, but on the increase. Vintages fluctuate greatly. Best in BURGENLAND, KAMPTAL, and the THERMENREGION (from growers Achs, BRÜNDLMAYER, Johanneshof, STIEGELMAR, UMATHUM, and WIENINGER).

Blauer Portugieser Light, fruity wines to drink slightly chilled when young. Mostly made for local consumption. Top producers: Fischer, Lust.

Blauer Zweigelt BLAUFRÄNKISCH-ST-LAURENT cross: high yields and rich colour. Lower yields and improved methods can produce some fine reds. Top producers: HEINRICH, Nittnaus, Pitnauer, Pöckl, UMATHUM.

Blaufränkisch (Lemberger in Germany, Kékfrankos in Hungary) Austria's red grape variety with the most potential, much planted in MITTELBURGENLAND: wines with gd body, peppery acidity, and a fruity cherry taste. Often blended with Cab Sauv. Best from Achs, Gesellmann, HEINRICH, Iby, Igler, Krutzler, Nittnaus, TRIEBAUMER.

Bouvier Indigenous grape, generally producing light wines with low acidity but plenty of aroma, esp gd for Beeren- and Trockenbeerenauslesen.

Bründlmayer, Willi r w sp ★★★→★★★★ 90 92 93 94 95 97 98 99 00 01 02 03 Leading LANGENLOIS-KAMPTAL estate. V.gd wines: both local (RIESLING, GRÜNER VELTLINER) and international styles, inc CHARDONNAY. Also Austria's best Sekt.

Burgenland Province and wine region (40,000 acres) in the E next to Hungarian border. Warm climate. Ideal conditions, esp for botrytis wines nr NEUSIEDLER SEE, also reds. Four wine areas: MITTELBURGENLAND, NEUSIEDLER SEE, NEUSIEDLERSEE-HÜGELLAND, and SÜDBURGENLAND.

Buschenschank The same as HEURIGE; often a country cousin.

Carnuntum r w Wine region since 1994, E of VIENNA, bordered by the Danube to the N. Best producers: Glatzer, G Markowitsch, Pitnauer.

Chardonnay Increasingly grown, mainly oaked. Also traditionally grown in STYRIA as MORILLON (usually unoaked): strong fruit taste, lively acidity. Esp BRÜNDLMAYER, Loimer, Malat, POLZ, SATTLER, STIEGELMAR, TEMENT, VELICH, WIENINGER.

Deutschkreutz r (w) MITTELBURGENLAND red wine area, esp for BLAUFRÄNKISCH.

Districtus Austriae Controllatus (DAC) Austria's first appellation system, introduced in 2003. Similar to France's AC and Italy's DOC.

Donauland (Danube) w (r) Wine region since 1994, just W of VIENNA. Inc KLOSTERNEUBURG S of Danube and WAGRAM N of the river. Mainly whites, esp GRÜNER VELTLINER. Best producers inc: Fritsch, Chorherren Klosterneuburg, Leth, Bernhard Ott, Wimmer-Czerny, R Zimmermann.

Dürnstein w Wine centre of the WACHAU with famous ruined castle. Mainly GRÜNER VELTLINER, RIESLING. Top growers: FREIE WEINGÄRTNER WACHAU, KNOLL, PICHLER, Schmidl.

Eisenstadt r w dr sw Capital of BURGENLAND and historic seat of Esterházy family. Major producer: Esterházy.

Falkenstein w Wine centre in the eastern WEINVIERTEL nr Czech border. Gd GRÜNER VELTLINER. Best producers: Jauk, Luckner, HEINRICH, and Josef Salomon.

Federspiel Medium quality level of the VINEA WACHAU categories, roughly corresponding to Kabinett. Fruity, elegant, dry wines.

Feiler-Artinger r w sw ★★★→★★★★ 91 92 93 94 95 96 97 98 99 00 01 02 03 Considered the outstanding RUST estate. Top AUSBRUCH dessert wines since 1993. Also gd dry whites and increasingly exciting reds.

Freie Weingärtner Wachau w (r) ★★★ **92 93 94 95 96 97 98 99 00** 02 03 Important and v.gd growers' co-op in DURNSTEIN. Excellent GRÜNER VELTLINER and RIESLING. Domaine Wachau range.

Gamlitz w Town in southern STYRIA. Growers inc Lackner-Tinnacher, SATTLER.

Gemischter Satz A blend of grapes (mostly white) grown, harvested, and vinified together. Traditional wine, still served in HEURIGEN.

Gobelsburg, Schloss ★★★ Renowned 86-acre estate in KAMPTAL revitalized since 1996. Excellent dry RIESLING and GRÜNER VELTLINER.

Gols r w dr sw Largest BURGENLAND wine commune (N shore of NEUSIEDLER SEE). Best producers: Achs, Beck, HEINRICH, Leitner, A&H Nittnaus, Renner, STIEGELMAR.

Grüner Veltliner Austria's national white grape (over a third of v'yd area). Fruity, racy, lively young wines. Can be distinguished, age-worthy. CHARDONNAY, watch out! Best: BRÜNDLMAYER, FREIE WEINGÄRTNER WACHAU, HIRTZBERGER, Högl, KNOLL, Loimer, MANTLER, NEUMAYER, NIGL, NIKOLAIHOF, PFAFFL, F X PICHLER, PRAGER, Schmelz.

G'spritzer Popular, refreshing summer drink, usually white-wine-based; made sparkling by adding soda or mineral water. Esp in HEURIGEN.

Gumpoldskirchen w r dr sw Resort village S of VIENNA, famous for HEURIGEN. Centre of THERMENREGION. Distinctive, tasty, often sweet wines from ZIERFANDLER and ROTGIPFLER grapes. Best producers: Biegler, Schellmann.

Heinrich, Gernot r w dr sw ★★→★★★ **92 93 94 96 97 98 99 00 01** 02 03 Young, modern estate in GOLS with Pannobile and (esp) red Gabarinza labels.

Heurige Wine of the most recent harvest, called "new wine" for one year, then classified as "old". Heurigen are wine houses where growers-cum-patrons serve wine by the glass or bottle with simple local food – an institution, esp in VIENNA.

Hirtzberger, Franz w ★★★★ **93 94 95 96 97 98 99 00 01** 02 03 Leading producer with 22 acres at SPITZ AN DER DONAU. Fine dry RIESLING and GRÜNER VELTLINER.

Horitschon MITTELBURGENLAND region for reds. Best: Anton Iby, WENINGER.

Illmitz w (r) dr sw SEEWINKEL region famous for Beeren- and Trockenbeeren-auslesen. Best from Angerhof, KRACHER, Martin Haider, Helmut Lang, OPITZ.

Jamek, Josef w ★★★★ **94 95 97 98 99 00 01** 02 03 Well-known WACHAU estate and restaurant. Pioneer of dry whites since 1950s. Recently back on top form.

Jurtschitsch/Sonnhof w (r) dr (sw) ★→★★ **94 95 97 98 99 00 01** 02 03 Domaine run by three brothers: gd whites (RIESLING, GRÜNER VELTLINER, CHARDONNAY).

Kamptal r w Wine region since 1994, along River Kamp N of WACHAU. Top v'yds: LANGENLOIS, STRASS, Zöbing. Best growers: BRÜNDLMAYER, Dolle, Ehn, Schloss Gobelsburg, Hiedler, Hirsch, JURTSCHITSCH, Loimer, Topf.

Kattus ★→★★ Producer of traditional Sekt in VIENNA.

Klöch w W STYRIA wine town famous for Traminer. Best from Stürgkh.

Kloster Und Wine-tasting centre in restored monastery nr KREMS.

Klosterneuburg r w Main wine town of DONAULAND. Rich in tradition with a famous Benedictine monastery and a wine college founded in 1860. Best producers: Stift Klosterneuburg, Zimmermann.

KMW Abbreviation for "Klosterneuburger Mostwaage" (must level), the unit used in Austria to measure the sugar content in grape juice.

Knoll, Emmerich w ★★★★ **95 96 97 98 99 00 01** 02 03 Traditional, highly regarded estate in LOIBEN producing showpiece GRÜNER VELTLINER and RIESLING.

Kollwentz-Römerhof w r dr (sw) ★★→★★★ **90 92 93 94 95 96 97 98 99 00** 01 02 03 Innovative producer nr EISENSTADT: Sauv Bl, Eiswein, gd reds.

Kracher, Alois w (r) dr (sw) ★★★★ **81 89 91 93 94 95 96 97 98 99 00 01** 02 03 First-class small ILLMITZ producer. Speciality: PRÄDIKATS (dessert), some barrique-aged (Nouvelle Vague), others not (Zwischen den Seen); gd reds since 1997.

Krems w (r) dr (sw) Ancient town, W of VIENNA. Capital of KREMSTAL. Best from Forstreiter, NIGL, SALOMON, Weingut Stadt Krems, Walzer.

Kremstal w (r) Wine region since 1994 esp for GRÜNER VELTLINER and RIESLING. Top growers: Malat, MANTLER, NIGL, SALOMON, S Moser, Weingut Stadt Krems.

Langenlois r w Wine town and region in KAMPTAL with 5,000 acres. Best producers: BRÜNDLMAYER, Ehn, Hiedler, JURTSCHITSCH, Loimer.

Lenz Moser ★★→★★★ Producer nr KREMS. LM III invented high-vine system. Also inc wines from Schlossweingut Malteser Ritterorden (wine estate of Knights of Malta): Mailberg (WEINVIERTEL), Klosterkeller Siegendorf (BURGENLAND).

Loiben w In lower, wider part of Danube Valley (WACHAU). Ideal conditions for RIESLING and GRÜNER VELTLINER. Top: Alzinger, FREIE WEINGÄRTNER, KNOLL, F X PICHLER.

Mantler, Josef w ★★→★★★ **90 95 96 97 98 99 00 01** 02 03 Leading estate in Gedersdorf nr KREMS. V.gd traditional RIESLING, GRÜNER VELTLINER, CHARDONNAY, and rare Roter Veltliner (Malvasia).

Messwein Mass wine: must have ecclesiastical approval (and natural must).

Mittelburgenland r (w) dr (sw) Wine region on Hungarian border protected by three hill ranges. Makes large quantities of red (especially BLAUFRÄNKISCH). Producers: Gesellmann, HEINRICH, Iby, Igler, P Kerschbaum, WENINGER.

Mörbisch r w dr sw Wine town on the W shore of NEUSIEDLER SEE just N of the Hungarian border. The top grower is Schönberger.

Morillon Name given in STYRIA to CHARDONNAY.

Müller-Thurgau See RIESLING-SYLVANER.

Muskat-Ottonel Grape for fragrant, often dry whites, interesting PRÄDIKATS.

Muskateller Rare, aromatic grape for dry whites. Best from STYRIA and WACHAU. Top growers: Gross, HIRTZBERGER, Lackner-Tinnacher, F X PICHLER, POLZ, SATTLER.

Neuburger Indigenous white grape with nutty flavour; mainly in the WACHAU (elegant, flowery), THERMENREGION (mellow and ample-bodied), and N BURGENLAND (strong, full). Best from Beck, FREIE WEINGÄRTNER, HIRTZBERGER.

Neumayer ★★★ **94 95 96 97 98 99 00 01** 02 03 The Neumayer brothers make powerful, pithy, dry GRÜNER VELTLINER and RIESLING at the best estate in the new TRAISENTAL area.

Neusiedler See Very shallow (max 1.8m deep) BURGENLAND lake on Hungarian border. Warm temperatures and autumn mists encourage botrytis. Gives name to wine territories of NEUSIEDLERSEE-HÜGELLAND and NEUSIEDLERSEE.

Neusiedlersee r w dr sw Area N and E of NEUSIEDLER SEE. Best growers: Achs, Beck, HEINRICH, Juris-Stiegelmar, KRACHER, Nittnaus, OPITZ, Pöckl, UMATHUM, VELICH.

Neusiedlersee-Hügelland r w dr sw Wine region W of NEUSIEDLER SEE based around OGGAU, RUST, and MORBISCH on the lake shores, and EISENSTADT in the foothills of the Leitha Mts. Best producers: FEILER-ARTINGER, KOLLWENTZ, Prieler, Schandl, Schönberger, Schröck, ERNST TRIEBAUMER, Wenzel.

Niederösterreich (Lower Austria) With 58% of Austria's v'yds: CARNUNTUM, DONAULAND, KAMPTAL, KREMSTAL, THERMENREGION, TRAISENTAL, WACHAU, WEINVIERTEL.

Nigl ★★★ w **92 93 94 95 96 97 98 99 00 01** 02 03 Top grower of KREMSTAL making sophisticated dry RIESLING and GRÜNER VELTLINER capable of long ageing.

Nikolaihof w ★★★ **90 91 92 94 95 97 98 99 00 01** 02 Estate built on Roman foundations. Superb RIESLING from Steiner Hund site, other wines v.gd and very traditional in style.

Nussdorf VIENNA district famous for HEURIGEN and v.gd Ried Nussberg.

Opitz, Willi ★★★ A tiny ILLMITZ estate specializing in late-harvest wines, including "Schilfmandl" and "Opitz One" from grapes dried on reeds from the NEUSIEDLER SEE.

Pfaffl ★★★ **90 93 94 95 96 97 98 99 00 01** 02 03 WEINVIERTEL estate in Stretten nr VIENNA. Best known for blended red "Excellence", but racy, dry GRÜNER VELTLINERS are no less impressive. Also runs nearby Schlossweingut Bockfliess estate.

Pichler, Franz Xavier w ★★★★ **90 92 93 94 95 96 97 98 99 00 01** 02 03 Top WACHAU producer with very intense, rich RIESLING and GRÜNER VELTLINER (esp Kellerberg). Widely recognized as one of Austria's best growers for dry wines.

Polz, Erich and Walter w ★★★ 92 93 95 96 97 98 99 00 01 02 03 S STYRIAN (Weinstrasse) growers; esp Hochgrassnitzberg: Sauv Bl, CHARDONNAY, Graugurgunder, WEISSBURGUNDER.

Prädikat, Prädikatswein Quality graded wines from Spätlese upwards (Spätlese, Auslese, Eiswein, Strohwein, Beerenauslese, AUSBRUCH, and Trockenbeerenauslese). See Germany, p.144.

Prager, Franz w ★★★★ 90 91 92 93 94 95 96 97 98 99 00 01 02 03 Together with JOSEF JAMEK, pioneer of top-quality WACHAU dry white. Now run by Anton Bodenstein; new RIESLING clones and great PRÄDIKAT wines.

Renomierte Weingüter Burgenland Association founded 1995 by top BURGENLAND producers to promote region's best wines; inc KRACHER, TRIEBAUMER, UMATHUM.

Retz r w Important town in W WEINVIERTEL. Esp Weinbauschule Retz.

Ried Single v'yd.

Riesling On its own always means German RIESLING. WELSCHRIESLING (unrelated) is labelled as such. Top growers: Alzinger, BRÜNDLMAYER, FREIE W WACHAU, HIRTZBERGER, Högl, KNOLL, NIGL, NIKOLAIHOF, PFAFFL, F X PICHLER, PRAGER, SALOMON.

Riesling-Sylvaner Name (wrongly) used for Müller-Thurgau (about 10% of Austria's grapes). Müller-Thurgau is actually Riesling x Chasselas de Courtillier. These things happen. Best producers: HIRTZBERGER, JURTSCHITSCH.

Rotgipfler Fragrant, indigenous grape of THERMENREGION. With ZIERFANDLER, makes lively, interesting wine. Esp Biegler, Schellmann, Stadelmann.

Rust w r dr sw BURGENLAND region, famous since 17th C for dessert AUSBRUCH; now also for red and dry white. Esp from FEILER-ARTINGER, Schandl, Heidi Schröck, ERNST TRIEBAUMER, Paul Triebaumer, Wenzel. Cercle Ruster Ausbruch producers focus on powerful sw wines from a wide range of grapes. Standards very high.

St-Laurent Traditional red grape, potentially v.gd, with cherry aroma, possibly related to Pinot N. Esp from Fischer, Mad, STIEGELMAR, UMATHUM.

Salomon-Undhof w ★★★ V.gd producer of RIESLING, WEISSBURGUNDER, Traminer in KREMS. Excellent quality since 1995.

Sattler, Willi w ★★→★★★ 92 93 94 95 96 97 98 99 00 01 02 03 Top S STYRIA grower. Esp for Sauv, MORILLON. Recent vintages less oaked, more balanced.

Schilcher Rosé wine from indigenous Blauer Wildbacher grapes (sharp, dry: high acidity). Speciality of W STYRIA. Try: Klug, Lukas, Reiterer, Strohmeier.

Schlumberger Largest sparkling winemaker in Austria (VIENNA); wine is bottle-fermented by unique "Méthode Schlumberger". Delicate and fruity.

Seewinkel ("Lake corner") Name given to the part of NEUSIEDLERSEE including Apetlon, ILLMITZ, and Podersdorf. Ideal conditions for botrytis.

Sepp Moser ★★★ 93 94 95 97 98 99 00 01 02 03 KREMSTAL estate (Rohrendorf) founded with original LENZ MOSER v'yds. Richly aromatic, elegant, dry RIESLING, GRÜNER VELTLINER, CHARDONNAY, Sauv Bl. Also gd reds from Apetlon in Neusiedlersee region.

Servus w BURGENLAND everyday light and mild, dry white-wine brand.

Smaragd Highest-quality category of VINEA WACHAU, similar to dry Spätlese.

Spätrot-Rotgipfler Typical THERMENREGION (Spätrot and ROTGIPFLER) wine.

Spitz an der Donau w WACHAU cool microclimate: esp from Singerriedel v'yd. Top growers are: HIRTZBERGER, FREIE WEINGARTNER, Högl, Lagler.

Steinfeder VINEA WACHAU quality category for very light, fragrant, dry wines.

Stiegelmar, Georg & Axl (Juris-Stiegelmar) w r dr sw ★→★★★ 93 95 96 97 98 99 00 01 02 03 GOLS growers: CHARDONNAY, Sauv Bl, reds, and unusual specialities.

Strass w (r) Centre of KAMPTAL region for gd Qualität white wines. Best prods: Dolle, Topf.

Styria (Steiermark) Southernmost wine region of Austria. Some gd dry whites, esp Sauv Bl. Inc SUDSTEIERMARK, SUD-OSTSTEIERMARK WESTSTEIERMARK (S, SE, W Styria).

Süd-Oststeiermark (SE Styria) w (r) STYRIAN region with islands of excellent v'yds. Best producers: Neumeister, Winkler-Hermaden.

Südburgenland r w Small S BURGENLAND wine region: gd red wines. Best producers: Krutzler, Wachter, Wiesler.

Südsteiermark (S Styria) w Best wine region of STYRIA: makes very popular whites (MORILLON, MUSKATELLER, WELSCHRIESLING, and Sauv Blanc). Top producers: Gross, Lackner-Tinnacher, POLZ, Prünte, SATTLER, Skoff, TEMENT, Tscheppe, Wohlmuth.

Tement, Manfred w ★★★ 90 92 93 94 97 98 99 00 01 02 03 Renowned estate on S STYRIA Weinstrasse for beautifully made, traditional "Steirisch Klassik" and gently oaked Sauv Bl and MORILLON from Ziereggste. World-class.

Thermenregion r w dr sw Wine/hot-springs region, S of VIENNA. Indigenous grapes (eg ZIERFANDLER, ROTGIPFLER) and gd reds from Baden, GUMPOLDSKIRCHEN Tattendorf, Traiskirchen areas. The top producers are: Alphart, Biegler, Fischer, Johanneshof, Schafler, Schellmann, Stadelmann.

Traditionsweingüter Association of KAMPTAL and KREMSTAL estates, committed to quality and v'yd classification. Inc BRÜNDLMAYER, Loimer, Malat, NIGL, SALOMON.

Traisental New area: 1,750 acres just S of KREMS on Danube. Dry whites similar to WACHAU. Top producers: Huber, NEUMAYER.

Triebaumer, Ernst r (w) dr sw ★★★ 90 92 93 94 95 97 98 99 00 01 02 03 RUST producer; some of Austria's best reds: BLAUFRÄNKISCH (Mariental), Cab Sauv/ Merlot blend. V.gd AUSBRUCH.

Umathum, Josef w r dr sw ★★★ 90 91 92 94 95 97 98 99 00 01 02 03 Distinguished NEUSIEDLERSEE producer. V.gd reds inc BLAUER BURGUNDER; gd whites.

Velich w SW BURGENLAND ★★★ Burgundian-style "Tiglat" CHARDONNAY (99 00 01) has 22 months in barrel. Since 1995 some of top PRÄDIKATS in the SEEWINKEL.

Vienna w (r) ("Wien" in German and on labels.) The Austrian capital is a wine region in its own right (1,500 v'yd acres in suburbs). Generally simple, lively wines, served in HEURIGEN: esp Bernreiter, MAYER, Schilling, WIENINGER.

Vinea Wachau WACHAU appellation started by winemakers in 1983 with three categories of dry wine: STEINFEDER, FEDERSPIEL, and powerful SMARAGD.

Wachau w Danube wine region W of KREMS: some of Austria's best wines, inc RIESLING, GRÜNER VELTLINER. Top producers: Alzinger, FREIE WEINGÄRTNER, HIRTZBERGER, Högl, JAMEK, KNOLL, NIKOLAIHOF, F X PICHLER, PRAGER.

Wagram r w Part of the Donauland wine region with loess terraces. Best producers: Fritsch, Leth, Bernhard Ott, Wimmer-Czerny.

Weinviertel "Wine Quarter" w (r) Largest Austrian wine region, between Danube and Czech border. First to adopt DAC appellation status. Mostly refreshing, light w, esp from Falkenstein, Poysdorf, RETZ. Best producers: Graf Hardegg, Gruber, Malteser Ritterorden, PFAFFL, Schwarzböck, Taubenschuss, Zull.

Weissburgunder (Pinot Bl) Ubiquitous: gd dry wines and PRÄDIKATS. Esp Beck, Fischer, Gross, HEINRICH, HIRTZBERGER, Lackner-Tinnacher, POLZ, TEMENT.

Welschriesling White grape, not related to RIESLING, grown in all wine regions: light, fragrant, young-drinking dry wines and gd PRÄDIKATS.

Weststeiermark (West Styria) p Small Austrian wine region specializing in SCHILCHER. Esp from Klug, Lukas, Reiterer, Strohmeier.

Wien See VIENNA.

Wieninger, Fritz w r ★★→★★★ 92 93 94 95 97 98 99 00 01 02 03 V.gd VIENNA-Stammersdorf grower: HEURIGE, CHARDONNAY, BLAUER BURGUNDER reds; esp gd GRÜNER VELTLINER and RIESLING.

Winzer Krems Wine-growers' co-op in KREMS: dependable, solid whites.

Zierfandler (Spätrot) White variety almost exclusive to the THERMENREGION. Blended with ROTGIPFLER: robust, lively, age-worthy wines. Best producers: Biegler, Schellmann, Stadelmann.

Central & Southeast Europe

More heavily shaded areas are the wine growing regions

To say that parts of this region are still in transition is an understatement. But new regional autonomies and new statehoods are being followed in many cases by higher aspirations in winemaking. In a few much-publicized cases this takes the form of international "flying winemakers" pitching their tents at vintage-time, usually to make wines acceptable to Western supermarkets from predictable grape varieties, occasionally to do far better. This affects indigenous winemaking, too – often with happy results, making fresher and fruitier wines of intriguingly different flavours.

The fifteen years since Communism have witnessed the decline of state firms and the emergence of new family- and corporate-owned wineries. These are now establishing their winemaking styles and market positions, with either fresh and fruity or more complex, aged wines. So far, Hungary, Bulgaria, Slovenia, and the Czech Republic have taken the lead in what has become an area to follow with fascination. The potential of other ex-Communist states has still to emerge, with Romania in particular catching up. But about Greece there is no doubt: the new age of wine has well and truly arrived.

In this section, references are arranged country by country, each shown on the map on this page. Included alongside regions are producers and other terms in the alphabetical listings.

Hungary

Hungary entered the Communist era with Eastern Europe's finest and most individual wines. It emerged with traditions severely battered. The past fifteen years have been revolutionary. Winemakers have invested capital and earnings into improving cellar equipment and procedures and expanding plantings of international grapes. The initial years of experiment have given way to proven winemaking techniques and definite wine styles.This is especially true for the reds of Villány, Szekszárd (the "z"s are silent), and Eger. Tokaji, the one undisputed great wine of Central European history, remains in full renaissance, and native grapes provide the backbone for the more traditional preference for fiery, hearty, full-bodied wines. The situation should continue to improve following accession to the EU in May 2004.

Alföld Hungary's Great Plain: much everyday wine (mostly international varieties) and some better. Incorporates 3 wine districts: HAJÓS-Baja, Csongrád, KUNSÁG.

Ászár-Neszmély Wine region in NW Hungary nr the Danube. International and native grapes.

Aszú Botrytis-shrivelled grapes and the sweet wine made from them, similar to Sauternes (see France). Used to designate both wine and shrivelled berries.

Aszú Eszencia Tokaj sw ★★★★ **57 63 93** 96 99 Second TOKAJI quality (see ESZENCIA). 7 PUTTONYOS-plus; should be superb amber elixir, like celestial butterscotch.

Árvay & Co New TOKAJI cellar (established 2003) headed by former DISZNÓKÓ winemaker János Árvay. First wines are on the market: ASZÚ (5/6 PUTTONYOS) and cuvée Edés Élet.

Badacsony w dr sw ★★→★★★ Wine district on the N shore of Lake BALATON, home to the native variety KÉKNYELÜ. The basalt soil can give rich, highly flavoured white wines; well-made Ries and SZÜRKEBARÁT have fine mineral flavours. The leader is SZEREMLEY'S SZT ORBÁN winery.

Balaton Hungary's inland sea, Europe's largest freshwater lake. Many gd wines take its name.

Balatonboglár r w dr sw ★★→★★★ Progressive winery on S shore of Lake BALATON in Dél-Balaton region. Decent whites (Chard, Sem, Muscat). Also *cuve close* sparkling. Owned by Henkell & Söhnlein.

Bikavér Eger r ★ "Bull's Blood", historic red wine of EGER: at best full-bodied and well-balanced, but highly variable in export version today. Now under supervision to protect identity and improve quality (see EGER). Mostly from KÉKFRANKOS, Cab Sauv, Cab Fr, Kekoporto, Merlot. Also made in SZEKSZÁRD.

Bock, József Family winemaker in VILLÁNY. Hearty reds, both varietal and blends.

Bor "Wine": *vörös* is red; *fehér* is white; *asztali* is table; *táj* is country, a section of the market that is currently growing.

Dégenfeld, Grof Large TOKAJI estate. Traditional-style wines, plus dry FURMINT.

Disznókö Important first-class TOKAJI estate, owned by French company AXA. Very modern style, Sauternes-influenced wines of great refinement and vigour.

Edes Sweet wine (but not as luscious as ASZÚ).

Eger r w dr sw ★→★★★ Best-known red-wine centre of N Hungary; Baroque city of cellars full of BIKAVÉR. Fresh LEÁNYKA (perhaps its best product), OLASZRIZLING, Chard, Cab Sauv. Top producers: Vilmos Thummerer (consistent BIKAVÉR), TIBOR GAL, Pók Tamás, Ostoros Bor, Béla Vincze, and the huge Egervin.

Eszencia ★★★★ The fabulous quintessence of TOKAJI: intensely sweet and aromatic from grapes wizened by botrytis. Properly grape juice of very low, if any, alcoholic strength, reputed to have miraculous properties: its sugar content can be over 750 grams per litre. In commerce, ASZÚ ESZENCIA takes its place.

Etyek-Buda Wine region nr Budapest. Source of modern-style wines, esp Chard and Sauv Bl. Leading producer: HUNGAROVIN.

Ezerjó Literally "thousand blessings". Widespread traditional variety. In MÓR, makes one of the country's top dry whites. Has great potential: fragrant with hint of grapefruit.

François President French-founded (1882) sparkling-wine brand now owned by HUNGAROVIN; winery at Budafok, nr Budapest. Vintage President very drinkable.

Furmint The classic grape of TOKAJI, with great flavour, acidity, and fire, also grown for table wine at Lake BALATON and in SOMLÓ.

Gál, Tibor EGER winemaker for barrique-aged BIKAVÉR, also oaked GIA Chard.

Gere, Attila Family winemaker in VILLÁNY with gd, forward-looking reds, esp oak-aged Cab Sauv (oo) and Cuvée Phoenix (oo).

Gundel TOKAJI venture at MÁD, making wines for famous Gundel's restaurant in Budapest. Also v'yds and cellar at EGER.

Hajós Pincék Alföld r ★ Charming village in S Hungary with 1,500 cellars. Mostly traditional, family production. Some quality lighter red wines can be found.

Hárslevelü "Linden-leaved" grape variety used at Debrö and as second grape of TOKAJI (compare with Sem/Sauv Bl in Sauternes). Gentle, mellow wine with a peach aroma.

Helvécia (Kecskemét) Historic ALFÖLD cellars. V'yds ungrafted: phylloxera bugs cannot negotiate sandy soil. Whites and rosés modernist; reds traditional.

Hétszölö Noble first-growth 116-acre TOKAJI estate owned by Grands Millésimes de France and Japanese Suntory. Second label, from purchased grapes: Dessewffy. Fordítás is halfway to ASZÚ in style.

Hilltop Neszmély Winery in ÁSZÁR-NESZMÉLY making international-style wines, inc Woodcutters White from homegrown Czerszegi Fuszeres hybrid.

Hungarovin Large company with cellars at Budafok nr Budapest: international varietals (Chard, Cab Sauv, Merlot), also *cuve close*, transfer, and classic sparkling. Owned by German sekt specialist Henkell.

Kadarka Traditional red grape for vast quantities in S, but can produce ample flavour and interesting maturity (esp at SZEKSZÁRD and VILLÁNY), and considered by some an essential component of BIKAVÉR.

Kékburgundi German Spätburgunder: Pinot N.

Kecskemét Major town of the ALFÖLD. Much everyday wine, some better.

Kékfrankos Hungarian for Blaufränkisch; reputedly related to Gamay. Most widely planted red variety. Gd light or full-bodied reds, esp at SOPRON. Used in BIKAVÉR at EGER.

Kéknyelü "Blue stalk". High-flavoured, low-yielding white grape making the best and "stiffest" wine of Mt BADACSONY. Best is flowery and spicy stuff. Top producer: SZEREMLEY (aromatic and fruity whites).

Királyudvar Promising new TOKAJI winery, formally opened in 2000 and directed by István SZEPSY. Wines inc dry and late-harvest FURMINT, Cuvee Ilona (early-bottled ASZÚ) and Jegbor (Eiswein).

Különleges Minöség Special quality: highest official grading.

Kunság Largest region in ALFÖLD (Great Plain). Gd KADARKA esp from Kiskörös.

Leányka "Little girl". Native Hungarian white grape. Admirable, aromatic, light, dry wine. Királyleányka ("Royal") is a different variety and supposedly superior.

Mád Old commercial centre of the TOKAJI region. Growers inc Vince Gergely, GUNDEL, József Monyok, ROYAL TOKAJI, SZEPSY.

Mátraalja w (r) ★★ District in foothills of Mátra range in N, nr Gyöngyös. Promising, dry SZÜRKEBARÁT, Chard, MUSKOTALY, Sauv Bl. Foreign investment from France, Germany, and Australia.

Mecsekalja S Hungary district, known for gd whites from PÉCS, esp sparkling.

Megyer, Château TOKAJI estate bought by Jean-Louis Laborde of Ch Clinet in

Pomerol. Also owns Ch PAJZOS. Megyer is the lighter wine. Quality is fair.

Mézes Mály In TARCAL. This and SZARVAS are historically the greatest v'yds of TOKAJI.

Minőségi Bor Quality wine. Hungary's *appellation contrôlée* (see France).

Mór N Hungary w ★★→★★★ Region long-famous for fresh, dry EZERJÓ. Now also Ries and Sauv Bl. Wines now mostly exported.

Muskotály Muscat; usually Ottonel. Muscat Bl à Petits Grains is Muscat Lunel. Makes light, but long-lived, wine in TOKAJ and EGER. A little goes into the TOKAJI blend. Very occasionally makes a wonderful ASZÚ wine solo.

Nagyburgundi Literally "great burgundy": indigenous grape often mistaken for KÉFRANKOS. Sound, solid wine, esp around VILLÁNY and SZEKSZÁRD.

Olaszrizling Hungarian name for the Italian Ries or Welschriesling. Better examples can have a burnt-almond aroma.

Oremus Ancient TOKAJ v'yd of founding Rakóczi family, owned by Spain's Vega Sicilia with HQ at Tolcsva. First-rate ASZÚ. Also a lesser TOKAJI grape.

Pajzos, Château B'x-owned TOKAJ estate with some fine ASZÚ. See MEGYER.

Pécs Mecsek w (r) ★→★★★ Major S wine city. Esp sp, OLASZRIZLING, Pinot Bl, etc.

Pincészet Winery.

Pinot Noir Normally means KÉKBURGUNDI.

Puttonyos Measure of sweetness in TOKAJI ASZÚ. A "puttony" is a 25-kilo measure, traditionally a hod of grapes. The number of "putts" per barrel (136 litres) of dry base wine or must determines the final richness of the wine, from 3 putts to 6 (3 putts = 60 g of sugar per litre, 4 = 90, 5 = 120, 6 = 150). ASZÚ ESZENCIA must have at least 180 g. The measuring of residual sugar has replaced actual puttonyos. See ESZENCIA for the *really* sticky stuff.

Royal Tokáji Wine Co Pioneer Anglo-Danish-Hungarian venture at MÁD. 200 acres, mainly first- or second-growth. First wine (90) a revelation: 91 and (esp) 93 led renaissance of TOKAJI. 95, 99, 00 to follow. I have to declare an interest as a founder.

Siklós City in S Hungary; part of VILLÁNY-SIKLÓS. Mainly small producers, known for whites: esp HÁRSLEVELŰ. Ripe, fruity Chard promising; also TRAMINI, OLASZRIZLING.

Somló N Hungary w ★★ Isolated small district N of BALATON: whites (formerly of high repute) from FURMINT and Juhfark ("sheep's tail") in both traditional barrel-fermented and fresh, fruity styles. Top producers inc Fekete, Inhauser.

Sopron W Hungary r ★★→★★★ Historic enclave S of Neusiedlersee (see Austria). Traditionally known for lighter reds like KÉKFRANKOS and Austrian-style sweet wines, but showing promise for whites such as Sauv Bl.

Szamorodni Literally "as it was born"; describes TOKAJI not sorted in the v'yd. Dry or (fairly) sweet, depending on proportion of ASZÚ grapes naturally present. Sold as an apéritif. In vintage TOKAJI ASZÚ yrs, the sweet style can offer some ASZÚ character at much less cost. Dry *szamorodni* is Hungary's sherry.

Száraz Dry, esp of TOKAJI SZAMORODNI.

Szarvas TOKAJI v'yd at Tarcal; a top site. Solely owned by TOKAJI TRADING HOUSE.

Szekszárd r ★★→★★★ District in S central Hungary; some of country's top reds from KÉKFRANKOS, Cab Sauv, Cab Fr, and Merlot. Also KADARKA which needs age (3–4 yrs); can also be botrytized ("Nemes Kadar"). Gd organic BIKAVÉR, Chard, and OLASZRIZLING. Quality wines are lighter, more delicate than those from VILLÁNY. Producers inc Vesztergombi, Peter Vida, Heimann.

Szent Orbán See SZEREMLEY.

Szepsy, István Legendary name and impeccable small production of long-ageing TOKAJI ASZÚ. See KIRÁLYUDVAR. Same family name as the man who created the ASZÚ method in 17th-C, though not related.

Szeremley, Huba Leader in BADACSONY. Ries, SZÜRKEBARÁT, KÉKNYELŰ, ZEUSZ are modern models. Fine KÉKFRANKOS from Tihány Peninsula. Szent Orbán is another label.

HUNGARY

Szürkebarát Literally "Grey Friar": Pinot Gr. Source of sw tourist wines from BALATON. But this is one of the best: wait for great dry wines.

Tarcal TOKAJI commune with 2 great first-growths and several gd producers.

Tiffán, Ede VILLÁNY grower, who with son Zsolt produces full-bodied, oaked reds.

Tokaj Trading House The formerly state-owned TOKAJI company, now reduced to 180 acres inc the magnificent SZARVAS v'yd. Also called Crown Estates. Castle Island is the brand for dry wines. Quality improving.

Tokajbor-Bene New TOKAJI cellar at Bodrogkeresztúr. To watch.

Tokaji Tokaj w dr sw ★★→★★★★ Tokaji is the wine (English spelling Tokay) and Tokaj the town. The ASZÚ is Hungary's famous liquorous sweet wine (since c.1600), comparable to a highly aromatic, dramatically vital Sauternes (see France) with a searing finish (and less alcohol), from hills in NE nr Slovakian border. Appellation covers 13,500 acres of the Tokajhegyalja. See ASZÚ, ESZENCIA, FURMINT, PUTTONYOS, SZAMORODNI. Also dry table wine of character.

Tramini Gewürztraminer, esp in SIKLÓS.

Villány-Siklós S wine region named after its two main towns. Villány makes mostly red, often gd quality B'x styles. Siklós makes mostly white. High-quality producers inc: BOCK, Csányi, GERE, Günzer, Malatinsky, Molnár, Polgar, TIFFÁN, and Vylyan.

Wille-Baumkauff, Márta Hungarian returnee goes MÁD with TOKAJI. Quality improves steadily.

Zemplen Ridge Or Zemplén Hegyhát. István SZEPSY and Anthony Hwang of KIRÁLYUDVAR think there's a market for less-concentrated TOKAJI for younger drinkers. First vintage was 02. Couldn't they just dilute to taste?

Zéta A cross of Bouvier and FURMINT used by some in ASZÚ production, also as varietal with a pear/green-apple flavour, but production waning.

Zeusz Recent variety for aromatic sweet whites.

Bulgaria

2001 was the first vintage under the new "French style" wine law, which introduced detailed regulations in the five wine regions. The drive for higher standards has been reflected by the increased demand for quality wines.

The Danube Plain regions specialize in fruity whites and reds at Svishtov, while further south, Lyaskovets and Pavlikeni produce some well-balanced reds. The Black Sea region is particularly suitable for the production of fresh, dry, and fruity whites at Targovishte, Shumen, and Pomorie. The largest and most productive region is the Thracian Valley with constant high temperatures producing rich reds, especially at Haskovo, Iambol, Sliven, and Assenovgrad. Struma Valley in the southwest is the hottest region, producing substantial reds of great longevity at Damianitsa and Harsovo.

Foreign investment in the modernization of established wineries continues, while newcomers are bringing a welcome diversity to the wine scene.

Assenovgrad r ★★ 01 Main MAVRUD-producing cellar near PLOVDIV. Should age well, esp the high-quality, limited edition "Boutique" series.

Blueridge r (w) ★★ Largest winery; in the town of Sliven. Owned by DOMAINE BOYAR and is the name used for its export wines. Successful winemaking team of Kapka Georgieva and Pavel Panov are now at SLIVEN and KORTEN.

Burgas w p (r) ★→★★ Black Sea port and source of rosé (the speciality), easy whites, and some gd young reds.

Cabernet Sauvignon Dark, vigorous, fruity, very drinkable young; best quality ages well. Gd examples: IAMBOL, SLIVEN, ROUSSE, SVISHTOV.

Chardonnay Was less successful than CABERNET SAUVIGNON. Gd results now from N and E. Very dry, full-flavoured wine. Recent wines promising, esp SHUMEN, SLIVEN, and POMORIE.

Controliran Like France's *appellation contrôlée*. New wine law published in 2000.

Country Wines Regional wines (cf French Vins de Pays), often 2-variety blends.

Damianitza r ★★ MELNIK winery specializing in native Melnik grape. Also excellent MERLOTS such as Redark (**01**).

Danube River dividing Bulgaria and Romania. ROUSSE and SVISHTOV v'yds benefit from its proximity, esp for reds.

A Bulgarian choice for 2005

Red Cab Sauv Tsar's Reserve 98 Iambol, Domaine Boyar Merlot Thracian Plain 01 Sliven, Stara Zagora Merlot 03, Sungurlare Cab Sauv 03.
White Targovishte Reserve Chard 01, Slaviantsi Reserve Chard 98, Vini Sliven Chard 02, Domaine Boyar Chard 03 Sliven, Vini Sliven Sauv Bl 02.
Native varieties Assenovgrad Mavrud 03, Blueridge Dimiat 01.

Dimiat The common native white grape, grown in the E towards the coast. Gd examples from BLUERIDGE (**01**), Black Sea Gold, and POMORIE.

Domaine Boyar Large company – a household name in Bulgaria. Exports as BLUERIDGE. See also KORTEN, SHUMEN, SLIVEN.

Gamza Red grape (Kadarka of Hungary) with potential esp from N region DANUBE plain. PAVLIKENI, NOVO SELO, and PLEVEN are specialists.

Harsovo Struma Valley region, esp for MELNIK.

Haskovo r (w) ★★ Recently privatized winery (with v'yds) in Thracian Plain region specializing in MERLOT; STAMBOLOVO, and SAKAR are satellite wineries.

Iambol r w ★→★★ Winery in Thracian Plain specializing in CABERNET SAUVIGNON and MERLOT. New owners: Vinprom Peshtera.

Karlovo Town located in the famous Valley of the Roses. Whites, esp MISKET. Recommended: Rose Valley Kabinet Reserves.

Khan Krum Satellite cellar of PRESLAV, whites esp Reserve CHARDONNAY.

Korten Boutique cellar of SLIVEN favouring traditional winemaking styles.

Mavrud Grape variety and darkly plummy red from S Bulgaria, esp ASSENOVGRAD. Can mature 20 yrs+. Considered the country's best indigenous red variety.

Melnik Village in SW and highly prized grape variety. Dense red; locals say it can be carried in a handkerchief. Needs 5 yrs+; lasts 15. Also ripe, ageworthy CABERNET SAUVIGNON.

Merlot Mainly planted in HASKOVO. Best: STAMBOLOVO, IAMBOL, Lyubimets, Elhovo in the S; SHUMEN, SVISHTOV in the N.

Misket Mildly aromatic indigenous grape; the basis for most country whites.

Muscat Ottonel Grown in E for mid-sweet, fruity white.

Novo Selo Gd red GAMZA from the N.

Oriachovitza r ★★ Satellite of STARA ZAGORA. Thracian Plain area for CONTROLIRAN CABERNET SAUVIGNON and MERLOT. Rich, savoury red best at 4–5 yrs. Recently gd Reserve CABERNET SAUVIGNON.

Pamid The light, soft, everyday red of the SE and NW.

Pavlikeni r Specializes in MERLOT and CABERNET SAUVIGNON.

Peruschtitza r Winery nr PLOVDIV. Reds only, esp MAVRUD, CABERNET SAUVIGNON, RUBIN.

Pleven N cellar for PAMID, GAMZA, CABERNET SAUVIGNON. Also a wine research station.

Plovdiv City in S; source of gd CABERNET SAUVIGNON and MAVRUD. Most winemaking at ASSENOVGRAD and PERUSCHTITZA. University's Food Technology Dept where many Bulgarian oenologists study.

Pomorie w (r) ★★ Black Sea winery in E. Esp CHARDONNAY and MUSKAT.

Preslav w ★★ Well-known cellar in Black Sea region. Best: CHARDONNAY Premium Oak 03. Also gd brandy.

HUNGARY/BULGARIA

Riesling Rhine Ries is grown, but most is Italiansky Riesling (Welschriesling) used for medium and dry wines.

Rkatziteli Russian variety, one of the most widely grown grapes in the world. Known as Rikat in Bulgaria. Widely used in white blends in NE.

Rubin Bulgarian cross (Nebbiolo x Syrah); often used in blends.

Sakar SE wine area for MERLOT, some of Bulgaria's best.

Sauvignon Blanc Grown in E and N, esp at SHUMEN and TARGOVISHTE.

Shumen w r ★★ Black Sea region and winery (owned by DOMAINE BOYAR), esp whites and New World-style reds. Barrique CHARDONNAY (**01**) and MERLOT (**00**).

Slaviantsi w (r) ★★ Esp MUSCAT, CHARDONNAY, MISKET, and Ugni Blanc. Best: Ashton Estate CHARDONNAY (**01**).

Sliven, Vini r (w) ★★ Big producer in the town of Sliven, owned by DOMAINE BOYAR. Esp for MERLOT, Pinot N (blended COUNTRY WINE), MISKET, and CHARDONNAY. Promising barrique-aged CABERNET SAUVIGNON. Best: Tweeda 02. Also see BLUERIGDE and KORTEN.

Stambolovo Satellite cellar of HASKOVO. MERLOT specialist.

Stara Zagora r Thracian Plain winery. Esp Reserve CABERNET SAUVIGNON and MERLOT.

Sungurlare Satellite of SLAVIANTSI. MISKET with delicate fragrance. Also CHARDONNAY.

Svishtov r ★★ N winery on DANUBE. Reds only, esp finely balanced CABERNET SAUVIGNON. Also gd rosé CABERNET SAUVIGNON (**01**).

Targovishte w ★★ Winery in E. Quality CHARDONNAY (inc barrel-fermented), Sauv Bl.

Traminer Increasingly grown in NE. Fine whites with hints of spice.

Slovenia

Slovenia joined the EU in May 2004. The traditional, conservative wine industry is wary of change but quality producers should now benefit from access to a bigger market. It is worth exploring the different styles of Slovenian wine now, when many are still great value by international standards. Slovenia is divided into three wine regions, subdivided into districts. The better ones are listed below. Wines are generally bottled by grape variety, although many producers are pushing their signature blends. Vintages do not vary greatly, yet among the most recent, 1997 and 2000 are considered exceptional. There are great hopes for 2003.

Barbara International ★→★★★ Sparklers of all types and price. NV Barbara and Miha are gd value, while No.1 Vintage is often Slovenia's best sparkling wine.

Batič ★★ Increasingly organic v'yd from VIPAVA. Top wine: CHARDONNAY; others v.gd.

Bjana ★★ Top GORIŠKA BRDA sparkling producer. Intense, full-bodied wines. Very popular in classier Ljubljana restaurants.

Cabernet Sauvignon Grown in PROMORSKI region, best in KOPER. Almost everybody in GORIŠKA BRDA and VIPAVA grows it. Decent quality.

Chardonnay Grown everywhere and generally gd. Also often unoaked, esp in PODRAVSKI.

Cviček Traditional pink blend of POSAVSKI. Low alcohol, high acid. Decent quality from co-op Krško, premium by Frelih (Cviček od fare).

Čurin ★★ Legendary pioneer of private wine growing from early 1970s onwards. Varietal whites and PREDIKATS of very high standards.

Gorice Name for hills with v'yds, used with different geographical names to denote districts in PODRAVSKI region.

Goriška Brda Slovenian part of Collio. Many v.gd producers, among them Blažič, Četrtič, Erzetič, Jakončič, Kabaj, Klinec, MOVIA, SIMČIČ, ŠČUREK, Stekar, etc. Slovenia's largest co-op of the same name produces several brands: Bagueri ★★★ (esp CHARDONNAY and MERLOT), Quercus ★★ (REBULA and Tokaji).

Haloze ★→★★★ Winery in Ptuj with a collection of vintages from 1917. Recent vintages less notable, but the 80s were fantastic (and still great value): look in particular for RENSKI RIZLING and TRAMINEC.

Izbor Auslese (see p.144).

Jagodni izbor Beerenauslese (see p.144).

Joannes ★★ Fine winery nr Maribor. Crisp, well-defined whites.

Klinec ★★★ V.gd GORIŠKA BRDA producer. Very fine red blend Quela and white Bela Quela.

Kogl ★★★★ Hilltop winery near Ormož tracing its history to 1542. Replanted in 1984. Whites are among Slovenia's best, either varietal (since 01 named Solo) or Duo, Trio, and Quartet blends. Reds since 00 (MODRI PINOT 02, Slovenia's purest Syrah). New red and white oaked blends Magna Domenica in 02. Exceptional PREDIKATS.

Kristančič Dušan ★★ Top producer from GORIŠKA BRDA, though recently less spectacular. Top CHARDONNAY and SIVI PINOT.

Koper PRIMORSKI coastal district, known for REFOŠK. SANTOMAS and VINAKOPER excel.

Kras PRIMORSKI district. Several gd TERAN producers. Inc Cŏtar, Lisjak Boris, RENČEL.

Kupljen Jože ★★→★★★ Quality dry wine pioneer near Ormož. Pinot N labelled Modri Burgundec; in better yrs as POZNA TRGATEV.

Laški Rizling Welschriesling. Slovenia's most planted variety, but now in decline.

Ledeno vino Icewine. Only in exceptional yrs and can be sublime.

Ljutomer Traditionally top wine district with neighbouring Ormož. Co-op called Ljutomerčan will definitely see better times, as its v'yds are among Slovenia's best.

Malvazija Underrated variety in KOPER. Slightly bitter yet generous flavour, which goes very well with seafood. M by VINAKOPER is incredible value. Also v.gd from Pucer, Rojac.

Merlot Planted widely in PRIMORSKI (except KRAS). Fairly gd, seldom outstanding.

Mlečnik ★★★ Disciple of Italy's Joško Gravner from VIPAVA. The closest anyone in Slovenia comes to organics. Best known for very long-lived CHARDONNAY, recently also for REBULA and Tokaji.

Modra frankinja Austria's Blaufränkisch. Fruity reds mostly in POSAVSKI, best as Metliška črnina by the Metlika co-op in the Bela krajina district.

Modri pinot Pinot Noir. Recently planted in all regions, with mixed results.

Movia ★★★★ Best-known Slovenian winery. Releases only mature vintages of its top wines: Veliko Rdeče (r) after 6 yrs and Belo (w) after 4. Different varieties in one v'yd for white blend Turno. Varietals: look for REBULA and possibly Slovenia's finest MODRI PINOT. Second wine: Villa Marija.

Ormož ★→★★★ Top wine district with Ljutomer. Co-op named Jeruzalem Ormož. Premium brand Holermuos (02), and gd Muscat sparkler.

Podravski Traditionally most respected Slovenian region in the NE. Recent comeback with aromatic whites and increasingly fine reds, mostly MODRI PINOT.

Posavski Conservative wine region in the SE, best known for CVIČEK.

Pozna trgatev Late harvest.

Predikat Wines made of botrytis-affected grapes with high sugar content. Term is taken from the German tradition and is used mostly in the PODRAVSKI region as POZNA TRGATEV, IZBOR, JAGODNI IZBOR, SUHI JAGODNI IZBOR, LEDENO VINO.

Primorski Region in the SW from the Adriatic to GORIŠKA BRDA. The most forward-looking Slovenian wine region for both reds and whites.

Radgonske gorice ★→★★★ District nr Austrian border, and co-op home to Radgonska Penina, Slovenia's best known sparkler. Vintage Zlata (golden) is drier and fuller, also ages well, NV Srebrna (silver) often off-dry. Also very popular sweet TRAMINEC and blend Janževec.

Rebula Traditional white variety of GORIŠKA BRDA. Can be exceptional.

Refošk Italy's Refosco. Dark and acidic red, a local favourite. Oaked and unoaked versions. Top by SANTOMAS.

Renčel ★★★★ Outstanding producer of TERAN (tiny quantities); also v.gd whites.

Renski Rizling Ries. PODRAVSKI only. Best: JOANNES, ORMOŽ, KOGL, Skaza Anton.

Santomas ★★★ High-quality mature REFOŠK and international-style CABERNET SAUVIGNON. Premium brands are Antonius and Grande Cuvée.

Simčič Edi ★★★ Highly reputed GORIŠKA BRDA producer. In particular look for CHARDONNAY, REBULA, SIVI PINOT. All reserve bottlings are very refined and harmonious. Very popular red blend, Duet.

Simčič Marjan ★★★ GORIŠKA BRDA producer of very high standards (CHARDONNAY, SIVI PINOT). REBULA-based blend Teodor is outstanding. A particular gem is Sauv Bl.

Sivi Pinot Italy's Pinot Grigio. Not particularly fine but top names can be v.gd.

Sčurek ★★→★★★ Very reliable GORIŠKA BRDA producer (CHARDONNAY, REBULA, Tokaji, Sauv Bl, Cab Fr). Very particular red and white blends Stara brajda and classy white Dugo.

Steyer ★★ Top name from RADGONSKE GORICE. Best known for TRAMINEC, recently also v.gd CHARDONNAY, RENSKI RIZLING, SIVI PINOT.

Suhi jagodni izbor Trockenbeerenauslese (see p.144). Extremely rare, notable examples by VINAG.

Šturm ★★★ Long-established, yet lone star of the Bela Krajina district in POSAVSKI. Red and white PREDIKATS, also gd varietal wines.

Teran 100% REFOŠK from KRAS. Alongside CVIČEK most popular Slovenian wine.

Traminec Gewurz, only in PODRAVSKI. Generally sweet – also as PREDIKAT.

Valdhuber ★★★ Dry wine pioneers in PODRAVSKI. Top wine is (dry!) TRAMINEC.

Vinag One of largest co-ops in Slovenia, with HQ and immense cellars in Maribor. Decent varietals and many older vintage PREDIKATS.

Vinakoper ★★★ Large company with own v'yds in KOPER. Many v.gd varietals: MALVAZIJA, CABERNET SAUVIGNON, REFOŠK. Premium brands: Capo d'Istria (varietals), Capris (blends). Sw Muscat and v.gd vin doux naturel-style Muscat Tartini.

Vinakras ★→★★★ Co-op producing decent-quality TERAN in large quantities. Matured TERAN is branded Teranton and is very different from its younger cousin.

Vipava ★★→★★★ District in PRIMORSKI region. Many fine producers: BATIČ, Lisjak Radivoj, MLEČNIK, Sutor, Tilia. Co-op of same name with premium brand Lanthieri ★★ (formerly Vipava 1894). Traditional blend Vrtovčan and more recent one with intriguing name Kindermacher. Several decent varietals.

Croatia

Communism and civil war have not helped the wine industry of Croatia. The economic situation is improving, but still tough, and foreign investment is not widespread. Wine areas are divided in two major regions: Kontinentalna (inland) and Primorska (coastal). There are many native varieties, especially in Dalmatia. In 2002, it was confirmed that Zinfandel/Primitivo originated from a native Dalmatian grape known locally as Crljenak. Most wine is consumed by Croats themselves.

Agrolaguna ★→★★ Co-op at Poreč, ISTRIA. Gd w and r, esp Cab Sauv.

Babić Dark, long-lived, native red from Primošten (DALMATIA). Can be excellent. Best by VINOPLOD. Unique v'yd site.

Badel ★→★★★ Big négociant and co-op. Wines and wineries from all over. Best are IVAN DOLAC, GRAŠEVINA Daruvar, Pošip Smokvica.

Chardonnay Grown in KONTINENTALNA HRVATSKA and ISTRIA. Usually gd.

Dalmacija-vino ★ Co-op at Split: range of DALMATIAN wines. V.gd Faros.

Dalmacija Dalmatia. The coast of Croatia, Zadar to Dubrovnik, inc islands. Home of many native varieties. Traditionally high in alcohol. V.gd reds; whites are old-fashioned but improving.

Dingač V'yd designation on PELJEŠAC'S steep southern slopes. Made from partially dried PLAVAC MALI, producing a full-bodied jammy red, but emerging as a robust, dry red that supports oak and bottle ageing. Highly esteemed and expensive. Look for Bura, Kiridžija, Matuško, Miličić, Skaramuča.

Enjingi, Ivan ★★★ Producer of excellent white from Požega. Sivi Pinot N, Graševina, Gewurz, botrytised wines. Interesting Zweigelt.

Graševina Local name for Welschriesling. Best from SLAVONIA. Look for Adžić, ENJINGI, KRAUTHAKER, Vinarija Daruvar, Djakovačka vina, KUTJEVO.

Grk Rare native w of Korčula. Oldest Croatian native. Try: Cebalo Branimir.

Grgić, Miljenko ★★★ Californian winemaker (see Grgich Hills, p.226) returns to his Croatian roots. Cellar on PELJEŠAC peninsula. Makes PLAVAC and POŠIP.

Hvar Island in mid-Dalmatia. Some excellent reds from PLAVAC MALI grapes from steep southern slopes. Interesting whites and reds from plateau. Look for ZLATAN PLAVAC, IVAN DOLAC, Faros, Zadruga Svirče.

Istria N Adriatic peninsula. Gd MALVAZIJA, CHARDONNAY, and Muscat. Look for Coronica, Degrassi, KOZLOVIĆ, MATOŠEVIĆ, and Ravalico. Also gd Merlot, Cab Sauv, and TERAN.

Istravino (Ivex) ★ Co-op based in Rijeka. Known for its sparkler.

Ivan Dolac V'yd area on S slopes of HVAR. V.gd dry red from PLAVAC MALI.

Kontinentalna Hrvatska Inland Croatia (N). Mostly for whites (GRAŠEVINA, Ries, CHARDONNAY). But gd reds (Pinot N, Merlot) emerging.

Kozlović ★★★ Advanced white producer from ISTRIA. Esp MALVAZIJA. Also reds.

Krauthaker, Vlado ★★★ V.gd whites from Kutjevo, esp CHARDONNAY and GRAŠEVINA. Reds are ★★.

Kutjevo Name shared by a town in SLAVONIJA and the ★★→★★★ co-op based there. V.gd Gewurz, GRAŠEVINA, and botrytis.

Malvazija Malvasia. Planted in ISTRIA. A pleiad of private producers made a shift from old-fashioned oxidized MALVAZIJA to some v.gd crisp wines.

Matošević, Ivica ★★★ Small producer from ISTRIA. Look for CHARDONNAY.

Miloš, Frano ★★ Producer from PELJEŠAC. Cult brand Stagnum (PLAVAC MALI).

Pelješac Beautiful peninsula and quality wine region in S DALMATIA. Some v.gd PLAVAC MALI, but mostly overrated. See GRGIĆ, MILOŠ, POSTUP, DINGAČ.

Plančić ★★ Producer of gd red and white on HVAR. Rare red Darnekuša.

Plavac Mali The best DALMATIAN red grape: wine of body, strength, and ageability. See DINGAČ, GRGIĆ, IVAN DOLAC, MILOŠ, POSTUP, ZLATAN OTOK. Promising at island of Brač (Murvica).

Polu... Polu-slatko is semi-sweet, polu-suho is semi-dry.

Postup V'yd designation just NW of DINGAČ. Medium- to full-bodied red.

Pošip Best DALMATIAN white, mostly on island of Korčula.

Prošek Almost port-like dessert wine from ISTRIA and DALMATIA: 15% abv.

Primorska Entire coastal Croatia, inc ISTRIA and DALMATIA.

Slavonija Sub-region in N Croatia for white. Try: ENJINGI, KRAUTHAKER, KUTJEVO.

Stolno vino Table wine. Some v.gd wines are designated as this.

Teran Stout, highly acidic, dark red of ISTRIA made from Refosco grape.

Vinoplod ★ Co-op from Sibenik in N DALMATIA. BABIĆ ★★★.

Vrhunsko vino New origin-based designation for top-quality wines.

Vugava Rare w of Vis (mid-DALMATIA). Linked to Viognier. Look for Lipanović.

Zdjelarević ★★ White wine producer from SLAVONIJA, esp CHARDONNAY.

Zlatan otok ★★★ HVAR-based winery producing top-quality red from PLAVAC MALI branded Zlatan Plavac. Gd white and rosé. Also v.gd PROŠEK.

Žlahtina Native white from island of Krk. Look for Katunar, Toljanić.

Bosnia and Herzegovina

Blatina Ancient MOSTAR red grape and wine from pebbled W bank of Neretva.

Kameno Vino White wine of unique irrigated desert v'yd in Neretva Valley.

Mostar Means "old bridge". Was Herzegovina's Islamic-looking wine centre, but cellars destroyed during the civil war. Ljubuski and Citluk are rebuilding. Potentially admirable ZILAVKA white and BLATINA red.

Samotok Light, red (rosé/*ruzica*) wine from run-off juice (and no pressing).

Zilavka White grape of MOSTAR. Potentially dry and pungent. Memorably fruity with a faint flavour of apricots.

Serbia

Serbia has its own Prokupac grape. Used alone it makes a light, fruity red; it is also often blended with Pinot Noir or Gamay. Some Cabernet Sauvignon and Merlot is also grown in the southeast.

Montenegro

13 July State-run co-op; high-tech Italian kit, nr Podgorica. VRANAC: high quality.

Crmnica Lakeside/coastal v'yds esp for Kadarka grape (see Macedonia).

Duklja Late-harvested, semi-sweet version of VRANAC.

Krstac Montenegro's top white grape and wine; esp from CRMNICA.

Merlot Since 1980: gd, wood-aged results.

Vranac Local vigorous and abundant red grape and wine. Value.

Macedonia

Recommended wineries: Povardarie-Negotine, Bovin-Negotino for Cab Sauv, Merlot, Pinot N, and VRANEC. Lozar-Veles for Sauv Bl, Chard, and Zilavka.

Belan White Grenache. Makes neutral blended wine.

Kadarka Major red grape of Hungary; here closer to its origins around L Ohrid.

Kratosija Locally favoured red grape; sound wines with gd potential.

Plovdina Native (S) grape for mild red, white; esp blended with tastier PROKUPAC.

Prokupac Serbian and Macedonian top red grape. Makes dark rosé (*ruzica*) and full red of character, esp at Zupa. PLOVDINA often added for smoothness.

Rkatsiteli Russian (white) grape often used in blends.

Temjanika Grape for spicy, semi-sweet whites.

Teran Transferred from Istria, but Macedonia's version is less stylish.

Tikves Much-favoured hilly v'yd region (20,000 acres). Esp for pleasant, dark-red KRATOSIJA; fresh, dry Smederevka – locally mixed with soda.

Traminac The Traminer. Also grown in Vojvodina and Slovenia.

Vardar Valley Brings the benefits of the Aegean Sea to inland v'yds.

Vranec Local name for Vranac of Montenegro (qv); indifferent quality.

Vrvno Vino Controlled origin designation for quality wines.

The Czech Republic & Slovakia

The Czech (Moravia and Bohemia) and Slovak republics had barely any tradition of exporting, but good wines have emerged since 1989. Foreign investment and advice bodes well for the future. The Czech Republic joined the EU in 2004. Outstanding vintages: 1997, 1999, 2000.

Moravia

Favourite wines in Prague for variety and value. Vineyards are situated along River Danube tributaries near the Austrian border and similar grapes are grown: Grüner Veltliner, Müller-Thurgau, Sauvignon Blanc, Traminer, St-Laurent, Pinot Noir, Pinot Blanc, Blauer Portugieser, Frankovka (Lemberger), Riesling,

Welschriesling. Look for: Mikros and Tanzberg from Mikulov (good white); Znovín in Znojmo (modern, internationally recognized); Vinné Sklepy Valtice (historic château; savoury white, aromatic red). Also: Vinselekt (Rakvice), Baloun (Velké Pavlovice), Moravíno and Reisten (Valtice), Viniblat (Blatnice), Sonberk (Pouzdřany), Springer (Bořetice), Špalkovi (Nový Šaldorf). Moravia also has sparkling: Sekt Domaine Petrák (Kobylí) and Znovín DeLuxe (Znojmo).

Bohemia

Winemaking since 9th century. Same latitude and similar wines to East Germany. Best made in the Elbe Valley (north of Prague) most notably at Melník (Riesling, Ruländer, Traminer, and interesting Pinot Noir). Vineyard renewal, esp round Prague, with small boutique wineries also emerging. Top wineries: **Karlštejn** (experimental research centre), **Litoměřice, Lobkowicz-Mělník** (oak-aged reds, barrel-fermented Chardonnay), **Lobkowicz-Roudnice** (Sylvaner, Pinot Noir), **Znoseky** (Riesling, Pinot Blanc, Muscat). Sparkling wine is mostly tank-fermented using grapes from Austria. Bohemia Sekt production in Starý Plzenec (Henkell-Söhnlein) and Soare is growing, thanks to foreign investment.

Slovakia

Vineyards now declining. Hungarian and international varieties, with best wines from Malo-Karpatská region (in foothills of Little Carpathians) and east Slovakia neighbouring Hungary's Tokaj. Other key districts: Malá Trna, Nové Mesto, Skalice, Bratislava, Pezinok, Modra. Leading producers: Château Belá, Malík, Masaryk, Matyšák, Movino, Mrva & Stanko, J J Ostrožovič, and Pavelka. For sparkling wine: Hubert, JE, and Pálffy Sekt.

Romania

Romania has a long winemaking tradition, but potential for quality was wasted during decades of supplying the USSR with cheap, sweet wine. Quantity is still the goal but modern equipment, foreign expertize, and a growing focus on vineyard management are seeing a fraction of Romania's vast potential realized. The full, soft reds from Dealul Mare (especially Pinot Noir) are gaining an international reputation. Further capital investment, as well as consistency, is still needed.

Alba Iulia Area in cool TIRNAVE region of TRANSYLVANIA, known for aromatic and off-dry white (RIESLING ITALIEN, FETEASCA, MUSKAT OTTONEL), bottle-fermented sparkling.

Aligoté Pleasantly fresh white from 24,000 acres.

Băbească Neagra Traditional red grape of the FOCSANI area, light body and colour. Literally "(black) grandmother grape".

Banat Plain on Serbia border. Workaday RIESLING ITALIEN, SAUVIGNON BLANC, MUSKAT OTTONEL, local Riesling de Banat; light red Cadarca, CABERNET SAUVIGNON, MERLOT.

Burgund Mare Name linked to Burgenland (Austria) where grape is called Blaufränkisch (Kékfrankos in Hungary).

Buzau Hills Gd reds (CABERNET SAUVIGNON, MERLOT, BURGUND MARE) from continuation of DEALUL MARE.

Cabernet Sauvignon Increasingly grown, esp at DEALUL MARE; dark, intense wines.

Carl Reh German-owned 2.5 million-litre winery in Oprisor.

Carpathian Winery DEALUL MARE. Excellent PINOT NOIR.

Chardonnay Some sweet styles, but modern dry and oak-aged styles, esp from MURFATLAR and TRANSYLVANIA increasingly available.

Cotnari N region with warm microclimate and gd botrytis. Famous (rare) light, sw wine from GRASA, FETEASCA ALBA, TĂMÎÎOASĂ, Francusa. Tastes like delicate TOKAJI.

Crisana W region inc historical Minis area (since 15th C): esp red Cadarca; crisp, white Mustoasa. Other areas: Silvania (esp FETEASCĂ), Diosig, Valea lui Mihai.

Dealul Mare "The big hill". Important, up-to-date, well-sited area in SE Carpathian foothills. Reds from FETEASCĂ NEAGRĂ, CABERNET SAUVIGNON, MERLOT, PINOT NOIR. Whites from TĂMÎÎOASĂ. French investment. Look for Dionis label.

Dobrogea Sunny, dry, Black Sea region. Inc MURFATLAR. Quality is gd.

DOC New classification for higher-quality wines replacing VS, VSO.

DOCG (Was VSOC) Top-range wines. CMD: late-harvest; CMI: late-harvest with noble rot; CIB is from selected nobly rotten grapes (like Beerenauslese).

Drăgăşani Region on River Olt S of Carpathian Mountains, since Roman times. Traditional and modern grapes (esp Sauv Bl). Gd MUSKAT OTTONEL.

Fetească White grape with spicy, faintly Muscat aroma. Two types: F Alba (same as Hungary's Leányka, ageworthy and with better potential esp when carefully handled; base for sp and sw COTNARI) and F Regala (gd for sp).

Fetească Neagră Red Fetească. Difficult to handle, but can give deep, full-bodied reds with gd character and ageing potential. "Black maiden grape".

Focsani Important MOLDAVIA region, inc Cotesti, Nicoresti, and Odobesti.

Grasă A form of the Hungarian Furmint grape grown in Romania and used in, among other wines, COTNARI. Prone to botrytis. Grasă means "fat".

Iaşi Region for fresh, acidic whites (FETEASCĂ ALBA, also RIESLING ITALIEN, ALIGOTE, and spumante-style MUSKAT OTTONEL): Bucium, Copu, Tomesti. Reds: MERLOT, CABERNET SAUVIGNON; top BABEASCA.

Jidvei Winery in the Carpathians (TÎRNAVE) among the country's northernmost V'yds. Gd whites: FETEASCĂ, Furmint, RIESLING ITALIEN, and SAUVIGNON BLANC.

Lechinta Transylvanian wine area. Local varieties noted for bouquet.

Merlot Romania's workhorse grape. Most widely planted red.

Murfatlar V'yds nr Black Sea, second-best botrytis conditions (see COTNARI): esp sweet CHARDONNAY and late-harvest CABERNET SAUVIGNON. Now also full, dry wines and sparkling.

Muscat Ottonel The E European Muscat, a speciality of Romania, esp in cool-climate TRANSYLVANIA and dry wines in MOLDAVIA.

Paulis Small estate cellar in town of same name. Oak-aged MERLOT a treasure.

Perla Semi-sw speciality of TÎRNAVE: RIESLING ITALIEN, FETEASCĂ, and MUSKAT OTTONEL.

Pinot Gris Widely grown in TRANSYLVANIA and MURFATLAR. Full, slightly aromatic wines, closer to Alsace than Italian Pinot Grigio in style.

Pinot Noir Grown in the S: can surprise with taste and character.

Prahova Winecellars Promising British venture (7 wineries in DEALUL MARE) using native and international grapes, inc Sangiovese. Try PINOT NOIR 99.

Premiat Reliable range of higher-quality wines for export.

Riesling Italien (Welschriesling) Widely planted. Most is poorly made, but there is potential.

Sauvignon Blanc Often Romania's tastiest white, esp blended with FETEASCĂ.

Tămîîoasă Românească Traditional white grape known as "frankincense" for its exotic scent and flavour. Pungent sweet wines often affected by botrytis.

Târnave (also Tîrnave) Transylvanian region (Romania's coolest), known for its PERLA and FETEASCĂ REGALA. Dry aromatic wines (esp PINOT GRIS, Gewurz) and sp.

Transylvania High central region. See ALBA IULIA, LECHINTA, TĂRNAVE.

Valea Călugărească "Valley of the Monks", part of DEALUL MARE. MERLOT, CABERNET SAUVIGNON, PINOT NOIR are admirable, as are RIESLING ITALIEN and PINOT GRIS.

Vin de Masa Most basic wine classification – for local drinking only.

Vinexport Established 1990, fast developing (80% of Romania's wine exports).

Vinterra Dutch/Romanian venture. MERLOT is gd.

Vrancea E region covering Panciu, Odobesti, Cotesti, and Nicoresti.

Greece

Since entry into the EC in 1981 Greece's antique wine industry has been transformed. Some is still fairly primitive, but a new system of appellations is in place, and recent years have seen an explosion of stylish and original wines. Well-made, authentically Greek wines are worth seeking out, and not only in Greece.

Aghiorghitiko Widely planted NEMEA red-wine grape. Very high potential.

Agioritikos Medium whites and rosés from Agios Oros (Mount Athos), Halkidiki's monastic peninsula. Brand name for TSANTALIS.

Alpha Estate ★★ Modern estate in cooler-climate Amindeo. First wine the barrel-aged 02 blend of Merlot, Syrah, and XINOMAVRO. New vibrant Sauv Bl (03).

Antonopoulos ★★→★★★ Highly reputed producer: MANTINIA, Adoli Ghis, unoaked, nutty Chard, Cab Sauv-Nea Dris (**97 98 00 01**). New concentrated aromatic Gris de Noir (03). To watch.

Arghyros ★★→★★★ Top SANTORINI producer with delicious (expensive) Vinsanto aged 20 yrs in cask. Current vintage: 85. Bone-dry white Ktima Arghyros 03.

Biblia Hora ★★→★★★ V'yds and villa-like winery near Kavala. Polished New World-style wines. Grapey Sauv Bl/Assyrtiko 03. Floral Syrah Rosé 03.

Boutari, J and Son ★→★★ Producers and merchants in NAOUSSA. Also v'yds and wineries in GOUMENISSA, MANTINIA, on SANTORINI and CRETE. New varietals: MOSCOFILERO 03 and AGHIORGHITIKO 01.

Calliga ★ KOURTAKIS-owned. Gd AGHIORGHITIKO sourced for Montenero and Rubis.

Cambas, Andrew ★ Brand owned by BOUTARI. V.gd value Chard and Cab Sauv.

Carras, Domaine ★★ Estate at Sithonia, Halkidiki, with its own AC (Côtes de Meliton). Old Vine Syrah 98. Under new management since 2000.

Cava Legal term for cask-aged still white and red wines. Eg Cava BOUTARI (NAOUSSA-NEMEA).

Cephalonia (Kephalonia) Ionian island: gd white ROBOLA and Muscat.

Creat-Olympias ★→★★ Emerging Cretan producer. V.gd value fruity white Xerolithia. Improving juicy red Mirabelo, cask-aged (r and w) Creta-Nobile 01.

Crete Improving quality. Led by Alexakis, Ekonomou, Lyrarakis.

Emery ★→★★ Historic RHODES producer, specializing in local varieties. Look for brands: Villare and GrandRose. Also gd quality, traditional-method sparkling.

Gaia ★★★ Top-quality NEMEA-based producer. Fruity Notios label. Leading AGHIORGHITIKO (03). Top wine Gaia Estate (**97 98 99 00 01**). Also unoaked and oaked Thalassitis from SANTORINI. Astonishing RETSINA Ritinitis Nobilis.

Gentilini ★★→★★★ Upmarket white ROBOLA from CEPHALONIA. New Syrah 01.

Gerovassiliou ★★★ Perfectionist miniature estate nr Salonika. Look for benchmark fruity blend Assyrtiko/Malagousia 03, smooth Syrah/Merlot blend 02, and top Viognier (03).

Goumenissa (AC) ★→★★ Oaked red from MACEDONIA. Esp BOUTARI, Ktima Tatsis.

Hatzimichalis, Domaine ★ Small estate and merchant in Atalanti. Huge range. Greek and French varieties. Top wine: red CAVA.

Katsaros ★★→★★★ Small organic winery of very high standards on Mount Olympus. Ktima has staying power. Cab Sauv/Merlot 01, supple Chard 03.

Kir-Yanni ★★ High-quality v'yds in Naoussa and at Amindeo. Vibrant white Samaropetra 02; gd Syrah 00; top Naoussa (XINOMAVRO single-v'yd) 00.

Kouros ★ Reliable, well-marketed white PATRAS and red NEMEA from KOURTAKIS.

Kourtakis, D ★★ Athenian merchant with mild RETSINA and gd dark NEMEA.

Ktima Estate, farm. Term not exclusive to wine.

Nico Lazaridis ★→★★ Family estate in Drama, NE of Salonika. Spectacular post-modernist winery. Rich Merlot 02. Top wine: Magiko Vouno w (03) r (00).

Lazaridis, Domaine Kostas ★→★★ Not to be confused with NICO LAZARIDIS. Quality Amethystos label. Top wine: unfiltered red CAVA 01.

Lemnos (AC) Aegean island: co-op dessert wines, deliciously fortified Muscat of Alexandria. New dry Muscats by Kyathos-Honas winery.

Macedonia Quality wine region in the N, for XINOMAVRO.

Malagousia Rediscovered perfumed white grape.

Mantinia (AC) High central PELOPONNESE region. Fresh, grapey MOSCOFILERO.

Matsa, Château ★★→★★★ Small Attica producer exploits native Greek varieties. Top wine: Savatiano Vieilles Vignes. Also stylish Laoutari, excellent MALAGOUSIA.

Mavrodaphne (AC) "Black laurel", and red grape. Cask-aged port/recioto-like, concentrated red; fortified to 15–22%. Speciality of PATRAS, N PELOPONNESE.

Mercouri ★★→★★★ PELOPONNESE family estate. Very fine Refosco, delicious RODITIS. New CAVA (01). Classy Refosco dal Penducolo rosso and dry MAVRODAPHNE blend.

Moscofilero Blanc de Gris Rose-scented high-quality, high-acid grape.

Naoussa (AC) r High-quality region for XINOMAVRO. One of two Greek regions where a "cru" notion may soon develop. Excellent vintages: 00 01.

Nemea (AC) r Region in E PELOPONNESE producing dark, spicy AGHIORGHITIKO wines. Often also the backbone of many (not always Greek) blends. High Nemea merits its own appellation. Koutsi front-runner for cru status.

Oenoforos ★★→★★★ Gd PELOPONNESE producer. Leading RODITIS white Asprolithi. Also elegant white Lagorthi, fresh Chard, subtle Cab Sauv, crisp Ries 03, and fine Syrah 01.

Papaïoannou ★★→★★★ Top NEMEA grower. Classy red (inc Pinot N); flavourful white. Top wine: Ktima Papaioannou Palea Klimata (old vines) 97 98 00.

Patras (AC) White wine (based on RODITIS) and wine town facing the Ionian Sea. Home of MAVRODAPHNE. Rio-Patras (AC) sweet Muscat.

Peloponnese Mountainous southern land mass of mainland Greece, with half of the country's v'yds, inc NEMEA, MANTINIA, and PATRAS.

Rapsani Interesting oaked red from Mt Ossa. Rasping until rescued by TSANTALI.

Retsina Attica speciality white with Aleppo pine resin added; oddly appropriate with certain Greek food. Domestic consumption now waning.

Rhodes Easternmost island. Home to creamy (dry) Athiri white grape. Top wines inc Caïr (co-op) Rodos 2400 and Emery's Villare. Also some sparkling.

Roditis White grape grown all over Greece. Many clones. Gd when yields are low.

Samos (AC) Island nr Turkey famed for sw, pale, golden Muscat. Esp (fortified) Anthemis 99, (sun-dried) Nectar. Rare old bottlings can be great.

Santorini Volcanic island N of CRETE: luscious, sweet Vinsanto (sun-dried grapes), mineral-laden, bone-dry white from fine Assyrtico grape. Oaked examples are gd. Top producers inc: ARGYROS, GAIA, SIGALAS.

Semeli, Château ★★ Estate nr Athens. Gd white and red, inc NEMEA.

Sigalas ★★→★★★ Top Santorini estate producing the leading oaked Santorini Oia Bareli (03). Stylish, golden-robed Vinsanto (01).

Skouras ★★ Innovative PELOPONNESE wines. Viognier (Cuvée Eclectic). Best wine: Megas Oenos red (00). Gd high NEMEA, Grande Cuvée (01).

Spiropoulos, Domaine ★★ Gd organic producer in MANTINIA. Improving oaky, red Porfyros (AGHIORGHITIKO, Cab Sauv, Merlot). Sparkling Odi Panos has potential.

Strofilia-Katogi ★ Predominantly Greek varieties, but also Chard, Cab Sauv, and floral Traminer.

Tsantalis ★→★★ Merchant/producer at Agios Pavlos. V'yds in NAOUSSA, Maronia, and RAPSANI. Full range of country and AC wines. New organic varietal Assyrtiko (03), Merlot (02), Cab Sauv (01).

Tselepos ★★→★★★ Top-quality MANTINIA producer and Greece's best Gewurz (03). Other wines: fresh, oaky Chard, solid NEMEA (01), v.gd Cab Sauv/

Merlot (00), stylish Merlot (00), single-v'yd Avlotopi Cab Sauv (01). Top wine: single-v'yd Kokinomylos Merlot (01).

Voyatzi Ktima ★★ Small estate nr Kozani. Fat white Malvasia Aromatica (03). Top red: Ktima Voyatzi (01) XINOMAVRO and Cab Sauv blend.

Xinomavro The tastiest of many indigenous Greek red grapes – though name means "acidic-black". Grown in the cooler N, it is the basis for NAOUSSA, GOUMENISSA, and Amindeo. High potential.

Zitsa Mountainous N. Epirius AC. Delicate Debina white, still or sparkling.

Cyprus

Cyprus's finest product is the historic sweet Commandaria – a watery version of which is often used as Communion wine in churches. For years wines were basic, but now upgrading has started. Vineyards are located in the foothills of the Troodos Mountains and until recently, only two local grapes were grown; now another twelve have emerged, alongside international varietals. Significantly, Cyprus has never had phylloxera. Today the majority of the island's wine is produced by four organizations: KEO, ETKO, SODAP, and Loel. Cyprus joined the EU in May 2004.

Commandaria Gd quality brown sweet wine traditionally produced in hills N of LIMASSOL. Region limited to 14 villages; principal village: Kalo Khorio. Made from sun-dried XYNISTERI and MAVRO grapes. Best (as old as 100 yrs) is superb. A limited quantity of vintage wine is exported.

ETKO Based in LIMASSOL. 16 different wines inc: Olympus, Cornaro Carignan, Cornaro Grenache, Semeli (all red) and Nefel (white). Best: Ino Cab Sauv.

KEO Large, go-ahead firm. Production moved from LIMASSOL to regional wineries. Range inc: Aphrodite (XYNISTERI), sp Bellapais, Rosella (fragrant pink), Heritage (rich oaked MARATHEFTICO), Othello (solid red), Domaine d'Ahera (velvety red). COMMANDARIA St John. Standard Dry White and Dry Red v.gd value.

Kokkineli Deep-coloured, semi-sweet rosé: the name is related to cochineal.

Limassol Southern wine port. Historically the home to all the large wineries.

Loel One of major producers. Reds: Orpho Negro, Hermes. Whites: varietal PALOMINO and Ries, also COMMANDARIA Alasia and brandies.

Maratheftico Vines of superior quality make concentrated red wine of tannin, colour, close to Cab Sauv; the future grape of Cyprus.

Mavro The black grape of Cyprus. Can produce quality if planted at high altitude; otherwise gives sound, acceptable wines.

Opthalmo Black grape (red/rosé): lighter, sharper than MAVRO.

Palomino Soft, dry white (LOEL, SODAP). Very drinkable ice-cold.

Pitsilia Region S of Mt Olympus. Some of best white and COMMANDARIA wines.

SODAP A co-op winery and one of the four largest producers. Wines inc: (w) Arsinoë (XYNISTERI), Artemis, Danae; (r) Afames, varietal Carignan, and Grenache. New range called Island Vines is modern, fresh, and inexpensive.

Xynisteri Native aromatic white grape of Cyprus, making delicate, fruity wines.

Malta

With accession to the EU in May 2004, producers are upgrading winemaking and labelling practices. Incentives have been instituted to boost locally grown wines. Other wines may be made from imported grapes. Meridiana's pioneering estate has Antinori support in making good Isis Chardonnay, Melqart Cabernet Sauvignon/Merlot, Nexus Merlot, an excellent Bel Syrah, and premium Celsius Cabernet Sauvignon Reserve. Marsovin and Delicata also feature.

GREECE/CYPRUS/MALTA

England & Wales

The UK wine industry is young (first commercial vintage 1954) and small, with 800 hectares and 300 growers producing 2.2 million bottles a year. Most wine is white – German crosses such as Bacchus, Reichensteiner, and Schönburger, and the French/US hybrid Seyval Blanc – although interesting reds from Rondo, Dornfelder, Regent, and Pinot Noir are also made. Some excellent bottle-fermented sparkling wines are now being made, the best using the classic Champagne varieties. Global warming seems to be helping this marginal region. Since 1994, the UK has had an official appellation system for still wines and the best are labelled as 'Quality Wine' or 'Regional Wine'; plain 'UK Table Wine' is best avoided. Beware 'British Wine' that is made from imported concentrate.

Bothy Abingdon Oxfordshire ★★ New owners now winning prizes. Renaissance 02 excellent. Range small, but improving. 03 should be gd.

Breaky Bottom East Sussex ★★ 99 01 Cult following. Makes very dry wines and improving range of sparkling wines. Seyval Blanc 01 and sparkling Cuvée Rémy Alexandre 99 worth trying. Wines improve with age.

Camel Valley Cornwall ★★★ 01 02 Gd quality, esp Cornwall Brut 99, Pinot N sparkling 01, Bacchus 02. Excellent facilities and very welcoming to visitors.

Denbies Surrey) ★★ 01 02 England's largest v'yd at 261 acres. Impressive winery: worth a visit. Surrey Gold 02, Rose Hill 02 gd. Sparkling improving.

New Wave Wines Ltd Kent ★★★ 00 01 02 Largest UK producer inc Curious Grape, Chapel Down, Tenterden, and Lamberhurst brands. Wide range of excellent wines. Pinot Bl 01, Rosé sparkling 01 both gold medal winners. Pinot N 00 best red.

Nyetimber W Sussex ★★★ 95 96 Best UK specialist sparkling-wine producer; uses classic Champagne varieties. Classic Cuvée 95 and Blanc de Blancs 96 both gold medal winners.

RidgeView E Sussex ★★★ 99 00 Specialist sparkling-wine producer using classic Champagne varieties and fast catching Nyetimber in quality stakes.

Sharpham Devon ★★★ 01 02 Produces consistently gd wines. Barrel Fermented and Dart Valley Reserve medal winners. Beenleigh made from (tunnel-grown) Cab Sauv and Merlot usually UK's best red.

Three Choirs Gloucestershire ★★ 99 00 01 02 UK's second-largest producer. Wines not always consistent, but Estate Reserve Bacchus, Phoenix, and Siegerrebe are v.gd. English Nouveau and sparkling worth trying.

Valley Berkshire ★★★ 97 98 99 00 01 02 UK's most successful producer with large range of serious quality wines. Oak-aged Fumé, Stanlake, and sparklers Heritage Rosé and Ascot worth trying. Makes for several other v'yds.

Other noteworthy producers
Barnsole All wines Quality and Regional status. Pilgrim's Harvest very good.
Davenport Good range of wines, including Limney sparkling. Organic from 2003.
Sandhurst Major supplier to New Wave. Red wines and Bacchus good.
Shawsgate Changed hands in 2003. Bacchus is a silver medal winner.
Tiltridge Small vineyard with good range, including Elgar and Seyval Oaked.
Warden Abbey Regular award winners. Try Bacchus and Warden Abbot.
Wickham Wines usually good. Especially Oaked Red and Special Release Fumé.

Asia, North Africa, & the Levant

Algeria As a combined result of Islam and the EU, once-massive v'yds continue to dwindle. Legislation in 2004 banning the import of alcohol casts more uncertainty. Red, white, and esp rosé of some quality and power come from coastal hills of Tlemcen, Mascara (gd red and white), Haut-Dahra (strong red, rosé), Zaccar, Tessala, Médéa, and Aïn-Bessem (Bouira esp gd). Sidi Brahim is a drinkable red brand. Cork also produced.

China China's enthusiasm for wine is unabated and national consumption increases each yr. Now the eleventh-largest producer of wine in the world, there are over 300 individual wineries across the N of the country. Wine regions are becoming more defined: the Bohai Bay area accounts for roughly 50% of production and is home to 2 premium areas: the Tianjin Coast and the Shandong Peninsular (best vintages: w 93 97 98 00 02; r 93 97 00 02). Viticulture is also expanding in the Shacheng District to the N of the Great Wall and in the Yellow River area in Anhui and Henan provinces. In addition, Chinese authorities recently introduced some internationally recognized standards, eg single vintage designations, place of origin. Around 80% of China's wine is produced by 3 companies: Changyu, Dynasty, and Great Wines. Best wines inc: single-v'yd Chard and Ries from Huadong; premium Cab Sauv, Merlot, Chenin Bl from Lou Lan Winery (Xinjiang); premium Cabs (Sauv and Fr) from Grace Winery (Shanxi). Others to watch: Kai Xuan Winery (Shandong); rice wine producer Maotai Winery (Hebei).

India Tiny industry based in 3 main areas: Maharashtra, Kamataka, and Punjab. Production is dominated by 3 companies. Chateau Indage (Maharashtra) is the largest and its range inc internationally known Omar Khayyám sparkling (Chard/Ugni Blanc) made with Piper Heidsieck's help. Grover Vineyards (Kamataka) also has an international consultant, Michel Rolland (see France). Sula (Maharashtra) has been operating since 1999 and produces 7 wines. One to watch: McDowell Winery (Bangalore).

Japan The wine industry is based in the Honshu prefecture of Yamanashi, W of Tokyo. Other significant regions: Nagano and Yamagata prefectures (N of Tokyo) and the N island of Hokkaido. Quality wine production is beset with climatic problems, esp heavy rainfall, though Hokkaido tends to escape the worst conditions and holds most promise for the future. Cultivation grew dramatically in the 1960s and 1970s, esp with hybrids, but one vinifera vine proved most popular: Koshu (discovered 1186), which produces light white wines. The past 20 yrs have seen an introduction of premium varieties and new viticultural techniques. Plantings of Chard, Cab Sauv, Cab Fr, Merlot – and recently Gewurz, Viognier, and Barbera – have created a new market for premium Japanese wines; quality can be high, but quantities are tiny. Labelling laws permit a small amount of genuine domestic wine to go a long way, so concentrates, must, and bulk wine are imported and used for fermenting or blending locally. Around 65% of production is accounted for by 5 giants: Mercian, Suntory, Sapporo (Polaire), Manns, and Kyowa Hakko Kogyo (Ste-Neige). The most interesting (and expensive) wines are Mann's Chard from Nagano, Mercian's Kikyogahara Merlot and Jyonohira Cab Sauv: real density and quality. Suntory also makes an interesting B'x blend and Sauternes-style wine. Smaller operations producing Koshu and/or European varieties inc: Ch Lumière, Marufuji, Grace, Asahi Yoshu, Kizan, Katsunuma Jozo, Alps, Takeda, Obuse Domaine Saga, Okuizumo, and Kobe Wines.

Morocco North Africa's best wine is produced from v'yds around Meknes and Fez (best known) and along the Atlantic coast (Rabat to Casablanca, light, fruity with a white "Gris" made from red grapes). V'yds have declined from 190,000 to 32,000 acres but big investment from French companies, such as William Pitters and Castel, is transforming the industry. Celliers de Meknes is the local leader but has now been joined by Cépages de Meknes, Cépages de Boulaouane, and SADAY in producing quality wines. Look for varietal reds, esp Syrah, and Sauv Bl. Also L'Excellence de Bonassia (aged Cab Sauv/Merlot blend), Domaine de Sahari, gd value Atlas Vineyards, El Baraka.

Tunisia Recent government initiatives plus an influx of foreign investment – Swiss (Ceptunis), Austrian (Dom Atlas), French (St Augustine), Italian (Dom Neferis) – and New World winemakers have seen a new wave of producers and labels emerge. Dom Hannon produces gd full-bodied reds, inc a premium Carignan (Tapsus), Shiraz, and Merlot. An AOC system endeavours to ensure quality for the strong domestic and growing export markets.

Turkey Most of Turkey's 1.5 million acres of v'yd produce table grapes; only 2% are for wine. Wines from Thrace, Anatolia, and the Aegean can be very drinkable. There are 60 commercial varieties; indigenous (eg w Narince, Emir; r Bogazkere, Oküzgözü) are used with Ries, Sem, Pinot N, Grenache, Carignan, and Gamay. Trakya (Thrace) white and Buzbag (E Anatolian) red are well-known standards of state producer Tekel (21 state wineries). Diren, Doluca, Kavaklidere, Taskobirlik are private firms; fair quality. Doluca's Kav from SE Anatolia is well made, as is Villa Doluca. Kavaklidere makes good Primeurs (white Cankaya, red Yakut) from local grapes. Buzbag is Turkey's most original and striking wine.

The Old Russian Empire

The 12 Commonwealth of Independent States (CIS) countries of the former USSR now produce a total of only 3% of the world's wine. Improvements since the 1991 revolution are slow but some producers are getting there.

Ukraine (inc Crimea) Second-largest wine-producer in the CIS. Crimea's first-class dessert and fortified wines were revealed in 1990 by the auction of old wines from the last Tsar's Massandra Collection, nr Yalta, where production continues. Classic brut sp from Novy Svet (founded 1890 by Prince Golitsyn, served at Tsar's coronation 1896). Wineries to watch: Inkermann, Magarach. Reds: potential (eg Massandra's Alushta). Whites: Aligoté; Artyomovskoe sp.

Georgia Possibly the oldest wine region of all: antique methods such as fermentation in clay vats (*kwevris*) still exist. Reluctant to modernize, but newer techniques used for exports (Mukuzani, Tsinandali). Kakheti (E) makes two-thirds of Georgia's wine, esp lively, savoury reds (Saperavi) and acceptable whites (Tibaani, Rkatsiteli, Gurjaani). Foreign investors: Pernod Ricard with GWS brand; US-owned Bagrationi has cheap, drinkable sp. As equipment, techniques, attitudes evolve (and if the new government reduces corruption), Georgia could be an export hit.

Moldova Most important in size and potential. Wine generates a third of Moldova's income. Wine regions: Bugeac (most important), Nistrean, Codrean, Northern. Grapes inc: Cab Sauv, Pinot N, Merlot, Saperavi, Ries, Chard, Pinot Gr, Aligoté, Rkatsiteli. Cab Sauv/Saperavi blends can be esp gd. Top wineries: Purkar, Cahul, Kazayak, Hincesti. Also gd: Cricova (its cellars are an impressive tourist attraction with some 120 km of tunnels). New World investment at Hincesti, and more recently by local company Vininvest, has brought modern winemaking practices. Moldova's most modern wines: Ryman's Hincesti Chard; Abastrele (w); Legenda (r). Most wineries are now privatized; progress has not been smooth, but is worth following. Appellations are now in force.

Russia Moscow and St Petersburg are waking up to wine, esp in restaurants. But things are not helped by imported cheap, bulk wine. Krasnodar on Northern Black Sea Coast produces 60% of Russia's wine (2003 a record harvest). Top producer: Fanagoria (Temruk) Merlot and Cab Sauv. Also look for fair Cab Sauv, Merlot, Saperavi, Ries, Rkatsiteli from Anapa and Temruk; sw Kagor and red Pontiskoe from Vityazevo Winery (Anapa). Abrau Durso brut (also Prince Golitsyn): classic sp since 1896. New small winery Karakezidi (Anapa) exports red Stretto with Caucasus oak.

The Levant

ASIA, NORTH AFRICA & THE LEVANT

Israel Continuing to show consistent improvement in quality. Many wines are quite exciting, particularly from cool climate, high altitude regions like Upper Galilee, Golan Heights, and Judean Hills.

Amphorae r w ★ Powerful, full-bodied Cab Sauv (01); gd value Rhyton (r).

Barkan r w Consistent Res Cab Sauv. Also owns Segal label (Chard).

Carmel r w sp No 1 producer and exporter founded in 1882 by a Rothschild. Undergoing dramatic revitalization. Gd wines at all levels. Excellent single-v'yd Ramat Arad Cab Sauv (00') and Zarit Cab Sauv.

Castel Judean Hills r w ★★★ Small family estate in mountains W of Jerusalem producing characterful, complex Cab Sauv/Merlot (97 98 99' 00') and an outstanding Chard (00 01). Great value second label Petit Castel.

Chateau Golan Golan Heights r w Shows promise. Deep, well-balanced Merlot.

Dalton Upper Galilee r w Sauv Bl is by some way the best in Israel.

Flam r ★★ Fine, concentrated Merlot (01). Young Classico is gd value.

Galil Mountain Upper Galilee r w Up-and-coming B'dx blend Yiron.

Harel Ayalon Valley r w Rich and buttery Clos de Gat Chard.

Margalit r ★→★★ Oaky, seductive Cab Fr and intense Special Res Cab Sauv (01).

Recanati r w Produces Cab Sauv, Chard, and Merlot; Res Chard is best.

Saslove r w Res Cab Sauv has ageing potential; easy-drinking Aviv full of flavour.

Tabor Galilee r w Gd whites, esp Sauv Bl.

Tishbi r w sp Family grower. Crisp, classic method sparkling wine.

Tzora r w Kibbutz winery. Stone Ridge best value. Ilan Misty Hills B'x blend.

Yarden Golan Heights r w sp ★★→★★★ Pioneering winery. New Pinot N, Syrah, and Chard from organic v'yds. Multi-layered Cab Sauv (97 99 00') and rare red Katzrin (90' 96 00') are highest quality.

Yatir Yatir Forest r ★★ Classy Cab Sauv/Merlot (01) with velvety finish.

Lebanon Small wine industry based in Beka'a Valley, E of Beirut. New wineries are challenging the old order. Some quality reds, made with French influence.

Chateau Musar r (w) ★★★ Splendid and unique Cab Sauv with Cinsault (91 94 97 99) improves with age. Old vintages were remarkable, will current ones go so long? Lighter red Hochar Père et Fils (Cinsault/Cab Sauv). Also oaky white from indigenous grape, Obaideh.

Clos St Thomas r (w) Small winery. Ch St Thomas is soft, fruity, rounded red.

Kefraya r w ★★ Fragrant Ch Kefraya Comte de M (97 98 99) blend of Cab Sauv/Mourvèdre/Syrah. Also fresh rosé and luscious dessert, Lacrima d'Oro.

Kouroum r w Petit Noir is a light but interesting blend of Cinsault and Grenache.

Ksara r w ★→★★ Established 1857 by Jesuits. Cuvée Millenaire Cab Sauv/Petit Verdot blend, herbs and spice (00); Reserve du Couvent red, light and fruity. Clean Chard. New World style.

Massaya r w ★ French-Lebanese collaboration. Gd Cab Sauv/Mourvèdre blend.

Wardy r w Promising winery. Gd Chard and Sauv Bl. Red label Ch les Cèdres.

North America

WASHINGTON
OREGON
CALIFORNIA
EASTERN STATES

California

Sierra Foothills
NEVADA
Anderson Valley
Clear Lake
Clear Lake
Sacramento
Lake Tahoe
Alexander Valley
Russian River Valley
Napa Valley
Sacramento
El Dorado
Sonoma Valley
Carneros
Amador
Lodi
Calaveras
San Francisco
Livermore Valley
Santa Clara Valley
Santa Cruz Mountains
Salinas
San Joaquin
Carmel Valley
Arroyo Seco
Fresno
San Lucas
Pacific Ocean
Paso Robles
CALIFORNIA
Edna Valley
Santa Maria Valley
SANTA BARBARA
Santa Ynez Valley
More heavily shaded areas are the wine growing regions
Santa Barbara
Los Angeles
Temecula

Thousands of acres of new vines were planted in California during the 1990s. The economy was booming and free-spending consumers were eager to try the latest trendy cult wine. However, as the economy stalled, the free spenders of the 1990s began pinching pennies. As new vineyards in the Central Coast and the Central Valley came into production, a wine surplus built up, peaking in early 2003.

At that point, savvy producers began buying up bulk wine and selling it at rock-bottom prices through discount wine and food chains. Consumers who had thought nothing of spending $40 or $50 on the latest must-drink Merlot were now buying cases of Charles Shaw, aka "Two-Buck Chuck", so called because it sold for $1.99 a bottle.

By 2004, the California wine glut was more or less over, but consumers were still bargain hunting. Vintners rushed brands to the market priced under $5 and for the first time in a decade, per capita wine consumption actually began to grow. One welcome trend was the sighting of bottlings of Pinot Noir selling for around $10. Most of these wines were made from young vine grapes grown in Santa Barbara and San Luis Obispo counties. These juicy juveniles were an agreeable alternative to more muscular Australian Shiraz.

Perhaps as a result of shopping for bargains, people are discovering that there is more to California than Napa and Sonoma. Regions once overlooked, such as Zinfandel from the Lodi AVA (American Viticultural Area) an hour's drive east of San Francisco Bay, are attracting a new kind of wine consumer, buying on flavour and price rather than trends inspired by high scores, although there are still plenty of trend chasers around. Lake County, north of Napa, is coming along as an outstanding source of mid-priced Cabernet Sauvignon, while the Central Coast is still recognized as prime Chardonnay country. Overall, California remains a good source of fruit-driven reds and oaky-toasty Chardonnay, although some producers are backing away from the over-oaked monsters of the 90s. Napa and Sonoma remain very much in the chase when it comes to world-class Cabernet, Merlot, and Pinot Noir.

The principal Californian vineyard areas

Central Coast

An umbrella region stretching from San Francisco Bay south almost to Los Angeles, including the following AVAs:

Arroyo Grande San Luis Obispo County. A coolish growing region with Pacific influence. Gd Pinot N, Viognier. Zin at warmer elevations away from the coast.

Arroyo Seco Monterey County. Excellent Ries both dry and late harvest, citrus Chard and Cab Sauv from warmer canyons in the Santa Lucia mountains.

Carmel Valley Monterey County. Resort area with small production of dense, concentrated Cab Sauv and Merlot on hillside v'yds and some gd Sauv Bl.

Edna Valley San Luis Obispo County. Cool winds whip through a gap in the coastal range off Morro Bay. Excellent minerally Chard.

Monterey County Wide range of soils and micro-climates gives great variety to Monterey Wines. See individual listings for best regions.

Paso Robles San Luis Obispo County. Large, productive area E of coastal range. Known for Zin. Promising plantings of Syrah and Rhône varieties.

Santa Lucia Highlands Monterey County. Newish AVA above the Salinas Valley, E of the Santa Lucia mountains. Excellent Syrah and Ries; promising Pinot N.

Santa Maria Valley Santa Barbara County. Outstanding Pinot N, gd Chard, Viognier, and Syrah.

Santa Ynez Valley Santa Barbara County. Like Santa Maria but with warmer inland regions. Rhône grapes, Pinot N, Chard in cool areas. Sauv Bl a gd bet.

North Coast

Encompasses Lake, Mendocino, Napa, Sonoma counties, all north of San Francisco. Ranges from very cool climate near San Francisco Bay to very warm interior regions. Soils vary from volcanic to sandy loam. Includes the following regions:

Alexander Valley Sonoma County. Fairly warm AVA bordering Russian River. Excellent Cab Sauv in a ripe, juicy style. Gd Sauv Bl near the river.

Anderson Valley Mendocino County. Cool valley opening to the Pacific along the Navarro River. Outstanding sparkling wine, v.gd Gewurz and Pinot N. Hillside v'yds above the fog produce terrific old-vine Zin.

Carneros Napa and Sonoma Counties. Very cool region bordering San Francisco Bay. Top site for Pinot N and Chard. V.gd sparkling wine.

Dry Creek Valley Sonoma County. Relatively warm region offering distinctive Zin and Sauv Bl, with Cab Sauv a winner on rocky hillsides.

Lake County Warm to hot mountainous region centred around Clear Lake, the largest natural lake in California. Good Zin, Sauv Bl nr the lake, and lush, fruity Cab Sauv on cooler hillsides.

Mendocino County Large region N of Sonoma County with a wide range of growing regions from hot interior valleys to the coast.

Mount Veeder Napa County. High altitude AVA (v'yds planted up to 2,400 feet) best known for concentrated Cab Sauv and rich Chard.

Napa Valley Best-known wine district, N of San Francisco Bay. With its relatively small size and large number of wineries, Napa's v'yd land has become most expensive outside Europe. Great diversity of soil, climate, and topography in such a small area can produce a wide range of wines, esp the red B'x varieties and Pinot N in cooler areas. Wines have achieved international acclaim and are priced to match.

Oakville Napa County. Located in mid-Valley, the heart of Cab Sauv County.

Redwood Valley Mendocino County. Warm interior region. Gd basic Cab Sauv, excellent Zin, everyday Chard and Sauv Bl. Also gd plantings of Syrah.

Russian River Valley Sonoma County. Very cool area, often fog-bound until noon. Maybe the best Pinot N in California; Zin and Cab Sauv on hillside v'yds. Green Valley is a small super-cool AVA within the Russian River AVA.

Rutherford, Rutherford Bench Napa County. Rivals Oakville as Cab Sauv heartland. Long-lived reds from hillside vineyards, lush and dazzling Merlots and other B'x reds closer to Napa River.

Sonoma Coast Sonoma County. Trendy new region borders the Pacific. Very cool climate, very poor soils. New plantings of Pinot N show great promise.

Sonoma Mountain Sonoma County. Part of the Sonoma Valley AVA. High-elevation v'yds ideal for powerful Cab Sauv.

Sonoma Valley This is Jack London's Valley of the Moon. Varied growing regions produce everything from Cab Sauv to Zin. Separated from Napa Valley by the Mayacamas mountains.

Spring Mountain Napa County. Part of the Mayacamas range. V.gd Cab Sauv with pockets of delicious Sauv Bl at lower elevations, plus good Ries.

Stags Leap Napa County. E of Napa River, distinctive Cab Sauv and Merlot.

Bay Area

Urban sprawl has wiped out most of the vineyards that once surrounded San Francisco Bay.

Contra Costa County Historic growing district E of the Bay now succumbing to homes and shopping malls. Remaining old vines make fine Zins, red Rhônes.

Livermore E and S of San Francisco Bay, valley soils are gravel and stone. Surprisingly gd Cab Sauv; outstanding Sauv Bl and Sem.

Marin County Old (1820s) growing region being revived with new plantings of Pinot N and Chard near the coast.

Santa Clara Valley Broad valley S of the Bay, once major wine district, now called Silicon Valley. Remnant areas like Hecker Pass can surprise today.

Santa Cruz County Pierce's Disease has wiped out many historic v'yds here, although a few remain, yielding gd Cab Sauv and some Pinot N.

Central Valley

About 60% of California's v'yds are in this huge region that runs N to S for several hundred miles, bounded by the Coastal mountains and the Sierra Nevada. Now shedding its image as a producer of low-quality jug wines, as Valley growers realize they must go for quality to keep up in the global market.

Clarksburg Sacramento, Solano, and Yola counties. Just outside the state capital Sacramento, running along the river. Viognier, Syrah, and Sauv Bl are strong.

Lodi San Joaquin and Sacramento counties. Ten years ago, this AVA began a push for quality. It has paid off in a major way. Strengths are Zin, Sauv Bl, Muscat (sweet), and fruit-forward Chard grown nr the Sacramento River.

Sacramento Valley Northern half of California's agricultural centrepiece makes affordable Rhône varietals from the Dunnigan Hills AVA.

San Joaquin Valley Hot heart of the Central Valley. Source of most jug, bag-in-a-box, and fortified dessert wine from the state. Many growers now process their own grapes, making fruity, easy-drinking varietals at a bargain price.

Sierra Foothills

Grapes were first planted here during Gold Rush days. Best regions include:

Amador County Warm region famous for old Zin v'yds producing jammy, intense wines with a signature metallic backnote, as well as crisp Sauv Bl. Top Rhône reds and Italian varietals are beginning to emerge.

Fiddletown Amador County. High elevation v'yds produce a more elegant, understated Zin than much of Amador.

Shenandoah Valley Amador County. Source of powerful Zins and increasingly well-regarded Syrah.

Recent vintages

Because of its size and wide range of microclimates, it is virtually impossible to produce a one-size-fits-all vintage report for California. California's climate is not as consistent as its "land of sunshine" reputation suggests, and although grapes ripen regularly, they are often subject to spring frosts, sometimes a wet harvest-time and (too often) drought. Wines from the Central Valley tend to be most consistent. The Central Coast region, with its much cooler maritime mesoclimate has a different pattern of vintage quality from the North Coast or Sierra Foothills. Rain is much less of a factor and arrives later, rarely before mid-December. Grapes ripen more slowly and are harvested 3–6 weeks later than inland regions such as Napa. That said, the following vintage assessment relies most heavily on evaluation of Cabernets and Zinfandels from North Coast regions. For Chardonnay, the best vintages are: 97 99 01 03.

2003 A difficult year all around. Spring was wet and cool, with a series of heat spikes during the summer and some harvest rains. The size of the crop is down and quality is spotty on the North Coast, better on the Central Coast. Careful grape selection could lead to an above-average vintage.

2002 Average winter rainfall and slightly delayed budbreak with some frost damage. Heavy rain in May, cool growing season but no rain until Nov. Average-sized crop with every indication of superior quality.

2001 Little winter rain, sporadic heat in March, severe April frost, hottest May on record, and no rain until Oct. Excellent quality.

2000 Scares included a threatened storm from the south in early Sept, but damage was minimal. Biggest harvest on record. OK quality.

1999 Very cold spring and summer created late harvest, but absence of fall rain left crop unscathed. High natural acids and a hot Oct made for intensely flavoured and coloured wines. Outstanding quality.

1998 Erratic harvest stumbled into Nov. Wines are adequate to dismal.

1997 Huge crop, but strongly flavoured and showing very well at present. Favourite vintage on record for growers; well appreciated by consumers.

1996 Tiny crop, with lots of structure, lacks aromatic charm. Age is helping.

1995 Tiny crop, great vitality but slow to unfold. Good Zinfandels, great Cabernets. Best vintage for cellaring since 90.

1994 Mild growing season; dry, late harvest. Superb Zinfandels, but a bit long in the tooth now; Cabernets are supple, wonderful for drinking right now.

1993 Modest, plain-faced, serviceable year in the North Coast, but spectacular in Sierra Foothills with concentrated Zinfandels, refreshing acidity. Drink up.

1992 Oddly inconsistent. Some empty. Some flavourful and vital.

1991 Very late harvest; very large crop: 30–50% bigger than normal and twice the size of tiny 90. Wines are lean, racy, most European-style in years.

1990 Picture-perfect California vintage and small crop: wonderful development and strong collectors' value. Cabernets magnificent.

California wineries

Acacia Carneros ★★★ (Chard) **95 99** 00 **01** 02 (Pinot N) **95 99 00** 01 02 CARNEROS pioneer in Chard and Pinot N, moving towards darker Pinot N fruit with emphasis on single-v'yd wines.

Alban Edna Valley ★★→★★★ Pioneer planter of Rhône varieties, and (with Calera) benchmark for Viognier, in California. Small quantities of excellent Grenache, Roussanne, Marsanne.

Alexander Valley Vineyards Sonoma ★★ Juicy approachable Cab Sauv. SinZin is a delight. Skip the whites.

Altamura Vineyards Napa ★★★ (Cab) 01 Elegant and luscious Cab Sauv. Sangiovese is one of the state's best.

Amador Foothills Winery ★★ Amador. Ripe and delicious Zin and bright Sauv Bl, often blended with Sem.

Andrew Murray Sta Barbara ★★★ **99 00 01** Small winery with a goal of producing only Rhône varietals. V'yds planted on slopes thus reducing yields. Gd Syrah, great Roussanne and Viognier.

Araujo Napa ★★★★ 95 97 **99** 01' Powerful, sleek Cab Sauv made from Eisele v'yd, was bottled for many years by JOSEPH PHELPS as a single-v'yd wine.

Armida Sonoma ★★ RUSSIAN RIVER VALLEY winery with solid Merlot, gd Pinot N, and a zippy Zin made from DRY CREEK VALLEY grapes.

Arrowood Sonoma ★★→★★★★ (Chard) **99 01** 02 (Cab) **85 87 90 91 94** 95 96 97 **99** 01 Now in the Mondavi stable but quality is still at the top. Supple Cab Sauv and a luscious Viognier.

Artesa Napa Carneros ★★ Former Codorniu NAPA has turned away from bubbly to still-wine production, showing steady improvement.

Arthur Earl Sta Barbara ★★ Small producer of Rhône and southern French varietals. V.gd Mourvédre.

Atlas Peak Napa ★★ Allied-Domecq-owned winery previously focused on Sangiovese and Sangiovese/Cab Sauv Consenso, now much more on Cab Sauv, from Antinori-owned v'yds in E hills.

Au Bon Climat Sta Barbara ★★★ (Chard) **96 99 01** 02 (Pinot N) **95** 99 01' Jim

Clendenen listens to his private drummer: ultra-toasty Chard, flavourful Pinot N, light-hearted Pinot Bl. Vita Nova label for B'x varieties, Podere dellos Olivos for Italianates. See also QUPÉ.

Babcock Vineyards Sta Barbara ★★★ Very cool location in W SANTA YNEZ VALLEY. Gd for Pinot N and Chard; "Eleven Oaks" Sauv Bl is one of California's better examples. New entry into Syrah is impressive.

Beaulieu Vineyard Napa ★★★★ (Cab) **58 65 73 78 85 90** 91 **95 97** 99' 01' Under André Tchelistcheff in the 1940s and 1950s, Beaulieu set the style for NAPA Cab Sauv. Now owned by Diageo Chateau and Estate Wines. Not the jewel it once was, but still quite gd, esp the Georges de Latour Private Reserve Cab Sauv. CARNEROS Chard also worth a look.

Bell Cellars Napa ★★★ Founded by South African Tony Bell, Cab Sauv has been consistently gd. Winery sold in 2002.

Benessere Napa ★★ Sangiovese is worth a try but Zin comes in tops.

Benziger Family Winery Sonoma ★★→★★★ Family began converting vines to biodynamic in the mid-1990s. Steady improvement in wines, esp Chard and a soft, delicious Merlot.

Beringer-Blass Napa (Chard) **99 00** 01 (Cab) 87 90 91 **94** 95 **97** 99' 01' A NAPA classic producing wines from Central and N Coast. Single-v'yd Cab Sauv Reserves are over the top, but marvellous. Velvety but powerful Howell Mountain Merlot. Look for Founder's Estate bargain line. Also owns CHATEAU ST-JEAN, CHATEAU SOUVERAIN, MERIDIAN, STAGS' LEAP WINERY, and TAZ. Part of the Mildara-Blass empire.

Pierce's Disease
This bacterial vine infection became a high-profile issue in 2000 when an energetic flying insect called the Glassy-winged Sharpshooter arrived, borne on ornamental plants. Some districts were particularly hard hit, but despite hysterical press announcements even small growers in those areas soldiered on, fighting back with insect sprays and careful v'yard management. Spread of the problem has since proven to be slow, especially with strict quarantine measures and careful checking of nursery shipments. New research at UC Davis and elsewhere continues, but at this point no solutions have been offered.

Bernardus Carmel Valley ★★★ Strong Meritage wines from densely planted high-altitude v'yd above the valley floor. Brilliant Sauv Bl.

Biale Napa ★★ Small Zin specialist using mostly NAPA fruit.

Boeger El Dorado ★★ First El Dorado winery after prohibition. Mostly estate wines. Attractive Merlot, Barbera, Zin, and a Meritage combining Cab Sauv, Cab Fr, and Petit Verdot. Wines more understated than many in SIERRA FOOTHILLS.

Bogle Vineyards Yolo ★ Major growers in the SACRAMENTO Delta, Bogle family makes attractive line of budget varietals and an excellent old-vine Zin.

Bonny Doon Sta Cruz Mtns ★★→★★★ Original Rhône Ranger Randall Grahm has expanded operations in S France and Italy. All wines now in screwcap. Best is Cigare Volant, his homage to Châteauneuf-du-Pape. Big House Red and Big House White are gd bargain quaffs. Brilliant Pacific Rim Riesling.

Bouchaine Vineyards Napa Carneros ★★→★★★ (Chard) 99 00 **01** (Pinot N) **00 01** Winery has had some ups and downs since its founding in 1980. Now on an up-swing with classic, sleek Chard and juicy Pinot N.

Bruce, David Sta Cruz Mtns ★★★ (Pinot) 95 97 **99** 00 (01) Long-time source of eccentric bruiser (now moderated) Chard. Pinot N (from own and SONOMA vines) is forte.

CALIFORNIA

Buehler Napa ★★ Inconsistent Cab Sauv has marred Buehler record. Gd t⚊ outstanding estate Zin and a Chard made from RUSSIAN RIVER grapes are worth looking for.

Buena Vista Napa Carneros ★★ (Chard) **99** 00 01 Has swapped a taste-the grapes style for one more heavily marked by winemaking: esp Chard.

Burgess Cellars Napa ★★ (Cab) **90** 95 97 99' (01) Emphasis on dark, weighty estate Cab Sauv made from hillside vines. Powerful Zin worth seeking out.

Bynum, Davis Sonoma ★★★ (Pinot N) 95 **99** 00 (01) Marvellous single-v'yd Pinot N from RUSSIAN RIVER VALLEY. Lean, minerally Chard is a treat.

Byron Vineyards Sta Barbara ★★★ (Chard) 96 **99** 00 **01'** (Pinot) 95 97 **99** 00 01 Founder Ken Brown is now winemaker under MONDAVI ownership. Brown is a Pinot specialist who has done outstanding work with that varietal, but don't neglect the Chard, which is splendid.

Cain Cellars Napa ★★★ (Cain Five) 85 87 90 94 **95** 97 99' (01) Stylish, supple Cain Five anchored in estate plantings of Cab Sauv and four B'x cousins on SPRING MOUNTAIN; Cain Cuvée (declassified Cain Five) can rival the big brother. Monterey Sauvignon Musqué from Ventana Vineyards also fine.

Cafaro Napa ★★★ Winemaker label for sturdy-to-solid Cab and Merlot.

Cakebread Napa ★★★ (Chard) 97 **99 00** 01 (Cab) **85 87 90 94** 95 97 99' **00 01'** Powerful Cab Sauv with well-integrated if sometimes obvious oak. One of the best Sauv Bls in the state. Chard sometimes too oaky.

Calera San Benito ★★★★ (Chard) 99 00 01 (Pinot) 95 96 97 **99 00** 01 Yale and Oxford graduate Josh Jensen went in search of the holy grail of Pinot N and found it in the dry, hot hills of San Benito, E of MONTEREY. Jensen makes three Pinot Ns named after v'yd blocks: Reed, Seleck, and Jensen. He also makes an intense, flowery Viognier.

Cambria Sta Barbara ★★ Part of KENDALL-JACKSON'S Artisans and Estates group. Chard routinely toasty, Pinot N more enticing.

Campion Winery Napa. Pinot N guru Larry Brooks (ex-SAINTSBURY) is making only Pinot N and only single-v'yd Pinot N. Very promising beginning.

Carmenet Sonoma ★★★→★★★★ (Cab blend) 87 90 **94** 95 99' 00 01 Ripe and concentrated mountain Cab Sauv. CHALONE-owned.

Carneros Creek Napa Carneros ★★★ (Pinot N) 95 96 97 **99** 00 01 One of the first to explore the potential of Pinot N in Carneros. Makes several different bottlings each year, inc a richer, deeper Signature Reserve. Pleasing Chard as well.

Caymus Napa ★★★→★★★★ (Cab) 87 **90 91 94** 95 96 **97 98 99'** 00 01 (02) The Caymus Special Selection Cab Sauv is consistently one of the best in California. It's a rich, intense wine, slow to mature. Also a quite gd regular bottling, balanced and a little lighter.

Cedar Mountain Winery Livermore. Top marks for powerful, long-lived Cab Sauv from estate v'yds. A range of delicious port-style dessert wines as well.

Ceja Vineyards Napa. Established in 1999 and already making a mark with balanced, focused Cab Sauv and delicious Chard.

Chalk Hill Sonoma ★★ Large estate that has been up and down over the years. Usually reliable Cab Sauv made for ageing and a pleasing Chard.

Chalone Monterey ★★★→★★★★ (Chard) 95 **99 00** 01 02 (Pinot) **99** 00 01 (02) Unique mountain estate on E edge of MONTEREY. Marvellous flinty Chard and rich, intense Pinot N. Also makes a gd Chenin Bl (unusual in California) and a tasty Pinot Bl. Chalone is publicly traded and also owns ACACIA, CARMENET, DYNAMITE VINEYARD, EDNA VALLEY VINEYARD, Echelon Gavilan, Jade Mountain, Moon Mountain, Provenance, and Canoe Ridge (Washington). (Lafite) Rothschilds are major shareholders.

Chappellet Napa ★★★ (Cab) 87 90 **94** 95 97 **99** 00 01' Beautiful amphitheatrical hill v'yd, with California's first modern winery building (1968). Ageworthy Cab Sauv has new grace-notes, esp Signature label. Chenin Bl: a NAPA classic now touched with oak (too bad). Pleasing, understated Chard; easy Sangiovese; gd Cab Fr, Merlot, Tocai Friulano, sweet Moelleux.

Château Montelena Napa ★★★ (Chard) 96 97 **99** 00 01' (Cab) 87 **90** 95 97 99' 00 01 (02)' Understated ageworthy Chard, and Calistoga Estate Cab Sauv modified after 1990 vintage but still tannic and able to age long term.

Château Potelle Napa ★★★ Ex-pat French couple produce quietly impressive Chard (Reserve edition toastier) and vigorous Cab Sauv from MOUNT VEEDER estate. Outrageously gd Zin from estate-owned v'yds in Paso Robles.

Château St Jean Sonoma ★★→★★★ Pioneered single-v'yd Chard in California under Richard Arrowood in the 1970s, still outstanding; gd Sauv Bl. Red wine now a priority. Cinq Cepage, made from the five B'x varieties, one of the best in the state. Owned by BERINGER-BLASS.

Château Souverain Sonoma ★★→★★★ (Cab) 87 **90** 95 97 99' Top-of-the-line CARNEROS Chard, ALEXANDER VALLEY Cab Sauv, and DRY CREEK VALLEY Zin, all with lots of oak – maybe too much in some cases. Owned by BERINGER-BLASS.

Chimney Rock Napa ★★★→★★★★ (Cab) **90 94 95** 97 **99** 00 01 Elegant STAGS LEAP District Cab Sauv on a steep upward curve under winemaker Doug Fletcher.

Christopher Creek Sonoma ★★★ **97 99** 00 01 Deep, intense Petite Sirah and pretty southern Rhône-style Syrah from estate grapes.

Cline Cellars Carneros ★★ Originally Contra Costa (important v'yds still there), now in SONOMA/CARNEROS and still dedicated mostly to husky Rhône Rangers (blends and varietals), eg Côtes d'Oakley, Mourvèdre.

Claiborne & Churchill San Luis Obispo. Owners have a love affair with Alsace. Outstanding dry Gewurz and just off-dry Ries.

Clos du Bois Sonoma ★★★ (Chard) **99** 00 01 (Cab) 87 **90 94** 95' 97 **99**' 00 01 Allied-Domecq operation producing 1.6 million cases annually. Winemaker Margaret Davenport. Single-v'yd Cab Sauv Briarcrest, Chard Calcaire v.gd.

Clos LaChance Santa Cruz. Newcomer showing gd Zin, bright Chard.

Clos Pegase Napa ★★→★★★ (Chard) 00 01 02 (Cab) **90** 91 **94** 95 **97 99**' 00 01 Post-modernist winery-cum-museum (or vice versa) makes a spare, wiry NAPA CARNEROS Chard and a sleek Cab Sauv from N NAPA grapes.

Clos du Val Napa ★★★→★★★★ (Cab) **85** 87 **90 94** 95 97 **99**' 00 01 (02) Bernard Portet and his staff create consistently elegant Cab Sauvs that are among the best ageing candidates in the state. Chard is a delight and a Sem/Sauv Bl blend called Ariadne is one of state's best whites.

Cohn, B R Sonoma ★★★ Mostly estate Cab Sauvs; hard-edged and awkward in the 1990s, now showing gd juicy base and ageing potential.

Constellation Huge NY firm, formerly known as Canandaigua. Owns and operates wineries in California, NY, Washington State, Chile, Australia, and New Zealand. Produces 75 million cases of wine annually. 2003 sales hit $US3.2 billion. Now number two to GALLO in California and long a power in bottom tier of market (Richard's Wild Irish Rose, Taylor California Cellars, etc). Lately reaching up, first tentatively with DUNNEWOOD, more aggressively with SIMI, now owns FRANCISCAN Estates, ESTANCIA, MOUNT VEEDER, and RAVENSWOOD.

Corison Napa ★★★ (Cab) **90 94** 95 97 99' 00 01 (02) Long-time winemaker at CHAPPELLET making supple, flavoursome Cab Sauv promising to age well.

Cosentino Napa ★★ (Meritage) 97 99' Irrepressible winemaker-owner always full tilt. Results sometimes odd, sometimes brilliant, never dull. Crystal Valley is a widely distributed down-market brand.

H Coturri & Sons Sonoma. Organic, no-sulphite wines. Sometimes gd Zin with an attitude. Has a cult following.

Cuvaison Napa ★★★ (Chard) 99 00 **01** 02 (Merlot) 95 **97** 98 99 00 Estate CARNEROS Chard steadily fine. Estate Cab Sauv is catching up to the Merlot.

Dalla Valle Napa ★★★★ 95 97 00 01 Hillside estate is that rare thing: a cult classic with a track record. Maya is a Cab Sauv-based brawny beauty, and Pietre Rosso, from Sangiovese, is a brilliant showcase for that varietal.

Dehlinger Sonoma ★★★★ (Pinot) **95** 97 **99** 00 01 02 Tom D focuses on ever plummier estate RUSSIAN RIVER VALLEY Pinot N, and rightly. Also Chard, Syrah.

Delicato Vineyards San Joaquin ★→★★ One-time CENTRAL VALLEY jug produce has moved up scale with purchase of MONTEREY v'yds and several new bottlings from LODI.

DeLoach Vineyards Sonoma ★★★ Fruit-rich Chard ever the mainstay of reliable RUSSIAN RIVER VALLEY winery. Gargantuan single-v'yd Zins (Papera, Pelletti) finding an audience. Now owned by Boisset.

Diamond Creek Napa ★★★★ (Cab S) 85 87 **90 94 95** 97 99' 00 01 (02) Austere, stunningly high-priced cult Cabs from hilly v'yd nr Calistoga go by names of v'yd blocks: Gravelly Meadow, Volcanic Hill, Red Block Terrace. Wines age beautifully.

Emerging California wine regions

One of the most exciting developments in California over the past few years has been the high quality of wine coming from regions once considered good only for jug wines or bulk wine production, and the high-quality wines coming from newer growing areas. In the Central Valley, growers and vintners from Lodi and the Fresno-Modesto area have upgraded the quality of the wines by paying more attention to vineyards and investing in new winery equipment. This has resulted in a new wave of fruit-forward wines for everyday consumption at reasonable prices. On the Central Coast, new vineyards planted to Chardonnay and Pinot Noir are producing fruit from young vines that can challenge lower-priced imports from Australia and Chile for both quality and price.

Domaine Carneros Carneros ★★★ Showy US outpost of Taittinger in CARNEROS echoes austere style of its parent in Champagne but with a delicious dollop of California fruit. Vintage Blanc de Blancs the luxury cuvée. Still Pinot N and Chard also impressive.

Domaine Chandon Napa ★★→★★★ Maturing v'yds, maturing style, broadening range taking Moët & Chandon's California arm to new heights. Look esp for NV Reserve, étoile Rosé. Still wines a recent and welcome addition.

Domaine de la Terre Rouge Amador County ★★★ Former retailer is a Rhône specialist with a strong stable of growers. Syrah, Mourvèdre, and Grenache are superb. Also makes a red blend and a white blend from Rhône varietals.

Dominus Napa ★★★★ 85 87 90 **96 97** 98 99 00 01 (02) Christian Moueix of Pomerol produces red B'x blend which is slow to open but ages beautifully; packed with power inside a silk glove. Big jump in quality in the mid-1990s.

Dry Creek Vineyard Sonoma ★★ Sauv (Fumé) Bl set standard for California for decades. Still impressive. Pleasing Chenin Bl made from Delta fruit. Gd Zin, with one bottling from Heritage vines.

Duckhorn Vineyards Napa ★★★★ (Merlot) **90 95 97 99'** 00 01 Known for dark, tannic, almost plummy-ripe, single-v'yd Merlots (esp Three Palms) and Cab Sauv-based blend Howell Mountain. New facility in ANDERSON VALLEY for Golden Eye Pinot N for an impressive start.

Dunn Vineyards Napa ★★★★ (Cab) **87 90 94 95** 97 99' 00 01 Owner-winemaker Randy Dunn makes dark, iconic Cab Sauv from Howell Mountain which ages magnificently, slightly milder from valley floor. 4,000 cult cases.

utton-Goldfield Western Sonoma Co ★★★ Adroitly crafted Burgundian varieties from several top sites. Owners have the v'yd smarts to reach four stars soon.

uxoup Sonoma. Quirky producer of excellent Rhône-style Syrah (don't look for Shiraz here) and inky, old-vine Charbono. A promising Sangiovese under the Gennaio label. Limited production but worth seeking out.

berle Winery San Luis Obispo ★★★ Burly ex-footballer makes Cab Sauv and Zin in his own image: plenty of knock-your-socks-off power but behind that gd balance and a supple concentration.

chelon Napa. Gd value CHALONE label featuring gd CENTRAL COAST Chard.

dna Valley Vineyard San Luis Obispo ★★ (Chard) 00 01 02 Decidedly toasty Chard from a joint venture of local grower and CHALONE. Pinot N best drunk soon after vintage. Recent Syrah impressive.

stancia FRANCISCAN label for gd value MONTEREY Chard, Sauv, Pinot N, Cab Sauv.

tude Napa ★★★→★★★★ (Pinot N) 99 00 01 02 Winemaking consultant Tony Soter makes an incredibly rich and silky Pinot N from CARNEROS fruit and a v.gd Cab Sauv. Now owned by BERINGER-BLASS, Soter will continue to run the winemaking side.

ar Niente Napa ★★★ (Chard) 99 00 01 02 (Cab) 94 95 97 99' 00 01 Opulence is the goal in both Cab Sauv and Chard from luxury NAPA estate.

arrell, Gary Sonoma ★★★★ After yrs of sharing working space at Davis Bynum while making legendary RUSSIAN RIVER Pinot N, Farrell now has his own winery. Also look for Zin and Chard.

errari-Carano Sonoma ★★★ Over-the-top winery draws on estate v'yds in NAPA and SONOMA to make range of above-average wines, Merlot being the best.

ess Parker Sta Barbara County ★★★ Owned by actor who played Daniel Boone on TV; son Eli is winemaker. Gd Chard in tropical-fruit style, impressive Pinot N and Syrah, surprisingly gd Ries. New release is Parker Station Pinot N, a luscious little wine made from young vines.

Fetzer Mendocino ★★★ A leader in the organic/sustainable viticulture movement, Fetzer has produced consistently gd value wines from least expensive range (Sundial, Valley Oaks) to brilliant Reserve wines. Fetzer also owns Bonterra Vineyards (all organic grapes) where Roussanne and Marsanne are the stars.

Ficklin Vineyards Madera. Lush and delicious port-style dessert wines made from the classic Portuguese varieties.

Fiddlehead ★★★→★★★★ Winemaker Kathy Joseph commutes between home/ office nr SACRAMENTO and two wineries where she contracts space: one in ARROYO GRANDE AVA, San Luis Obispo; the other in Oregon. She has recently formed a partnership for limited-production Santa Maria Pinot N with BERINGER-BLASS. Her Pinot N is always the top and she also makes several bottlings of Sauv Bl, inc a minerally B'x-style.

Firestone Sta Barbara ★★ (Chard) 00 01 02 (Merlot) 95 97 99 00 Fine Chard overshadows but does not outshine delicious Ries.

Fisher Sonoma ★★ Hill-top SONOMA grapes for often-fine Chard; NAPA grapes dominate steady Cab Sauv.

Flora Springs Wine Co Napa ★★★ (Chard) 00 01 02 (Trilogy) 90 95 97 99 00 01 (02) Best here are the two Meritage wines, a red blend called Trilogy and a white called Soliloquy. Juicy Merlot also worth a look. Chard can be too oaky.

Folie à Deux Napa ★★ Valley doyen Richard Peterson and winemaker Scott Harvey have extraordinary Amador Zins and underrated NAPA Cab Sauvs.

Foppiano Sonoma ★★ Long-established wine family turns out fine reds (esp Petite Sirah, Zin) under family name. Responsible for leading the mini-renaissance in "petty sir". Whites labelled Fox Mountain.

Forman Napa ★★★ The winemaker who brought STERLING its first fame in the

1970s now makes excellent Cab Sauv and Chard on his own.

Foxen Sta Barbara ★★★ (Pinot) 97 **99** 00 01 Tiny winery nestled between SAN YNEZ and SANTA MARIA VALLEYS. Always bold, frequently brilliant Pinot overshadows stylish Chard.

Franciscan Vineyard Napa ★★★ (Cab) 85 87 90 **94** 95 97 **99'** 00 01 Soli producer of reliable Cab Sauv and Merlot, complex yet supple Charc Austere Cab Sauv and red Meritage from MOUNT VEEDER label. Now owne by CONSTELLATION. Will quality stay high?

Franzia San Joaquin ★ Penny-saver wines under Franzia, Corbett Canyon NAPA Ridge. Charles Shaw ("Two-Buck Chuck") and other labels. Larges bag-in-box producer.

Freemark Abbey Napa ★★★ (Chard) **00 01** 02 (Cab Sauv) **85** 87 90 91 92 94 9 97 **99'** 00 01 (02) Underrated but consistent producer of inexhaustible stylish Cab Sauvs (esp single-v'yd Sycamore and Bosché) of great depth V.gd, deliciously true-to-variety Chard.

Frog's Leap Napa ★★→★★★ (Cab S) 87 90 **94** 95 97 **99'** 00 01 (02) Small winery charming as its name (and T-shirts), and mostly organic to boot. Lean minerally Sauv Bl, toasty Chard, spicy Zin. Supple and delicious Merlot tops the briary Cab Sauv.

Gallo, E & J San Joaquin ★★ Having mastered the world of commodity wines this huge family firm (the world's second biggest after CONSTELLATION) is now unleashing a blizzard of regional varietals under such names as Anapauma, Marcellina, Turning Leaf, Zabaco, and more, some from Modesto, some via GALLO SONOMA, all mostly forgettable.

Gallo Sonoma Sonoma ★★→★★★ (Chard) **00 01** 02 (Cab) **94 95 97 99** 00 01 DRY CREEK VALLEY winery bottles several wines from SONOMA, NORTH COAST. Cab Sauv can be v.gd, esp the single-v'yd ones. SONOMA line impressive for gd value wines.

Geyser Peak Sonoma ★★→★★★ Owned by distiller Jim Beam, but Aussie winemaker Daryl Groom (who came when Penfolds was a partner) has a free hand. Big, toasty Chard, powerful, sleek Cab Sauv, and juicy Shiraz top the charts. A blend of B'x reds compares with best from anywhere.

Gloria Ferrer Sonoma Carneros ★★★ Built by Spain's Freixenet for sparkling wine, now producing spicy Chard and bright, silky Pinot N, all from CARNEROS fruit. Bubbly quality remains high, esp the Royal Cuvée, inspired by a visit from King Juan Carlos of Spain.

Goosecross Cellars Napa. Spicy and lively Chard. Reds are coming along.

Grace Family Vineyard Napa. Stunning Cab Sauv. Shaped for long ageing. One of the few cult wines that is actually worth the price.

Green & Red Vineyards Napa. Zingy and long-lasting Zin from Pope Valley.

Greenwood Ridge Mendocino ★★★ Winery well above the floor of ANDERSON VALLEY made its name as producer of off-dry, perfumy Ries. Reds, esp Cab Sauv and Pinot N, now moving up fast.

Grgich Hills Cellars Napa ★★★★ (Chard) 95 96 97 98 **99' 00** 01 02 Vastly underrated NAPA producer of supple Chard (which can age) balanced and elegant Cab Sauv, and a jammy, ripe Zin made from SONOMA grapes. Sauv Bl in a minerally style is gd.

Groth Vineyards Napa ★★★★ (Cab) 85 87 90 **94** 95 97 **99'** 00 01 (02) OAKVILLE estate Cab Sauv has been consistently 4-star quality for a decade, with big, wrap-around flavours made for ageing. Chard also excellent.

Guenoc Vineyards Lake County ★★ Ambitious winery/v'yd in its own AVA just N of NAPA county line. Property once owned by English actress and close personal friend of Edward VII, Lillie Langtry. Supple, long-lived reds from B'x varietals, bright and lean Sauv Bl, serious Petite Sirah.

undlach-Bundschu Sonoma ★★ (Cab) 95 97 99' 00 01 Pioneer name solidly revived by fifth generation. Versatile Rhinefarm estate v'yd signals memorably individual Gewurz, Merlot, Zin. Much-improved Cab Sauv recently from hillside vines.

agafen Napa ★★ One of the first serious kosher producers. Esp Chard and crisp Sauv Bl.

ahn Estate Monterey ★★ Drawing on v'yds in the SANTA LUCIA HIGHLANDS and ARROYO SECO, Hahn makes consistently gd Cab Sauv and reasonably priced Chard.

andley Cellars Mendocino ★★→★★★ (Chard) 97 99 01' 02 Winemaker Mila Handley makes excellent ANDERSON VALLEY Chard, Gewurz, Pinot N, plus (tiny lots) classic sp and Meunier. Also v.gd DRY CREEK VALLEY Sauv, Chard from her family's vines.

anzell Sonoma ★★★→★★★★ (Chard) 96 99' 00 01 02 Small producer of outstanding terroir-driven Chard and Pinot N from estate vines. Always gd, quality level has risen in past few years.

arlan Estate Napa ★★★★ (Cab) 94 95 97 99' 00 (02) Concentrated, sleek Cab Sauv from small estate in hills W of OAKVILLE earning its right to luxury prices.

arrison Napa ★★ 94 95 96 97' 99' 01' Nicely located nr LONG VINEYARDS and the cult Cab Sauv of Bryant family. Predictably specializing in Cab Sauv.

artford Court Sonoma ★★★ Part of KENDALL JACKSON's Artisans & Estates group shows promise with single-v'yd Pinot Ns, tight coastal-grown Chard, and wonderful old-vine RUSSIAN RIVER Zins.

artwell Napa ★★★ High-end image, small producer with gd Cab Sauv potential.

IDV Carneros Chard from grower Larry Hyde's v'yd in conjunction with Aubert de Villaine of Romanee Conti. First releases promising.

leitz Napa ★★★★ (Cab) 74 78 90 91 97 99' 01 (02) Rich yet supple and deeply flavoured, minty Cab Sauv from Martha's Vineyard. Bella Oaks and newer Trailside Vineyard rival but don't beat Martha.

leller Estate Carmel Valley Monterey ★★→★★★ (Cab) 95 96 97 99 Dark and powerful wines (esp the past few years as vines mature) are acquiring something of a cult status for long life. Chenin Bl is charming.

less Collection, The Napa ★★★ (Chard) 00 01 02 (Cab) 94 95 97 99 00 01 A winery-cum-museum in former Mont La Salle winery, owned by Swiss art collector Donald Hess. Cab Sauvs often underrated but offer supple balance and long wrap-around flavours. Chard crisp and bright. Budget Hess Select label gives v.gd value for money.

lill Winery, William Napa ★★ Allied-Domecq property on the rise with subtle (for California) Chard; even more with flavourful, silky Cab Sauv.

lobbs, Paul Sonoma Co ★★★ Excellent winemaker, well known for consulting with Catena in Argentina, buying top Chard grapes in CARNEROS, Cab Sauv in NAPA, and Pinot N in RUSSIAN RIVER for own label. First releases show high promise.

lop Kiln Sonoma ★★ Inky and rich Zin from RUSSIAN RIVER and a burly Petite Sirah are best bets.

lusch Vineyards Mendocino ★★ Has ANDERSON VALLEY v'yd for often fine Pinot N and Ukiah v'yd for sometimes gd Sauv Bl, Cab Sauv.

ron Horse Vineyards Sonoma ★★★(★)Chard) 99 00 01 02 RUSSIAN RIVER family estate producing some of California's best bubbly, inc a series of late-disgorged beauties. Chard from cool RUSSIAN RIVER VALLEY is outstanding and an above-average Cab Sauv from ALEXANDER VALLEY v'yds.

Sonoma ★★★ Born part of JORDAN, now on its own in RUSSIAN RIVER VALLEY. Creamy classic-method Brut the foundation. Also still Pinot N worth a look.

Jade Mountain Napa ★★ After sale to CHALONE, pursuing lofty goals using Rhône varieties, esp Syrah, Mourvèdre.

Jekel Vineyards Arroyo Seco Monterey ★★ Ripe juicy Ries used to be most noteworthy item. It remains quaffable, but red B'x blends from estate v'yds have improved dramatically. Owned by Brown-Forman.

Jessie's Grove Lodi ★★ Old Zin vines work well for farming family's new venture

Jordan Sonoma ★★★★ (Cab) 87 90 **94 95** 97 **99'** 00 01 (02) Extravagant ALEXANDER VALLEY estate models its Cab Sauv on supplest B'x. And it lasts. Chard moving away from oaky-toast to a leaner Burgundy model.

Justin Paso Robles ★★ Former investment banker with little auberge operation making impressive blended reds, esp. Meritage called Isoceles.

Kautz-Ironstone Lodi and Calaveras County ★★ Showplace destination in SIERRA FOOTHILLS attracts visitors from all over the state. Honestly priced broad range led by fine Cab Fr.

Karly Amador ★★ Gd source of SIERRA FOOTHILLS Zin.

Keegan Cellars Napa ★★ Eugenia Keegan makes small amounts of v'yd designated Pinot N which show great promise.

Keenan Winery, Robert Napa ★★ Winery on SPRING MOUNTAIN: supple, restrained Cab Sauv, Merlot; also Chard.

Kendall-Jackson Lake County ★★→★★★ Staggeringly successful style aimed at widest market: esp broadly sourced off-dry toasty Chard. Even more noteworthy for the development of a diversity of wineries under the umbrella of KENDALL-JACKSON's Artisans & Estates.

Kenwood Vineyards Sonoma ★★ (Jack London Cab) 87 **90 95** 97 98 **99'** 00 01 Single-v'yd Cab Sauv, Zin (several) the high points. Sauv Bl is very reliable value. Owned by KORBEL.

Kistler Vineyards Sonoma ★★★ (Chard) 98 99' **00** 01' Still chasing the Burgundian model of single v'yd Pinot N, most from RUSSIAN RIVER, with mixed success. Chards very toasty, buttery.

Konigsgaard Napa ★★★ Small production of Chard, Syrah and Roussanne from former Newton winemaker

Korbel Sonoma ★★ Long-established sparkling specialist emphasizes bold fruit flavours, intense fizz; Natural tops the line. Distributed by Brown-Forman.

Krug, Charles Napa ★★ Historically important winery with sound wines. Cabs at head of list. CK-Mondavi is a relentlessly sweet commodity brand.

Kunde Estate Sonoma ★★★ Long-time large grower has become solid producer with buttery Chard, flavourful Sauv Bl, peachy Viognier and silky Merlot.

La Jota Napa ★★ Huge, long-lived Cab Sauv from Howell Mountain. Owned by Markham Vineyards.

Lambert Bridge Sonoma Dry Creek ★★★ Seductive Merlot, zesty Zin and brilliant Sauv Bl in a "B'x meets New Zealand" style. Winery on the way up, for sure.

Lamborn Howell Mountain Napa ★★★ V'yd planted on historic 19th-C site. Big juicy Zin, Cab Sauv coming along for this deserving cult winery.

Landmark Sonoma ★★ (Chard) **00** 01 02 Early promise of elegant Burgundian-style Chard blunted by oaky-toasty flavours for a time in the late 1990s. Recent bottlings seem to be back on track.

Lang & Reed Napa ★★★ Specialist focusing on delicious Loire-style Cab Fr.

Laurel Glen Sonoma ★★★★ (Cab) **90** 91 **94 95** 97 99' 00 01 (02) Floral, well-etched Cab Sauv with a sense of place from steep v'yd in SONOMA MOUNTAIN sub-AVA. Steadily improving into 4-star territory.

Lava Cap El Dorado ★★ Gd v'yd site on volcanic soils. Sleek, lean Chard, peppery Zin. Gd value for price.

Lipartia Cellars Napa Howell Mountain ★★★ Deeply concentrated Cab Sauv which promises long cellar life.

Livingston Moffett St Helena Napa ★★★ Noteworthy Cab Sauv from Rutherford Ranch v'yds. Recent Syrah shows promise.

Lockwood Monterey ★★ Large v'yd in S Salinas Valley, offering gd value in Chard, Sauv Bl. Shale Creek is second label.

Lohr, J Central Coast ★→★★ Large, wide-reaching firm at peak with PASO ROBLES Cab Sauv Seven Oaks. Recent series of Meritage-style reds best yet. Commodity line sub-titled Cypress.

Lolonis Mendocino ★★ Pre-Prohibition Mendo growers, founded winery in 1982. Gd, solid Zin, Merlot, spicy Chard.

Long Meadow W Mtns Napa ★★★ Elegant, silky Cab Sauv better with each vintage. V'yd is organically farmed. Potential cult beauty from winemaker Cathy CORISON.

Long Vineyards Napa ★★★ (Chard) **99 00** 01 02 (Cab) **87 90 91 94 95** 97 99' 00 01 Owned by legendary winemakers Robert and Zelma Long, small estate produces luscious Chard and velvety Ries for top prices.

Longoria Winery Santa Barbara (★★→★★★) Rick Longoria makes brilliant Pinot N from top v'yds in the area.

MacRostie Sonoma Carneros ★★ Toasty, ripe Chard with some complexity is flagship. Also well-oaked Merlot, Pinot N.

Marcassin Sonoma Coast. Cult consultant Helen Turley's own tiny label. Worth so much at auction that few ever drink it. Concentrated Chard and dense Pinot N. Those who like the style give it rave reviews. Those who don't, don't. Chard is so densely concentrated, those who do taste it never forget.

Markham Napa ★★★ (Merlot) **94 95 97 98 99** 01' Way underrated producer of balanced, elegant Merlot and solid Cab Sauv.

Martinelli Russian River ★★★ Family growers from fog-shrouded western hills, famous for old-vine Jackass Hill Vineyard Zin. Sought after small production of Pinot N and Chard made under Helen Turley's consulting eye.

Martini, Louis M Napa ★★★ Long history making surprisingly ageworthy Cab Sauv, Zin, and Barbera from fine v'yds (Monte Rosso, Los Vinedos, Glen Oaks, etc) in NAPA and SONOMA. Has been on the down side for several years. May be on the way back after purchase by GALLO in 2002.

Matanzas Creek Sonoma (Chard) **99 00 01** (Merlot) **94 95 97 99** 01' Excellent Sauv Bl has slipped of late. Merlot outstanding. Owned by KENDALL-JACKSON.

Mayacamas Napa ★★★ Pioneer boutique v'yd with rich Chard and firm (but no longer steel-hard) Cab Sauv, capable of long ageing. Some Sauv Bl and Pinot N.

McDowell Valley Vineyards Mendocino ★★ Grower-label for family with hearts set on Rhône varieties, esp ancient-vine Syrah and Grenache.

Meridian San Luis Obispo ★★ Gd value Santa Barbara Chard, PASO ROBLES Cab Sauv. Owned by BERINGER-BLASS.

Mettler Family Vineyards Lodi ★★ Long-time growers are now producing a sleek and tangy Cab Sauv and a powerful Petite Sirah. On the way up.

Merry Edwards Russian River ★★★★ Superstar consultant has planted her own Pinot N v'yd in RUSSIAN RIVER district and buys in grapes from other v'yds. Has quickly established the brand as one of the top Pinot N producers in California.

Merryvale Napa ★★★ Best at Cab Sauv and Merlot, which have elegant balance and supple finish. Chard being revitalized under new winemaker Stephen Test, moving away from oaky-toast to a more complex Burgundian model.

Michael, Peter Sonoma ★★★ Stunning, complex Chard from Howell Mountain in a powerful style, and a more supple ALEXANDER VALLEY bottling. Cab Sauv on the tight side.

Michel-Schlumberger Sonoma ★★ Excellent ageing potential in supple Cab

Sauv usually blended with Merlot from hillside vines.

Milano Mendocino ★★ Small producer of Zin, Cab Sauv, worth seeking out.

Mirassou Central Coast ★★ Sixth-generation grower and pioneer in MONTERE (Salinas). Sold brand to GALLO but retained v'yds.

Mondavi, Robert Napa ★★→★★★★ Brilliant innovator now applying lessons to varietals for every purse. From top: NAPA VALLEY Reserves (bold, prices to match), NAPA VALLEY appellation series (eg CARNEROS Chard, OAKVILLE Cab Sauv, etc), NAPA VALLEY (basic production), Coastal Series (eg CENTRAL COAST Chard, NORTH COAST Zin etc), RM-Woodbridge (California appellation fo basic production, also pricier "Twin Oaks" line). Also OPUS ONE, BYRON Calitterra (Chile), Luce and Ornelia (Italy). Some critics feel that the second generation has lost focus on Napa and is spread too thin.

Monteviña Amador ★★ Ripe and fruit-forward Sierra Zin and one of state's best Barberas. Owned by SUTTER HOME. Top of line called Terra d'Oro.

Monticello Cellars Napa ★★★ (Cab) **87 90 94 95** 97 **99** 00 01 Consistently worth seeking out. Basic line under Monticello label, reserves under Corley. Both inc Chard, Cab Sauv.

Morgan Monterey ★★★ Winemaker-owner. Top-end single-v'yd Pinot Ns and Chards from v.gd SANTA LUCIA HIGHLANDS v'yds. Esp fine unoaked Chard called Metallico. V'yds now farmed organically.

Mumm Napa Valley Napa ★★★ Joint venture with Seagram offers stylish bubbly esp delicious Blanc de Noirs and a rich, complex DVX single-v'yd fizz.

Murphy-Goode Sonoma ★★ Large ALEXANDER VALLEY estate. Sauv Bl, Zin are tops Merlot better than average. New Tin Roof (screwtop) line offers refreshing Sauv Bl and Chard sans oak, in contrast to lavishly oaked Reserve line.

Nalle Sonoma ★★★(★) Doug Nalle makes lovely Zins from Dry Creek fruit, tha are juicy and delicious when young and will also mature gracefully for years.

Navarro Vineyards Mendocino ★★→★★★ From ANDERSON VALLEY, splendidly ageworthy Chard, perhaps the grandest Gewurz in state. Even more special: late-harvest Ries, Gewurz. Pinot N in two styles, homage to Burgundy from ANDERSON VALLEY grapes, a brisk and juicy bottling from bought-in grapes. Only self-deprecating prices keep this from being cult favourite of big-shot collectors.

Nevada City Sierra Foothills ★★ Wide range of tourism-designed offerings distrac from extraordinary Cab Fr.

Newlan Yountville, Napa. Reliable producer with fine value Cab Sauv (worth ageing in gd vintages).

Newton Vineyards Napa ★★★★ (Cab) **87 91 94 95 97** 99' 00 01 (02) (Merlot) **86 87 88 90 91 95** 97 99 00 01 (02) Mountain estate makes some of California's best Merlot in several bottlings. Lush Chard and a supple Cab Sauv.

Neyers Napa ★★★ Gd quality overall; great Syrah and a lovely Chard.

Niebaum-Coppola Estate Napa ★★★(★) (Rubicon) **84 85 91 94 95 96 97**' 98 99' 00 01 (02) "Godfather" Coppola has proven he is as serious abou making wine as making movies. Now owns the historic Inglenook Estate v'yd and winery (but not the brand). Flagship Rubicon ranks with the state's best B'x red blends. Edizone Pennino concentrates on delightfuly old-fashioned Zin; gd value Diamond series always worth a look.

Ojai Ventura Co ★★★ Former AU BON CLIMAT partner Adam Tolmach on his own since early 1990s makes wide range of excellent wines, esp Syrah.

Opus One Napa ★★★★ (Cab) 85 87 **90** 91 **94 95 97**' 99' 00 01 Joint venture o MONDAVI and Baronne Philippine de Rothschild. Sometimes outstanding bu even the best never reaches the level of Mondavi Reserve. B'x need not fear.

Pacific Echo Anderson Valley ★★ Formerly Scharffenberger, now Pommery owned, sparkling wine. Some loss of quality in the last few years.

Pahlmeyer Napa ★★★ Cultish producer of dense, tannic Cab Sauv and more supple, fruity Merlot.

Paradigm Napa ★★★ Westside OAKVILLE v'yd with an impressive Merlot and a bright, supple Cab Sauv.

Paraiso Springs Monterey ★★ Up and comer owned by large grower in Salinas, making luscious Ries and Pinot Bl. More recently bright and balanced Pinot N from SANTA LUCIA HIGHLANDS fruit.

Patz & Hall Napa ★★→★★★ Reputation for CARNEROS Chard from individual v'yds firmly established around crisp structure and opulent winemaking. Pinot N also inviting.

Peachy Canyon Paso Robles ★★ Big bold Zin is a story worth telling.

Pedroncelli Sonoma ★★ Old-hand in DRY CREEK producing agreeable Zin, Cab Sauv, and a solid Chard.

Perry Creek Eldorado ★★ An extraordinary Syrah from high-elevation vines and above-average Cab Sauv.

Phelps, Joseph Napa ★★★★ (Cab Sauv) 85 87 90 91 **94 95** 97 **98** 99' Deluxe winery, beautiful v'yd: impeccable standards. V.gd Chard, Cab Sauv (esp Backus), and Cab Sauv-based Insignia. Also look for fine Rhône series under Vin du Mistral label.

Philips, R H Yolo, Dunnigan Hills ★→★★ The only winery in the Dunnigan Hills AVA makes a wide range of wines. Excellent job with Rhône varieties under the EXP label and gd value Toasted Head Chard. Also excellent old-vine Zin sourced from v'yds in the suburbs of Los Angeles.

Pine Ridge Napa ★★→★★★ Tannic and concentrated Cab Sauvs from several NAPA AVAs are worthy of ageing. The just off-dry Chenin Bl is a treat.

Preston Sonoma Dry Creek Valley ★★★ Lou Preston is a demanding terroirist, making outstanding DRY CREEK VALLEY icons like Zin and fruity, marvellous Barbera. His Sauv Bl is a delicious fusion of "New Zealand meets SONOMA".

Pride Mountain Spring Mountain, Napa ★★★ Top hillside location contributes bright fruit characters to fine B'x variety offerings with significant ageing potential.

Provenance Oakville Napa ★★★ Lovely, elegant, and supple Cab Sauv from heart of NAPA estate; owned by CHALONE.

Quady Winery San Joaquin ★★ Imaginative Madera Muscat dessert wines, inc celebrated orangey Essencia, rose-petal-flavoured Elysium, and Moscato d'Asti-like Electra.

Quintessa Napa ★★★(★) Splendid new estate on Silverado Trail, linked to FRANCISCAN. Early releases of red Meritage-style show tremendous promise.

Quivira Sonoma ★★ Sauv Bl, Zin, and others, from Dry Creek Valley estate. More enamoured of oak than v'yd in recent vintages.

Qupé Sta Barbara ★★→★★★ Never-a-dull-moment cellar-mate of AU BON CLIMAT. Marsanne, Pinot Bl, Syrah are all well worth trying.

Rafanelli, A Sonoma ★★★ (Cab) **90 94 95** 97' 99 00 01 (Zin) **97 99 00** 01' Hearty, fetchingly rustic DRY CREEK Zin; Cab Sauv of striking intensity.

Rasmussen, Kent Carneros ★★→★★★ Crisp and lingering Chard and delicious Pinot N are worth looking for. Ramsay is an alternate label for small production lots.

Ravenswood Sonoma ★★★ Zin Master Joel Peterson is a pioneer striking single-v'yd Zin and affordable line of SONOMA and Vintners Reserve Zin and Merlot. Will quality remain at peak under CONSTELLATION ownership? Too soon to tell.

Raymond Vineyards and Cellar Napa ★★★ (Cab) 87 **90 94 95** 97 99 00 01 Much under-rated Cab Sauv from family v'yds. Potential for long-term ageing.

NB Vintages in colour are those you should choose first for drinking in 2005.

CALIFORNIA

Renwood Amador ★★ Gd Zin and Syrah from foothill v'yds. Has the potential to perform better.

Ridge Sta Cruz Mts ★★★★ (Cab) **85 87 90 94 95 97** 99' 00 01 Winery of highest repute among connoisseurs. Drawing from NAPA (York Creek) and its own mountain v'yd (Montebello) for lithe, harmonious Cab Sauvs, worthy of long maturing, and from SONOMA, NAPA, and PASO ROBLES for amazing Zin. Outstanding Chard from wild-yeast fermentation is often overlooked.

Rios-Lovell Livermore ★★ New producer with an outstanding Petite Sirah and better-than-average Zin.

Rochioli, J Sonoma ★★★(★) (Pinot N) **95 96 97 98 99** 00 01 Long-time RUSSIAN RIVER grower sells most of fruit to GARY FARRELL and other top Pinot N producers, but makes several own label Pinot Ns every year which are simply super. Also v.gd Zin.

Roederer Estate Mendocino ★★★★ ANDERSON VALLEY branch of Champagne house (established 1988). Supple, elegant house style. Easily one of the top three sparklers in California and hands-down the best rosé. Top-of-the-line luxury cuvée l'Ermitage superb.

Rosenblum Cellars San Francisco Bay ★★→★★★ Makes 7–8 single-v'yd Zins in any given year sourced from all over the state, many from old vines. Quality varies, but always well above average.

Rubissow-Sargent Mt Veeder, Napa ★★ Gd quality Cab Sauv built to last.

Rutz Cellars Russian River Valley Sonoma ★★→★★★ Outstanding Chard from select RUSSIAN RIVER v'yds. Super Pinot N with more guts than most. Keep an eye on Rutz.

Saddleback Cellars Napa ★★★ Owner-winemaker Nils Venge is a legend in NAPA. Lush Zin and long-lived Cab Sauv.

St Amant Lodi ★★ LODI producer could soon earn third star, esp with old-vine Zin and a nifty Syrah.

St Clement Napa ★★→★★★ (Cab) **85 87 90 91 94 95 97** 99' 00 01 (02) Supple, long-lived Oroppas, a Cab Sauv-based blend, is the go-to wine here. Merlot and Chard also outstanding. Owned by BERINGER-BLASS.

St Francis Sonoma ★★★ (Merlot) **95 97 99** 00 01' (Zin) **97 99** 00' 01 Deep and concentrated Cab Sauv, fruity and lively Merlot with lashings of oak. Go for the old-vine Zin.

St-Supéry Napa ★★★ Sleek and graceful Merlot; Cab Sauv can be outstanding as is red Meritage. Sauv Bl one of best in state. Sources some grapes from warmer Pope Valley E of NAPA VALLEY. French-owned (SKALLI).

Saintsbury Carneros ★★★ (Chard) **97 99 00** 01' (02) (Pinot) **97 99 00** 01 Outstanding Pinot N, more dense than most from CARNEROS. Chard full flavoured and oak-shy. Garnet Pinot N, made from younger vines, is a treat.

Sanford Sta Barbara ★★★ (Pinot) **96 97 98 99** 00 01 Pinot N pioneer in Santa Barbara. Wines can be forward and intense, but with a few years in bottle take on a supple richness. Sauv Bl is a beauty.

Sattui, V Napa ★★ King of direct-only sales (ie winery door or mail order). Wines made in a rustic, drink-now style. Reds are best, esp Cab Sauv, Zin.

Sausal Sonoma ★★ ALEXANDER VALLEY estate noted for its Zin and Cab Sauv. Century Vine Zin is a stunning example of old-vine Zin.

Scherrer Sonoma ★★★ Ripe, California-style Pinot N and Chard from RUSSIAN RIVER, as well as mouth-filling old-vine Zin from ALEXANDER VALLEY.

Schramsberg Napa ★★★★ One of California's top sparkling producers and the first to make a true methodé champenoise in the state in commercial quantity. Historic caves. Reserve is splendid; Blanc de Noir outstanding (2–10 yrs). Luxury cuvée J Schram is America's Krug.

Schug Cellars Carneros ★★★ German-born and trained owner-winemaker dabbles in other types, but CARNEROS Chard and Pinot N are his main interests and wines. Pinot N is always near the top.

Screaming Eagle Napa ★★★★ Grower + consulting oenologist = small lots of cult Cab Sauv at luxury prices.

Sebastiani Sonoma ★ Former jug wine king has tried to go upscale with single-v'yd wines.

Seghesio Sonoma ★★★ Concentrating now on superb, ageworthy Zins from own old v'yds in ALEXANDER and DRY CREEK VALLEYS, but don't overlook smaller lots of Sangiovese Vitigno Toscano.

Selene Napa ★★★ Ace winemaker Mia Klein makes rich and concentrated Merlot and brilliant Sauv Bl from her new winery.

Sequoia Grove Napa ★★★ Estate Cab Sauvs are intense and long-lived. Chard is a cut above and can age.

Shafer Vineyards Napa ★★★★ (Cab) 90 91 94 95 97' 99 00 01 (Merlot) 87 80 91 95 97 99 01 Always in the top range for Merlot; Cab Sauv also getting steadily better, esp the Hillside Select from STAGS LEAP. CARNEROS Chard (Red Shoulder Ranch) breaking out of oak shackles. Also look for Firebreak, a single-v'yd Sangiovese.

Sierra Vista El Dorado ★★(★) Dedicated Rhôneist in SIERRA FOOTHILLS. Dedicated "Rhônigade" at high elevation. Style is elegant, mid-weight, and fruit driven, with emphasis on varietal typicity.

Signorello Napa ★★★ Fairly high-end Cab Sauvs and Chards, noteworthy Pinot N from RUSSIAN RIVER, v.gd Sem/Sauv Bl blend is best value. All could do with a bit less oak.

Silver Oak Napa/Sonoma ★★★ Separate wineries in NAPA and ALEXANDER VALLEYS make Cab Sauv only. Owners have ridden extreme American-oaked style to pinnacle of critical acclaim among those who admire such wines.

Silverado Vineyards Napa ★★★ (Cab) 90 94 95 97 99 00 01 (02) Showy hilltop STAGS LEAP district winery offering supple Cab Sauv, lean and minerally Chard, and distinctive Sangiovese.

Simi Sonoma ★★ Up-and-down historic winery makes a wide range of varietals. Long-lived Cab Sauv and v.gd Chard still the heart of the matter. White Meritage 'Sendal' is super.

Sinskey Vineyards, Robert Napa ★★★ Ex-ACACIA partner started winery. Chard with a gd acidic bite and luscious Pinot N are the highlights.

Smith-Madrone Napa High up on SPRING MOUNTAIN, the Smith brothers craft a superb off-dry Ries and a lean Chard.

Sonoma-Cutrer Vineyards Sonoma ★★ (Chard) 97 99 00 01' Chard specialist in oaky-toasty territory is in a down period just now. Owned by Brown-Forman.

Spencer Roloson ★★ Negociant producer of stylish Zin and Temp. Worth watching.

Spottswoode Napa ★★★★ (Cab) 87 91 94 95 97 99 01 (02) Firm, resonant luxury Cab Sauv from small St Helena v'yd. Supple, polished Sauv.

Spring Mountain Napa ★★→★★★ Famed on TV as "Falcon Crest", a mountain estate now concentrating on wine. Excellent Cab Sauv and outstanding Sauv Bl from estate vines.

Stag's Leap Wine Cellars Napa ★★→★★★★ (Cask 23) 78 84 87 90 91 94 95 97 99' Celebrated v'yd for silky, seductive Cab Sauvs (SLV, Fay, top-of-line Cask 23) and Merlots. Gd Chard is often overlooked. Hawk Crest is budget line made from mostly MENDOCINO grapes.

Stags' Leap Winery ★★ Historic estate being revived by BERINGER-BLASS. Important for Petite Sirah.

Staglin Napa ★★ (Cab) 90 94 95 97 99 Silky and elegant Cab Sauv from

Rutherford Bench originally developed for BEAULIEU when André Tchelistcheff was the wine wizard there.

Steele Wines Lake ★★→★★★ Jed Steele is a genius at sourcing v'yds for a series of single-v'yd wines under main label and a second label called Shooting Star. Chard can get a little oaky, but Pinot N and some speciality wines, like Washington State Lemberge, are outstanding.

Sterling Napa ★★→★★★ Scenic NAPA estate now owned by Diageo Chateau and Estate Wines. Gd basic Chard and understated single-v'yd Cab Sauv. But Sterling has never seemed to fulfil potential.

Stony Hill Napa ★★★ (Chard) **93 96 97 99** 00 01' Hilly v'yd and winery for many of California's top Chards over the past 30 yrs.

Storybook Mountain Napa ★★★ Napa's only dedicated Zin specialist makes taut and tannic Estate and Reserve wines from Calistoga v'yd.

Strong Vineyard, Rodney Sonoma ★★ (Cab) **90 94 95 97 99** 00 01 Cab Sauv from single-v'yd bottlings often three stars; gd RUSSIAN RIVER Pinot N.

Sutter Home Napa ★ Famous for white Zin and rustic Amador red Zin. Trying to move up-scale with Signature Series and M Trinchero brands.

Swan, Joseph Sonoma ★★★ (Zin) **95 97 99** 00 01' Long-time RUSSIAN RIVER producer of intense Zin and classy Pinot N.

Tablas Creek Paso Robles ★★★ Joint venture between owners of Château Beaucastel and importer Robert Hass. V'yd based on cuttings from Châteauneuf v'yds. First results promising.

Talbott, R Monterey ★★→★★★ Chard from single v'yds in MONTEREY is the name of the game. Approach is Burgundian and several bottlings reach 3-star level.

Tanner, Lane Santa Barbara ★★★ (Pinot N) **93 94 95 96 97** 98 99 Owner-winemaker with often superb single-v'yd Pinot N (Bien Nacido, Sierra Madre Plateau) reflecting terroir with a quiet, understated elegance.

The Terraces Napa ★★★ High above the Silverado trail, this is the home of outstanding Zin and Cab Sauv with supple style.

Torres Estate, Marimar Sonoma ★★★ (Chard) **97 99'** 00 01 (Pinot N) **97** 99 00 01 Sister of Catalan hero. Edgy Chard (ages magnificently), lovely Pinot N from RUSSIAN RIVER VALLEY. New Pinot N plantings on coast will likely go 4-star. V'yds now farmed organically.

Trefethen Napa ★★★ (Chard) **96 97 98 98** 00 01' Respected family winery. Gd off-dry Ries, tense Chard for ageing (late-released Library wines show how well). Cab Sauv shows increasing depths.

Truchard Carneros ★★→★★★ From the warmer, inner-end of CARNEROS comes one of the flavoury, firmly built Merlots that give the AVA identity. Cab Sauv and Syrah even better.

Turley Napa ★★★ Former partner in FROG'S LEAP, now specializing in hefty, heady, single-v'yd Zin and Petite Sirah from old vines.

Ventana Monterey ★★ 1978 winery, showcase for owner's v'yds: watch for Chard and Sauv Bl from Musqué clone. Exciting new Syrah and Temp.

Viansa Sonoma ★★ Wines pay homage to Sam SEBASTIANI'S ancestors with blended, varietal Italianates, inc such rarities (for California) as Arneis, Dolcetto, and Freisa.

Vino Noceto Amador ★★ Sangiovese one of the best in California.

Wellington Sonoma ★★ Vivid old-vine Zin and sleek, powerful Cab Sauv from selected v'yds.

Wente Vineyards Livermore and Monterey ★★ Historic specialist in whites, esp Livermore Sauv Bl and Sem. But Livermore estate Cab Sauv is also v.gd. Monterey sweet Ries can be exceptional. A little classic sparkling.

Wild Horse Winery San Luis Obispo ★★ (Pinot) **95 96 97 99** 00 01' Solid producer of Merlot and Pinot N from CENTRAL COAST grapes, now owned by

Geyser Peak.

Williams Selyem Sonoma ★★★ (Pinot) **90 92 93 96 97** 99 00 01' Intense smoky RUSSIAN RIVER Pinot N, esp Rochioli and Allen v'yds. Now reaching to SONOMA COAST, MENDOCINO for grapes.

Young, Robert Sonoma ★★★ Outstanding Chard, Cab Sauv from famed v'yd, source of CHATEAU ST JEAN Chard for many years.

York Creek Spring Mtn, Napa ★★★ Exceptional v'yd owned by Fritz Maytag, father of microbrew revolution in US. Sells to RIDGE and now has own label.

Zaca Mesa Sta Barbara ★★ Now turning away from Chard and Pinot N to concentrate on Rhône grapes (esp Marsanne and Syrah) and blends (Cuvée Z) grown on estate.

ZD Napa ★★ (Chard) 98 **99** 00 **01'** Lusty Chard tattooed by American oak is ZD signature wine.

The Pacific Northwest

The wine country of the Pacific Northwest spans three adjoining states. Oregon has more than 15,000 acres of vines, concentrated in the Willamette Valley, south of Portland. Washington's 35,000 acres of vineyard are concentrated in the warmer, drier half of the state, east of the Cascade mountain range. Idaho's wine country lies just east of Washington's, along the Snake River.

The grapes of Burgundy and Alsace do well in Oregon; Dijon clones of Chardonnay and Pinot Noir promise earlier ripening and potentially more complex wines. Across the Columbia River in eastern Washington, the warmer, drier climate of the Columbia Valley allows thicker-skinned varieties (Merlot, Cabernet Sauvignon, Cabernet Franc, and the hot new favourite, Syrah) to ripen well. These same varieties also grow well in the warmer southern appellations of Oregon, and in Idaho.

The largest wineries of the Pacific Northwest seem small in comparison to those in California. Most of the more than 460 wineries – a number that increases every year – produce fewer than 30,000 cases of wine annually, and many wineries make only 2,000 to 5,000 cases. Washington's Walla Walla Valley continues to be the most glamorous and rapidly expanding appellation, growing from ten producers in 1995 to more than 60 wineries by 2003 and more than doubling vineyard plantings within the same period.

Recent vintages

2003 A potentially mixed vintage after a season of heat and water stress.

2002 Wines with full expression and elegance.

2001 Lower acidity and less concentration than previous three years.

2000 Solid vintage. High yields, concentrated, structured wines. Now – 2010.

1999 Superb. Perfect growing season produced balanced wines. Now – 2008.

1998 Excellent throughout. Reduced yields and greater concentration in Oregon (now or soon); quantity and quality in Washington (hold).

Oregon

Abacela Vineyards Umpqua Valley ★★→★★★ **97 98** 99' 00 **02** New producer; and one to watch: Temp, Dolcetto, Cab Fr, and Syrah stand out.

Adelsheim Vineyard Yamhill County ★→★★ 91 92 93 94 95 **96** 97 **98** 99' 00' Smoothly balanced Pinot N. New Dijon clone Chard, Ries, top Pinots Gr and Bl: clean, bracing. Also fruity Merlot.

Amity Willamette ★ **97 98 99** 00 Top Gewurz, Ries, Pinot Bl. Patchy Pinot N.

Andrew Rich (Tabula Rasa) Willamette ★ Small producer; wide range: Pinot

N, Washington Cab Sauv, Chenin, Sauv Bl, rosé, and Gewurz Icewine.

Archery Summit Yamhill Co ★★★ **93 94 95' 96** 97 **98'** 99' 00' Flashy sibling of NAPA winery Pine Ridge. Very impressive oaky Pinot N.

Argyle Yamhill County ★→★★ (sp) **89 91 93 94** 96 98 99' 00 01 02 NW's best sp (inc NV), consistently well made. Also fine Ries, Chard, high-quality Pinot N.

Beaux Frères Yamhill County ★★ **91 92 93 94 95** 96 97 98 99' 00' **02'** Produces an excellent, structured Pinot N; showing more finesse in recent yrs. Part-owned by Robert Parker Jr.

Bethel Heights Willamette ★★ **91 92 93 94 95 96 97 98** 99' 00' 02' Deftly made Pinot N from estate nr Salem. Also notable Chard, Pinot Bl, Pinot Gr.

Brick House Yamhill County ★★ **93 94 95 96** 97 **98** 99' 00 Dynamic, organic property operated by former CBS news correspondent. Very Burgundian style. Small quantities of v.gd Pinot N, Gamay, and barrel-fermented Chard.

Cameron Yamhill County ★→★★ **93 94 95** 96 97 98' 99' Eclectic producer of Pinot N, Chard: some great. Also v.gd Pinot Bl.

Chehalem Yamhill County ★→★★ **91 92 93 94 95 96** 97 **98** 99' 02' (w 00') Top-quality Pinot N, Chard, Pinot Gr, Ries. Reserve Pinot N.

Cooper Mountain Willamette ★ Steadily increasing quality. Pinot N, Chard, Pinot Gr, Pinot Bl. Certified biodynamic v'yds.

Cristom N Willamette ★→★★ **92' 93 94 95** 96 97 98' 99' 00' **02'** Delicious Pinot N and buttery-smooth Chard. Try the barrel-fermented Viognier.

Domaine Drouhin Willamette ★→★★★ **91 92 93'** **94 95 96** 97 **98' 99'** 00' Superb estate-grown Pinot N from one of the first families of Burgundy. Laurène Reserve silky and elegant, equally fine Chard **96 97 98 99'** 00' 01' 02'. Also very fine new Louise cuvée.

Domaine Serene Willamette ★★★ **98'** 99' 00 Big, jammy wines. Small production. Look for Evenstead Reserve Pinot N; new Rockblock Syrah is also worth finding.

Elk Cove Vineyards Willamette ★ **98** 99' Quality range of wines featuring Pinot N, Pinot Gr, Chard, Ries. Excellent dessert wine Ultima.

Erath Vineyards Yamhill County ★ **93'** 94 95 96 97 **98** 99 00 V.gd Chard, Pinot Gr, Gewurz, Pinot Bl. Esp lovely old Pinot N **76** and Ries **76**. New winemaker in 2002.

Evesham Wood Nr Salem Willamette ★→★★ Small family winery; fine Pinot N (**91 92 93 94 95** 96 97 **98 99** 00' 01' 02), Pinot Gris, and dry Gewurz. Limited production of Cuvée J in high demand. Newly organic v'yds.

Eyrie Vineyards, The Willamette ★→★★ Pioneer (1965) winery with Burgundian convictions. Older vintages of Pinot N are treasures (**75' 76' 80 83 86 89 90**); Chards and Pinot Gr: rich yet crisp. All wines age beautifully.

Firesteed ★ Large-volume producer of value-priced Pinot N and a fine DOC Barbera d'Asti (made in Italy).

Ken Wright Cellars Yamhill County ★★ **93 94 95 96** 97 **98'** 99 01 02' Floral Pinot N that has a cult following. Also v.gd Chard and Melon de Bourgogne.

King Estate S Willamette ★ **98** 99' 01 02' Huge beautiful NAPA-like estate. V.gd Pinot Gr; Chard and Pinot N improving; fruit sourced from all over, inc Cab Sauv, Merlot, and Zin. New estate wines top.

Lange Winery Yamhill County ★ **98** 99' **00 02'** Small family winery; excellent reserve Pinot N; Pinot Gr is solid but Res reveals a heavy hand with oak.

Lemelson Yamhill County ★→★★ 99' **00' 01 02** New, well-financed operation producing well-structured fine wines.

Panther Creek Willamette ★→★★ **94' 95** 96 97 **98'** 99' 00' 01 02' Concentrated, meaty, single v'yd Pinot N and pleasant Melon de Bourgogne. Purchased grapes from top v'yds, inc Shea.

Patricia Green Cellars Yamhill County ★→★★ Wines of great pizazz and expression from former TORII MOR winemaker. Lovely wines in all vintages.

Ponzi Vineyards Willamette Valley ★→★★ **94 95 96** 97 **98'** 99' 00' 02' Small pioneering winery almost in Portland, well known for Pinot Gr, Chard, Pinot N. Also well-made Arneis and Dolcetto.

Rex Hill Willamette ★→★★ **93 94 95** 96 97 **98'** 99' 00' 02' Excellent Pinot N, Pinot Gr, and Chard from several N Willamette vineyards. Reserves are among Oregon's best; great value King's Ridge label. New winemaker 2002.

St-Innocent Willamette ★→★★ **98 99 00 01 02** Gaining reputation for big, delicious, forward Pinot N; pleasant but slightly bitter whites.

Tracking down Northwest wines

Portland Wildwood (1221 NW 21st Avenue, tel 503-248-9663) Quintessential Northwest restaurant, with a dynamite wine list.

Oregon Wines on Broadway (515 SW Broadway, tel 503-288-4655) Wine bar/shop with daily selections of Pinot N for tasting.

Dundee Ponzi Wine Bar (100 7th Street, tel 503-554-1500) Focuses on Ponzi's wines, but has a broad selection of hard-to-find releases from other producers.

Seattle McCarthy & Schiering Wine Merchants (2401-B Queen Anne Ave. N, tel 206-282-8500; 6500 Ravenna Ave. NE, tel 206-524-9500) A stellar line-up of top NW names. Owner Dan McCarthy is co-author of "A Pocket Guide to the Wines of Washington, Oregon & Idaho".

Walla Walla Whitehouse Crawford (55 West Cherry St, tel 509-525-2222) THE place to eat in newly hip Walla Walla. Fabulous wood-fired food and an encyclopedic wine list.

McMinnville The International Pinot Noir Celebration (tel 1-800-775-4762; info@ipnc.org) held each July at Linfield College. A collegial, semi-educational wine and food extravaganza that brings together the world's top Pinot producers to mingle with retailers and regular folk. Best place to taste a wide range of Pinot N across a vintage.

Sokol Blosser Willamette ★→★★ **93 94 95 96** 97 **98'** 99' 00' 01 02' Much improved. Look for Pinot N. Evolution NV is also notable.

Torii Mor Yamhill County ★★→★★★ 93 94 95 96 97 98' 99' 00' Several gd single-v'yd Pinot N bottlings. New winemaker in 2000. First $100 bottle in Oregon.

Tyee S Willamette ★ Small, family-owned and run winery is esp gd with dry Gewurz, Ries, and Pinot Bl. Pinot N improving.

Willakenzie Estate Yamhill County ★→★★ **98' 99'** 00 02' First wines released 1996; delicious Pinots Gr and Bl, Chard, Pinot N. Well-financed, state-of-the-art facility; French owner and new winemaker.

Willamette Valley Vineyards Willamette ★→★★ **98'** 99' 00 01 02 Huge winery near Salem. Moderate- to very high-quality Chard, Ries, Pinot N. Amazing range from commercial to top flight. Also owns and produces v.gd Griffin Creek and Tualatin brands. New winemaker; needs watching.

Washington & Idaho

Andrew Will Puget Sound (Washington) ★★ ★★★★ **89 90 91 92 93 94 95 96 97 98'** 99' 00' 01 02 Exceptional Cab Sauv, Merlot, and barrel-fermented Chard from best E Washington grapes.

Arbor Crest Spokane ★→★★ New life from 1999 when oenologist daughter returned; tremendous talent just now showing in the wines.

Barnard Griffin Pasco, Columbia Valley (Washington) ★→★★ Small producer: well-made Merlot, Chard (esp barrel-fermented), Sem, Sauv Bl. Top Syrah.

Bookwalter Columbia Valley ★ 00' 01 02 Older estate with new life thanks to consultant Zelma Long. Rich, balanced wines, well-priced.

Canoe Ridge Walla Walla (Columbia Valley) ★ (Chard, Merlot) **95 96 97 98** 99 00 Owned by CHALONE (California). V.gd Chard and Merlot, also fine Gewurz.

Cayuse Walla Walla ★★→★★★ **98'** 99' 00' 01' 02' Striking Rhône-styles; a real sense of place. Cult following.

Château Ste-Michelle Woodinville (Washington) ★→★★★ Ubiquitous regional giant is Washington's largest winery; also owns COLUMBIA CREST, Northstar (top Merlot), Domaine Ste-Michelle, and Snoqualmie. Major E Washington v'yd holdings, first-rate equipment, and skilled winemakers keep wide range of varieties in front ranks. V'yd-designated Cab Sauv, Merlot, and Chard. Successful ventures with Antinori (Col Solare) and Ernst Loosen (Eroica).

Chinook Wines Yakima Valley (Washington) ★ Owner-winemakers purchase local grapes for sturdy Chard, Cab Sauv, Merlot, and Syrah. Look for Cab Fr.

Columbia Crest Columbia Valley ★→★★ Separately run CHÂTEAU STE-MICHELLE label for delicious, well-made, top-value wines. Cab Sauv, Merlot, Syrah, and Sauv Bl best. Also v.gd reserve wines.

Columbia Winery Woodinville ★ (Cab) **79 83 85 87 88 89 90 91 92 93** 94 95 **96** 97 **98** 99 Pioneer (1962, as Associated Vintners) and still a leader. Balanced, stylish, understated single-v'yd wines, esp Syrah and Viognier.

DeLille Cellars Woodinville ★★→★★★ **96' 97 98'** 99 00 01 02 Exciting winery for v.gd red B'x blends: ageworthy Chaleur Estate, D2 (more forward, affordable). Excellent barrel-fermented Sauv Bl/Sem. Look for new Syrah, Doyenne.

Dunham Cellars Walla Walla ★★ **95 96 97** 98' 99 00 01' 02 Young, exciting wines. Cab Sauv and Sem/Chard well extracted and elegant; lovely Syrah.

Glen Fiona Walla Walla ★★ **99 00 01'** Gd Syrahs and Syrah blends, esp a new Syrah/Cinsault/Counoise cuvée.

Gordon Brothers Columbia Valley ★→★★ Tiny cellar; consistent, balanced Chard (Reserve **91**), Merlot, Cab Sauv. Recently improving: new winemaker.

Hedges Cellars Yakima Valley ★→★★ Made its name exporting its wines to Europe and Scandinavia. Now boasts fine v'yd (Red Mountain), château-style winery, delicious Cab Sauv, Merlot, Sauv Bl.

Hogue Cellars, The Yakima Valley ★ Large well-established producer known for excellent, gd value wines, esp Ries, Chard, Merlot, Cab Sauv. Produces quintessential Washington Sauv Bl.

Indian Creek Idaho ★ **98** Top-quality Pinot N.

Kiona Vineyards Yakima Valley ★ Solid Red Mountain producer since 1980. V.gd quality/value Lemberger, Syrah, Cab Sauv.

Leonetti Walla Walla ★★★ **93 94** 95 **96'** 97 98' 99' 00' 01 02 The Washington estate in highest demand – a major collectable wine. Harmonious, individual Cab Sauv: fine and big-boned. Merlot: bold, ageworthy.

A choice of Pacific Northwest wines for 2005

Patricia Green Sauvignon Blanc	**Glen Fiona** Cuvee Parallel 46
Andrew Will Merlot Klipsun	**Woodward Canyon** Estate
Chehalem Riesling	**Adelsheim** Tocai Friulano

L'Ecole No 41 Walla Walla ★→★★ **91 92 93 94 95 96'** 97 98' 99' 00' 01 02 Blockbuster reds (Merlot, Cab Sauv, and super Meritage blend) with jammy, ageworthy fruit. Gd barrel-fermented Sem.

Matthews Cellars Woodinville ★→★★ **96' 97** 98' 99 Smaller producer of mouth-filling B'x blends since 1993. New Sem is worth hunting down.

McCrea Puget Sound ★→★★ Small winery for gd Viognier, Syrah, and Grenache. Experiments with Rhône blends continue.

Quilceda Creek Vintners Puget Sound ★★★ **87 88 89 90 91 92 93** 94 95 96' 97

98' **99 00 01 02** Expertly crafted, ripe, well-oaked Cab Sauv from Columbia Valley grapes is the speciality. Exceptional finesse and ageability. Winemaker is the nephew of the legendary André Tchelistcheff.

Reininger Walla Walla ★★ 99' 00' 01 02 Small, focused producer of top wines. Super Syrah.

Rose Creek Vineyards S Idaho ★ Small family winery; gd esp for Chard.

Ste Chapelle Caldwell (Idaho) Pleasant, forward Chard, Ries, Cab Sauv, Merlot, and Syrah from local and E Washington v'yds. Attractive sparkling wine: gd value and improving quality.

Vickers Vineyard Idaho ★ Lovely rich, barrel-fermented Chard.

Waterbrook Walla Walla ★→★★ **93** 94 95 96 97 98 99 00 Stylish, distinctive Chard, Sauv Bl, Cab Sauv, and Merlot from a winery that has hit its stride.

Woodward Canyon Walla Walla ★★ **93 94 95 96** 97 98 99' 00' 01 02 Quality-driven, loyally followed. Ripe, intense, but elegant Cab, Chard, and blends. Fabulous estate blend worth hunting down.

East of the Rockies

Producers in New York (there are now 179 in nine AVAs) and other eastern states, as well as Ohio (90 in five AVAs) traditionally made wine from hardy native grapes and French-American hybrids. Today, consumer taste plus cellar and vineyard technology largely bypass these. Chardonnay, Riesling, and Cabernet Sauvignon are now firmly established. Pinot Noir is emerging with some notable results, and Cabernet Franc and Merlot appear overall to be the East's most promising reds. There are some exciting early results with Viognier and Gewurztraminer. Progress, from Virginia to Ohio, is accelerating as the wines gain recognition outside their own immediate region.

Allegro Pennsylvania ★★ 02 03 Produces a worthy Chard and a Cab Sauv-based B'x style blend.

Anthony Road Finger Lakes 01 02 03 Fine Ries and superb late-harvest VIGNOLES.

Bedell Long Island ★★★ 00 01 02 Excellent Merlot and Cab Sauv.

Biltmore Estate ★★ 01 02 03 Largest of North Carolina's 38 wineries with Vanderbilt mansion, the state's largest. Look for Chard and sparkling.

Chaddsford Pennsylvania ★★★ 00 01 02 03 Solid producer since 1982: esp for gd Pinot Gr and B'x-style red blend.

Chamard ★★ 00 01 02 03 Connecticut's best winery, owned by Tiffany chairman. Top Chard. AVA is Southeastern New England.

Clinton Vineyards Hudson River ★★ **02 03** Clean, dry Seyval; gd sparkling version.

Debonné Vineyards Lake Erie ★★ 02 03 Largest OHIO estate winery. Chard, Ries, Pinot Gr and some hybrids: Chambourcin and Vidal.

Chateau LaFayette Reneau Finger Lakes 00 (02) **01** 03 Stylish Chard, Ries, and Cab Sauv from established producer. Stunning lakeside setting.

Constellation See California.

Finger Lakes Beautiful upstate NY cool region, source of most of state's wines. Top wineries: ANTHONY ROAD, CHATEAU LAFAYETTE RENEAU, DR FRANK, FOX RUN, GLENORA, Kings Ferry, Red Newt, Shalestone, STANDING STONE, Swedish Hill, and H WEIMER.

Firelands Lake Erie ★★ 02 03 Ohio estate making Chard, Cab Sauv, Gewurz, Pinot Gr, sparkling Ries, and Pinot N.

Fox Run Finger Lakes ★★★ 00 01 02 Continues to set the pace for serious winemaking; some of the region's best Chard, Gewurz, Ries, and Pinot N.

Frank, Dr Konstantin (Vinifera Wine Cellars) Finger Lakes ★★★ 98 **00 01** 02 03 Influential winery. The late Dr F was a pioneer in growing European vines in the FINGER LAKES. Excellent Ries, Gewurz; gd Chard, Cab Sauv, and Pinot N. Also v.gd Chateau Frank sparkling.

Glenora Wine Cellars Finger Lakes ★★ **01** 02 Makes gd sparkling wine, Chard, and Ries. Restaurant and inn with scenic lake views.

Hamptons, The (Aka South Fork) LONG ISLAND AVA. The top winery is moneyed WOLLFER ESTATE. Showcase Duck Walk is owned by PINDAR.

Hudson River Region America's oldest wine growing district (17 producers) and NY's first AVA. Straddles the river, two hours' drive N of Manhattan.

Lake Erie Largest grape-growing district in the eastern US; 25,000 acres along shore of Lake Erie, inc portions of New York, Pennsylvania, and OHIO. 90% is CONCORD (mostly used for commercial juice and jelly). Also name of a tri-state AVA: NY's sector has eight wineries, Pennsylvania's seven and Ohio's 26. Ohio's Harpersfield sets standards for quality.

Lamoreaux Landing Finger Lakes ★★★ **00 01** 02 Promising Chard, Ries, and Cab Fr from striking Greek-revival winery.

Lenz ★★★ **01** 02 03 Classy winery of NORTH FORK AVA. Fine austere Chard in the Chablis mode, also Gewurz, Merlot, and sparkling wine.

Long Island Exciting wine region E of the Rockies and a hothouse of experimentation. Currently 3,000 acres, all *vinifera* (35% Merlot) and three AVAs (LONG ISLAND, NORTH FORK, THE HAMPTONS). Most of its 29 wineries are on the North Fork. Best varieties: Chard, Cab Sauv, Merlot. A long growing season; almost frost-free. Promising new wineries inc: Martha Clara, Old Field (first wine sold 2002), Sherwood House (Chard and Merlot), Raphael.

Michigan In addition to fine cool climate Ries, impressive Gewurz, Pinot N, and Cab Fr are emerging; 40 commercial wineries and four AVAs. Best inc: St-Julien Wine Co, Ch Grand Traverse, Peninsula Cellars (esp dry Gewurz), and Tabor Hill. Mawby Vyds and Ch Chantal known for sparkling wine from Chard, Pinot N, and Pinot Meunier. Fenn Valley and Lemon Creek have large regional following. Black Star Farms, a showplace with inn, creamery and distillery. Up and coming Dom Berrien and Willow.

Millbrook Hudson River ★★★ **01** 02 03 Dedicated viticulture and savvy marketing has lifted spiffy whitewashed Millbrook in big old barn into NY's firmament. Burgundian Chards; Cab Fr can be delicious.

North Fork LONG ISLAND AVA (of three). Top wineries: Bedell, Macari, Lieb, LENZ, PALMER, PAUMANOK, PELLEGRINI, PINDAR. 2.5 hrs' drive from Manhattan.

Ohio 90 wineries, five AVAs, notably LAKE ERIE and Ohio Valley.

Palmer Long Island ★★★ **01** 02 03 Superior NORTH FORK producer and byword in Darwinian metropolitan market. High profile due to perpetual-motion marketing. Tasty Chard, Sauv Bl, and Chinon-like Cab Fr.

Paumanok Long Island ★★★ **01** 02 03 Rising NORTH FORK winery; impressive Ries, Merlot, Cab Sauv, Chard; outstanding Chenin Bl; savoury late-harvest Sauv Bl.

Pellegrini Long Island ★★★ **99** 00 **01** 02 03 An enchantingly designed winery on NORTH FORK. Opulent Merlot, stylish Chard, Bordeaux-like Cab Sauv. Inspired winemaking. Exceptionally flavourful wines.

Pindar Vineyards Long Island ★★★ 00 **01** 03 A 287-acre operation at NORTH FORK (Island's largest). Wide range of blends and popular varietals, inc Chard, Merlot, sparkling, v.gd B'x-style red blend, Mythology. Popular with tourists.

Red Newt Finger Lakes ★★★ **01** 02 03 Turns out top Chard, Ries, Cab Fr, Merlot, and B'x-inspired red blend. Popular bistro.

Sakonnet SE New England ★★ **01** 02 03 Largest New England winery, based in Little Compton, Rhode Island. Very drinkable wines inc Chard, Vidal, dry Gewurz, Cab Fr, and Pinot N. Delicious sparkling Brut cuvée.

Standing Stone Finger Lakes ★★ 00 **01** 02 One of the region's finest wineries with v.gd Ries, Gewurz, and B'x-type blend.

omasello New Jersey ★★ **00 01** 02 Gd Chambourcin, Cab Sauv, and Merlot.

Unionville Vineyards New Jersey ★★ **01** 02 03 Lovely Ries and gd red blend.

Wagner Vineyards Finger Lakes ★★ **01** 02 03 Barrel-fermented Chard, dry and sweet Ries and Icewine. Attracts many visitors.

Westport Rivers SE New England ★★ **01** 02 03 Massachusetts house established in 1989. Gd Chard and elegant sparkling.

Wiemer, Hermann J Finger Lakes ★★→★★★ **00 01** 02 03 Creative, German-born winemaker. Outstanding Ries, inc v.gd sp and late harvest. V.gd Chard.

Wolffer Estate Long Island ★★★ **00 01** 02 Modish Chard and Merlot from German-born winemaker. Proof that gd wine can be made on the South Fork.

Wollersheim ★★ Wisconsin winery specializing in variations of Maréchal Foch. Prairie Fumé (Seyval Bl) is a commercial success.

Southern & central states

Missouri A blossoming industry with over 40 producers in three AVAs: Augusta (first in the US), Hermann, and Ozark Highlands. Best wines are Seyval Bl, Vidal, Vignoles (sweet and dry versions) and Chambourcin. The top estate is Stone Hill in Hermann (since 1847). Look for its rich red made from Norton grape variety – Hermannhof (1852) is also drawing notice for the same. Other notable wineries: St James for Vignoles and Norton; Mount Pleasant in Augusta for rich "port" and nice sparkling wine; Adam Puchta for good Riefenstaher; Augusta Winery for Chambourcin, Cynthia; Blumenhof makes attractive blends; Les Bourgeois, also with dining; Montelle; Röbller.

Maryland Has 11 wineries in two AVAs. Catoctin AVA is the main growing area for Cab Sauv and Chard; Linganore is the second AVA. Best-known producer is Boordy Vineyards, making good Seyval, Chard, Cab Sauv, and sparkling wine. Basignani for good Cab Sauv, Chard, and Seyval. Fiore's Chambourcin is interesting.

Georgia The rate of new vine plantings here (hybrid and vinifera) is among the highest in the east. Look for: Three Sisters (Dahlonega), Habersham V'yds, and Chateau Elan (Braselton) which features southern splendour with v'yds, wine, and a resort.

> **Region to watch: Virginia**
> With 84 bonded wineries and six AVAs, Virginia is turning out some of the best wines in the eastern US. The modern winemaking era, which began mid-1980s, now encompasses virtually every part of the state, including Loudoun County just a few miles north of Washington DC. Wines include praiseworthy Cabernet Franc, Chardonnay, Cabernet Sauvignon, Merlot, and Viognier. Among the top producers are Barboursville, Breaux, Chrysalis, Horton, Jefferson, Kluge, Linden, Veritas, Villa Appalaccia, and Valhalla. Up-and-coming wineries: Blenheim, Keswick, and King.

The Southwest & the Rockies
Texas

The fifth-largest wine-producing state in the US has over 40 bonded wineries and seven AVAs. The best wines compare well with California.

Becker Vineyards ★★★ Stonewall. V.gd Cab Sauv, Chard, Ries, Chenin Bl.

La Buena Vida Vineyards ★ Tasting room in Grapevine (nr Dallas). Produces tables wines under brands of Springtown, Walnut Creek Cellars, and La Buena Vida. V.gd Walnut Creek "ports".

Cap Rock ★★★ Nr Lubbock. Reliably gd varietals: Cab Sauv, Chard. Well-crafted blends, esp Cabernet Royale.

Cross Timbers Nr Dallas. Gd Cab Sauv and Merlot.

Delaney Vineyards ★★ Nr Dallas. V.gd Sauv Bl; gd Chard and Merlot.

Dry Comal (TX Hill Country) Gd Merlot and Chard.

Haak Vineyard & Winery (Galveston County) ★ Both vinifera and hybrids with v.gd Blanc du Bois.

Llano Estacado ★★★ Nr Lubbock. The pioneer (since 1976) continues on award winning track with Chard (esp Cellar Select), Chenin Bl, and Zin. V.gd blends esp Signature Series and Viviano.

Messina Hof Wine Cellars ★★★ Nr Bryan. Most award-winning wines in the state Excellent Ries, Chard (Private Reserve), Merlot, and Cab Sauv. V.gd port-style wines. Has restaurant and deluxe B&B.

Pheasant Ridge Nr Lubbock. V.gd Chard and Chenin Bl; promising Pinot N.

Sister Creek Boerne. Boutique winery with v.gd Pinot N, Chard, Muscat Canelli.

Ste-Genevieve ★ Fort Stockton. Largest Texas winery, linked with Domaines Cordier (France). Well-made NV wines, esp Sauv Bl. Now has premium label Escondido Valley wines, esp Chard, Cab Sauv, and Syrah.

Spicewood Gd Sem and Cab Fr.

New Mexico, etc

New Mexico Continues to show promise with more emphasis on *vinifera* grapes, though some French hybrids are still used (historic Mission grape is produced at Tularosa Winery). Over 30 wineries, three AVAs. Black Mesa: ★ V.gd Cab Sauv, Pinot Gr, Merlot; gd blends, esp Coyote (r). Casa Rondeña ★★ V.gd Cab Fr and Sangiovese. Corrales: ★★ Gd blends; v.gd Cab Sauv. Gruet: ★★★ Excellent sp and v.gd Chard and Pinot N. Jory: v.gd Sauv B and Zin. La Chiripada: ★★ V.gd Ries and blends, some with hybrids; gd port-style wine. La Querencia: ★→★★ new in 2002, winning medals with Lemberger, Cab Fr, and Chambourcin. Milagro V'yds: v.gd Chard and Cab Sauv. Ponderosa Valley: ★★ V.gd Ries, gd Pinot N, Merlot, and blends, esp Summer Sage and Jemez Red. Santa Fe V'yds: ★ v.gd Sauv Bl and Merlot. La Viña: ★★ V.gd Chard and Zin; gd blends, esp Rojo Loco. St Clair, Blue Teal V'yds, Mademoiselle V'yds, DH Lescombes, and Santa Rita Cellars all under winemaker Florent Lescombes have a gd variety of wines.

Colorado Focus is on vinifera grapes, with over 600 acres planted, mostly on the Western Slope. Has over 40 wineries and two AVAs. Leading producers include: Carlson Cellars: ★★★ v.gd Gewurz and Ries. Canyon Wind: gd Chard and Merlot. Cottonwood Cellars: rich Cab Sauv; gd Merlot and Chard. Garfield Estates: promising Merlot, Cab Fr, v.gd Sauv Bl. Grande River ★★→★★★ v.gd Chard; gd Merlot, Sem, Syrah, Viognier. Plum Creek: ★ gd Chard and Merlot. Terror Creek: ★★ small with gd Pinot N, Ries, Gewurz. Trail Ridge: gd Gewurz and Ries.

Arizona Progress has been made in overall quality and the number of wineries. Success with Rhône and Mediterranean grape varieties: Sangiovese, Syrah, Petite Sirah show promise. Callaghan Vineyards: ★★ Excellent Temp-based Padres, v.gd Syrah, Cab Sauv, and blends, esp Caitlin's selection. Dos Cabezas: ★ V.gd Cab Sauv, Petite Sirah, Sangiovese. Kokopelli: Arizona's largest winery, makes sound, reasonably priced wines.

Oklahoma The region has expanded to over 15 wineries, with some emphasis on native American grapes. Stone Bluff Cellars: gd Vignoles, Cynthiana, and blends. Nuyaka Creek winery: gd Chard and fruit wines.

Utah Improved state wine regulations may bolster winery/grape growth. Spanish Valley (Moab) is the source of gd Ries and Cab Sauv.

Nevada Pahrump Valley nr Las Vegas has v.gd Chard, Cab Sauv, and Symphony. Tahoe Ridge (Minden) shows promise.

Canada

British Columbia

This expanding and significant part of the Canadian wine industry has grown up since the 1970s. The biggest concentration of wineries is in the splendid Okanagan Valley around a vast lake, 150 miles east of Vancouver, in climatic conditions not very different from eastern Washington. There are 50 wineries and four appellations (Okanagan Valley, Frasier Valley, Similkameen Valley, and Vancouver Island).

Blue Mountain 98 00 01 02 03 Outstanding Pinots (N, Gr, Bl) and sparkling.

Burrowing Owl 00 01 02 03 Excellent Chard and Pinot Gr; promising reds.

Calona Vineyards ★★ 00 01 02 03 Large winery. Gd Pinot Bl and Merlot.

Cedar Creek ★★★ 00 01 02 03 Outstanding Chard, Pinot Bl, Pinot N. Tapas-style restaurant.

Mission Hill ★→★★★ 00 01 02 03 Acclaimed Reserve Chard, Pinot Bl, Syrah. Notable collection of antiques and tapestries.

Quails' Gate ★★ 00 01 02 03 Chard, Pinot N, Ries, Late Harvest Optima.

Sumac Ridge ★★ 00 01 02 Gewurz, Sauv Bl, sparkling among region's best. Notable Meritage and Merlot. (Owned by VINCOR.)

Ontario

The main eastern Canada wine region, on Niagara Peninsula, Pelee Island, and LAKE ERIE north shore: 80 wineries. Three small boutique wineries (Thirty Bench, Malivoire, Thirteenth Street) are raising the quality bar here. Riesling, Chardonnay, Cabernet Franc, Pinot Noir show potential for longevity. Icewine is the international flagship of region. Gewurztraminer and Pinot Gris showing promise. 2002 vintage generally stellar.

Andres 00 01 **02** 03 Second-largest Canadian winery. Owns HILLEBRAND and Peller Estates.

Cave Spring Cellars ★★★ 01 **02** 03 Ontario boutique: sophisticated Chard, Ries, and Gamay. Big restaurant, popular tourist stop, 28-room inn.

Château des Charmes ★★★ 00 01 **02** 03 Show-place château-style winery. Fine Chard, Viognier, Cab Sauv, sparkling.

Henry of Pelham ★★★ 00 01 **02** 03 Elegant Chard and Ries; Cab Sauv/Merlot, distinctive Baco Noir, Icewine.

Hillebrand Estates ★→★★★ 00 01 **02** 03 Attracting attention with Ries, sparkling, and B'x-style red blend. Handsome restaurant.

Inniskillin ★★★★ 00 01 **02** 03 Important (VINCOR-owned) producer that spearheaded birth of modern Ontario wine industry. Skilful burgundy-style Chard, Pinot N; also B'x-style red. V.gd Ries, Icewine (inc sp), Pinot Gr.

Konzelmann ★★★ Top Ries, Chard, and Icewine.

Peninsula Ridge ★★★ 00 01 **02** 03 Established in 2000, already showing gd Chard, Merlot, and delicious Icewine. Restaurant with panoramic view of Lake Ontario.

Vincor International ★→★★ Fourth-largest company in N America. (California's RH PHILLIPS; Washington's HOGUE CELLARS.) Premium wines, varietals, blends. Owns Jackson-Triggs, INNISKILLIN (Chard, Cab Sauv), Sumac Ridge, also Goundrey (Australia) and Kim Crawford (New Zealand).

Vineland Estates ★★★ 00 01 **02** 03 Gd producer; dry and semi-dry Ries, Gewurz much admired. VIDAL Icewine: gd, Chard, Cab Sauv, Sauv Bl, and B'x-style red. Excellent restaurant and tasting room.

Vintners Quality Alliance Canada's appellation body, started in Ontario but now inc British Columbia. Its rigid standards have rapidly raised respect and awareness of Canadian wines. VQA enacted into Ontario law in 2000.

Central & South America

More heavily shaded areas
are the wine growing regions

Chile

It's true, Chilean wine can be boring, if made using grapes from over-cropped, over-irrigated young vines on fertile soils. But thanks to increased respect for *terroir*, and more sensitive winemaking, the best Chilean wines now have a complexity and flavour that has more in common with southern Europe than other parts of the New World. Indeed *terroir*-driven premium wines from Viña Errazuriz took three of the top four places in a bench-mark tasting held in Berlin in 2004, against top wines from Bordeaux and Tuscany (see p.246).

Carmenère, the old Bordeaux grape that the Chileans misidentified as Merlot for many years, is hailed as a unique selling point. On its own, it can be rather one-dimensional, but the oily spice notes it lends to Bordeaux blends can be very attractive. Cabernet Sauvignon remains the most important grape variety, although Syrah is also proving successful, particular on hillside sites. Whites lag behind. It's just too warm in most parts of the 300-mile long Central Valley to the south of Santiago which is home to most vineyards (virtually all irrigated, mostly ungrafted). But in regions closer to the coast such as (from north to south) Limari, Casablanca and Leyda or much further south such as Bío-Bío, decent Chardonnay and Sauvignon Blanc (and Pinot Noir) can now be found.

Recent vintages

Most wines are ready to drink on release, although the better reds improve for up to five years. Curiously, odd years have been best for reds in recent vintages.

2003 Warm, low-yielding year. High-quality reds; whites may lack crispness.

2002 Good in Maipo and Aconcagua, more patchy further south due to rain.

2001 Near-perfect conditions, generally lower yields, very high quality.

2000 Large, cool vintage. Good vineyard managers made excellent aromatic wines.

1999 Low yields and drought produced concentrated (some slightly baked) reds.

1998 Cool, El Niño-affected season; erratic ripening and high yields.

Aconcagua Northernmost quality wine region. Inc CASABLANCA, Panquehue, Leyda.

Almaviva See BARON PHILIPPE DE ROTHSCHILD.

Antiyal ★★★ New MAIPO venture from Alvaro Espinoza, making fine and complex red from organically grown fruit.

Apaltagua ★★→★★★ Carmenère specialist drawing on old-vine fruit from Apalta (Colchagua). Grial is rich, herbal flagship wine.

Baron Philippe de Rothschild ★★★→★★★★ B'x company making gd Mapa varietal range, better Escudo Rojo red blend, and expensive but classy, claret-style Almaviva, the latter a MAIPO joint venture with CONCHA Y TORO.

Bío-Bío Southernmost quality wine region. Potential for gd whites and Pinot N.

Calina, Viña ★★ Kendall-Jackson (see California) venture. Better reds (esp Selección de Las Lomas Cab Sauv) than whites, with silky Elite Cab Sauv the pick. El Caliz is gd, intro-level range.

Caliterra ★★→★★★ Sister winery of ERRÁZURIZ. Chard and Sauv Bl improving (more CASABLANCA grapes), reds becoming less one-dimensional; esp Reserva range. California's Mondavi is partner for the v.gd Arboleda wines (Cab Sauv, Syrah, Carmenère, Merlot, Chard) and Seña (★★★★), a Cab Sauv/Merlot/Carmenère blend launched in 1997.

Cánepa, José ★★ Back on song after upheavals in mid-1990s; lemony Sem and spicy Zin among the more unusual wines, juicy berryish Malbec and fragrant Syrah Reserve among the best.

Carmen, Viña ★★→★★★ MAIPO winery under same ownership as SANTA RITA. Ripe, fresh Special Res (CASABLANCA) Chard and deliciously light Late-harvest MAIPO Sem top whites. Reds even better; esp RAPEL Merlots, MAIPO Petite Sirah, and Cab Sauvs, esp Gold Reserve. Now does v.gd MAIPO Syrah/Cab Sauv and has an organic range called Nativa.

Carta Vieja ★★ MAULE winery owned by one family for six generations. Reds, esp Cab Sauv and Merlot, better than whites; but Antigua Selección Chard is gd.

Casa Lapostolle ★★★ Money from the family of Grand Marnier and advice from Michel Rolland (see France) result in fine range. B'x-style Sauv Bl is gd, but reds, led by stunning (but pricey) Merlot-based Clos Apalta, are even better.

Casablanca Cool-climate region between Santiago and coast. Little water: drip irrigation essential. Top-class Chard, Sauv Bl; promising Merlot, Pinot N.

Casablanca, Viña ★★★ Sister winery to SANTA CAROLINA. RAPEL and MAIPO fruit used for some reds; but better wines – Merlot, Sauv Bl, Chard, Gewurz – come from Santa Isabel Estate in CASABLANCA. Look for new super-cuvée Neblus.

Casa Silva ★★ Colchagua estate offering pithy Classic Sem, spicy, chunky Reserva Merlot, and top-of-the-range Quinta Generación Red and White; the white is a very successful blend of Chard, Sauv Gr, and Viognier.

Concha y Toro ★→★★★★ Mammoth but quality-minded operation, gd value. Top wines: increasingly subtle Amelia Chard (CASABLANCA); rich, chocolatey Marqués de Casa Concha Merlot (RAPEL); inky Don Melchor Cab Sauv (RAPEL); and silky Terrunyo Pinot N (CASABLANCA). Impressive Winemaker

Lot. Copper Range, Trio, Explorer, and Casillero del Diablo (inc fine new Viognier) offer v.gd value. See also BARON PHILIPPE DE ROTHSCHILD.

Cono Sur ★★→★★★ Chimbarongo winery owned by CONCHA Y TORO for v.gd Pinot N (local and CASABLANCA fruit). Also dense, fruity Cab Sauv, delicious Viognier, and spicy Zin. New innovations under Visión label, top releases appear as "20 Barrels" selection. Second label Isla Negra.

Cousiño Macul ★★→★★★ Established firm, recently relocated from historic MAIPO estate to establish new v'yds in Buin. Fresher, more modern styles since 2001. Long-lived Antiguas Res Cab Sauv; top wine Finis Terrae (B'x blend).

Domus ★★★ MAIPO single-v'yd venture making gd Chard and v.gd Cab Sauv. Patrick Valette (see EL PRINCIPAL).

Echeverría ★★ Boutique Curicó (MAULE) winery producing reliable Reserve Cab Sauv, v.gd oaked and unoaked Chard and improving Sauv Bl.

Edwards, Luís Felipé ★★ Colchagua (RAPEL) winery; citrus Chard, silky Reserve Cab Sauv. Wines now made by an ex-Penfolds winemaker.

El Principal, Viña ★★★ Excellent Pirque (MAIPO) estate making complex B'x blends under the guidance of Patrick Valette of Ch Berliquet in St Emilion. El Principal is top wine, Memorias the impressive second cuvée.

Errázuriz ★★★ Main winery in Panquehue district of ACONCAGUA. First-class range, inc complex, mealy Wild Ferment Chard (now partnered by a Pinot N); brooding Syrah; Chile's best Sangiovese; earthy, plummy Merlot; fine Cab Sauv topped by Don Maximiano Reserve. Award-winning premium wines Viñedo Chadwick (00), Seña (00 01) excellent but pricey. Also see CALITERRA.

Falernia, Viña Winery in far N Elqui Valley where fruit flavours are extreme. So far Sauv Bl and Merlot are very tasty.

Fortuna, Viña La ★★ Established winery in Lontué Valley. Attractive range.

Francisco de Aguirre, Viña ★★ Promising Cabs Sauv and Fr and Chard under the Palo Alto label from the northerly region of Valle de Limari.

Gracia de Chile ★★ Winery with v'yds from ACONCAGUA down to BÍO-BÍO. Cab Sauv Reserva R is best; gd Pinot N and Chard. Plans for Mourvèdre and Syrah.

Haras de Pirque ★★ New estate in Pirque (MAIPO). Smoky Sauv Bl, stylish Chard, dense Cab Sauv/Merlot. Joint venture with Tuscany's Antinori (see Italy).

Larose, Viña de ★ RAPEL venture by Médoc Ch Larose-Trintaudon under the Las Casas del Toqui and Viña Alamosa labels. Promising top-end Leyenda Chard and red blend.

Leyda, Viña ★★ Sole winery in Leyda (see introduction p.244), producing elegant Chard and lush Pinot N. Also decent MAIPO Cab Sauv and RAPEL Merlot.

Maipo Famous wine region close to Santiago. Chile's best Cab Sauvs often come from higher eastern sub-regions such as Pirque and Puente Alto.

Maule Southernmost region in Central Valley. Claro, Loncomilla, Tutuven Valleys.

Montes ★★→★★★ Alpha Cab Sauv can be brilliant; Merlot, Syrah, and Malbec also fine; Chard v.gd. B'x blend Montes Alpha M is improving with each vintage, while Folly Syrah is outstanding – the best in Chile.

MontGras ★★→★★★★ State-of-the-art Colchagua winery with fine limited-edition wines, inc Syrah and Zin. High-class flagship Ninquen Cab Sauv.

Morande ★★ Vast range inc César, Cinsault, Bouschet, Carignan. Limited Edition used for top wines, inc a spicy Syrah/Cab Sauv and inky Malbec. Gd value.

Odfjell ★→★★★★ MAIPO-based, Norwegian-owned red specialist. Top wine rich but elegant Aliara Cab Sauv; Orzada range, inc perfumed Cab Fr and plummy Carignan (both MAULE) also v.gd.

Paul Bruno ★★ MAIPO joint venture of Paul Pontallier and Bruno Prats from B'x with Chilean Felipé de Solminihac and Ghislain de Montgolfier of Champagne Bollinger. Flagship wine improving as vines age. Also promising Sol de Sol Chard from BÍO-BÍO.

Pérez Cruz ★★★ New MAIPO winery with Alvaro Espinoza (see ANTIYAL) in charge of winemaking. Debut 2002 reds inc fresh but spicy Syrah. Stylish Liguai (Cab Sauv/Syrah/Carmenère) is uniformly excellent.

Porta, Viña ★★ MAIPO winery under same ownership as GRACIA DE CHILE, offering reliable range inc supple, spicy Cab Sauv.

Rapel Central quality region divided into Colchagua and Cachapoal valleys. Source of great Merlot. Watch out for sub-region Marchihue in the future.

La Rosa, Viña ★★ Reliable, if seldom exciting, RAPEL Chard, Merlot, and Cab Sauv under La Palmeria and Cornellana labels. Don Reca Merlot is the star.

San Pedro ★★→★★★ Massive Curicó-based producer. Gato and 35 South (35 Sur) are reliable top-sellers. Best wines: Castillo de Molina and 1865 reds.

Santa Carolina, Viña ★★→★★★ Historic bodega; increasingly impressive and complex wines. All MAIPO Reserve wines are gd, inc a rich, limey Sauv Bl. Barrica Selection range, inc earthy Carmenère and supple Syrah, is better still. New Cab Sauv/Merlot/Syrah VSC is complex and excellent value.

Santa Inés ★★ Successful small family winery in Isla de MAIPO making ripe, blackcurranty Legado de Armida Cab Sauv. Also labelled as De Martino.

Santa Mónica ★→★★★ Rancagua (RAPEL) winery; the best label is Tierra del Sol. Ries, Sém, and Merlot under Santa Mónica label also gd.

Santa Rita ★★→★★★★ Long-established, quality-conscious MAIPO bodega. Range in ascending quality: 120, Reserva, Medalla Real, Floresta (inc fine red blends and v.gd Sauv Bl), Casa Real. Best: Casa Real MAIPO Cab Sauv; but Triple C (Cab Sauv/Cab Fr/Carmenère) nearly as gd.

Selentia New Chilean/Spanish venture. Reserve Special Cab Sauv is fine.

Seña See CALITERRA.

Tarapacá, Viña ★★ MAIPO winery improved after investment, but inconsistent.

Terramater ★★ Wines from throughout Central Valley, inc v.gd Altum range.

Terranoble ★★→★★★ Talca winery specializing in grassy Sauv Bl and light, peppery Merlot. Range now inc v.gd spicy Carmenère Gran Reserva.

Torreón de Paredes ★★ Attractive, crisp Chard, ageworthy Reserve Cab Sauv from this RAPEL bodega. Flagship Don Amedo Cab Sauv could be better.

Torres, Miguel ★★★ Pioneering Curicó winery with fresh whites and gd reds, esp sturdy Manso del Velasco single-v'yd Cab Sauv and Cariñena-based Cordillera. See also Spain.

Undurraga ★★ Traditional MAIPO estate known for its Pinot N. Top wines: Reserva Chard, refreshing, limey Gewurz, peachy Late Harvest Sem.

Valdivieso ★★ Major producer with new Lontué winery. Single-v'yd Cab Fr, Merlot, Malbec, and NV blend Caballo Loco are pick of the range. Reserve bottlings also gd, but quality more erratic among the cheaper wines.

Vascos, Los ★★→★★★ Lafite-Rothschild venture making Cab Sauv in B'x mould. Recent vintages show more fruit than earlier efforts. Top wines: Le Dix and Grande Réserve.

Veramonte ★★ CASABLANCA-based operation of Agustín Huneeus (formerly of California winery Franciscan); whites from CASABLANCA fruit, red from Central Valley grapes – all gd. Top wine: Primus red blend.

Villard ★★ Sophisticated wines made by French-born Thierry Villard. Gd MAIPO reds, esp heady Merlot, Equis Cab Sauv, and CASABLANCA whites. Also very alluring CASABLANCA Pinot N.

Viñedos Organicos Emiliana (VOE) ★★→★★★ Organic/biodynamic arm of Santa Emiliana (part of CONCHA Y TORO), with Alvaro Espinoza (see ANTIYAL) as consultant. Novas varietal range has tasty entry-level wines, while complex, heady red blend Coyam is a stunning bargain.

Viu Manent ★★ Emerging Colchagua winery; best of fine range are plummy Cab Sauv, exotic Merlot, and dense, fragrant Viu 1. Look for Syrah in the future.

Argentina

Much of Argentina may still be under an economic cloud, but there is a new confidence about the wine industry. The devalued peso has made the country attractive to export markets and overseas investors, and this, allied with continuing leaps in wine quality, makes a winning combination. A healthy tension between local and foreign winemaking talent ensures that quality continues to improve. The warm, dry climate, watered by snow-melt from the Andes, makes grape-growing relatively easy, although hail is a threat. Vineyard conditions are determined more by altitude than latitude. Mendoza is the most important area and Malbec remains the most successful grape variety. Decent Cabernet Sauvignon exists, Syrah shows promise, and a few producers are finally taking advantage of the mature vineyards of Tempranillo, Sangiovese, and Bonarda. Chardonnay and Sauvignon Blanc can be very fair, but spicy Torrontés makes the most distinctive wines; though not to everyone's taste.

Recent vintages

As a general rule, whites and cheaper reds should be drunk as young as possible.

2003 Frosts and hail, but otherwise the vintage was fine and dry.

2002 A good vintage, resulting in the best wines for more than a decade.

2001 Quality is variable, but some very good reds.

2000 Rain and hail caused problems, but some excellent reds.

1999 A drought year. Some rich, full-bodied red wines.

1998 The El Niño vintage. Dilute, occasionally unripe reds, but some are good.

Achaval Ferrer ★★★→★★★★ MENDOZA. Super-concentrated Finca Altamira Malbec and Quimera Malbec/Cab Sauv/Merlot blend.

La Agrícola ★ Dynamic MENDOZA estate producing gd value Santa Julia range, led by new blend "Magna" and better "Q" label (impressive Malbec, Merlot, Temp). Terra Organica organic wines: gd but not great.

Alta Vista ★★★ French-owned MENDOZA venture specializing in Malbec. Dense, spicy Alto among best wines in the country. Also fresh, zesty Torrontés.

Altos las Hormigas ★★★ Italian-owned Malbec specialist, wines made by consultant Alberto Antonini (ex-Italy's Antinori). Top wine: Viña las Hormigas.

Anubis ★★ Joint venture between Alberto Antonini and Susana Balbo, making exciting juicy reds, esp Malbec.

Arizù, Leoncio ★★ Small MENDOZA (Maipù) bodega with three tiers of quality – Viña Paraiso, Luigi Bosca, and Finca Los Nobles. High standards with esp gd Los Nobles Malbec/Verdot and Cab Sauv/Bouchet.

Balbi, Bodegas ★★ Allied-Domecq-owned San Raphael producer. Juicy Malbec, Chard, and delicious Syrah (red and rosé). Red blend Barbaro also v.gd.

Bianchi, Valentin ★ San Rafael red specialist. Familia Bianchi (Cab Sauv) is excellent flagship. Gd value Elsa's Vineyard inc meaty Barbera. Pithy Sauv Bl.

Canale, Bodegas Humberto ★★ Premier Río Negro winery known for its Sauv Bl and Pinot N, but Merlot and Malbec (esp Black River label) are the stars.

Catena ★→★★★★ Style can be a little international, but quality is always gd. Range rises from Malambo through Argento, Alamos Ridge, Catena, Catena Alta, to flagship Nicolas Catena Zapata and a new trio of fine single-v'yd Malbecs. Also red blend Caro made with the Rothschilds of Lafite.

Clos de los Siete ★★ Seven parcels of French-owned vines in MENDOZA, run by Michel Rolland (see France). A juicy Malbec already exists, but each site will produce its own wine.

Chandon, Bodegas ★→★★ Makers of Baron B and M Chandon sparklers under Moët & Chandon supervision; promising Pinot N/Chard blend. See TERRAZAS.

Dominio del Plata ★→★★★ EX-CATENA husband-and-wife pair Susana Balbo and Pedro Marchevsky produce superior wines under the Crios, Susana Balbo, and BenMarco labels.

Doña Paula ★ Luján de Cuyo estate owned by Santa Rita (see Chile) making dense, structured Malbec.

Etchart ★★→★★★ Pernod-Ricard owned, two wineries: SALTA and MENDOZA. Reds from both regions gd, topped by plummy Cafayate Cab Sauv.

Fabre Montmayou ★★ French-owned Luján de Cuyo (MENDOZA) bodega; fine reds and advice from Michel Rolland (see France). Also decent Chard.

Finca La Anita ★★→★★★ MENDOZA estate making high-class reds, esp Syrah and Malbec, and intriguing whites, inc Sem and Tocai Friulano.

Finca Colomé ★★★ SALTA bodega known for very Rhône-like Cab Sauv/Merlot blend. New owner California's Hess Collection is still to release its first wines.

Finca Flichman ★★ Old company: two wineries in MENDOZA now owned by Portugal's Sogrape. Gd value Syrah. Top wine: Dedicato blend.

Finca El Retiro ★★ MENDOZA bodega making gd Malbec Bonarda and Temp. See ALTOS LAS HORMIGAS.

Lurton, Bodegas J & F ★→★★ MENDOZA venture of Jacques and François Lurton. Juicy, concentrated Piedra Negra Malbec heads range; also has decent Pinot Gr, Malbec, and Cab Sauv.

Masi Tupungato ★★→★★★★ MENDOZA enterprise for the well-known Valpolicella producer (see Italy). Passo Doble is fine Ripasso-style Malbec/Corvino blend, Corbec is even better Amarone lookalike from Corvina and Malbec.

Mendoza Most important province for wine (over 70% of plantings). Best sub-regions: Agrelo, Tupungato, Luján de Cuyo, and Maipú.

Navarro Correas ★★ Gd if sometimes over-oaked reds, esp Col Privada Cab Sauv. Also reasonable whites, inc very oaky Chard and Deutz-inspired fizz.

Nieto Senetiner, Bodegas ★★ Luján de Cuyo-based bodega. Gd value under Valle de Vistalba label, plus recently introduced top-of-range Cadus reds.

Norton, Bodegas ★★★ Old bodega, now Austrian-owned. Gd whites and v.gd reds, esp chunky Malbec and Privada blend (Merlot/Cab Sauv/Malbec).

O Fournier ★→★★★ Spanish-owned Valle de Uco bodega making impressive Temp-based wines. Best wines are Temp/Merlot/Malbec blends Crux.

Patagonia, Viña ★→★★ Owned by Concha y Toro of Chile, making gd value international Malbec, Syrah, Cab Sauv, Merlot, Chard under Trivento label.

Peñaflor ★→★★★ Argentina's biggest wine company. Labels inc Andean Vineyards and for finer wines, TRAPICHE.

Río Negro Promising new area in Patagonia.

Salentein, Bodegas ★★ Ambitious new Valle de Uco (MENDOZA) bodega, already succeeding with Cab Sauv, Malbec, Merlot, and (under the Primus label) Pinot N. Entry-level wines appear as Finca El Portillo or La Pampa.

Salta Northerly province with the world's highest v'yds. Sub-region Cafayate renowned for Torrontés.

San Pedro de Yacochuya ★★★ SALTA collaboration between Michel Rolland (see France) and the ETCHART family. Ripe but fragrant Torrontés, dense, earthy Malbec, and powerful, stunning Yacochuya Malbec from oldest vines.

San Telmo ★★ Modern Seagram-owned winery making fresh, full-flavoured Chard, Chenin Bl, Merlot. Best: Malbec and Cab Sauv Cruz de Piedra-Maipú.

Santa Ana, Bodegas ★ Old-established family firm at Guaymallen, MENDOZA. Malbec Reserva is pick of a wide but rather uninspiring range.

Tacuil, Bodegas ★★★ New SALTA venture for Raul Davalos, former owner of FINCA COLMÉ. 33 de Davalos is excellent spicy Cab Sauv/Malbec blend.

Terrazas ★★→★★★★ CHANDON enterprise for still wines made from Malbec, Cab Sauv, Chard, Syrah. Three ranges: entry-level Alto (juicy Cab Sauv is the

star), mid-price Reserva, and top-of-the-tree Gran Terrazas. Also join
venture with Ch Cheval Blanc of B'x making superb Cheval des Andes blend.

Torino, Michel ★★ Rapidly improving organic Cafayate enterprise, esp Cab Sauv.

Trapiche ★★→★★★ Premium label of PEÑAFLOR. Labels in ascending quality
order are Astica, Trapiche (pick is Oak Cask Syrah), Fond de Cave (gd
Malbec Reserva), Medalla (plummy Cab Sauv), and pricey red blend Iscay.

Val de Flores ★★★★ Another Michel Rolland-driven enterprise close to CLOS DE
LOS SIETE (MENDOZA) for compelling yet elegant old-vine Malbec.

Viniterra ★→★★ Clean, modern wines under Omnium, Bykos, Viniterra labels.

Weinert, Bodegas ★→★★ Potentially fine reds, esp Cavas de Weinert blend
(Cab Sauv/Merlot/Malbec), are often spoiled by extended ageing in old oak.

Other Central & South American wines

Bolivia With a generally hot, humid climate, annual domestic consumption of
just one bottle per capita, only 2,000 ha of grapes (most destined for fiery
aguardiente brandy), and only 10 wineries, this is not a major wine producer.
Even so, wines from **Vinos y Viñedos La Concepción**, especially the Cab
Sauvs, are good and show what is possible. The vineyards, 1,000 km S of La
Paz, lie at altitudes of up to 2,800 m, making them the highest in the world.

Brazil New plantings of better grapes are transforming a big, booming industry
with an increasing home market. International investment, especially in Rio
Grande do Sul and Santana do Liuramento, notably from France and Italy,
are significant, and point to possible exports. The sandy Frontera region and
Sierra Gaucha hills (Italian-style sparkling) are to watch. More than two crops
a year are possible in some equatorial vineyards. So far quality from these
has been basic, but look out for fruits of a new project involving Portuguese
winemaker Rui Reguinga. Of the wines that do leave Brazil, 95% are made
by the massive **Vinicola Aurora (Bento Gonçalves)**. Look for **Amazon** label.

Mexico Oldest Latin American wine industry is reviving, with investment from
abroad (eg Freixenet, Martell, Domecq) and California influence via UC Davis.
Best in Baja California (85% of total), Querétaro, and on the Aguascalientes
and Zacatecas plateaux. Top Baja C producers are **Casa de Piedra** (very
impressive Temp/Cab Sauv), **L A Cetto** (Valle de Guadaloupe, the largest, esp
for Cab Sauv, Nebbiolo, Petite Sirah), **Bodegas Santo Tomás** (now working
with California's Wente Brothers to make Duetto, using grapes from both
sides of the border), **Monte Xanic** (with Napa-award winning Cab Sauv),
Bodegas San Antonio, and **Cavas de Valmar**. The premium Chard and Cab
Sauv from Monterrey-based **Casa Madero** are also good. **Marqués de Aguayo**
is the oldest (1593), now only for brandy.

Peru Viña Tacama near Ica (top wine region) exports some pleasant wines, esp
the Gran Vino Blanco white; also Cab Sauv and classic-method sparkling.
Chincha, Moquegua, and Tacha regions are slowly making progress. But
phylloxera is a serious problem.

Uruguay Uruguay's point of difference is Tannat, the rugged and tannic grape
responsible for Madiran in SW France. Tannat alone produces a sturdy,
plummy red, better blended with more supple Merlot and Cab Fr. A few
producers offer decent Gewurz and Chard, while the promising **De Lucca** has
Roussanne and Syrah. Five different viticultural zones were established in
1992, but the name of the producer is the more important. **Carrau/Castel
Pujol** is among the most impressive wineries. Its Amat Gran Tradición 1752
and Las Violetas Reserva show Tannat at its most fragrant. Other wineries
inc: Bruzzone & Sciutto, Casa Filguera, Castillo Viejo, Los Cerros de San Juan,
Dante Irurtia, Juanicó, Pisano, Carlos Pizzorno, and Stagnari.

Australia

Heavier shaded areas are the wine growing regions

The influence of Australia in the modern wine world is out of all proportion to the size of its vineyards. They represent less than 4% of global production, yet Australian wines, ideas, and names are on all wine-lovers' lips. In seventeen years, its exports have grown from eight to 508 million litres and the number of wineries has climbed to over 1,700. Even growers in the south of France listen to Australian winemakers. Australia has mastered easy-drinking wine and is making some of the world's very best.

Its classics are Shiraz, Semillon, and Riesling. In the 1970s they were joined by Cabernet Sauvignon, Merlot, Chardonnay, and Pinot Noir. In the 1990s, Sauvignon Blanc, Grenache, and Mourvèdre were rediscovered. Next seem to be Tempranillo and Pinot Gris. Cool fermentation and the use of new barrels accompanied a general move to cooler areas. For a while, excessive oak flavour was a common problem. Moderation is now the fashion – and sparkling wine of highly satisfactory quality is a new achievement.

Australia faces a major challenge in managing its own helter-skelter growth. Take-over battles and big company egos do not help. Australia has to find ways to more than double its exports over the next ten years without damaging its reputation. Chardonnay was its flag-bearer in the 1980s and 1990s; it is now betting on Shiraz doing the trick in the current decade. The debate is whether supermarket brands or truly fine wines are the key to Australia's future.

AUSTRALIA

Recent vintages

New South Wales
2003 Continued drought broken by heavy rain in Jan/Feb; variable outcomes.

2002 Heavy Feb rain caused problems in all but two areas. Riverina outstanding.

2001 Extreme summer heat and ill-timed rain set the tone; remarkably, Hunter Valley Semillon shone.

2000 A perfect growing season for the Hunter Valley, but dire for the rest of the state; extreme heat followed by vintage rain.

1999 Another Hunter success; rain when needed. Other regions variable.

1998 Good to excellent everywhere; good winter rain, warm, dry summer.

1997 Heavy rain bedevilled the Hunter; Mudgee, Orange and Canberra all starred.

1996 Yields varied, but very good wine in most regions.

1995 Severe drought slashed yields and stressed fruit; good at best.

1994 Hunter heatwaves and fires followed by torrential rain didn't help; good red wines elsewhere, particularly Mudgee.

1993 Unusually cool, wet spring and summer diminished quality; excellent autumn saved Canberra and Hilltops.

1992 Continuation of the 1991 drought followed by brief vintage flooding soured Hunter, Mudgee, and Cowra; others fared rather better.

Victoria
2003 Overall, fared better than other states, except for bushfire-ravaged Alpine Valleys.

2002 Extremely cool weather led to tiny yields, but wines of high quality.

2001 Did not escape the heat; a fair-to-good red vintage, whites more variable.

2000 Southern and central regions flourished in warm and dry conditions; terrific reds. Northeast poor; vintage rain.

1999 Utterly schizophrenic; Yarra disastrous (vintage rain); some other southern and central regions superb; northeast up and down.

1998 Drought and Oct frost did not spoil an outstanding year in all regions, notably for Shiraz, Cabernet Sauvignon, and Merlot.

1997 Few, but very high-quality grapes, especially Pinot Noir in the south.

1996 Extremely variable. Far southwest, Grampians, and Bendigo did well.

1995 Disappointing; hot summer, wet autumn. Grampains and Geelong good.

1994 Quality saved by a glorious Indian summer; good to excellent throughout.

1993 Cooler red-wine regions fared best.

1992 Magnificent for Yarra; gd elsewhere, equable growing conditions.

South Australia
2003 A curate's egg. The good: Limestone Coast and Clare Riesling (yet again); the bad: rain-split Shiraz.

2002 Very cool weather led to much reduced yields in the South, and to a great Riverland vintage in both yield and quality. Fine Riesling again.

2001 Far better than 2000; Clare Valley Riesling an improbable success.

2000 The culmination of a four-year drought impacted on both yield and quality, the Limestone Coast zone faring the best.

1999 Continuing drought was perversely spoiled by ill-timed March rainfall; Limestone Coast and Clare reds the few bright spots.

1998 Very dry year. Overall quality of reds superb, esp south of Adelaide.

1997 On-again, off-again weather upset vines and vignerons alike, with the exception of Eden and Clare Valley Riesling. Yields down overall.

1996 Classic vintage, classic wines, succulent, and long-lived.

1995 Reduced yields and quality, the low yields averting disaster.

994 A long, cool, and dry growing season produced excellent white wines across the state, and elegant reds with above-average yields.

993 A warm and dry March and below-average yields saved the day.

992 Vintage rain in all regions except McLaren Vale and Langhorne Creek spoiled what might have been a good vintage.

Western Australia

2003 An in-between year, with ill-timed rainfall nipping greatness in the bud.

2002 Best since 84 in Swan District. In the south quality is variable.

2001 Great Southern, the best vintage since 95; good elsewhere.

2000 Margaret River excellent; variation elsewhere, the Swan Valley ordinary.

1999 An outstanding vintage for Margaret River and Swan reds (best in over a decade) and pretty handy elsewhere, other than the Great Southern.

1998 The Swan Valley shone again, elsewhere in the state a rainy vintage.

1997 Good reds from Margaret River and Riesling from Great Southern.

1996 The Swan Valley was cooked, but the warm year was a blessing for Margaret River and Great Southern, with lovely Cabernet the pick.

1995 Very low yields balanced by quality in the south and Margaret River.

1994 Perfect conditions for Great Southern (superb) and Margaret River.

1993 Best Swan Valley whites for decades. Excellent whites, useful reds elsewhere.

1992 A mild growing season produced good wines in the south.

Adelaide Hills SA) Spearheaded by PETALUMA: cool, 450-m sites in Mt Lofty ranges.

Alkoomi Mt Barker r w ★★★ (Ries) **94' 96' 99 01** 02 (Cab Sauv) **93' 94'** 97 99 01' 25-yr veteran producing fine steely Ries and potent long-lived reds.

Allandale Hunter Valley r w ★★ Small winery without v'yds, buying selected local and Hilltops grapes. Quality can be gd, esp Chard.

Alpine Valleys Vic Geographically similar to KING VALLEY and similar use of grapes.

Amberley Estate Margaret R r w ★★ Successful maker of a full range of regional styles with Chenin Bl the commercial engine.

Angove's SA r w (br) ★→★★ Large long-established MURRAY VALLEY family business. Gd-value whites, esp Chard.

Ashbrook Estate Margaret R r w ★★★ Minimum of fuss; consistently makes 8,000 cases of exemplary Sem, Chard, Sauv Bl, Verdelho, and Cab Sauv.

Ashton Hills Adelaide Hills r w (sp) ★★★ Fine racy long-lived Ries and compelling Pinot N crafted by Stephen George from 20-yr-old v'yds.

Bailey's NE Vic r w br ★★ Rich, old-fashioned reds of great character, esp Shiraz, and magnificent dessert Muscat (★★★★) and "Tokay". Part of BERINGER BLASS.

Balnaves of Coonawarra r w ★★★ Grape-grower since 1975; winery since 1996. V.gd Chard; excellent Shiraz, Merlot, Cab Sauv.

Bannockburn Geelong r w ★★★ (Chard) **96' 97' 98' 00** 02' 03' (Pinot N) **94' 97** 99' **00** 02' 03 Intense, complex Chard and Pinot N made using Burgundian techniques.

Banrock Station Riverland SA r w ★→★★ 3950 acre property on Murray River, 600 acre v'yd, owned by HARDY. Impressive budget wines.

Barossa SA Australia's most important winery (but not v'yd) area; grapes from diverse sources make diverse wines. Local specialities: very old vine Shiraz and Grenache.

Barwang Hilltops r w ★★ Owned by MCWILLIAMS; Stylish estate wines.

Bass Phillip Gippsland Vic r ★★★→★★★★ (Pinot N) **95 96'** 97' **98' 00'** 02' 03 Tiny amounts of stylish, eagerly sought-after Pinot N in 3 quality grades; very Burgundian in style.

Bay of Fires N Tas ★★→★★★ r w sp Pipers River outpost of HARDYS empire; stylish table wines and essential components for Hardy Arras super-cuvée sparkler.

AUSTRALIA

Beggar's Belief Shiraz S Aus Blackberries, rum, oak in a stand-a-spoon-up tincture.

Bendigo Vic Widespread small v'yds, some v.gd quality. Notable estates Balgownie and Passing Clouds.

Beringer Blass Barossa r w (sp, sw, br) ★★★ (Cab Sauv blend) **90' 91' 93 94 96' 97 98'** 00 02 Founded by the ebullient Wolf Blass, now swallowed up by massive multinational. It is well-served by winemakers Chris Hatch (chief) and Caroline Dunn (reds).

Best's Grampians r w ★★→★★★ (Shiraz) **91 92' 93 94'** 96 97' 98' 99' 00' 03 Conservative old family winery; v.gd mid-weight reds. Thomson Family Shiraz from 120-yr-old vines is superb.

Big Rivers Zone NSW & Vic The continuation of South Australia's RIVERLAND inc the Murray Darling Perricoota and Swan Hill Regions.

Botobolar Mudgee r w ★★ Marvellously eccentric little organic winery.

Bowen Estate Coonawarra r w ★★★ **90' 91' 94' 96' 98'** 99 01 02' Small winery: intense Cab Sauv, spicy Shiraz, no longer too alcoholic.

Brand's of Coonawarra Coonawarra r w ★★★ **90' 91' 94' 96'** 98' 99 01 02 Owned by McWILLIAMS. Going from strength to strength esp with super-premium Stentiford's SHIRAZ and Patron's Cab Sauv.

Brangayne of Orange Orange r w ★★ Reflects potential of relatively new region. Wines of great finesse inc Chard, Sauv Bl, and Shiraz.

Bremerton Langhorne Creek r w ★★ Regularly produces attractively priced red wines with silky, soft mouth-feel and stacks of flavour.

Brokenwood Hunter Valley r w ★★★ (Shiraz) **87' 91' 93' 94'** 95' 98' 99 00' Exciting Cab Sauv; Shiraz since 1973 – Graveyard Shiraz outstanding. Sem and Cricket Pitch Sem/Sauv Bl fuel sales.

Brookland Valley Margaret R r w ★★→★★★ Superbly sited winery and restaurant doing great things, esp with Sauv Bl. Half-share owned by HARDYS.

Brown Brothers King Valley r w dr br sp sw ★→★★★ (Noble Ries) **94' 96' 97** 98 99' Old family firm, with new ideas. Wide range of delicate, varietal wines, many from cool mountain districts, inc Chard and Ries. Dry white Muscat is outstanding. Cab Sauv blend is best red.

Buring, Leo Barossa w ★★→★★★ (Ries) **75' 79' 84' 91' 92 94' 95 97 99'** 02' 03 Old Ries specialist, part of SOUTHCORP. Great with age (even great age), esp releases under Leonay label.

Cabernet Sauvignon 29,573 ha, 257,223 tonnes. Grown in all wine regions, best in COONAWARRA. From herbaceous green pepper in coolest regions through blackcurrant and mulberry, to dark chocolate and redcurrant in warmer areas.

Campbells of Rutherglen NE Vic r br (w) ★★ Smooth ripe reds and gd fortified wines, the latter in youthful, fruity style other than Merchant Prince Muscat.

Canberra District NSW Both quality and quantity on the increase; altitude-dependent, site selection important.

Cape Mentelle Margaret R r w ★★★ (Cab Sauv) **83' 91' 93' 94' 95'** 96 99' 00 Robust Cab Sauv can be magnificent, Chard even better; also Zin and very popular Sauv Bl/Sem. LVMH Veuve Clicquot owner; also Mountadam (BAROSSA) and Cloudy Bay (see New Zealand).

Capel Vale Geographe WA r w ★★★ Very successful with gd whites, inc Ries. Also top-end Shiraz and Cab Sauv.

Casella Riverina r w ★ The [yellow tail] phenomenon has swept all before it with multi-million case sales in US; like Fanta, soft and sweet.

Central Ranges Zone NSW Encompasses MUDGEE, ORANGE, and Cowra regions, expanding in high altitude, moderately cool to warm climates.

Chain of Ponds Adelaide Hills r w ★★ Impeccably made, full, flavoursome wines vinified by PENFOLDS. Sem, Sauv Bl, and Chard to the fore. Elegant Amadeus Cab Sauv is also gd.

Chalkers Crossing Hilltops r w ★★→★★★ New winery with beautifully balanced cool climate wines.

Chambers' Rosewood NE Vic br (r w) ★★→★★★ Viewed with MORRIS as the greatest maker of "Tokay" and Muscat.

Chapel Hill McL Vale r w ★★ (r) Now owned by Swiss Schmidheiny group with multinational wine interests inc Napa's Cuvaison in California.

Chardonnay 21,724 ha, 256,328 tonnes. Best-known for fast-developing buttery, peachy, sometimes syrupy wines, but cooler regions produce more elegant, tightly structured, age-worthy examples. Oak, too, is now less heavy-handed.

> **New varieties staking a claim**
> An unlikely trio of Riesling, Sauvignon Blanc and Merlot is rattling the cage of Chardonnay, Cabernet Sauvignon and Shiraz, however important the latter three varieties may be. The hitherto false dawn of the "Riesling Revival" is now an objective fact; Merlot is still rushing on like a mountain stream; and Sauvignon Blanc defies all logic (and the competition from Marlborough) as the newly-adopted market darling.

Charles Melton Barossa r w (sp) ★★★ Tiny winery with bold, luscious reds, esp Nine Popes, an old-vine Grenache and Shiraz blend.

Cheviot Bridge Central Vic High Country r w ★★ Fast-moving part of new corporate empire which bought the Long Flat brand from TYRRELL (for Aus$14m).

Clare Valley SA Small high-quality area 90 miles N of Adelaide, best for Ries (glorious in 2002); also Shiraz and Cab Sauv.

Clarendon Hills Mclaren Vale r (w) ★★★ Monumental (and expensive) reds from small parcels of contract grapes around Adelaide.

Clonakilla Canberra District r w ★★★ Deserved leader of the Shiraz Viognier brigade. Ries and other wines also v.gd.

Coldstream Hills Yarra Valley r w (sp) ★★★ (Chard) 88' 92' 96' 97 98 00' 02' 03 (Pinot N) **91' 92' 96' 97** 00' 02' 03 (Cab Sauv) **91' 92'** 94 97' 98' 00' Established in 1985 by wine critic James Halliday. Delicious Pinot N to drink young and Reserve to age leads Australia. V.gd Chard (esp res wines), fruity Cab Sauv, and Cab Sauv/Merlot, and (from 97) Merlot. Acquired by SOUTHCORP in 1996.

Coonawarra SA Southernmost and perhaps finest v'yds of state: most of Australia's best Cab Sauv; successful Chard, Ries, and Shiraz. Newer arrivals inc Murdock and Reschke.

Coriole McLaren Vale r w ★★→★★★ (Shiraz) **90' 91' 94' 96'** 98' 99' 00 02' To watch, esp for old-vine Shiraz Lloyd Reserve.

Craiglee Macedon Vic r w ★★★ (Shiraz) **86' 88' 90' 91' 92 93 94'** 97' 98' 00' 02' Re-creation of famous 19th-C estate. Fragrant, peppery Shiraz, Chard.

Cranswick Estates Riverina r w ★ Large winery firmly aimed at export market with accent on value. Acquired by EVANS & TATE in 2002.

Croser See PETALUMA.

Cullen Wines Margaret R r w ★★★★ (Chard) **96' 97 98 99'** 00' 01 (Cab Sauv/Merlot) **76' 84' 86' 87' 90' 91' 94'** 95' 96' 99' 01' Vanya Cullen makes strongly structured Cab Sauv/Merlot (Australia's best), substantial but subtle Sem/Sauv Bl, and bold Chard: all real characters.

Dalwhinnie Pyrenees r w ★★★ (Chard) **99' 00'** 02' (Reds) **93 94' 95'** 97 98' 99' 00' 01 02 Concentrated, rich Chard and Shiraz. Cab Sauv the best in PYRENEES.

d'Arenberg McLaren Vale r w (rsw br sp) ★★→★★★ Old firm with new lease of life; sumptuous Shiraz and Grenache, fine Chard with lots of whacky labels.

Deakin Estate Murray Darling r w ★ Part of Katnook group producing 550,000 cases of very decent varietal table wines.

De Bortoli Griffith NSW r w dr sw (br) ★→★★★ (Noble Sem) 82' 87' 91' 94 95' 96' 97' 99' 00' 02 Irrigation-area winery. Standard red and white but splendid sweet botrytized Sauternes-style Noble Sem. See also next entry.

De Bortoli Yarra Valley r w ★★→★★★ (Chard) 96' 97 98 99 00' 01' 02' (Cab Sauv) 92' 94' 97 98' 99 00' 02' YARRA VALLEY's largest producer. Main label is more than adequate; second label Gulf Station and third label Windy Peak v.gd value. 400, 000 c/s.

Delatite Central Vic r w (sp) ★★ (Ries) 93' 97' 99 00 01 02' Rosalind Ritchie makes appropriately willowy and feminine Ries, Gewurz, and Cab Sauv from this very cool mountainside v'yd.

Devil's Lair Margaret R r w ★★★ Opulently concentrated Chard and Cab Sauv/Merlot. Fifth Leg is trendy second label. Part of SOUTHCORP.

Diamond Valley Yarra Valley r w ★★→★★★ (Pinot) 96' 97 98' 99' 00 02' 03 Outstanding Pinot N in significant quantities; other wines gd, esp Chard.

Domaine Chandon Yarra Valley sp (r w) ★★★ Classic sparkling wine from grapes grown in the cooler wine regions, with strong support from owner Moët & Chandon. Successful in UK under GREEN POINT label (also used for table wine).

Dominique Portet Yarra Valley r w ★★ After a 25-yr career at Taltarni, now in his own winery for the first time. Much is expected.

Dromana Estate Mornington Peninsula r w ★★→★★★ (Chard) 98' 99 00' 01 02' 03 Light, fragrant Cab Sauv, Pinot N, and Chard. Now taking Italian varieties (grown elsewhere) very seriously.

Elderton Barossa r w (sp br) ★★ Old v'yds; flashy, rich, oaked Cab Sauv and Shiraz.

Evans Family Hunter Valley r w ★★★ (Chard) 98' 99' 00' 01 02 Excellent Chard from small v'yd owned by family of Len Evans. Fermented in new oak. Repays cellaring. See also TOWER ESTATE.

Evans & Tate Margaret River r w ★★★ (Cab) 91' 92' 94 95' 96' 99' 00 Fine elegant Sem, Chard, Cab Sauv, Merlot from MARGARET RIVER, Redbrook. Stock-exchange listing underpins continued growth.

Ferngrove Vineyards Great Southern r w ★★★ Cattle farmer Murray Burton's syndicate has established over 988 acres of vines since 1997; great Ries.

Fox Creek Mclaren V r (w) ★★→★★★ Produces 35,000 cases of flashy, full-flavoured wines, which are inveterate wine show winners.

Freycinet Tasmania r w (sp) ★★★ (Pinot N) 91' 94' 97 98 00' 01' 02' 03 E coast winery producing voluptuous, rich Pinot N, gd Chard.

Regions: Geographical Indications

The process of formally defining the boundaries of the zones, regions, and sub-regions, known compendiously as Geographic Indications (GIs), continues. These correspond to the French ACs and AVAs in the US. It means every aspect of the labelling of Australian wines has a legal framework which, in all respects, complies with EC laws and requirements. The guarantee of quality comes through the mandatory analysis certificate for, and the tasting (by expert panels) of, each and every wine exported from Australia.

Gapsted Wines Alpine Valleys (Vic) r w ★★ Brand of large winery which crushes grapes for 50 growers.

Geelong Vic Once-famous area destroyed by phylloxera, re-established in the mid-1960s. Very cool, dry climate: firm table wines from gd-quality grapes. Names inc BANNOCKBURN, SCOTCHMAN'S HILL, By Farr, Curlewis.

Geoff Merrill McLaren Vale r w ★★ Ebullient maker of Geoff Merrill, Mt Hurtle, Cockatoo Ridge. A questing enthusiast; his best are excellent, others unashamedly mass-market oriented. TAHBILK owns 50%.

Geoff Weaver Adelaide Hills r w ★★★ 20 acre estate at Lenswood. Very fine Sauv Bl, Chard, Ries, and Cab Sauv/Merlot blend. Marvellous label design.

Giaconda Beechworth r w ★★★ (Chard) 91 92' 93 94' 96' 97' 98 99' 00' 02' Australia's answer to Kistler (see California). Chard is considered by many to be the best in Australia – certainly the 96 is one of all time greats. Pinot N is very variable.

Goulburn Valley Vic Very old (TAHBILK) and relatively new (MITCHELTON) wineries in temperate mid-Victoria region; full-bodied table wines.

Goundrey Wines Great Southern WA r w ★★ Recent expansion has caused quality to become variable. Acquired by Canada's Vincorp in 2003.

Grampians Vic Region previously known as Great Western. Temperate region in central W of state. High quality.

Granite Belt Qld High-altitude, (relatively) cool region just N of NSW border Esp spicy Shiraz and rich Sem.

Granite Hills Macedon r w ★★→★★★ 30-yr-old family v'yd and winery has regained original class with fine elegant Ries and spicy Shiraz.

Grant Burge Barossa r w (sp sw br) ★★→★★★ 110,000 cases of silky-smooth reds and whites from the best grapes of Burge's large v'yd holdings.

Greenock Creek Barossa r ★★★ Soaring prices and iconic status for Shiraz thanks to Robert Parker and US buyers.

Great Southern WA Remote, cool area; FERNGROVE, GOUNDREY, and PLANTAGENET are the largest wineries.

Grenache 2,528 ha, 26,280 tonnes. Produces thin wine if over-cropped, but can do much better. Growing interest in old BAROSSA and MCLAREN VALE plantings.

Grosset Clare r w ★★★→★★★★ (Ries) 90' 93' 94' 95' 97' 99' 00' 01 02' (Gaia) 90' 91 92' 94' 95 96' 98' 99' 01 02 Fastidious winemaker. Foremost Australian Ries, lovely Chard, Pinot N, and exceptional Gaia Cab Sauv/Merlot from dry v'yd high on Mt Horrocks.

Hanging Rock Macedon (Vic) r w sp ★→★★★ (Shiraz) 90 91' 92' 97' 98' 99 00' Eclectic: budget varietal wines; huge Heathcote Shiraz; complex sparkler.

Hardys r w sp (rsw) ★★→★★★★★ (Eileen Chard) 97 98 99' 00 01 ("Vintage Port") 46' 51' 54' 56' 58' 75 77 82 84' 96' Historic company blending wines from several areas. Best are Eileen Hardy and Thomas Hardy series and (Australia's best) "Vintage Ports". REYNELLA's restored buildings are group HQ. Merged with US Constellation group in 2003 to create the world's largest wine group. See also BAY OF FIRES.

Heathcote Divorce from BENDIGO in 2003 led to formal recognition of this Shiraz-specialist region; JASPER HILL the big name.

Heggies Eden Valley r w dr (sw w) ★★ (Ries) 92 95 98 99 00 01' V'yd at 500 m owned by S SMITH & SONS, but separately marketed.

Henschke Barossa r w ★★★★ (Shiraz) 58' 61' 64' 67' 68' 80' 81 84' 86' 90' 90' 91' 93' 96' 98' (Cab Sauv) 78' 80' 85 86' 88 90' 91' 92 93 94 96' 98' 99 01 02' A 125-yr-old family business, perhaps Australia's best, known for delectable Hill of Grace (Shiraz), v.gd Cab Sauv and red blends, and value whites, inc Ries. Lenswood v'yds in ADELAIDE HILLS add excitement. Fervent advocate of screwcaps for reds too.

Hollick Coonawarra r w (sp) ★★ (Cab Sauv/Merlot) 90 91' 92 93 96' 98' 99 01 02 Gd Chard and Ries. Much-followed reds, esp Ravenswood.

Houghton Swan Valley r w ★→★★★ The most famous old winery of WA. Soft, ripe Supreme is top-selling, age-worthy white; a national classic. Also excellent Cab Sauv, Verdelho, Shiraz, etc. sourced from MARGARET RIVER and GREAT SOUTHERN. See HARDYS.

Howard Park Mount Barker and Margaret River r w ★★★ (Ries) 93 94' 95' 96' 97' 98' 99' 02 (Cab Sauv) 86' 88' 90' 92 94' 96' 98' 99' 02 Scented Ries,

Chard; spicy Cab Sauv. Second label: Madfish Bay is excellent value.

Hunter Valley NSW Great name in NSW. Broad, soft, earthy Shiraz and gentle Sem that live for 30 yrs. Cab Sauv not important; Chard is.

Huntington Estate Mudgee r w ★★★ (Cab Sauv) **91 93 94' 95' 96'** 97' 99' 02' Small winery; the best in MUDGEE. Fine Cab Sauv, v.gd Shiraz. Underpriced.

Jasper Hill Heathcote r w ★★★→★★★★ (Shiraz) **83' 85' 86' 90' 91' 92'** 96' 97' 98' 99' 00 01' 02 Emily's Paddock Shiraz/Cab Fr blend and Georgia's Paddock Shiraz from dry-land estate are intense, long-lived, much admired.

Jim Barry Clare r w ★★→★★★ Some great v'yds provide gd Ries, McCrae Wood Shiraz, and convincing Grange challenger The Armagh.

Kaesler Barossa r (w) ★★→★★★ Old Bastard Shiraz (Aus$155) outranks Old Vine Shiraz (a mere Aus$60). Wine in the glass pretty gd too.

Katnook Estate Coonawarra r w (sp sw w) ★★★ (Cab Sauv) **86** 90' 91' **92 93** 96' 98' 99 02' (03) Excellent, pricey Cab Sauv and Chard. Also Ries and Sauv Bl.

Keith Tulloch Hunter r w ★★★ Ex-Rothbury winemaker fastidiously crafting elegant yet complex Sem, Shiraz, etc.

Killikanoon Clare V ★★→★★★ r w Strongly regional Ries and Shiraz have been awesome performers in shows over past few yrs.

King Valley Vic Important alpine region. 15,000 tonnes chiefly for purchasers outside the region. Some wineries of its own.

Knappstein Wines Clare r w ★★→★★★ Reliable Cab Sauv/Merlot and Cab Sauv. Owned by LION NATHAN.

Knappstein Lenswood Vineyards r w ★★★ Estate now sole occupation of Tim KNAPPSTEIN making subtle Sauv Bl, powerful Chard, and Pinot N.

Lake Breeze Langhorne Ck r (w) ★★ Long-term grape-growers turned winemakers producing succulently smooth Shiraz and Cab Sauv.

Lake's Folly Hunter Valley r w ★★★★ (Chard) **94 95 96 97' 98** 99 00' 01 (Cab Sauv) **69 81 89' 91 93'** 97' 98' 99 00' Founded by Max Lake, the pioneer of HUNTER Cab Sauv. New owners since 2000. Cab Sauv and Chard are very fine, complex.

Lamont Swan V r w ★★ Winery and superb restaurant owned by Corin Lamont (daughter of legendary Jack Mann) and husband. Delicious wines.

Lark Hill Canberra District r w ★★ Most consistent CANBERRA producer, making esp attractive Ries, pleasant Chard, and surprising Pinot N.

Leasingham Clare r w ★★→★★★ Important mid-sized quality winery bought by HARDYS in 1987. Gd Ries, Shiraz, and Cab Sauv/Malbec. Various labels.

Leeuwin Estate Margaret River r w ★★★★ (Chard) **83' 85' 87' 89 90 92' 94 95' 96** 97' 98 **99'** 00 01' (02) Leading W Australia estate, lavishly equipped. Superb, ageworthy (and expensive) Chard, Sauv Bl and Cab Sauv. Artists' Labels are very fine. Also gd Ries.

Limestone Coast Zone SA Important zone inc COONAWARRA, PADTHAWAY Wrattonbully, Mount Benson, Robe, Mount Gambier, and Bordertown.

Lindemans Originally Hunter Valley, now everywhere r w ★→★★★ (COONAWARRA Red) **86' 90' 91' 96'** 98' 99 01 02' One of the oldest firms, now a giant owned by SOUTHCORP. V.gd Chard and COONAWARRA reds (eg Limestone Ridge, Pyrus).

Lion Nathan New Zealand brewery and big investor in Australian wine. Owns PETALUMA, STONIER, TATACHILLA and KNAPPSTEIN.

Macedon and Sunbury Vic Adjacent regions, Macedon at higher elevation, Sunbury nr Melbourne airport. CRAIGLEE, HANGING ROCK, VIRGIN HILLS, GRANITE HILLS.

Majella Coonawarra r (w) ★★★ Rising to the top of COONAWARRA cream. "The Malleea" is outstanding Cab Sauv/Shiraz super-premium red. Shiraz and Cab Sauv also v.gd.

Margan Family Winemakers Hunter r w ★★ Highly successful winemaker inc fascinating House of Certain Views brand.

Margaret River WA Temperate coastal area, 174 miles S of Perth, with superbly elegant wines . Australia's most vibrant tourist wine (and surfing) region.

McGuigan Simeon Hunter Valley ★→★★ Nominal Hunter base of Australia's fifth-largest wine group, recently adding MIRANDA scalp to its collection.

McLaren Vale SA Historic region on the southern outskirts of Adelaide. Big, alcoholic flavoursome reds have great appeal to US market.

Names to watch in 2005	
Clare Valley S Australia	Brilliant 2002 Rieslings
Cullen Margaret River	Chardonnay and Merlot
De Bortoli Yarra Valley	Consistently delivers
Devil's Lair Margaret River	Vineyard expansion coming on-stream
Ferngrove Great Southern	Huge potential; 400 ha of vineyards
O'Leary Walker Clare Valley	Some hype, even more performance
Tasmania generally	Global warming is just the ticket
Taylors Clare Valley	Spectacular improvement
Tower Estate Hunter Valley	Len Evans's pride and joy

McWilliam's Hunter Valley and Riverina r w (sw br) ★★→★★★ (Elizabeth Sem) 84' 86' **87' 89'** 93 94' 95 96 98 99' 00' Famous family of HUNTER VALLEY winemakers at Mount Pleasant: Shiraz and Sem. Also pioneer in RIVERINA: Cab Sauv and Ries. Recent show results demonstrate high standards. Elizabeth (sold at 4 yrs) and Lovedale (6 yrs) Sems are quite superb. Hanwood (RIVERINA) v.gd value.

Merlot The darling of the new millennium; from 9,000 tonnes in 1996 to 104,423 tonnes in 2003. Grown everywhere, but shouldn't be.

Miramar Mudgee r w ★★ Some of MUDGEE's best white wines, esp Chard; long-lived Cab Sauv and Shiraz.

Miranda Riverina r w (sww) ★→★★ V'yds and wineries in RIVERINA, KING VALLEY and BAROSSA underpin this major producer, now part of MCGUIGAN SIMEON.

Mitchell Clare r w ★★→★★★ (Ries) 90' 92 94' 95 00' 01' 02' 03' Small family winery for excellent Cab Sauv and very stylish dry Ries.

Mitchelton Goulburn Valley r w (sw w) ★★→★★★ Substantial winery, acquired by PETALUMA in 1992. A wide range inc v.gd wood-matured Marsanne, Shiraz; GOULBURN VALLEY Blackwood Park Ries is one of Australia's best-value wines.

Moorilla Estate Tasmania r w (sp) ★★★ (Ries) 93 94' 95' 97' 99 00' 01' 02 Senior winery on outskirts of Hobart on Derwent River: v.gd Ries, Traminer, and Chard; Pinot N now in the ascendant.

Moorooduc Estate Mornington Peninsula r w ★★★ Stylish and sophisticated (wild yeast, etc.) producer of top-flight Chard and Pinot N.

Mornington Peninsula Vic Exciting wines in new cool coastal area 25 miles S of Melbourne. 2,470 acres. Wineries inc DROMANA, STONIER, TEN MINS BY TRACTOR.

Morris NE Vic (r w) ★★→★★★★ Old winery at Rutherglen for some of Australia's greatest dessert Muscats and "Tokays"; also gd low-priced table wine.

Moss Wood Margaret R r w ★★★★ (Sem) 92' 94' 95' 97' 98' 99 01 (Cab Sauv) 75' 80' 85' **87 90' 91'** 94 95' 96' 98 99' 01 To many, the best MARGARET RIVER winery (29 acres). Sem, Cab Sauv, Pinot N and Chard, all with rich fruit flavours.

Mount Horrocks Clare w r ★★★→★★★★ Finest dry Ries and sweet Cordon Cut in separate range from GROSSET winery.

Mount Langi Ghiran Grampians r w ★★★ (Shiraz) 88 90' **91 92** 93' 95 96' 98' 99' 01 (03) Esp for superb, rich, peppery, Rhône-like Shiraz, one of Australia's best cool-climate versions. Now owned by YERING STATION.

Mount Mary Yarra Valley r w ★★★★ (Pinot N) 94 95 96' 97' **98** 99' 00' 02' (Cab Sauv/Cab Fr/Merlot) 84' 85' 86' 88' 90' 92' **93'** 94 95' 96' 97' 98' 99

oo' o2 Dr John Middleton is a perfectionist making tiny amounts of suave
Chard, vivid Pinot N, and (best of all) Cab Sauv blend: Australia's most B'dx-
like "claret". All will age impeccably.

New wineries to watch

Adelaide Hills Setanta Fantastic packaging.

Barossa Valley Hann Wines Immaculate Viognier, Merlot. **Mitolo Wines** Slick marketing, clever winemaking.

Canberra District Brindabella Hills Research scientist makes cool climate wines.

Clare Valley Kirrihill Estate Rapidly expanding 7000-tonne winery. **Wilson Vineyard** Outstanding Ries.

Coonawarra Punters Corner Clever name, gd quality and v.gd wine. **Ladbroke Grove** Change of ownership, excellent results.

Geelong Curlewis Classy, wild Pinot N. **Farr Rising** Pinot N and Chard by Nick, son of Gary Farr of Bannockburn. **Jindalee Estate** Large, schizophrenic Riverland varietals and quality Geelong Fettlers Rest label.

Geographe Hackersley Part grape grower, part winemaker; supple, smooth wines. **Willow Bridge** New 1200-tonne winery, 70 ha v'yds.

Great Southern Garlands 3500 c/s making quality leaps. **West Cape Howe Wines** Important winemaker for self and others making full range of varietals.

Heathcote Wild Duck Creek Estate Celebrated producer of Duck Muck, etc. **Red Edge** Super-concentrated reds in tiny quantities .

Henty Crawford River Diamond clear Ries. **Tarrington Estate** Scare Pinot N to die for.

Hunter Valley Pepper Tree Vinyards Here and Coonawarra; great reds. **Scarborough** Excellent, rich Sem and Chard.

Macedon Bindi Icon Pinot N. **Curly Flat** Aspirational; gd Chard and Pinot N.

McLaren Vale Gemtree Vinyards Great v'yd resources. **Tapestry** Prior Chapel Hill owners making magic. **Ulithorne** Outstanding Shiraz.

Margaret River Carbunup Crest Glorious, cheap Shiraz. **Flying Fish Cove** Exceptional reds for own label and others. **Cape Grace** Great Shiraz and Cab Sauv. **Gralyn** 30-yr-old v'yd; top reds. **Higher Plane** Freakish attention to detail. **Suckfizzle** Feisty winemaker Janice McDonald is not Gargantua; v.gd Sauv Bl and Sem/Sauv Bl blend.

Mornington Peninsula Eldridge Estate V.gd Chard, Pinot N, Gamay. **Montalto** Scaling the heights; Ries, Chard, Pinot N. **Kooyong** Winemaker Sandro Mosele, a touch of genius.

Perth Hills Millbrook Winery State of the art newcomer. **Western Range Wines** Five growers own one winery; value and quality.

Rutherglen All Saints Great fortified "Tokay" and Muscat. **Warrabilla** Enormous red wines, esp Durif.

Tasmania Apsley Gorge; Domaine A; Elsewhere Vineyard; Meadowbank; Tamar Ridge; Wellington All top flight producers of Chard, Pinot N and/or Ries.

Yarra Valley Giant Steps Former Devil's Lair owner Phil Sexton does it all again. **Shelmerdine Vineyards** Substantial new venture by industry heavyweight Stephen Shelmerdine. **Toolangi Vineyards** Top class Chard and Pinot N.

Mountadam Barossa r w (sp) ★★★ High EDEN VALLEY winery of Adam Wynn. Chard is rich, voluptuous, and long. Other labels inc David Wynn and Eden Ridge. Acquired by CAPE MENTELLE 2000.

Mudgee NSW Small, isolated area 168 miles NW of Sydney. Big reds, surprisingly fine Sem, and full Chard.

Murdock Coonawarra r ★★★ Long-term grower now making classic Cab Sauv.

Murray Valley SA, Vic & NSW Vast irrigated v'yds. Principally making "cask" table wines. 40% of total Australian wine production.

Nepenthe Adelaide Hills r w ★★→★★★ One of a handful of new wineries in the region. State-of-the-art kit, excellent v'yds, skilled winemaking, and sophisticated wines (esp Sauv Bl, Chard, and Sem).

Ninth Island See PIPER'S BROOK.

O'Leary Walker Wines Clare r w ★★★ Two whizz-kids have mid-life crisis and leave BERINGER BLASS to do their own thing – very well.

Orange NSW Cool-climate region giving lively Chard, Cab Sauv, Merlot, Shiraz.

Orlando (Gramp's) Barossa r w sp (br sw w) ★★→★★★ (St Hugo Cab) **86' 88 90' 96 98'** 99 01 02' Great pioneering company, now owned by Pernod-Ricard. Full range from best-selling Jacob's Creek to excellent Jacaranda Ridge Cab Sauv from COONAWARRA. See also WYNDHAM ESTATE.

Padthaway SA Large v'yd area developed as overspill of COONAWARRA. Cool climate; excellent Chard (esp LINDEMANS and HARDYS) and Shiraz (ORLANDO).

Paringa Estate Mornington Peninsula r w ★★★ Maker of quite spectacular Chard, Pinot N, and (late-picked) Shiraz winning innumerable trophies.

Parker Estate Coonawarra r ★★★ Small estate making v.gd Cab Sauv, esp Terra Rossa First Growth, with Andrew Pirie recently ensconced CEO.

Pemberton WA Region between MARGARET RIVER and GREAT SOUTHERN; initial enthusiasm for Pinot N replaced by Merlot and Shiraz.

Penfolds Originally Adelaide, now everywhere r w (sp br) ★★→★★★★ (Grange) **52' 53' 55' 62' 63' 66' 67 71' 75 76 80 83 85 86' 88** 90' 91' 92 94' 95 96' 97 98' (Bin 707) **64 76' 78 80 84' 86' 88' 90' 91** 92 94' 96' 98' 99 Ubiquitous and excellent: in BAROSSA VALLEY, CLARE, COONAWARRA, RIVERINA, etc. Consistently Australia's best red wine company, if you can decode its labels. Its Grange (was called "Hermitage") is deservedly ★★★★. Penfold's Yattarna Chard ("White Grange") was released in 98. Bin 707 Cab Sauv not far behind. Other bin-numbered wines (eg. Kalimna Bin 28 Shiraz) can be outstanding.

Penley Estate Coonawarra r w ★★★ High-profile, no-expense-spared, winery. Rich, textured, fruit-and-oak Cab Sauv; Shiraz/Cab Sauv blend; Chard.

Perth Hills WA Fledgling area 19 miles E of Perth with a larger number of growers on mild hillside sites. Millbrook and Western Range best.

Petaluma Adelaide Hills r w sp ★★★★ (Ries) **80' 82 84' 86' 87** 94' **96'** 97 99' 00' 01' **02'** 03' (Chard) **94' 95' 96' 00** 02' (Cab Sauv) **79' 86' 88' 90' 91' 93 95' 97** 98' 99 00' 02 A rocket-like 1980s success with COONAWARRA Cab Sauv, ADELAIDE HILLS Chard, Croser CLARE VALLEY Ries, all processed at winery in ADELAIDE HILLS. Created by the fearsome intellect and energy of Brian Croser. Red wines richer from 1988 on. Owns KNAPPSTEIN, MITCHELTON, Smithbrook, and STONIER. Fell prey to Lion Nathan 2002; quality so far unaffected.

Peter Lehmann Wines Barossa r w (sp br sw w) ★★→★★★ Defender of BAROSSA faith; fought off Allied-Domecq by marriage with Swiss Hess group. Consistently well-priced wines in substantial quantities. Try Stonewell Shiraz and dry Ries, esp with age.

Pierro Margaret River r w ★★★ (Chard) **90' 94 95' 96'** 99' 00' 01' Highly rated producer of expensive, tangy Sem/Sauv Bl and v.gd barrel-fermented Chard.

Pipers Brook Tasmania r w sp ★★★ (Ries) **84' 85 89' 93' 94' 95' 96' 98'** 99' 00' 01' (Chard) **92' 93' 94' 95'** 97 **99'** 00' (02') Cool-area pioneer; v.gd Ries, Pinot N, restrained Chard and sp from Tamar Valley. Lovely labels. Second label: Ninth Island. Bought HEEMSKERK, Rochecombe in 1998; has 35% of Tasmanian wine industry. Acquired 2002 by Belgian Kreglinger family, owners of Vieux Château Certan.

Pinot Noir 4,414 ha, 21,341 tonnes. Mostly used in sparkling. Exciting wines from S Victoria, TASMANIA, and ADELAIDE HILLS; plantings are increasing.

Pirramimma McLaren V r w ★★ Low-profile, century-old family business with first-class v'yds making underpriced wines inc excellent Petit Verdot.

Plantagenet Mount Barker r w (sp) ★★★ (Reds) **92' 93' 94' 95'** 98 99 The region's elder statesman: wide range of varieties, esp rich Chard, Shiraz, and vibrant, potent Cab Sauv.

Poets Corner Mudgee r w ★★ Reliable underrated producer of Chard, Shiraz, and Cab Sauv. Also Montrose and Henry Lawson labels.

Primo Estate Adelaide Plains r w dr (w sw) ★★★ Joe Grilli is a miracle-worker given the climate; successes inc v.gd botrytized Ries, tangy Colombard, and potent Joseph Cab Sauv/Merlot.

Pyrenees Vic Central Vic region producing rich, minty reds and some interesting whites, esp a Marsanne/Roussanne blend.

Red Hill Estate Mornington Peninsula r w sp ★★→★★★ One of the larger and more important wineries; notably elegant wines.

Redman Coonawarra r ★→★★ Famous old name in COONAWARRA; red specialist: Shiraz, Cab Sauv, Cab Sauv/Merlot. Wine fails to do justice to v'yd quality.

Reynell McLaren Vale r rsw w ★★→★★★★ Brand bought by HARDYS in 1982. Historic winery, Chateau Reynella, serves as HQ for HARDYS group. V.gd "Basket-pressed" red table wines; superb vintage "Port".

Richmond Grove Barossa r w ★→★★★ Master winemaker John Vickery produces great Ries at bargain prices; other wines are OK. Owned by ORLANDO WYNDHAM.

Riesling 3,962ha, 27,838 tonnes. Has a special place in the BAROSSA, EDEN and CLARE valleys. Usually made bone-dry; can be glorious with up to 20 yrs bottle-age. Screwcaps now only accepted closure.

Riverina NSW Large-volume irrigated zone centred around Griffith. Gd-quality "cask" wines (esp white) and great sweet, botrytized Sem. Watch for reduced yields and better quality, eg. the marvellous 02 wines.

Robert Channon Wines Granite Belt (Queensland) r w ★★ Lawyer turned vigneron has 17 acres of permanently netted, immaculately trained v'yd producing v.gd Verdelho (plus usual others).

Rockford Barossa r w sp ★★→★★★★ Small producer. Range of individual wines, from old, low-yielding v'yds; reds best, also iconic sparkling Black Shiraz.

Rosemount Estate Upper Hunter, McLaren Vale, Coonawarra r w (sp) ★★→★★★★ Rich, Roxburgh Chard, MCLAREN VALE Balmoral Syrah, MUDGEE Mountain Blue Cab Sauv/Shiraz, and COONAWARRA Cab Sauv lead the wide range. Merged with SOUTHCORP in 2001. Links with Mondavi, too (see California).

Rosevears Estate N Tasmania r w ★★ Spectacularly sited winery/restaurant complex by Tamar River. Chard, Pinot N, and Cab Sauv/Merlot under Rosevears and Notley Gorge labels.

Rothbury Estate Hunter Valley r w ★★ Fell prey to BERINGER BLASS in 1996 after long bitter fight by original founder Len Evans (since departed). Has made long-lived Sem and Shiraz and rich, buttery, early-drinking COWRA Chard to gd effect. Old Evans fans should see EVANS FAMILY and TOWER ESTATE.

Rutherglen & Glenrowan Vic 2 of 5 regions in the NE Victorian Zone justly famous for weighty reds and magnificent, fortified dessert wines.

Rymill Coonawarra ★★ Descendants of John Riddoch carrying on the gd work of the founder of COONAWARRA. Strong, dense Shiraz and Cab Sauv esp noteworthy.

St Hallett Barossa r w ★★★ (Old Block) **86' 88' 90' 91' 92' 93'** 94' 95 96' 98' 99 02' Rejuvenated winery. 60+-yr-old vines give splendid Old Block Shiraz. Rest of range is smooth and stylish. LION NATHAN-owned.

St Sheila's SA p sw sp **36 22 38** Full-bodied fizzer. Ripper grog, too.

Saltram Barossa r w ★★→★★★ Mamre Brook (Shiraz, Cab Sauv, Chard) and No 1 Shiraz are leaders. Metala is associated Stonyfell label for Langhorne Creek Cab Sauv/Shiraz. A BERINGER BLASS brand.

Sandalford Swan Valley r w (br) ★→★★★ Fine old winery with contrasting styles of red and white single-grape wines from SWAN and MARGARET RIVER areas. Sandalera is amazing long-aged sweet white.

Sauvignon Blanc 2,914 ha, 25,567 tonnes. Usually not as distinctive as in New Zealand, but amazingly popular. Made in many different styles, from bland to pungent.

Scotchman's Hill Geelong r w ★★ Relative newcomer making significant quantities of stylish Pinot N and gd Chard.

Semillon 6,610 ha, 100,785 tonnes. Before the arrival of Chard, Sem was the HUNTER VALLEY'S answer to South Australia's Ries. Traditionally made without oak and extremely long-lived. Brief affair with oak terminated.

Seppelt Barossa, Grampians, Padthaway, etc. r w sp br (sw w) ★★★ (Shiraz) 56' 71' **85' 86' 90 91' 92** 93' 96' 97' 98' 99' 03' Far-flung producer of important wines under various labels inc Great Western; also new range of Victoria-sourced table wines. Top sparkling is highly regarded "Salinger". Another part of SOUTHCORP.

Sevenhill Clare r w (br) ★★ Owned by the Jesuitical Manresa Society since 1851. Consistently gd wine; Shiraz and Ries can be outstanding.

Seville Estate Yarra Valley r w ★★★ (Shiraz) 76' 85' **88 91' 94** 97' 00' 02' 03 Tiny winery owned by BROKENWOOD shareholders; Chard, Shiraz, Pinot N, Cab Sauv.

Shadowfax Vineyard Geelong Vic r w ★★ Stylish new winery, part of historic Werribee Park, also hotel based on 1880s Mansion. Gd Pinot Noir.

Shantell Yarra Valley r w ★★→★★★ Under-rated producer with 30-yr-old v'yd. Sem, Chard, Pinot N, and Cab Sauv.

Shaw & Smith McLaren Vale w (r) ★★★ Founded by Martin Shaw and Australia's first MW, Michael Hill Smith. Crisp Sauv Bl, v.gd unoaked Chard, complex, barrel-ferm Reserve Chard, and new Merlot.

Shiraz 37,031 ha, 326,866 tonnes. Hugely flexible: velvety/earthy in the HUNTER; spicy, peppery, and Rhône-like in central and S Victoria; or brambly, rum-sweet and luscious in BAROSSA and environs (eg. PENFOLDS' Grange).

Sirromet Queensland Coast r w ★★ A striking (247-acre) 75,000-case winery, with a 200-seat restaurant. Biggest of many such new ventures.

South Burnett Now Queensland's second region with 11 wineries and more births imminent, symptomatic of whole SE corner of the state.

Southcorp The former giant of the industry; but a fallen idol in the stock market. Owns PENFOLDS, LINDEMANS, SEPPELT, Seaview, WYNNS, and ROSEMOUNT.

Sparkling wines: top Australian producers	
Yarrabank	Greenpoint/Domaine Chandon
Hardy Arras	Jansz
Clover Hill	Croser

Southern NSW Zone (NSW) inc CANBERRA, Gundagai, Hilltops, and Tumbarumba.

S Smith & Sons (alias Yalumba) Barossa r w sp br (sw w) ★★→★★★ Big old family firm with considerable verve. Full spectrum of high-quality wines, inc HILL-SMITH ESTATE, HEGGIES and YALUMBA. Signature Res are best. Angas Brut, a gd-value sparkling wine, and Oxford Landing Chard are now world brands.

Stanton & Killeen Rutherglen br r ★★★ Grandson Chris Killeen has a modernist palate, making a great dry red, outstanding "Vintage Port", and Muscat.

Stonehaven PADTHAWAY r w ★★ First large (Aus$20m) winery in PADTHAWAY region built by HARDYS servicing whole LIMESTONE COAST ZONE production.

Stonier Wines Morn Pen r w ★★★ (Chard) 97 98 00' 01' 02 03 (Pinot N) 97 99 00' 02' 03 Consistently v.gd; Reserves outstanding. 70% owned by PETALUMA.

Swan Valley WA Located N of Perth. Birthplace of wine in the W. Hot climate makes strong, low-acid table wines.

Tahbilk Goulburn Valley r w ★★→★★★ (Marsanne) **79' 89' 92' 95 98' 99** 00' 01 03 (Shiraz) **81 84' 86' 88 91'** 95' 97 98 99' 00 Beautiful historic family estate: reds for long ageing, also Ries and Marsanne. Reserve Cab Sauv outstanding; value for money ditto. Rare 1860 vines Shiraz, too.

Taltarni Grampians/Avoca r w (sp) ★★ New management and winemaking team producing more sophisticated reds, esp Cepahs.

Tapanappa New COONAWARRA collaboration between Brian CROSER, Bollinger and J-M Cazes of Paulliac. To watch.

Tarrawarra Yarra Valley r w ★★★ (Chard) **97 98' 00'** 02' (Pinot N) **96 98 00'** 02' Multimillion-dollar investment with idiosyncratic, expensive Chard and robust, long-lived Pinot N. Tin Cows is the second label.

Tasmania Production bounced back in 2003, but still tiny. Great potential for Chard, Pinot N, and Ries in cool climate.

Tatachilla McLaren V r w ★★→★★★ Significant (250,000 case) production of nice whites and v.gd reds. Acquired by LION NATHAN in 2002.

Taylors Wines Clare r w ★★→★★★ 250,000 case production of much-improved Ries, Shiraz, and Cab Sauv – esp under St Andrew's label.

Ten Minutes by Tractor Mornington Peninsula r w ★★ Amusing name and sophisticated packaging links 3 family v'yds which are – yes, you've guessed. Sauv Bl, Chard, and Pinot N are all gd.

Terroir in Australia

Terroir – the conjunction of soil, subsoil, slope, aspect, altitude, and all the elements of site climate – is as alive and well in Australia as it is anywhere else in the world. This vast continent offers a range of terroirs greater than any other country other than the US, sustaining the creation of styles ranging from the finest bottle-fermented sparkling wines to the richest fortified wines. But over the past five years, and into the future, there has been a move from warmer to cooler climates, and a progressive matching of terroir and variety. Thus Hunter Valley Semillon; Yarra Valley Pinot Noir; Coonawarra Cabernet Sauvignon; Barossa/ McLaren Vale Grenache; Clare Valley Riesling; Margaret River Chardonnay.

T'Gallant Mornington Peninsula w (r) ★★ Improbable name and avant garde labels for Australia's top Pinot Gris/Grigio producer. Also makes a fragrant unwooded Chard. Quixotic acquisition by BERINGER BLASS.

Torbreck Barossa ★★→★★★★ r (w) The most stylish of the cult wineries beloved of the US; focus on old-vine Rhône varieties.

Tower Estate r w ★★★→★★★★ Newest venture of Len Evans (and financial partners) offering luxury convention facilities and portfolio of 10 wines made from grapes grown in the best parts of Australia. Impressive.

Trentham Estate Múrray Darling (r) w ★★ 55,000 c/s of family-grown and made sensibly priced wines from "boutique" winery on R Murray; gd restaurant, too.

Turkey Flat Barossa Valley r p ★★★ Icon producer of rosé, Grenache, and Shiraz from core of 150-yr-old v'yd's. Top Stuff.

Tyrrell's Hunter Valley r w ★★★ (Sem Vat 1) **77' 86' 87' 93' 94' 95' 96'** 98 99' 00' (Chard Vat 47) **73' 79' 92' 95' 97' 98' 99'** 00' 01 **02** (Shiraz Vats) **75' 79' 81' 87 91'** 92' **94' 96' 97** 98' 99' 00' 02 Some of the best traditional HUNTER VALLEY wines, Shiraz and Sem. Pioneered Chard with big, rich Vat 47 – still a classic. Also Pinot N.

Upper Hunter NSW Established in early 1960s; irrigated vines (mainly whites), lighter and quicker developing than Lower Hunter's.

Vasse Felix Margaret River r w ★★★ (Cab Sauv) **89 91 94 95' 96'** 97 99' 00' 01 o2 With CULLEN, pioneer of MARGARET RIVER. Elegant Cab Sauv, notable for mid-weight balance.

Verdelho Old white grape re-emerging in some light, aromatic wines and Chard blends. Worth trying.

Virgin Hills Macedon Ranges r ★★★ 73' 74' 76' 81' 82 88 91' 92' 98' 00' 01' Tiny supplies of one red (a Cab Sauv/Shiraz/Malbec blend) of legendary style and balance. Rapid ownership changes unsettling.

Voyager Estate Margaret River r w ★★★ 30,000 cases of estate-grown, rich, and powerful Sem, Sauv Bl, Chard, and Cab Sauv/Merlot.

Wendouree Clare r ★★★★ 78 79 83 86 89' 90' 91' 92 93 94' 96' 98' 99' 01 (02') Treasured maker (tiny quantities) of Australia's most powerful and concentrated reds based on Shiraz, Cab Sauv, Mourvedre, and Malbec; immensely long-lived.

Westfield Swan Valley w r ★→★★ John Kosovich's Cab Sauv, Chard, and Verdelho show particular finesse for a hot climate, but has also developed a new v'yd in the much cooler PEMBERTON region.

Wirra Wirra McLaren Vale r w (sp sw w) ★★★ (Cab Sauv) 86 90' 91' 92 95 96' 98' 99 02' High-quality wines making a big impact. Angelus is superb, top-of-the-range Cab Sauv, ditto RSW Shiraz.

Wyndham Estate Mudgee NSW r w (sp) ★→★★ Aggressive, large HUNTER and MUDGEE group with brands: Craigmoor, Hunter Estate, MONTROSE, and Richmond Grove. ORLANDO WYNDHAM is owned by Pernod Ricard.

Wynns Coonawarra r w ★★★ (Shiraz) 55' 63 86' 88' 90' 91' 93 94' 96' 98' 99 (02') (Cab Sauv) 57' 60' 82' 85' 86' 90' 91' 94' 96' 97 98' 99' 00 (02') SOUTHCORP-owned COONAWARRA classic. Ries, Chard, Shiraz, and Cab Sauv are all v.gd, esp John Riddoch Cab Sauv, and Michael Shiraz.

Yalumba See S SMITH & SONS.

Yarra Burn Yarra Valley r w sp ★★→★★★ Estate making Sem, Sauv Bl, Chard, sparkling Pinot N, Pinot N, and Cab Sauv. Acquired by HARDYS in 1995, with changes now underway. Bastard Hill Chard and Pinot N legitimate flag-bearers.

Yarra Ridge Yarra Valley r w ★★→★★★ Chard, Cab Sauv, Sauv Bl, Pinot N, all with flavour and finesse at appealing prices. Owned by BERINGER BLASS.

Yarra Valley Superb historic area nr Melbourne. Growing emphasis on very successful Pinot N and sparkling.

Yarra Yarra Yarra Valley r w ★★★ Recently increased to 7 ha giving greater access to fine Sem/Sauv Bl and Cab Sauv, each in classic B'dx style.

Yarra Yering Yarra Valley r w ★★★→★★★★ (Dry Reds) 81' 82' 83 84 85 90' 91' 93' 94' 95 96' 97' 98 99' 00' 01 02' Best-known Lilydale boutique winery. Esp: powerful Pinot N; deep, herby Cab Sauv (Dry Red No 1); Shiraz (Dry Red No 2). Luscious, daring flavours in red and white. Also fortified "Port-Sorts" from the correct grapes.

Yellowglen Bendigo/Ballarat sp ★★ High-flying sparkling winemaker owned by BERINGER-BLASS. Recent improvement in quality, with top-end brands like Vintage Brut, Cuvée Victoria, and "Y".

Yeringberg Yarra Valley r w ★★★ (Marsanne) 91' 92 94' 95 97 98 00' 02' 03 (Cab Sauv) 76' 80' 81' 84 86 88' 90 91' 92 93 94' 97' 98 99 00' 02 Dreamlike, historic estate still in the hands of founding family. Makes minute quantities of very high-quality Marsanne, Roussanne, Chard, Cab Sauv, and Pinot N.

Yering Station/Yarrabank r w sp ★★★ Yarra Valley On site of Victoria's first v'yd; replanted after 80-yr gap. Extraordinary joint venture: Yering Station table wines (Reserve Chard, Pinot N, Shiraz, Viognier); Yarrabank (esp fine sparkling wines for Champagne Devaux).

Zema Estate Coonawarra r ★★→★★★ One of last bastions of hand pruning in COONAWARRA; silkily powerful, disarmingly straightforward reds.

AUSTRALIA

New Zealand

More heavily shaded areas
are the wine growing regions

Since the mid-1980s, New Zealand has made its name for wines (mainly white) of a quality no one had anticipated, well able to compete with those of Australia, California, or indeed France. In 1982, it exported 12,000 cases; in 2003, over 3 million. There are now over 50,000 vineyard acres. White grapes still prevail, though red are catching up. Sauvignon Blanc and Chardonnay are most extensively planted (over half the national total). Pinot Noir, Merlot, and Cabernet Sauvignon are well-established, with sizeable pockets of Riesling, Semillon, Pinot Gris (newly fashionable), Gewurztraminer, Cabernet Franc, Malbec, and Syrah. Intense fruit and crisp acidity are the hallmarks of New Zealand. Nowhere matches Marlborough Sauvignon for pungency. Chardonnay shines throughout the country, while Riesling's stronghold is the South Island. Marlborough has also proved itself with fine fizz. Claret-style reds (increasingly Merlot-based) from Hawke's Bay and Auckland are of improving, at best outstanding, quality. Pinot Noir makes wonderful wines in Martinborough and South Island.

Recent vintages

2003 Frost-affected season, yielding the lightest crop yet. Unripe flavours in some wines; excellent intensity in others.

2002 Bumper crop (50% heavier than previous record). Outstanding Chardonnay and variable reds in Hawkes Bay.

2001 Very dry in the South, wet in the North. Tiny crop in Hawkes Bay and Gisborne. Marlborough Sauv Blanc of variable quality. Pinot Noir excellent.

2000 Cool, wet spring and summer, saved by an Indian summer. Low yields. Aromatic whites – good intensity and vigour. Pinot Noir better than Cabernet Sauvignon.

1999 Average in Gisborne and Hawkes Bay, but drier and better in Marlborough.

1998 Widespread drought. Richly alcoholic wines with low acidity. Tropical fruit-flavoured Marlborough Sauv Blanc and powerful Hawkes Bay reds.

Akarua Central Otago ★★ Large v'yd at Bannockburn, producing classy, exuberantly fruity Pinot N, flinty Chard, and Pinot Gr.

Allan Scott Marlborough ★★ Attractive Ries, Chard, Sauv Bl; top label Prestige.

Ata Rangi Martinborough ★★★ Small but highly respected winery. Outstanding Pinot N (**99 00 01** 02). Rich, concentrated Craighall Chard. Increasingly impressive Cab Sauv/Merlot/Syrah blend Célèbre.

Auckland (r) **99 00' 02** (w) **00' 02** Largest city in NZ. Henderson, Huapai, Kumeu, Matakana, Clevedon, Waiheke Island districts – top reds – nearby.

Babich Henderson (Auckland) ★★→★★★ Mid-size family firm, established 1916; quality, value. AUCKLAND, HAWKE'S BAY, and MARLBOROUGH v'yds. Refined, slow-maturing Irongate Chard (**00'** 01) and Cab Sauv/Merlot (single-v'yd).

Black Ridge Central Otago ★→★★ One of the world's southernmost wineries. Noted for rich, soft Pinot N, also gd Chard, Ries, and Gewurz.

Brancott Vineyards ★★→★★★ Brand used by MONTANA in US market.

Brookfield Hawke's Bay ★★ One of region's top v'yds: outstanding "gold label" Cab Sauv/Merlot; rich Chard, Pinot Gr, and Gewurz.

Cable Bay Waiheke Island ★★ Sizeable newcomer, first vintage 2002. Classy Waiheke Chard and subtle, finely textured MARLBOROUGH Sauv Bl.

Cairnbrae Marlborough ★★ Recently bought by SACRED HILL; quality Sauv Bl, Ries.

Canterbury (r) **01' 02** 03 (w) **01' 02** 03 NZ's seventh-largest wine region; v'yds at Waipara and nr Christchurch. Long, dry summers favour Pinot N, Chard, Ries.

Canterbury House Waipara ★→★★ Sizeable N Canterbury winery, US-owned, best known for fresh, punchy Sauv Bl and honey-sweet Noble Ries.

Carrick Central Otago ★★ Emerging Bannockburn winery with flinty, flavourful whites (Pinot Gr, Sauv Bl, Chard) and rich, velvety Pinot N.

Cellier Le Brun Marlborough ★★ Small winery: v.gd bottle-fermented sparkler, esp Vintage (97) and Blanc de Blancs (97). Terrace Road table wines also gd.

Central Otago (r) **01 02'** (w) **01 02'** Fast-expanding, cool, mountainous region in S of South Island. Ries and Pinot Gr promising; Pinot N perfumed and silky, with notably intense character.

Chard Farm Central Otago ★★ Fresh, vibrant Ries, Pinot Gr, and Pinot N.

Church Road Hawke's Bay ★★→★★★ MONTANA winery. Wines inc rich Chard and elegant Merlot/Cab Sauv. Top reserve wines; prestige, claret-style red, Tom.

Clearview Hawke's Bay ★★→★★★ Very small producer. Burly, flavour-packed Res Chard; dark, rich Res Cab Fr, Res Merlot, Old Olive Block (Cab Sauv blend).

Cloudy Bay Marlborough ★★★ Owned by the vast LVMH group. Large-volume Sauv Bl, Chard, and Pinot N are v.gd. Pelorus sp impressive. Rarer Gewurz, Late-Harvest Ries, and Te Koko (oak-aged Sauv Bl) now the greatest wines.

Collard Brothers Auckland ★★ Long-established, small family winery. Whites, esp Rothesay Vineyard Chard.

Cooper's Creek Auckland ★★ Excellent Swamp Res Chard, gd MARLBOROUGH Sauv Bl.

Corbans Auckland ★→★★★ Established 1902, bought by MONTANA in 2000. Key brands: Corbans (esp Cottage Block and Private Bin), STONELEIGH (MARLBOROUGH), Huntaway Res, LONGRIDGE, Robard & Butler. Quality from basic to outstanding.

Craggy Range Hawke's Bay ★★→★★★ New winery with large v'yds in HAWKE'S BAY and MARLBOROUGH. Immaculate Sauv Bl and Chard; complex Merlot.

Crossroads Hawke's Bay ★→★★ Small winery. Gd Sauv Bl, but flagship is rich Talisman red (blended from unspecified varieties).

Delegat's Auckland ★★ Mid-size family winery. V'yds at HAWKE'S BAY and MARLBOROUGH. Res Chard, Merlot, and Cab Sauv/Merlot offer v.gd quality and value. OYSTER BAY brand: deep-flavoured Chard and Sauv Bl.

Deutz Auckland ★★★ Champagne company gives name and technical aid to fine sp from MARLBOROUGH by MONTANA. NV: lively, yeasty, flinty. Vintage Blanc de Blancs: rich and creamy.

Domaine Georges Michel Marlborough ★ French-owned, based at former Merlen winery. Sauv Bl of varying quality and crisp, appley Chablis-like Chard.

Dry River Martinborough ★★★ Tiny winery. Penetrating, long-lived Chard, Ries, Pinot Gr (NZ's finest), Gewurz (ditto), and powerful Pinot N (**99 00 01** 02).

Esk Valley Hawke's Bay ★★→★★★ Now owned by VILLA MARIA. Some of NZ's most voluptuous Merlot-based reds (esp Res label **98' 99 00'** 01 02), v.gd dry Merlot rosé, Chenin Bl, satisfying Chards, and Sauv Bl.

A choice from New Zealand for 2005

Merlot Villa Maria Reserve (01), CJ Pask Reserve (00), Esk Valley Reserve blend Merlot/Cab Sauv/Malbec (00)

Pinot Noir Ata Rangi (02), Felton Road Block 3 (02), Akarua (02), Wither Hills (02)

Chardonnay Morton Estate Black Label (00), Te Mata Elston (02), Millton Clos de Ste Anne (02)

Sauvignon Blanc Saint Clair Reserve (03), Cloudy Bay (03), Palliser Estate (03)

Riesling Pegasus Bay Waipara (03), Allan Scott Marlborough (03), Seifried Winemaker's Collection Nelson (03), Babich Marlborough (02)

Sparkling Nautilus Cuvée Marlborough NV, Lindauer Grandeur, Pelorus (99)

Sweet wines Alpha Domus Noble Selection Semillon (00), Forrest Botrytised Riesling (02), Pegasus Bay Aria Late Picked Riesling (02)

Fairhall Downs Marlborough ★★ Rich, vibrantly fruity whites, notably weighty, peachy, spicy Pinot Gr and scented, pure, deep-flavoured Sauv Bl.

Felton Road Central Otago ★★★ Star winery in warm Bannockburn area. Pinot N Block 3 and Ries outstanding; excellent Chard and regular Pinot N.

Firstland Waikato ★★ US-owned winery, previously De Redcliffe. Hotel du Vin attached. Gd MARLBOROUGH whites. Improving HAWKE'S BAY reds.

Forrest Marlborough ★★ Mid-size winery; fragrant, ripe Chard, Sauv Bl, and Ries; stylish HAWKE'S BAY Cornerstone Vineyard Cab Sauv/Merlot/Malbec.

Framingham Marlborough ★★ Aromatic whites, notably Ries (Classic is slightly sweet, intense, and zesty; Dry is even finer). Rich, bone-dry Sauv Bl.

Fromm Marlborough ★★★ Swiss-founded, focusing on very powerful red wines. Fine Pinot N, esp under Fromm Vineyard and Clayvin Vineyard labels.

Gibbston Valley Central Otago ★★ Pioneer winery with popular restaurant. Greatest strength is Pinot N, esp fleshy, firm Reserve (**99' 00 01 02'**). Racy local whites (Chard, Ries, Pinot Gr, Sauv Bl).

Giesen Estate Canterbury ★ German family winery. Gd, slightly honeyed Ries, but bulk of production is now average-quality MARLBOROUGH Sauv Bl.

Gisborne (r) **00'** (w) **00 02'** NZ's third-largest region. Key strength is Chard (typically deliciously fragrant, ripe, and soft in its youth). Abundant rain and fertile soils ideal for heavy croppers, esp Müller-Thurgau. Reds typically light, but Merlot shows promise.

Goldwater Waiheke Island ★★★ Region's pioneer Cab Sauv/Merlot (**99' 00'**) is still one of NZ's finest: Médoc-like finesse, concentration, and structure. Also crisp, citrus Chard and pungent Sauv Bl, both grown in MARLBOROUGH.

Gravitas Marlborough ★★ Exciting new company, owned by UK-based NZer Martyn Nicholls. First 02 vintage yielded exceptionally rich Sauv and Chard.

Greenhough Nelson ★★→★★★ One of region's top producers, with immaculate and deep-flavoured Ries, Sauv, Chard, and Pinot N. Top label: Hope Vineyard.

Grove Mill Marlborough ★★→★★★ Attractive whites, inc vibrant Chard; excellent Ries, Sauv, and slightly sweet Pinot Gr. Gd, lower-tier Sanctuary brand.

Hawke's Bay (r) **98' 99' 00'** 01 02' (w) **00' 02'** NZ's second-largest region. Long history of winemaking in sunny climate, shingly and heavier soils.

Full, rich Cab Sauv and Merlot-based reds in gd vintages; Syrah a rising star; powerful Chard; rounded Sauv Bl.

Highfield Marlborough ★★ Japanese-owned with quality Ries, Chard, Sauv Bl, and Pinot N. Also piercing, flinty, yeasty Elstree sparkling.

Huia Marlborough ★★ Mouth-filling, subtle wines that age well, inc savoury, rounded Chard and perfumed, well-spiced Gewurz.

Hunter's Marlborough ★★→★★★ Top name in intense, immaculate Sauv Bl. Fine, delicate Chard. Excellent sp, Ries, Gewurz; light, elegant Pinot N.

Isabel Estate Marlborough ★★★ Family estate with limey clay soil. Outstanding Pinot N, Sauv Bl, and Chard, all with impressive depth and finesse.

Jackson Estate Marlborough ★★→★★★ Rich Sauv Bl, gd Chard (esp weighty Res), and attractive Dry Ries.

Kaituna Valley Canterbury ★★→★★★ Small producer with v'yds nr Christchurch and in MARLBOROUGH. Consistently powerful, multi award-winning Pinot N.

Kemblefield Hawke's Bay ★→★★ US-owned winery. Solid reds; ripely herbal, oak-aged Sauv Bl; soft, peppery Gewurz; and fleshy, lush Chard.

Kim Crawford Hawke's Bay ★★ Founded 1996 by ex-COOPER'S CREEK winemaker; sold in 2003 to Vincor (Canada). Numerous labels, inc: rich GISBORNE Chard; robust, unoaked MARLBOROUGH Chard; Sauv Bl; and vibrant, supple Cab Fr.

Kumeu River Auckland ★★→★★★ Rich, mealy Kumeu Chard (02'); single-v'yd Mate's Vineyard Chard even more opulent. Rest of range solid. Inc: fresh, pure Pinot Gr; oaky, savoury Pinot N. Second label: Kumeu River Village.

Lake Chalice Marlborough ★★ Small producer with bold, creamy-rich, softly textured Chard, and powerful Cab Sauv and Merlot. Also Ries and Sauv Bl of gd quality. Platinum is premium label.

Lawson's Dry Hills Marlborough ★★→★★★ Weighty wines with rich, intense flavours. Distinguished Sauv Bl and Gewurz; gd Pinot Gr and Ries.

Lincoln Auckland ★ Long-established family winery. Gd value varietals of sound quality: buttery GISBORNE Chard (top label Reserve).

Lindauer See MONTANA.

Linden Hawke's Bay ★→★★ Smallish producer with soft, buttery Chard, ripely herbal Sauv Bl, smooth, berryish Merlot, and Cab Sauv.

Longridge Former CORBANS brand, now MONTANA-owned. Reliable, moderately priced wines (inc citrusy Chard) typically, but not always, from HAWKE'S BAY.

Margrain Martinborough ★★ Small winery with firm, concentrated Chard, Ries, Pinot Gr, Merlot, and Pinot N, all of which reward bottle-age.

Marlborough (r) **00 01' 02** (w) **01' 03** NZ's largest region (half of all plantings). Sunny, warm days and cool nights give intense, crisp whites. Amazingly intense Sauv Bl, from sharp, green capsicum to ripe tropical fruit. Fresh, limey Ries, very promising Pinot Gr and Gewurz. High-quality sparkling.

Martinborough (r) **01** 03 (w) **01 02** 03 Small, high-quality area in S WAIRARAPA (foot of North Island). Warm summers, dry autumns, gravelly soils. Success with white grapes (Chard, Sauv Bl, Ries, Gewurz, Pinot Gr), but most renowned for sturdy, rich Pinot N.

Martinborough Vineyard Martinborough ★★★ Distinguished small winery; one of NZ's top Pinot Noirs (**00 01**). Rich, biscuity Chard and intense Ries.

Matakana Estate Auckland ★→★★ Largest producer in Matakana district. Since 1998, average to gd Chard, Pinot Gr, Sem, Syrah, and Merlot/Cab Sauv blend. Volume label: Goldridge.

Matariki Hawke's Bay ★★→★★★ Stylish, concentrated white and red, extensive v'yds in stony Gimblett Road. Rich, ripe Sauv Bl; robust, spicy Quintology red blend.

Matawhero Gisborne ★→★★ Formerly NZ's top Gewurz specialist. Now has wide range (also Chard, Sauv Bl, and Cab Sauv/Merlot) of often gd quality.

Matua Valley Auckland ★★→★★★ Highly rated mid-size winery with v'yds in 4 regions. Excellent oaked Matheson Sauv Bl. Top range Ararimu inc fat, savoury Chard and dark, rich Merlot/Cab Sauv. Numerous attractive GISBORNE (esp Judd Chard), HAWKE'S BAY, and MARLBOROUGH wines (Shingle Peak).

Mills Reef Bay of Plenty ★★→★★★ The Preston family produces impressive wines from HAWKE'S BAY grapes. Top Elspeth range inc lush, barrel-fermented Chard and dense, rich B'x-style reds. Reserve range also impressive.

Millton Gisborne ★★→★★★ Region's top small winery: mostly organic. Top Opou Vineyard Ries and soft, savoury Chard. Robust, complex dry Chenin Bl.

Mission Hawke's Bay ★→★★ NZ's oldest wine producer, established 1851, still run by Catholic Society of Mary. Solid varietals: sweetish, perfumed Ries is esp gd value. Reserve range inc excellent B'x-style reds, Sem, Ries, Chard.

Montana Auckland ★→★★★ NZ wine giant, over 50% market share after buying CORBANS in 2000. Wineries in AUCKLAND, GISBORNE, HAWKE'S BAY, and MARLBOROUGH. Extensive co-owned v'yds. Famous for MARLBOROUGH whites, inc top-value Sauv Bl, Ries, and Chard (Reserve range esp gd). Strength in sp, inc DEUTZ, and stylish, fine-value LINDAUER. Elegant CHURCH ROAD reds and quality Chard. Bought by UK-based Allied-Domecq in 2001.

Morton Estate Bay of Plenty ★★ Respected mid-size producer with v'yds in HAWKE'S BAY and MARLBOROUGH. Refined Black Label Chard is one of NZ's best (**00'**). White Label Chard also gd. Brilliant Coniglio Chard is NZ's priciest.

Mount Riley Marlborough ★→★★★ Fast-growing company with extensive v'yds and new winery. Beautifully balanced, easy-drinking Chard; piercing Ries; punchy Sauv Bl and dark, flavoursome Cab Sauv/Merlot. All gd value.

Mt Difficulty Central Otago ★★ Quality producer in relatively hot Bannockburn area. Powerful, toasty Chard, flinty Ries and very refined, intense Pinot N.

Muddy Water Waipara ★★ Small, high-quality producer since 1996 with beautifully intense Ries, minerally Chard, and savoury, subtle Pinot N.

Nautilus Marlborough ★★ Small range of distributors Négociants (NZ), owned by S Smith & Son of Australia (cf Yalumba). Top wines inc Sauv Bl and fragrant, yeasty, smooth sparkler. Lower-tier wines: Twin Islands.

Nelson (r) **01 02'** (w) **01 02'** Small region W of MARLBOROUGH; climate a little wetter. Clay soils of Upper Moutere hills and silty Waimea Plains. Strengths in whites, esp Ries, Sauv Bl, and Chard. Pinot N is the best red.

Neudorf Nelson ★★★ One of NZ's top boutique wineries. Strapping, creamy-rich Chard (**00 01 02'**). Superb Pinot N, Sauv Bl, and Ries.

Nga Waka Martinborough ★★ Dry, steely whites of high quality. Outstanding Sauv Bl; piercingly flavoured Ries; robust, savoury Chard.

Ngatarawa Hawke's Bay ★★→★★★ Mid-sized. Top Alwyn Reserve range, inc powerful Chard, Cab Sauv, and Merlot. Mid-range Glazebrook also excellent.

Nobilo Auckland ★→★★ NZ's second-largest wine company, now owned by Hardy's (see Australia). MARLBOROUGH Sauv Bl is gd, but sharply priced. Superior varietals labelled Icon. V.gd Drylands Sauv Bl. Cheaper wines labelled Fernleaf and Fall Harvest.

Okahu Estate Northland ★→★★ NZ's northernmost winery, at Kaitaia. Hot, humid climate. Warm, ripe reds; complex Reserve Clifton Chard (multi-region blend).

Omaka Springs Marlborough ★→★★ Small producer with punchy, herbaceous Sauv Bl, solid Ries, Chard, and Merlot. Reserve Chard and Pinot N impressive.

Oyster Bay See DELEGAT'S.

Palliser Estate Martinborough ★★→★★★ One of the area's largest and best wineries. Superb tropical-fruit-flavoured Sauv Bl, excellent Chard, Ries, and Pinot N. Top wines: Palliser Estate. Lower tier: Pencarrow.

Pask, C J Hawke's Bay ★★→★★★ Mid-size winery, extensive v'yds. Gd to excellent Chard. Cab Sauv and Merlot-based reds fast improving. Rich, complex Reserves.

Pegasus Bay Waipara ★★→★★★ Small but distinguished range: notably taut, cool-climate Chard; lush, complex, oaked Sauv Bl/Sem; and zingy Ries. Cab Sauv-based reds are region's finest. Pinot N lush and silky.

Peregrine Central Otago ★★ Emerging star with steely, incisive Ries; fleshy, rich Pinot Gr and Gewurz; and distinguished, gd value Pinot N.

> **The best Pinot Noirs from New Zealand**
> Pinot Noir is the hot Kiwi red, yielding perfumed, supple, richly varietal wines in Martinborough and several South Island regions, notably Central Otago but also (recently) Marlborough. Quantities are small but rising swiftly, and the best are of exciting quality. Top labels include Ata Rangi, Martinborough Vineyard, Dry River, Palliser (all Martinborough); Fromm, Isabel, Seresin, Villa Maria Reserve, Wither Hills (Marlborough); Kaituna Valley (Marlborough and Canterbury); Neudorf and Greenhough Hope Vineyard (Nelson); Mountford, Pegasus Bay (Canterbury); Felton Road, Gibbston Valley Reserve, Peregrine, Quartz Reef (Central Otago).

Providence Auckland ★★★ Rare Merlot-based red from Matakana district. Perfumed, lush and silky, very high-priced.

Quartz Reef Central Otago ★★ Quality producer with weighty, flinty Pinot Gr; substantial rich Pinot N; yeasty, lingering, Champagne-like sparkler, Chauvet.

Rippon Vineyard Central Otago ★→★★ Stunning v'yd. Fine-scented, very fruity Pinot N and slowly evolving whites, inc steely, appley Ries.

Robard & Butler Former CORBANS brand, now MONTANA-owned. Low-priced varietals.

Sacred Hill Hawke's Bay ★★ Sound Whitecliff varietals; gd, oaked Res Sauv Bl (Barrel Fermented and Sauvage). Gd Basket Press Merlot and barrel-fermented Chard. Distinguished Rifleman's Reserve Chard.

Saint Clair Marlborough ★★→★★★ Fast-growing, export-led producer with substantial v'yds. Prolific award winner. Sauv Bl, fragrant Ries, easy Chard, and plummy, early-drinking Merlot. Rich Reserve Sauv Blanc, Chard, Merlot.

St Helena Canterbury ★ The region's oldest winery, founded nr Christchurch in 1978. Light, supple Pinot N (Reserve is bolder). Chard variable but gd in better vintages. Cheap, earthy, savoury Pinot Bl is fine value.

Seifried Estate Nelson ★★ Region's only mid-size winery, founded by an Austrian. Known initially for well-priced Ries and Gewurz; now also producing gd value, often excellent Sauv Bl and Chard. Best wines: Winemaker's Collection.

Selaks ★→★★ Mid-size family firm bought by in NOBILO 1998. Sauv Bl and Chard are its strengths, but the reds are plain.

Seresin Marlborough ★★→★★★ Established by NZ film producer Michael S. Stylish. Immaculate Sauv, Chard, Pinots N and Gr, Ries, Noble Ries.

Sherwood Canterbury ★→★★ Tart austere Ries, Chard, and two Pinot Ns, notably fresh, plummy, berryish Reserve. Bold, peachy, nutty Reserve Chard.

Shingle Peak See MATUA VALLEY.

Sileni Hawke's Bay ★★ Major new winery (from 1998) with extensive v'yds and very classy Merlot/Cab Sauv, Chard, and Sem. Most top wines labelled Estate Selection; then Cellar Selection.

Soljans Auckland ★ Long-established small family winery. Gd, supple Pinotage.

Spy Valley Marlborough ★★ Fast-growing company with extensive v'yds, first vintage 00. Ries, Gewurz, and Pinot Gr are esp gd.

Stonecroft Hawke's Bay ★★→★★★ Small winery. Dark, concentrated Syrah, more Rhône than Australian. Also v.gd red blend Ruhanui, Chard, Gewurz.

Stoneleigh Former CORBANS brand, now MONTANA-owned. Impressive MARLBOROUGH whites and Pinot N, esp Rapaura Reserve.

Stonyridge Waiheke Island ★★★★ Boutique winery. Famous for exceptional

272 |

B'x-style red, Larose (**94 96 97** 99 00). Dark, perfumed, and magnificently concentrated, it matures well for a decade. Airfield is second label.

Te Awa Farm Hawke's Bay ★★ US-owned large estate v'yd. Classy Frontier Chard and Boundary (Merlot-based blend), gd larger volume Longlands labels.

Te Kairanga Martinborough ★★ One of district's larger wineries. Big, flinty Chard (richer Reserve), perfumed, supple Pinot N (complex and powerful Reserve).

Te Mata Hawke's Bay ★★★→★★★★ Prestigious winery. Fine, powerful Elston Chard; v.gd oaked Cape Crest Sauv Bl; stylish Coleraine Cab Sauv/Merlot (**95'** 98' 00'). Second label Awatea blend v.gd with less new oak.

Te Motu Waiheke Island ★★ Top wine of Waiheke Vineyards, owned by the Dunleavy and Buffalora families. Dark, concentrated, brambly red of v.gd quality, first vintage 93. Dunleavy Cab Sauv/Merlot is second label.

The best Sauvignon Blancs from New Zealand
Marlborough produces inimitably zesty and explosively flavoured Sauvignon Blancs, best drunk young (6–18 months). Hawke's Bay's more robust, ripely herbaceous, and rounded Sauvignons are less punchy, but better suited to barrel maturation. Classic labels include Montana Brancott Estate, Cloudy Bay, Hunter's, Goldwater, Grove Mill, Isabel, Lawson's Dry Hills, Palliser, Vavasour, Villa Maria Reserve, Saint Clair Wairau Reserve, Seresin, Wither Hills, and Whitehaven.

Thornbury ★★ V'yds in HAWKE'S BAY and MARLBOROUGH. Best known for weighty, rich, tropical fruit-flavoured MARLBOROUGH Sauv Bl.

Torlesse Waipara ★→★★ Small, gd value Canterbury producer of weighty, concentrated Sauv Bl; fresh, flinty Ries; and firm, toasty, citrus Chard.

Trinity Hill Hawke's Bay ★★ Part-owned by John Hancock (ex-MORTON ESTATE). Firm, concentrated reds since 96, and elegant Chard.

Unison Hawke's Bay ★★→★★★ Red specialist with dark, spicy, flavour-crammed blends of Merlot, Cab Sauv, and Syrah. Selection label is oak-aged longest.

Vavasour Marlborough ★★ Based in Awatere Valley. Immaculate, intense Chard and Sauv Bl; promising Pinot N. Dashwood is second label.

Vidal Hawke's Bay ★★→★★★ Established in 1905 by a Spaniard, now part of VILLA MARIA. Reserves (Chard, Cab Sauv/Merlot) uniformly high standard.

Villa Maria Auckland ★★→★★★ One of NZ's 3 largest wine companies, inc VIDAL and ESK VALLEY. Owned by George Fistonich. Top range: Reserve (Noble Ries NZ's most awarded sweet white); Cellar Selection: middle-tier (less oak); third-tier Private Bin wines can be excellent and top value (esp Ries, Sauv Bl, Gewurz). Brilliant track record in competitions.

Waipara Springs Canterbury ★★ Small producer with lively, cool climate Ries, Sauv Bl, and Chard; concentrated Reserve Pinot N.

Waipara West Canterbury ★★ Co-owned by London-based Kiwi wine distributor Paul Tutton. Finely scented lively Ries; freshly acidic, herbaceous Sauv Bl; firm citrus Chard; and increasingly ripe and substantial Pinot N.

Wairarapa NZ's Fifth-largest wine region. See MARTINBOROUGH.

Wairau River Marlborough ★★ Intense Sauv Bl; flinty, toasty Chard.

Wellington Capital city and name of region; inc WAIRARAPA, Te Horo, MARTINBOROUGH.

West Brook Auckland ★★ Long-established under-rated, richly flavoured Chard, Sauv Bl, and Ries. Top wines labelled Blue Ridge.

Whitehaven Marlborough ★★ Excellent wines: racy Ries; scented, delicate, lively Sauv Bl; flavourful, easy Chard.

Wither Hills Marlborough ★★★ Established by former DELEGAT's winemaker Brent Marris, sold to Lion Nathan in 2002. Exceptional Chard, Sauv Bl. Serious, concentrated, spicy Pinot N.

South Africa

Why is South Africa no longer an also-ran beside top New World wine producers? There's been a marked leap in quality in the last two or three years. The leading reds are more finely tuned, their tannins riper and better rounded. Whites too, at the top end, especially Sauvignon Blancs, are fresher, less blowsy – though most, including Chardonnays, are still best drunk young. Almost across the board, the best advice is to go for youth. Even among serious reds, real quality shines – and lurks, there are scores of new producers each year now – most frequently in wines that are well under 10 years old.

All this is partly the pay-off for a decade of incremental upgrading in vineyards. But perhaps even more important, in the years since the end of apartheid sanctions, an invasion of new domestic and foreign investors. A younger Cape generation have also wrested the controls from an establishment that often confused tradition with quality. South Africa was cramped, too, by inertia after its long isolation from world markets, the comfort of subsidies, fixed local prices, and production quota guarantees.

South Africa is the eighth-largest producer in the world, with the kind of intense internal rivalry that's propelled quality in California and Australia; and, using modern vineyard canopy management and virus-controlling regimens, grape quality and selection has improved beyond all recognition. Exports have soared, increasing tenfold since 1994. The stylistic debates now are about how to achieve elegance rather than flamboyance; there is a real attempt to make Cape Shiraz, or Syrah, more European and less jammy; growers are teasing more of the grape (than oak, for example) into the bottle; are working to broaden varietal choices, and to match climates and soils to grapes.

In fact, international pundits and visiting wine gurus are starting to list the Cape as among the most exciting of all New World wine regions, a judgement perhaps not entirely unrelated to its magnificent mountain-to-ocean vistas, the charming old Cape Dutch architecture, and much-improved culinary scene.

Recent vintages

2003 Excellent: hot, dry, generally disease-free. Concentrated, rich reds, for longer keeping. Heatwave mid-harvest denied whites some fresh, tropical flavours. Cape dry whites best drunk within 2–3 years.

2002 Wet, mildewy start then a long heatwave in many districts; most top growers made reds of good colour and fruit.

2001 Lower-than-average yields, concentrated fruit. Among the better recent red vintages. Big wines, deep colours, should keep well.

2000 Third successive year of high temperatures, then isolated hailstorms. General improvement in vineyard management yielded promising reds.

1999 Prolonged heatwave prior to harvest pushed up alcohol; some massive, unbalanced wines

1998 Searingly hot, dry vintage from outset, curtailing season. Low yields helped quality. Big, high-alcohol reds.

1997 Longest, coolest season in decades, allowing for gradual ripening; fine red year.

African Terroir Wines ★★ Big, Swiss-owned STELLENBOSCH- and PAARL-based winery. Widely sourced grapes, several gd value ranges. Azania Syrah **01 02**; Out of Africa Shiraz **01 02** 03; Winds of Change range has gd Sauv Bl.

Allesverloren r ★★ Old family estate in Swartland W of Cape Town. Both Cab Sauv **99** oo and Shiraz **00 01** less rugged than before. Local acclaim for smooth, sweet port style **89 90, 93 96 97**.

Anthony de Jager Wines r ★★★ Fairview Estate winemaker's own label; intriguing, complex Shiraz/Viognier blend Homtini **00** 02.

Asara St'bosch r w ★★ Old estate, recent makeover (formerly Verdun). Fine reds. Bell Tower Cab Sauv/Merlot 97 98' is flagship. Outstanding CHENIN BLANC dessert botrytis.

Avontuur St'bosch r w sw ★★ Reputation for dense lemony Chard, fruity oaked Reserve PINOTAGE **99** 00 01. Gd sparkling Brut NV, from Pinot N/Chard. Barrel-aged, botrytis Ries "Above Royalty".

Axe Hill r sw ★★★ Outstanding tiny specialist producer of vintage port style at Calitzdorp. Touriga Nacional, Tinta Barroca **97** 98 99 00 01.

Backsberg r w sw ★→★★ Large PAARL estate reclaiming former reputation with 2002 releases. Top is new Babylonstoren B'x blend 02, Chard, Viognier. Gd value under other labels. Also outstanding cask-aged Sydney Back brandy.

Beaumont r w ★★ Walker Bay. Small, family-run winery, with reputation for Rhône-style reds: Shiraz **99 01** 02; dense, dark Mourvèdre **99 01** 02. Gd PINOTAGE Reserve **99 00** 01, Chard, and old vine CHENIN BLANC.

Bellingham r w ★→★★ Gd reds in premium "Spitz" range. Cab Fr **99'**, PINOTAGE **96 99**, Shiraz **98 99 00** 02. Popular whites (all DYA), Chard, Sauv Bl, and Chard/Sauv Bl blend Sauvenay.

Beyerskloof St'bosch r ★★→★★★ Small specialist grower. Deep-flavoured Cab Sauv/Merlot blend **97 98 99 00** 01; PINOTAGE **98 99 00** 01; PINOTAGE Res 02. Also interesting Cape blend (Pinotage/Cab Sauv/Merlot) Synergy 02.

Boekenhoutskloof r w ★★★ Franschhoek. A Cape star, with spicy Syrah **97' 98 99 00** 01'; acclaimed Cab Sauv **97 98** 99' 00; new blend Chocolate Block 02 is supple, rich-flavoured Grenache/Cab Sauv/Viognier/Cinsault mix. Also excellent Sem. Gd value second label Porcupine Ridge.

Boplaas r w sw ★→★★★ Estate in dry, hot Karoo. Earthy, deep Cape Vintage Res port style **86 91 94 96 97 99'**, fortified Muscadels, and Cape Tawny Port NV.

Boschendal r w sp ★★ Cape's biggest estate nr Franschhoek (recently sold to foreign/local black joint venture). Gd whites, inc bold Res Chard, Sauv Bl. V.gd Shiraz **97 98 99**; renamed Syrah 01. Also B'x blend Grand Reserve 97

98 99 00, Res Cab Sauv 00, Merlot **97 98 99 01**.

Bouchard-Finlayson Walker Bay r w ★★★ Leading Pinot N producer: Galpin Peak **97 99 00 01** 02 and Tête de Cuvée **99 01'** 02. Excellent Chard sp "Missionvale" label, also Kaaimansgat **01 02 03**. V.gd Sauv Bl (DYA).

Buitenverwachting r w sp ★★→★★★ Historic German-owned estate in Constantia suburbs of Cape Town. Stand-out Sauv Bl, generally DYA, Chard **02 03**, B'x blend Christine **96 98 99** 00', Cab Sauv **95 99** 00, Merlot **95 99** 01.

Cabrière Estate Franschhoek ★★ Gd NV sparklers under Pierre Jourdan label (Brut Sauvage, Chard/Pinot N, and Belle Rosé Pinot N). Also fine Pinot N in some years **94 00**.

Cape Point Vineyards Cape Point r w ★★ Atlantic on both sides of these v'yds on the Peninsula. Outstanding Sauv Bl (DYA), Sauv Bl/Sem, Sem dessert.

Cederberg Wines r w ★★→★★★ High Cape v'yds. Scintillating, fruity, crisp whites: Sauv Bl, Reserve CHENIN BLANC. Superb Cab Sauv-based blend "V Generations" **00'** 01.

Château Libertas Big-selling blend of mainly Cab Sauv made by STELLENBOSCH FARMERS' WINERY.

Chenin Blanc Most widely planted grape; very adaptable. Sometimes v.gd; much upgrading by leading growers, inc with barrel-fermentation, to improve ageability. Generally, short-lived; lasts better when sweet.

Clos Malverne St'bosch ★★ Small estate, with reputation for PINOTAGE Res **97 98 99 00** 01, Cab Sauv/Merlot/PINOTAGE blend "Auret" **97 98 99 01**.

Constantia Once the world's most famous sweet, Muscat-based wines (both red and white), from the Cape. See KLEIN CONSTANTIA.

Constantia Uitsig r w ★★ Specializing in Chard Res, Sem Res, Cab Sauv/Merlot 00 from premium Constantia v'yds (with top restaurant of same name).

Cordoba St'bosch r w ★★→★★★ Highly regarded winery/v'yds on Helderberg mountains. Stylish Cab Fr-based claret blend labelled Crescendo **97 98 99 00'**; plus ripe, rich Merlot **96 97 98 01'**.

Darling Cellars r w sw ★→★★ Atlantic Coast W of Cape Town, Onyx label tops large range which also inc: PINOTAGE, Shiraz, Grenache, gd Cab Sauv. Gd value DC range.

De Krans Estate ★→★★ Karoo semi-desert v'yds make rich, full Vintage Reserve port style. Best **91 94 95 97** 99. Also traditional fortified sw r and Muscadels.

De Toren St'bosch r ★★★ Among Cape's finest new labels. B'x blend Fusion V **99 00 01**. Obssesive v'yd management and berry selection make for elegance and complexity.

De Trafford Wines St'bosch r w ★★★ Exceptional small-scale artisan specializing in unfiltered, natural yeast fermentation B'x blend "Elevation 393" **98 99 00** 01; Cab Sauv **97 98 99** 00 01; Shiraz **98'** 00 01; Merlot **00'** 01 02). Also dry CHENIN BLANC in oak and dessert CHENIN BLANC Vin de Paille worth cellaring.

De Wetshof Robertson w sw ★★ Large-scale producer, inc Chards of varying style – top are flagship barrel-selected Bateleur **01 02 03** and Finesse 02 **03**. Also Sauv Bl, Gewurz, Danie de Wet Rhine Ries, Edeloes botrytis dessert. Exports own-brand Chard for supermarkets.

Delaire Winery St'bosch r w ★★ Mountain v'yds at Helshoogte Pass. Rich Chard **01 02 03**, massive Cab Sauv Botmaskop 98 **00** 02, Merlot **98** 00.

Delheim St'bosch r w dr sw ★→★★★ Family winery. Acclaimed Vera Cruz Shiraz **98** 00 **01**; plummy Grand Res B'x blend **96 97** 98 **99** 00. Gd Cab Sauv **98 99** 00; also Chard and Sauv Bl. Outstanding botrytis Steen, Edelspatz.

Domaines Paradyskloof r w ★★★ Highly rated STELLENBOSCH properties inc Vriesenhof, Talana Hill, and Paradyskloof labels. Run by Cape wine (and rugby) character, Jan Boland Coetzee. Winning approving notices for Pinot N **00** 01. Firm B'x blend flagship Kallista **95 97 98 99** 00 01, Cab Sauv **95 97 98**

99 00, gd Chard. Gd B'x blend Talana Hill (**99** 01') Chard.

Dornier Wines St'bosch r w ★★ Massive new foreign investment, promising start with B'x blend, Cab Sauv/Cab Fr/Merlot/Shiraz 02; excellent flinty core to fruity CHENIN BLANC/Sem/Sauv Bl **03**.

Durbanville Hills r w ★★ Maritime-cooled v'yds. Fine reds: single-v'yd Caapman Cab Sauv/Merlot **99**. Premium range Cab Sauv, Merlot, PINOTAGE, Shiraz all **99 00 01**. Several gd Sauv Bl and Chard labels (DYA).

Edelkeur ★★★ Excellent, intensely sw, noble rot white from CHENIN BLANC by NEDERBURG – like all full-blown botrytis desserts, officially designated Noble Late Harvest.

Eikendal Vineyards r w sw ★→★★ Swiss-owned 100-acre v'yds, winery on Helderburg, STELLENBOSCH. Merlot **98 99 00 01** 02. Consistently gd Chard **01 02** 03; Cab Sauv Res **94 96 99** 00.

Ernie Els r ★★★ South Africa's golfing great's rich aromatic B'x blend **00** 01' with fruit from Helderburg/STELLENBOSCH v'yds. Made at Rust en Vrede.

Estate Wine Official term for wines grown and made (not necessarily bottled)

A choice from South Africa for 2005

Cabernet Franc Raats Family, Warwick

Cabernet Sauvignon/Bordeaux-style blends Morgenster, Cordoba Crescendo, Rust en Vrede, Vergelegen V, De Toren, Etienne Le Riche, Jordan Cobblers Hill, Thelema, Rustenberg, Boukenhoutskloof, Rudera, Rupert & Rothschild, Morgenhof

Cape Red blend Flagstone, Beyerskloof, Kaapzicht, Warwick

Merlot Spice Route, Thelema, De Trafford, Steenberg, Morgenhof Reserve, Fleur du Cap (unfiltered)

Pinotage Spice Route, Newton Johnson, Beyerskloof, Kaapzicht, Uiterwyk, Nitida, Warwick, Kanonkop, L'Avenir

Pinot Noir Flagstone (Poetry Collection), Paul Cluver, Domaines Paradyskloof, Bouchard-Finalyson, Hamilton Russell

Ruby Cabernet Flagstone Ruby in the Dust

Shiraz/Syrah The Foundry, Fairview (Solitude, Beacon Rock), Anthony de Jager, Beaumont, Boekenhoutskloof, Hartenberg, Neil Ellis

Chardonnay Kumala (Journey's End), Glen Carlou, Bouchard Finlayson, L'Avenir, Neil Ellis, Jordan, Hamilton Russell, Thelema, Vergelegen

Chenin Blanc Rudera, Beaumont, Kanu, Cederberg, Ken Forrester, De Trafford, L'Avenir

Dry White Blends Fleur du Cap, Vergelegen, Dornier

Semillon Steenberg, Stellenzicht, Constantia Uitsig, Nitida, Boekenhoutskloof

Sauvignon Blanc Neil Ellis, Cederberg, Durbanville Hills, Nitida, Klein Constantia, Steenberg, Vergelegen Reserve, Thelema, Zondernaam, Havana Hills, Fleur du Cap

Dessert Asara, Ken Forrester Chenin Bl T, Kanu, De Trafford

Sparkling Desiderius (J C Le Roux), Villiera (Brut Natural Chardonnay), Graham Beck Brut, Blanc de Blancs

---

exclusively on registered estates. Not a quality designation.

Fairview r w dr sw ★★→★★★★ Cutting-edge Cape winery. Eclectic ranges inc many labels, styles of Shiraz-based reds (five labels and growing). Top range Red Seal, with outstanding Solitude, Beacon Rock, Cyril Back, Jackalsfontein (all Shiraz, all **01 02** 03); two Pinotages: Primo, Amos **00 01**; Pegleg Carignan **01 02** 03; Akkerbos Chard; Oom Pegel Sem. Regular labels inc gd Viognier **00 01 02** 03. Successful with Rhône-style blends (w r p) cheekily named Goats do Roam and Goat-Roti.

Flagstone r w ★★→★★★ Fast-rising Cape star. Best labels are The Berrio Sauv Bl (DYA); Cab Sauv **01**; Ruby in the Dust **02'**, Longitude Shiraz/Merlot/PINOTAGE **00** 02, Bowwood Cab Sauv/Merlot 02; Poetry Collection Pinot N **00**.

Fleur du Cap r w sw ★★→★★★ Recently improved wines from giant producer Distell at STELLENBOSCH, inc v.gd Unfiltered Collection. Gd Cab Sauv **96 98 00** 01, Merlot **96 98 00** 01; outstanding dry White Blend (Chard/Sauv Bl/Sem/ Viognier) **02'**. Also fine Gewurz, botrytis CHENIN BLANC, Chard, and Sauv Bl (DYA).

Gilga Wines St'bosch r ★★→★★★ A hit with intense spicy Syrah **98 00 01** 02.

Glen Carlou r w ★★★ Top Cape winery, v'yds at PAARL, recently bought out by Donald Hess (See California). Outstanding Chard Res **00 01 02 03**; B'x blend Grand Classique **95 97 98** 99' 00 01; full Pinot N **96 98 00** 01; spicy Shiraz **00 01** 02. Gd "port" **98**.

Graceland Vineyards St'bosch r ★★ Very promising unfiltered Cab Sauv **00** 01, Merlot **99 00** 01.

Graham Beck Winery Robertson r w sp ★★→★★★ Avant-garde properties producing classy MÉTHODE CAP CLASSIQUE bubblies: Brut RD NV; Blanc de Blancs Chard **93 96 97 98**; well-regarded Chard **00 01 02 03**. Cult-status Shiraz The Ridge **97 98 99 00** 01'. Cornerstone Cab Sauv **98 99** 01 and Old Road Pinotage **98 99** 00'. Also claret-style blend The William 99 00.

Grangehurst St'bosch r ★★→★★★ Small, top red specialist, buying in grapes. Outstanding Cape blend Nikela **97 98 99** (Cab Sauv, PINOTAGE, Merlot). Gd PINOTAGE **95 97 98** 00 and concentrated Cab Sauv/Merlot **95 96 97 98** 00'.

Groot Constantia r w ★→★★ Historic government-owned estate nr Cape Town. Superlative red and white Muscat desserts in early 19th C. Gd Cab Sauv/ Merlot Gouverneur's Reserve **97 99** 00 01, PINOTAGE **97 99** 00 01, Merlot **01**, Chard Reserve **00 01 02**, sw Weisser (Rhine) Ries **98 99 01**. Also "port" style and sparkling Chard.

Hamilton Russell Vineyards Walker Bay r w ★★★ Cape's "burgundy" specialist estate at Hermanus. Fine Pinot N **96 97 98 99 00** 01'. Classy Chard **97 98 99** 00 01 02. Small yields, French-inspired vinification, careful barrelling.

Hartenberg St'bosch r w ★★→★★★ Respected producer of Shiraz **96 97 00** 01. Lately laurels also for Merlot **00** 01 and Cab Sauv **00** 01. Zin **97 99** 00 01; Chard and sw Weisser (Rhine) Ries.

Havana Hills Durbanville r w ★★→★★★ Top coastal winery nr Cape Town. Best are Bisweni and Reserve Du Plessis range, both with deep-flavoured Cab Sauv **00** 01 and Merlot **00** 01 02. Also Shiraz **00** 01 02; excellent Sauv Bl (DYA).

Hazendal r w ★→★★ Old STELLENBOSCH estate. Flagship is Cab Sauv/Shiraz **97 98 99** 00 01. Also sparklers, PINOTAGE, and CHENIN BLANC.

Hidden Valley St'bosch r ★★★ Small Devon Valley v'yd. Outstanding PINOTAGE **96 97** 00. Classic Cab Sauv **99** 00.

J C le Roux St'bosch sp ★→★★★ Gd, large sparkling wine house. Top is Desiderius **96 97**; also Pinot N **90 96**; Blanc de Blancs Chard, long (5–9 yrs) maturation in bottle. Well-priced Pinot N/Chard NV blend Pongràcz MÉTHODE CAP CLASSIQUE.

Jordan Vineyards St'bosch r w ★★★ A Cape star. Excellent Chards **00 01 02** and Res **02'**. Cab Sauv blend Cobbler's Hill **97 98 99** 00'; Cab Sauv **98 99** 00'; Merlot **99 00 01** 02; v.gd Sauv Bl (DYA) and barrel-fermented CHENIN BLANC. California-trained husband-and-wife team Gary and Cathy Jordan.

J P Bredell St'bosch ★★ Rich, dark, deep Vintage Res port style (Tinta Barocca and Souzão) **91 95 97** 98. Also PINOTAGE **96 98 99**.

Kaapzicht Estate St'bosch r w ★★→★★★ Regularly tops local listings with Steytler range PINOTAGE **98 99 00** 01' and Vision blend (Pinotage/Cab Sauv/ Merlot) **98 00** 01'; well-crafted Cab Sauv **96 97 98 99** 00 01'.

Kanonkop St'bosch r ★★★ Grand local status, international plaudits for oak-finished PINOTAGE **91 94 97 98 99** 00 01. Equally distinctive, emphatic B'x-style blend Paul Sauer **89 91 94 95 97 98' 99** 00 01 and Cab Sauv **89 91 94 95 97 98 99'** 00 01.

Kanu Wines St'bosch r w sw ★★ Fine Cab Sauv Limited Release **98** 99 01'; Merlot **98 99 00 01**; barrel-aged, new-style CHENIN BLANC; v.gd Chard **01 02 03**; and Sauv Bl (DYA); botrytis dessert wine Kia Ora **99** 01.

Ken Forrester Vineyards St'bosch ★★→★★★ Helderberg producer (and restaurateur at 96 Winery Rd). Oustanding CHENIN BLANC from 30-yr-old+ bush vines sp under Family Reserve **97 98 00 01 02**. V.gd Sauv Bl (DYA). Botrytis CHENIN BLANC named T **00 01'**. Now a serious Syrah grower, with selection labels, topped by elegant Gypsy and Family Reserve, both **01** 02.

Klein Constantia Estate r w sw ★★ →★★★ Standout neighbour of more historic Groot Constantia with a Cape icon: from 1986, Vin de Constance revived 18th-C Constantia legend (mint/lime/coffee aromas) dessert from Muscat de Frontignan **93 94 95 96 97 98 99** 00. Bold, crisp Sauv Bl, DYA but can hang in for years; solid Chard **99 00 01** 03. Taut B'x-style blend Marlbrook **95 96 97** 99 00. Ageworthy, just off-dry Ries **01** 03.

Kleine Zalze St'bosch r w ★★ Gd reds inc Cab Sauv **99** 00 and Merlot 00. Barrel-fermented CHENIN BLANC and Chard **01 02 03**.

Kumala r w sp ★→★★ Gd value, many-tiered range by British-based Western Wines; biggest-selling Cape brand in UK (2 million cases p.a.). From 2004 entered the domestic South Africa market. Journey's End Cab Sauv **01** and Chard **01'** top lists. Also Kumala Res range, inc sound Cab Sauv 03, Merlot, PINOTAGE, Shiraz, Chard, Sauv Bl, and Chard Brut, MÉTHODE CAP CLASSIQUE.

KWV International Paarl r w sw ★→★★★ The Kooperatieve Wijnbouwers Vereniging, formerly South Africa's national wine co-op. Range of gd-to-excellent wines, esp Cathedral Cellar: Cab Sauv **95 96 97 99** 00, Merlot **96 97 98 99 00**, PINOTAGE **95 96 97 99**. B'x blend Triptych **94 95 96 97 98 99** 00, Shiraz **97 98 99** 00, Chard **01 02**. Regular KWV labels inc traditional blend (Shiraz/Merlot/Cab Sauv) Roodeberg, a legendary name in Cape wine **97 98' 99** 01, and a vast range of dry whites. Also sherry and port styles Vintage Port **97'**, Millenium Vintage Port **99**, Full Ruby NV. KWV-run La Borie Estate Shiraz Jean Taillefert **01**, Cab Sauv **96 98** 01. Also luxurious, fortified dessert from PINOTAGE, Pineau de Laborie, and classic MÉTHODE CAP CLASSIQUE bubbly **96 98**.

La Motte r w ★★ Lavishly appointed Rupert family estate nr Franschhoek. Gd reds: B'x-style blend Millennium **95 97** 98 **99** and Shiraz **95 96 97** 98 **99** 00.

L'Avenir St'bosch ★★→★★★ Outstanding estate. Leading producer of PINOTAGE **97 98 99 00 01** 02 and top, rich, sturdy Cape CHENIN BLANC **99 00 01 02**; Cab Sauv **95 97 99 00** 01, Chard **02 03**, and Sauv Bl (DYA). Also botrytis dessert Vin de Meurveur

Landskroon Estate r w ★→★★ Old (eight generations) family property in PAARL. Recently upgraded reds with Paul de Villiers Cab Sauv **99 01**; gd range of other Cab Sauv, Merlot, Shiraz **00 01**. Outstanding port style **96 97 98** 99.

Lanzerac St'bosch r w ★★ Big venture now under newly created Christo Wiese Portfolio inc old v'yds (and grand hotel) at Lanzerac and a vast spread at nearby Lourensford/Somerset West. Lanzerac Range Merlot **99 00** 01 and Cab Sauv **98 99**. Promising Five Heirs and Eden Crest for future.

Le Bonheur Estate St'bosch r w ★★ Minerally B'x blend Prima **97 98 99**, Cab Sauv **97 98** 99, and big-bodied Sauv Bl (DYA).

Le Riche Wines St'bosch r ★★→★★★ Outstanding boutique wines, hand-crafted by respected Etienne le Riche: Cab Sauv Res **97 98 99 00** 01, Cab Sauv **97 99** 00, Cab Sauv/Merlot **99 00 01**.

Linton Park Wellington r w ★★ British-owned venture producing warm, rich reds that reflect the sunny, hot climate→area: best are the Reserves – Shiraz

01 02, Cab Sauv 01, and Merlot **01**.

Longridge Winery St'bosch r w ★★ Forward, powerful reds: Cab Sauv 00 01, PINOTAGE **00 01**, Merlot **01**. Always gd Chard.

Long Mountain Wine ★→★★ Pernod-Ricard label, buying grapes from co-ops under peripatetic Aussie Robin Day and local Jacques Kruger. Well-priced Cab Sauv, Ruby Cab, Cab Sauv/Merlot Res, Chard, CHENIN BLANC.

L'Ormarins Estate r w sw ★★ One of two beautiful Rupert family estates nr Franschhoek. Best red is B'x blend Optima **96 97** 98 00'. Cab Sauv **91 94 99**.

Meerlust Estate St'bosch r w ★★→★★★ Prestigious old estate. Hannes Myburgh is eighth generation to own Meerlust. Fine – stressing elegance over impact – Rubicon B'x blend **91 92 95 97 98 99** 00; Merlot **91 95 96 97 99** 00'. Pinot N Reserve **96 97 98 99** 00'. Ripe, heavy Chard **99 00 01 02**.

Meinert Wines St'bosch r ★★→★★★ Two fine blends, Devon Crest (B'x) and Synchronicity (Cab Sauv/Cab Fr/Merlot/PINOTAGE) **00** 01. Merlot **98 00** 01 from Devon Valley v'yds. Owned by consultant Martin Meinert.

Méthode Cap Classique South African term for classic-method sparkling wine.

Morgenhof Estate St'bosch r w sw ★★→★★★ French-owned estate on a roll. Outstanding Merlot Res **98' 00** 01'. B'x blend Première Sélection **96 97 98 99** 00. Cab Sauv Res **98 01**. Also v.gd Chard **03**, CHENIN BLANC **01 02**, Sauv Bl (DYA); port style LBV **95**, and Vintage **98** 00. Brut Res **90 00** from Chard/Pinot N.

Morgenster Estate St'bosch r ★★★ Serious new Italian investment with Pierre Lurton consulting. Cab Fr-based B'x blend is fine; supple proprietary label, debut 00. Elegant second label B'x blend (Merlot/Cab Sauv/Cab Fr) **98 99** 00 01.

Mulderbosch Vineyards St'bosch r w ★★★ Penetrating Sauv Bl – DYA, but can last; two Chards, one oak-fermented 00' **01 02**, other fresh, less oaky **98 00 01**. V.gd barrel-fermented CHENIN BLANC Steen op Hout **99 00** 01'. Easy, B'x-style blend, Faithful Hound **94 97 98 00** 01.

Muratie Estate r ★★ Old STELLENBOSCH estate. B'x blend Ansela **96 97 98** 01, gd Shiraz **01** 02, and Cab Sauv 00 01. Sumptuous vintage port **98** 99, ruby-style NV "port" – all Portuguese varieties. Fortified Muscat Amber, with loyal following since 1925. Gd Chard Isabella.

Nederburg Paarl r w p dr sw s/sw sp ★→★★ Large winery established 1937. Own grapes and suppliers. Makeover in progress under Romanian Razvan Macici. Improving Classic reds inc Edelrood blend **99 00 01** and Cab Sauv **00** 01. Also Chard, Sauv Bl, Ries, and sparklers. Small quantities of Limited Vintage, Private Bins for auction, some outstanding (Private Bin PINOTAGE **97 99** 00; Shiraz **00** 01). A 1970s' pioneer of botrytis sw wines. Stages Cape's biggest annual wine event, the Nederburg Auction. See also EDELKEUR.

Neethlingshof St'bosch r w sw ★★ Large estate, many labels. Lord Neethling range Laurentius Shiraz/Cab Sauv blend **97 98**; Cab Sauv **97 98 99**; PINOTAGE **99** 00'; standard Cab Sauv **94 96 97 98 99** 00; Cape blend 01; Shiraz **98 99 00** 01; Chard; excellent Gewurz, and blush Blanc de Noirs. Champion botrytis wines from Weisser Riesling.

Neil Ellis Wines St'bosch r w ★★★ Among most respected Cape names. Full, forthright wines from widely sourced grapes, vinified at Jonkershoek Valley. Top-flight Res V'yd Selection Cab Sauv **97 98 99** 00 01, Shiraz **97 98 99 00** 01'. Premium STELLENBOSCH range: Cab Sauv **94 96 97 99** 00 01', PINOTAGE **98 99 00** 01 Shiraz **97 98 99** 00, Cab Sauv/Merlot 97 98 99. Always excellent Sauv Bl, inc Groenkloof (DYA), and full bold Chards from STELLENBOSCH and Elgin **01' 02**.

Newton-Johnson Wines r w ★★→★★★ Sourcing grapes widely, supplemented by own harvests/labels: family-run winery at Walker Bay. Among few v.gd Cape Pinot N growers with 00' **01** 02. Also Cab Sauv **98 99 00** 01, PINOTAGE **98 00 01** 02, lemony Chard, and intense Sauv Bl: Sandstone and regular (DYA). Gd value Cape Bay labels.

Nitida Cellars r w Durbanville ★★ Small v.gd range: Cab Sauv **00** 01; PINOTAGE 01 02; B'x blend Calligraphy **00 01**; Sauv Bl (DYA) and excellent Sem **02 03**.

Overgaauw Estate St'bosch r w ★★ Old (1783) family estate. Excellent Merlot **98 99** 01 and B'x blend Tria Corda **97 98 99** 01, v.gd Cab Sauv **97 98 99 00** 01. Also two excellent port styles: Cape Vintage **91 97 98'** and Reserve **97**.

Paarl Town 30 miles NE of Cape Town and the wine district around it.

Paul Cluver Estate r w ★★ Gd Pinot N **98 00 01 02'** and Cab Sauv 00 01 from fashionable Elgin region, E of Cape Town. Also elegant Chard, botrytis dessert, and off-dry Rhine Weisser Ries **00 01 03'**. Stylish, aromatic off-dry Gewurz.

Pinotage South African red grape cross of Pinot N and Cinsault, "born" in 1926. Can be delicious – intriguing boiled-sweets and banana flavours – and has shown potential if carefully matured in oak. But coarse, estery flamboyance can dominate (and often does). Now featuring in growing number of "Cape blends", a local term sometimes used to differentiate these from B'x blends where Pinotage is usually absent. (Not yet legislated stipulation though.)

Plaisir de Merle r w ★★ Grand, Distell-owned cellar, v'yds nr PAARL. Approachable Merlot **99 00 01**, weightier Grand Plaisir B'x blend 01.

Quoin Rock St'bosch r w ★★★ Lavish winery aiming for cult status. Debut with rich, plush Merlot 01; elegant dry white flagship Oculus 01 02; also clean-cut Chard and Sauv Bl from v'yds at cooler, southerly Cape Agulhas region.

Raats Family St'bosch r w ★★ Promising new label, deep-scented, minerally Cab Franc 01 and two outstanding CHENIN BLANCS **02 03**.

Radford-Dale r w ★★ Aussie Ben Radford and Briton Alex Dale source grapes for small-scale premium exports as The Winery venture. Initial Merlot **00** 01, unfiltered Shiraz 01, and Chard **00 01 02**. Also Vinum Cab Sauv and Chard.

Rickety Bridge Franschhoek r w ★★ V.gd Shiraz **97 98** 00 01 and Cab Sauv/Merlot flagship Paulinas Reserve **96** 00 01'. Also gd Chard and Sem.

Robertson District Inland from Cape. Mainly dessert (notably Muscat) and white wines. Determined effort now to increase red v'yds.

R&R at Fredericksburg Winery r w ★★→★★★ Top v'yds, cellar at Simondium, PAARL. Joint venture between Baron Edmond Rothschild (not the First Growth family) and Rupert, two old French and South African wine families. Mellow, soft Cab Sauv/Cab Fr/Merlot **97 98 99** 00 01 named Baron Edmond since 1998. Chard Baroness Nadine **99 00 01** a deep-flavoured classic.

Rudera Wines St'bosch r w ★★→★★★ Among best of new crop Cape names. Classy Cab Sauv **00**, Syrah 01; three CHENIN BLANCS, fresh, oak-fermented, and botrytis, all outstanding **01 02**.

Rustenberg Wines r w ★★★→★★★★ Prestigious old STELLENBOSCH estate, founded 300 yrs ago, making wine continuously for more than a hundred. Flagship is single-v'yd Peter Barlow Cab Sauv **97 98 99** 01 02; Rustenberg B'x blend John X Merriman **97 98 99 00** 01. Outstanding Chard Five Soldiers **01 02** 03. Also top second label Brampton, Cab Sauv/Merlot **98 99 00 01** 02, plus Chard, Sauv Bl.

Rust en Vrede Estate r ★★★ Estate just E of STELLENBOSCH: best-known for strong, individual, mainly Cab Sauv blend Rust en Vrede Estate Wine, superb in latest releases **91 94 96 97 98 99** 00 01. Solid Cab Sauv **91 94 96** 98 99 and Shiraz **94 96 97** 98.

Sadie Family Wines Swartland r ★★★ Outstanding Columella (Shiraz/ Mourvèdre) 00 01 is set to become Cape benchmark. Also an intriguing Viognier/ Chard/CHENIN BLANC blend from **02**. Star winemaker Eben Sadie.

Saxenburg Wines St'bosch r w dr sw sp ★★→★★★ Swiss-owned v'yds and winery jointly run with French Château Capion. Distinctive, powerful Cape reds: Private Collection Shiraz **95 96 97 98 99** 00' and Shiraz Saxenburg Select **98 00** 01. Robust, deep-flavoured PINOTAGE **96 98 99 00** 01, Cab

Sauv **94 95 97 99 00 01**. Also Merlot, Chard, Sauv Bl, and sweet Gewurz.

Seidelberg Estate r w ★★ PAARL. Major revamp of beautifully situated v'yds, (formerly De Leuwen Jagt) with Reserve Merlot **99 00 01**, Syrah **01**, Chard **01 02**, and CHENIN BLANC **01 02 03**.

Simonsig Estate St'bosch r w sp sw ★★ Malan family winery. Extensive range inc: red blend Tiara **94 95 97 98 99 00 01**; Frans Malan Reserve, mainly PINOTAGE **98 99 00 01**; Red Hill PINOTAGE **99 00 01**; Syrah Res Merindol **97 98 99 00**; v.gd Chard **00 01 02**; dessert style Gewurz. First (30 yrs ago) Cape MÉTHODE CAP CLASSIQUE, Kaapse Vonkel brut from Pinot N/Chard.

Simonsvlei International r w p sw sp ★ One of South Africa's best-known co-op cellars, just outside PAARL. Many tiers of quality, from Hercules Paragon (Merlot) to Mount Marble.

Spice Route Wine Company r w ★★→★★★ Malmesbury, fashionable West Coast region. Very intense, dark, rich flagship Syrah **98 99 00 01**, Merlot **98 99 00 01'**, PINOTAGE **98 99 00 01**; full, barrel-fermented CHENIN BLANC **99 02 03**.

Spier Cellars St'bosch r w ★★ A Wine Corp label. Expanding labels under premium Private Collection Cab Sauv **98 00 01**, Merlot **98 99 00 01**. Promising new dry whites inc: Sem, Viognier, CHENIN BLANC, fresh Sauv Bl, and dessert botrytis.

Springfield Estate Robertson ★★→★★★ Distinctive wines from whole-berry and wild yeast fermentation. Two v.gd softer style Cab Sauvs, unfiltered, unfined: Whole Berry **98 99 00 01'** and Méthode Anciènne (wild yeast) **98**; B'x blend Cab Fr/Merlot/Petit Verdot **01**. Also crisp Sauv Bl (DYA), and rich, wild, yeast Chard under Méthode Anciènne **00 01 02 03**.

Steenberg Vineyards Constantia r w ★★★ Serious, elegant Merlot **98 99 00 01 02** and red blend Catharina **97 99 00 01**. Consistently outstanding Sauv Bls: flinty Res **00 01 02 03** and fruitier Regular **00 01 02 03**. Two lasting Sems (**00 01 02**), oaked and unoaked. Gd sparkling Brut 1682 NV. Also Nebbiolo **01 02**.

Stellenbosch Oak-shaded university town, second oldest in South Africa, and demarcated wine district 30 miles E of Cape Town. Heart of the wine industry – the Napa of the Cape. Many top estates, especially for reds, tucked into mountain valleys and wine routes, many restaurants.

Stellenbosch Farmers' Winery (SFW) World's fifth-largest winery, part of SA's biggest wine conglomerate Distell: equivalent of 14 million cases p.a. Ranges inc NEDERBURG; top is ZONNEBLOEM. Wide selection of mid- and low-price wines.

Stellenbosch Vineyards ★→★★ Big regional venture by some 150 growers (from former co-ops Welmoed, Eersterivier, Helderberg, Bottelary). Top range is Genesis Cab Sauv **00 01**; big, juicy Merlot **99 00 01**; v.gd Shiraz **97 98 99 00'**, Chard. Kumkani label features tropical-fruit Sauv Bl and gd value reds, inc Shiraz (DYA). Gd value wines, inc CHENIN BLANC-based dry white Versus.

Stellenzicht St'bosch ★★ Modern winery, neat mountainside v'yds. V.gd Syrah **94 95 97 98 99 00 01**, well-regarded B'x blend Stellenzicht **94 95 97 98 99 00 01**, PINOTAGE **98 99 01**, Sem Res **00 01 02**. Golden Triangle range inc gd Cab Sauv, Malbec, PINOTAGE, Shiraz.

The Foundry St'bosch r ★★★ Sources grapes in STELLENBOSCH and PAARL. Among new names re-writing Cape pecking order. Outstanding, rich, intense Syrah **01' 02**.

Thelema Mountain Vineyards St'bosch r w ★★★→★★★★ Winemaker Gyles Webb and Thelema have been top international names for more than a decade. Cab Sauv **91 92 93 94 95 97 98 99 00' 01**, Merlot **97 98 99 00 01**, ultra-rich Merlot Res **99' 00**. Elegant Shiraz **00 01'**, Chard **99 00 01 03**, Sauv Bl (DYA). Individual, spicy, rich Chard named Ed's Reserve **99 00 02**. Immaculate v'yds.

Tokara St'bosch r w Ultra-modern winery, newly planted v'yds under direction of Gyles Webb (THELEMA). First releases due 2004/2005. Second label ZONDERNAAM Sauv Bl **02 03** (DYA) won best white in SAA airline tastings in 2002/3. Also gd Cab Sauv **00 01** and PINOTAGE **01**.

Uiterwyk Estate r w ★★ Old estate SW of STELLENBOSCH. De Waal is top range, inc striking single-v'yd PINOTAGE Top of the Hill 96 97 00 01. V.gd Estate Wine Cab Sauv-based blend (inc PINOTAGE) 94 96 97 98 99 00, Shiraz 01. Also Viognier, Chard, Sauv Bl.

Veenwouden r ★★★ Immaculate family-run PAARL property owned by Geneva-based opera singer Deon Van der Walt. Outstanding Merlot 97 98 99 00 01 and B'x blend Veenwouden Classic 96 97 98 99 00. Chard Special Reserve from 02.

Vergelegen St'bosch r w ★★★→★★★★ One of Cape's oldest wine farms (founded 1700) in Helderberg and hottest names. Talented, outspoken winemaker André van Rensburg is brilliant, complex, like his reds: new flagship "V" Cab Sauv 01 is a dark, rich powerhouse aiming for Cape icon status; B'x blend Vergelegen 98 99' 00 01', Cab Sauv 97 98 99 00 01', Merlot 98 99 00 01, exceptional spicy Shiraz 01'. Estate White is taut, elegant Sauv Bl/Sem barrel-fermented 01 02'. Superb fresh, lemony Chard Res 99 00 01 02 03 and racy Sauv Bl Reserve. Cracker dessert: Noble Late Harvest Sem 98 00.

Vergenoegd r w sw ★★ Old STELLENBOSCH family estate. B'x blend 95 97 98 99 00 01, Cab Sauv 95 98 00, Shiraz 96 97 98 00 01. Vintage port style 93 94 95 96 97 00.

Villiera Wines St'bosch r w sp ★★→★★★ Big family-run winery with excellent quality range, inc five MÉTHODE CAP CLASSIQUE bubblies: Brut Natural Chard 98 99 00', virtually organic; Vintage Brut 95; Tradition Brut NV and Rosé NV; Monro Brut Première Cuvée 95 96. Sound reds: B'x blend Cru Monro 96 97 98 99 00, unusual Merlot/PINOTAGE 98 00 01, Merlot Res 98 99, single-v'yd spicy Shiraz 99 00 01 02. Consistently gd and gd value Bush Vine Sauv Bl (DYA); dry CHENIN BLANC; dessert botrytis CHENIN BLANC (00); port style 95 97 98'.

Vredendal Cooperative r w dr sw ★ South Africa's largest co-op winery in warm Olifants River region. Improving reds, inc Shiraz Mt Maskam. Huge range, mostly white. Big exporter of various supermarket labels.

Warwick Estate St'bosch r w ★★→★★★ Consistently gd B'x blend Trilogy 95 97 98 99 00' 01 and Cape blend Three Ladies 97 98 99 01'. Fine individual Cab Fr 94 95 97 98 00 01'. Top Old Bush Vine PINOTAGE 97 98 00 01 from 25-yr-old vines. V.gd Chard.

Waterford St'bosch r w ★★ Showpiece winery. Kevin Arnold Shiraz (lately with Mourvèdre) 98 99 00 01 02, Cab Sauv 99 00 01 02'. V.gd Sauv Bl (DYA) and Chard 02.

Welgemeend Estate Paarl r ★★ Boutique estate: B'x-style blend 96 97 98 00. Amade blend 98 00. Malbec-based blend Douelle 96 97 98 00.

WhaleHaven Wines Walker Bay r w ★★ Local reputation for Pinot N Oak Valley 97 98 99 00 01; cool-climate, limey crispness in Chard.

Wine Corp Umbrella group at STELLENBOSCH, controlling SPIER CELLARS, Longridge, Savanha, Capelands.

Wine of Origin The Cape's "*appellation contrôlée*", but without French crop-yield restrictions. Certifies the following: vintage, variety, region of origin.

Woolworths Top supermarket chain with expansive selection. Many of Cape's best producers are regular suppliers.

Worcester Demarcated wine district round BREEDE and Hex river valleys, E of PAARL. Many co-op cellars. Mainly dessert wines, brandy, dry whites.

Zondernaam (meaning "no name" in Afrikaans) Award-winning second label of Tokara. Excellent Sauv Bl 02 03 (DYA). Also gd Cab Sauv 00 01, PINOTAGE 01.

Zonnebloem r w sw ★★ (Cab Sauv) STELLENBOSCH FARMERS' WINERY's top wines, with Fine Art range: Shiraz/Malbec 01, Cab Sauv/Shiraz 01. Gd value standard range inc Merlot 99 00 02, Shiraz 99 00 01 02, and Cab Sauv 94 95 98 99 01. B'x blend Laureat 94 96 97 98 00 01', PINOTAGE 98 99 00 01, Sauv Bl (DYA), Chard 02 03. Also popular Blanc de Blanc Sauv Bl/CHENIN BLANC blend.

A little learning...

A few technical words

The jargon of laboratory analysis is often seen on back-labels. It creeps menacingly into newspapers and magazines. What does it mean? This hard-edged wine-talk, unsympathetic as it is to most lovers of wine, is very briefly explained below.

The most frequent technical references are to the ripeness of grapes at picking; the resultant alcohol and sugar content of the wine; various measures of its acidity; the sulphur dioxide used as a preservative; and occasionally the amount of "dry extract"– the sum of all the things that give wine its character. And about the barrels.

The **sugar** in wine is mainly glucose and fructose, with traces of arabinose, xylose and other sugars that are not fermentable by yeast, but can be attacked by bacteria. Each country has its own system for measuring the sugar content or ripeness of grapes, known in English as the **"must weight"**. The chart below relates the three principal systems (German, French, American) to each other, to specific gravity, and to the potential alcohol of the wine if all the sugar is fermented.

Sugar to alcohol: potential strength

Specific Gravity	°Oechsle	Baumé	Brix	% Potential Alcohol v/v
1.065	65	8.8	15.8	8.1
1.070	70	9.4	17.0	8.8
1.075	75	10.1	18.1	9.4
1.080	80	10.7	19.3	10.0
1.085	85	11.3	20.4	10.6
1.090	90	11.9	21.5	12.1
1.095	95	12.5	22.5	13.0
1.100	100	13.1	23.7	13.6
1.105	105	13.7	24.8	14.3
1.110	110	14.3	25.8	15.1
1.115	115	14.9	26.9	15.7
1.120	120	15.5	28.0	16.4

Residual sugar is the sugar left after fermentation has finished or been stopped, measured in grams per litre. A dry wine has virtually none.

Alcohol content (mainly ethyl alcohol) is expressed in per cent by volume of the total liquid. (Also known as "degrees".) Table wines are usually between 11.5° and 13.5°, though up to 15° is increasingly seen.

Acidity is both fixed and volatile. **Fixed acidity** consists principally of tartaric, malic and citric acids, all found in the grape, and lactic and succinic acids, produced during fermentation. **Volatile acidity** consists mainly of acetic acid, which is rapidly formed by bacteria in the presence of oxygen. A small amount of volatile acidity is inevitable and even attractive. With a larger amount the wine becomes "pricked"– to use the Shakespearian term. It turns to vinegar. Acidity may be natural, in warm regions it may also be added.

Total acidity is fixed and volatile acidity combined. As a rule of thumb, for a well-balanced wine it should be in the region of one gram per thousand for each 10° Oechsle (see table on p.283).

Barriques Too much of the flavour of many modern wines is added in the form of oak; either from ageing and/or fermenting in barrels (the newer the barrel the stronger the influence) or from the addition of oak chips or – at worst – oak essence. Newcomers to wine can easily be beguiled by the vanilla-like scent and flavour into thinking they have bought something luxurious rather than something cosmetically flavoured. But barrels are expensive; real ones are only used for wines with the inherent quality to benefit long-term. French oak is classic and most expensive; especially that from the Allier, the famous Tronçais forest, Burgundy, the Vosges, Nevers, and Limoges. Each supposedly has a different flavour and influence – which can be altered by "toasting" the inside to different degrees when the barrel is constructed. American oak has a strong vanilla flavour. Baltic oak is more neutral.

Malolactic fermentation is often referred to as a secondary fermentation, and can occur naturally or be induced. The process involves converting tart malic acid into softer lactic acid. Unrelated to alcoholic fermentation, "*la malo*" can add complexity and flavour to both red and white wines. In hotter climates where natural acidity may be low canny operators avoid it.

Micro-oxygenation is a widely used technique that allows the wine controlled contact with oxygen during maturation. This mimics the effect of barrel-ageing, reduces the need for racking, and helps to stabilize the wine.

pH is a measure of the strength of the acidity: the lower the figure the more acid. Wine usually ranges from pH 2.8 to 3.8. High pH can be a problem in hot climates. Lower pH gives better colour, helps stop bacterial spoilage and allows more of the SO_2 to be free and active as a preservative.

Sulphur dioxide (SO_2) is added to prevent oxidation and other accidents in winemaking. Some of it combines with sugars etc and is **"bound"**. Only the **"free" SO_2** is effective as a preservative. **Total SO_2** is controlled by law according to the level of residual sugar: the more sugar, the more SO_2 is needed.

Tannins are the focus of attention for red winemakers intent on producing softer, more approachable wines. Later picking, and picking by tannin ripeness rather than sugar levels gives riper, silkier tannins.

Toast refers to the burning of the inside of the barrel. "High toast" gives the wine caramel-like flavours.

Organic and Biodynamic wines

There is no such thing as "organic wine" under EU law, only wine made from organically grown grapes. (US law is different.) That means no chemicals may be used in the vineyard, although an exception is made for Bordeaux mixture (copper sulphate plus lime) which is effective against downy mildew.

Biodynamism goes further. Based on the theories of Rudolf Steiner, biodynamism views the soil and the vine as part of a larger whole embracing the planets and the cosmos. Chemicals are forbidden (again, with the exception of Bordeaux mixture) and instead vines and soil are treated with homeopathic quantities of preparations dynamised (stirred in water) by hand to harness cosmic forces. Converts (including many top Burgundy domaines) report healthier vines and better ripening. The unconverted may see it as quackery. What we need is research to show rational reasons why it works, as it seems to do.

And the score is...

It seems that America and the rest of the world will never agree about the idea of scoring wines. America is seemingly besotted with the 100-point scale devised by Robert Parker, based on the strange US school system in which 50 = 0. Arguments that taste is too various, too subtle, too evanescent, too wonderful to be reduced to a pseudo-scientific set of numbers fall on deaf ears. Arguments that the accuracy implied by giving one wine a score of 87 and another 88 is a chimera don't get much further. Numbers are too useful to investors.

European critics do use numbers, but smaller, less dramatic ones. A 20-point system is popular among professionals; others use a 7-point scale, and the magazine *Decanter* a 5-star system which works well for its readers. Amateurs (the French word fits wine-lovers perfectly) will always be sceptical about claims of total precision. The pleasure principle is the one they believe in.

The Johnson System

I offer a tried and tested alternative way of registering how much *you* like a wine. The Johnson System reflects the enjoyment (or lack of it) that each wine offered at the time it was drunk with inescapable honesty. Here it is:

One sniff	the minimum score. Emphatically no thanks
One sip	one step up
Two sips	faint interest (or disbelief)
A half glass	slight hesitation
One glass	tolerance, even general approval

Individuals will vary in their scoring after this (they do with points systems, too). You should assume that you are drinking without compunction – without your host pressing you or the winemaker glowering at you. But you have time and you are thirsty.

Two glasses	means you quite like it
	(or there is nothing else to drink);
Three glasses	you find it more than acceptable;
Four	it tickles your fancy;
One bottle	means satisfaction:
A second bottle	is the real thumbs up.

The steps grow higher now:

A full dozen	means you are not going to miss out on this one... and so on.
	The logical top score in the Johnson System is, of course, the whole vineyard.

Quick reference vintage charts

These charts give a picture of the range of qualities made in the principal "classic" areas (every year has its relative successes and failures) and a guide to whether the wine is ready to drink or should be kept. Generalizations are unavoidable.

☞ drink up	Ⴘ needs keeping
Ұ can be drunk with pleasure now, but the better wines will continue to improve	⋔ avoid
	o no good
	10 best

Germany / Italy / Spain

Vintage	Rhine		Mosel		Piedmont reds		Tuscan reds		Rioja	
2003	6–9	Ⴘ	6–9	Ⴘ	6–8	Ⴘ	6–8	Ⴘ	6–7	Ⴘ
2002	7–8	Ⴘ	7–8	Ⴘ	5–6	Ⴘ	5–7	Ⴘ	6–7	Ⴘ
2001	7–9	Ⴘ	8–10	Ⴘ	8–9	Ⴘ	6–7	Ұ	7–9	Ⴘ
2000	5–8	Ⴘ	5–8	Ⴘ	7–8	Ⴘ	6–7	Ұ	7–8	Ⴘ
99	7–10	Ұ	7–10	Ұ	8–10	Ⴘ	8–10	Ⴘ	6–7	Ұ
98	6–9	Ұ	6–9	Ұ	7–8	Ұ	6–7	Ұ	7–8	Ұ
97	7–9	Ұ	7–10	Ұ	7–8	Ұ	7–9	Ұ	5–7	Ұ
96	7–9	Ұ	6–8	Ұ	8–10	Ұ	5–7	Ұ	7–9	Ұ
95	7–10	☞	8–10	☞	6–8	Ұ	6–8	Ұ	8–10	☞
94	5–7	☞	6–10	☞	4–5	☞	4–5	☞	8–10	☞
93	5–8	☞	6–9	☞	6–8	☞	6–8	☞	4–5	☞
92	5–9	☞	5–9	☞	2–4	⋔	2–4	⋔	6–8	☞
91	5–7	☞	5–7	☞	4–5	⋔	4–6	☞	7–9	☞

Australia / Champagne / Port

Vintage	Shiraz		Chardonnay		Vintage			Vintage (97 = declared)	
2003	5–7	Ⴘ	5–7	Ⴘ	2003	7–8	Ⴘ	2003	N/A	Ⴘ
2002	5–8	Ұ	5–8	Ұ	2002	7–9	Ⴘ	2002	4–5	Ⴘ
2001	6–8	Ұ	5–7	Ұ	2001	1–3		2001	6–7	Ⴘ
2000	6–8	Ұ	7–9	☞	2000	7–9	Ⴘ	2000	8–10	Ⴘ
99	7–9	☞	5–7	☞	99	6–8	Ⴘ	99	4–6	Ⴘ
98	7–9	Ұ	7–9	☞	98	5–7	Ⴘ	98	4–6	Ⴘ
97	6–8	Ұ	8–10	☞	97	5–7	Ұ	97	8–10	Ⴘ
96	8–10	Ұ	4–7	☞	96	8–10	Ұ	96	4–6	Ұ
95	8–10	☞	3–5	⋔	95	7–9	Ұ	95	4–6	Ұ
94	6–8	☞	7–9	☞	94	2–4		94	8–9	Ⴘ
93	5–7	☞	5–7	☞	93	5–6	Ұ	93	2–5	Ұ
92	6–8	☞	6–8	☞	92	5–7	Ұ	92	8–9	Ⴘ

California / New Zealand / S.Africa

Vintage	Cabernet		Chardonnay		Red		White		Red	
2003	6–7	Ⴘ	6–7	Ⴘ	6–8	Ұ	6–8	Ұ	7–9	Ұ
2002	6–8	Ⴘ	6–8	Ұ	6–8	Ұ	6–8	Ұ	6–8	Ұ
2001	6–8	Ⴘ	5–7	Ұ	5–7	Ұ	6–8	Ұ	6–8	☞
2000	6–7	Ұ	5–8	Ұ	6–8	Ұ	7–9	☞	4–6	☞
99	7–9	Ұ	5–8	Ұ	6–8	☞	7–9	☞	6–8	☞

France

Vintage	Red Bordeaux		White Bordeaux		Alsace
	Médoc/Graves	Pom/St-Em	Sauternes & sw	Graves & dry	
2003	5-9	5-8	7-8	6-7	6-7
2002	6-8	5-8	7-8	7-8	7-8
2001	6-8	7-8	8-10	7-9	6-8
2000	8-10	7-9	6-8	6-8	8-10
99	5-7	5-8	6-9	7-10	6-8
98	5-8	6-9	5-8	5-9	7-9
97	5-7	4-7	7-9	4-7	7-9
96	6-8	5-7	7-9	7-10	8-10
95	7-9	6-9	6-8	5-9	6-9
94	5-8	5-8	4-6	5-8	6-9
93	4-6	5-7	2-5	5-7	6-8
92	3-5	3-5	3-5	4-8	5-7
91	3-6	2-4	2-5	6-8	3-5
90	8-10	8-10	8-10	7-8	7-9
89	6-9	7-9	8-10	6-8	7-10
88	6-8	7-9	7-10	7-9	8-10
87	5-7	5-7	2-5	7-10	7-8
86	6-9	5-8	7-10	7-9	7-8
85	7-9	7-9	6-8	5-8	7-10

France continued

Vintage	Burgundy			Rhône	
	Côte d'Or red	Côte d'Or white	Chablis	Rhône (N)	Rhône (S)
2003	6-8	6-7	6-7	5-7	6-8
2002	7-8	7-8	7-8	4-6	5-5
2001	6-8	7-9	6-8	7-8	7-9
2000	7-8	6-9	7-9	6-8	7-9
99	7-10	5-7	5-8	7-9	6-9
98	5-8	5-7	7-8	6-8	7-9
97	5-8	5-8	7-9	7-9	5-8
96	6-8	7-9	5-10	5-7	4-6
95	7-9	7-9	6-9	6-8	6-8
94	5-8	5-7	4-7	6-7	5-7
93	6-8	5-6	5-8	3-6	4-9
92	3-6	5-8	4-6	4-6	3-6
91	3-6	4-6	6-9	6-9	4-5
90	7-10	8-10	6-9	6-9	7-9

Beaujolais 02, 00, 99 Crus will keep. **Mâcon-Villages** (white) Drink 02, 01, 00, now or can wait. **Loire** (Sweet Anjou and Touraine) best recent vintages: 02, 97, 96, 93, 90, 89, 88, 85; Bourgueil, Chinon, Saumur-Champigny: 02, 00, 99, 97. **Upper Loire** (Sancerre, Pouilly-Fumé): 02, 00, 99, 98, 97 **Muscadet** 02, 01, 00, 99: DYA.

The right temperature

No single aspect of serving wine makes or mars it so easily as getting the temperature right. White wines almost invariably taste dull and insipid served warm and red wines have disappointingly little scent or flavour served cold. The chart below gives an indication of what is generally found to be the most satisfactory temperature for serving each class of wine.

	°F	°C	
	68	20	
	66	19	
Room temperature	64	18	
	63	17	Best red wines especially Bordeaux
Red burgundy	61	16	
	59	15	Chianti, Zinfandel, Côtes du Rhône
Best white burgundy, port, madeira	57	14	
	55	13	Standard daily reds
	54	12	Lighter red wines eg Beaujolais
Ideal cellar Sherry	52	11	
	50	10	
Champagne, Most dry white wines, Fino sherry, Tokaji Aszú	48	9	Rosés, Lambrusco
	46	8	
Domestic fridge	45	7	
	43	6	
	41	5	Most sweet white wines, Sparkling wines
	39	4	
	37	3	
	35	2	
	33	1	
	32	0	

wine
catalogue

The following titles are just a selection
from the Mitchell Beazley Wine List and
are available from all good bookstores.

To order direct from the publisher
in the UK call our Credit Card Hotline
number: **01903 828800**

In the USA call Phaidon Press Inc
on 1877 Phaidon (toll-free)

In Canada call McArthur & Co
Publishing Ltd on 416 408 4007

Alternatively visit our website on
www.mitchell-beazley.com

MITCHELL BEAZLEY

The Hugh Johnson List

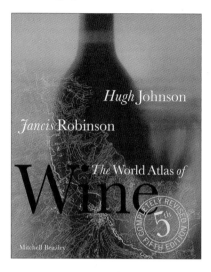

THE WORLD ATLAS OF WINE *5th Edition*

HUGH JOHNSON & JANCIS ROBINSON

For this brand new extended edition of the best-selling *World Atlas of Wine*, Hugh Johnson has teamed up with Jancis Robinson to create the most comprehensive revision of the book so far. The maps, text, photographs, and illustrations have all been extensively updated, with additional pages dedicated to the fastest developing wine regions of the 1990s. In keeping with the *Atlas's* reputation for cartographic excellence, all the maps have been digitally updated and in some cases extended, and thirty new maps detail the vineyards in the wine world's emerging regions.

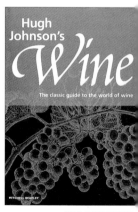

HUGH JOHNSON'S WINE

The classic guide to the world of wine
HUGH JOHNSON

For an accessible, all-round guide to the complex world of wine, *Hugh Johnson's Wine* covers everything from how wine is made to detailed tours of the wine regions, explaining what makes a "great" wine and how to select the right wine when dining out or entertaining at home.

THE WORLD ATLAS OF WINE
ISBN: 1 84000 332 4
£35/us$50/cn$75 Hardback 352 pages

HUGH JOHNSON'S WINE
ISBN: 0 85533 039 2
£14.99/us$24.95/cn$34.95
Hardback 272 pages

To order: UK 01903 828800 / USA 1877 Phaidon (toll-free)/Canada 416 408 4007 McArthur

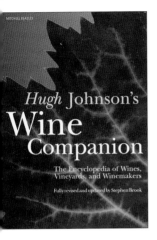

HUGH JOHNSON'S WINE COMPANION

The Encyclopedia of Wines, Vineyards and Winemakers
5th Edition

HUGH JOHNSON

This new fifth edition is the most up-to-date, comprehensive, authoritative, and easy-to-use source of information on the world's wines and winemakers. It presents a unique approach to wine producers, combining detailed background information with practical advice on how to enjoy wine to the full. Extensively revised and updated by Stephen Brook, it leaves few questions about wine unanswered.

HUGH JOHNSON'S THE STORY OF WINE
New Illustrated Edition

Written by the world's best-selling wine author, this new illustrated edition is an enthralling read, tracing the story of wine from the bacchanalian splendour of the ancient world through the upheavals of the middle ages to the present day. Updated to include the latest developments in wine, this edition features a selection of archive photographs never seen before.

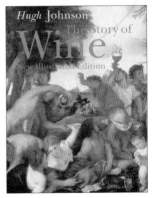

"Hugh Johnson's masterpiece; combining his gifts as writer, taster and historian to superb effect. Quirky, informative and extremely readable." TIM ATKIN MW

HUGH JOHNSON'S WINE COMPANION
ISBN: 1 84000 704 4
£35 / US $50 / CN $50 Hardback 592 pages

HUGH JOHNSON'S THE STORY O F WINE
ISBN: 1 84000 972 1
£30 / US $40 / CN $60 Hardback 256 pages

To order: UK 01903 828800 / USA 1877 Phaidon (toll-free)/Canada 416 408 4007 McArthur

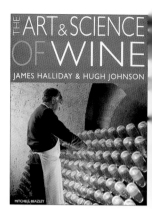

HUGH JOHNSON'S
HOW TO ENJOY YOUR WINE

Everything you need to know to get the most from wine

HUGH JOHNSON

Aimed at those who already enjoy a glass of wine, but who want to deepen their understanding of it. Hugh Johnson explains everything you need to know about handling wine in all social situations. With tips and guidance on all aspects of storing, serving, and tasting wine.

THE ART & SCIENCE OF WINE

HUGH JOHNSON & JAMES HALLIDAY

An approachable guide to the process behind winemaking. Hugh Johnson and James Halliday examine how nature, art, and science combine to provide the infinite variety of the world's wines; from the vineyard, vatroom, and cellar to the bottle.

HUGH JOHNSON'S
CELLAR BOOK

HUGH JOHNSON

Keep cellar records in order with this indispensable book. Useful tips on storing, opening, enjoying and recording wine. Followed by how to plan a cellar. The *Cellar Book* also includes space for personal notes.

HUGH JOHNSON'S HOW TO ENJOY YOUR WINE
ISBN: 1 84000 074 0
£9.99 Hardback
120 pages
*This edition not available from Phaidon/McArthurs

THE ART & SCIENCE OF WINE
ISBN: 1 85732 422 6
£15.99 Paperback
232 pages
*This edition not available from Phaidon/McArthur

HUGH JOHNSON'S CELLAR BOOK
ISBN: 1 84000 093 7
£18.99/us$29.95/cn$40
Hardback 224 pages

Special leather bound edition
ISBN: 1 84000 094
£80/us $120 Hardback

To order: **UK 01903 828800** / **USA 1877 Phaidon (toll-free)/Canada 416 408 4007 McArthur**

PLANET WINE
A Grape by Grape Visual Guide to the Contemporary Wine World
STUART PIGOTT

Hang on to your seat for a whistle-stop, grape-by-grape tour of our wine planet. Combining witty words and provocative pictures Stuart Pigott explains why a single grape variety can make very different tasting wines – showing how you too can taste the world in a glass of wine.

RIESLING RENAISSANCE
FREDDY PRICE

The Riesling grape has recently undergone an incredible leap in reputation, establishing itself once again as one of the world's greatest wines. Freddy Price documents this renaissance, celebrating Riesling's fascinating history and covering the nine countries and fifteen regions that produce Riesling – from the cool-climate, steep slopes of the Mosel Valley to the hot, dry plains of Australia.

THE NEW SPAIN
A Complete Guide to Contemporary Spanish Wine
JOHN RADFORD

This brand-new, second edition is the only up-to-date, illustrated, reference book to Spanish wines available. Revealing the recent progress and huge developments in Spain's wine laws, John Radford takes the reader on a region-by-region tour of Spain's rapidly changing vineyards and wineries.

PLANET WINE	RIESLING RENAISSANCE	THE NEW SPAIN
ISBN: 1 84000 776 1	ISBN: 1 84000 777 X	ISBN: 1 84000 928 4
£16.99 / US $29.95 / CN $39.95	£25 / US $40 / CN $60	£25 / US $40 / CAN $60
Hardback 160 pages	Hardback 192 pages	Hardback 224 pages

To order: **UK 01903 828800 / USA 1877 Phaidon (toll-free)/Canada 416 408 4007 McArthur**

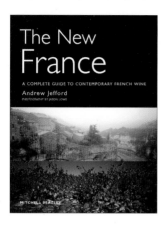

THE NEW FRANCE
ANDREW JEFFORD

This groundbreaking and authoritative book on French wine draws on painstaking research by leading wine writer Andrew Jefford, who has travelled extensively in each of France's fourteen wine regions to investigate the personalities and producers who have masterminded the resurgence of the French wine industry. Includes vintage charts and fifteen full-colour maps.

TOURING IN WINE COUNTRY
SERIES EDITOR HUGH JOHNSON

Each book in this best-selling series offers a comprehensive and inspirational guide to travelling in the world's top wine regions. Evocative descriptions of wine routes are accompanied by detailed maps showing the route and surrounding vineyards. Each title also includes the author's recommendations for hotels, restaurants, and producers.

BORDEAUX
ISBN: 1 84000 246 8

BURGUNDY
ISBN: 1 84000 245 X

NORTHWEST ITALY
ISBN: 1 85732 864 7

PROVENCE
ISBN: 1 84000 046 5

TUSCANY
ISBN: 1 84000 247 6

£12.99/US$19.95/CN$21.95
Paperback

THE NEW FRANCE
ISBN: 1 84000 410 X
£30/US$45/CN$70 Hardback 256 pages

To order: UK 01903 828800 / USA 1877 Phaidon (toll-free)/Canada 416 408 4007 McArthur

Mitchell Beazley Wine Guides

This series offers consumer guides that cover the key wine-producing countries and regions around the world. Each guide details the wine laws, producers, and their wines; there are also vintage and wine tasting guides.

New

WINE GUIDES
£9.99/us$14.95/cn$21.95 Hardback

WINES OF ITALY
BURTON ANDERSON
ISBN: 1 84000 861 X

WINES OF BORDEAUX
DAVID PEPPERCORN
ISBN: 1 84000 862 8

WINES OF CALIFORNIA
STEPHEN BROOK
ISBN: 1 84000 393 6

WINES OF AUSTRALIA
JAMES HALLIDAY
ISBN: 1 84000 708 7

WINES OF BURGUNDY
SERENA SUTCLIFFE
ISBN: 1 84000 709 5

WINES OF SPAIN
JAN READ
ISBN: 1 84000 710 9

MICHAEL BROADBENT'S WINETASTING
MICHAEL BROADBENT
ISBN: 1 84000 854 7

MICHAEL BROADBENT'S WINE VINTAGES
MICHAEL BROADBENT
ISBN: 1 84000 853 9

New

POCKET GUIDES
£8.99/us$14.95/cn$21.95 Hardback

WINES OF NEW ZEALAND
MICHAEL COOPER
ISBN: 1 84000 020 1

SCOTCH WHISKY
CHARLES MACLEAN
ISBN: 1 84000 990 X

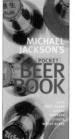

MICHAEL JACKSON'S POCKET BEER BOOK
MICHAEL JACKSON

This handy guide will keep beer lovers abreast of the world's best breweries and their beers.

MICHAEL JACKSON
ISBN: 1 84000 252 2
£8.99 Hardback 208 pages
*This edition not available from Phaidon/McArthur

To order: **UK** 01903 828800 / **USA** 1877 Phaidon (toll-free)/**Canada** 416 408 4007 McArthur

MITCHELL BEAZLEY CLASSIC WINE LIBRARY

SERIES EDITOR MARGARET RAND

This definitive series is aimed at the wine trade, professionals, and serious consumers who buy a wide range of wines of above-average quality on a regular basis. Each book provides in-depth coverage of the regions and/or communes, wine law, terroir, grape varieties, production details, vineyard areas and key producers. Written by a collection of the world's most prestigious wine authors.

New

COGNAC
ISBN: 1 84000 903 9
£20 / US $29.95 / CN $39.95
Hardback c300 pages

SHERRY
ISBN: 1 84000 923 3
£20 / US $29.95 / CN $39.95
Hardback c300 pages

THE WINES OF GREECE
ISBN: 1 84000 897 0
£20 / US $29.95 / CN $39.95
Hardback c300 pages

PORT AND THE DOURO
ISBN: 1 84000 943 8
£20 / US $29.95 / CN $39.95
Hardback c350 pages

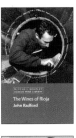

THE WINES OF RIOJA
ISBN: 1 84000 940 3
£20 / US $29.95 / CN $39.95
Hardback c300 pages

BIODYNAMIC WINES
ISBN: 1 84000 964 0
£20 / US $29.95 / CN $39.95
Hardback c300 pages

THE WINES OF THE SOUTH OF FRANCE
ISBN: 1 84000 793 1
£25 / US $37.50 / CN $50
Paperback 752 pages

BAROLO TO VALPOLICELLA
ISBN: 1 84000 901 2
£20 / US $29.95 / CN $39.95
Hardback 374 pages